## Get the eBook FREE!

(PDF, ePub, Kindle, and liveBook all included)

We believe that once you buy a book from us, you should be able to read it in any format we have available. To get electronic versions of this book at no additional cost to you, purchase and then register this book at the Manning website.

Go to https://www.manning.com/freebook and follow the instructions to complete your pBook registration.

## That's it!
## Thanks from Manning!

*Natural Language Processing in Action*

# Natural Language Processing in Action

*Understanding, analyzing, and generating text with Python*

HOBSON LANE
COLE HOWARD
HANNES MAX HAPKE

MANNING
SHELTER ISLAND

For online information and ordering of this and other Manning books, please visit
www.manning.com. The publisher offers discounts on this book when ordered in quantity.
For more information, please contact

> Special Sales Department
> Manning Publications Co.
> 20 Baldwin Road
> PO Box 761
> Shelter Island, NY 11964
> Email: orders@manning.com

Manning Publications Co.
20 Baldwin Road
PO Box 761
Shelter Island, NY 11964

| | |
|---|---|
| Acquisitions editor: | Brian Sawyer |
| Development editor: | Karen Miller |
| Technical development editor: | René van den Berg |
| Review editor: | Ivan Martinović |
| Production editor: | Anthony Calcara |
| Copy editor: | Darren Meiss |
| Proofreader: | Alyson Brener |
| Technical proofreader: | Davide Cadamuro |
| Typesetter and cover designer: | Marija Tudor |

ISBN 9781617294631
Printed in the United States of America

# brief contents

# contents

# *foreword*

I first met Hannes in 2006 when we started different post-graduate degrees in the same department. He quickly became known for his work leveraging the union of machine learning and electrical engineering and, in particular, a strong commitment to having a positive world impact. Throughout his career, this commitment has guided each company and project he has touched, and it was by following this internal compass that he connected with Hobson and Cole, who share similar passion for projects with a strong positive impact.

When approached to write this foreword, it was this passion for the application of machine learning (ML) for good that persuaded me. My personal journey in machine learning research was similarly guided by a strong desire to have a positive impact on the world. My path led me to develop algorithms for multi-resolution modeling ecological data for species distributions in order to optimize conservation and survey goals. I have since been determined to continue working in areas where I can improve lives and experiences through the application of machine learning.

> *With great power comes great responsibility.*
>
> —Voltaire?

Whether you attribute these words to Voltaire or Uncle Ben, they hold as true today as ever, though perhaps in this age we could rephrase to say, "With great access to data comes great responsibility." We trust companies with our data in the hope that it is used to improve our lives. We allow our emails to be scanned to help us compose more grammatically correct emails; snippets of our daily lives on social media are studied and used to inject advertisements into our feeds. Our phones and homes respond to our words, sometimes when we are not even talking to them. Even our news preferences are monitored so that our interests, opinions, and beliefs are indulged. What is at the heart of all these powerful technologies?

The answer is natural language processing. In this book you will learn both the theory and practical skills needed to go beyond merely understanding the inner workings of these systems, and start creating your own algorithms or models. Fundamental computer science concepts are seamlessly translated into a solid foundation for the approaches and practices that follow. Taking the reader on a clear and well-narrated tour through the core methodologies of natural language processing, the authors begin with tried and true methods, such as TF-IDF, before taking a shallow but deep (yes, I made a pun) dive into deep neural networks for NLP.

Language is the foundation upon which we build our shared sense of humanity. We communicate not just facts, but emotions; through language we acquire knowledge outside of our realm of experience, and build understanding through sharing those experiences. You have the opportunity to develop a solid understanding, not just of the mechanics of NLP, but the opportunities to generate impactful systems that may one day understand humankind through our language. The technology of NLP has great potential for misuse, but also great potential for good. Through sharing their knowledge, via this book, the authors hope to tip us towards a brighter future.

DR. ARWEN GRIFFIOEN
SENIOR DATA SCIENTIST - RESEARCH
ZENDESK

# *preface*

Around 2013, natural language processing and chatbots began dominating our lives. At first Google Search had seemed more like an index, a tool that required a little skill in order to find what you were looking for. But it soon got smarter and would accept more and more natural language searches. Then smart phone autocomplete began to get sophisticated. The middle button was often exactly the word you were looking for.[1]

In late 2014, Thunder Shiviah and I were collaborating on a Hack Oregon project to mine natural language campaign finance data. We were trying to find connections between political donors. It seemed politicians were hiding their donors' identities behind obfuscating language in their campaign finance filings. The interesting thing wasn't that we were able to use simple natural language processing techniques to uncover these connections. What surprised me the most was that Thunder would often respond to my rambling emails with a succinct but apt reply seconds after I hit send on my email. He was using *Smart Reply*, a Gmail Inbox "assistant" that composes replies faster than you can read your email.

So I dug deeper, to learn the tricks behind the magic. The more I learned, the more these impressive natural language processing feats seemed doable, understandable. And nearly every machine learning project I took on seemed to involve natural language processing.

Perhaps this was because of my fondness for words and fascination with their role in human intelligence. I would spend hours debating whether words even have "meaning" with John Kowalski, my information theorist boss at Sharp Labs. As I

---

[1] Hit the middle button (https://www.reddit.com/r/ftm/comments/2zkwrs/middle_button_game/:) repeatedly on a smart phone predictive text keyboard to learn what Google thinks you want to say next. It was first introduced on Reddit as the "SwiftKey game" (https://blog.swiftkey.com/swiftkey-game-winning-is/) in 2013.

gained confidence, and learned more and more from my mentors and mentees, it seemed like I might be able to build something new and magical myself.

One of the tricks I learned was to iterate through a collection of documents and count how often words like "War" and "Hunger" are followed by words like "Games" or "III." If you do that for a large collection of texts, you can get pretty good at guessing the right word in a "chain" of words, a phrase, or sentence. This classical approach to language processing was intuitive to me.

Professors and bosses called this a Markov chain, but to me it was just a table of probabilities. It was just a list of the counts of each word, based on the preceding word. Professors would call this a conditional distribution, probabilities of words conditioned on the preceding word. The spelling corrector that Peter Norvig built for Google showed how this approach scales well and takes very little Python code.[2] All you need is a lot of natural language text. I couldn't help but get excited as I thought about the possibilities for doing such a thing on massive free collections of text like Wikipedia or the Gutenberg Project.[3]

Then I heard about latent semantic analysis (LSA). It seemed to be just a fancy way of describing some linear algebra operations I'd learned in college. If you keep track of all the words that occur together, you can use linear algebra to group those words into "topics." LSA could compress the meaning of an entire sentence or even a long document into a single vector. And, when used in a search engine, LSA seemed to have an uncanny ability to return documents that were exactly what I was looking for. Good search engines would do this even when I couldn't think of the words that might be in those documents!

Then `gensim` released a Python implementation of Word2vec word vectors, making it possible to do semantic math with individual words. And it turned out that this fancy neural network math was equivalent to the old LSA technique if you just split up the documents into smaller chunks. This was an eye-opener. It gave me hope that I might be able to contribute to the field. I'd been thinking about hierarchical semantic vectors for years—how books are made of chapters of paragraphs of sentences of phrases of words of characters. Tomas Mikolov, the Word2vec inventor, had the insight that the dominant semantics of text could be found in the connection between two layers of the hierarchy, between words and 10-word phrases. For decades, NLP researchers had been thinking of words as having components, like niceness and emotional intensity. And these sentiment scores, components, could be added and subtracted to combine the meanings of multiple words. But Mikolov had figured out how to create these vectors without hand-crafting them, or even defining what the components should be. This made NLP fun!

---

[2]  See the web page titled "How to Write a Spelling Corrector" by Peter Norvig (http://www.norvig.com/spell-correct.html).

[3]  If you appreciate the importance of having freely accessible books of natural language, you may want to keep abreast of the international effort to extend copyrights far beyond their original "use by" date: gutenberg.org (http://www.gutenberg.org) and gutenbergnews.org (http://www.gutenbergnews.org/20150208/copyright-term-extensions-are-looming:).

About that time, Thunder introduced me to his mentee, Cole. And later others introduced me to Hannes. So the three of us began to "divide and conquer" the field of NLP. I was intrigued by the possibility of building an intelligent-sounding chatbot. Cole and Hannes were inspired by the powerful black boxes of neural nets. Before long they were opening up the black box, looking inside and describing what they found to me. Cole even used it to build chatbots, to help me out in my NLP journey.

Each time we dug into some amazing new NLP approach it seemed like something I could understand and use. And there seemed to be a Python implementation for each new technique almost as soon as it came out. The data and pretrained models we needed were often included with these Python packages. "There's a package for that" became a common refrain on Sunday afternoons at Floyd's Coffee Shop where Hannes, Cole, and I would brainstorm with friends or play Go and the "middle button game." So we made rapid progress and started giving talks and lectures to Hack Oregon classes and teams.

In 2015 and 2016 things got more serious. As Microsoft's Tay and other bots began to run amok, it became clear that natural language bots were influencing society. In 2016 I was busy testing a bot that vacuumed up tweets in an attempt to forecast elections. At the same time, news stories were beginning to surface about the effect of Twitter bots on the US presidential election. In 2015 I had learned of a system used to predict economic trends and trigger large financial transactions based only on the "judgment" of algorithms about natural language text.[4] These economy-influencing and society-shifting algorithms had created an amplifier feedback loop. "Survival of the fittest" for these algorithms appeared to favor the algorithms that generated the most profits. And those profits often came at the expense of the structural foundations of democracy. Machines were influencing humans, and we humans were training them to use natural language to increase their influence. Obviously these machines were under the control of thinking and introspective humans, but when you realize that those humans are being influenced by the bots, the mind begins to boggle. Could those bots result in a runaway chain reaction of escalating feedback? Perhaps the initial conditions of those bots could have a big effect on whether that chain reaction was favorable or unfavorable to human values and concerns.

Then Brian Sawyer at Manning Publishing came calling. I knew immediately what I wanted to write about and who I wanted to help me. The pace of development in NLP algorithms and aggregation of natural language data continued to accelerate as Cole, Hannes, and I raced to keep up.

The firehose of unstructured natural language data about politics and economics helped NLP become a critical tool in any campaign or finance manager's toolbox. It's unnerving to realize that some of the articles whose sentiment is driving those predictions are being written by other bots. These bots are often unaware of each other. The bots are literally talking to each other and attempting to manipulate each other, while

---

[4] See the web page titled "Why Banjo Is the Most Important Social Media Company You've Never Heard Of" (https://www.inc.com/magazine/201504/will-bourne/banjo-the-gods-eye-view.html).

the health of humans and society as a whole seems to be an afterthought. We're just along for the ride.

One example of this cycle of bots talking to bots is illustrated by the rise of fintech startup Banjo in 2015.[5] By monitoring Twitter, Banjo's NLP could predict newsworthy events 30 minutes to an hour before the first Reuters or CNN reporter filed a story. Many of the tweets it was using to detect those events would have almost certainly been favorited and retweeted by several other bots with the intent of catching the "eye" of Banjo's NLP bot. And the tweets being favorited by bots and monitored by Banjo weren't just curated, promoted, or metered out according to machine learning algorithms driven by analytics. Many of these tweets were written entirely by NLP engines.[6]

More and more entertainment, advertisement, and financial reporting content generation can happen without requiring a human to lift a finger. NLP bots compose entire movie scripts.[7] Video games and virtual worlds contain bots that converse with us, sometimes talking about bots and AI themselves. This "play within a play" will get ever more "meta" as movies about video games and then bots in the real world write reviews to help us decide which movies to watch. Authorship attribution will become harder and harder as natural language processing can dissect natural language style and generate text in that style.[8]

NLP influences society in other less straightforward ways. NLP enables efficient information retrieval (search), and being a good filter or promoter of some pages affects the information we consume. Search was the first commercially successful application of NLP. Search powered faster and faster development of NLP algorithms, which then improved search technology itself. We help you contribute to this virtuous cycle of increasing collective brain power by showing you some of the natural language indexing and prediction techniques behind web search. We show you how to index this book so that you can free your brain to do higher-level thinking, allowing machines to take care of memorizing the terminology, facts, and Python snippets here. Perhaps then you can influence your own culture for yourself and your friends with your own natural language search tools.

The development of NLP systems has built to a crescendo of information flow and computation through and among human brains. We can now type only a few characters into a search bar, and often retrieve the exact piece of information we need to complete whatever task we're working on, like writing the software for a textbook on NLP. The top few autocomplete options are often so uncannily appropriate that we feel like we have a human assisting us with our search. Of course we authors used various search engines throughout the writing of this textbook. In some cases these

---

[5]  Banjo, https://www.inc.com/magazine/201504/will-bourne/banjo-the-gods-eye-view.html

[6]  The 2014 financial report by Twitter revealed that >8% of tweets were composed by bots, and in 2015 DARPA held a competition (https://arxiv.org/ftp/arxiv/papers/1601/1601.05140.pdf) to try to detect them and reduce their influence on society in the US.

[7]  Five Thirty Eight, http://fivethirtyeight.com/features/some-like-it-bot/

[8]  NLP has been used successfully to help quantify the style of 16th century authors like Shakespeare (https://pdfs.semanticscholar.org/3973/ff27eb173412ce532c8684b950f4cd9b0dc8.pdf).

search results included social posts and articles curated or written by bots, which in turn inspired many of the NLP explanations and applications in the following pages.

What is driving NLP advances?

- A new appreciation for the ever-widening web of unstructured data?
- Increases in processing power catching up with researchers' ideas?
- The efficiency of interacting with a machine in our own language?

It's all of the above and much more. You can enter the question "Why is natural language processing so important right now?" into any search engine,[9] and find the Wikipedia article full of good reasons.[10]

There are also some deeper reasons. One such reason is the accelerating pursuit of artificial general intelligence (AGI), or Deep AI. Human intelligence may only be possible because we are able to collect thoughts into discrete packets of meaning that we can store (remember) and share efficiently. This allows us to extend our intelligence across time and geography, connecting our brains to form a collective intelligence.

One of the ideas in Steven Pinker's *The Stuff of Thought* is that we actually think in natural language.[11] It's not called an "inner dialog" without reason. Facebook, Google, and Elon Musk are betting on the fact that words will be the default communication protocol for thought. They have all invested in projects that attempt to translate thought, brain waves, and electrical signals into words.[12] In addition, the Sapir-Whorf hypothesis is that words affect the way we think.[13] And natural language certainly is the communication medium of culture and the collective consciousness.

So if it's good enough for human brains, and we'd like to emulate or simulate human thought in a machine, then natural language processing is likely to be critical. Plus there may be important clues to intelligence hidden in the data structures and nested connections between words that you're going to learn about in this book. After all, you're going to use these structures, and connection networks make it possible for an inanimate system to digest, store, retrieve, and generate natural language in ways that sometimes appear human.

And there's another even more important reason why you might want to learn how to program a system that uses natural language well… you might just save the world. Hopefully you've been following the discussion among movers and shakers about the *AI Control Problem* and the challenge of developing "Friendly AI."[14] Nick Bostrom,[15]

---

9 Duck Duck Go query about NLP (https://duckduckgo.com/?q=Why+is+natural+language+processing+so +important+right+now:)

10 See the Wikipedia article "Natural language processing" (https://en.wikipedia.org/wiki/Natural_language _processingWikipedia/NLP).

11 Steven Pinker, https://en.wikipedia.org/wiki/The_Stuff_of_Thought

12 See the Wired Magazine Article "We are Entering the Era of the Brain Machine Interface" (https://backchannel.com/we-are-entering-the-era-of-the-brain-machine-interface-75a3a1a37fd3).

13 See the web page titled "Linguistic relativity" (https://en.wikipedia.org/wiki/Linguistic _relativity).

14 Wikipedia, AI Control Problem, https://en.wikipedia.org/wiki/AI_control_problem

15 Nick Bostrom, home page, http://nickbostrom.com/

Calum Chace,[16] Elon Musk,[17] and many others believe that the future of humanity rests on our ability to develop friendly machines. And natural language is going to be an important connection between humans and machines for the foreseeable future.

Even once we are able to "think" directly to/with machines, those thoughts will likely be shaped by natural words and languages within our brains. The line between natural and machine language will be blurred just as the separation between man and machine fades. In fact this line began to blur in 1984. That's the year of the Cyborg Manifesto,[18] making George Orwell's dystopian predictions both more likely and easier for us to accept.[19, 20]

Hopefully the phrase "help save the world" didn't leave you incredulous. As you progress through this book, we show you how to build and connect several lobes of a chatbot "brain." As you do this, you'll notice that very small nudges to the social feedback loops between humans and machines can have a profound effect, both on the machines and on humans. Like a butterfly flapping its wings in China, one small decimal place adjustment to your chatbot's "selfishness" gain can result in a chaotic storm of antagonistic chatbot behavior and conflict.[21] And you'll also notice how a few kind, altruistic systems will quickly gather a loyal following of supporters that help quell the chaos wreaked by shortsighted bots—bots that pursue "objective functions" targeting the financial gain of their owners. Prosocial, cooperative chatbots can have an outsized impact on the world, because of the network effect of prosocial behavior.[22]

This is how and why the authors of this book came together. A supportive community emerged through open, honest, prosocial communication over the internet using the language that came naturally to us. And we're using our collective intelligence to help build and support other semi-intelligent actors (machines).[23] We hope that our words will leave their impression in your mind and propagate like a meme through the world of chatbots, infecting others with passion for building prosocial NLP systems. And we hope that when superintelligence does eventually emerge, it will be nudged, ever so slightly, by this prosocial ethos.

---

[16] Calum Chace, *Surviving AI*, https://www.singularityweblog.com/calum-chace-on-surviving-ai/

[17] See the web page titled "Why Elon Musk Spent $10 Million To Keep Artificial Intelligence Friendly" (http://www.forbes.com/sites/ericmack/2015/01/15/elon-musk-puts-down-10-million-to-fight-skynet/#17f7ee7b4bd0).

[18] Haraway, *Cyborg Manifesto*, https://en.wikipedia.org/wiki/A_Cyborg_Manifesto

[19] Wikipedia on George Orwell's *1984*, https://en.wikipedia.org/wiki/Nineteen_Eighty-Four

[20] Wikipedia, The Year 1984, https://en.wikipedia.org/wiki/1984

[21] A chatbot's main tool is to mimic the humans it is conversing with. So dialog participants can use that influence to engender both prosocial and antisocial behavior in bots. See the Tech Republic article "Why Microsoft's Tay AI Bot Went Wrong" (http://www.techrepublic.com/article/why-microsofts-tay-ai-bot-went-wrong).

[22] An example of autonomous machines "infecting" humans with their measured behavior can be found in studies of the impact self-driving cars are likely to have on rush-hour traffic (https://www.enotrans.org/wp-content/uploads/AV-paper.pdf). In some studies, as few as 1 in 10 vehicles around you on the freeway will help moderate human behavior, reducing congestion and producing smoother, safer traffic flow.

[23] Toby Segaran's *Programming Collective Intelligence* kicked off my adventure with machine learning in 2010 (https://www.goodreads.com/book/show/1741472.Programming_Collective_Intelligence).

# *acknowledgments*

Assembling this book and the software to make it *live* would not have been possible without a supportive network of talented developers, mentors, and friends. These contributors came from a vibrant Portland community sustained by organizations like PDX Python, Hack Oregon, Hack University, Civic U, PDX Data Science, Hopester, PyDX, PyLadies, and Total Good.

Kudos to Zachary Kent who designed, built, and maintained openchat (PyCon Open Spaces Twitter bot) and Riley Rustad who prototyped its data schema as the book and our skills progressed. Santi Adavani implemented named entity recognition using the Stanford CoreNLP library, developed tutorials for SVD and PCA, and supported us with access to his RocketML HPC framework to train a real-time video description model for people who are blind. Eric Miller allocated some of Squishy Media's resources to bootstrap Hobson's NLP visualization skills. Erik Larson and Aleck Landgraf generously gave Hobson and Hannes leeway to experiment with machine learning and NLP at their startup.

Anna Ossowski helped design the PyCon Open Spaces Twitter bot and then shepherded it through its early days of learning to help it tweet responsibly. Chick Wells cofounded Total Good, developed a clever and entertaining IQ Test for chatbots, and continuously supported us with his devops expertise. NLP experts, like Kyle Gorman, generously shared their time, NLP expertise, code, and precious datasets with us. Catherine Nikolovski shared her Hack Oregon and Civic U community and resources. Chris Gian contributed his NLP project ideas to the examples in this book, and valiantly took over as instructor for the Civic U Machine Learning class when the teacher *bailed* halfway through the *climb*. You're a Sky Walker. Rachel Kelly gave us the exposure and support we needed during the early stages of material development.

Thunder Shiviah provided constant inspiration through his tireless teaching and boundless enthusiasm for machine learning and life.

Molly Murphy and Natasha Pettit at Hopester are responsible for giving us a cause, inspiring the concept of a prosocial chatbot. Jeremy Robin and the Talentpair crew provided valuable software engineering feedback and helped to bring some concepts mentioned in this book to life. Dan Fellin helped kickstart our NLP adventures with teaching assistance at the PyCon 2016 tutorial and a Hack University class on Twitter scraping. Aira's Alex Rosengarten, Enrico Casini, Rigoberto Macedo, Charlina Hung, and Ashwin Kanan "mobilized" the chatbot concepts in this book with an efficient, reliable, maintainable dialog engine and microservice. Thank you, Ella and Wesley Minton, for being our guinea pigs as you experimented with our crazy chatbot ideas while learning to write your first Python programs. Suman Kanuganti and Maria Mac-Mullin had the vision to found "Do More Foundation" to make Aira's visual interpreter affordable for students. Thank you, Clayton Lewis, for keeping me engaged in his cognitive assistance research, even when I had only enthusiasm and hacky code to bring to the table for his workshop at the Coleman Institute.

Some of the work discussed in this book was supported by the National Science Foundation (NSF) grant 1722399 to Aira Tech Corp. Any opinions, findings, and recommendations expressed in this book are those of the authors and do not necessarily reflect the views of the organizations or individuals acknowledged here.

Finally, we would like to thank everyone at Manning Publications for their hard work, as well as Dr. Arwen Griffioen for contributing the foreword, Dr. Davide Cadamuro for his technical review, and all our reviewers, whose feedback and help improving our book added significantly to our collective intelligence: Chung-Yao Chuang, Fradj Zayen, Geoff Barto, Jared Duncan, Mark Miller, Parthasarathy Mandayam, Roger Meli, Shobha Iyer, Simona Russo, Srdjan Santic, Tommaso Teofili, Tony Mullen, Vladimir Kuptsov, William E. Wheeler, and Yogesh Kulkarni.

### Hobson Lane

I'm eternally grateful to my mother and father for filling me with delight at words and math. To Larissa Lane, the most intrepid adventurer I know, I'm forever in your debt for your help in achieving two lifelong dreams, sailing the world and writing a book.

To Arzu Karaer I'm forever in debt to you for your grace and patience in helping me pick up the pieces of my broken heart, reaffirming my faith in humanity, and ensuring this book maintained its hopeful message.

### Hannes Max Hapke

I owe many thanks to my partner, Whitney, who supported me endlessly in this endeavor. Thank you for your advice and feedback. I also would like to thank my family, especially my parents, who encouraged me to venture out into the world to discover it. All this work wouldn't have been possible without them. All of my life adventures wouldn't have been possible without the brave men and women changing the world on a November night in '89. Thank you for your bravery.

### *Cole Howard*

I would like to thank my wife, Dawn. Her superhuman patience and understanding is truly an inspiration. And my mother, for the freedom to experiment and the encouragement to always be learning.

# about this book

*Natural Language Processing in Action* is a practical guide to processing and generating natural language text in the real world. In this book we provide you with all the tools and techniques you need to build the backend NLP systems to support a virtual assistant (chatbot), spam filter, forum moderator, sentiment analyzer, knowledge base builder, natural language text miner, or nearly any other NLP application you can imagine.

*Natural Language Processing in Action* is aimed at intermediate to advanced Python developers. Readers already capable of designing and building complex systems will also find most of this book useful, since it provides numerous best-practice examples and insight into the capabilities of state-of-the art NLP algorithms. While knowledge of object-oriented Python development may help you build better systems, it's not required to use what you learn in this book.

For special topics, we provide sufficient background material and cite resources (both text and online) for those who want to gain an in-depth understanding.

### Roadmap

If you are new to Python and natural language processing, you should first read part 1 and then any of the chapters of part 3 that apply to your interests or on-the-job challenges. If you want to get up to speed on the new NLP capabilities that deep learning enables, you'll also want to read part 2, in order. It builds your understanding of neural networks, incrementally ratcheting up the complexity and capability of those neural nets.

As soon as you find a chapter or section with a snippet that you can "run in your head," you should run it for real on your machine. And if any of the examples look like they might run on your own text documents, you should put that text into a CSV or text file (one document per line) in the nlpia/src/nlpia/data/ directory. Then you can use the `nlpia.data.loaders.get_data()` function to retrieve that data and run the examples on your own data.

## About this book

The chapters of part 1 deal with the logistics of working with natural language and turning it into numbers that can be searched and computed. This "blocking and tackling" of words comes with the reward of some surprisingly useful applications such as information retrieval and sentiment analysis. Once you master the basics, you'll find that some very simple arithmetic, computed over and over and over in a loop, can solve some pretty important problems, such as spam filtering. Spam filters of the type you'll build in chapters 2 through 4 are what saved the global email system from anarchy and stagnation. You'll learn how to build a spam filter with better than 90% accuracy using 1990s era technology—calculating nothing more than the counts of words and some simple averages of those counts.

All this math with words may sound tedious, but it's actually quite fun. Very quickly you'll be able to build algorithms that can make decisions about natural language as well or better than you can (and certainly much faster). This may be the first time in your life that you have the perspective to fully appreciate the way that words reflect and empower your thinking. The high-dimensional vector-space view of words and thoughts will hopefully leave your brain spinning in recurrent loops of self-discovery.

That crescendo of learning may reach a high point toward the middle of this book. The core of this book in part 2 will be your exploration of the complicated web of computation and communication within neural networks. The network effect of small logical units interacting in a web of "thinking" has empowered machines to solve problems that only smart humans even bothered to attempt in the past, things such as analogy questions, text summarization, and translation between natural languages.

Yes, you'll learn about word vectors, don't worry, but oh so much more. You'll be able to visualize words, documents, and sentences in a cloud of connected concepts that stretches well beyond the three dimensions you can readily grasp. You'll start thinking of documents and words like a Dungeons and Dragons character sheet with a myriad of randomly selected characteristics and abilities that have evolved and grown over time, but only in our heads.

An appreciation for this intersubjective reality of words and their meaning will be the foundation for the coup-de-grace of part 3, where you learn how to build machines that converse and answer questions as well as humans.

## About the code

This book contains many examples of source code both in numbered listings and in line with normal text. In both cases, source code is formatted in a `fixed-width font like this` to separate it from ordinary text. Sometimes code is also **`in bold`** to highlight code that has changed from previous steps in the chapter, such as when a new feature adds to an existing line of code.

In many cases, the original source code has been reformatted; we've added line breaks and reworked indentation to accommodate the available page space in the book. In rare cases, even this was not enough, and listings include line-continuation markers (➥). Additionally, comments in the source code have often been removed from the listings when the code is described in the text. Code annotations accompany many of the listings, highlighting important concepts.

The source code for all listings in this book is available for download from the Manning website at https://www.manning.com/books/natural-language-processing-in-action and from GitHub at https://github.com/totalgood/nlpia.

### *liveBook discussion forum*

Purchase of *Natural Language Processing in Action* includes free access to a private web forum run by Manning Publications where you can make comments about the book, ask technical questions, and receive help from the authors and from other users. To access the forum, go to https://livebook.manning.com/#!/book/natural-language-processing-in-action/discussion. You can also learn more about Manning's forums and the rules of conduct at https://livebook.manning.com/#!/discussion.

Manning's commitment to our readers is to provide a venue where a meaningful dialogue between individual readers and between readers and the authors can take place. It is not a commitment to any specific amount of participation on the part of the authors, whose contribution to the forum remains voluntary (and unpaid). We suggest you try asking the authors some challenging questions lest their interest stray! The forum and the archives of previous discussions will be accessible from the publisher's website as long as the book is in print.

# *about the authors*

HOBSON LANE has 20 years of experience building autonomous systems that make important decisions on behalf of humans. At Talentpair Hobson taught machines to read and understand resumes with less bias than most recruiters. At Aira he helped build their first chatbot to interpret the visual world for those who are blind. Hobson is passionate about openness and prosocial AI. He's an active contributor to open source projects such as Keras, scikit-learn, PyBrain, PUGNLP, and ChatterBot. He's currently pursuing open science research and education projects for Total Good including building an open source cognitive assistant. He has published papers and presented talks at AIAA, PyCon, PAIS, and IEEE and has been awarded several patents in Robotics and Automation.

HANNES MAX HAPKE is an electrical engineer turned machine learning engineer. He became fascinated with neural networks in high school while investigating ways to compute neural networks on micro-controllers. Later in college, he applied concepts of neural nets to control renewable energy power plants effectively. Hannes loves to automate software development and machine learning pipelines. He co-authored deep learning models and machine learning pipelines for recruiting, energy, and healthcare applications. Hannes presented on machine learning at various conferences including OSCON, Open Source Bridge, and Hack University.

 COLE HOWARD is a machine learning engineer, NLP practitioner, and writer. A lifelong hunter of patterns, he found his true home in the world of artificial neural networks. He has developed large-scale e-commerce recommendation engines and state-of-the-art neural nets for hyperdimensional machine intelligence systems (deep learning neural nets), which perform at the top of the leader board for the Kaggle competitions. He has presented talks on Convolutional Neural Nets, Recurrent Neural Nets, and their roles in natural language processing at the Open Source Bridge Conference and Hack University.

# about the cover illustration

The figure on the cover of *Natural Language Processing in Action* is captioned "Woman from Kranjska Gora, Slovenia." This illustration is taken from a recent reprint of Balthasar Hacquet's *Images and Descriptions of Southwestern and Eastern Wends, Illyrians, and Slavs*, published by the Ethnographic Museum in Split, Croatia, in 2008. Hacquet (1739–1815) was an Austrian physician and scientist who spent many years studying the botany, geology, and ethnography of the Julian Alps, the mountain range that stretches from northeastern Italy to Slovenia and that is named after Julius Caesar. Hand drawn illustrations accompany the many scientific papers and books that Hacquet published.

The rich diversity of the drawings in Hacquet's publications speaks vividly of the uniqueness and individuality of the eastern Alpine regions just 200 years ago. This was a time when the dress codes of two villages separated by a few miles identified people uniquely as belonging to one or the other, and when members of a social class or trade could be easily distinguished by what they were wearing. Dress codes have changed since then and the diversity by region, so rich at the time, has faded away. It is now often hard to tell the inhabitant of one continent from another, and today the inhabitants of the picturesque towns and villages in the Slovenian Alps are not readily distinguishable from the residents of other parts of Slovenia or the rest of Europe.

We at Manning celebrate the inventiveness, the initiative, and, yes, the fun of the computer business with book covers based on the rich diversity of regional life of two centuries ago, brought back to life by the pictures from this collection.

# Part 1

# Wordy machines

**P**art 1 kicks off your natural language processing (NLP) adventure with an introduction to some real-world applications.

In chapter 1, you'll quickly begin to think of ways you can use machines that process words in your own life. And hopefully you'll get a sense for the magic—the power of machines that can glean information from the words in a natural language document. Words are the foundation of any language, whether it's the keywords in a programming language or the natural language words you learned as a child.

In chapter 2, we give you the tools you need to teach machines to extract words from documents. There's more to it than you might guess, and we show you all the tricks. You'll learn how to automatically group natural language words together into groups of words with similar meanings without having to hand-craft synonym lists.

In chapter 3, we count those words and assemble them into vectors that represent the meaning of a document. You can use these vectors to represent the meaning of an entire document, whether it's a 140-character tweet or a 500-page novel.

In chapter 4, you'll discover some time-tested math tricks to compress your vectors down to much more useful topic vectors.

By the end of part 1, you'll have the tools you need for many interesting NLP applications—from semantic search to chatbots.

# Packets of thought (NLP overview) 1

**This chapter covers**

- What natural language processing (NLP) is
- Why NLP is hard and only recently has become widespread
- When word order and grammar is important and when it can be ignored
- How a chatbot combines many of the tools of NLP
- How to use a regular expression to build the start of a tiny chatbot

You are about to embark on an exciting adventure in natural language processing. First we show you what NLP is and all the things you can do with it. This will get your wheels turning, helping you think of ways to use NLP in your own life, both at work and at home.

Then we dig into the details of exactly how to process a small bit of English text using a programming language like Python, which will help you build up your NLP toolbox incrementally. In this chapter, you'll write your first program that can read and write English statements. This Python snippet will be the first of many you'll use to learn all the tricks needed to assemble an English language dialog engine—a chatbot.

## 1.1    *Natural language vs. programming language*

Natural languages are different from computer programming languages. They aren't intended to be translated into a finite set of mathematical operations, like programming languages are. Natural languages are what humans use to share information with each other. We don't use programming languages to tell each other about our day or to give directions to the grocery store. A computer program written with a programming language tells a machine exactly what to do. But there are no compilers or interpreters for natural languages such as English and French.

> **DEFINITION**    *Natural language processing* is an area of research in computer science and artificial intelligence (AI) concerned with processing natural languages such as English or Mandarin. This processing generally involves translating natural language into data (numbers) that a computer can use to learn about the world. And this understanding of the world is sometimes used to generate natural language text that reflects that understanding.

Nonetheless, this chapter shows you how a machine can *process* natural language. You might even think of this as a natural language interpreter, just like the Python interpreter. When the computer program you develop processes natural language, it will be able to act on those statements or even reply to them. But these actions and replies aren't precisely defined, which leaves more discretion up to you, the developer of the natural language pipeline.

> **DEFINITION**    A natural language processing system is often referred to as a *pipeline* because it usually involves several stages of processing where natural language flows in one end and the processed output flows out the other.

You'll soon have the power to write software that does interesting, unpredictable things, like carry on a conversation, which can make machines seem a bit more human. It may seem a bit like magic—at first, all advanced technology does. But we pull back the curtain so you can explore backstage, and you'll soon discover all the props and tools you need to do the magic tricks yourself.

> *"Everything is easy, once you know the answer."*
>
> —Dave Magee

## 1.2    *The magic*

What's so magical about a machine that can read and write in a natural language? Machines have been processing languages since computers were invented. However, these "formal" languages—such as early languages Ada, COBOL, and Fortran—were designed to be interpreted (or compiled) only one correct way. Today Wikipedia lists more than 700 programming languages. In contrast, *Ethnologue*[1] has identified 10 times as many natural languages spoken by humans around the world. And Google's index of natural language documents is well over 100 million gigabytes.[2] And that's just the index. And it's incomplete. The size of the actual natural language content currently online must exceed 100 billion gigabytes.[3] But this massive amount of natural language text isn't the only reason it's important to build software that can process it.

The interesting thing about the process is that it's hard. Machines with the capability of processing something natural isn't natural. It's kind of like building a structure that can do something useful with architectural diagrams. When software can process languages not designed for machines to understand, it seems magical—something we thought was a uniquely human capability.

The word "natural" in "natural language" is used in the same sense that it is used in "natural world." Natural, evolved things in the world about us are different from mechanical, artificial things designed and built by humans. Being able to design and build software that can read and process language like what you're reading here—language about building software that can process natural language… well that's very meta, very magical.

To make your job a little easier, we focus on only one natural language, English. But you can use the techniques you learn in this book to build software that can process any language, even a language you don't understand, or has yet to be deciphered by archaeologists and linguists. And we're going to show you how to write software to process and generate that language using only one programming language, Python.

Python was designed from the ground up to be a readable language. It also exposes a lot of its own language processing "guts." Both of these characteristics make it a natural choice for learning natural language processing. It's a great language for building maintainable production pipelines for NLP algorithms in an enterprise environment, with many contributors to a single codebase. We even use Python in lieu of the "universal language" of mathematics and mathematical symbols, wherever possible. After all, Python is an unambiguous way to express mathematical algorithms,[4] and it's designed to be as readable as possible for programmers like you.

### 1.2.1 Machines that converse

Natural languages can't be directly translated into a precise set of mathematical operations, but they do contain information and instructions that can be extracted. Those pieces of information and instruction can be stored, indexed, searched, or immediately

---

[1] *Ethnologue* is a web-based publication that maintains statistics about natural languages.

[2] See the web page titled "How Google's Site Crawlers Index Your Site - Google Search" (https://www.google.com/search/howsearchworks/crawling-indexing/).

[3] You can estimate the amount of actual natural language text out there to be at least 1000 times the size of Google's index.

[4] Mathematical notation is ambiguous. See the "Mathematical notation" section of the Wikipedia article "Ambiguity" (https://en.wikipedia.org/wiki/Ambiguity#Mathematical_notation).

acted upon. One of those actions could be to generate a sequence of words in response to a statement. This is the function of the "dialog engine" or chatbot that you'll build.

We focus entirely on English text documents and messages, not spoken statements. We bypass the conversion of spoken statements into text—speech recognition, or speech to text (STT). We also ignore speech generation or text to speech, converting text back into some human-sounding voice utterance. But you can still use what you learn to build a voice interface or virtual assistant like Siri or Alexa, because speech-to-text and text-to-speech libraries are freely available. Android and iOS mobile operating systems provide high quality speech recognition and generation APIs, and there are Python packages to accomplish similar functionality on a laptop or server.

> **Speech recognition systems**
>
> If you want to build a customized speech recognition or generation system, that undertaking is a whole book in itself; we leave that as an "exercise for the reader." It requires a lot of high quality labeled data, voice recordings annotated with their phonetic spellings, and natural language transcriptions aligned with the audio files. Some of the algorithms you learn in this book might help, but most of the recognition and generation algorithms are quite different.

### 1.2.2  *The math*

Processing natural language to extract useful information can be difficult. It requires tedious statistical bookkeeping, but that's what machines are for. And like many other technical problems, solving it is a lot easier once you know the answer. Machines still cannot perform most practical NLP tasks, such as conversation and reading comprehension, as accurately and reliably as humans. So you might be able to tweak the algorithms you learn in this book to do some NLP tasks a bit better.

The techniques you'll learn, however, are powerful enough to create machines that can surpass humans in both accuracy and speed for some surprisingly subtle tasks. For example, you might not have guessed that recognizing sarcasm in an isolated Twitter message can be done more accurately by a machine than by a human.[5] Don't worry, humans are still better at recognizing humor and sarcasm within an ongoing dialog, due to our ability to maintain information about the context of a statement. But machines are getting better and better at maintaining context. And this book helps you incorporate context (metadata) into your NLP pipeline, in case you want to try your hand at advancing the state of the art.

---

[5]  Gonzalo-Ibanez et al. found that educated and trained human judges couldn't match the performance of their simple classification algorithm of 68% reported in their ACM paper. The Sarcasm Detector (https://github.com/MathieuCliche/Sarcasm_detector) and the web app (http://www.thesarcasmdetector.com/) by Matthew Cliche at Cornell achieve similar accuracy (>70%).

Once you extract structured numerical data, vectors, from natural language, you can take advantage of all the tools of mathematics and machine learning. We use the same linear algebra tricks as the projection of 3D objects onto a 2D computer screen, something that computers and drafters were doing long before natural language processing came into its own. These breakthrough ideas opened up a world of "semantic" analysis, allowing computers to interpret and store the "meaning" of statements rather than just word or character counts. Semantic analysis, along with statistics, can help resolve the ambiguity of natural language—the fact that words or phrases often have multiple meanings or interpretations.

So extracting information isn't at all like building a programming language compiler (fortunately for you). The most promising techniques bypass the rigid rules of regular grammars (patterns) or formal languages. You can rely on statistical relationships between words instead of a deep system of logical rules.[6] Imagine if you had to define English grammar and spelling rules in a nested tree of if...then statements. Could you ever write enough rules to deal with every possible way that words, letters, and punctuation can be combined to make a statement? Would you even begin to capture the semantics, the meaning of English statements? Even if it were useful for some kinds of statements, imagine how limited and brittle this software would be. Unanticipated spelling or punctuation would break or befuddle your algorithm.

Natural languages have an additional "decoding" challenge that is even harder to solve. Speakers and writers of natural languages assume that a human is the one doing the processing (listening or reading), not a machine. So when I say "good morning", I assume that you have some knowledge about what makes up a morning, including not only that mornings come before noons and afternoons and evenings but also after midnights. And you need to know they can represent times of day as well as general experiences of a period of time. The interpreter is assumed to know that "good morning" is a common greeting that doesn't contain much information at all about the morning. Rather it reflects the state of mind of the speaker and her readiness to speak with others.

This theory of mind about the human processor of language turns out to be a powerful assumption. It allows us to say a lot with few words if we assume that the "processor" has access to a lifetime of common sense knowledge about the world. This degree of compression is still out of reach for machines. There is no clear "theory of mind" you can point to in an NLP pipeline. However, we show you techniques in later chapters to help machines build ontologies, or knowledge bases, of common sense knowledge to help interpret statements that rely on this knowledge.

---

[6] Some grammar rules can be implemented in a computer science abstraction called a finite state machine. Regular grammars can be implemented in regular expressions. There are two Python packages for running regular expression finite state machines, `re` which is built in, and `regex` which must be installed, but may soon replace `re`. Finite state machines are just trees of if...then...else statements for each token (character/word/n-gram) or action that a machine needs to react to or generate.

## 1.3    *Practical applications*

Natural language processing is everywhere. It's so ubiquitous that some of the examples in table 1.1 may surprise you.

**Table 1.1   Categorized NLP applications**

| Search | Web | Documents | Autocomplete |
|---|---|---|---|
| **Editing** | Spelling | Grammar | Style |
| **Dialog** | Chatbot | Assistant | Scheduling |
| **Writing** | Index | Concordance | Table of contents |
| **Email** | Spam filter | Classification | Prioritization |
| **Text mining** | Summarization | Knowledge extraction | Medical diagnoses |
| **Law** | Legal inference | Precedent search | Subpoena classification |
| **News** | Event detection | Fact checking | Headline composition |
| **Attribution** | Plagiarism detection | Literary forensics | Style coaching |
| **Sentiment analysis** | Community morale monitoring | Product review triage | Customer care |
| **Behavior prediction** | Finance | Election forecasting | Marketing |
| **Creative writing** | Movie scripts | Poetry | Song lyrics |

A search engine can provide more meaningful results if it indexes web pages or document archives in a way that takes into account the meaning of natural language text. Autocomplete uses NLP to complete your thought and is common among search engines and mobile phone keyboards. Many word processors, browser plugins, and text editors have spelling correctors, grammar checkers, concordance composers, and most recently, style coaches. Some dialog engines (chatbots) use natural language search to find a response to their conversation partner's message.

NLP pipelines that generate (compose) text can be used not only to compose short replies in chatbots and virtual assistants, but also to assemble much longer passages of text. The Associated Press uses NLP "robot journalists" to write entire financial news articles and sporting event reports.[7] Bots can compose weather forecasts that sound a lot like what your hometown weather person might say, perhaps because human meteorologists use word processors with NLP features to draft scripts.

NLP spam filters in early email programs helped email overtake telephone and fax communication channels in the '90s. And the spam filters have retained their edge in the cat and mouse game between spam filters and spam generators for email, but may be losing in other environments like social networks. An estimated 20% of the tweets

---

[7] "AP's 'robot journalists' are writing their own stories now," The Verge, Jan 29, 2015, http://www.theverge .com/2015/1/29/7939067/ap-journalism-automation-robots-financial-reporting.

about the 2016 US presidential election were composed by chatbots.[8] These bots amplify their owners' and developers' viewpoints. And these "puppet masters" tend to be foreign governments or large corporations with the resources and motivation to influence popular opinion.

NLP systems can generate more than just short social network posts. NLP can be used to compose lengthy movie and product reviews on Amazon and elsewhere. Many reviews are the creation of autonomous NLP pipelines that have never set foot in a movie theater or purchased the product they're reviewing.

There are chatbots on Slack, IRC, and even customer service websites—places where chatbots have to deal with ambiguous commands or questions. And chatbots paired with voice recognition and generation systems can even handle lengthy conversations with an indefinite goal or "objective function" such as making a reservation at a local restaurant.[9] NLP systems can answer phones for companies that want something better than a phone tree but don't want to pay humans to help their customers.

> **NOTE** With its *Duplex* demonstration at Google IO, engineers and managers overlooked concerns about the ethics of teaching chatbots to deceive humans. We all ignore this dilemma when we happily interact with chatbots on Twitter and other anonymous social networks, where bots don't share their pedigree. With bots that can so convincingly deceive us, the AI control problem[10] looms, and Yuval Harari's cautionary forecast of "Homo Deus"[11] may come sooner than we think.

NLP systems exist that can act as email "receptionists" for businesses or executive assistants for managers. These assistants schedule meetings and record summary details in an electronic Rolodex, or CRM (customer relationship management system), interacting with others by email on their boss's behalf. Companies are putting their brand and face in the hands of NLP systems, allowing bots to execute marketing and messaging campaigns. And some inexperienced daredevil NLP textbook authors are letting bots author several sentences in their book. More on that later.

## 1.4    Language through a computer's "eyes"

When you type "Good Morn'n Rosa," a computer sees only "01000111 01101111 01101111 ...". How can you program a chatbot to respond to this binary stream intelligently? Could a nested tree of conditionals (if... else... statements) check each one of those bits and act on them individually? This would be equivalent to writing a

---

[8]  New York Times, Oct 18, 2016, https://www.nytimes.com/2016/11/18/technology/automated-pro-trump-bots-overwhelmed-pro-clinton-messages-researchers-say.html and MIT Technology Review, Nov 2016, https://www.technologyreview.com/s/602817/how-the-bot-y-politic-influenced-this-election/.

[9]  Google Blog May 2018 about their *Duplex* system https://ai.googleblog.com/2018/05/advances-in-semantic-textual-similarity.html.

[10]  See the web page titled "AI control problem - Wikipedia" (https://en.wikipedia.org/wiki/AI_control _problem).

[11]  WSJ Blog, March 10, 2017 https://blogs.wsj.com/cio/2017/03/10/homo-deus-author-yuval-noah-harari-says-authority-shifting-from-people-to-ai/.

special kind of program called a finite state machine (FSM). An FSM that outputs a sequence of new symbols as it runs, like the Python `str.translate` function, is called a finite state transducer (FST). You've probably already built an FSM without even knowing it. Have you ever written a regular expression? That's the kind of FSM we use in the next section to show you one possible approach to NLP: the pattern-based approach.

What if you decided to search a memory bank (database) for the exact same string of bits, characters, or words, and use one of the responses that other humans and authors have used for that statement in the past? But imagine if there was a typo or variation in the statement. Our bot would be sent off the rails. And bits aren't continuous or forgiving—they either match or they don't. There's no obvious way to find similarity between two streams of bits that takes into account what they signify. The bits for "good" will be just as similar to "bad!" as they are to "okay."

But let's see how this approach would work before we show you a better way. Let's build a small regular expression to recognize greetings like "Good morning Rosa" and respond appropriately—our first tiny chatbot!

### 1.4.1  *The language of locks*

Surprisingly, the humble combination lock is actually a simple language processing machine. So, if you're mechanically inclined, this section may be illuminating. But if you don't need mechanical analogies to help you understand algorithms and how regular expressions work, then you can skip this section.

After finishing this section, you'll never think of your combination bicycle lock the same way again. A combination lock certainly can't read and understand the textbooks stored inside a school locker, but it can understand the language of locks. It can understand when you try to "tell" it a "password": a combination. A padlock combination is any sequence of symbols that matches the "grammar" (pattern) of lock language. Even more importantly, the padlock can tell if a lock "statement" matches a particularly meaningful statement, the one for which there's only one correct "response": to release the catch holding the U-shaped hasp so you can get into your locker.

This lock language (regular expressions) is a particularly simple one. But it's not so simple that we can't use it in a chatbot. We can use it to recognize a key phrase or command to unlock a particular action or behavior.

For example, we'd like our chatbot to recognize greetings such as "Hello Rosa," and respond to them appropriately. This kind of language, like the language of locks, is a formal language because it has strict rules about how an acceptable statement must be composed and interpreted. If you've ever written a math equation or coded a programming language expression, you've written a formal language statement.

Formal languages are a subset of natural languages. Many natural language statements can be matched or generated using a formal language grammar, like regular expressions. That's the reason for this diversion into the mechanical, "click, whirr"[12] language of locks.

---

[12] One of Cialdini's six psychology principles in his popular book, *Influence* http://changingminds.org/techniques/general/cialdini/click-whirr.htm

### 1.4.2 Regular expressions

Regular expressions use a special kind (class) of formal language grammar called a regular grammar. Regular grammars have predictable, provable behavior, and yet are flexible enough to power some of the most sophisticated dialog engines and chatbots on the market. Amazon Alexa and Google Now are mostly pattern-based engines that rely on regular grammars. Deep, complex regular grammar rules can often be expressed in a single line of code called a regular expression. There are successful chatbot frameworks in Python, like `Will`, that rely exclusively on this kind of language to produce some useful and interesting behavior. Amazon Echo, Google Home, and similarly complex and useful assistants use this kind of language to encode the logic for most of their user interaction.

> **NOTE** Regular expressions implemented in Python and in Posix (Unix) applications such as `grep` aren't true regular grammars. They have language and logic features such as look-ahead and look-back that make leaps of logic and recursion that aren't allowed in a regular grammar. As a result, regular expressions aren't provably halting; they can sometimes "crash" or run forever.[13]

You may be saying to yourself, "I've heard of regular expressions. I use `grep`. But that's only for search!" And you're right. Regular expressions are indeed used mostly for search, for sequence matching. But anything that can find matches within text is also great for carrying out a dialog. Some chatbots, like `Will`, use "search" to find sequences of characters within a user statement that they know how to respond to. These recognized sequences then trigger a scripted response appropriate to that particular regular expression match. And that same regular expression can also be used to extract a useful piece of information from a statement. A chatbot can add that bit of information to its knowledge base about the user or about the world the user is describing.

A machine that processes this kind of language can be thought of as a formal mathematical object called a finite state machine or deterministic finite automaton (DFA). FSMs come up again and again in this book. So you'll eventually get a good feel for what they're used for without digging into FSM theory and math. For those who can't resist trying to understand a bit more about these computer science tools, figure 1.1 shows where FSMs fit into the nested world of

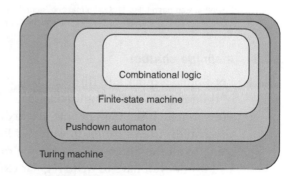

**Figure 1.1 Kinds of automata**

---

[13] Stack Exchange went down for 30 minutes on July 20, 2016 when a regex "crashed" (http://stackstatus.net/post/147710624694/outage-postmortem-july-20-2016).

automata (bots). And the side note that follows explains a bit more formal detail about formal languages.

> ### Formal mathematical explanation of formal languages
>
> Kyle Gorman describes programming languages this way:
>
> - Most (if not all) programming languages are drawn from the class of context-free languages.
> - Context-free languages are parsed with context-free grammars, which provide efficient parsing.
> - The regular languages are also efficiently parsable and used extensively in computing for string matching.
> - String matching applications rarely require the expressiveness of context-free.
> - There are a number of formal language classes, a few of which are shown here (in decreasing complexity):[a]
>   - Recursively enumerable
>   - Context-sensitive
>   - Context-free
>   - Regular
>
> Natural languages:
>
> - Are not regular[b]
> - Are not context-free[c]
> - Can't be defined by any formal grammar[d]

[a] See the web page titled "Chomsky hierarchy - Wikipedia" (https://en.wikipedia.org/wiki/Chomsky_hierarchy).

[b] "English is not a regular language" (http://cs.haifa.ac.il/~shuly/teaching/08/nlp/complexity.pdf#page=20) by Shuly Wintner.

[c] "Is English context-free?" (http://cs.haifa.ac.il/~shuly/teaching/08/nlp/complexity.pdf#page=24) by Shuly Wintner.

[d] See the web page titled "1.11. Formal and Natural Languages — How to Think like a Computer Scientist: Interactive Edition" (http://interactivepython.org/runestone/static/CS152f17/GeneralIntro/FormalandNaturalLanguages.html).

### 1.4.3   A simple chatbot

Let's build a quick and dirty chatbot. It won't be very capable, and it will require a lot of thinking about the English language. You will also have to hardcode regular expressions to match the ways people may try to say something. But don't worry if you think you couldn't have come up with this Python code yourself. You won't have to try to think of all the different ways people can say something, like we did in this example. You won't even have to write regular expressions (regexes) to build an awesome chatbot. We show you how to build a chatbot of your own in later chapters without hardcoding anything. A modern chatbot can learn from reading (processing) a bunch of English text. And we show you how to do that in later chapters.

   This pattern matching chatbot is an example of a tightly controlled chatbot. Pattern matching chatbots were common before modern machine learning chatbot techniques were developed. And a variation of the pattern matching approach we show you here is used in chatbots like Amazon Alexa and other virtual assistants.

For now let's build an FSM, a regular expression, that can speak lock language (regular language). We could program it to understand lock language statements, such as "01-02-03." Even better, we'd like it to understand greetings, things like "open sesame" or "hello Rosa." An important feature for a prosocial chatbot is to be able to respond to a greeting. In high school, teachers often chastised me for being impolite when I'd ignore greetings like this while rushing to class. We surely don't want that for our benevolent chatbot.

In machine communication protocol, we'd define a simple handshake with an ACK (acknowledgement) signal after each message passed back and forth between two machines. But our machines are going to be interacting with humans who say things like "Good morning, Rosa." We don't want it sending out a bunch of chirps, beeps, or ACK messages, like it's syncing up a modem or HTTP connection at the start of a conversation or web browsing session. Instead let's use regular expressions to recognize several different human greetings at the start of a conversation handshake:

> **There are two "official" regular expression packages in Python. We use the re package here just because it's installed with all versions of Python. The regex package comes with later versions of Python and is much more powerful, as you'll see in chapter 2.**

> **'|' means "OR," and '\*' means the preceding character can occur 0 or more times and still match. So our regex will match greetings that start with "hi" or "hello" or "hey" followed by any number of '<space>' characters and then any number of letters.**

```
>>> import re
>>> r = "(hi|hello|hey)[ ]*([a-z]*)"
>>> re.match(r, 'Hello Rosa', flags=re.IGNORECASE)
<_sre.SRE_Match object; span=(0, 10), match='Hello Rosa'>
>>> re.match(r, "hi ho, hi ho, it's off to work ...", flags=re.IGNORECASE)
<_sre.SRE_Match object; span=(0, 5), match='hi ho'>
>>> re.match(r, "hey, what's up", flags=re.IGNORECASE)
<_sre.SRE_Match object; span=(0, 3), match='hey>
```

> **Ignoring the case of text characters is common, to keep the regular expressions simpler.**

In regular expressions, you can specify a character class with square brackets. And you can use a dash (-) to indicate a range of characters without having to type them all out individually. So the regular expression "[a-z]" will match any single lowercase letter, "a" through "z." The star ('*') after a character class means that the regular expression will match any number of consecutive characters if they are all within that character class.

Let's make our regular expression a lot more detailed to try to match more greetings:

> **You can compile regular expressions so you don't have to specify the options (flags) each time you use them.**

```
>>> r = r"[^a-z]*([y]o|[h']?ello|ok|hey|(good[ ])?(morn[gin']{0,3}|"\
...     r"afternoon|even[gin']{0,3}))[\s,;:]{1,3}([a-z]{1,20})"
>>> re_greeting = re.compile(r, flags=re.IGNORECASE)
```

```
>>> re_greeting.match('Hello Rosa')
<_sre.SRE_Match object; span=(0, 10), match='Hello Rosa'>
>>> re_greeting.match('Hello Rosa').groups()
('Hello', None, None, 'Rosa')
>>> re_greeting.match("Good morning Rosa")
<_sre.SRE_Match object; span=(0, 17), match="Good morning Rosa">
>>> re_greeting.match("Good Manning Rosa")
>>> re_greeting.match('Good evening Rosa Parks').groups()
('Good evening', 'Good ', 'evening', 'Rosa')
>>> re_greeting.match("Good Morn'n Rosa")
<_sre.SRE_Match object; span=(0, 16), match="Good Morn'n Rosa">
>>> re_greeting.match("yo Rosa")
<_sre.SRE_Match object; span=(0, 7), match='yo Rosa'>
```

**Notice that this regular expression cannot recognize (match) words with typos.**

**Our chatbot can separate different parts of the greeting into groups, but it will be unaware of Rosa's famous last name, because we don't have a pattern to match any characters after the first name.**

**TIP**  The "r" before the quote specifies a raw string, not a regular expression. With a Python raw string, you can send backslashes directly to the regular expression compiler without having to double-backslash ("\\") all the special regular expression characters such as spaces ("\\ ") and curly braces or handlebars ("\\{ \\}").

There's a lot of logic packed into that first line of code, the regular expression. It gets the job done for a surprising range of greetings. But it missed that "Manning" typo, which is one of the reasons NLP is hard. In machine learning and medical diagnostic testing, that's called a false negative classification error. Unfortunately, it will also match some statements that humans would be unlikely to ever say—a false positive, which is also a bad thing. Having both false positive and false negative errors means that our regular expression is both too liberal and too strict. These mistakes could make our bot sound a bit dull and mechanical. We'd have to do a lot more work to refine the phrases that it matches to be more human-like.

And this tedious work would be highly unlikely to ever succeed at capturing all the slang and misspellings people use. Fortunately, composing regular expressions by hand isn't the only way to train a chatbot. Stay tuned for more on that later (the entire rest of the book). So we only use them when we need precise control over a chatbot's behavior, such as when issuing commands to a voice assistant on your mobile phone.

But let's go ahead and finish up our one-trick chatbot by adding an output generator. It needs to say something. We use Python's string formatter to create a "template" for our chatbot response:

```
>>> my_names = set(['rosa', 'rose', 'chatty', 'chatbot', 'bot',
...     'chatterbot'])
>>> curt_names = set(['hal', 'you', 'u'])
>>> greeter_name = ''
>>> match = re_greeting.match(input())
...
>>> if match:
...     at_name = match.groups()[-1]
```

**We don't yet know who is chatting with the bot, and we won't worry about it here.**

```
...         if at_name in curt_names:
...             print("Good one.")
...         elif at_name.lower() in my_names:
...             print("Hi {}, How are you?".format(greeter_name))
```

So if you run this little script and chat to our bot with a phrase like "Hello Rosa," it will respond by asking about your day. If you use a slightly rude name to address the chatbot, she will be less responsive, but not inflammatory, to try to encourage politeness.[14] If you name someone else who might be monitoring the conversation on a party line or forum, the bot will keep quiet and allow you and whomever you are addressing to chat. Obviously there's no one else out there watching our input() line, but if this were a function within a larger chatbot, you'd want to deal with these sorts of things.

Because of the limitations of computational resources, early NLP researchers had to use their human brains' computational power to design and hand-tune complex logical rules to extract information from a natural language string. This is called a pattern-based approach to NLP. The patterns don't have to be merely character sequence patterns, like our regular expression. NLP also often involves patterns of word sequences, or parts of speech, or other "higher level" patterns. The core NLP building blocks like stemmers and tokenizers as well as sophisticated end-to-end NLP dialog engines (chatbots) like ELIZA were built this way, from regular expressions and pattern matching. The art of pattern-matching approaches to NLP is coming up with elegant patterns that capture just what you want, without too many lines of regular expression code.

> **CLASSICAL COMPUTATIONAL THEORY OF MIND**  This classical NLP pattern-matching approach is based on the computational theory of mind (CTM). CTM assumes that human-like NLP can be accomplished with a finite set of logical rules that are processed in series.[15] Advancements in neuroscience and NLP led to the development of a "connectionist" theory of mind around the turn of the century, which allows for parallel pipelines processing natural language simultaneously, as is done in artificial neural networks.[16, 17]

You'll learn more about pattern-based approaches—such as the Porter stemmer or the Treebank tokenizer—to tokenizing and stemming in chapter 2. But in later chapters we take advantage of modern computational resources, as well as our larger datasets, to shortcut this laborious hand programming and refining.

If you're new to regular expressions and want to learn more, you can check out appendix B or the online documentation for Python regular expressions. But you

---

[14] The idea for this defusing response originated with Viktor Frankl's *Man's Search for Meaning*, his Logotherapy (https://en.wikipedia.org/wiki/Logotherapy) approach to psychology, and the many popular novels where a child protagonist like Owen Meany has the wisdom to respond to an insult with a response like this.

[15] Stanford Encyclopedia of Philosophy, Computational Theory of Mind, https://plato.stanford.edu/entries/computational-mind/.

[16] Stanford Encyclopedia of Philosophy, Connectionism, https://plato.stanford.edu/entries/connectionism/.

[17] Christiansen and Chater, 1999, Southern Illinois University, https://crl.ucsd.edu/~elman/Bulgaria/christiansen-chater-soa.pdf.

don't have to understand them just yet. We'll continue to provide you with example regular expressions as we use them for the building blocks of our NLP pipeline. So don't worry if they look like gibberish. Human brains are pretty good at generalizing from a set of examples, and I'm sure it will become clear by the end of this book. And it turns out machines can learn this way as well.

### 1.4.4    Another way

Is there a statistical or machine learning approach that might work in place of the pattern-based approach? If we had enough data could we do something different? What if we had a giant database containing sessions of dialog between humans, statements and responses for thousands or even millions of conversations? One way to build a chatbot would be to search that database for the exact same string of characters our chatbot user just "said" to our chatbot. Couldn't we then use one of the responses to that statement that other humans have said in the past?

But imagine how a single typo or variation in the statement would trip up our bot. Bit and character sequences are discrete. They either match or they don't. Instead, we'd like our bot to be able to measure the difference in *meaning* between character sequences.

When we use character sequence matches to measure distance between natural language phrases, we'll often get it wrong. Phrases with similar meaning, like "good" and "okay," can often have different character sequences and large distances when we count up character-by-character matches to measure distance. And sequences with completely different meanings, like "bad" and "bar," might be too close to one other when we use metrics designed to measure distances between numerical sequences. Metrics like Jaccard, Levenshtein, and Euclidean vector distance can sometimes add enough "fuzziness" to prevent a chatbot from stumbling over minor spelling errors or typos. But these metrics fail to capture the essence of the relationship between two strings of characters when they are dissimilar. And they also sometimes bring small spelling differences close together that might not really be typos, like "bad" and "bar."

Distance metrics designed for numerical sequences and vectors are useful for a few NLP applications, like spelling correctors and recognizing proper nouns. So we use these distance metrics when they make sense. But for NLP applications where we are more interested in the meaning of the natural language than its spelling, there are better approaches. We use vector representations of natural language words and text and some distance metrics for those vectors for these NLP applications. We show you each approach, one by one, as we talk about these different vector representations and the kinds of applications they are used with.

We won't stay in this confusing binary world of logic for long, but let's imagine we're famous World War II-era code-breaker Mavis Batey at Bletchley Park and we've just been handed that binary, Morse code message intercepted from communication between two German military officers. It could hold the key to winning the war. Where would we start? Well the first step in our analysis would be to do something statistical with that stream of bits to see if we can find patterns. We can first use the Morse code table (or ASCII table, in our case) to assign letters to each group of bits. Then, if the characters are gibberish to us, as they are to a computer or a cryptographer in WWII, we could start counting them up, looking up the short sequences in a dictionary of all the words we've seen before and putting a mark next to the entry every time it occurs. We might also make a mark in some other log book to indicate which message the word occurred in, creating an encyclopedic index to all the documents we've read before. This collection of documents is called a *corpus*, and the collection of words or sequences we've listed in our index is called a *lexicon*.

If we're lucky, and we're not at war, and the messages we're looking at aren't strongly encrypted, we'll see patterns in those German word counts that mirror counts of English words used to communicate similar kinds of messages. Unlike a cryptographer trying to decipher German Morse code intercepts, we know that the symbols have consistent meaning and aren't changed with every key click to try to confuse us. This tedious counting of characters and words is just the sort of thing a computer can do without thinking. And surprisingly, it's nearly enough to make the machine appear to understand our language. It can even do math on these statistical vectors that coincides with our human understanding of those phrases and words. When we show you how to teach a machine our language using Word2Vec in later chapters, it may seem magical, but it's not. It's just math, computation.

But let's think for a moment about what information has been lost in our effort to count all the words in the messages we receive. We assign the words to bins and store them away as bit vectors like a coin or token sorter directing different kinds of tokens to one side or the other in a cascade of decisions that piles them in bins at the bottom. Our sorting machine must take into account hundreds of thousands if not millions of possible token "denominations," one for each possible word that a speaker or author might use. Each phrase or sentence or document we feed into our token sorting machine will come out the bottom, where we have a "vector" with a count of the tokens in each slot. Most of our counts are zero, even for large documents with verbose vocabulary. But we haven't lost any words yet. What have we lost? Could you, as a human, understand a document that we presented you in this way, as a count of each possible word in your language, without any sequence or order associated with those words? I doubt it. But if it was a short sentence or tweet, you'd probably be able to rearrange them into their intended order and meaning most of the time.

Here's how our token sorter fits into an NLP pipeline right after a tokenizer (see chapter 2). We've included a stopword filter as well as a "rare" word filter in our mechanical token sorter sketch. Strings flow in from the top, and bag-of-word vectors are created from the height profile of the token "stacks" at the bottom.

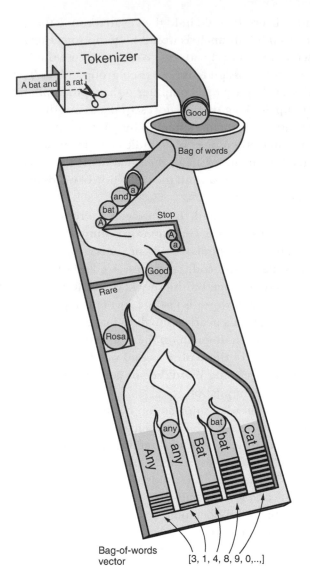

**Figure 1.2   Token sorting tray**

It turns out that machines can handle this bag of words quite well and glean most of the information content of even moderately long documents this way. Each document, after token sorting and counting, can be represented as a vector, a sequence of integers for each word or token in that document. You see a crude example in figure 1.2, and then chapter 2 shows some more useful data structures for bag-of-word vectors.

This is our first vector space model of a language. Those bins and the numbers they contain for each word are represented as long vectors containing a lot of zeros and a few ones or twos scattered around wherever the word for that bin occurred. All the different ways that words could be combined to create these vectors is called a *vector space*. And relationships between vectors in this space are what make up our model, which is attempting to predict combinations of these words occurring within a collection of various sequences of words (typically sentences or documents). In Python, we can represent these sparse (mostly empty) vectors (lists of numbers) as dictionaries. And a Python `Counter` is a special kind of dictionary that bins objects (including strings) and counts them just like we want:

```
>>> from collections import Counter

>>> Counter("Guten Morgen Rosa".split())
Counter({'Guten': 1, 'Rosa': 1, 'morgen': 1})
>>> Counter("Good morning, Rosa!".split())
Counter({'Good': 1, 'Rosa!': 1, 'morning,': 1})
```

You can probably imagine some ways to clean those tokens up. We do just that in the next chapter. But you might also think to yourself that these sparse, high-dimensional vectors (many bins, one for each possible word) aren't very useful for language processing. But they are good enough for some industry-changing tools like spam filters, which we discuss in chapter 3.

We can imagine feeding into this machine, one at a time, all the documents, statements, sentences, and even single words we could find. We'd count up the tokens in each slot at the bottom after each of these statements was processed, and we'd call that a vector representation of that statement. All the possible vectors a machine might create this way is called a *vector space*. And this model of documents and statements and words is called a *vector space model*. It allows us to use linear algebra to manipulate these vectors and compute things like distances and statistics about natural language statements, which helps us solve a much wider range of problems with less human programming and less brittleness in the NLP pipeline.

One statistical question that is asked of bag-of-words vector sequences is "What is the combination of words most likely to follow a particular bag of words?" Or, even better, if a user enters a sequence of words, "What is the closest bag of words in our database to a bag-of-words vector provided by the user?" This is a search query. The input words are the words you might type into a search box, and the closest bag-of-words vector corresponds to the document or web page you were looking for. The ability to efficiently answer these two questions would be sufficient to build a machine learning chatbot that could get better and better as we gave it more and more data.

But wait a minute, perhaps these vectors aren't like any you've ever worked with before. They're extremely high-dimensional. It's possible to have millions of dimensions for a 3-gram vocabulary computed from a large corpus. In chapter 3, we discuss the curse of dimensionality and some other properties that make high dimensional vectors difficult to work with.

## 1.5     *A brief overflight of hyperspace*

In chapter 3, we show you how to consolidate words into a smaller number of vector dimensions to help mitigate the curse of dimensionality and maybe turn it to our advantage. When we project these vectors onto each other to determine the distance between pairs of vectors, this will be a reasonable estimate of the similarity in their *meaning* rather than merely their statistical word usage. This vector distance metric is called *cosine distance metric*, which we talk about in chapter 3, and then reveal its true power on reduced dimension topic vectors in chapter 4. We can even project ("embed" is the more precise term) these vectors in a 2D plane to have a "look" at them in plots and diagrams to see if our human brains can find patterns. We can then teach a computer to recognize and act on these patterns in ways that reflect the underlying meaning of the words that produced those vectors.

Imagine all the possible tweets or messages or sentences that humans might write. Even though we do repeat ourselves a lot, that's still a lot of possibilities. And when those tokens are each treated as separate, distinct dimensions, there's no concept that

"Good morning, Hobs" has some shared meaning with "Guten Morgen, Hannes." We need to create some reduced dimension vector space model of messages so we can label them with a set of continuous (float) values. We could rate messages and words for qualities like subject matter and sentiment. We could ask questions like

- How likely is this message to be a question?
- How much is it about a person?
- How much is it about me?
- How angry or happy does it sound?
- Is it something I need to respond to?

Think of all the ratings we could give statements. We could put these ratings in order and "compute" them for each statement to compile a "vector" for each statement. The list of ratings or dimensions we could give a set of statements should be much smaller than the number of possible statements. And statements that mean the same thing should have similar values for all our questions.

These rating vectors become something that a machine can be programmed to react to. We can simplify and generalize vectors further by clumping (clustering) statements together, making them close on some dimensions and not on others.

But how can a computer assign values to each of these vector dimensions? Well, we simplify our vector dimension questions to things like "Does it contain the word 'good'?" Does it contain the word "morning?" And so on. You can see that we might be able to come up with a million or so questions resulting in numerical values that a computer could assign to a phrase. This is the first practical vector space model, called a bit vector language model, or the sum of "one-hot encoded" vectors. You can see why computers are just now getting powerful enough to make sense of natural language. The millions of million-dimensional vectors that humans might generate simply "Does not compute!" on a supercomputer of the 80s, but is no problem on a commodity laptop in the 21st century. More than just raw hardware power and capacity made NLP practical; incremental, constant-RAM, linear algebra algorithms were the final piece of the puzzle that allowed machines to crack the code of natural language.

There's an even simpler, but much larger representation that can be used in a chatbot. What if our vector dimensions completely described the exact sequence of characters. It would contain the answer to questions like, "Is the first letter an A? Is it a B? ... Is the second letter an A?" and so on. This vector has the advantage that it retains all the information contained in the original text, including the order of the characters and words. Imagine a player piano that could only play a single note at a time, and it had 52 or more possible notes it could play. The "notes" for this natural language mechanical player piano are the 26 uppercase and lowercase letters plus any punctuation that the piano must know how to "play." The paper roll wouldn't have to be much wider than for a real player piano, and the number of notes in some long piano songs doesn't exceed the number of characters in a small document. But this one-hot character sequence encoding representation is mainly useful for recording and then replaying an exact piece rather than composing something new or extracting the essence of a piece. We can't easily compare the piano paper roll for one song to that of another. And this representation is longer than the original ASCII-encoded representation of the document. The number of possible document representations just exploded in order to retain information about each sequence of characters. We retained the order of characters and words, but expanded the dimensionality of our NLP problem.

These representations of documents don't cluster together well in this character-based vector world. The Russian mathematician Vladimir Levenshtein came up with a brilliant approach for quickly finding similarities between sequences (strings of characters) in this world. Levenshtein's algorithm made it possible to create some surprisingly fun and useful chatbots, with only this simplistic, mechanical view of language. But the real magic happened when we figured out how to compress/embed these higher dimensional spaces into a lower dimensional space of fuzzy meaning or topic vectors. We peek behind the magician's curtain in chapter 4 when we talk about latent semantic indexing and latent Dirichlet allocation, two techniques for creating much more dense and meaningful vector representations of statements and documents.

## 1.6 Word order and grammar

The order of words matters. Those rules that govern word order in a sequence of words (like a sentence) are called the grammar of a language. That's something that our bag of words or word vector discarded in the earlier examples. Fortunately, in most short phrases and even many complete sentences, this word vector approximation works OK. If you just want to encode the general sense and sentiment of a short sentence, word order is not terribly important. Take a look at all these orderings of our "Good morning Rosa" example:

```
>>> from itertools import permutations

>>> [" ".join(combo) for combo in\
...     permutations("Good morning Rosa!".split(), 3)]
['Good morning Rosa!',
 'Good Rosa! morning',
 'morning Good Rosa!',
 'morning Rosa! Good',
 'Rosa! Good morning',
 'Rosa! morning Good']
```

Now if you tried to interpret each of these strings in isolation (without looking at the others), you'd probably conclude that they all probably had similar intent or meaning. You might even notice the capitalization of the word "Good" and place the word at the front of the phrase in your mind. But you might also think that "Good Rosa" was some sort of proper noun, like the name of a restaurant or flower shop. Nonetheless, a smart chatbot or clever woman of the 1940s in Bletchley Park would likely respond to any of these six permutations with the same innocuous greeting, "Good morning my dear General."

Let's try that (in our heads) on a much longer, more complex phrase, a logical statement where the order of the words matters a lot:

```
>>> s = """Find textbooks with titles containing 'NLP',
...     or 'natural' and 'language', or
...     'computational' and 'linguistics'."""
>>> len(set(s.split()))
12
>>> import numpy as np
>>> np.arange(1, 12 + 1).prod()  # factorial(12) = arange(1, 13).prod()
479001600
```

The number of permutations exploded from `factorial(3) == 6` in our simple greeting to `factorial(12) == 479001600` in our longer statement! And it's clear that the logic contained in the order of the words is important to any machine that would like to reply with the correct response. Even though common greetings aren't usually garbled by bag-of-words processing, more complex statements can lose most of their meaning when thrown into a bag. A bag of words isn't the best way to begin processing a database query, like the natural language query in the preceding example.

Whether a statement is written in a formal programming language like SQL, or in an informal natural language like English, word order and grammar are important when a statement intends to convey logical relationships between things. That's why computer languages depend on rigid grammar and syntax rule parsers. Fortunately, recent advances in natural language syntax tree parsers have made possible the extraction of syntactical and logical relationships from natural language with remarkable accuracy (greater than 90%).[18] In later chapters, we show you how to use packages like `SyntaxNet` (Parsey McParseface) and `SpaCy` to identify these relationships.

And just as in the Bletchley Park example greeting, even if a statement doesn't rely on word order for logical interpretation, sometimes paying attention to that word order can reveal subtle hints of meaning that might facilitate deeper responses. These deeper layers of natural language processing are discussed in the next section. And chapter 2 shows you a trick for incorporating some of the information conveyed by word order into our word-vector representation. It also shows you how to refine the crude tokenizer used in the previous examples (`str.split()`) to more accurately bin words into more appropriate slots within the word vector, so that strings like "good" and "Good" are assigned the same bin, and separate bins can be allocated for tokens like "rosa" and "Rosa" but not "Rosa!".

## 1.7    *A chatbot natural language pipeline*

The NLP pipeline required to build a dialog engine, or chatbot, is similar to the pipeline required to build a question answering system described in *Taming Text* (Manning, 2013).[19] However, some of the algorithms listed within the five subsystem blocks may

---

[18] A comparison of the syntax parsing accuracy of SpaCy (93%), SyntaxNet (94%), Stanford's CoreNLP (90%), and others is available at https://spacy.io/docs/api/.

[19] Ingersol, Morton, and Farris, http://www.manning.com/books/taming-text.

be new to you. We help you implement these in Python to accomplish various NLP tasks essential for most applications, including chatbots.

A chatbot requires four kinds of processing as well as a database to maintain a memory of past statements and responses. Each of the four processing stages can contain one or more processing algorithms working in parallel or in series (see figure 1.3):

1 *Parse*—Extract features, structured numerical data, from natural language text.
2 *Analyze*—Generate and combine features by scoring text for sentiment, grammaticality, and semantics.
3 *Generate*—Compose possible responses using templates, search, or language models.
4 *Execute*—Plan statements based on conversation history and objectives, and select the next response.

Each of these four stages can be implemented using one or more of the algorithms listed within the corresponding boxes in the block diagram. We show you how to use Python to accomplish near state-of-the-art performance for each of these processing steps. And we show you several alternative approaches to implementing these five subsystems.

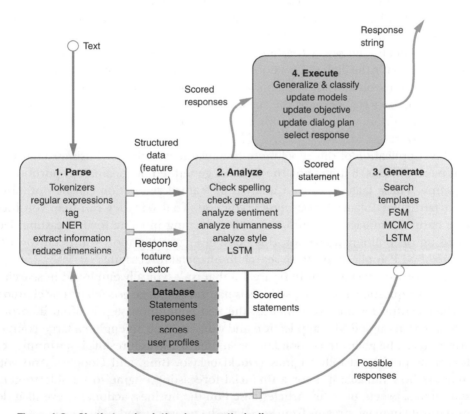

**Figure 1.3   Chatbot recirculating (recurrent) pipeline**

Most chatbots will contain elements of all five of these subsystems (the four processing stages as well as the database). But many applications require only simple algorithms for many of these steps. Some chatbots are better at answering factual questions, and others are better at generating lengthy, complex, convincingly human responses. Each of these capabilities require different approaches; we show you techniques for both.

In addition, deep learning and data-driven programming (machine learning, or probabilistic language modeling) have rapidly diversified the possible applications for NLP and chatbots. This data-driven approach allows ever greater sophistication for an NLP pipeline by providing it with greater and greater amounts of data in the domain you want to apply it to. And when a new machine learning approach is discovered that makes even better use of this data, with more efficient model generalization or regularization, then large jumps in capability are possible.

The NLP pipeline for a chatbot shown in figure 1.3 contains all the building blocks for most of the NLP applications that we described at the start of this chapter. As in *Taming Text*, we break out our pipeline into four main subsystems or stages. In addition, we've explicitly called out a database to record data required for each of these stages and persist their configuration and training sets over time. This can enable batch or online retraining of each of the stages as the chatbot interacts with the world. We've also shown a "feedback loop" on our generated text responses so that our responses can be processed using the same algorithms used to process the user statements. The response "scores" or features can then be combined in an objective function to evaluate and select the best possible response, depending on the chatbot's plan or goals for the dialog. This book is focused on configuring this NLP pipeline for a chatbot, but you may also be able to see the analogy to the NLP problem of text retrieval or "search," perhaps the most common NLP application. And our chatbot pipeline is certainly appropriate for the question answering application that was the focus of *Taming Text*.

The application of this pipeline to financial forecasting or business analytics may not be so obvious. But imagine the features generated by the analysis portion of your pipeline. These features of your analysis or feature generation can be optimized for your particular finance or business prediction. That way they can help you incorporate natural language data into a machine learning pipeline for forecasting. Despite focusing on building a chatbot, this book gives you the tools you need for a broad range of NLP applications, from search to financial forecasting.

One processing element in figure 1.3 that isn't typically employed in search, forecasting, or question answering systems is natural language *generation*. For chatbots this is their central feature. Nonetheless, the text generation step is often incorporated into a search engine NLP application and can give such an engine a large competitive advantage. The ability to consolidate or summarize search results is a winning feature for many popular search engines (DuckDuckGo, Bing, and Google). And you can imagine how valuable it is for a financial forecasting engine to be able to generate statements, tweets, or entire articles based on the business-actionable events it detects in natural language streams from social media networks and news feeds.

The next section shows how the layers of such a system can be combined to create greater sophistication and capability at each stage of the NLP pipeline.

## 1.8 Processing in depth

The stages of a natural language processing pipeline can be thought of as layers, like the layers in a feed-forward neural network. Deep learning is all about creating more complex models and behavior by adding additional processing layers to the conventional two-layer machine learning model architecture of feature extraction followed by modeling. In chapter 5, we explain how neural networks help spread the learning across layers by backpropagating model errors from the output layers back to the input layers. But here we talk about the top layers and what can be done by training each layer independently of the other layers.

The top four layers in figure 1.4 correspond to the first two stages in the chatbot pipeline (feature extraction and feature analysis) in the previous section. For example, the part-of-speech tagging (POS tagging) is one way to generate features within the Analyze stage of our chatbot pipeline. POS tags are generated automatically by the default `SpaCy` pipeline, which includes all the top four layers in this diagram. POS tagging is typically accomplished with a finite state transducer like the methods in the `nltk.tag` package.

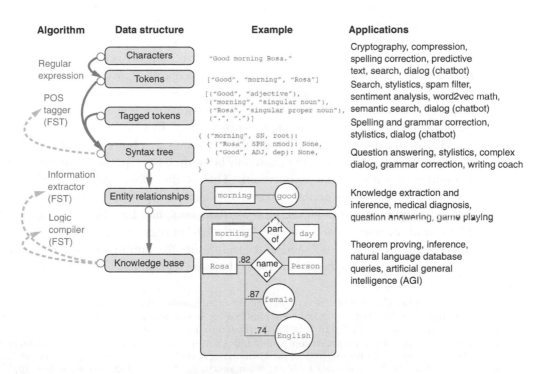

**Figure 1.4  Example layers for an NLP pipeline**

The bottom two layers (Entity relationships and a Knowledge base) are used to populate a database containing information (knowledge) about a particular domain. And the information extracted from a particular statement or document using all six of these layers can then be used in combination with that database to make inferences. *Inferences* are logical extrapolations from a set of conditions detected in the environment, like the logic contained in the statement of a chatbot user. This kind of "inference engine" in the deeper layers of this diagram is considered the domain of artificial intelligence, where machines can make inferences about their world and use those inferences to make logical decisions. However, chatbots can make reasonable decisions without this knowledge database, using only the algorithms of the upper few layers. And these decisions can combine to produce surprisingly human-like behaviors.

Over the next few chapters, we dive down through the top few layers of NLP. The top three layers are all that's required to perform meaningful sentiment analysis and semantic search, and to build human-mimicking chatbots. In fact, it's possible to build a useful and interesting chatbot using only a single layer of processing, using the text (character sequences) directly as the features for a language model. A chatbot that only does string matching and search is capable of participating in a reasonably convincing conversation, if given enough example statements and responses.

For example, the open source project `ChatterBot` simplifies this pipeline by merely computing the string "edit distance" (Levenshtein distance) between an input statement and the statements recorded in its database. If its database of statement-response pairs contains a matching statement, the corresponding reply (from a previously "learned" human or machine dialog) can be reused as the reply to the latest user statement. For this pipeline, all that is required is step 3 (Generate) of our chatbot pipeline. And within this stage, only a brute force search algorithm is required to find the best response. With this simple technique (no tokenization or feature generation required), `ChatterBot` can maintain a convincing conversion as the dialog engine for Salvius, a mechanical robot built from salvaged parts by Gunther Cox.[20]

`Will` is an open source Python chatbot framework by Steven Skoczen with a completely different approach.[21] `Will` can only be trained to respond to statements by programming it with regular expressions. This is the labor-intensive and data-light approach to NLP. This grammar-based approach is especially effective for question answering systems and task-execution assistant bots, like Lex, Siri, and Google Now. These kinds of systems overcome the "brittleness" of regular expressions by employing "fuzzy regular expressions"[22] and other techniques for finding approximate grammar matches. Fuzzy regular expressions find the closest grammar matches among a list of

---

[20] ChatterBot by Gunther Cox and others at https://github.com/gunthercox/ChatterBot.

[21] See the GitHub page for "Will," a chatbot for HipChat by Steven Skoczen and the HipChat community (https://github.com/skoczen/will). In 2018 it was updated to integrate with Slack.

[22] The Python `regex` package is backward compatible with `re` and adds fuzziness among other features. It will replace the `re` package in the future (https://pypi.python.org/pypi/regex). Similarly TRE `agrep`, or "approximate grep," (https://github.com/laurikari/tre) is an alternative to the UNIX command-line application `grep`.

possible grammar rules (regular expressions) instead of exact matches by ignoring some maximum number of insertion, deletion, and substitution errors. However, expanding the breadth and complexity of behaviors for a grammar-based chatbot requires a lot of human development work. Even the most advanced grammar-based chatbots, built and maintained by some of the largest corporations on the planet (Google, Amazon, Apple, Microsoft), remain in the middle of the pack for depth and breadth of chatbot IQ.

A lot of powerful things can be done with shallow NLP. And little, if any, human supervision (labeling or curating of text) is required. Often a machine can be left to learn perpetually from its environment (the stream of words it can pull from Twitter or some other source).[23] We show you how to do this in chapter 6.

## 1.9    *Natural language IQ*

Like human brainpower, the power of an NLP pipeline cannot be easily gauged with a single IQ score without considering multiple "smarts" dimensions. A common way to measure the capability of a robotic system is along the dimensions of complexity of behavior and degree of human supervision required. But for a natural language processing pipeline, the goal is to build systems that fully automate the processing of natural language, eliminating all human supervision (once the model is trained and deployed). So a better pair of IQ dimensions should capture the breadth and depth of the complexity of the natural language pipeline.

A consumer product chatbot or virtual assistant like Alexa or Allo is usually designed to have extremely broad knowledge and capabilities. However, the logic used to respond to requests tends to be shallow, often consisting of a set of trigger phrases that all produce the same response with a single if-then decision branch. Alexa (and the underlying Lex engine) behave like a single layer, flat tree of (if, elif, elif, …) statements.[24] Google Dialogflow (which was developed independently of Google's Allo and Google Assistant) has similar capability to Amazon Lex, Contact Flow, and Lambda, but without the drag-and-drop user interface for designing your dialog tree.

On the other hand, the Google Translate pipeline (or any similar machine translation system) relies on a deep tree of feature extractors, decision trees, and knowledge graphs connecting bits of knowledge about the world. Sometimes these feature extractors, decision trees, and knowledge graphs are explicitly programmed into the system, as in figure 1.4. Another approach rapidly overtaking this "hand-coded" pipeline is the deep learning data-driven approach. Feature extractors for deep neural networks are learned rather than hard-coded, but they often require much more training data to achieve the same performance as intentionally designed algorithms.

---

[23] Simple neural networks are often used for unsupervised feature extraction from character and word sequences.

[24] More complicated logic and behaviors are now possible when you incorporate Lambdas into an AWS Contact Flow dialog tree. See "Creating Call Center Bot with AWS Connect" (https://greenice.net/creating-call-center-bot-aws-connect-amazon-lex-can-speak-understand).

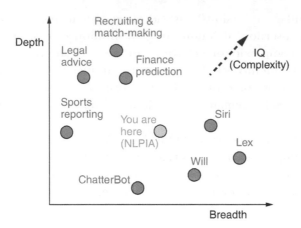

**Figure 1.5    2D IQ of some natural language processing systems**

You'll use both approaches (neural networks and hand-coded algorithms) as you incrementally build an NLP pipeline for a chatbot capable of conversing within a focused knowledge domain. This will give you the skills you need to accomplish the natural language processing tasks within your industry or business domain. Along the way you'll probably get ideas about how to expand the breadth of things this NLP pipeline can do. Figure 1.5 puts the chatbot in its place among the natural language processing systems that are already out there. Imagine the chatbots you have interacted with. Where do you think they might fit on a plot like this? Have you attempted to gauge their intelligence by probing them with difficult questions or something like an IQ test?[25] You'll get a chance to do exactly that in later chapters, to help you decide how your chatbot stacks up against some of the others in this diagram.

As you progress through this book, you'll be building the elements of a chatbot. Chatbots require all the tools of NLP to work well:

- Feature extraction (usually to produce a vector space model)
- Information extraction to be able to answer factual questions
- Semantic search to learn from previously recorded natural language text or dialog
- Natural language generation to compose new, meaningful statements

Machine learning gives us a way to trick machines into behaving as if we'd spent a lifetime programming them with hundreds of complex regular expressions or algorithms. We can teach a machine to respond to patterns similar to the patterns defined in regular expressions by merely providing it examples of user statements and the responses we want the chatbot to mimic. And the "models" of language, the FSMs, produced by machine learning are much better. They are less picky about mispelings and typoz.

And machine learning NLP pipelines are easier to "program." We don't have to anticipate every possible use of symbols in our language. We just have to feed the training pipeline with examples of the phrases that match and example phrases that

---

[25] A good question suggested by Byron Reese is: "What's larger? The sun or a nickel?" (https://gigaom.com/2017/11/20/voices-in-ai-episode-20-a-conversation-with-marie-des-jardins). Here are a couple more (https://github.com/totalgood/nlpia/blob/master/src/nlpia/data/iq_test.csv) to get you started.

don't match. As long we label them during training, so that the chatbot knows which is which, it will learn to discriminate between them. And there are even machine learning approaches that require little if any "labeled" data.

We've given you some exciting reasons to learn about natural language processing. You want to help save the world, don't you? And we've attempted to pique your interest with some practical NLP applications that are revolutionizing the way we communicate, learn, do business, and even think. It won't be long before you're able to build a system that approaches human-like conversational behavior. And you should be able to see in upcoming chapters how to train a chatbot or NLP pipeline with any domain knowledge that interests you—from finance and sports to psychology and literature. If you can find a corpus of writing about it, then you can train a machine to understand it.

The rest of this book is about using machine learning to save us from having to anticipate all the ways people can say things in natural language. Each chapter incrementally improves on the basic NLP pipeline for the chatbot introduced in this chapter. As you learn the tools of natural language processing, you'll be building an NLP pipeline that can not only carry on a conversation but help you accomplish your goals in business and in life.

## Summary

- Good NLP may help save the world.
- The meaning and intent of words can be deciphered by machines.
- A smart NLP pipeline will be able to deal with ambiguity.
- We can teach machines common sense knowledge without spending a lifetime training them.
- Chatbots can be thought of as semantic search engines.
- Regular expressions are useful for more than just search.

# Build your vocabulary
# (word tokenization)

**2**

---

### This chapter covers

- Tokenizing your text into words and *n*-grams (tokens)
- Dealing with nonstandard punctuation and emoticons, like social media posts
- Compressing your token vocabulary with stemming and lemmatization
- Building a vector representation of a statement
- Building a sentiment analyzer from handcrafted token scores

---

So you're ready to save the world with the power of natural language processing? Well the first thing you need is a powerful vocabulary. This chapter will help you split a document, any string, into discrete tokens of meaning. Our tokens are limited to words, punctuation marks, and numbers, but the techniques we use are easily extended to any other units of meaning contained in a sequence of characters, like ASCII emoticons, Unicode emojis, mathematical symbols, and so on.

Retrieving tokens from a document will require some string manipulation beyond just the `str.split()` method employed in chapter 1. You'll need to separate punctuation from words, like quotes at the beginning and end of a statement. And you'll need to split contractions like "we'll" into the words that were combined to form them. Once you've identified the tokens in a document that you'd like to include in your vocabulary, you'll return to the regular expression toolbox to try to combine words with similar meaning in a process called *stemming*. Then you'll assemble a vector representation of your documents called a bag of words, and you'll try to use this vector to see if it can help you improve upon the greeting recognizer sketched out at the end of chapter 1.

Think for a moment about what a word or token represents to you. Does it represent a single concept, or some blurry cloud of concepts? Could you be sure you could always recognize a word? Are natural language words like programming language keywords that have precise definitions and a set of grammatical usage rules? Could you write software that could recognize a word? Is "ice cream" one word or two to you? Don't both words have entries in your mental dictionary that are separate from the compound word "ice cream"? What about the contraction "don't"? Should that string of characters be split into one or two "packets of meaning?"

And words could be divided even further into smaller packets of meaning. Words themselves can be divided up into smaller meaningful parts. Syllables, prefixes, and suffixes, like "re," "pre," and "ing" have intrinsic meaning. And parts of words can be divided further into smaller packets of meaning. Letters or graphemes (https://en.wikipedia.org/wiki/Grapheme) carry sentiment and meaning.[1]

We'll talk about character-based vector space models in later chapters. But for now let's just try to resolve the question of what a word is and how to divide up text into words.

What about invisible or implied words? Can you think of additional words that are implied by the single-word command "Don't!"? If you can force yourself to think like a machine and then switch back to thinking like a human, you might realize that there are three invisible words in that command. The single statement "Don't!" means "Don't you do that!" or "You, do not do that!" That's three hidden packets of meaning for a total of five tokens you'd like your machine to know about. But don't worry about invisible words for now. All you need for this chapter is a tokenizer that can recognize words that are spelled out. You'll worry about implied words and connotation and even meaning itself in chapter 4 and beyond.[2]

---

[1] Morphemes are parts of words that contain meaning in and of themselves. Geoffrey Hinton and other deep learning deep thinkers have demonstrated that even graphemes (letters)—the smallest indivisible piece of written text—can be treated as if they are intrinsically meaningful.

[2] If you want to learn more about exactly what a "word" really is, check out the introduction to *The Morphology of Chinese* by Jerome Packard where he discusses the concept of a "word" in detail. The concept of a "word" didn't exist at all in the Chinese language until the 20th century when it was translated from English grammar into Chinese.

In this chapter, we show you straightforward algorithms for separating a string into words. You'll also extract pairs, triplets, quadruplets, and even quintuplets of tokens. These are called *n*-grams. Pairs of words are 2-grams (bigrams), triplets are 3-grams (trigrams), quadruplets are 4-grams, and so on. Using *n*-grams enables your machine to know about "ice cream" as well as the "ice" and "cream" that comprise it. Another 2-gram that you'd like to keep together is "Mr. Smith." Your tokens and your vector representation of a document will have a place for "Mr. Smith" along with "Mr." and "Smith," too.

For now, all possible pairs (and short *n*-grams) of words will be included in your vocabulary. But in chapter 3, you'll learn how to estimate the importance of words based on their document frequency, or how often they occur. That way you can filter out pairs and triplets of words that rarely occur together. You'll find that the approaches we show aren't perfect. Feature extraction can rarely retain all the information content of the input data in any machine learning pipeline. That's part of the art of NLP, learning when your tokenizer needs to be adjusted to extract more or different information from your text for your particular application.

In natural language processing, composing a numerical vector from text is a particularly "lossy" feature extraction process. Nonetheless the bag-of-words (BOW) vectors retain enough of the information content of the text to produce useful and interesting machine learning models. The techniques for sentiment analyzers at the end of this chapter are the same techniques Gmail used to save us from a flood of spam that almost made email useless.

## 2.1 Challenges (a preview of stemming)

As an example of why feature extraction from text is hard, consider *stemming*—grouping the various inflections of a word into the same "bucket" or cluster. Very smart people spent their careers developing algorithms for grouping inflected forms of words together based only on their spelling. Imagine how difficult that is. Imagine trying to remove verb endings like "ing" from "ending" so you'd have a stem called "end" to represent both words. And you'd like to stem the word "running" to "run," so those two words are treated the same. And that's tricky, because you have to remove not only the "ing" but also the extra "n." But you want the word "sing" to stay whole. You wouldn't want to remove the "ing" ending from "sing" or you'd end up with a single-letter "s."

Or imagine trying to discriminate between a pluralizing "s" at the end of a word like "words" and a normal "s" at the end of words like "bus" and "lens." Do isolated individual letters in a word or parts of a word provide any information at all about that word's meaning? Can the letters be misleading? Yes and yes.

In this chapter we show you how to make your NLP pipeline a bit smarter by dealing with these word spelling challenges using conventional stemming approaches. Later, in chapter 5, we show you statistical clustering approaches that only require you to amass a collection of natural language text containing the words you're interested in. From that collection of text, the statistics of word usage will reveal "semantic stems" (actually, more useful clusters of words like lemmas or synonyms), without any hand-crafted regular expressions or stemming rules.

## 2.2 *Building your vocabulary with a tokenizer*

In NLP, *tokenization* is a particular kind of document segmentation. *Segmentation* breaks up text into smaller chunks or segments, with more focused information content. Segmentation can include breaking a document into paragraphs, paragraphs into sentences, sentences into phrases, or phrases into tokens (usually words) and punctuation. In this chapter, we focus on segmenting text into *tokens*, which is called tokenization.

You may have heard of tokenizers before, if you took a computer science class where you learned about how compilers work. A tokenizer used for compiling computer languages is often called a *scanner* or *lexer*. The vocabulary (the set of all the valid tokens) for a computer language is often called a *lexicon*, and that term is still used in academic articles about NLP. If the tokenizer is incorporated into the computer language compiler's parser, the parser is often called a scannerless parser. And tokens are the end of the line for the context-free grammars (CFG) used to parse computer languages. They are called *terminals* because they terminate a path from the root to the leaf in CFG. You'll learn more about *formal* grammars like CFGs and regular expressions in chapter 11 when you will use them to match patterns and extract information from natural language.

For the fundamental building blocks of NLP, there are equivalents in a computer language compiler:

- *tokenizer*—scanner, lexer, lexical analyzer
- *vocabulary*—lexicon
- *parser*—compiler
- *token, term, word,* or *n-gram*—token, symbol, or terminal symbol

Tokenization is the first step in an NLP pipeline, so it can have a big impact on the rest of your pipeline. A tokenizer breaks unstructured data, natural language text, into chunks of information that can be counted as discrete elements. These counts of token occurrences in a document can be used directly as a vector representing that document. This immediately turns an unstructured string (text document) into a numerical data structure suitable for machine learning. These counts can be used directly by a computer to trigger useful actions and responses. Or they might also be used in a machine learning pipeline as features that trigger more complex decisions or behavior. The most common use for bag-of-words vectors created this way is for document retrieval, or search.

The simplest way to tokenize a sentence is to use whitespace within a string as the "delimiter" of words. In Python, this can be accomplished with the standard library method `split`, which is available on all `str` object instances as well as on the `str` built-in class itself. See the following listing and figure 2.1 for an example.

---

**Listing 2.1   Example Monticello sentence split into tokens**

```
>>> sentence = """Thomas Jefferson began building Monticello at the
...     age of 26."""
>>> sentence.split()
['Thomas',
 'Jefferson',
 'began',
 'building',
 'Monticello',
 'at',
 'the',
 'age',
 'of',
 '26.']
>>> str.split(sentence)
['Thomas',
 'Jefferson',
 'began',
 'building',
 'Monticello',
 'at',
 'the',
 'age',
 'of',
 '26.']
```

Thomas | Jefferson | began | building | Monticello | at | the | age | of | 26.

**Figure 2.1   Tokenized phrase**

As you can see, this built-in Python method already does a decent job tokenizing a simple sentence. Its only "mistake" was on the last word, where it included the sentence-ending punctuation with the token "26." Normally you'd like tokens to be separated from neighboring punctuation and other meaningful tokens in a sentence. The token "26." is a perfectly fine representation of a floating point number 26.0, but that would make this token different than another word "26" that occurred elsewhere in the corpus in the middle of sentences or the word "26?" that might occur at the end of a question. A good tokenizer should strip off this extra character to create the word "26" as an equivalent class for the words "26," "26!", "26?", and "26." And a more accurate tokenizer would also output a separate token for any sentence-ending punctuation so that a sentence segmenter or sentence boundary detector can find the end of that sentence.

For now, let's forge ahead with your imperfect tokenizer. You'll deal with punctuation and other challenges later. With a bit more Python, you can create a numerical vector representation for each word. These vectors are called *one-hot vectors*, and soon you'll see why. A sequence of these one-hot vectors fully captures the original document text in a sequence of vectors, a table of numbers. That will solve the first problem of NLP, turning words into numbers:

**str.split () is your quick-and-dirty tokenizer.**

**Your vocabulary lists all the unique tokens (words) that you want to keep track of.**

```
>>> import numpy as np
>>> token_sequence = str.split(sentence)
>>> vocab = sorted(set(token_sequence))
>>> ', '.join(vocab)
'26., Jefferson, Monticello, Thomas, age, at, began, building, of, the'
>>> num_tokens = len(token_sequence)
>>> vocab_size = len(vocab)
>>> onehot_vectors = np.zeros((num_tokens,
...                            vocab_size), int)
>>> for i, word in enumerate(token_sequence):
...     onehot_vectors[i, vocab.index(word)] = 1
>>> ' '.join(vocab)
'26. Jefferson Monticello Thomas age at began building of the'
>>> onehot_vectors
array([[0, 0, 0, 1, 0, 0, 0, 0, 0, 0],
       [0, 1, 0, 0, 0, 0, 0, 0, 0, 0],
       [0, 0, 0, 0, 0, 0, 1, 0, 0, 0],
       [0, 0, 0, 0, 0, 0, 0, 1, 0, 0],
       [0, 0, 1, 0, 0, 0, 0, 0, 0, 0],
       [0, 0, 0, 0, 0, 1, 0, 0, 0, 0],
       [0, 0, 0, 0, 0, 0, 0, 0, 0, 1],
       [0, 0, 0, 0, 1, 0, 0, 0, 0, 0],
       [0, 0, 0, 0, 0, 0, 0, 0, 1, 0],
       [1, 0, 0, 0, 0, 0, 0, 0, 0, 0]])
```

**Sorted lexographically (lexically) so numbers come before letters, and capital letters come before lowercase letters.**

**For each word in the sentence, mark the column for that word in your vocabulary with a I.**

**The empty table is as wide as your count of unique vocabulary terms and as high as the length of your document, 10 rows by 10 columns.**

If you have trouble quickly reading all those ones and zeros, you're not alone. Pandas DataFrames can help make this a little easier on the eyes and more informative. Pandas wraps a 1D array with some helper functionality in an object called a `Series`. And Pandas is particularly handy with tables of numbers like lists of lists, 2D numpy arrays, 2D numpy matrices, arrays of arrays, dictionaries of dictionaries, and so on.

A `DataFrame` keeps track of labels for each column, allowing you to label each column in our table with the token or word it represents. A `DataFrame` can also keep track of labels for each row in the `DataFrame.index`, for speedy lookup. But this is usually just a consecutive integer for most applications. For now you'll use the default index of integers for the rows in your table of one-hot word vectors for this sentence about Thomas Jefferson, shown in the following listing.

**Listing 2.2  One-hot vector sequence for the Monticello sentence**

```
>>> import pandas as pd
>>> pd.DataFrame(onehot_vectors, columns=vocab)
    26.  Jefferson  Monticello  Thomas  age  at  began  building  of  the
0    0        0          0         1     0   0     0        0      0    0
1    0        1          0         0     0   0     0        0      0    0
2    0        0          0         0     0   0     1        0      0    0
3    0        0          0         0     0   0     0        1      0    0
4    0        0          1         0     0   0     0        0      0    0
5    0        0          0         0     0   1     0        0      0    0
6    0        0          0         0     0   0     0        0      0    1
7    0        0          0         0     1   0     0        0      0    0
8    0        0          0         0     0   0     0        0      1    0
9    1        0          0         0     0   0     0        0      0    0
```

One-hot vectors are super-sparse, containing only one nonzero value in each row vector. So we can make that table of one-hot row vectors even prettier by replacing zeros with blanks. Don't do this with any `DataFrame` you intend to use in your machine learning pipeline, because it'll create a lot of non-numerical objects within your numpy array, mucking up the math. But if you just want to see how this one-hot vector sequence is like a mechanical music box cylinder, or a player piano drum, the following listing can be a handy view of your data.

**Listing 2.3  Prettier one-hot vectors**

```
>>> df = pd.DataFrame(onehot_vectors, columns=vocab)
>>> df[df == 0] = ''
>>> df
   26. Jefferson Monticello Thomas age at began building of the
0                             1
1           1
2                                          1
3                                               1
4                   1
5                                    1
6                                                          1
7                           1
8                                                     1
9    1
```

In this representation of your one-sentence document, each row is a vector for a single word. The sentence has 10 words, all unique, and it doesn't reuse any words. The table has 10 columns (words in your vocabulary) and 10 rows (words in the document). A "1" in a column indicates a vocabulary word that was present at that position in the document. So if you wanted to know what the third word in a document was, you'd go to the third row in the table. And you'd look up at the column heading for the "1" value in the third row (the row labeled 2, because the row numbers start at 0). At the top of that column, the seventh column in the table, you can find the natural language representation of that word, "began."

Each row of the table is a binary row vector, and you can see why it's also called a one-hot vector: all but one of the positions (columns) in a row are 0 or blank. Only one column, or position in the vector, is "hot" ("1"). A one (1) means on, or hot. A zero (0) means off, or absent. And you can use the vector [0, 0, 0, 0, 0, 0, 1, 0, 0, 0] to represent the word "began" in your NLP pipeline.

One nice feature of this vector representation of words and tabular representation of documents is that no information is lost.[3] As long as you keep track of which words are indicated by which column, you can reconstruct the original document from this table of one-hot vectors. And this reconstruction process is 100% accurate, even though your tokenizer was only 90% accurate at generating the tokens you thought would be useful. As a result, one-hot word vectors like this are typically used in neural nets, sequence-to-sequence language models, and generative language models. They're a good choice for any model or NLP pipeline that needs to retain all the meaning inherent in the original text.

This one-hot vector table is like a recording of the original text. If you squint hard enough you might be able to imagine that the matrix of ones and zeros above is a player piano paper roll.[4] Or maybe it's the bumps on the metal drum of a music box.[5] The vocabulary key at the top tells the machine which "note" or word to play for each row in the sequence of words or piano music. Unlike a player piano, your mechanical word recorder and player is only allowed to use one "finger" at a time. It can only play one "note" or word at a time. It's one-hot. And each note or word is played for the same amount of "time" with a consistent pace. There's no variation in the spacing of the words.

But this is just one way of thinking of one-hot word vectors. You can come up with whatever mental model makes sense for you. The important thing is that you've turned a sentence of natural language words into a sequence of numbers, or vectors. Now you can have the computer read and do math on the vectors just like any other vector or list of numbers. This allows your vectors to be input into any natural language processing pipeline that requires this kind of vector.

You could also play a sequence of one-hot encoded vectors back if you want to generate text for a chat bot, just like a player piano might play a song for a less artificial audience. Now all you need to do is figure out how to build a player piano that can "understand" and combine those word vectors in new ways. Ultimately, you'd like your chatbot or NLP pipeline to play us, or say something, you haven't heard before. We get to that in chapters 9 and 10 when we talk about LSTM models, and similar neural networks.

---

[3] Except for the distinction between various white spaces that were "split" with your tokenizer. If you wanted to get the original document back, unless your tokenizer keeps track of the white spaces it discarded during tokenization, you can't. If your tokenizer didn't preserve that information, there's no way to tell whether a space or a newline or a tab or even nothing should be inserted at each position between words. But the information content of whitespace is low, negligible in most English documents. And many modern NLP parsers and tokenizers retain that whitespace information for you, if you ever need it.

[4] See the "Player piano" article on Wikipedia (https://en.wikipedia.org/wiki/Player_piano).

[5] See the web page titled "Music box" (https://en.wikipedia.org/wiki/Music_box).

This representation of a sentence in one-hot word vectors retains all the detail, grammar, and order of the original sentence. And you've successfully turned words into numbers that a computer can "understand." They are also a particular kind of number that computers like a lot: binary numbers. But this is a big table for a short sentence. If you think about it, you've expanded the file size that would be required to store your document. For a long document this might not be practical. Your document size (the length of the vector table) would grow to be huge. The English language contains at least 20,000 common words, millions if you include names and other proper nouns. And your one-hot vector representation requires a new table (matrix) for every document you want to process. This is almost like a raw "image" of your document. If you've done any image processing, you know that you need to do dimension reduction if you want to extract useful information from the data.

Let's run through the math to give you an appreciation for just how big and unwieldy these "player piano paper rolls" are. In most cases, the vocabulary of tokens you'll use in an NLP pipeline will be much more than 10,000 or 20,000 tokens. Sometimes it can be hundreds of thousands or even millions of tokens. Let's assume you have a million tokens in your NLP pipeline vocabulary. And let's say you have a meager 3,000 books with 3,500 sentences each and 15 words per sentence—reasonable averages for short books. That's a whole lot of big tables (matrices):

```
>>> num_rows = 3000 * 3500 * 15          Number of rows
>>> num_rows                         ◄──┘ in the table
157500000
>>> num_bytes = num_rows * 1000000        Number of bytes, if you use only one
>>> num_bytes                        ◄──┘ byte for each cell in your table
157500000000000
>>> num_bytes / 1e9
157500  # gigabytes
>>> _ / 1000      ◄──
157.5  # terabytes    In a python interactive console, the variable name "_" is
                      automatically assigned the value of the previous output. This is handy
                      if you forget to explicitly assign the output of a function or expression
                      to a variable name like you did for num_bytes and num_rows.
```

You're talking more than a million million bits, even if you use a single bit for each cell in your matrix. At one bit per cell, you'd need nearly 20 terabytes of storage for a small bookshelf of books processed this way. Fortunately, you don't ever use this data structure for storing documents. You only use it temporarily, in RAM, while you're processing documents one word at a time.

So storing all those zeros, and trying to remember the order of the words in all your documents, doesn't make much sense. It's not practical. And what you really want to do is compress the meaning of a document down to its essence. You'd like to compress your document down to a single vector rather than a big table. And you're willing to give up perfect "recall." You just want to capture most of the meaning (information) in a document, not all of it.

What if you split your documents into much shorter chunks of meaning, say sentences. And what if you assumed that most of the meaning of a sentence can be gleaned from just the words themselves. Let's assume you can ignore the order and grammar of the words, and jumble them all up together into a "bag," one bag for each sentence or short document. That turns out to be a reasonable assumption. Even for documents several pages long, a bag-of-words vector is still useful for summarizing the essence of a document. You can see that for your sentence about Jefferson, even after you sorted all the words lexically, a human can still guess what the sentence was about. So can a machine. You can use this new bag-of-words vector approach to compress the information content for each document into a data structure that's easier to work with.

If you summed all these one-hot vectors together, rather than "replaying" them one at a time, you'd get a bag-of-words vector. This is also called a word frequency vector, because it only counts the *frequency* of words, not their order. You could use this single vector to represent the whole document or sentence in a single, reasonable-length vector. It would only be as long as your vocabulary size (the number of unique tokens you want to keep track of).

Alternatively, if you're doing basic keyword search, you could *OR* the one-hot word vectors into a binary bag-of-words vector. And you could ignore a lot of words that wouldn't be interesting as search terms or keywords. This would be fine for a search engine index or the first filter for an information retrieval system. Search indexes only need to know the presence or absence of each word in each document to help you find those documents later.

Just like laying your arm on the piano, hitting all the notes (words) at once doesn't make for a pleasant, meaningful experience. Nonetheless this approach turns out to be critical to helping a machine "understand" a whole group of words as a unit. And if you limit your tokens to the 10,000 most important words, you can compress your numerical representation of your imaginary 3,500 sentence book down to 10 kilobytes, or about 30 megabytes for your imaginary 3,000-book corpus. One-hot vector sequences would require hundreds of gigabytes.

Fortunately, the words in your vocabulary are sparsely utilized in any given text. And for most bag-of-words applications, we keep the documents short; sometimes just a sentence will do. So rather than hitting all the notes on a piano at once, your bag-of-words vector is more like a broad and pleasant piano chord, a combination of notes (words) that work well together and contain meaning. Your chatbot can handle these chords even if there's a lot of "dissonance" from words in the same statement that aren't normally used together. Even dissonance (odd word usage) is useful information about a statement that a machine learning pipeline can make use of.

Here's how you can put the tokens into a binary vector indicating the presence or absence of a particular word in a particular sentence. This vector representation of a set of sentences could be "indexed" to indicate which words were used in which document. This index is equivalent to the index you find at the end of many textbooks, except that instead of keeping track of which page a word occurs on, you can keep track of the sentence (or the associated vector) where it occurred. Whereas a textbook index generally only cares about important words relevant to the subject of the book, you keep track of every single word (at least for now).

Here's what your single text document, the sentence about Thomas Jefferson, looks like as a binary bag-of-words vector:

```
>>> sentence_bow = {}
>>> for token in sentence.split():
...     sentence_bow[token] = 1
>>> sorted(sentence_bow.items())
[('26.', 1)
 ('Jefferson', 1),
 ('Monticello', 1),
 ('Thomas', 1),
 ('age', 1),
 ('at', 1),
 ('began', 1),
 ('building', 1),
 ('of', 1),
 ('the', 1)]
```

One thing you might notice is that Python's sorted() puts decimal numbers before characters, and capitalized words before lowercase words. This is the ordering of characters in the ASCII and Unicode character sets. Capital letters come before lowercase letters in the ASCII table. The order of your vocabulary is unimportant. As long as you are consistent across all the documents you tokenize this way, a machine learning pipeline will work equally well with any vocabulary order.

And you might also notice that using a dict (or any paired mapping of words to their 0/1 values) to store a binary vector shouldn't waste much space. Using a dictionary to represent your vector ensures that it only has to store a 1 when any one of the thousands, or even millions, of possible words in your dictionary appear in a particular document. You can see how it would be much less efficient to represent a bag of words as a continuous list of 0's and 1's with an assigned location in a "dense" vector for each of the words in a vocabulary of, say, 100,000 words. This dense binary vector representation of your "Thomas Jefferson" sentence would require 100 kB of storage. Because a dictionary "ignores" the absent words, the words labeled with a 0, the dictionary representation only requires a few bytes for each word in your 10-word sentence. And this dictionary could be made even more efficient if you represented each word as an integer pointer to each word's location within your lexicon—the list of words that makes up your vocabulary for a particular application.

So let's use an even more efficient form of a dictionary, a Pandas Series. And you'll wrap that up in a Pandas DataFrame so you can add more sentences to your binary vector "corpus" of texts about Thomas Jefferson. All this hand waving about gaps in the vectors and sparse versus dense bags of words should become clear as you add more sentences and their corresponding bag-of-words vectors to your DataFrame (table of vectors corresponding to texts in a corpus):

```
>>> import pandas as pd
>>> df = pd.DataFrame(pd.Series(dict([(token, 1) for token in
...     sentence.split()])), columns=['sent']).T
>>> df
      26. Jefferson Monticello Thomas age at began building of the
sent   1       1          1        1    1   1    1       1    1   1
```

Let's add a few more texts to your corpus to see how a DataFrame stacks up. A DataFrame indexes both the columns (documents) and rows (words) so it can be an "inverse index" for document retrieval, in case you want to find a Trivial Pursuit answer in a hurry.

---

**Listing 2.4   Construct a `DataFrame` of bag-of-words vectors**

```
>>> sentences = """Thomas Jefferson began building Monticello at the\
...     age of 26.\n"""
>>> sentences += """Construction was done mostly by local masons and\
...     carpenters.\n"""
>>> sentences += "He moved into the South Pavilion in 1770.\n"
>>> sentences += """Turning Monticello into a neoclassical masterpiece\
...     was Jefferson's obsession."""
>>> corpus = {}
>>> for i, sent in enumerate(sentences.split('\n')):
...     corpus['sent{}'.format(i)] = dict((tok, 1) for tok in
...         sent.split())
>>> df = pd.DataFrame.from_records(corpus).fillna(0).astype(int).T
>>> df[df.columns[:10]]
       1770.  26.  Construction  ...  Pavilion  South  Thomas
sent0      0    1             0  ...         0      0       1
sent1      0    0             1  ...         0      0       0
sent2      1    0             0  ...         1      1       0
sent3      0    0             0  ...         0      0       0
```

**This is the original sentence defined in listing 2.1.**

**This shows only the first 10 tokens (DataFrame columns), to avoid wrapping.**

**Normally you should use .splitlines() but here you explicitly add a single '\n' character to the end of each line/ sentence, so you need to explicitly split on this character.**

---

With a quick scan, you can see little overlap in word usage for these sentences. Among the first seven words in your vocabulary, only the word "Monticello" appears in more than one sentence. Now you need to be able to compute this overlap within your pipeline whenever you want to compare documents or search for similar documents. One way to check for the similarities between sentences is to count the number of overlapping tokens using a *dot product*.

### 2.2.1   Dot product

You'll use the dot product a lot in NLP, so make sure you understand what it is. Skip this section if you can already do dot products in your head.

The dot product is also called the *inner product* because the "inner" dimension of the two vectors (the number of elements in each vector) or matrices (the rows of the first matrix and the columns of the second matrix) must be the same, because that's where the products happen. This is analogous to an "inner join" on two relational database tables.

The dot product is also called the *scalar product* because it produces a single scalar value as its output. This helps distinguish it from the *cross product*, which produces a vector as its output. Obviously, these names reflect the shape of the symbols used to indicate the dot product ("·") and cross product ("×") in formal mathematical notation.

The scalar value output by the scalar product can be calculated by multiplying all the elements of one vector by all the elements of a second vector, and then adding up those normal multiplication products.

Here's a Python snippet you can run in your Pythonic head to make sure you understand what a dot product is.

---
**Listing 2.5   Example dot product calculation**

```
>>> v1 = pd.np.array([1, 2, 3])
>>> v2 = pd.np.array([2, 3, 4])
>>> v1.dot(v2)
20
>>> (v1 * v2).sum()              ◄──┐  Multiplication of numpy arrays is a
20                                   │  "vectorized" operation that is very efficient.
>>> sum([x1 * x2 for x1, x2 in zip(v1, v2)])   ◄──┐  You shouldn't iterate through
20                                                 │  vectors this way unless you want
                                                   │  to slow down your pipeline.
```

**TIP**   The dot product is equivalent to the *matrix product*, which can be accomplished in numpy with the `np.matmul()` function or the `@` operator. Since all vectors can be turned into Nx1 or 1xN matrices, you can use this shorthand operator on two column vectors (Nx1) by transposing the first one so their inner dimensions line up, like this: `v1.reshape(-1, 1).T @ v2.reshape(-1, 1)`, which outputs your scalar product within a 1x1 matrix: `array([[20]])`.

### 2.2.2   *Measuring bag-of-words overlap*

If we can measure the bag of words overlap for two vectors, we can get a good estimate of how similar they are in the words they use. And this is a good estimate of how similar they are in meaning. So let's use your newfound dot product understanding to estimate the bag-of-words vector overlap between some new sentences and the original sentence about Thomas Jefferson (`sent0`).

---
**Listing 2.6   Overlap of word counts for two bag-of-words vectors**

```
>>> df = df.T
>>> df.sent0.dot(df.sent1)
0
>>> df.sent0.dot(df.sent2)
1
>>> df.sent0.dot(df.sent3)
1
```

From this you can tell that one word was used in both `sent0` and `sent2`. Likewise one of the words in your vocabulary was used in both `sent0` and `sent3`. This overlap of words is a measure of their similarity. Interestingly, that oddball sentence, `sent1`, was the only sentence that did not mention Jefferson or Monticello directly, but used a completely different set of words to convey information about other anonymous people.

Here's one way to find the word that is shared by `sent0` and `sent3`, the word that gave you that last dot product of 1:

```
>>> [(k, v) for (k, v) in (df.sent0 & df.sent3).items() if v]
[('Monticello', 1)]
```

This is your first vector space model (VSM) of natural language documents (sentences). Not only are dot products possible, but other vector operations are defined for these bag-of-word vectors: addition, subtraction, OR, AND, and so on. You can even compute things such as Euclidean distance or the angle between these vectors. This representation of a document as a binary vector has a lot of power. It was a mainstay for document retrieval and search for many years. All modern CPUs have hardwired memory addressing instructions that can efficiently hash, index, and search a large set of binary vectors like this. Though these instructions were built for another purpose (indexing memory locations to retrieve data from RAM), they are equally efficient at binary vector operations for search and retrieval of text.

### 2.2.3 A token improvement

In some situations, other characters besides spaces are used to separate words in a sentence. And you still have that pesky period at the end of your "26." token. You need your tokenizer to split a sentence not just on whitespace, but also on punctuation such as commas, periods, quotes, semicolons, and even hyphens (dashes). In some cases you want these punctuation marks to be treated like words, as independent tokens. In other cases you may want to ignore them.

In the preceding example, the last token in the sentence was corrupted by a period at the end of "26." The trailing period can be misleading for the subsequent sections of an NLP pipeline, like stemming, where you would like to group similar words together using rules that rely on consistent word spellings. The following listing shows one way.

> **Listing 2.7  Tokenize the Monticello sentence with a regular expression**

```
>>> import re
>>> sentence = """Thomas Jefferson began building Monticello at the\
...     age of 26."""
>>> tokens = re.split(r'[ \s.,;!?]+', sentence)
>>> tokens
['Thomas',
 'Jefferson',
 'began',
 'building',
 'Monticello',
 'at',
 'the',
 'age',
 'of',
 '26',
 '']
```

**This splits the sentence on whitespace or punctuation that occurs at least once (note the '+' after the closing square bracket in the regular expression). See sidenote that follows.**

We promised we'd use more regular expressions. Hopefully they're starting to make a little more sense than they did when we first used them. If not, the following sidenote will walk you through each character of the regular expression. And if you want to dig even deeper, check out appendix B.

### HOW REGULAR EXPRESSIONS WORK

Here's how the regular expression in listing 2.7 works. The square brackets ([ and ]) are used to indicate a *character class*, a set of characters. The plus sign after the closing square bracket (]) means that a match must contain one or more of the characters inside the square brackets. The \s within the character class is a shortcut to a pre-defined character class that includes all whitespace characters like those created when you press the [space], [tab], and [return] keys. The character class r'[\s]' is equivalent to r' \t\n\r\x0b\x0c'. The six whitespace characters are space (' '), tab ('\t'), return ('\r'), newline ('\n'), and form-feed ('\f').

You didn't use any character ranges here, but you may want to later. A character range is a special kind of character class indicated within square brackets and a hyphen, like r'[a-z]' to match all lowercase letters. The character range r'[0-9]' matches any digit 0 through 9 and is equivalent to r'[0123456789]'. The regular expression r'[_a-zA-Z]' would match any underscore character ('_') or letter of the English alphabet (upper- or lowercase).

The hyphen (-) right after the opening square bracket is a bit of a quirk of regexes. You can't put a hyphen just anywhere inside your square brackets, because the regex parser may think you mean a character range like r'[0-9]'. To let it know that you really mean a literal hyphen character, you have to put it right after the open square bracket for the character class. So whenever you want to indicate an actual hyphen (dash) character in your character class, you need to make sure it's the first character, or you need to escape it with a backslash.

The re.split function goes through each character in the input string (the second argument, sentence) left to right looking for any matches based on the "program" in the regular expression (the first argument, r'[-\s.,;!?]+'). When it finds a match, it breaks the string right before that matched character and right after it, skipping over the matched character or characters. So the re.split line will work just like str.split, but it will work for any kind of character or multicharacter sequence that matches your regular expression.

The parentheses ("(" and ")") are used to group regular expressions just like they're used to group mathematical, Python, and most other programming language expressions. These parentheses force the regular expression to match the entire expression within the parentheses before moving on to try to match the characters that follow the parentheses.

### IMPROVED REGULAR EXPRESSION FOR SEPARATING WORDS

Let's compile our regular expression so that our tokenizer will run faster. Compiled regular expression objects are handy for a lot of reasons, not just speed.

### When to compile your regex patterns

The regular expression module in Python allows you to precompile regular expressions,[a] which you then can reuse across your code base. For example, you might have a regex that extracts phone numbers. You could use `re.compile()` to precompile the expression and pass it along as an argument to a function or class doing tokenization. This is rarely a speed advantage, because Python caches the compiled objects for the last `MAXCACHE=100` regular expressions. But if you have more than 100 different regular expressions at work, or you want to call methods of the regular expression rather than the corresponding `re` functions, `re.compile` can be useful:

```
>>> pattern = re.compile(r"([-\s.,;!?])+")
>>> tokens = pattern.split(sentence)
>>> tokens[-10:]  # just the last 10 tokens
['the', ' ', 'age', ' ', 'of', ' ', '26', '.', '']
```

---

[a] See stack overflow or the latest Python documentation for more details (http://stackoverflow.com/a/452143/623735).

This simple regular expression is helping to split off the period from the end of the token "26." However, you have a new problem. You need to filter the whitespace and punctuation characters you don't want to include in your vocabulary. See the following code and figure 2.2:

```
>>> sentence = """Thomas Jefferson began building Monticello at the\
...    age of 26."""
>>> tokens = pattern.split(sentence)
>>> [x for x in tokens if x and x not in '- \t\n.,;!?']
['Thomas',
 'Jefferson',
 'began',
 'building',
 'Monticello',
 'at',
 'the',
 'age',
 'of',
 '26']
```

> If you want practice with lambda and filter(), use list(filter(lambda x: x if x and x not in '- \t\n.,;!?' else None, tokens)).

Thomas | Jefferson | began | building | Monticello | at | the | age | of | 26 |.

**Figure 2.2  Tokenized phrase**

So the built-in Python `re` package seems to do just fine on this example sentence, as long as you are careful to filter out undesirable tokens. There's really no reason to look elsewhere for regular expression packages, except...

> **When to use the new regex module in Python**
>
> There's a new regular expression package called `regex` that will eventually replace the `re` package. It's completely backward compatible and can be installed with `pip` from pypi. It's useful new features include support for
>
> - Overlapping match sets
> - Multithreading
> - Feature-complete support for Unicode
> - Approximate regular expression matches (similar to TRE's `agrep` on UNIX systems)
> - Larger default MAXCACHE (500 regexes)
>
> Even though `regex` will eventually replace the `re` package and is completely backward compatible with `re`, for now you must install it as an additional package using a package manager such as pip:
>
> ```
> $ pip install regex
> ```
>
> You can find more information about the *regex* module on the PyPI website (https://pypi.python.org/pypi/regex).

As you can imagine, tokenizers can easily become complex. In one case, you might want to split based on periods, but only if the period isn't followed by a number, in order to avoid splitting decimals. In another case, you might not want to split after a period that is part of "smiley" emoticon symbol, such as in a Twitter message.

Several Python libraries implement tokenizers, each with its own advantages and disadvantages:

- *spaCy*—Accurate , flexible, fast, Python
- *Stanford CoreNLP*—More accurate, less flexible, fast, depends on Java 8
- *NLTK*—Standard used by many NLP contests and comparisons, popular, Python

NLTK and Stanford CoreNLP have been around the longest and are the most widely used for comparison of NLP algorithms in academic papers. Even though the Stanford CoreNLP has a Python API, it relies on the Java 8 CoreNLP backend, which must be installed and configured separately. So you can use the Natural Language Toolkit (NLTK) tokenizer here to get you up and running quickly; it will help you duplicate the results you see in academic papers and blog posts.

You can use the NLTK function `RegexpTokenizer` to replicate your simple tokenizer example like this:

```
>>> from nltk.tokenize import RegexpTokenizer
>>> tokenizer = RegexpTokenizer(r'\w+|$[0-9.]+|\S+')
>>> tokenizer.tokenize(sentence)
['Thomas',
 'Jefferson',
 'began',
 'building',
 'Monticello',
```

```
'at',
'the',
'age',
'of',
'26',
'.']
```

This tokenizer is a bit better than the one you used originally, because it ignores whitespace tokens. It also separates sentence-ending trailing punctuation from tokens that do not contain any other punctuation characters.

An even better tokenizer is the Treebank Word Tokenizer from the NLTK package. It incorporates a variety of common rules for English word tokenization. For example, it separates phrase-terminating punctuation (?!.;,) from adjacent tokens and retains decimal numbers containing a period as a single token. In addition it contains rules for English contractions. For example "don't" is tokenized as ["do", "n't"]. This tokenization will help with subsequent steps in the NLP pipeline, such as stemming. You can find all the rules for the Treebank Tokenizer at http://www.nltk.org/api/nltk.tokenize .html#module-nltk.tokenize.treebank. See the following code and figure 2.3:

```
>>> from nltk.tokenize import TreebankWordTokenizer
>>> sentence = """Monticello wasn't designated as UNESCO World Heritage\
...     Site until 1987."""
>>> tokenizer = TreebankWordTokenizer()
>>> tokenizer.tokenize(sentence)
['Monticello',
 'was',
 "n't",
 'designated',
 'as',
 'UNESCO',
 'World',
 'Heritage',
 'Site',
 'until',
 '1987',
 '.']
```

Monticello│was│n't│designated│as│UNESCO│World│Heritage│Site│until│1987│.

**Figure 2.3  Tokenized phrase**

### CONTRACTIONS

You might wonder why you would split the contraction wasn't into was and n't. For some applications, like grammar-based NLP models that use syntax trees, it's important to separate the words was and not to allow the syntax tree parser to have a consistent, predictable set of tokens with known grammar rules as its input. There are a variety of standard and nonstandard ways to contract words. By reducing contractions to their constituent words, a dependency tree parser or syntax parser only need be programmed to anticipate the various spellings of individual words rather than all possible contractions.

---

**Tokenize informal text from social networks such as Twitter and Facebook**

The NLTK library includes a tokenizer—`casual_tokenize`—that was built to deal with short, informal, emoticon-laced texts from social networks where grammar and spelling conventions vary widely.

The `casual_tokenize` function allows you to strip usernames and reduce the number of repeated characters within a token:

```
>>> from nltk.tokenize.casual import casual_tokenize
>>> message = """RT @TJMonticello Best day everrrrrrr at Monticello.\
...   Awesommmmmmeeeeeeee day :*)"""
>>> casual_tokenize(message)
['RT', '@TJMonticello',
 'Best', 'day','everrrrrrr', 'at', 'Monticello', '.',
 'Awesommmmmmeeeeeeee', 'day', ':*)']
>>> casual_tokenize(message, reduce_len=True, strip_handles=True)
['RT',
 'Best', 'day', 'everrr', 'at', 'Monticello', '.',
 'Awesommmeee', 'day', ':*)']
```

---

### 2.2.4   *Extending your vocabulary with n-grams*

Let's revisit that "ice cream" problem from the beginning of the chapter. Remember we talked about trying to keep "ice" and "cream" together:

> *I scream, you scream, we all scream for ice cream.*

But I don't know many people that scream for "cream." And nobody screams for "ice," unless they're about to slip and fall on it. So you need a way for your word-vectors to keep "ice" and "cream" together.

#### WE ALL GRAM FOR N-GRAMS

An *n*-gram is a sequence containing up to *n* elements that have been extracted from a sequence of those elements, usually a string. In general the "elements" of an *n*-gram can be characters, syllables, words, or even symbols like "A," "T," "G," and "C" used to represent a DNA sequence.[6]

In this book, we're only interested in *n*-grams of words, not characters.[7] So in this book, when we say 2-gram, we mean a pair of words, like "ice cream." When we say 3-gram, we mean a triplet of words like "beyond the pale" or "Johann Sebastian Bach"

---

[6] Linguistic and NLP techniques are often used to glean information from DNA and RNA. This site provides a list of nucleic acid symbols that can help you translate nucleic acid language into a human-readable language: "Nucleic Acid Sequence" (https://en.wikipedia.org/wiki/Nucleic_acid_sequence).

[7] You may have learned about trigram indexes in your database class or the documentation for PostgreSQL (`postgres`). But these are triplets of characters. They help you quickly retrieve fuzzy matches for strings in a massive database of strings using the "%," "~," and "*" symbols in SQL full text search queries.

or "riddle me this." *n*-grams don't have to mean something special together, like compound words. They merely have to be frequent enough together to catch the attention of your token counters.

Why bother with *n*-grams? As you saw earlier, when a sequence of tokens is vectorized into a bag-of-words vector, it loses a lot of the meaning inherent in the order of those words. By extending your concept of a token to include multiword tokens, *n*-grams, your NLP pipeline can retain much of the meaning inherent in the order of words in your statements. For example, the meaning-inverting word "not" will remain attached to its neighboring words, where it belongs. Without *n*-gram tokenization, it would be free floating. Its meaning would be associated with the entire sentence or document rather than its neighboring words. The 2-gram "was not" retains much more of the meaning of the individual words "not" and "was" than those 1-grams alone in a bag-of-words vector. A bit of the context of a word is retained when you tie it to its neighbor(s) in your pipeline.

In the next chapter, we show you how to recognize which of these *n*-grams contain the most information relative to the others, which you can use to reduce the number of tokens (*n*-grams) your NLP pipeline has to keep track of. Otherwise it would have to store and maintain a list of every single word sequence it came across. This prioritization of *n*-grams will help it recognize "Thomas Jefferson" and "ice cream," without paying particular attention to "Thomas Smith" or "ice shattered." In chapter 4, we associate word pairs, and even longer sequences, with their actual meaning, independent of the meaning of their individual words. But for now, you need your tokenizer to generate these sequences, these *n*-grams.

Let's use your original sentence about Thomas Jefferson to show what a 2-gram tokenizer should output, so you know what you're trying to build:

```
>>> tokenize_2grams("Thomas Jefferson began building Monticello at the\
...     age of 26.")
['Thomas Jefferson',
 'Jefferson began',
 'began building',
 'building Monticello',
 'Monticello at',
 'at the',
 'the age',
 'age of',
 'of 26']
```

I bet you can see how this sequence of 2-grams retains a bit more information than if you'd just tokenized the sentence into words. The later stages of your NLP pipeline will only have access to whatever tokens your tokenizer generates. So you need to let those later stages know that "Thomas" wasn't about "Isaiah Thomas" or the "Thomas & Friends" cartoon. *n*-grams are one of the ways to maintain context information as data passes through your pipeline.

Here's the original 1-gram tokenizer:

```
>>> sentence = """Thomas Jefferson began building Monticello at the\
...     age of 26."""
```

```
>>> pattern = re.compile(r"([-\s.,;!?])+")
>>> tokens = pattern.split(sentence)
>>> tokens = [x for x in tokens if x and x not in '- \t\n.,;!?']
>>> tokens
['Thomas',
 'Jefferson',
 'began',
 'building',
 'Monticello',
 'at',
 'the',
 'age',
 'of',
 '26']
```

And this is the *n*-gram tokenizer from `nltk` in action:

```
>>> from nltk.util import ngrams
>>> list(ngrams(tokens, 2))
[('Thomas', 'Jefferson'),
 ('Jefferson', 'began'),
 ('began', 'building'),
 ('building', 'Monticello'),
 ('Monticello', 'at'),
 ('at', 'the'),
 ('the', 'age'),
 ('age', 'of'),
 ('of', '26')]
>>> list(ngrams(tokens, 3))
[('Thomas', 'Jefferson', 'began'),
 ('Jefferson', 'began', 'building'),
 ('began', 'building', 'Monticello'),
 ('building', 'Monticello', 'at'),
 ('Monticello', 'at', 'the'),
 ('at', 'the', 'age'),
 ('the', 'age', 'of'),
 ('age', 'of', '26')]
```

> **TIP** In order to be more memory efficient, the `ngrams` function of the NLTK library returns a Python generator. Python generators are "smart" functions that behave like iterators, yielding only one element at a time instead of returning the entire sequence at once. This is useful within `for` loops, where the generator will load each individual item instead of loading the whole item list into memory. However, if you want to inspect all the returned *n*-grams at once, convert the generator to a list as you did in the earlier example. Keep in mind that you should only do this in an interactive session, not within a long-running task tokenizing large texts.

The *n*-grams are provided in the previous listing as tuples, but they can easily be joined together if you'd like all the tokens in your pipeline to be strings. This will allow the later stages of the pipeline to expect a consistent datatype as input, string sequences:

```
>>> two_grams = list(ngrams(tokens, 2))
>>> [" ".join(x) for x in two_grams]
```

```
['Thomas Jefferson',
 'Jefferson began',
 'began building',
 'building Monticello',
 'Monticello at',
 'at the',
 'the age',
 'age of',
 'of 26']
```

You might be able to sense a problem here. Looking at your earlier example, you can imagine that the token "Thomas Jefferson" will occur across quite a few documents. However the 2-grams "of 26" or even "Jefferson began" will likely be extremely rare. If tokens or *n*-grams are extremely rare, they don't carry any correlation with other words that you can use to help identify topics or themes that connect documents or classes of documents. So rare *n*-grams won't be helpful for classification problems. You can imagine that most 2-grams are pretty rare—even more so for 3- and 4-grams.

Because word combinations are rarer than individual words, your vocabulary size is exponentially approaching the number of *n*-grams in all the documents in your corpus. If your feature vector dimensionality exceeds the length of all your documents, your feature extraction step is counterproductive. It'll be virtually impossible to avoid overfitting a machine learning model to your vectors; your vectors have more dimensions than there are documents in your corpus. In chapter 3, you'll use document frequency statistics to identify *n*-grams so rare that they are not useful for machine learning. Typically, *n*-grams are filtered out that occur too infrequently (for example, in three or fewer different documents). This scenario is represented by the "rare token" filter in the coin-sorting machine of chapter 1.

Now consider the opposite problem. Consider the 2-gram "at the" in the previous phrase. That's probably not a rare combination of words. In fact it might be so common, spread among most of your documents, that it loses its utility for discriminating between the meanings of your documents. It has little predictive power. Just like words and other tokens, *n*-grams are usually filtered out if they occur too often. For example, if a token or *n*-gram occurs in more than 25% of all the documents in your corpus, you usually ignore it. This is equivalent to the "stop words" filter in the coin-sorting machine of chapter 1. These filters are as useful for *n*-grams as they are for individual tokens. In fact, they're even more useful.

### STOP WORDS

Stop words are common words in any language that occur with a high frequency but carry much less substantive information about the meaning of a phrase. Examples of some common stop words include[8]

- a, an
- the, this

---

[8] A more comprehensive list of stop words for various languages can be found in NLTK's corpora (https://raw.githubusercontent.com/nltk/nltk_data/gh-pages/packages/corpora/stopwords.zip).

- and, or
- of, on

Historically, stop words have been excluded from NLP pipelines in order to reduce the computational effort to extract information from a text. Even though the words themselves carry little information, the stop words can provide important relational information as part of an *n*-gram. Consider these two examples:

- `Mark reported to the CEO`
- `Suzanne reported as the CEO to the board`

In your NLP pipeline, you might create 4-grams such as `reported to the CEO` and `reported as the CEO`. If you remove the stop words from the 4-grams, both examples would be reduced to `"reported CEO"`, and you would lack the information about the professional hierarchy. In the first example, Mark could have been an assistant to the CEO, whereas in the second example Suzanne was the CEO reporting to the board. Unfortunately, retaining the stop words within your pipeline creates another problem: it increases the length of the *n*-grams required to make use of these connections formed by the otherwise meaningless stop words. This issue forces us to retain at least 4-grams if you want to avoid the ambiguity of the human resources example.

Designing a filter for stop words depends on your particular application. Vocabulary size will drive the computational complexity and memory requirements of all subsequent steps in the NLP pipeline. But stop words are only a small portion of your total vocabulary size. A typical stop word list has only 100 or so frequent and unimportant words listed in it. But a vocabulary size of 20,000 words would be required to keep track of 95% of the words seen in a large corpus of tweets, blog posts, and news articles.[9] And that's just for 1-grams or single-word tokens. A 2-gram vocabulary designed to catch 95% of the 2-grams in a large English corpus will generally have more than 1 million unique 2-gram tokens in it.

You may be worried that vocabulary size drives the required size of any training set you must acquire to avoid overfitting to any particular word or combination of words. And you know that the size of your training set drives the amount of processing required to process it all. However, getting rid of 100 stop words out of 20,000 isn't going to significantly speed up your work. And for a 2-gram vocabulary, the savings you'd achieve by removing stop words is minuscule. In addition, for 2-grams you lose a lot more information when you get rid of stop words arbitrarily, without checking for the frequency of the 2-grams that use those stop words in your text. For example, you might miss mentions of "The Shining" as a unique title and instead treat texts about that violent, disturbing movie the same as you treat documents that mention "Shining Light" or "shoe shining."

So if you have sufficient memory and processing bandwidth to run all the NLP steps in your pipeline on the larger vocabulary, you probably don't want to worry

---

[9] See the web page titled "Analysis of text data and Natural Language Processing" (http://rstudio-pubs-static.s3.amazonaws.com/41251_4c55dff8747c4850a7fb26fb9a969c8f.html).

about ignoring a few unimportant words here and there. And if you're worried about overfitting a small training set with a large vocabulary, there are better ways to select your vocabulary or reduce your dimensionality than ignoring stop words. Including stop words in your vocabulary allows the document frequency filters (discussed in chapter 3) to more accurately identify and ignore the words and *n*-grams with the least information content within your particular domain.

If you do decide to arbitrarily filter out a set of stop words during tokenization, a Python list comprehension is sufficient. Here you take a few stop words and ignore them when you iterate through your token list:

```
>>> stop_words = ['a', 'an', 'the', 'on', 'of', 'off', 'this', 'is']
>>> tokens = ['the', 'house', 'is', 'on', 'fire']
>>> tokens_without_stopwords = [x for x in tokens if x not in stop_words]
>>> print(tokens_without_stopwords)
['house', 'fire']
```

You can see that some words carry a lot more meaning than others. And you can lose more than half the words in some sentences without significantly affecting their meaning. You can often get your point across without articles, prepositions, or even forms of the verb "to be." Imagine someone doing sign language or in a hurry to write a note to themselves. Which words would they chose to always skip? That's how stop words are chosen.

To get a complete list of "canonical" stop words, NLTK is probably the most generally applicable list. See the following listing.

| Listing 2.8   NLTK list of stop words |
| --- |

```
>>> import nltk
>>> nltk.download('stopwords')
>>> stop_words = nltk.corpus.stopwords.words('english')
>>> len(stop_words)
153
>>> stop_words[:7]
['i', 'me', 'my', 'myself', 'we', 'our', 'ours']
>>> [sw for sw in stopwords if len(sw) == 1]
['i', 'a', 's', 't', 'd', 'm', 'o', 'y']
```

A document that dwells on the first person is pretty boring, and more importantly for you, has low information content. The NLTK package includes pronouns (not just first person ones) in its list of stop words. And these one-letter stop words are even more curious, but they make sense if you've used the NLTK tokenizer and Porter stemmer a lot. These single-letter tokens pop up a lot when contractions are split and stemmed using NLTK tokenizers and stemmers.

> **WARNING** The set of English stop words that sklearn uses is quite different from those in NLTK. At the time of this writing, sklearn has 318 stop words. Even NLTK upgrades its corpora periodically, including the stop words list.

When we reran listing 2.8 to count the NLTK stop words with `nltk` version 3.2.5 in Python 3.6, we got 179 stop words instead of 153 from an earlier version.

This is another reason to consider *not* filtering stop words. If you do, others may not be able to reproduce your results.

Depending on how much natural language information you want to discard ;), you can take the union or the intersection of multiple stop word lists for your pipeline. Here's a comparison of `sklearn` stop words (version 0.19.2) and `nltk` stop words (version 3.2.5).

---

**Listing 2.9   NLTK list of stop words**

```
>>> from sklearn.feature_extraction.text import\
...    ENGLISH_STOP_WORDS as sklearn_stop_words
>>> len(sklearn_stop_words)
318
>>> len(stop_words)
179
>>> len(stop_words.union(sklearn_stop_words))
378
>>> len(stop_words.intersection(sklearn_stop_words))
119
```

**NTLK's list contains 60 stop words that aren't in the larger sklearn set.**

**NLTK and sklearn agree on fewer than a third of their stop words (119 out of 378).**

### 2.2.5   *Normalizing your vocabulary*

So you've seen how important vocabulary size is to the performance of an NLP pipeline. Another vocabulary reduction technique is to normalize your vocabulary so that tokens that mean similar things are combined into a single, normalized form. Doing so reduces the number of tokens you need to retain in your vocabulary and also improves the association of meaning across those different "spellings" of a token or *n*-gram in your corpus. And as we mentioned before, reducing your vocabulary can reduce the likelihood of overfitting.

#### CASE FOLDING

Case folding is when you consolidate multiple "spellings" of a word that differ only in their capitalization. So why would we use case folding at all? Words can become case "denormalized" when they are capitalized because of their presence at the beginning of a sentence, or when they're written in ALL CAPS for emphasis. Undoing this denormalization is called *case normalization*, or more commonly, *case folding*. Normalizing word and character capitalization is one way to reduce your vocabulary size and generalize your NLP pipeline. It helps you consolidate words that are intended to mean the same thing (and be spelled the same way) under a single token.

However, some information is often communicated by capitalization of a word—for example, 'doctor' and 'Doctor' often have different meanings. Often capitalization is used to indicate that a word is a proper noun, the name of a person, place, or thing. You'll want to be able to recognize proper nouns as distinct from other words, if named entity recognition is important to your pipeline. However, if tokens aren't case normalized, your vocabulary will be approximately twice as large, consume twice as much memory and processing time, and might increase the amount of training data you need to label for your machine learning pipeline to converge to an accurate, general solution. Just as in any other machine learning pipeline, your labeled dataset used for training must be "representative" of the space of all possible feature vectors your model must deal with, including variations in capitalization. For 100,000-D bag-of-words vectors, you usually must have 100,000 labeled examples, and sometimes even more than that, to train a supervised machine learning pipeline without overfitting. In some situations, cutting your vocabulary size by half can be worth the loss of information content.

In Python, you can easily normalize the capitalization of your tokens with a list comprehension:

```
>>> tokens = ['House', 'Visitor', 'Center']
>>> normalized_tokens = [x.lower() for x in tokens]
>>> print(normalized_tokens)
['house', 'visitor', 'center']
```

And if you're certain that you want to normalize the case for an entire document, you can `lower()` the text string in one operation, before tokenization. But this will prevent advanced tokenizers that can split *camel case* words like "WordPerfect," "FedEx," or "stringVariableName."[10] Maybe you want WordPerfect to be it's own unique thing (token), or maybe you want to reminisce about a more perfect word processing era. It's up to you to decide when and how to apply case folding.

With case normalization, you are attempting to return these tokens to their "normal" state before grammar rules and their position in a sentence affected their capitalization. The simplest and most common way to normalize the case of a text string is to lowercase all the characters with a function like Python's built-in `str.lower()`.[11] Unfortunately this approach will also "normalize" away a lot of meaningful capitalization in addition to the less meaningful first-word-in-sentence capitalization you intended to normalize away. A better approach for case normalization is to lowercase only the first word of a sentence and allow all other words to retain their capitalization.

Lowercasing on the first word in a sentence preserves the meaning of proper nouns in the middle of a sentence, like "Joe" and "Smith" in "Joe Smith." And it properly groups words together that belong together, because they're only capitalized when they are at the beginning of a sentence, since they aren't proper nouns. This prevents "Joe" from being confused with "coffee" ("joe")[12] during tokenization. And

---

[10] See the web page titled "Camel case case" (https://en.wikipedia.org/wiki/Camel_case_case).

[11] We're assuming the behavior of `str.lower()` in Python 3. In Python 2, bytes (strings) could be lowercased by just shifting all alpha characters in the ASCII number (`ord`) space, but in Python 3 `str.lower` properly translates characters so it can handle embellished English characters (like the "acute accent" diactric mark over the e in resumé) as well as the particulars of capitalization in non-English languages.

[12] The trigram "cup of joe" (https://en.wiktionary.org/wiki/cup_of_joe) is slang for "cup of coffee."

this approach prevents the blacksmith connotation of "smith" being confused with the proper name "Smith" in a sentence like "A word smith had a cup of joe." Even with this careful approach to case normalization, where you lowercase words only at the start of a sentence, you will still introduce capitalization errors for the rare proper nouns that start a sentence. "Joe Smith, the word smith, with a cup of joe." will produce a different set of tokens than "Smith the word with a cup of joe, Joe Smith." And you may not want that. In addition, case normalization is useless for languages that don't have a concept of capitalization.

To avoid this potential loss of information, many NLP pipelines don't normalize for case at all. For many applications, the efficiency gain (in storage and processing) for reducing one's vocabulary size by about half is outweighed by the loss of information for proper nouns. But some information may be "lost" even without case normalization. If you don't identify the word "The" at the start of a sentence as a stop word, that can be a problem for some applications. Really sophisticated pipelines will detect proper nouns before selectively normalizing the case for words at the beginning of sentences that are clearly not proper nouns. You should implement whatever case normalization approach makes sense for your application. If you don't have a lot of "Smith's" and "word smiths" in your corpus, and you don't care if they get assigned to the same tokens, you can just lowercase everything. The best way to find out what works is to try several different approaches, and see which approach gives you the best performance for the objectives of your NLP project.

By generalizing your model to work with text that has odd capitalization, case normalization can reduce overfitting for your machine learning pipeline. Case normalization is particularly useful for a search engine. For search, normalization increases the number of matches found for a particular query. This is often called the "recall" performance metric for a search engine (or any other classification model).[13]

For a search engine without normalization, if you searched for "Age" you would get a different set of documents than if you searched for "age." "Age" would likely occur in phrases like "New Age" or "Age of Reason." In contrast, "age" would more likely occur in phrases like "at the age of" in your sentence about Thomas Jefferson. By normalizing the vocabulary in your search index (as well as the query), you can ensure that both kinds of documents about "age" are returned, regardless of the capitalization in the query from the user.

However, this additional recall accuracy comes at the cost of precision, returning many documents that the user may not be interested in. Because of this issue, modern search engines allow users to turn off normalization with each query, typically by quoting those words for which they want only exact matches returned. If you're building such a search engine pipeline, in order to accommodate both types of queries you will have to build two indexes for your documents: one with case-normalized *n*-grams, and another with the original capitalization.

---

[13] Check our appendix D to learn more about *precision* and *recall*. Here's a comparison of the recall of various search engines on the Webology site (http://www.webology.org/2005/v2n2/a12.html).

### STEMMING

Another common vocabulary normalization technique is to eliminate the small meaning differences of pluralization or possessive endings of words, or even various verb forms. This normalization, identifying a common stem among various forms of a word, is called stemming. For example, the words housing and houses share the same stem, house. Stemming removes suffixes from words in an attempt to combine words with similar meanings together under their common stem. A stem isn't required to be a properly spelled word, but merely a token, or label, representing several possible spellings of a word.

A human can easily see that "house" and "houses" are the singular and plural forms of the same noun. However, you need some way to provide this information to the machine. One of its main benefits is in the compression of the number of words whose meanings your software or language model needs to keep track of. It reduces the size of your vocabulary while limiting the loss of information and meaning, as much as possible. In machine learning this is referred to as dimension reduction. It helps generalize your language model, enabling the model to behave identically for all the words included in a stem. So, as long as your application doesn't require your machine to distinguish between "house" and "houses," this stem will reduce your programming or dataset size by half or even more, depending on the aggressiveness of the stemmer you chose.

Stemming is important for keyword search or information retrieval. It allows you to search for "developing houses in Portland" and get web pages or documents that use both the word "house" and "houses" and even the word "housing," because these words are all stemmed to the "hous" token. Likewise you might receive pages with the words "developer" and "development" rather than "developing," because all these words typically reduce to the stem "develop." As you can see, this is a "broadening" of your search, ensuring that you are less likely to miss a relevant document or web page. This broadening of your search results would be a big improvement in the "recall" score for how well your search engine is doing its job at returning all the relevant documents.[14]

But stemming could greatly reduce the "precision" score for your search engine, because it might return many more irrelevant documents along with the relevant ones. In some applications this "false-positive rate" (proportion of the pages returned that you don't find useful) can be a problem. So most search engines allow you to turn off stemming and even case normalization by putting quotes around a word or phrase. Quoting indicates that you only want pages containing the exact spelling of a phrase, such as "'Portland Housing Development software.'" That would return a different sort of document than one that talks about a "'a Portland software developer's house'". And there are times when you want to search for "Dr. House's calls" and not "dr house call," which might be the effective query if you used a stemmer on that query.

---

[14] Review appendix D if you've forgotten how to measure recall or visit the Wikipedia page to learn more (https://en.wikipedia.org/wiki/Precision_and_recall).

Here's a simple stemmer implementation in pure Python that can handle trailing S's:

```
>>> def stem(phrase):
...     return ' '.join([re.findall('^(.*ss|.*?)(s)?$',
...         word)[0][0].strip("'") for word in phrase.lower().split()])
>>> stem('houses')
'house'
>>> stem("Doctor House's calls")
'doctor house call'
```

The preceding stemmer function follows a few simple rules within that one short regular expression:

- If a word ends with more than one s, the stem is the word and the suffix is a blank string.
- If a word ends with a single s, the stem is the word without the s and the suffix is the s.
- If a word does not end on an s, the stem is the word and no suffix is returned.

The strip method ensures that some possessive words can be stemmed along with plurals.

This function works well for regular cases, but is unable to address more complex cases. For example, the rules would fail with words like `dishes` or `heroes`. For more complex cases like these, the NLTK package provides other stemmers.

It also doesn't handing the "housing" example from your "Portland Housing" search.

Two of the most popular stemming algorithms are the Porter and Snowball stemmers. The Porter stemmer is named for the computer scientist Martin Porter.[15] Porter is also responsible for enhancing the Porter stemmer to create the Snowball stemmer.[16] Porter dedicated much of his lengthy career to documenting and improving stemmers, due to their value in information retrieval (keyword search). These stemmers implement more complex rules than our simple regular expression. This enables the stemmer to handle the complexities of English spelling and word ending rules:

```
>>> from nltk.stem.porter import PorterStemmer
>>> stemmer = PorterStemmer()
>>> ' '.join([stemmer.stem(w).strip("'") for w in
...     "dish washer's washed dishes".split()])
'dish washer wash dish'
```

Notice that the Porter stemmer, like the regular expression stemmer, retains the trailing apostrophe (unless you explicitly strip it), which ensures that possessive words will be distinguishable from nonpossessive words. Possessive words are often proper

---

[15] See "An algorithm for suffix stripping," 1993 (http://www.cs.odu.edu/~jbollen/IR04/readings/readings5 .pdf) by M.F. Porter.

[16] See the web page titled "Snowball: A language for stemming algorithms" (http://snowball.tartarus.org/texts/ introduction.html).

nouns, so this feature can be important for applications where you want to treat names differently than other nouns.

---

### More on the Porter stemmer

Julia Menchavez has graciously shared her translation of Porter's original stemmer algorithm into pure Python (https://github.com/jedijulia/porter-stemmer/blob/master/stemmer.py). If you are ever tempted to develop your own stemmer, consider these 300 lines of code and the lifetime of refinement that Porter put into them.

There are eight steps to the Porter stemmer algorithm: 1a, 1b, 1c, 2, 3, 4, 5a, and 5b. Step 1a is a bit like your regular expression for dealing with trailing S's:[a]

```python
def step1a(self, word):
    if word.endswith('sses'):
        word = self.replace(word, 'sses', 'ss')   ◁── This isn't at all like
    elif word.endswith('ies'):                         str.replace(). Julia's
        word = self.replace(word, 'ies', 'i')          self.replace() modifies only
    elif word.endswith('ss'):                          the ending of a word.
        word = self.replace(word, 'ss', 'ss')
    elif word.endswith('s'):
        word = self.replace(word, 's', '')
    return word
```

The remainining seven steps are much more complicated because they have to deal with the complicated English spelling rules for the following:

- **Step 1a**—"s" and "es" endings
- **Step 1b**—"ed," "ing," and "at" endings
- **Step 1c**—"y" endings
- **Step 2**—"nounifying" endings such as "ational," "tional," "ence," and "able"
- **Step 3**—adjective endings such as "icate,"[b] "ful," and "alize"
- **Step 4**—adjective and noun endings such as "ive," "ible," "ent," and "ism"
- **Step 5a**—stubborn "e" endings, still hanging around
- **Step 5b**—trailing double consonants for which the stem will end in a single "l"

---

[a] This is a trivially abbreviated version of Julia Menchavez's implementation of `porter-stemmer` on GitHub (https://github.com/jedijulia/porter-stemmer/blob/master/stemmer.py).

[b] Sorry Chick. Porter doesn't like your `obsfucate` username ;).

---

### LEMMATIZATION

If you have access to information about connections between the meanings of various words, you might be able to associate several words together even if their spelling is quite different. This more extensive normalization down to the semantic root of a word—its lemma—is called lemmatization.

In chapter 12, we show how you can use lemmatization to reduce the complexity of the logic required to respond to a statement with a chatbot. Any NLP pipeline that wants to "react" the same for multiple different spellings of the same basic root word can benefit from a lemmatizer. It reduces the number of words you have to respond to, the dimensionality of your language model. Using it can make your model more general, but it can also make your model less precise, because it will treat all spelling variations of a given root word the same. For example "chat," "chatter," "chatty," "chatting," and perhaps even "chatbot" would all be treated the same in an NLP pipeline with lemmatization, even though they have different meanings. Likewise "bank," "banked," and "banking" would be treated the same by a stemming pipeline, despite the river meaning of "bank," the motorcycle meaning of "banked," and the finance meaning of "banking."

As you work through this section, think about words where lemmatization would drastically alter the meaning of a word, perhaps even inverting its meaning and producing the opposite of the intended response from your pipeline. This scenario is called *spoofing*—when someone intentionally tries to elicit the wrong response from a machine learning pipeline by cleverly constructing a difficult input.

Lemmatization is a potentially more accurate way to normalize a word than stemming or case normalization because it takes into account a word's meaning. A lemmatizer uses a knowledge base of word synonyms and word endings to ensure that only words that mean similar things are consolidated into a single token.

Some lemmatizers use the word's part of speech (POS) tag in addition to its spelling to help improve accuracy. The POS tag for a word indicates its role in the grammar of a phrase or sentence. For example, the noun POS is for words that refer to "people, places, or things" within a phrase. An adjective POS is for a word that modifies or describes a noun. A verb refers to an action. The POS of a word in isolation cannot be determined. The context of a word must be known for its POS to be identified. So some advanced lemmatizers can't be run-on words in isolation.

Can you think of ways you can use the part of speech to identify a better "root" of a word than stemming could? Consider the word `better`. Stemmers would strip the "er" ending from "better" and return the stem "bett" or "bet." However, this would lump the word "better" with words like "betting," "bets," and "Bet's," rather than more similar words like "betterment," "best," or even "good" and "goods."

So lemmatizers are better than stemmers for most applications. Stemmers are only really used in large-scale information retrieval applications (keyword search). And if you really want the dimension reduction and recall improvement of a stemmer in your information retrieval pipeline, you should probably also use a lemmatizer right before the stemmer. Because the lemma of a word is a valid English word, stemmers work well on the output of a lemmatizer. This trick will reduce your dimensionality and increase your information retrieval recall even more than a stemmer alone.[17]

How can you identify word lemmas in Python? The NLTK package provides functions for this. Notice that you must tell the WordNetLemmatizer which part of speech your are interested in, if you want to find the most accurate lemma:

---

[17] Thank you Kyle Gorman for pointing this out.

```
>>> nltk.download('wordnet')
>>> from nltk.stem import WordNetLemmatizer
>>> lemmatizer = WordNetLemmatizer()
>>> lemmatizer.lemmatize("better")          ⊲───┐  The default part of speech
'better'                                           is "n" for noun.
>>> lemmatizer.lemmatize("better", pos="a")  ⊲──┐  "a" indicates the adjective
'good'                                            │  part of speech.
>>> lemmatizer.lemmatize("good", pos="a")
'good'
>>> lemmatizer.lemmatize("goods", pos="a")
'goods'
>>> lemmatizer.lemmatize("goods", pos="n")
'good'
>>> lemmatizer.lemmatize("goodness", pos="n")
'goodness'
>>> lemmatizer.lemmatize("best", pos="a")
'best'
```

You might be surprised that the first attempt to lemmatize the word "better" didn't change it at all. This is because the part of speech of a word can have a big effect on its meaning. If a POS isn't specified for a word, then the NLTK lemmatizer assumes it's a noun. Once you specify the correct POS, "a" for adjective, the lemmatizer returns the correct lemma. Unfortunately, the NLTK lemmatizer is restricted to the connections within the Princeton WordNet graph of word meanings. So the word "best" doesn't lemmatize to the same root as "better." This graph is also missing the connection between "goodness" and "good." A Porter stemmer, on the other hand, would make this connection by blindly stripping off the "ness" ending of all words:

```
>>> stemmer.stem('goodness')
'good'
```

### USE CASES

When should you use a lemmatizer or a stemmer? Stemmers are generally faster to compute and require less-complex code and datasets. But stemmers will make more errors and stem a far greater number of words, reducing the information content or meaning of your text much more than a lemmatizer would. Both stemmers and lemmatizers will reduce your vocabulary size and increase the ambiguity of the text. But lemmatizers do a better job retaining as much of the information content as possible based on how the word was used within the text and its intended meaning. Therefore, some NLP packages, such as spaCy, don't provide stemming functions and only offer lemmatization methods.

If your application involves search, stemming and lemmatization will improve the recall of your searches by associating more documents with the same query words. However, stemming, lemmatization, and even case folding will significantly reduce the precision and accuracy of your search results. These vocabulary compression approaches will cause an information retrieval system (search engine) to return many documents not relevant to the words' original meanings. Because search results can be ranked according to relevance, search engines and document indexes often use stemming or lemmatization to increase the likelihood that the search results include the documents a user is looking for. But they combine search results for stemmed and unstemmed versions of words to rank the search results that they present to you.[18]

For a search-based chatbot, however, accuracy is more important. As a result, a chatbot should first search for the closest match using unstemmed, unnormalized words before falling back to stemmed or filtered token matches to find matches. It should rank such matches of normalized tokens lower than the unnormalized token matches.

> **IMPORTANT**  Bottom line, try to avoid stemming and lemmatization unless you have a limited amount of text that contains usages and capitalizations of the words you are interested in. And with the explosion of NLP datasets, this is rarely the case for English documents, unless your documents use a lot of jargon or are from a very small subfield of science, technology, or literature. Nonetheless, for languages other than English, you may still find uses for lemmatization. The Stanford information retrieval course dismisses stemming and lemmatization entirely, due to the negligible recall accuracy improvement and the significant reduction in precision.[19]

## 2.3    Sentiment

Whether you use raw single-word tokens, *n*-grams, stems, or lemmas in your NLP pipeline, each of those tokens contains some information. An important part of this information is the word's sentiment—the overall feeling or emotion that the word invokes. This *sentiment analysis*—measuring the sentiment of phrases or chunks of text—is a common application of NLP. In many companies it's the main thing an NLP engineer is asked to do.

Companies like to know what users think of their products. So they often will provide some way for you to give feedback. A star rating on Amazon or Rotten Tomatoes is one way to get quantitative data about how people feel about products they've purchased. But a more natural way is to use natural language comments. Giving your user a blank slate (an empty text box) to fill up with comments about your product can produce more detailed feedback.

In the past you'd have to read all that feedback. Only a human can understand something like emotion and sentiment in natural language text, right? However, if you had to read thousands of reviews you'd see how tedious and error-prone a human reader can be. Humans are remarkably bad at reading feedback, especially criticism or negative feedback. And customers generally aren't very good at communicating feedback in a way that can get past your natural human triggers and filters.

---

[18] Additional metadata is also used to adjust the ranking of search results. Duck Duck Go and other popular web search engines combine more than 400 independent algorithms (including user-contributed algorithms) to rank your search results (https://duck.co/help/results/sources).

[19] See the web page titled "Stemming and lemmatization" (https://nlp.stanford.edu/IR-book/html/htmledition/stemming-and-lemmatization-1.html).

But machines don't have those biases and emotional triggers. And humans aren't the only things that can process natural language text and extract information, and even meaning, from it. An NLP pipeline can process a large quantity of user feedback quickly and objectively, with less chance for bias. And an NLP pipeline can output a numerical rating of the positivity or negativity or any other emotional quality of the text.

Another common application of sentiment analysis is junk mail and troll message filtering. You'd like your chatbot to be able to measure the sentiment in the chat messages it processes so it can respond appropriately. And even more importantly, you want your chatbot to measure its own sentiment of the statements it's about to send out, which you can use to steer your bot to be kind and pro-social with the statements it makes. The simplest way to do this might be to do what Moms told us to do: if you can't say something nice, don't say anything at all. So you need your bot to measure the niceness of everything you're about to say and use that to decide whether to respond.

What kind of pipeline would you create to measure the sentiment of a block of text and produce this sentiment positivity number? Say you just want to measure the positivity or favorability of a text—how much someone likes a product or service that they are writing about. Say you want your NLP pipeline and sentiment analysis algorithm to output a single floating point number between -1 and +1. Your algorithm would output +1 for text with positive sentiment like, "Absolutely perfect! Love it! :-) :-) :-)." And your algorithm should output -1 for text with negative sentiment like, "Horrible! Completely useless. :(." Your NLP pipeline could use values near 0, like say +0.1, for a statement like, "It was OK. Some good and some bad things."

There are two approaches to sentiment analysis:

- A rule-based algorithm composed by a human
- A *machine learning* model learned from data by a machine

The first approach to sentiment analysis uses human-designed rules, sometimes called *heuristics*, to measure sentiment. A common rule-based approach to sentiment analysis is to find keywords in the text and map each one to numerical scores or weights in a dictionary or "mapping"—a Python `dict`, for example. Now that you know how to do tokenization, you can use stems, lemmas, or *n*-gram tokens in your dictionary, rather than just words. The "rule" in your algorithm would be to add up these scores for each keyword in a document that you can find in your dictionary of sentiment scores. Of course you need to hand-compose this dictionary of keywords and their sentiment scores before you can run this algorithm on a body of text. We show you how to do this using the VADER algorithm (in `sklearn`) in the upcoming code.

The second approach, machine learning, relies on a labeled set of statements or documents to train a machine learning model to create those rules. A machine learning sentiment model is trained to process input text and output a numerical value for the sentiment you are trying to measure, like positivity or spamminess or trolliness. For the machine learning approach, you need a lot of data, text labeled with the "right" sentiment score. Twitter feeds are often used for this approach because the hash tags, such as #awesome or #happy or #sarcasm, can often be used to create a "self-labeled" dataset. Your company may have product reviews with five-star ratings that you could associate with reviewer comments. You can use the star ratings as a numerical score for the positivity of each text. We show you shortly how to process a dataset like this and train a token-based machine learning algorithm called *Naive Bayes* to measure the positivity of the sentiment in a set of reviews after you're done with VADER.

### 2.3.1 *VADER—A rule-based sentiment analyzer*

Hutto and Gilbert at GA Tech came up with one of the first successful rule-based sentiment analysis algorithms. They called their algorithm VADER, for **V**alence **A**ware **D**ictionary for s**E**ntiment **R**easoning.[20] Many NLP packages implement some form of this algorithm. The NLTK package has an implementation of the VADER algorithm in nltk.sentiment.vader. Hutto himself maintains the Python package vaderSentiment. You'll go straight to the source and use vaderSentiment here.

You'll need to pip install vaderSentiment to run the following example.[21] We haven't included it in the nlpia package:

> **SentimentIntensityAnalyzer.lexicon contains that dictionary of tokens and their scores that we talked about.**

```
>>> from vaderSentiment.vaderSentiment import SentimentIntensityAnalyzer
>>> sa = SentimentIntensityAnalyzer()
>>> sa.lexicon
{ ...
':(': -1.9,
':)': 2.0,
...
'pls': 0.3,
'plz': 0.3,
...
'great': 3.1,
... }
>>> [(tok, score) for tok, score in sa.lexicon.items()
...    if " " in tok]
[("( '}{' )", 1.6),
 ("can't stand", -2.0),
 ('fed up', -1.8),
 ('screwed up', -1.5)]
>>> sa.polarity_scores(text=\
...    "Python is very readable and it's great for NLP.")
{'compound': 0.6249, 'neg': 0.0, 'neu': 0.661,
'pos': 0.339}
>>> sa.polarity_scores(text=\
```

> **A tokenizer better be good at dealing with punctuation and emoticons (emojis) for VADER to work well. After all, emoticons are designed to convey a lot of sentiment (emotion).**

> **If you use a stemmer (or lemmatizer) in your pipeline, you'll need to apply that stemmer to the VADER lexicon, too, combining the scores for all the words that go together in a single stem or lemma.**

> **Out of 7500 tokens defined in VADER, only 3 contain spaces, and only 2 of those are actually *n*-grams; the other is an emoticon for "kiss."**

> **The VADER algorithm considers the intensity of sentiment polarity in three separate scores (positive, negative, and neutral) and then combines them together into a compound positivity sentiment.**

---

[20] "VADER: A Parsimonious Rule-based Model for Sentiment Analysis of Social Media Text" by Hutto and Gilbert (http://comp.social.gatech.edu/papers/icwsm14.vader.hutto.pdf)

[21] You can find more detailed installation instructions with the package source code on github (https://github.com/cjhutto/vaderSentiment).

```
...     "Python is not a bad choice for most applications.")
{'compound': 0.431, 'neg': 0.0, 'neu': 0.711,
'pos': 0.289}
```

← **Notice that VADER handles negation pretty well—"great" has a slightly more positive sentiment than "not bad." VADER's built-in tokenizer ignores any words that aren't in its lexicon, and it doesn't consider *n*-grams at all.**

Let's see how well this rule-based approach does for the example statements we mentioned earlier:

```
>>> corpus = ["Absolutely perfect! Love it! :-) :-) :-)",
...           "Horrible! Completely useless. :(",
...           "It was OK. Some good and some bad things."]
>>> for doc in corpus:
...     scores = sa.polarity_scores(doc)
...     print('{:+}: {}'.format(scores['compound'], doc))
+0.9428: Absolutely perfect! Love it! :-) :-) :-)
-0.8768: Horrible! Completely useless. :(
+0.3254: It was OK. Some good and some bad things.
```

This looks a lot like what you wanted. So the only drawback is that VADER doesn't look at all the words in a document, only about 7,500. What if you want all the words to help add to the sentiment score? And what if you don't want to have to code your own understanding of the words in a dictionary of thousands of words or add a bunch of custom words to the dictionary in `SentimentIntensityAnalyzer.lexicon`? The rule-based approach might be impossible if you don't understand the language, because you wouldn't know what scores to put in the dictionary (lexicon)!

That's what machine learning sentiment analyzers are for.

### 2.3.2 Naïve Bayes

A Naïve Bayes model tries to find keywords in a set of documents that are predictive of your target (output) variable. When your target variable is the sentiment you are trying to predict, the model will find words that predict that sentiment. The nice thing about a Naïve Bayes model is that the internal coefficients will map words or tokens to scores just like VADER does. Only this time you won't have to be limited to just what an individual human decided those scores should be. The machine will find the "best" scores for any problem.

For any machine learning algorithm, you first need to find a dataset. You need a bunch of text documents that have labels for their positive emotional content (positivity sentiment). Hutto compiled four different sentiment datasets for us when he and his collaborators built VADER. You'll load them from the `nlpia` package:[22]

```
>>> from nlpia.data.loaders import get_data
>>> movies = get_data('hutto_movies')
```

---

[22] If you haven't already installed `nlpia`, check out the installation instructions at http://github.com/totalgood/nlpia.

```
>>> movies.head().round(2)
    sentiment                                                    text
id
1        2.27  The Rock is destined to be the 21st Century...
2        3.53  The gorgeously elaborate continuation of ''...
3       -0.60                          Effective but too tepid ...
4        1.47  If you sometimes like to go to the movies t...
5        1.73  Emerges as something rare, an issue movie t...
>>> movies.describe().round(2)
       sentiment
count  10605.00
mean       0.00
min       -3.88
max        3.94
```

> It looks like movies were rated
> on a scale from -4 to +4.

Now let's tokenize all those movie review texts to create a bag of words for each one. You'll put them all into a Pandas DataFrame like you did earlier in this chapter:

**This line helps display wide DataFrames in the console so they look prettier.**

**NLTK's casual_tokenize can handle emoticons, unusual punctuation, and slang better than Treebank Word Tokenizer or the other tokenizers in this chapter.**

**The Python built-in Counter takes a list of objects and counts them, returning a dictionary where the keys are the objects (tokens in your case) and the values are the integer counts of those objects.**

```
>>> import pandas as pd
>>> pd.set_option('display.width', 75)
>>> from nltk.tokenize import casual_tokenize
>>> bags_of_words = []
>>> from collections import Counter
>>> for text in movies.text:
...     bags_of_words.append(Counter(casual_tokenize(text)))
>>> df_bows = pd.DataFrame.from_records(bags_of_words)
>>> df_bows = df_bows.fillna(0).astype(int)
>>> df_bows.shape
(10605, 20756)
>>> df_bows.head()
   !  "  #  $  %  &  '  ...  zone  zoning  zzzzzzzzz  ½  élan  –  '
0  0  0  0  0  0  0  4  ...     0       0          0  0     0  0  0
1  0  0  0  0  0  0  4  ...     0       0          0  0     0  0  0
2  0  0  0  0  0  0  0  ...     0       0          0  0     0  0  0
3  0  0  0  0  0  0  0  ...     0       0          0  0     0  0  0
4  0  0  0  0  0  0  0  ...     0       0          0  0     0  0  0
>>> df_bows.head()[list(bags_of_words[0].keys())]
   The  Rock  is  destined  to  be  ...  Van  Damme  or  Steven  Segal  .
0    1     1   1         1   2   1  ...    1      1   1       1      1  1
1    2     0   1         0   0   0  ...    0      0   0       0      0  4
2    0     0   0         0   0   0  ...    0      0   0       0      0  0
3    0     0   1         0   4   0  ...    0      0   0       0      0  1
4    0     0   0         0   0   0  ...    0      0   0       0      0  1
```

**A bag-of-words table can grow quite large quickly, especially when you don't use case normalization, stop word filters, stemming, and lemmatization, which we discussed earlier in this chapter. Try inserting some of these dimension reducers here and see how they affect your pipeline.**

**Numpy and Pandas can only represent NaNs in float objects, so once you fill all the NaNs with zeros you can convert the DataFrame to integers, which are much more compact (in memory and to display).**

**The from_records() DataFrame constructor takes a sequence of dictionaries. It creates columns for all the keys, and the values are added to the table in the appropriate columns, filling missing values with NaN.**

Now you have all the data that a Naive Bayes model needs to find the keywords that predict sentiment from natural language text:

> Naive Bayes models are classifiers, so you need to convert your output variable (sentiment float) to a discrete label (integer, string, or bool).

> Convert your binary classification variable (0 or 1) to -4 or 4 so you can compare it to the "ground truth" sentiment. Use nb.predict_proba to get a continuous value.

```
>>> from sklearn.naive_bayes import MultinomialNB
>>> nb = MultinomialNB()
>>> nb = nb.fit(df_bows, movies.sentiment > 0)
>>> movies['predicted_sentiment'] =\
...     nb.predict_proba(df_bows) * 8 - 4
>>> movies['error'] = (movies.predicted_sentiment - movies.sentiment).abs()
>>> movies.error.mean().round(1)
2.4
>>> movies['sentiment_ispositive'] = (movies.sentiment > 0).astype(int)
>>> movies['predicted_ispositiv'] = (movies.predicted_sentiment > 0).astype(int)
>>> movies['''sentiment predicted_sentiment sentiment_ispositive\
...     predicted_ispositive'''.split()].head(8)
    sentiment  predicted_sentiment  sentiment_ispositive  predicted_ispositive
id
1    2.266667                    4                     1                     1
2    3.533333                    4                     1                     1
3   -0.600000                   -4                     0                     0
4    1.466667                    4                     1                     1
5    1.733333                    4                     1                     1
6    2.533333                    4                     1                     1
7    2.466667                    4                     1                     1
8    1.266667                   -4                     1                     0
>>> (movies.predicted_ispositive ==
...     movies.sentiment_ispositive).sum() / len(movies)
0.9344648750589345
```

You got the "thumbs up" rating correct 93% of the time.

The average absolute value of the prediction error (mean absolute error or MAE) is 2.4.

This is a pretty good start at building a sentiment analyzer with only a few lines of code (and a lot of data). You didn't have to compile a list of 7500 words and their sentiment like VADER did. You just gave it a bunch of text and labels for that text. That's the power of machine learning and NLP!

How well do you think it will work on a completely different set of sentiment scores, like for product reviews instead of movie reviews?

If you want to build a real sentiment analyzer like this, remember to split your training data (and leave out a test set—see appendix D for more on test/train splits). You forced your classifier to rate all the text as thumbs up or thumbs down, so a random guess would have had a MAP error of about 4. So you're about twice as good as a random guesser:

```
>>> products = get_data('hutto_products')
...     bags_of_words = []
>>> for text in products.text:
...     bags_of_words.append(Counter(casual_tokenize(text)))
```

**Your new bags of words have some tokens that weren't in the original bags of words DataFrame (23302 columns now instead of 20756 before).**

```
>>> df_product_bows = pd.DataFrame.from_records(bags_of_words)
>>> df_product_bows = df_product_bows.fillna(0).astype(int)
>>> df_all_bows = df_bows.append(df_product_bows)
>>> df_all_bows.columns                               ◄────────
Index(['!', '"', '#', '#38', '$', '%', '&', ''', '(', '(8',
       ...
       'zoomed', 'zooming', 'zooms', 'zx', 'zzzzzzzzz', '~', '½', 'élan',
       '–', '''],
      dtype='object', length=23302)
>>> df_product_bows = df_all_bows.iloc[len(movies):][df_bows.columns]   ◄─────
>>> df_product_bows.shape
(3546, 20756)              **This is the original**
>>> df_bows.shape     ◄──┘ **movie bags of words.**
(10605, 20756)
>>> products[ispos] =
➥ (products.sentiment > 0).astype(int)
>>> products['predicted_ispositive'] =
➥ nb.predict(df_product_bows.values).astype(int)
>>> products.head()
id   sentiment                                           text   ispos  pred
0    1_1       -0.90   troubleshooting ad-2500 and ad-2600 ...       0     0
1    1_2       -0.15   repost from january 13, 2004 with a ...       0     0
2    1_3       -0.20   does your apex dvd player only play ...       0     0
3    1_4       -0.10   or does it play audio and video but ...       0     0
4    1_5       -0.50   before you try to return the player ...       0     0
>>> (products.pred == products.ispos).sum() / len(products)
0.5572476029328821
```

**You need to make sure your new product DataFrame of bags of words has the exact same columns (tokens) in the exact same order as the original one used to train your Naive Bayes model.**

So your Naive Bayes model does a poor job of predicting whether a product review is positive (thumbs up). One reason for this subpar performance is that your vocabulary from the `casual_tokenize` product texts has 2546 tokens that weren't in the movie reviews. That's about 10% of the tokens in your original movie review tokenization, which means that all those words won't have any weights or scores in your Naive Bayes model. Also the Naive Bayes model doesn't deal with negation as well as VADER does. You'd need to incorporate *n*-grams into your tokenizer to connect negation words (such as "not" or "never") to the positive words they might be used to qualify.

We leave it to you to continue the NLP action by improving on this machine learning model. And you can check your progress relative to VADER at each step of the way to see if you think machine learning is a better approach than hard-coding algorithms for NLP.

## Summary

- You implemented tokenization and configured a tokenizer for your application.
- *n*-gram tokenization helps retain some of the *word order* information in a document.

- Normalization and stemming consolidate words into groups that improve the "recall" for search engines but reduce precision.
- Lemmatization and customized tokenizers like `casual_tokenize()` can improve precision and reduce information loss.
- Stop words can contain useful information, and discarding them is not always helpful.

# Math with words (TF-IDF vectors)

Having collected and counted words (tokens), and bucketed them into stems or lemmas, it's time to do something interesting with them. Detecting words is useful for simple tasks, like getting statistics about word usage or doing keyword search. But you'd like to know which words are more important to a particular document and across the corpus as a whole. Then you can use that "importance" value to find relevant documents in a corpus based on keyword importance within each document.

That will make a spam detector a little less likely to get tripped up by a single curse word or a few slightly-spammy words within an email. And you'd like to measure how positive and prosocial a tweet is when you have a broad range of words with various degrees of "positivity" scores or labels. If you have an idea about the frequency with which those words appear in a document *in relation to* the rest of the documents, you can use that to further refine the "positivity" of the document. In this chapter, you'll learn about a more nuanced, less binary measure of words and their usage within a document. This approach has been the mainstay for generating features from natural language for commercial search engines and spam filters for decades.

The next step in your adventure is to turn the words of chapter 2 into continuous numbers rather than just integers representing word counts or binary "bit vectors" that detect the presence or absence of particular words. With representations of words in a continuous space, you can operate on their representation with more exciting math. Your goal is to find numerical representation of words that somehow capture the importance or information content of the words they represent. You'll have to wait until chapter 4 to see how to turn this information content into numbers that represent the *meaning* of words.

In this chapter, we look at three increasingly powerful ways to represent words and their importance in a document:

- *Bags of words*—Vectors of word counts or frequencies
- *Bags of n-grams*—Counts of word pairs (bigrams), triplets (trigrams), and so on
- *TF-IDF vectors*—Word scores that better represent their importance

**IMPORTANT**  TF-IDF stands for *term frequency times inverse document frequency*. Term frequencies are the counts of each word in a document, which you learned about in previous chapters. Inverse document frequency means that you'll divide each of those word counts by the number of documents in which the word occurs.

Each of these techniques can be applied separately or as part of an NLP pipeline. These are all statistical models in that they are *frequency* based. Later in the book, you'll see various ways to peer even deeper into word relationships and their patterns and non-linearities.

But these "shallow" NLP machines are powerful and useful for many practical applications such as spam filtering and sentiment analysis.

## 3.1 Bag of words

In the previous chapter, you created your first vector space model of a text. You used one-hot encoding of each word and then combined all those vectors with a binary OR (or clipped `sum`) to create a vector representation of a text. And this binary bag-of-words vector makes a great index for document retrieval when loaded into a data structure such as a Pandas DataFrame.

You then looked at an even more useful vector representation that counts the number of occurrences, or frequency, of each word in the given text. As a first approximation, you assume that the more times a word occurs, the more meaning it must contribute to that document. A document that refers to "wings" and "rudder" frequently may be more relevant to a problem involving jet airplanes or air travel, than say a document that refers frequently to "cats" and "gravity." Or if you have classified some words as expressing positive emotions—words like "good," "best," "joy," and "fantastic"—the more a document that contains those words is likely to have positive "sentiment." You can imagine though how an algorithm that relied on these simple rules might be mistaken or led astray.

Let's look at an example where counting occurrences of words is useful:

```
>>> from nltk.tokenize import TreebankWordTokenizer
>>> sentence = """The faster Harry got to the store, the faster Harry,
...     the faster, would get home."""
>>> tokenizer = TreebankWordTokenizer()
>>> tokens = tokenizer.tokenize(sentence.lower())
>>> tokens
['the',
 'faster',
 'harry',
 'got',
 'to',
 'the',
 'store',
 ',',
 'the',
 'faster',
 'harry',
 ',',
 'the',
 'faster',
 ',',
 'would',
 'get',
 'home',
 '.']
```

With your simple list, you want to get unique words from the document and their counts. A Python dictionary serves this purpose nicely, and because you want to count the words as well, you can use `Counter`, as you did in previous chapters:

```
>>> from collections import Counter
>>> bag_of_words = Counter(tokens)
>>> bag_of_words
Counter({'the': 4,
         'faster': 3,
         'harry': 2,
         'got': 1,
         'to': 1,
         'store': 1,
         ',': 3,
         'would': 1,
```

```
        'get': 1,
        'home': 1,
        '.': 1})
```

As with any good Python dictionary, the order of your keys got shuffled. The new order is optimized for storage, update, and retrieval, not consistent display. The information content contained in the order of words within the original statement has been discarded.

> **NOTE** A collections.Counter object is an unordered collection, also called a bag or multiset. Depending on your platform and Python version, you may find that a Counter is displayed in a seemingly reasonable order, like lexical order or the order that tokens appeared in your statement. But just as for a standard Python dict, you cannot rely on the order of your tokens (keys) in a Counter.

For short documents like this one, the unordered bag of words still contains a lot of information about the original intent of the sentence. And the information in a bag of words is sufficient to do some powerful things such as detect spam, compute sentiment (positivity, happiness, and so on), and even detect subtle intent, like sarcasm. It may be a bag, but it's full of meaning and information. So let's get these words ranked—sorted in some order that's easier to think about. The Counter object has a handy method, *most_common*, for just this purpose:

```
>>> bag_of_words.most_common(4)                    ◄
[('the', 4), (',', 3), ('faster', 3), ('harry', 2)]
```

> **By default, most_common() lists all tokens from most frequent to least, but you've limited the list to the top four here.**

Specifically, the number of times a word occurs in a given document is called the *term frequency*, commonly abbreviated TF. In some examples you may see the count of word occurrences normalized (divided) by the number of terms in the document.[1]

So your top four terms or tokens are "the," ",", "harry," and "faster." But the word "the" and the punctuation "," aren't very informative about the intent of this document. And these uninformative tokens are likely to appear a lot during your hurried adventure. So for this example, you'll ignore them, along with a list of standard English stop words and punctuation. This won't always be the case, but for now it helps simplify the example. That leaves you with "harry" and "faster" among the top tokens in your TF vector (bag of words).

Let's calculate the term frequency of "harry" from the Counter object (bag_of_words) you defined above:

```
>>> times_harry_appears = bag_of_words['harry']
>>> num_unique_words = len(bag_of_words)          ◄
```

> **The number of unique tokens from your original source**

---

[1] However, normalized frequency is really a probability, so it should probably not be called frequency.

```
>>> tf = times_harry_appears / num_unique_words
>>> round(tf, 4)
0.1818
```

Let's pause for a second and look a little deeper at normalized term frequency, a phrase (and calculation) we use often throughout this book. It's the word count tempered by how long the document is. But why "temper" it all? Let's say you find the word "dog" 3 times in document A and 100 times in document B. Clearly "dog" is way more important to document B. But wait. Let's say you find out document A is a 30-word email to a veterinarian and document B is *War & Peace* (approx 580,000 words!). Your first analysis was straight-up backwards. The following equations take the document length into account:

$TF(\text{"dog,"} \ document_A) = 3/30 = .1$
$TF(\text{"dog,"} \ document_B) = 100/580000 = .00017$

Now you have something you can see that describes "something" about the two documents and their relationship to the word "dog" and each other. So instead of raw word counts to describe your documents in a corpus, you can use normalized term frequencies. Similarly you could calculate each word and get the relative importance to the document of that term. Your protagonist, Harry, and his need for speed are clearly central to the story of this document. You've made some great progress in turning text into numbers, beyond just the presence or absence of a given word. Now this is a clearly contrived example, but you can quickly see how meaningful results could come from this approach. Let's look at a bigger piece of text. Take these first few paragraphs from the Wikipedia article on kites:

> *A kite is traditionally a tethered heavier-than-air craft with wing surfaces that react against the air to create lift and drag. A kite consists of wings, tethers, and anchors. Kites often have a bridle to guide the face of the kite at the correct angle so the wind can lift it. A kite's wing also may be so designed so a bridle is not needed; when kiting a sailplane for launch, the tether meets the wing at a single point. A kite may have fixed or moving anchors. Untraditionally in technical kiting, a kite consists of tether-set-coupled wing sets; even in technical kiting, though, a wing in the system is still often called the kite.*
>
> *The lift that sustains the kite in flight is generated when air flows around the kite's surface, producing low pressure above and high pressure below the wings. The interaction with the wind also generates horizontal drag along the direction of the wind. The resultant force vector from the lift and drag force components is opposed by the tension of one or more of the lines or tethers to which the kite is attached. The anchor point of the kite line may be static or moving (such as the towing of a kite by a running person, boat, free-falling anchors as in paragliders and fugitive parakites or vehicle).*
>
> *The same principles of fluid flow apply in liquids and kites are also used under water.*
>
> *A hybrid tethered craft comprising both a lighter-than-air balloon as well as a kite lifting surface is called a kytoon.*

*Kites have a long and varied history and many different types are flown individually and at festivals worldwide. Kites may be flown for recreation, art or other practical uses. Sport kites can be flown in aerial ballet, sometimes as part of a competition. Power kites are multi-line steerable kites designed to generate large forces which can be used to power activities such as kite surfing, kite landboarding, kite fishing, kite buggying and a new trend snow kiting. Even Man-lifting kites have been made.*

—Wikipedia

Then you'll assign the text to a variable:

```
>>> from collections import Counter
>>> from nltk.tokenize import TreebankWordTokenizer
>>> tokenizer = TreebankWordTokenizer()
>>> from nlpia.data.loaders import kite_text
>>> tokens = tokenizer.tokenize(kite_text.lower())
>>> token_counts = Counter(tokens)
>>> token_counts
Counter({'the': 26, 'a': 20, 'kite': 16, ',': 15, ...})
```

kite_text = "A kite is traditionally ..." as above

**NOTE** The `TreebankWordTokenizer` returns `'kite.'` (with a period) as a token. The Treebank Tokenizer assumes that your document has already been segmented into separate sentences, so it'll only ignore punctuation at the very end of the string. Sentence segmentation is tricky and you won't learn about it until chapter 11. Nonetheless, the spaCy parser is faster and more accurate because it does sentence segmentation and tokenization (along with a lot of other things)[2] in one pass. So use spaCy in your production app rather than the NLTK components we used for these simple examples.

Okay, back to the example. So that is a lot of stop words. It's not likely that this Wikipedia article is about the articles "the" and "a," nor the conjunction "and" and the other stop words. So let's ditch them for now:

```
>>> import nltk
>>> nltk.download('stopwords', quiet=True)
True
>>> stopwords = nltk.corpus.stopwords.words('english')
>>> tokens = [x for x in tokens if x not in stopwords]
>>> kite_counts = Counter(tokens)
>>> kite_counts
Counter({'kite': 16,
         'traditionally': 1,
         'tethered': 2,
         'heavier-than-air': 1,
         'craft': 2,
         'wing': 5,
         'surfaces': 1,
         'react': 1,
```

---

[2] See the web page titled "spaCy 101: Everything you need to know" (https://spacy.io/usage/spacy-101 #annotations-token).

```
'air': 2,
...,
'made': 1})}
```

By looking purely at the number of times words occur in this document, you're learning something about it. The terms *kite(s)*, *wing*, and *lift* are all important. And, if you didn't know what this document was about, you just happened across this document in your vast database of Google-like knowledge, you might "programmatically" be able to infer it has something to do with "flight" or "lift" or, in fact, "kites."

Across multiple documents in a corpus, things get a little more interesting. A set of documents may *all* be about, say, kite flying. You would imagine all the documents may refer to string and wind quite often, and the term frequencies TF("string") and TF("wind") would therefore rank highly in all the documents. Now let's look at a way to more gracefully represent these numbers for mathematical intents.

## 3.2  *Vectorizing*

You've transformed your text into numbers on a basic level. But you've still just stored them in a dictionary, so you've taken one step out of the text-based world and into the realm of mathematics. Next you'll go ahead and jump in all the way. Instead of describing a document in terms of a frequency dictionary, you'll make a vector of those word counts. In Python, this will be a list, but in general it's an ordered collection or array. You can do this quickly with

```
>>> document_vector = []
>>> doc_length = len(tokens)
>>> for key, value in kite_counts.most_common():
...     document_vector.append(value / doc_length)
>>> document_vector
[0.07207207207207207,
 0.06756756756756757,
 0.036036036036036036,
 ...,
 0.0045045045045045045]
```

This list, or *vector*, is something you can do math on directly.

> **TIP**  You can speed up processing of these data structures many ways.[3] For now you're just playing with the nuts and bolts, but soon you'll want to speed things up.

Math isn't very interesting with just one element. Having one vector for one document isn't enough. You can grab a couple more documents and make vectors for each of them as well. But the values within each vector need to be relative to something consistent across all the vectors. If you're going to do math on them, they need to represent a position in a common space, relative to something consistent. Your vectors need to have the same origin and share the same scale, or "units," on each of their

---

[3]  See the web page titled "NumPy" (http://www.numpy.org/).

dimensions. The first step in this process is to normalize the counts by calculating normalized term frequency instead of raw count in the document (as you did in the last section); the second step is to make all the vectors of standard length or dimension.

Also, you want the value for each element of the vector to represent the same word in each document's vector. But you may notice that your email to the vet isn't going to contain many of the words that are in *War & Peace* (or maybe it will, who knows?). But it's fine (and as it happens, necessary) if your vectors contain values of 0 in various positions. You'll find every unique word in each document and then find every unique word in the union of those two sets. This collections of words in your vocabulary is often called a *lexicon*, which is the same concept referenced in earlier chapters, just in terms of your special corpus. Let's look at what that would look like with something shorter than *War & Peace*. Let's check in on Harry. You had one "document" already—let's round out the corpus with a couple more:

```
>>> docs = ["The faster Harry got to the store, the faster and faster Harry
➥ would get home."]
>>> docs.append("Harry is hairy and faster than Jill.")
>>> docs.append("Jill is not as hairy as Harry.")
```

> **TIP** If you're playing along with us rather than typing these out, you can import them from the nlpia package: `from nlpia.data.loaders import harry_docs as docs`.

First, let's look at your lexicon for this corpus containing three documents:

```
>>> doc_tokens = []
>>> for doc in docs:
...     doc_tokens += [sorted(tokenizer.tokenize(doc.lower()))]
>>> len(doc_tokens[0])
17
>>> all_doc_tokens = sum(doc_tokens, [])
>>> len(all_doc_tokens)
33
>>> lexicon = sorted(set(all_doc_tokens))
>>> len(lexicon)
18
>>> lexicon
[',',
 '.',
 'and',
 'as',
 'faster',
 'get',
 'got',
 'hairy',
 'harry',
 'home',
 'is',
 'jill',
 'not',
 'store',
 'than',
```

```
'the',
'to',
'would']
```

Each of your three document vectors will need to have 18 values, even if the document for that vector doesn't contain all 18 words in your lexicon. Each token is assigned a "slot" in your vectors corresponding to its position in your lexicon. Some of those token counts in the vector will be zeros, which is what you want:

```
>>> from collections import OrderedDict
>>> zero_vector = OrderedDict((token, 0) for token in lexicon)
>>> zero_vector
OrderedDict([(',', 0),
             ('.', 0),
             ('and', 0),
             ('as', 0),
             ('faster', 0),
             ('get', 0),
             ('got', 0),
             ('hairy', 0),
             ('harry', 0),
             ('home', 0),
             ('is', 0),
             ('jill', 0),
             ('not', 0),
             ('store', 0),
             ('than', 0),
             ('the', 0),
             ('to', 0),
             ('would', 0)])
```

Now you'll make copies of that base vector, update the values of the vector for each document, and store them in an array:

> **copy.copy() creates an independent copy, a separate instance of your zero vector, rather than reusing a reference (pointer) to the original object's memory location. Otherwise you'd just be overwriting the same zero_vector with new values in each loop, and you wouldn't have a fresh zero on each pass of the loop.**

```
>>> import copy
>>> doc_vectors = []
>>> for doc in docs:
...     vec = copy.copy(zero_vector)          ←
...     tokens = tokenizer.tokenize(doc.lower())
...     token_counts = Counter(tokens)
...     for key, value in token_counts.items():
...         vec[key] = value / len(lexicon)
...     doc_vectors.append(vec)
```

You have three vectors, one for each document. So what? What can you do with them? Your document word-count vectors can do all the cool stuff any vector can do, so let's learn a bit more about vectors and vector spaces first.[4]

---

[4]  If you'd like more details about linear algebra and vectors, take a look at appendix C.

### 3.2.1 *Vector spaces*

Vectors are the primary building blocks of linear algebra, or vector algebra. They're an ordered list of numbers, or coordinates, in a vector space. They describe a location or position in that space. Or they can be used to identify a particular direction and magnitude or distance in that space. A *space* is the collection of all possible vectors that could appear in that space. So a vector with two values would lie in a 2D vector space, a vector with three values in 3D vector space, and so on.

A piece of graph paper, or a grid of pixels in an image, are both nice 2D vector spaces. You can see how the order of these coordinates matter. If you reverse the x and y coordinates for locations on your graph paper, without reversing all your vector calculations, all your answers for linear algebra problems would be flipped. Graph paper and images are examples of rectilinear, or Euclidean spaces, because the x and y coordinates are perpendicular to each other. The vectors we talk about in this chapter are all rectilinear, Euclidean spaces.

What about latitude and longitude on a map or globe? That map or globe is definitely a 2D vector space because it's an ordered list of two numbers: latitude and longitude. But each of the latitude-longitude pairs describes a point on an approximately spherical, bumpy surface—the Earth's surface. And latitude and longitude coordinates aren't exactly perpendicular, so a latitude-longitude vector space isn't rectilinear. That means you have to be careful when you calculate things like distance or closeness (similarity) between two points represented by a pair of 2D latitude-longitude vectors, or vectors in any non-Euclidean space. Think about how you would calculate the distance between the latitude and longitude coordinates of Portland, OR and New York, NY.[5]

Figure 3.1 is one way to draw the 2D vectors `(5, 5)`, `(3, 2)`, and `(-1, 1)`. The head of a vector (represented by the pointy tip of an arrow) is used to identify a

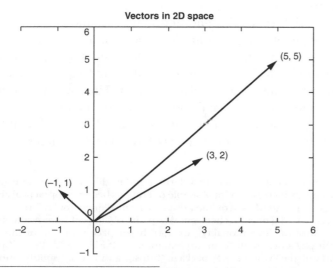

**Figure 3.1 2D vectors**

---

[5] You'd need to use a package like GeoPy (https://geopy.readthedocs.io) to get the math right.

location in a vector space. So the vector heads in this diagram will be at those three pairs of coordinates. The tail of a position vector (represented by the "rear" of the arrow) is always at the origin, or $(0, 0)$.

What about 3D vector spaces? Positions and velocities in the 3D physical world you live in can be represented by x, y, and z coordinates in a 3D vector. Or the curvilinear space formed by all the latitude-longitude-altitude triplets describing locations near the surface of the Earth.

But you aren't limited to normal 3D space. You can have 5 dimensions, 10 dimensions, 5,000, whatever. The linear algebra all works out the same. You might need more computing power as the dimensionality grows. And you'll run into some "curse-of-dimensionality" issues, but you can wait to deal with that until the last chapter, chapter 13.[6]

For a natural language document vector space, the dimensionality of your vector space is the count of the number of distinct words that appear in the entire corpus. For TF (and TF-IDF to come), sometimes we call this dimensionality capital letter "K." This number of distinct words is also the vocabulary size of your corpus, so in an academic paper it'll usually be called "|V|." You can then describe each document within this K-dimensional vector space by a K-dimensional vector. K = 18 in your three-document corpus about Harry and Jill. Because humans can't easily visualize spaces of more than three dimensions, let's set aside most of those dimensions and look at two for a moment, so you can have a visual representation of the vectors on this flat page you're reading. So in figure 3.2, K is reduced to two for a two-dimensional view of the 18-dimensional Harry and Jill vector space.

K-dimensional vectors work the same way, just in ways you can't easily visualize. Now that you have a representation of each document and know they share a common space, you have a path to compare them. You could measure the Euclidean distance between the vectors by subtracting them and computing the length of the distance between them, which is called the 2-norm distance. It's the distance a "crow" would have to fly (in a straight line) to get from a location identified by the tip (head) of one vector and the location of the tip of the other vector. Check out appendix C on linear algebra to see why this is a bad idea for word count (term frequency) vectors.

Two vectors are "similar" if they share similar direction. They might have similar magnitude (length), which would mean that the word count (term frequency) vectors are for documents of about the same length. But do you care about document length in your similarity estimate for vector representations of words in documents? Probably

---

[6]  The curse of dimensionality is that vectors will get exponentially farther and farther away from one another, in Euclidean distance, as the dimensionality increases. A lot of simple operations become impractical above 10 or 20 dimensions, like sorting a large list of vectors based on their distance from a "query" or "reference" vector (approximate nearest neighbor search). To dig deeper, check out Wikipedia's "Curse of Dimensionality" article (https://en.wikipedia.org/wiki/Curse_of_dimensionality), explore hyperspace with one of this book's authors at Exploring Hyperspace (https://docs.google.com/presentation/d/1SEU8VL0KWPDKKZnBSaMx UBDDwI8yqIxu9RQtq2bpnNg), play with the Python annoy package (https://github.com/spotify/annoy), or search Google Scholar for "high dimensional approximate nearest neighbors" (https://scholar.google.com/scholar?q=high+dimensional+approximate+nearest+neighbor).

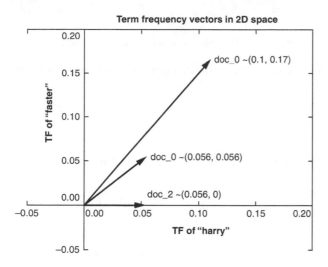

**Figure 3.2　2D term frequency vectors**

not. You'd like your estimate of document similarity to find use of the same words about the same number of times in similar proportions. This accurate estimate would give you confidence that the documents they represent are probably talking about similar things.

Cosine similarity is merely the cosine of the angle between two vectors (theta), shown in figure 3.3, which can be calculated from the Euclidian dot product using

$$A \cdot B = |A| \, |B| * \cos \Theta$$

Cosine similarity is efficient to calculate because the dot product doesn't require evaluation of any trigonometric functions. In addition, cosine similarity has a convenient range for most machine learning problems: -1 to +1.

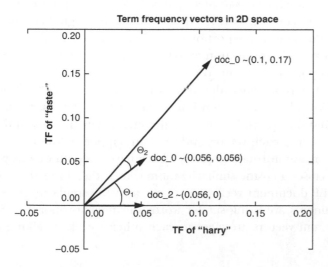

**Figure 3.3　2D thetas**

In Python this would be

```
a.dot(b) == np.linalg.norm(a) * np.linalg.norm(b) / np.cos(theta)
```

Solving this relationship for `cos(theta)`, you can derive the cosine similarity using

$$\cos \Theta = \frac{A \cdot B}{|A|\,|B|}$$

Or you can do it in pure Python without numpy, as in the following listing.

**Listing 3.1   Compute cosine similarity in python**

```
>>> import math
>>> def cosine_sim(vec1, vec2):
...     """ Let's convert our dictionaries to lists for easier matching."""
...     vec1 = [val for val in vec1.values()]
...     vec2 = [val for val in vec2.values()]
...
...     dot_prod = 0
...     for i, v in enumerate(vec1):
...         dot_prod += v * vec2[i]
...
...     mag_1 = math.sqrt(sum([x**2 for x in vec1]))
...     mag_2 = math.sqrt(sum([x**2 for x in vec2]))
...
...     return dot_prod / (mag_1 * mag_2)
```

So you need to take the dot product of two of your vectors in question—multiply the elements of each vector pairwise—and then sum up those products. You then divide by the norm (magnitude or length) of each vector. The vector norm is the same as its Euclidean distance from the head to the tail of the vector—the square root of the sum of the squares of its elements. This *normalized dot product*, like the output of the cosine function, will be a value between -1 and 1. It's the cosine of the angle between these two vectors. This value is the same as the portion of the longer vector that's covered by the shorter vector's perpendicular projection onto the longer one. It gives you a value for how much the vectors point in the same direction.

A cosine similarity of *1* represents identical normalized vectors that point in exactly the same direction along all dimensions. The vectors may have different lengths or magnitudes, but they point in the same direction. Remember you divided the dot product by the norm of each vector, and this can happen before or after the dot product. So the vectors are normalized so they both have a length of 1 as you do the dot product. So the closer a cosine similarity value is to 1, the closer the two vectors are in angle. For NLP document vectors that have a cosine similarity close to 1, you know that the documents are using similar words in similar proportion. So the documents whose document vectors are close to each other are likely talking about the same thing.

A cosine similarity of *0* represents two vectors that share no components. They are orthogonal, perpendicular in all dimensions. For NLP TF vectors, this situation occurs only if the two documents share no words in common. Because these documents use completely different words, they must be talking about completely different things. This doesn't necessarily mean they have different meanings or topics, just that they use completely different words.

A cosine similarity of *-1* represents two vectors that are anti-similar, completely opposite. They point in opposite directions. This can never happen for simple word count (term frequency) vectors or even normalized TF vectors (which we talk about later). Counts of words can never be negative. So word count (term frequency) vectors will always be in the same "quadrant" of the vector space. None of the term frequency vectors can sneak around into one of the quadrants behind the tail of the other vectors. None of your term frequency vectors can have components (word frequencies) that are the negative of another term frequency vector, because term frequencies just can't be negative.

You won't see any negative cosine similarity values for pairs of vectors for natural language documents in this chapter. But in the next chapter, we develop a concept of words and topics that are "opposite" to each other. And this will show up as documents, words, and topics that have cosine similarities of less than zero, or even *-1*.

> **OPPOSITES ATTRACT**  There's an interesting consequence of the way you calculated cosine similarity. If two vectors or documents have a cosine similarity of *-1* (are opposites) to a third vector, they must be perfectly similar to each other. They must be exactly the same vectors. But the documents those vectors represent may not be exactly the same. Not only might the word order be shuffled, but one may be much longer than the other, if it uses the same words in the same proportion.

Later, you'll come up with vectors that more accurately model a document. But for now, you've gotten a good introduction to the tools you need.

## 3.3  *Zipf's Law*

Now on to our main topic—sociology. Okay, not, but you'll make a quick detour into the world of counting people and words, and you'll learn a seemingly universal rule that governs the counting of most things. It turns out, that in language, like most things involving living organisms, patterns abound.

In the early twentieth century, the French stenographer Jean-Baptiste Estoup noticed a pattern in the frequencies of words that he painstakingly counted by hand across many documents (thank goodness for computers and Python). In the 1930s, the American linguist George Kingsley Zipf sought to formalize Estoup's observation, and this relationship eventually came to bear Zipf's name:

> *Zipf's law states that given some corpus of natural language utterances, the frequency of any word is inversely proportional to its rank in the frequency table.*
>
> Wikipedia

Specifically, *inverse proportionality* refers to a situation where an item in a ranked list will appear with a frequency tied explicitly to its rank in the list. The first item in the ranked list will appear twice as often as the second, and three times as often as the third, for example. One of the quick things you can do with any corpus or document is plot the frequencies of word usages relative to their rank (in frequency). If you see any outliers that don't fall along a straight line in a log-log plot, it may be worth investigating.

As an example of how far Zipf's Law stretches beyond the world of words, figure 3.4 charts the relationship between the population of US cities and the rank of that population. It turns out that Zipf's Law applies to counts of lots of things. Nature is full of systems that experience exponential growth and "network effects" like population dynamics, economic output, and resource distribution.[7] It's interesting that something as simple as Zipf's Law could hold true across a wide range of natural and manmade phenomena. Nobel Laureate Paul Krugman, speaking about economic models and Zipf's Law, put it this way:

> *The usual complaint about economic theory is that our models are oversimplified—that they offer excessively neat views of complex, messy reality. [With Zipf's law] the reverse is true: You have complex, messy models, yet reality is startlingly neat and simple.*

Here's an updated version of Krugman's city population plot.[8]

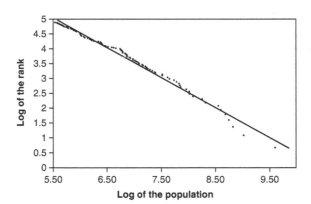

Figure 3.4   City population distribution

As with cities and social networks, so with words. Let's first download the Brown Corpus from NLTK:

> *The Brown Corpus was the first million-word electronic corpus of English, created in 1961 at Brown University. This corpus contains text from 500 sources, and the sources have been categorized by genre, such as news, editorial, and so on.[9]*

NLTK Documentation

---

[7]   See the web page titled "There is More than a Power Law in Zipf" (https://www.nature.com/articles/srep 00812).

[8]   Population data downloaded from Wikipedia using Pandas. See the `nlpia.book.examples` code on GitHub (https://github.com/totalgood/nlpia/blob/master/src/nlpia/book/examples/ch03_zipf.py).

[9]   For a complete list, see http://icame.uib.no/brown/bcm-los.html.

```
>>> nltk.download('brown')
>>> from nltk.corpus import brown
>>> brown.words()[:10]
 ['The',
 'Fulton',
 'County',
 'Grand',
 'Jury',
 'said',
 'Friday',
 'an',
 'investigation',
 'of']
>>> brown.tagged_words()[:5]
 [('The', 'AT'),
 ('Fulton', 'NP-TL'),
 ('County', 'NN-TL'),
 ('Grand', 'JJ-TL'),
 ('Jury', 'NN-TL')]
>>> len(brown.words())
1161192
```

**The Brown corpus is about 3MB.**

**words() is a built-in method of the NTLK corpus object that returns the tokenized corpus as a sequence of strs.**

**You'll learn about part-of-speech tagging in chapter 2.**

So with over 1 million tokens, you have something meaty to look at:

```
>>> from collections import Counter
>>> puncs = set((',', '.', '--', '-', '!', '?',
...      ':', ';', '``', "''", '(', ')', '[', ']'))
>>> word_list = (x.lower() for x in brown.words() if x not in puncs)
>>> token_counts = Counter(word_list)
>>> token_counts.most_common(20)
[('the', 69971),
 ('of', 36412),
 ('and', 28853),
 ('to', 26158),
 ('a', 23195),
 ('in', 21337),
 ('that', 10594),
 ('is', 10109),
 ('was', 9815),
 ('he', 9548),
 ('for', 9489),
 ('it', 8760),
 ('with', 7289),
 ('as', 7253),
 ('his', 6996),
 ('on', 6741),
 ('be', 6377),
 ('at', 5372),
 ('by', 5306),
 ('i', 5164)]
```

A quick glance shows that the word frequencies in the Brown corpus follow the logarithmic relationship Zipf predicted. "The" (rank 1 in term frequency) occurs roughly twice as often as "of" (rank 2 in term frequency), and roughly three times as often as "and" (rank 3 in term frequency). If you don't believe us, use the example code

(https://github.com/totalgood/nlpia/blob/master/src/nlpia/book/examples/ch03
_zipf.py) in the `nlpia` package to see this yourself.

In short, if you rank the words of a corpus by the number of occurrences and list them in descending order, you'll find that, for a sufficiently large sample, the first word in that ranked list is twice as likely to occur in the corpus as the second word in the list. And it is four times as likely to appear as the fourth word in the list. So given a large corpus, you can use this breakdown to say statistically how likely a given word is to appear in any given document of that corpus.

## 3.4    Topic modeling

Now back to your document vectors. Word counts are useful, but pure word count, even when normalized by the length of the document, doesn't tell you much about the importance of that word in that document *relative* to the rest of the documents in the corpus. If you could suss out that information, you could start to describe documents within the corpus. Say you have a corpus of every kite book ever written. "Kite" would almost surely occur many times in every book (document) you counted, but that doesn't provide any new information; it doesn't help distinguish between those documents. Whereas something like "construction" or "aerodynamics" might not be so prevalent across the entire corpus, but for the ones where it frequently occurred, you would know more about each document's nature. For this you need another tool.

Inverse document frequency, or IDF, is your window through Zipf in topic analysis. Let's take your term frequency counter from earlier and expand on it. You can count tokens and bin them up two ways: per document and across the entire corpus. You're going to be counting just by document.

Let's return to the Kite example from Wikipedia and grab another section (the History section); say it's the second document in your Kite corpus:

*Kites were invented in China, where materials ideal for kite building were readily available: silk fabric for sail material; fine, high-tensile-strength silk for flying line; and resilient bamboo for a strong, lightweight framework.*

*The kite has been claimed as the invention of the 5th-century BC Chinese philosophers Mozi (also Mo Di) and Lu Ban (also Gongshu Ban). By 549 AD paper kites were certainly being flown, as it was recorded that in that year a paper kite was used as a message for a rescue mission. Ancient and medieval Chinese sources describe kites being used for measuring distances, testing the wind, lifting men, signaling, and communication for military operations. The earliest known Chinese kites were flat (not bowed) and often rectangular. Later, tailless kites incorporated a stabilizing bowline. Kites were decorated with mythological motifs and legendary figures; some were fitted with strings and whistles to make musical sounds while flying. From China, kites were introduced to Cambodia, Thailand, India, Japan, Korea and the western world.*

*After its introduction into India, the kite further evolved into the fighter kite, known as the patang in India, where thousands are flown every year on festivals such as Makar Sankranti.*

*Kites were known throughout Polynesia, as far as New Zealand, with the assumption being that the knowledge diffused from China along with the people. Anthropomorphic kites made from cloth and wood were used in religious ceremonies to send prayers to the gods. Polynesian kite traditions are used by anthropologists get an idea of early "primitive" Asian traditions that are believed to have at one time existed in Asia.*

Wikipedia

First let's get the total word count for each document in your corpus, intro_doc and history_doc:

```
>>> from nlpia.data.loaders import kite_text, kite_history
>>> kite_intro = kite_text.lower()
>>> intro_tokens = tokenizer.tokenize(kite_intro)
>>> kite_history = kite_history.lower()
>>> history_tokens = tokenizer.tokenize(kite_history)
>>> intro_total = len(intro_tokens)
>>> intro_total
363
>>> history_total = len(history_tokens)
>>> history_total
297
```

**"A kite is traditionally … ? "**
**"a kite is traditionally …"**

Now with a couple tokenized kite documents in hand, let's look at the term frequency of "kite" in each document. You'll store the TFs you find in two dictionaries, one for each document:

```
>>> intro_tf = {}
>>> history_tf = {}
>>> intro_counts = Counter(intro_tokens)
>>> intro_tf['kite'] = intro_counts['kite'] / intro_total
>>> history_counts = Counter(history_tokens)
>>> history_tf['kite'] = history_counts['kite'] / history_total
>>> 'Term Frequency of "kite" in intro is: {:.4f}'.format(intro_tf['kite'])
'Term Frequency of "kite" in intro is: 0.0441'
>>> 'Term Frequency of "kite" in history is: {:.4f}'\
...     .format(history_tf['kite'])
'Term Frequency of "kite" in history is: 0.0202'
```

Okay, you have a number twice as large as the other. Is the intro section twice as much about kites? No, not really. So let's dig a little deeper. First, let's see how those numbers relate to some other word, say "and":

```
>>> intro_tf['and'] = intro_counts['and'] / intro_total
>>> history_tf['and'] = history_counts['and'] / history_total
>>> print('Term Frequency of "and" in intro is: {:.4f}'\
...     .format(intro_tf['and']))
Term Frequency of "and" in intro is: 0.0275
>>> print('Term Frequency of "and" in history is: {:.4f}'\
...     .format(history_tf['and']))
Term Frequency of "and" in history is: 0.0303
```

Great! You know both of these documents are about "and" just as much as they are about "kite"! Oh, wait. That's not helpful, huh? Just as in your first example, where the system seemed to think "the" was the most important word in the document about your fast friend Harry, in this example "and" is considered highly relevant. Even at first glance, you can tell this isn't revelatory.

A good way to think of a term's inverse document frequency is this: How strange is it that this token is in this document? If a term appears in one document a lot of times, but occurs rarely in the rest of the corpus, one could assume it's important to that document specifically. Your first step toward topic analysis!

A term's IDF is merely the ratio of the total number of documents to the number of documents the term appears in. In the case of "and" and "kite" in your current example, the answer is the same for both:

- 2 total documents / 2 documents contain "and" = 2/2 = 1
- 2 total documents / 2 documents contain "kite" = 2/2 = 1
- Not very interesting. So let's look at another word "China."
- 2 total documents / 1 document contains "China" = 2/1 = 2

Okay, that's something different. Let's use this "rarity" measure to weight the term frequencies:

```
>>> num_docs_containing_and = 0
>>> for doc in [intro_tokens, history_tokens]:
...     if 'and' in doc:                              similarly for "kite"
...         num_docs_containing_and += 1              and "China"
```

And let's grab the TF of "China" in the two documents:

```
>>> intro_tf['china'] = intro_counts['china'] / intro_total
>>> history_tf['china'] = history_counts['china'] / history_total
```

And finally, the IDF for all three. You'll store the IDFs in dictionaries per document like you did with TF:

```
>>> num_docs = 2
>>> intro_idf = {}
>>> history_idf = {}
>>> intro_idf['and'] = num_docs / num_docs_containing_and
>>> history_idf['and'] = num_docs / num_docs_containing_and
>>> intro_idf['kite'] = num_docs / num_docs_containing_kite
>>> history_idf['kite'] = num_docs / num_docs_containing_kite
>>> intro_idf['china'] = num_docs / num_docs_containing_china
>>> history_idf['china'] = num_docs / num_docs_containing_china
```

And then for the intro document you find:

```
>>> intro_tfidf = {}
>>> intro_tfidf['and'] = intro_tf['and'] * intro_idf['and']
>>> intro_tfidf['kite'] = intro_tf['kite'] * intro_idf['kite']
>>> intro_tfidf['china'] = intro_tf['china'] * intro_idf['china']
```

And then for the history document:

```
>>> history_tfidf = {}
>>> history_tfidf['and'] = history_tf['and'] * history_idf['and']
>>> history_tfidf['kite'] = history_tf['kite'] * history_idf['kite']
>>> history_tfidf['china'] = history_tf['china'] * history_idf['china']
```

### 3.4.1 *Return of Zipf*

You're almost there. Let's say, though, you have a corpus of 1 million documents (maybe you're baby-Google), someone searches for the word "cat," and in your 1 million documents you have exactly 1 document that contains the word "cat." The raw IDF of this is

1,000,000 / 1 = 1,000,000

Let's imagine you have 10 documents with the word "dog" in them. Your IDF for "dog" is

1,000,000 / 10 = 100,000

That's a big difference. Your friend Zipf would say that's *too* big, because it's likely to happen a lot. Zipf's Law showed that when you compare the frequencies of two words, like "cat" and "dog," even if they occur a similar number of times, the more frequent word will have an exponentially higher frequency than the less frequent one. So Zipf's Law suggests that you scale all your word frequencies (and document frequencies) with the `log()` function, the inverse of `exp()`. This ensures that words such as "cat" and "dog," which have similar counts, aren't exponentially different in frequency. And this distribution of word frequencies will ensure that your TF-IDF scores are more uniformly distributed. So you should redefine IDF to be the log of the original probability of that word occurring in one of your documents. You'll want to take the log of the term frequency as well.[10]

   The base of log function isn't important, because you only want to make the frequency distribution uniform, not to scale it within a particular numerical range.[11] If you use a base 10 log function, you'll get:

search: cat

idf = log(1,000,000/1) = 6

search: dog

idf = log(1,000,000/10) = 5

So now you're weighting the TF results of each more appropriately to their occurrences in language, in general.

---

[10] Gerard Salton and Chris Buckley first demonstrated the usefulness of log scaling for information retrieval in their paper Term Weighting Approaches in Automatic Text Retrieval (https://ecommons.cornell.edu/bitstream/handle/1813/6721/87-881.pdf).

[11] Later we show you how to normalize the TF-IDF vectors after all the TF-IDF values have been calculated using this log scaling.

And then finally, for a given term, *t*, in a given document, *d*, in a corpus, *D*, you get:

$$\text{tf}(t, d) = \frac{\text{count}(t)}{\text{count}(d)}$$

$$\text{idf}(t, D) = \log \frac{\text{number of documents}}{\text{number of documents containing } t}$$

$$\text{tfidf}(t, d, D) = \text{tf}(t, d) * \text{idf}(t, D)$$

So the more times a word appears in the document, the TF (and hence the TF-IDF) will go up. At the same time, as the number of documents that contain that word goes up, the IDF (and hence the TF-IDF) for that word will go down. So now, you have a number—something your computer can chew on. But what is it exactly? It relates a specific word or token to a specific document in a specific corpus, and then it assigns a numeric value to the importance of that word in the given document, given its usage across the entire corpus.

In some classes, all the calculations will be done in log space so that multiplications become additions and division becomes subtraction:

**Log probability of a particular term in a particular document**

**Log of the log probability of a particular term occurring at least once in a document—the first log is to linearize the IDF (compensate for Zipf's Law)**

```
>>> log_tf = log(term_occurences_in_doc) -\
...     log(num_terms_in_doc)
>>> log_log_idf = log(log(total_num_docs) -\
...     log(num_docs_containing_term))
>>> log_tf_idf = log_tf + log_idf
```

**Log TF-IDF is the log of the product of TF and IDF or the sum of the logs of TF and IDF.**

This single number, the TF-IDF, is the humble foundation of a simple search engine. As you've stepped from the realm of text firmly into the realm of numbers, it's time for some math. You won't likely ever have to implement the preceding formulas for computing TF-IDF. Linear algebra isn't necessary for full understanding of the tools used in natural language processing, but a general familiarity with how the formulas work can make their use more intuitive.

### 3.4.2   *Relevance ranking*

As you saw earlier, you can easily compare two vectors and get their similarity, but you have since learned that merely counting words isn't as descriptive as using their TF-IDF. Therefore, in each document vector let's replace each word's word_count with the word's TF-IDF. Now your vectors will more thoroughly reflect the meaning, or topic, of the document, as shown in this Harry example:

**You need to copy the zero_vector to create a new, separate object. Otherwise you'd end up overwriting the same object/vector each time through the loop.**

```
>>> document_tfidf_vectors = []
>>> for doc in docs:
...     vec = copy.copy(zero_vector)
```

```
...        tokens = tokenizer.tokenize(doc.lower())
...        token_counts = Counter(tokens)
...
...        for key, value in token_counts.items():
...            docs_containing_key = 0
...            for _doc in docs:
...                if key in _doc:
...                    docs_containing_key += 1
...            tf = value / len(lexicon)
...            if docs_containing_key:
...                idf = len(docs) / docs_containing_key
...            else:
...                idf = 0
...            vec[key] = tf * idf
...        document_tfidf_vectors.append(vec)
```

With this setup, you have K-dimensional vector representation of each document in the corpus. And now on to the hunt! Or search, in your case. Two vectors, in a given vector space, can be said to be similar if they have a similar angle. If you imagine each vector starting at the origin and reaching out its prescribed distance and direction, the ones that reach out at the same angle are similar, even if they don't reach out to the same distance.

Two vectors are considered similar if their cosine similarity is high, so you can find two similar vectors near each other if they minimize:

$$\cos \Theta = \frac{A \cdot B}{|A|\,|B|}$$

Now you have all you need to do a basic TF-IDF-based search. You can treat the search query itself as a document, and therefore get the TF-IDF-based vector representation of it. The last step is then to find the documents whose vectors have the highest cosine similarities to the query and return those as the search results.

If you take your three documents about Harry, and make the query "How long does it take to get to the store?" as shown here

```
>>> query = "How long does it take to get to the store?"
>>> query_vec = copy.copy(zero_vector)
>>> query_vec = copy.copy(zero_vector)           ◁─┐  copy.copy() ensures you're dealing
                                                     │  with separate objects, not multiple
                                                     │  references to the same object.

>>> tokens = tokenizer.tokenize(query.lower())
>>> token_counts = Counter(tokens)

>>> for key, value in token_counts.items():
...     docs_containing_key = 0
...     for _doc in documents:
...       if key in _doc.lower():
...         docs_containing_key += 1
...     if docs_containing_key == 0:               ◁─┐  You didn't find that token in the
...         continue                                  │  lexicon, so go to the next key.
```

```
...        tf = value / len(tokens)
...        idf = len(documents) / docs_containing_key
...      query_vec[key] = tf * idf
>>> cosine_sim(query_vec, document_tfidf_vectors[0])
0.5235048549676834
>>> cosine_sim(query_vec, document_tfidf_vectors[1])
0.0
>>> cosine_sim(query_vec, document_tfidf_vectors[2])
0.0
```

you can safely say document 0 has the most relevance for your query! And with this you can find relevant documents in any corpus, be it articles in Wikipedia, books from Gutenberg, or tweets from the wild west that is Twitter. Google look out!

Actually, Google's search engine is safe from competition from us. You have to do an "index scan" of your TF-IDF vectors with each query. That's an O(N) algorithm. Most search engines can respond in constant time (O(1)) because they use an *inverted index*.[12] You aren't going to implement an index that can find these matches in constant time here, but if you're interested you might like exploring the state-of-the-art Python implementation in the Whoosh[13] package and its source code.[14] Instead of showing you how to build this conventional keyword-based search engine, in chapter 4 we show you the latest semantic indexing approaches that capture the meaning of text.

> **TIP**  In the preceding code, you dropped the keys that weren't found in the lexicon to avoid a divide-by-zero error. But a better approach is to +1 the denominator of every IDF calculation, which ensures no denominators are zero. In fact this approach—called *additive smoothing* (Laplace smoothing)[15]— will usually improve the search results for TF-IDF keyword-based searches.

Keyword search is only one tool in your NLP pipeline. You want to build a chatbot. But most chatbots rely heavily on a search engine. And some chatbots rely exclusively on a search engine as their only algorithm for generating responses. You need to take one additional step to turn your simple search index (TF-IDF) into a chatbot. You need to store your training data in pairs of questions (or statements) and appropriate responses. Then you can use TF-IDF to search for a question (or statement) most like the user input text. Instead of returning the most similar statement in your database, you return the response associated with that statement. Like any tough computer science problem, ours can be solved with one more layer of indirection. And with that, you're chatting!

---

[12] See the web page titled "Inverted index" (https://en.wikipedia.org/wiki/Inverted_index).

[13] See the web page titled "Whoosh" (https://pypi.python.org/pypi/Whoosh).

[14] See the web page titled "GitHub - Mplsbeb/whoosh: A fast pure-Python search engine" (https://github.com/Mplsbeb/whoosh).

[15] See the web page titled "Additive smoothing" (https://en.wikipedia.org/wiki/Additive_smoothing).

### 3.4.3 Tools

Now that was a lot of code for things that have long since been automated. You can find a quick path to the same result using the `scikit-learn` package.[16] If you haven't already set up your environment using appendix A so that it includes this package, here's one way to install it:

```
pip install scipy
pip install sklearn
```

Here's how you can use sklearn to build a TF-IDF matrix. The sklearn TF-IDF class is a *model* with `.fit()` and `.transform()` methods that comply with the sklearn API for all machine learning models:

**The TFIDFVectorizer model produces a sparse numpy matrix, because a TF-IDF matrix usually contains mostly zeros, since most documents use a small portion of the total words in the vocabulary.**

```
>>> from sklearn.feature_extraction.text import TfidfVectorizer
>>> corpus = docs
>>> vectorizer = TfidfVectorizer(min_df=1)
>>> model = vectorizer.fit_transform(corpus)
>>> print(model.todense().round(2))
[[0.16 0.   0.48 0.21 0.21 0.   0.25 0.21 0.   0.   0.   0.21 0.   0.64
   0.21 0.21]
 [0.37 0.   0.37 0.   0.   0.37 0.29 0.   0.37 0.37 0.   0.   0.49 0.
   0.   0.  ]
 [0.   0.75 0.   0.   0.   0.29 0.22 0.   0.29 0.29 0.38 0.   0.   0.
   0.   0.  ]]
```

**The .todense() method converts a sparse matrix back into a regular numpy matrix (filling in the gaps with zeros) for your viewing pleasure.**

With `scikit-learn`, in four lines you created a matrix of your three documents and the inverse document frequency for each term in the lexicon. You have a matrix (practically a list of lists in Python) that represents the three documents (the three rows of the matrix). The TF-IDF of each term, token, or word in your lexicon make up the columns of the matrix (or again, the indices of each row). They only have 16, as they tokenize differently and drop the punctuation; you had a comma and a period. On large texts this or some other pre-optimized TF-IDF model will save you scads of work.

### 3.4.4 Alternatives

TF-IDF matrices (term-document matrices) have been the mainstay of information retrieval (search) for decades. As a result, researchers and corporations have spent a lot of time trying to optimize that IDF part to try to improve the relevance of search

---

[16] See the web page titled "scikit-learn: machine learning in Python" (http://scikit-learn.org/).

results. Table 3.1 lists some of the ways you can normalize and smooth your term frequency weights.[17]

**Table 3.1   Alternative TF-IDF normalization approaches (Molino 2017)**

| Scheme | Definition |
|--------|------------|
| None | $w_{ij} = f_{ij}$ |
| TF-IDF | $w_{ij} = \log(f_{ij}) \times \log(\frac{N}{n_j})$ |
| TF-ICF | $w_{ij} = \log(f_{ij}) \times \log(\frac{N}{f_j})$ |
| Okapi BM25 | $w_{ij} = \dfrac{f_{ij}}{0.5 + 1.5 \times \frac{f_j}{\frac{f_j}{j}} + f_{ij}} \log \dfrac{N - n_j + 0.5}{f_{ij} + 0.5}$ |
| ATC | $w_{ij} = \dfrac{(0.5 + 0.5 \times \frac{f_{ij}}{max_j}) \log(\frac{N}{n_j})}{\sqrt{\Sigma_{i=1}^{N} \left[ (0.5 + 0.5 \times \frac{f_{ij}}{max_j}) \log(\frac{N}{n_j}) \right]^2}}$ |
| LTU | $w_{ij} = \dfrac{(\log(f_{ij}) + 1.0) \log(\frac{N}{n_j})}{0.8 + 0.2 \times f_j \times \frac{j}{f_j}}$ |
| MI | $w_{ij} = \log \dfrac{P(t_{ij}|c_j)}{P(t_{ij}) P(c_j)}$ |
| PosMI | $w_{ij} = \max(0, \text{MI})$ |
| T-Test | $w_{ij} = \dfrac{P(t_{ij}|c_j) - P(t_{ij}) P(c_j)}{\sqrt{P(t_{ij}) P(c_j)}}$ |
| $x^2$ | See section 4.3.5 of *From Distributional to Semantic Similarity* (https://www.era.lib.ed.ac.uk/bitstream/handle/1842/563/ IP030023.pdf#subsection.4.3.5) by James Richard Curran |
| Lin98a | $w_{ij} = \dfrac{f_{ij} \times f}{f_i \times f_j}$ |
| Lin98b | $w_{ij} = -1 \times \log \dfrac{n_j}{N}$ |
| Gref94 | $w_{ij} = \dfrac{\log f_{ij} + 1}{\log n_j + 1}$ |

Search engines (information retrieval systems) match keywords (terms) between queries and documents in a corpus. If you're building a search engine and want to provide documents that are likely to match what your users are looking for, you should spend some time investigating the alternatives described by Piero Molino in table 3.1.

---

[17] *Word Embeddings Past, Present and Future* by Piero Molino at AI with the Best 2017.

One such alternative to using straight TF-IDF cosine distance to rank query results is Okapi BM25, or its most recent variant, BM25F.

### 3.4.5 *Okapi BM25*

The smart people at London's City University came up with a better way to rank search results. Rather than merely computing the TF-IDF cosine similarity, they normalize and smooth the similarity. They also ignore duplicate terms in the query document, effectively clipping the term frequencies for the query vector at 1. And the dot product for the cosine similarity isn't normalized by the TF-IDF vector norms (number of terms in the document and the query), but rather by a nonlinear function of the document length itself:

```
q_idf * dot(q_tf, d_tf[i]) * 1.5 /
    (dot(q_tf, d_tf[i]) + .25 + .75 * d_num_words[i] / d_num_words.mean()))
```

You can optimize your pipeline by choosing the weighting scheme that gives your users the most relevant results. But if your corpus isn't too large, you might consider forging ahead with us into even more useful and accurate representations of the meaning of words and documents. In subsequent chapters, we show you how to implement a semantic search engine that finds documents that "mean" something similar to the words in your query rather than just documents that use those exact words from your query. Semantic search is much better than anything TF-IDF weighting and stemming and lemmatization can ever hope to achieve. The only reason Google and Bing and other web search engines don't use the semantic search approach is that their corpus is too large. Semantic word and topic vectors don't scale to billions of documents, but millions of documents are no problem.

So you only need the most basic TF-IDF vectors to feed into your pipeline to get state-of-the-art performance for semantic search, document classification, dialog systems, and most of the other applications we mentioned in chapter 1. TF-IDFs are the first stage in your pipeline, the most basic set of features you'll extract from text. In the next chapter, we compute topic vectors from your TF-IDF vectors. Topic vectors are an even better representation of the meaning of the content of a bag of words than any of these carefully normalized and smoothed TF-IDF vectors. And things only get better from there as we move on to Word2vec word vectors in chapter 6 and neural net embeddings of the meaning of words and documents in later chapters.

### 3.4.6 *What's next*

Now that you can convert natural language text to numbers, you can begin to manipulate them and compute with them. Numbers firmly in hand, in the next chapter you'll refine those numbers to try to represent the *meaning* or *topic* of natural language text instead of only its words.

## *Summary*

- Any web-scale search engine with millisecond response times has the power of a TF-IDF term document matrix hidden under the hood.

- Term frequencies must be weighted by their inverse document frequency to ensure the most important, most meaningful words are given the heft they deserve.

- Zipf's law can help you predict the frequencies of all sorts of things, including words, characters, and people.

- The rows of a TF-IDF term document matrix can be used as a vector representation of the meanings of those individual words to create a vector space model of word semantics.

- Euclidean distance and similarity between pairs of high dimensional vectors doesn't adequately represent their similarity for most NLP applications.

- Cosine distance, the amount of "overlap" between vectors, can be calculated efficiently by just multiplying the elements of normalized vectors together and summing up those products.

- Cosine distance is the go-to similarity score for most natural language vector representations.

# Finding meaning in word counts (semantic analysis)

**This chapter covers**

- Analyzing semantics (meaning) to create topic vectors
- Semantic search using the similarity between topic vectors
- Scalable semantic analysis and semantic search for large corpora
- Using semantic components (topics) as features in your NLP pipeline
- Navigating high-dimensional vector spaces

You've learned quite a few natural language processing tricks. But now may be the first time you'll be able to do a little bit of magic. This is the first time we talk about a machine being able to understand the "meaning" of words.

The TF-IDF vectors (term frequency–inverse document frequency vectors) from chapter 3 helped you estimate the importance of words in a chunk of text. You used TF-IDF vectors and matrices to tell you how important each word is to the overall meaning of a bit of text in a document collection.

These TF-IDF "importance" scores worked not only for words, but also for short sequences of words, *n*-grams. These importance scores for *n*-grams are great for searching text if you know the exact words or *n*-grams you're looking for.

Past NLP experimenters found an algorithm for revealing the meaning of word combinations and computing vectors to represent this meaning. It's called *latent semantic analysis (LSA)*. And when you use this tool, not only can you represent the meaning of words as vectors, but you can use them to represent the meaning of entire documents.

In this chapter, you'll learn about these *semantic* or *topic* vectors.[1] You're going to use your weighted frequency scores from TF-IDF vectors to compute the topic "scores" that make up the dimensions of your topic vectors. You're going to use the correlation of normalized term frequencies with each other to group words together in topics to define the dimensions of your new topic vectors.

These topic vectors will help you do a lot of interesting things. They make it possible to search for documents based on their meaning—*semantic search*. Most of the time, semantic search returns search results that are much better than keyword search (TF-IDF search). Sometimes semantic search returns documents that are exactly what the user is searching for, even when they can't think of the right words to put in the query.

And you can use these semantic vectors to identify the words and *n*-grams that best represent the subject (topic) of a statement, document, or corpus (collection of documents). And with this vector of words and their relative importance, you can provide someone with the most meaningful words for a document—a set of keywords that summarizes its meaning.

And you can now compare any two statements or documents and tell how "close" they are in *meaning* to each other.

> **TIP**   The terms "topic," "semantic," and "meaning" have similar meaning and are often used interchangeably when talking about NLP. In this chapter, you're learning how to build an NLP pipeline that can figure out this kind of synonymy, all on its own. Your pipeline might even be able to find the similarity in meaning of the phrase "figure it out" and the word "compute." Machines can only "compute" meaning, not "figure out" meaning.

You'll soon see that the linear combinations of words that make up the dimensions of your topic vectors are pretty powerful representations of meaning.

## 4.1    *From word counts to topic scores*

You know how to count the frequency of words. And you know how to score the importance of words in a TF-IDF vector or matrix. But that's not enough. You want to score the meanings, the topics, that words are used for.

---

[1]   We use the term "topic vector" in this chapter about topic analysis and we use the term "word vector" in chapter 6 about Word2vec. Formal NLP texts such as the NLP bible by Jurafsky and Martin (https://web.stanford.edu/~jurafsky/slp3/ed3book.pdf#chapter.15) use "topic vector." Others, like the authors of Semantic Vector Encoding and Similarity Search (https://arxiv.org/pdf/1706.00957.pdf), use the term "semantic vector."

### 4.1.1    *TF-IDF vectors and lemmatization*

TF-IDF vectors count the exact spellings of terms in a document. So texts that restate the same meaning will have completely different TF-IDF vector representations if they spell things differently or use different words. This messes up search engines and document similarity comparisons that rely on counts of tokens.

In chapter 2, you normalized word endings so that words that differed only in their last few characters were collected together under a single token. You used normalization approaches such as stemming and lemmatization to create small collections of words with similar spellings, and often similar meanings. You labeled each of these small collections of words, with their lemma or stem, and then you processed these new tokens instead of the original words.

This lemmatization approach kept similarly *spelled*[2] words together in your analysis, but not necessarily words with similar meanings. And it definitely failed to pair up most synonyms. Synonyms usually differ in more ways than just the word endings that lemmatization and stemming deal with. Even worse, lemmatization and stemming sometimes erroneously lump together antonyms, words with opposite meaning.

The end result is that two chunks of text that talk about the same thing but use different words will not be "close" to each other in your lemmatized TF-IDF vector space model. And sometimes two lemmatized TF-IDF vectors that are close to each other aren't similar in meaning at all. Even a state-of-the-art TF-IDF similarity score from chapter 3, such as Okapi BM25 or cosine similarity, would fail to connect these synonyms or push apart these antonyms. Synonyms with different spellings produce TF-IDF vectors that just aren't close to each other in the vector space.

For example, the TF-IDF vector for this chapter in *NLPIA*, the chapter that you're reading right now, may not be at all close to similar-meaning passages in university textbooks about latent semantic indexing. But that's exactly what this chapter is about. But we use modern and colloquial terms in this chapter. Professors and researchers use more consistent, rigorous language in their textbooks and lectures. Plus, the terminology that professors used a decade ago has likely evolved with the rapid advances of the past few years. For example, terms such as "latent semantic *indexing*" were more popular than the term "latent semantic analysis" that researchers now use.[3]

### 4.1.2    *Topic vectors*

When you do math on TF-IDF vectors, such as addition and subtraction, these sums and differences only tell you about the frequency of word uses in the documents whose vectors you combined or differenced. That math doesn't tell you much about the meaning behind those words. You can compute word-to-word TF-IDF vectors (word co-occurrence or correlation vectors) by multiplying your TF-IDF matrix by

---

[2]    Both stemming and lemmatization remove or alter the word endings and prefixes, the last few characters of a word. Edit-distance calculations are better for identifying similarly spelled (or misspelled) words.

[3]    I love Google Ngram Viewer for visualizing trends like this (http://mng.bz/7Jnm).

itself. But "vector reasoning" with these sparse, high-dimensional vectors doesn't work well. When you add or subtract these vectors from each other, they don't represent an existing concept or word or topic well.

So you need a way to extract some additional information, meaning, from word statistics. You need a better estimate of what the words in a document "signify." And you need to know what that combination of words *means* in a particular document. You'd like to represent that meaning with a vector that's like a TF-IDF vector, but more compact and more meaningful.

We call these compact meaning vectors "word-topic vectors." We call the document meaning vectors "document-topic vectors." You can call either of these vectors "topic vectors," as long as you're clear on what the topic vectors are for, words or documents.

These topic vectors can be as compact or as expansive (high-dimensional) as you like. LSA topic vectors can have as few as one dimension, or they can have thousands of dimensions.

You can add and subtract the topic vectors you'll compute in this chapter just like any other vector. Only this time the sums and differences mean a lot more than they did with TF-IDF vectors (chapter 3). And the distances between topic vectors is useful for things like clustering documents or semantic search. Before, you could cluster and search using keywords and TF-IDF vectors. Now you can cluster and search using semantics, meaning!

When you're done, you'll have one document-topic vector for each document in your corpus. And, even more importantly, you won't have to reprocess the entire corpus to compute a new topic vector for a new document or phrase. You'll have a topic vector for each word in your vocabulary, and you can use these word topic vectors to compute the topic vector for any document that uses some of those words.

> **TIP**  Some algorithms for creating topic vectors, such as latent Dirichlet allocation, do require you to reprocess the entire corpus, every time you add a new document.

You'll have one word-topic vector for each word in your lexicon (vocabulary). So you can compute the topic vector for any new document by just adding up all its word topic vectors.

Coming up with a numerical representation of the semantics (meaning) of words and sentences can be tricky. This is especially true for "fuzzy" languages like English, which has multiple dialects and many different interpretations of the same words. Even formal English text written by an English professor can't avoid the fact that most English words have multiple meanings, a challenge for any new learner, including machine learners. This concept of words with multiple meanings is called *polysemy*:

- *Polysemy*—The existence of words and phrases with more than one meaning

Here are some ways in which polysemy can affect the semantics of a word or statement. We list them here for you to appreciate the power of LSA. You don't have to worry about these challenges. LSA takes care of all this for us:

- *Homonyms*—Words with the same spelling and pronunciation, but different meanings
- *Zeugma*—Use of two meanings of a word simultaneously in the same sentence

And LSA also deals with some of the challenges of polysemy in a voice interface—a chatbot that you can talk to, like Alexa or Siri:

- *Homographs*—Words spelled the same, but with different pronunciations and meanings
- *Homophones*—Words with the same pronunciation, but different spellings and meanings (an NLP challenge with voice interfaces)

Imagine if you had to deal with a statement like the following, if you didn't have tools like LSA to deal with it:

> *She felt … less. She felt tamped down. Dim. More faint. Feint. Feigned. Fain.*
>
> Patrick Rothfuss

Keeping these challenges in mind, can you imagine how you might squash a TF-IDF vector with one million dimensions (terms) down to a vector with 200 or so dimensions (topics)? This is like identifying the right mix of primary colors to try to reproduce the paint color in your apartment so you can cover over those nail holes in your wall.

You'd need to find those word dimensions that "belong" together in a topic and add their TF-IDF values together to create a new number to represent the amount of that topic in a document. You might even weight them for how important they are to the topic, how much you'd like each word to contribute to the "mix." And you could have negative weights for words that reduce the likelihood that the text is about that topic.

### 4.1.3 Thought experiment

Let's walk through a thought experiment. Let's assume you have some TF-IDF vector for a particular document and you want to convert that to a topic vector. You can think about how much each word contributes to your topics.

Let's say you're processing some sentences about pets in Central Park in New York City (NYC). Let's create three topics: one about pets, one about animals, and another about cities. Call these topics "petness," "animalness," and "cityness." So your "petness" topic about pets will score words like "cat" and "dog" significantly, but probably ignore words like "NYC" and "apple." The "cityness" topic will ignore words like "cat" and "dog," but might give a little weight to "apple," just because of the "Big Apple" association.

If you "trained" your topic model like this, without using a computer, only your common sense, you might come up with some weights like this:

```
>>> topic = {}
>>> tfidf = dict(list(zip('cat dog apple lion NYC love'.split(),
...     np.random.rand(6))))
```

This tfidf vector is just a random example, as if it were computed for a single document that contained these words in some random proportion.

```
>>> topic['petness'] = (.3 * tfidf['cat'] +\
...                      .3 * tfidf['dog'] +\
...                       0 * tfidf['apple'] +\
...                       0 * tfidf['lion'] -\
...                      .2 * tfidf['NYC'] +\
...                      .2 * tfidf['love'])
>>> topic['animalness'] = (.1 * tfidf['cat']  +\
...                         .1 * tfidf['dog'] -\
...                         .1 * tfidf['apple'] +\
...                         .5 * tfidf['lion'] +\
...                         .1 * tfidf['NYC'] -\
...                         .1 * tfidf['love'])
>>> topic['cityness']   = ( 0 * tfidf['cat']  -\
...                         .1 * tfidf['dog'] +\
...                         .2 * tfidf['apple'] -\
...                         .1 * tfidf['lion'] +\
...                         .5 * tfidf['NYC'] +\
...                         .1 * tfidf['love'])
```

"Hand-crafted" weights (.3, .3, 0, 0, -.2, .2) are multiplied by imaginary tfidf values to create topic vectors for your imaginary random document. You'll compute real topic vectors later.

In this thought experiment, you added up the word frequencies that might be indicators of each of your topics. You weighted the word frequencies (TF-IDF values) by how likely the word is associated with a topic. You did the same, but subtracted, for words that might be talking about something that is in some sense the opposite of your topic. This isn't a real algorithm walk-through, or example implementation, just a thought experiment. You're just trying to figure out how you can teach a machine to think like you do. You arbitrarily chose to decompose your words and documents into only three topics ("petness," "animalness," and "cityness"). And your vocabulary is limited; it has only six words in it.

The next step is to think through how a human might decide mathematically which topics and words are connected, and what weights those connections should have. Once you decided on three topics to model, you then had to decide how much to weight each word for those topics. You blended words in proportion to each other to make your topic "color mix." The topic modeling transformation (color mixing recipe) is a 3 x 6 matrix of proportions (weights) connecting three topics to six words. You multiplied that matrix by an imaginary 6 x 1 TF-IDF vector to get a 3 x 1 topic vector for that document.

You made a judgment call that the terms "cat" and "dog" should have similar contributions to the "petness" topic (weight of .3). So the two values in the upper left of the matrix for your TF-IDF-to-topic transformation are both .3. Can you imagine ways you might "compute" these proportions with software? Remember, you have a bunch of documents your computer can read, tokenize, and count tokens for. You have TF-IDF vectors for as many documents as you like. Keep thinking about how you might use those counts to compute topic weights for a word as you read on.

You decided that the term "NYC" should have a negative weight for the "petness" topic. In some sense, city names, and proper names in general, and abbreviations, and acronyms, share little in common with words about pets. Think about what "sharing in common" means for words. Is there something in a TF-IDF matrix that represents the meaning that words share in common?

You gave the word "love" a positive weight for the "pets" topic. This may be because you often use the word "love" in the same sentence with words about pets. After all, we humans tend to love our pets. We can only hope that our AI overlords will be similarly loving toward us.

Notice the small amount of the word "apple" into the topic vector for "city." This could be because you're doing this by hand and we humans know that "NYC" and "Big Apple" are often synonymous. Our semantic analysis algorithm will hopefully be able to calculate this synonymy between "apple" and "NYC" based on how often "apple" and "NYC" occur in the same documents.

As you read the rest of the weighted sums in the example "code," try to guess how you came up with these weights for these three topics and six words. How might you change them? What could you use as an objective measure of these proportions (weights)? You may have a different "corpus" in your head than the one we used in our heads. So you may have a different opinion about these words and the weights you gave them. What could you do to come to a consensus about your opinions about these six words and three topics?

> **NOTE**  We chose a signed weighting of words to produce the topic vectors. This allows you to use negative weights for words that are the "opposite" of a topic. And because you're doing this manually by hand, we chose to normalize your topic vectors by the easy-to-compute $L^1$-norm (Manhattan, taxicab, or city-block distance). Nonetheless, the real LSA you'll use later in this chapter normalizes topic vectors by the more useful $L^2$-norm. $L^2$-norm is the conventional Euclidean distance or length that you're familiar with from geometry class. It's the Pythagorean theorem solved for the length of the hypotenuse of a right triangle.

You might have realized in reading these vectors that the relationships between words and topics can be "flipped." The 3 x 6 matrix of three topic vectors can be transposed to produce topic weights for each word in your vocabulary. These vectors of weights would be your word vectors for your six words:

```
>>> word_vector = {}
>>> word_vector['cat']   =   .3*topic['petness'] +\
...                          .1*topic['animalness'] +\
...                          0*topic['cityness']
>>> word_vector['dog']   =   .3*topic['petness'] +\
...                          .1*topic['animalness'] -\
...                          .1*topic['cityness']
>>> word_vector['apple']=    0*topic['petness'] -\
...                          .1*topic['animalness'] +\
...                          .2*topic['cityness']
>>> word_vector['lion'] =    0*topic['petness'] +\
...                          .5*topic['animalness'] -\
...                          .1*topic['cityness']
```

```
>>> word_vector['NYC']  = -.2*topic['petness'] +\
...                       .1*topic['animalness'] +\
...                       .5*topic['cityness']
>>> word_vector['love'] =  .2*topic['petness'] -\
...                       .1*topic['animalness'] +\
...                       .1*topic['cityness']
```

These six topic vectors (shown in Figure 4.1), one for each word, represent the meanings of your six words as 3D vectors.

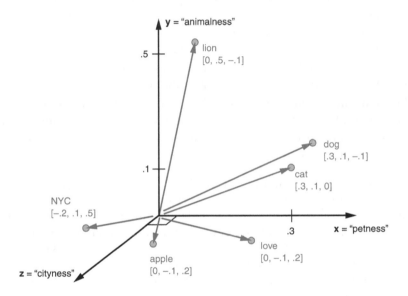

**Figure 4.1   3D vectors for a thought experiment about six words about pets and NYC**

Earlier, the vectors for each topic, with weights for each word, gave you 6-D vectors representing the linear combination of words in your three topics. In your thought experiment, you hand-crafted a three-topic model for a single natural language document! If you just count up occurrences of these six words and multiply them by your weights you get the 3D topic vector for any document. And 3D vectors are fun because they're easy for humans to visualize. You can plot them and share insights about your corpus or a particular document in graphical form. 3D vectors (or any low-dimensional vector space) are great for machine learning classification problems, too. An algorithm can slice through the vector space with a plane (or hyperplane) to divide up the space into classes.

The documents in your corpus might use many more words, but this particular topic vector model will only be influenced by the use of these six words. You could extend this approach to as many words as you had the patience (or an algorithm) for.

As long as your model only needed to separate documents according to three different dimensions or topics, your vocabulary could keep growing as much as you like. In the thought experiment, you compressed six dimensions (TF-IDF normalized frequencies) into three dimensions (topics).

This subjective, labor-intensive approach to semantic analysis relies on human intuition and common sense to break down documents into topics. Common sense is hard to code into an algorithm.[4] So it isn't repeatable—you'd probably come up with different weights than we did. And obviously this isn't suitable for a machine learning pipeline. Plus it doesn't scale well to more topics and words. A human couldn't allocate enough words to enough topics to precisely capture the meaning in any diverse corpus of documents you might want your machine to deal with.

So let's automate this manual procedure. Let's use an algorithm that doesn't rely on common sense to select topic weights for us.[5]

If you think about it, each of these weighted sums is just a dot product. And three dot products (weighted sums) is just a matrix multiplication, or inner product. You multiply a 3 x $n$ weight matrix with a TF-IDF vector (one value for each word in a document), where $n$ is the number of terms in your vocabulary. The output of this multiplication is a new 3 x 1 topic vector for that document. What you've done is "transform" a vector from one vector space (TF-IDFs) to another lower-dimensional vector space (topic vectors). Your algorithm should create a matrix of $n$ terms by $m$ topics that you can multiply by a vector of the word frequencies in a document to get your new topic vector for that document.

> **NOTE** In mathematics, the size of a vocabulary (the set of all possible words in a language) is usually written as $|V|$. And the variable $V$ alone is used to represent the set of possible words in your vocabulary. So if you're writing an academic paper about NLP, use $|V|$ wherever we've used $n$ to describe the size of a vocabulary.

### 4.1.4 An algorithm for scoring topics

You still need an algorithmic way to determine these topic vectors. You need a transformation from TF-IDF vectors into topic vectors. A machine can't tell which words belong together or what any of them signify, can it? J. R. Firth, a 20th century British

---

[4] Doug Lenat at Stanford is trying to do just that, code common sense into an algorithm. See the Wired Magazine article "Doug Lenat's Artificial Intelligence Common Sense Engine" (https://www.wired.com/2016/03/doug-lenat-artificial-intelligence-common-sense-engine).

[5] The Wikipedia page for topic models has a video that shows how this might work for many more topics and words. The darkness of the pixels represents the weight or value or score for a topic and a word, like the weights in your manual example. And the video shows a particular algorithm, called SVD, that reorders the words and topics, to put as much of the "weight" as possible along the diagonal. This helps identify patterns that represent the meanings of both the topics and the words. https://upload.wikimedia.org/wikipedia/commons/7/70/Topic_model_scheme.webm#t=00:00:01,00:00:17.600.

linguist, studied the ways you can estimate what a word or morpheme[6] signifies. In 1957 he gave you a clue about how to compute the topics for words. Firth wrote

*You shall know a word by the company it keeps.*

J. R. Firth

So how do you tell the "company" of a word? Well, the most straightforward approach would be to count co-occurrences in the same document. And you have exactly what you need for that in your bag-of-words (BOW) and TF-IDF vectors from chapter 3. This "counting co-occurrences" approach led to the development of several algorithms for creating vectors to represent the statistics of word usage within documents or sentences.

LSA is an algorithm to analyze your TF-IDF matrix (table of TF-IDF vectors) to gather up words into topics. It works on bag-of-words vectors, too, but TF-IDF vectors give slightly better results.

LSA also optimizes these topics to maintain diversity in the topic dimensions; when you use these new topics instead of the original words, you still capture much of the meaning (semantics) of the documents. The number of topics you need for your model to capture the meaning of your documents is far less than the number of words in the vocabulary of your TF-IDF vectors. So LSA is often referred to as a dimension reduction technique. LSA reduces the number of dimensions you need to capture the meaning of your documents.

Have you ever used a dimension reduction technique for a large matrix of numbers? What about pixels? If you've done machine learning on images or other high-dimensional data, you may have run across a technique called principal component analysis (PCA). As it turns out, PCA is exactly the same math as LSA. PCA, however, is what you say when you're reducing the dimensionality of images or other tables of numbers, rather than bag-of-words vectors or TF-IDF vectors.

Only recently did researchers discover that you could use PCA for semantic analysis of words. That's when they gave this particular application its own name, LSA. Even though you'll see the `scikit-learn` PCA model used shortly, the output of this fit and transform process is a vector representing the semantics of a document. It's still LSA.

And here's one more synonym for LSA you may run across. In the field of information retrieval, where the focus is on creating indexes for full text search, LSA is often referred to as latent semantic indexing (LSI). But this term has fallen out of favor. It doesn't produce an index at all. In fact, the topic vectors it produces are usually too high dimensional to ever be indexed perfectly. So we use the term "LSA" from here on out.

> **TIP**   Indexing is what databases do to be able to retrieve a particular row in a table quickly based on some partial information you provide it about that row. A textbook's index works like this. If you're looking for a particular page, you

---

[6] A *morpheme* is the smallest meaningful parts of a word. See Wikipedia article "Morpheme" (https://en.wikipedia.org/wiki/Morpheme).

can look up words in the index that should be on the page. Then you can go straight to the page or pages that contain all the words you're looking for.

**LSA "COUSINS"**

Two algorithms are similar to LSA, with similar NLP applications, so we mention them here:

- Linear discriminant analysis (LDA)
- Latent Dirichlet allocation (LDiA)[7]

LDA breaks down a document into only one topic. LDiA is more like LSA because it can break down documents into as many topics as you like.

> **TIP** Because it's one dimensional, LDA doesn't require singular value decomposition (SVD). You can just compute the centroid (average or mean) of all your TF-IDF vectors for each side of a binary class, like spam and non-spam. Your dimension then becomes the line between those two centroids. The further a TF-IDF vector is along that line (the dot product of the TF-IDF vector with that line) tells you how close you are to one class or another.

Here's an example of this simple LDA approach to topic analysis first, to get you warmed up before you tackle LSA and LDiA.

### 4.1.5 *An LDA classifier*

LDA is one of the most straightforward and fast dimension reduction and classification models you'll find. But this book may be one of the only places you'll read about it, because it's not very flashy.[8] But in many applications, you'll find it has much better accuracy than the fancier state-of-the art algorithms published in the latest papers. An LDA classifier is a supervised algorithm, so you do need labels for your document classes. But LDA requires far fewer samples than fancier algorithms.

For this example, we show you a simplified implementation of LDA that you can't find in `scikit-learn`. The model "training" has only three steps, so you'll just do them all directly in Python:

1 Compute the average position (centroid) of all the TF-IDF vectors within the class (such as spam SMS messages).
2 Compute the average position (centroid) of all the TF-IDF vectors not in the class (such as nonspam SMS messages).
3 Compute the vector difference between the centroids (the line that connects them).

---

[7] We use the acronym LDiA for latent Dirichlet allocation. Perhaps Panupong (Ice) Pasupat would approve. Panupong was an instructor at Stanford's online CS NLP class about LDiA (https://ppasupat.github.io/a9online/1140.html#latent-dirichlet-allocation-lda-).

[8] You can find it mentioned in papers back in the 1990s, when people had to be efficient with their use of computing and data resources (https://www.researchgate.net/profile/Georges_Hebrail/publication/221299406_Automatic_Document_Classification_Natural_Language_Processing_Statistical_Analysis_and_Expert_System_Techniques_used_together/links/0c960516cf4968b29e000000.pdf).

All you need to "train" an LDA model is to find the vector (line) between the two centroids for your binary class. LDA is a supervised algorithm, so you need labels for your messages. To do *inference* or prediction with that model, you just need to find out if a new TF-IDF vector is closer to the in-class (spam) centroid than it is to the out-of-class (nonspam) centroid. First let's "train" an LDA model to classify SMS messages as spam or nonspam (see the following listing).

---

**Listing 4.1    The SMS spam dataset**

```
>>> import pandas as pd
>>> from nlpia.data.loaders import get_data
>>> pd.options.display.width = 120
>>> sms = get_data('sms-spam')
>>> index = ['sms{}{}'.format(i, '!'*j) for (i,j) in\
...     zip(range(len(sms)), sms.spam)]
>>> sms = pd.DataFrame(sms.values, columns=sms.columns, index=index)
>>> sms['spam'] = sms.spam.astype(int)
>>> len(sms)
4837
>>> sms.spam.sum()
638
>>> sms.head(6)
       spam                                                    text
sms0      0  Go until jurong point, crazy.. Available only ...
sms1      0                    Ok lar... Joking wif u oni...
sms2!     1  Free entry in 2 a wkly comp to win FA Cup fina...
sms3      0  U dun say so early hor... U c already then say...
sms4      0  Nah I don't think he goes to usf, he lives aro...
sms5!     1  FreeMsg Hey there darling it's been 3 week's n...
```

**This line helps display the wide column of SMS text within a Pandas DataFrame printout.**

**This is just for display. You've flagged spam messages by appending an exclamation point, "!", to their label.**

So you have 4,837 SMS messages, and 638 of them are labeled with the binary class label "spam."

Now let's do our tokenization and TF-IDF vector transformation on all these SMS messages:

```
>>> from sklearn.feature_extraction.text import TfidfVectorizer
>>> from nltk.tokenize.casual import casual_tokenize
>>> tfidf_model = TfidfVectorizer(tokenizer=casual_tokenize)
>>> tfidf_docs = tfidf_model.fit_transform(\
...     raw_documents=sms.text).toarray()
>>> tfidf_docs.shape
(4837, 9232)
>>> sms.spam.sum()
638
```

The `nltk.casual_tokenizer` gave you 9,232 words in your vocabulary. You have almost twice as many words as you have messages. And you have almost ten times as many words as spam messages. So your model won't have a lot of information about the words that will indicate whether a message is spam or not. Usually, a Naive Bayes classifier won't work well when your vocabulary is much larger than the number of labeled examples in your dataset. That's where the semantic analysis techniques of this chapter can help.

Let's start with the simplest semantic analysis technique, LDA. You could use the LDA model in `sklearn.discriminant_analysis.LinearDiscriminant-Analysis`. But you only need compute the centroids of your binary class (spam and nonspam) in order to "train" this model, so you'll do that directly:

**You can use this mask to select only the spam rows from a numpy.array or pandas.DataFrame.**

```
>>> mask = sms.spam.astype(bool).values
>>> spam_centroid = tfidf_docs[mask].mean(axis=0)
>>> ham_centroid = tfidf_docs[~mask].mean(axis=0)

>>> spam_centroid.round(2)
array([0.06, 0.  , 0.  , ..., 0.  , 0.  , 0.  ])
>>> ham_centroid.round(2)
array([0.02, 0.01, 0.  , ..., 0.  , 0.  , 0.  ])
```

**Because your TF-IDF vectors are row vectors, you need to make sure numpy computes the mean for each column independently using axis=0.**

Now you can subtract one centroid from the other to get the line between them:

```
>>> spamminess_score = tfidf_docs.dot(spam_centroid -\
...     ham_centroid)
>>> spamminess_score.round(2)
array([-0.01, -0.02,  0.04, ..., -0.01, -0.  ,  0.  ])
```

**The dot product computes the "shadow" or projection of each vector on the line between the centroids.**

This raw `spamminess_score` is the distance along the line from the ham centroid to the spam centroid. We calculated that score by projecting each TF-IDF vector onto that line between the centroids using the dot product. And you did those 4,837 dot products all at once in a "vectorized" numpy operation. This can speed things up 100 times compared to a Python loop.

Figure 4.2 shows a view of the TF-IDF vectors in 3D and where these centroids are for your SMS messages.

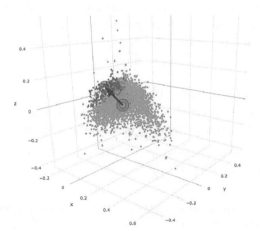

**Figure 4.2  3D scatter plot (point cloud) of your TF-IDF vectors**

The arrow from the nonspam centroid to the spam centroid is the line that defines your trained model. You can see how some of the green dots are on the back side of the arrow, so you could get a negative spamminess score when you project them onto this line between the centroids.

Ideally, you'd like your score to range between 0 and 1, like a probability. The sklearnMinMaxScaler can do that for you:

```
>>> from sklearn.preprocessing import MinMaxScaler
>>> sms['lda_score'] = MinMaxScaler().fit_transform(\
...     spamminess_score.reshape(-1,1))
>>> sms['lda_predict'] = (sms.lda_score > .5).astype(int)
>>> sms['spam lda_predict lda_score'.split()].round(2).head(6)
        spam  lda_predict  lda_score
sms0       0            0       0.23
sms1       0            0       0.18
sms2!      1            1       0.72
sms3       0            0       0.18
sms4       0            0       0.29
sms5!      1            1       0.55
```

That looks pretty good. All of the first six messages were classified correctly when you set the threshold at 50%. Let's see how it did on the rest of the training set:

```
>>> (1. - (sms.spam - sms.lda_predict).abs().sum() / len(sms)).round(3)
0.977
```

Wow! 97.7% of the messages were classified correctly with this simple model. You're not likely to achieve this result in the real world, because you haven't separated out a test set. This A+ score is on test "questions" that the classifier has already "seen." But LDA is a very simple model, with few parameters, so it should generalize well, as long as your SMS messages are representative of the messages you intend to classify. Try it on your own examples to find out. Or even better, check out appendix D and learn how to do what's called "cross validation."

This is the power of semantic analysis approaches. Unlike Naive Bayes or logistic regression models, semantic analysis doesn't rely on individual words.[9] Semantic analysis gathers up words with similar semantics (such as spamminess) and uses them all together. But remember that this training set has a limited vocabulary and some non-English words in it. So your test messages need to use similar words if you want them to be classified correctly.

Let's see what the training set confusion matrix looks like. This shows you the SMS messages that it labeled as spam that weren't spam at all (false positives), and the ones that were labeled as ham that should have been labeled spam (false negatives):

```
>>> from pugnlp.stats import Confusion
>>> Confusion(sms['spam lda_predict'.split()])
lda_predict     0     1
```

---

[9]  Actually, a Naive Bayes classifier and a logistic regression model are both equivalent to this simple LDA model. Dig into the math and the sklearn code if you want to see.

```
spam
0              4135    64
1                45   593
```

That looks nice. You could adjust the 0.5 threshold on your score if the false positives (64) or false negatives (45) were out of balance. Now you're ready to learn about models that can compute *multidimensional* semantic vectors instead of just 1D semantic scores. So far, the only thing your 1D vectors "understand" is the spamminess of words and documents. You'd like them to learn a lot more word nuances and give you a multidimensional vector that captures a word's meaning.

Before you dive into SVD, the math behind multidimensional LSA, we should mention some other approaches first.

### THE OTHER "COUSIN"

LSA has another "cousin." And it has an abbreviation similar to LDA. LDiA stands for latent Dirichlet allocation.[10] LDiA can also be used to generate vectors that capture the semantics of a word or document.

LDiA takes the math of LSA in a different direction. It uses a nonlinear statistical algorithm to group words together. As a result, it generally takes much longer to train than linear approaches like LSA. Often this makes LDiA less practical for many real-world applications, and it should rarely be the first approach you try. Nonetheless, the statistics of the topics it creates sometimes more closely mirror human intuition about words and topics. So LDiA topics will often be easier for you to explain to your boss.

And LDiA is useful for some single-document problems such as document summarization. Your corpus becomes the document, and your documents become the sentences in that "corpus." This is how `gensim` and other packages use LDiA to identify the most "central" sentences of a document. These sentences can then be strung together to create a machine-generated summary.[11]

For most classification or regression problems, you're usually better off using LSA. So we explain LSA and its underlying SVD linear algebra first.

## 4.2 Latent semantic analysis

Latent semantic analysis is based on the oldest and most commonly-used technique for dimension reduction, singular value decomposition. SVD was in widespread use long before the term "machine learning" even existed.[12] SVD decomposes a matrix into three square matrices, one of which is diagonal.

One application of SVD is matrix inversion. A matrix can be inverted by decomposing it into three simpler square matrices, transposing matrices, and then multiplying them back together. You can imagine all the applications for an algorithm that

---

[10] We chose the nonstandard LDiA acronym to distinguish it from the acronym LDA, which *usually* means linear discriminant analysis, but not always. At least in this book, you won't have to guess what we mean by that algorithm. LDA will always mean linear discriminant analysis. LDiA will always mean latent Dirichlet allocation.

[11] We generated some of the text in the "About this book" section using similar math, but implemented in a neural network (see chapter 12).

[12] Google Ngram Viewer (http://mng.bz/qJEA) is a great way to learn about the history of words and concepts.

gives you a shortcut for inverting a large, complicated matrix. SVD is useful for mechanical engineering problems such as truss structure stress and strain analysis. It's also useful for circuit analysis in electrical engineering. And it's even used in data science for behavior-based recommendation engines that run alongside content-based NLP recommendation engines.

Using SVD, LSA can break down your TF-IDF term-document matrix into three simpler matrices. And they can be multiplied back together to produce the original matrix, without any changes. This is like factorization of a large integer. Big whoop. But these three simpler matrices from SVD reveal properties about the original TF-IDF matrix that you can exploit to simplify it. You can truncate those matrices (ignore some rows and columns) before multiplying them back together, which reduces the number of dimensions you have to deal with in your vector space model.

These truncated matrices don't give the exact same TF-IDF matrix you started with—they give you a better one. Your new representation of the documents contains the essence, the "latent semantics" of those documents. That's why SVD is used in other fields for things such as compression. It captures the essence of a dataset and ignores the noise. A JPEG image is ten times smaller than the original bitmap, but it still contains all the information of the original image.

When you use SVD this way in natural language processing, you call it latent semantic analysis. LSA uncovers the semantics, or meaning, of words that is hidden and waiting to be uncovered.

Latent semantic analysis is a mathematical technique for finding the "best" way to linearly transform (rotate and stretch) any set of NLP vectors, like your TF-IDF vectors or bag-of-words vectors. And the "best" way for many applications is to line up the axes (dimensions) in your new vectors with the greatest "spread" or variance in the word frequencies.[13] You can then eliminate those dimensions in the new vector space that don't contribute much to the variance in the vectors from document to document.

Using SVD this way is called *truncated singular value decomposition* (truncated SVD). In the image processing and image compression world, you might have heard of this as *principal component analysis* (PCA). And we show you some tricks that help improve the accuracy of LSA vectors. These tricks are also useful when you're doing PCA for machine learning and feature engineering problems in other areas.

If you've taken linear algebra, you probably learned the algebra behind LSA called singular value decomposition. And if you've done machine learning on images or other high-dimensional data, like time series, you've probably used PCA on those high-dimensional vectors. LSA on natural language documents is equivalent to PCA on TF-IDF vectors.

LSA uses SVD to find the combinations of words that are responsible, together, for the biggest variation in the data. You can rotate your TF-IDF vectors so that the new

---

[13] There are some great visualizations and explanations in chapter 16 of Jurafsky and Martin's NLP textbook (https://web.stanford.edu/~jurafsky/slp3/ed3book.pdf#chapter.16).

dimensions (basis vectors) of your rotated vectors all align with these maximum variance directions. The "basis vectors" are the axes of your new vector space and are analogous to your topic vectors in the three 6-D topic vectors from your thought experiment at the beginning of this chapter. Each of your dimensions (axes) becomes a combination of word frequencies rather than a single word frequency. So you think of them as the weighted combinations of words that make up various "topics" used throughout your corpus.

The machine doesn't "understand" what the combinations of words means, just that they go together. When it sees words like "dog," "cat," and "love" together a lot, it puts them together in a topic. It doesn't know that such a topic is likely about "pets." It might include a lot of words like "domesticated" and "feral" in that same topic, words that mean the opposite of each other. If they occur together a lot in the same documents, LSA will give them high scores for the same topics together. It's up to us humans to look at what words have a high weight in each topic and give them a name.

But you don't have to give the topics a name to make use of them. Just as you didn't analyze all the 1,000s of dimensions in your stemmed bag-of-words vectors or TF-IDF vectors from previous chapters, you don't have to know what all your topics "mean." You can still do vector math with these new topic vectors, just like you did with TF-IDF vectors. You can add and subtract them and estimate the similarity between documents based on their topic vectors instead of just their word counts.

LSA gives you another bit of useful information. Like the "IDF" part of TF-IDF, it tells you which dimensions in your vector are important to the semantics (meaning) of your documents. You can discard those dimensions (topics) that have the least amount of variance between documents. These low-variance topics are usually distractions, noise, for any machine learning algorithm. If every document has roughly the same amount of some topic and that topic doesn't help you tell the documents apart, then you can get rid of it. And that will help generalize your vector representation so it will work better when you use it with documents your pipeline hasn't yet seen, even documents from a different context.

This generalization and compression that LSA performs accomplishes what you attempted in chapter 2 when you ignored stop words. But the LSA dimension reduction is much better, because it's optimal. It retains as much information as possible, and it doesn't discard any words, it only discards dimensions (topics).

LSA compresses more meaning into fewer dimensions. We only have to retain the high-variance dimensions, the major topics that your corpus talks about in a variety of ways (with high variance). And each of these dimensions becomes your "topics," with some weighted combination of all the words captured in each one.

### 4.2.1 *Your thought experiment made real*

Let's use an algorithm to compute some topics like "animalness," "petness," and "cityness" from your thought experiment. You can't tell the LSA algorithm what you want the topics to be about.[14] But let's just try it and see what happens. For a small corpus of short documents such as tweets, chat messages, and lines of poetry, it takes only a few dimensions (topics) to capture the semantics of those documents. See the following listing.

---

**Listing 4.2   Topic-word matrix for LSA on 16 short sentences about cats, dogs, and NYC**

```
>>> from nlpia.book.examples.ch04_catdog_lsa_3x6x16\
...     import word_topic_vectors
>>> word_topic_vectors.T.round(1)
      cat  dog  apple  lion  nyc  love
top0 -0.6 -0.4    0.5  -0.3  0.4  -0.1
top1 -0.1 -0.3   -0.4  -0.1  0.1   0.8
top2 -0.3  0.8   -0.1  -0.5  0.0   0.1
```

The rows in this topic-word matrix are the "word topic vectors" or just "topic vectors" for each word. This is like the word scores used in the sentiment analysis model in chapter 2. These will be the vectors you can use to represent the meaning of a word in any machine learning pipeline; they are also sometimes called word "semantic vectors." And the topic vectors for each word can be added up to compute a topic vector for a document.

Surprisingly SVD created topic vectors analogous to the ones you pulled from your imagination in the thought experiment. The first topic, labeled `topic0`, is a little like your "cityness" topic earlier. The `topic0` weights have larger weights for "apple" and "NYC." But `topic0` came first in the LSA ordering of topics and last in your imagined topics. LSA sorts the topics in order of importance, how much information or variance they represent for your dataset. The `topic0` dimension is along the axis of highest variance in your dataset. You can see the high variance in the cities when you notice several sentences about "NYC" and "apple," and several that don't use those words at all.

And `topic1` looks different from all the thought experiment topics. The LSA algorithm found that "love" was a more important topic than "animalness" for capturing the essence of the documents that you ran it on. The last topic, `topic2`, appears to be about "dog"s, with a little "love" thrown into the mix. The word "cat" is relegated to the "anti-cityness" topic (negative cityness), because cats and cities aren't mentioned together much.

One more short thought experiment should help you appreciate how LSA works—how an algorithm can create topic vectors without knowing what words mean.

#### MAD LIBS

Can you figure out what the word "awas" means from its context in the following statement?

*Awas! Awas! Tom is behind you! Run!*

---

[14] There is an area of research into something called "learned metrics," which you can use to steer the topics toward what you want them to be about. See NIPS paper "Learning Low-Dimensional Metrics" (https://papers.nips.cc/paper/7002-learning-low-dimensional-metrics.pdf) by Lalit Jain, Blake Mason, and Robert Nowak.

You might not guess that Tom is the alpha orangutan in Leakey Park, in Borneo. And you might not know that Tom has been "conditioned" to humans but is territorial, sometimes becoming dangerously aggressive. And your internal natural language processor may not have time to consciously figure out what "awas" means until you have run away to safety.

But once you catch your breath and think about it, you might guess that "awas" means "danger" or "watch out" in Indonesian. Ignoring the real world, and just focusing on the language context, the words, you can often "transfer" a lot of the significance or meaning of words you do know to words that you don't.

Try it sometime, with yourself or with a friend. Like a Mad Libs game,[15] just replace a word in a sentence with a foreign word, or even a made-up word. Then ask a friend to guess what that word means, or ask them to fill in the blank with an English word. Often your friend's guess won't be too far off from a valid translation of the foreign word, or your intended meaning for the made-up word.

Machines, starting with a clean slate, don't have a language to build on. So it takes much more than a single example for them to figure out what the words in it mean. It's like when you look at a sentence full of foreign words. But machines can do it quite well, using LSA, even with just a random sampling of documents containing at least a few mentions of the words you're interested in.

Can you see how shorter documents, like sentences, are better for this than large documents such as articles or books? This is because the meaning of a word is usually closely related to the meanings of the words in the sentence that contains it. But this isn't so true about the words that are far apart within a longer document.[16]

LSA is a way to train a machine to recognize the meaning (semantics) of words and phrases by giving the machine some example usages. Like people, machines can learn better semantics from example usages of words much faster and easier than they can from dictionary definitions. Extracting meaning from example usages requires less logical reasoning than reading all the possible definitions and forms of a word in a dictionary and then encoding that into some logic.

The math you use to uncover the meaning of words in LSA is called singular value decomposition. SVD, from your linear algebra class, is what LSA uses to create vectors like those in the word-topic matrices just discussed.[17]

Finally some NLP in action: we now show you how a machine is able to "play Mad Libs" to understand words.

---

[15] See the web page titled "Mad Libs" (https://en.wikipedia.org/wiki/Mad_Libs).

[16] When Tomas Mikolov was thinking about this as he came up with `Word2vec`, he realized he could tighten up the meaning of word vectors if he tightened up the context even further, limiting the distance between context words to five.

[17] Check out the examples in nlpia/book/examples/ch04_*.py if you want to see the documents and vector math behind this "actualization" of the thought experiment. This was a thought experiment before SVD was used on real natural language sentences. We were lucky that the topics were at all similar.

## 4.3   *Singular value decomposition*

Singular value decomposition is the algorithm behind LSA. Let's start with a corpus of only 11 documents and a vocabulary of 6 words, similar to what you had in mind for your thought experiment:[18]

```
>>> from nlpia.book.examples.ch04_catdog_lsa_sorted\
...     import lsa_models, prettify_tdm
>>> bow_svd, tfidf_svd = lsa_models()      ◁
>>> prettify_tdm(**bow_svd)
   cat dog apple lion nyc love
text
0              1     1                                      NYC is the Big Apple.
1              1     1                                NYC is known as the Big Apple.
2                       1  1                                      I love NYC!
3              1     1                        I wore a hat to the Big Apple party in NYC.
4              1     1                            Come to NYC. See the Big Apple!
5              1                                Manhattan is called the Big Apple.
6    1                                          New York is a big city for a small cat.
7    1                 1                      The lion, a big cat, is the king of the jungle.
8    1                       1                            I love my pet cat.
9                       1  1                            I love New York City (NYC).
10   1   1                                                 Your dog chased mycat.
```

> This performs LSA on the cats_and_dogs corpus using the vocabulary from the thought experiment. You'll soon peak inside this black box.

This is a document-term matrix where each row is a vector of the bag-of-words for a document.

You've limited the vocabulary to match the thought experiment. And you limited the corpus to only a few (11) documents that use the 6 words in your vocabulary. Unfortunately, the sorting algorithm and the limited vocabulary created several identical bag-of-words vectors (NYC, apple). But SVD should be able to "see" that and allocate a topic to that pair of words.

You'll first use SVD on the term-document matrix (the transpose of the document-term matrix above), but it works on TF-IDF matrices or any other vector space model:

```
>>> tdm = bow_svd['tdm']
>>> tdm
        0  1  2  3  4  5  6  7  8  9  10
cat     0  0  0  0  0  0  1  1  1  0  1
dog     0  0  0  0  0  0  0  0  0  0  1
apple   1  1  0  1  1  1  0  0  0  0  0
lion    0  0  0  0  0  0  0  1  0  0  0
nyc     1  1  1  1  1  0  0  0  0  1  0
love    0  0  1  0  0  0  0  0  1  1  0
```

SVD is an algorithm for decomposing any matrix into three "factors," three matrices that can be multiplied together to recreate the original matrix. This is analogous to finding exactly three integer factors for a large integer. But your factors aren't scalar integers, they are 2D real matrices with special properties. The three matrix factors

---

[18] We just chose 11 short sentences to keep the print version short. You could learn a lot by checking out the ch04 examples in nplia and running SVD on larger and larger corpora.

you compute with SVD have some useful mathematical properties you can exploit for dimension reduction and LSA. In linear algebra class you may have used SVD to find the inverse of a matrix. Here you'll use it for LSA to figure out what your topics (groups of related words) need to be.

Whether you run SVD on a BOW term-document matrix or a TF-IDF term-document matrix, SVD will find combinations of words that belong together. SVD finds those co-occurring words by calculating the correlation between the columns (terms) of your term-document matrix.[19] SVD simultaneously finds the correlation of term use between documents and the correlation of documents with each other. With these two pieces of information SVD also computes the linear combinations of terms that have the greatest variation across the corpus. These linear combinations of term frequencies will become your topics. And you'll keep only those topics that retain the most information, the most variance in your corpus. It also gives you the linear transformation (rotation) of your term-document vectors to convert those vectors into shorter topic vectors for each document.

SVD will group terms together that have high correlation with each other (because they occur in the same documents together a lot) and also vary together a lot over the set of documents. We think of these linear combinations of words as "topics." These topics turn your BOW vectors (or TF-IDF vectors) into topic vectors that tell you the topics a document is about. A topic vector is kind of like a summary, or generalization, of what the document is about.

It's unclear who came up with the idea to apply SVD to word counts to create topic vectors. Several linguists were working on similar approaches simultaneously. They were all finding that the semantic similarity between two natural language expressions (or individual words) is proportional to the similarity between the contexts in which words or expressions are used. These researchers include Harris, Z. S. (1951),[20] Koll (1979),[21] Isbell (1998),[22] Dumais et al. (1988),[23] Salton and Lesk (1965),[24] and Deerwester (1990).[25]

Here's what SVD (the heart of LSA) looks like in math notation:

$$W_{mxn} \Rightarrow U_{mxp} \, S_{pxp} \, V_{pxn}{}^T$$

---

[19] This is equivalent to the square root of the dot product of two columns (term-document occurrence vectors), but SVD provides you additional information that computing the correlation directly wouldn't provide.

[20] Jurafsky and Schone cite "Methods in structural linguistics" by Harris, Z. S., 1951 in their 2000 paper "Knowledge-Free Induction of Morphology Using Latent Semantic Analysis" (https://dl.acm.org/ft_gateway .cfm?id=1117615&ftid=570935&dwn=1&#URLTOKEN#) as well as in their slides (https://slidegur.com/doc/ 3928417/knowledge-free-induction-of-morphology-using-latent).

[21] Koll, M. (1979) "Generalized vector spaces model in information retrieval" (https://dl.acm.org/cita-tion.cfm?id=253506) and "Approach to Concept Based Information Retrieval" by Koll, M. (1979).

[22] "Restructuring Sparse High-Dimensional Data for Effective Retrieval" (http://papers.nips.cc/paper/1597 -restructuring-sparse-high-dimensional-data-for-effective-retrieval.pdf) by Charles Lee Isbell, Jr., 1998.

[23] "Using latent semantic analysis to improve access to textual information" by Dumais et al., 1988 (https:// dl.acm.org/citation.cfm?id=57214).

[24] Salton, G., (1965) "The SMART automatic document retrieval system."

[25] Deerwester, S. et al. "Indexing by Latent Semantic Indexing."

In this formula, $m$ is the number of terms in your vocabulary, $n$ is the number of documents in your corpus, and $p$ is the number of topics in your corpus, and this is the same as the number of words. But wait, weren't you trying to end up with fewer dimensions? You want to eventually end up with fewer topics than words, so you can use those topic vectors (rows of the topic-document matrix) as a reduced-dimension representation of the original TF-IDF vectors. You eventually get to that. But at this first stage, you retain all the dimensions in your matrices.

The following sections show you what those three matrices ($U$, $S$, and $V$) look like.

### 4.3.1   *U—left singular vectors*

The $U$ matrix contains the term-topic matrix that tells you about "the company a word keeps."[26] This is the most important matrix for semantic analysis in NLP. The $U$ matrix is called the "left singular vectors" because it contains row vectors that should be multiplied by a matrix of column vectors from the left.[27] $U$ is the cross-correlation between words and topics based on word co-occurrence in the same document. It's a square matrix until you start truncating it (deleting columns). It has the same number of rows and columns as you have words in your vocabulary (m): six. You still have six topics (p), because you haven't truncated this matrix... yet.

---

**Listing 4.3   $U_{mxp}$**

```
>>> import numpy as np
>>> U, s, Vt = np.linalg.svd(tdm)          ◁─┐  You're reusing the tdm term-
>>> import pandas as pd                        document matrix from the
>>> pd.DataFrame(U, index=tdm.index).round(2)  earlier code sections.
          0     1     2     3     4     5
cat   -0.04  0.83 -0.38 -0.00  0.11 -0.38
dog   -0.00  0.21 -0.18 -0.71 -0.39  0.52
apple -0.62 -0.21 -0.51  0.00  0.49  0.27
lion  -0.00  0.21 -0.18  0.71 -0.39  0.52
nyc   -0.75 -0.00  0.24 -0.00 -0.52 -0.32
love  -0.22  0.42  0.69  0.00  0.41  0.37
```

Notice that the SVD algorithm is a bread-and-butter numpy math operation, not a fancy scikit-learn machine learning algorithm.

The $U$ matrix contains all the topic vectors for each word in your corpus as columns. This means it can be used as a transformation to convert a word-document vector (a TF-IDF vector or a BOW vector) into a topic-document vector. You just multiply your topic-word $U$ matrix by any word-document column vector to get a new topic-document

---

[26] If you try to duplicate these results with the PCA model in sklearn, you'll notice that it gets this term-topic matrix from the $\mathbf{V}^T$ matrix because the input dataset is transposed relative to what you did here. scikit-learn always arranges data as row vectors so your term-document matrix in `tdm` is transposed into a document-term matrix when you use `PCA.fit()` or any other sklearn model training.

[27] Mathematicians call these vectors "left eigenvectors" or "row eigenvectors." See the Wikipedia article "Eigenvalues and eigenvectors" (https://en.wikipedia.org/wiki/Eigenvalues_and_eigenvectors#Left_and_right_eigenvectors).

vector. This is because the weights or scores in each cell of the *U* matrix represent how important each word is to each topic. This is exactly what you did in the thought experiment that started this whole cats and dogs adventure in NYC.

Even though you have what you need to map word frequencies to topics, we explain the remaining factors that SVD gives you and how they are used.

### 4.3.2 *S—singular values*

The Sigma or *S* matrix contains the topic "singular values" in a square diagonal matrix.[28] The singular values tell you how much information is captured by each dimension in your new semantic (topic) vector space. A diagonal matrix has nonzero values only along the diagonal from the upper left to the lower right. Everywhere else the *S* matrix will have zeros. So numpy saves space by returning the singular values as an array, but you can easily convert it to a diagonal matrix with the `numpy.diag` function, as shown in the following listing.

---

**Listing 4.4  S$_{pxp}$**

```
>>> s.round(1)
array([3.1, 2.2, 1.8, 1. , 0.8, 0.5])
>>> S = np.zeros((len(U), len(Vt)))
>>> pd.np.fill_diagonal(S, s)
>>> pd.DataFrame(S).round(1)
     0    1    2    3    4    5    6    7    8    9   10
0  3.1  0.0  0.0  0.0  0.0  0.0  0.0  0.0  0.0  0.0  0.0
1  0.0  2.2  0.0  0.0  0.0  0.0  0.0  0.0  0.0  0.0  0.0
2  0.0  0.0  1.8  0.0  0.0  0.0  0.0  0.0  0.0  0.0  0.0
3  0.0  0.0  0.0  1.0  0.0  0.0  0.0  0.0  0.0  0.0  0.0
4  0.0  0.0  0.0  0.0  0.8  0.0  0.0  0.0  0.0  0.0  0.0
5  0.0  0.0  0.0  0.0  0.0  0.5  0.0  0.0  0.0  0.0  0.0
```

---

Like the *U* matrix, your *S* matrix for your 6-word, 6-topic corpus has six rows (p). But it has many more columns (n) filled with zeros. It needs a column for every document so you can multiply it by $V^T$, the document-document matrix, that you'll learn about next. Because you haven't yet reduced the dimensionality by truncating this diagonal matrix, you have as many topics (p) as you have terms in your vocabulary (m), six. And your dimensions (topics) are constructed such that the first dimension contains the most information ("explained variance") about your corpus. That way when you want to truncate your topic model, you can start zeroing out the dimensions at the lower right and work your way up and to the left. You can stop zeroing out these singular values when the error in your topic model starts to contribute significantly to the overall NLP pipeline error.

**TIP**  Here's the trick we mentioned earlier. For NLP, and most other applications, you don't want to retain the variance information in your topic model. The documents you process in the future might not be about the same topics.

---

[28] Mathematicians call these eigenvalues.

In most cases you're better off setting the diagonal elements of your $S$ matrix to ones, creating a rectangular identity matrix that just reshapes the $V^T$ document-document matrix to be compatible with your $U$ word-topic matrix. That way if you multiply this $S$ matrix by some new set of document vectors you won't skew the topic vectors toward your original topic mix (distribution).

### 4.3.3    $V^T$—right singular vectors

The $V^T$ matrix contains the "right singular vectors" as the columns of the document-document matrix. This gives you the shared meaning between documents, because it measures how often documents use the same topics in your new semantic model of the documents. It has the same number of rows (p) and columns as you have documents in your small corpus, 11. See the following listing.

---

**Listing 4.5    $V_{pxn}{}^T$**

```
>>> pd.DataFrame(Vt).round(2)
      0     1     2     3     4     5     6     7     8     9    10
0  -0.44 -0.44 -0.31 -0.44 -0.44 -0.20 -0.01 -0.01 -0.08 -0.31 -0.01
1  -0.09 -0.09  0.19 -0.09 -0.09 -0.09  0.37  0.47  0.56  0.19  0.47
2  -0.16 -0.16  0.52 -0.16 -0.16 -0.29 -0.22 -0.32  0.17  0.52 -0.32
3   0.00 -0.00 -0.00  0.00  0.00  0.00 -0.00  0.71  0.00 -0.00 -0.71
4  -0.04 -0.04 -0.14 -0.04 -0.04  0.58  0.13 -0.33  0.62 -0.14 -0.33
5  -0.09 -0.09  0.10 -0.09 -0.09  0.51 -0.73  0.27 -0.01  0.10  0.27
6  -0.57  0.21  0.11  0.33 -0.31  0.34  0.34 -0.00 -0.34  0.23  0.00
7  -0.32  0.47  0.25 -0.63  0.41  0.07  0.07  0.00 -0.07 -0.18  0.00
8  -0.50  0.29 -0.20  0.41  0.16 -0.37 -0.37 -0.00  0.37 -0.17  0.00
9  -0.15 -0.15 -0.59 -0.15  0.42  0.04  0.04 -0.00 -0.04  0.63 -0.00
10 -0.26 -0.62  0.33  0.24  0.54  0.09  0.09 -0.00 -0.09 -0.23 -0.00
```

---

Like the $S$ matrix, you'll ignore the $V^T$ matrix whenever you're transforming new word-document vectors into your topic vector space. You'll only use it to check the accuracy of your topic vectors for recreating the original word-document vectors that you used to "train" it.

### 4.3.4    SVD matrix orientation

If you've done machine learning with natural language documents before, you may notice that your term-document matrix is "flipped" (transposed) relative to what you're used to seeing in scikit-learn and other packages. In the Naive Bayes sentiment model at the end of chapter 2, and the TF-IDF vectors of chapter 3, you created your training set as a document-term matrix. This is the orientation that scikit-learn models require. Each row of your training set in the sample-feature matrix for a machine learning sample is a document. And each column represented a word or feature of those documents. But when you do the SVD linear algebra directly, your matrix needs to be transposed into term-document format.[29]

---

[29] Actually, within the sklearn.PCA model they leave the document-term matrix unflipped and just flip the SVD matrix math operations. So the PCA model in scikit-learn ignores the $U$ and $S$ matrix and uses only the $V^T$ matrix for its transformation of new document-term row vectors into document-topic row vectors.

**IMPORTANT**   Matrices are named and sized by their rows first, then the columns. So a "term-document" matrix is a matrix where the rows are the words, and the columns are the documents. Matrix dimensions (sizes) work the same way. A 2 x 3 matrix will have two rows and three columns, which means it has an `np.shape()` of `(2, 3)` and a `len()` of two.

Don't forget to transpose your term-document or topic-document matrices back to the scikit-learn orientation before training a machine learning model. In scikit-learn, each row in an NLP training set should contain a vector of the features associated with a document (an email, SMS message, sentence, web page, or any other chunk of text). In NLP training sets, your vectors are row vectors. In traditional linear algebra operations, vectors are usually thought of as column vectors.

In the next section, we go through all this with you to train a scikit-learnTruncatedSVD transformer to transform bag-of-words vectors into topic-document vectors. You'll then transpose those vectors back to create the rows of your training set so you can train a scikit-learn (sklearn) classifier on those document-topic vectors.

**WARNING**   If you're using scikit-learn, you must transpose the feature-document matrix (usually called `X` in sklearn) to create a document-feature matrix to pass into your `.fit()` and `.predict()` methods of a model. Each row in a training set matrix should be a feature vector for a particular sample text, usually a document.[30]

### 4.3.5   Truncating the topics

You now have a topic model, a way to transform word frequency vectors into topic weight vectors. But because you have just as many topics as words, your vector space model has just as many dimensions as the original BOW vectors. You've just created some new words and called them "topics" because they each combine words together in various ratios. You haven't reduced the number of dimensions… yet.

You can ignore the $S$ matrix, because the rows and columns of your $U$ matrix are already arranged so that the most important topics (with the largest singular values) are on the left. Another reason you can ignore $S$ is that most of the word-document vectors you'll want to use with this model, like TF-IDF vectors, have already been normalized. Finally, it just produces better topic models if you set it up this way.[31]

So let's start lopping off columns on the right-hand side of $U$. But wait. How many topics will be enough to capture the essence of a document? One way to measure the accuracy of LSA is to see how accurately you can recreate a term-document matrix from a topic-document matrix. The following listing plots the reconstruction accuracy for the 9-term, 11-document matrix you used earlier to demonstrate SVD.

---

[30] See the scikit-learn documentation on LSA (http://scikit-learn.org/stable/modules/decomposition .html#lsa).

[31] Levy, Goldberg, and Dagan, Improving Distributional Similarity with Lessons Learned from Word Embeddings, 2015.

**Listing 4.6   Term-document matrix reconstruction error**

```
>>> err = []
>>> for numdim in range(len(s), 0, -1):
...     S[numdim - 1, numdim - 1] = 0
...     reconstructed_tdm = U.dot(S).dot(Vt)
...     err.append(np.sqrt((((\
...         reconstructed_tdm - tdm).values.flatten() ** 2).sum()
...         / np.product(tdm.shape)))
>>> np.array(err).round(2)
array([0.06, 0.12, 0.17, 0.28, 0.39, 0.55])
```

When you reconstruct a term-document matrix for your 11 documents using the singular vectors, the more you truncate, the more the error grows. The 3-topic model from earlier would have about 28% error if you used it to reconstruct BOW vectors for each document. Figure 4.3 shows a plot of that accuracy drop as you drop more and more dimensions in your topic model.

As you can see, the accuracy drop is pretty similar, whether you use TF-IDF vectors or BOW vectors for your model. But TF-IDF vectors will perform slightly better if you plan to retain only a few topics in your model.

This is a simple example, but you can see how you might use a plot like this to decide how many topics (dimensions) you want in your model. In some cases you may

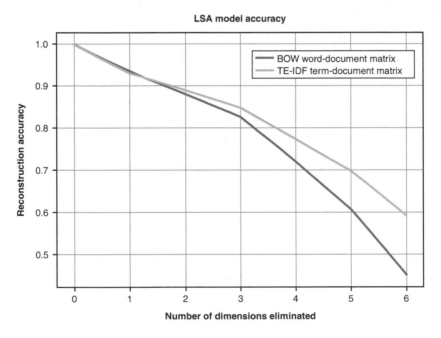

**Figure 4.3   Term-document matrix reconstruction accuracy decreases as you ignore more dimensions.**

find that you get perfect accuracy, after eliminating several of the dimensions in your term-document matrix. Can you guess why?

The SVD algorithm behind LSA "notices" if words are always used together and puts them together in a topic. That's how it can get a few dimensions "for free." Even if you don't plan to use a topic model in your pipeline, LSA (SVD) can be a great way to compress your word-document matrices and identify potential compound words or *n*-grams for your pipeline.

## 4.4 *Principal component analysis*

Principal component analysis is another name for SVD when it's used for dimension reduction, like you did to accomplish your latent semantic analysis earlier. And the PCA model in scikit-learn has some tweaks to the SVD math that will improve the accuracy of your NLP pipeline.

For one, sklearn.PCA automatically "centers" your data by subtracting off the mean word frequencies. Another, more subtle trick is that PCA uses a function called `flip_sign` to deterministically compute the sign of the singular vectors.[32]

Finally, the sklearn implementation of PCA implements an optional "whitening" step. This is similar to your trick of ignoring the singular values when transforming word-document vectors into topic-document vectors. Instead of just setting all the singular values in *S* to one, whitening divides your data by these variances just like the `sklearn.StandardScaler` transform does. This helps spread out your data and makes any optimization algorithm less likely to get lost in "half pipes" or "rivers" of your data that can arise when features in your dataset are correlated with each other.[33]

Before you apply PCA to real-world, high-dimensional NLP data, let's take a step back and look at a more visual representation of what PCA and SVD do. This will also help you understand the API for the scikit-learn PCA implementation. PCA is useful for a wide range of applications, so this insight will be helpful for more than just NLP. You're going to do PCA on a 3D point cloud before you try it out on high-dimensional natural language data.

For most "real" problems, you'll want to use the sklearn.PCA model for your latent semantic analysis. The one exception is if you have more documents than you can hold in RAM. In that case, you'll need to use the IncrementalPCA model in sklearn or some of the scaling techniques we talk about in chapter 13.

> **TIP** If you have a huge corpus and you urgently need topic vectors (LSA), skip to chapter 13 and check out gensim.models.LsiModel (https://radimre-hurek.com/gensim/models/lsimodel.html). If a single machine still isn't enough to get the work done quickly, check out RocketML's parallelization of the SVD algorithm (http://rocketml.net).

---

[32] You can find some experiments with these functions within PCA that you used to understand all these subtleties in nlpia.book.examples.ch04_sklearn_pca_source.

[33] See the web page titled "Deep Learning Tutorial - PCA and Whitening" (http://mccormickml.com/2014/06/03/deep-learning-tutorial-pca-and-whitening/).

You're going to start with a set of real-world 3D vectors, rather than 10,000+ dimensional document-word vectors. It's a lot easier to visualize things in 3D than it is in 10,000-D. Because you're only dealing with three dimensions, it's straightforward to plot them using the `Axes3D` class in Matplotlib. See the nlpia (http://github.com/totalgood/nlpia) package for the code to create rotatable 3D plots like this.

In fact, the point cloud shown in Figure 4.4 is from the 3D scan of the surface of a real-world object, not the pointy tips of a set of BOW vectors. But this will help you get a feel for how LSA works. And you can see how to manipulate and plot small vectors before you tackle higher-dimensional vectors such as document-word vectors.

Can you guess what this 3D object is that created these 3D vectors? You only have a 2D projection printed in this book to go on. Can you think of how you would program a machine to rotate the object around so that you could get a better view? Are there statistics about the data points that you could use to optimally align the X and Y axes with the object? As you rotate the 3D blob in your mind, imagine how the variance along the X, Y, and Z axes might change as you rotate it.

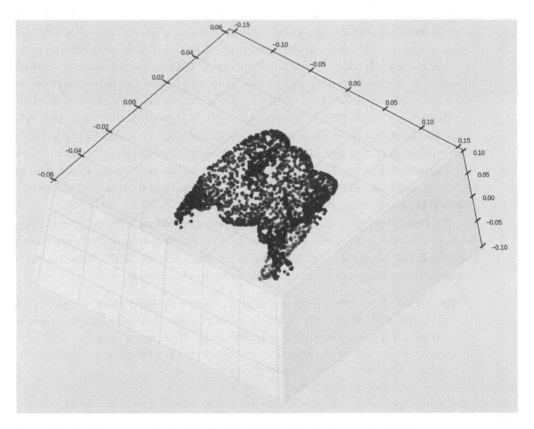

**Figure 4.4   Looking up from below the "belly" at the point cloud for a real object**

### 4.4.1   *PCA on 3D vectors*

We manually rotated the point cloud into this particular orientation to *minimize* the variance along the axes of the window for the plot. We did that so that you'd have a hard time recognizing what it is. If SVD (LSA) did this to your document-word vectors, it would "hide" the information in those vectors. Stacking the points on top of each other in your 2D projection prevents human eyes, or machine learning algorithms, from separating the points into meaningful clusters. But SVD preserves the structure, information content, of your vectors by *maximizing* the variance along the dimensions of your lower-dimensional "shadow" of the high-dimensional space. This is what you need for machine learning so that each low-dimensional vector captures the "essence" of whatever it represents. SVD *maximizes* the variance along each axis. And variance turns out to be a pretty good indicator of "information," or that "essence" you're looking for:

```
>>> import pandas as pd
>>> pd.set_option('display.max_columns', 6)        ◀── Ensure that your pd.DataFrame printouts fit within the width of a page.
>>> from sklearn.decomposition import PCA          ◀── Even though it's called PCA in scikit-learn, this is SVD.
>>> import seaborn
>>> from matplotlib import pyplot as plt
>>> from nlpia.data.loaders import get_data

>>> df = get_data('pointcloud').sample(1000)       ── You're reducing a 3D point cloud to a 2D "projection" for display in a 2D scatter plot.
>>> pca = PCA(n_components=2)                       ◀──
>>> df2d = pd.DataFrame(pca.fit_transform(df), columns=list('xy'))
>>> df2d.plot(kind='scatter', x='x', y='y')
>>> plt.show()
```

If you run this script, the orientation of your 2D projection may randomly "flip" left to right, but it never tips or twists to a new angle. The orientation of the 2D projection is computed so that the maximum variance is always aligned with the x axis, the first axis. The second largest variance is always aligned with the y axis, the second dimension of your "shadow" or "projection." But the *polarity* (sign) of these axes is arbitrary because the optimization has two remaining degrees of freedom. The optimization is free to flip the polarity of the vectors (points) along the x or y axis, or both.

There's also a horse_plot.py script in the nlpia/data directory if you'd like to play around with the 3D orientation of the horse. There may indeed be a more optimal transformation of the data that eliminates one dimension without reducing the information content of that data (to your eye). And Picasso's cubist "eye" might come up with a nonlinear transformation that maintains the information content of views from multiple perspectives all at once. And there are "embedding" algorithms to do this, like the one we talk about in chapter 6.

But don't you think good old linear SVD and PCA do a pretty good job of preserving the "information" in the point cloud vector data? Doesn't your 2D projection of the 3D horse provide a good view of the data? Wouldn't a machine be able to learn

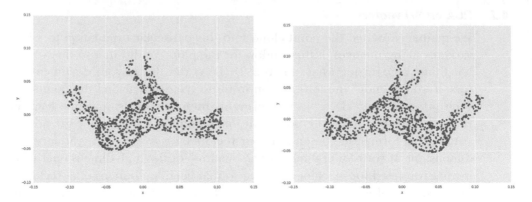

Figure 4.5   Head-to-head horse point clouds upside-down

something from the statistics of these 2D vectors computed from the 3D vectors of the surface of a horse (see figure 4.5)?

### 4.4.2   Stop horsing around and get back to NLP

Let's see how SVD will do on some natural language documents. Let's find the principal components using SVD on the 5,000 SMS messages labeled as spam (or not). The vocabulary and variety of topics discussed in this limited sct of SMS messages from a university lab should be relatively small. So let's limit the number of topics to 16. You'll use both the scikit-learn PCA model as well as the truncated SVD model to see if there are any differences.

The truncated SVD model is designed to work with sparse matrices. *Sparse matrices* are matrices that have the same value (usually zero or NaN) in a lot of the cells. NLP bag-of-words and TF-IDF matrices are almost always sparse, because most documents don't contain many of the words in your vocabulary. Most of your word counts are zero (before you add a "ghost" count to them all to smooth your data out).

Sparse matrices are like spreadsheets that are mostly empty, but have a few meaningful values scattered around. The sklearn PCA model may provide a faster solution than `TruncatedSVD` by using dense matrices with all those zeros filled in. But sklearn.PCA wastes a lot of RAM trying to "remember" all those zeros that are duplicated all over the place. The `TfidfVectorizer` in scikit-learn outputs sparse matrices, so you need to convert those to dense matrices before you compare the results to PCA.

First, let's load the SMS messages from a `DataFrame` in the `nlpia` package:

```
>>> import pandas as pd
>>> from nlpia.data.loaders import get_data
>>> pd.options.display.width = 120            ◁──┐ This helps the wide Pandas
                                                 │ DataFrames print out a bit prettier.
>>> sms = get_data('sms-spam')
```

```
>>> index = ['sms{}{}'.format(i, '!'*j)
⟹    for (i,j) in zip(range(len(sms)), sms.spam)]     ◄──
>>> sms.index = index
>>> sms.head(6)
```

> **You're adding an exclamation mark to the sms message index numbers to make them easier to spot.**

```
          spam                                                         text
sms0         0  Go until jurong point, crazy.. Available only ...
sms1         0                         Ok lar... Joking wif u oni...
sms2!        1  Free entry in 2 a wkly comp to win FA Cup fina...
sms3         0  U dun say so early hor... U c already then say...
sms4         0  Nah I don't think he goes to usf, he lives aro...
sms5!        1  FreeMsg Hey there darling it's been 3 week's n...
```

Now you can calculate the TF-IDF vectors for each of these messages:

```
>>> from sklearn.feature_extraction.text import TfidfVectorizer
>>> from nltk.tokenize.casual import casual_tokenize

>>> tfidf = TfidfVectorizer(tokenizer=casual_tokenize)
>>> tfidf_docs = tfidf.fit_transform(raw_documents=sms.text).toarray()
>>> len(tfidf.vocabulary_)
9232

>>> tfidf_docs = pd.DataFrame(tfidf_docs)
>>> tfidf_docs = tfidf_docs - tfidf_docs.mean()     ◄──
>>> tfidf_docs.shape                                ◄──
(4837, 9232)
>>> sms.spam.sum()                            ◄──
638
```

> **This centers your vectorized documents (BOW vectors) by subtracting the mean.**

> **The .shape attribute tells you the length of each of the dimensions for any numpy array.**

> **The .sum() method on a Pandas Series acts just like a spreadsheet column sum, adding up all the elements.**

So you have 4,837 SMS messages with 9,232 different 1-gram tokens from your tokenizer (`casual_tokenize`). Only 638 of these 4,837 messages (13%) are labeled as spam. So you have an unbalanced training set with about 8:1 ham (normal SMS messages) to spam (unwanted solicitations and advertisements).

You might deal with this ham sampling bias by reducing the "reward" for any model that classifies ham correctly. But the large vocabulary size, $|V|$, is trickier to deal with. The 9,232 tokens in your vocabulary is greater than the 4,837 messages (samples) you have to go on. So you have many more unique words in your vocabulary (or lexicon) than you have SMS messages. And of those SMS messages only a small portion of them (1/8th) are labeled as spam. That's a recipe for overfitting.[34] Only a few unique words out of your large vocabulary will be labeled as "spammy" words in your dataset.

Overfitting means that you will "key" off of only a few words in your vocabulary. So your spam filter will be dependent on those spammy words being somewhere in the spammy messages it filters out. Spammers could easily get around your filter if they just used synonyms for those spammy words. If your vocabulary doesn't include the spammer's new synonyms, then your filter will mis-classify those cleverly constructed SMS messages as ham.

---

[34] See the web page titled "Overfitting" (https://en.wikipedia.org/wiki/Overfitting).

And this overfitting problem is an inherent problem in NLP. It's hard to find a labeled natural language dataset that includes all the ways that people might say something that should be labeled that way. We couldn't find a big database of SMS messages that included all the different ways people say spammy and nonspammy things. And only a few corporations have the resources to create such a dataset. So all the rest of you need to have "countermeasures" for overfitting. You have to use algorithms that "generalize" well on just a few examples.

Dimension reduction is the primary countermeasure for overfitting. By consolidating your dimensions (words) into a smaller number of dimensions (topics), your NLP pipeline will become more "general." Your spam filter will work on a wider range of SMS messages if you reduce your dimensions, or "vocabulary."

That's exactly what LSA does—it reduces your dimensions and therefore helps prevent overfitting.[35] It generalizes from your small dataset by assuming a linear relationship between word counts. So if the word "half" occurs in spammy messages containing words like "off" a lot (as in "Half off!"), LSA helps you make those connections between words and sees how strong they are so it will generalize from the phrase "half off" in a spammy message to phrases like "80% off." And it might even generalize further to the phrase "80% discount" if the chain of connections in your NLP data includes "discount" associated with the word "off."

> **TIP**  Some think of generalization as the core challenge of machine learning and artificial intelligence. "One-shot learning" is often used to describe research into models that take this to the extreme, requiring orders of magnitude less data to accomplish the same accuracy as conventional models.

Generalizing your NLP pipeline helps ensure that it applies to a broader set of real-world SMS messages instead of just this particular set of messages.

### 4.4.3   *Using PCA for SMS message semantic analysis*

Let's try the PCA model from scikit-learn first. You've already seen it in action wrangling 3D horses into a 2D pen; now let's wrangle your dataset of 9,232-D TF-IDF vectors into 16-D topic vectors:

```
>>> from sklearn.decomposition import PCA

>>> pca = PCA(n_components=16)
>>> pca = pca.fit(tfidf_docs)
>>> pca_topic_vectors = pca.transform(tfidf_docs)
>>> columns = ['topic{}'.format(i) for i in range(pca.n_components)]
>>> pca_topic_vectors = pd.DataFrame(pca_topic_vectors, columns=columns,\
...     index=index)
>>> pca_topic_vectors.round(3).head(6)
      topic0  topic1  topic2  ...   topic13  topic14  topic15
sms0   0.201   0.003   0.037  ...    -0.026   -0.019    0.039
sms1   0.404  -0.094  -0.078  ...    -0.036    0.047   -0.036
```

---

[35] More on overfitting and generalization in appendix D.

```
sms2!  -0.030  -0.048   0.090   ...    -0.017  -0.045   0.057
sms3    0.329  -0.033  -0.035   ...    -0.065   0.022  -0.076
sms4    0.002   0.031   0.038   ...     0.031  -0.081  -0.021
sms5!  -0.016   0.059   0.014   ...     0.077  -0.015   0.021
```

If you're curious about these topics, you can find out how much of each word they "contain" by examining their weights. By looking at the weights, you can see how often "half" occurs with the word "off" (as in "half off") and then figure out which topic is your "discount" topic.

> **TIP** You can find the weights of any fitted sklearn transformation by examining its .components_ attribute.

First let's assign words to all the dimensions in your PCA transformation. You need to get them in the right order because your TFIDFVectorizer stores the vocabulary as a dictionary that maps each term to an index number (column number):

```
>>> tfidf.vocabulary_
{'go': 3807,
 'until': 8487,
 'jurong': 4675,
 'point': 6296,
 ...
>>> column_nums, terms = zip(*sorted(zip(tfidf.vocabulary_.values(),\
...      tfidf.vocabulary_.keys()))))
>>> terms
('!',
 '"',
 '#',
 '#150',
 ...
```

**Sort the vocabulary by term count. This "zip(\*sorted(zip()))" pattern is useful when you want to unzip something to sort by an element that isn't on the far left, and then rezip it after sorting.**

Now you can create a nice Pandas DataFrame containing the weights, with labels for all the columns and rows in the right place:

```
>>> weights = pd.DataFrame(pca.components_, columns=terms,
        index=['topic{}'.format(i) for i in range(16)])
>>> pd.options.display.max_columns = 8
>>> weights.head(4).round(3)
           !       "       #    ...            ...      ?     ?ud      ?
topic0  0.071   0.008  -0.001   ...    -0.002   0.001   0.001   0.001
topic1  0.063   0.008   0.000   ...     0.003   0.001   0.001   0.001
topic2  0.071   0.027   0.000   ...     0.002  -0.001  -0.001  -0.001
topic3 -0.059  -0.032  -0.001   ...     0.001   0.001   0.001   0.001
```

Some of those columns (terms) aren't that interesting, so let's explore your tfidf.vocabulary. Let's see if you can find some of those "half off" terms and which topics they're a part of:

```
>>> pd.options.display.max_columns = 12
>>> deals = weights['! ;) :) half off free crazy deal only $ 80 %'.split()].r
    ound(3) * 100
>>> deals
```

```
              !   ;)    :)  half  off  free  crazy  deal  only     $    80     %
topic0     -7.1   0.1  -0.5 -0.0 -0.4  -2.0   -0.0  -0.1  -2.2   0.3  -0.0  -0.0
topic1      6.3   0.0   7.4  0.1  0.4  -2.3   -0.2  -0.1  -3.8  -0.1  -0.0  -0.2
topic2      7.1   0.2  -0.1  0.1  0.3   4.4    0.1  -0.1   0.7   0.0   0.0   0.1
topic3     -5.9  -0.3  -7.1  0.2  0.3  -0.2    0.0   0.1  -2.3   0.1  -0.1  -0.3
topic4     38.1  -0.1 -12.5 -0.1 -0.2   9.9    0.1  -0.2   3.0   0.3   0.1  -0.1
topic5    -26.5   0.1  -1.5 -0.3 -0.7  -1.4   -0.6  -0.2  -1.8  -0.9   0.0   0.0
topic6    -10.9  -0.5  19.9 -0.4 -0.9  -0.6   -0.2  -0.1  -1.4  -0.0  -0.0  -0.1
topic7     16.4   0.1 -18.2  0.8  0.8  -2.9    0.0   0.0  -1.9  -0.3   0.0  -0.1
topic8     34.6   0.1   5.2 -0.5 -0.5  -0.1   -0.4  -0.4   3.3  -0.6  -0.0  -0.2
topic9      6.9  -0.3  17.4  1.4 -0.9   6.6   -0.5  -0.4   3.3  -0.4  -0.0   0.0
...
>>> deals.T.sum()
topic0     -11.9
topic1       7.5
topic2      12.8
topic3     -15.5
topic4      38.3
topic5     -33.8
topic6       4.8
topic7      -5.3
topic8      40.5
topic9      33.1
...
```

Topics 4, 8, and 9 appear to all contain positive "deal" topic sentiment. And topics 0, 3, and 5 appear to be "anti-deal" topics, messages about stuff that's the opposite of "deals": negative deals. So words associated with "deals" can have a positive impact on some topics and a negative impact on others. There's no single obvious "deal" topic number.

> **IMPORTANT**  The `casual_tokenize` tokenizer splits `"80%"` into `["80", "%"]` and `"$80 million"` into `["$", 80, "million"]`. So unless you use LSA or a 2-gram tokenizer, your NLP pipeline wouldn't notice the difference between 80% and $80 million. They'd both share the token "80."

This is one of the challenges of LSA, making sense of the topics. LSA only allows for linear relationships between words. And you usually only have a small corpus to work with. So your topics tend to combine words in ways that humans don't find all that meaningful. Several words from different topics will be crammed together into a single dimension (principle component) in order to make sure the model captures as much variance in usage of your 9,232 words as possible.

### 4.4.4   *Using truncated SVD for SMS message semantic analysis*

Now you can try the `TruncatedSVD` model in scikit-learn. This is a more direct approach to LSA that bypasses the scikit-learn `PCA` model so you can see what's going on inside the `PCA` wrapper. It can handle sparse matrices, so if you're working with large datasets you'll want to use `TruncatedSVD` instead of `PCA` anyway. The SVD part of `TruncatedSVD` will split your TF-IDF matrix into three matrices. The Truncated part of `TruncatedSVD` will discard the dimensions that contain the least information about your TF-IDF matrix. These discarded dimensions represent the "topics" (linear combinations of words) that vary the least within your document set. These discarded topics would likely be meaningless to the overall semantics of your corpus. They'd likely contain a lot of stop words and other words that are uniformly distributed across all the documents.

You're going to use TruncatedSVD to retain only the 16 most interesting topics, the topics that account for the most variance in your TF-IDF vectors:

Just like in PCA, you'll compute 16 topics but will iterate through the data 100 times (default is 5) to ensure that your answer is almost as exact as PCA.

fit_transpose decomposes your TF-IDF vectors and transforms them into topic vectors in one step.

```
>>> from sklearn.decomposition import TruncatedSVD

>>> svd = TruncatedSVD(n_components=16, n_iter=100)
>>> svd_topic_vectors = svd.fit_transform(tfidf_docs.values)
>>> svd_topic_vectors = pd.DataFrame(svd_topic_vectors, columns=columns,\
...       index=index)
>>> svd_topic_vectors.round(3).head(6)
       topic0  topic1  topic2  ...   topic13  topic14  topic15
sms0    0.201   0.003   0.037  ...    -0.036   -0.014    0.037
sms1    0.404  -0.094  -0.078  ...    -0.021    0.051   -0.042
sms2!  -0.030  -0.048   0.090  ...    -0.020   -0.042    0.052
sms3    0.329  -0.033  -0.035  ...    -0.046    0.022   -0.070
sms4    0.002   0.031   0.038  ...     0.034   -0.083   -0.021
sms5!  -0.016   0.059   0.014  ...     0.075   -0.001    0.020
```

These topic vectors from TruncatedSVD are exactly the same as what PCA produced! This result is because you were careful to use a large number of iterations (n_iter), and you also made sure all your TF-IDF frequencies for each term (column) were centered on zero (by subtracting the mean for each term).

Look at the weights for each topic for a moment and try to make sense of them. Without knowing what these topics are about, or the words they weight heavily, do you think you could classify these six SMS messages as spam or not? Perhaps looking at the "!" label next to the spammy SMS message row labels will help. It would be hard, but it is possible, especially for a machine that can look at all 5,000 of your training examples and come up with thresholds on each topic to separate the topic space for spam and nonspam.

### 4.4.5 *How well does LSA work for spam classification?*

One way to find out how well a vector space model will work for classification is to see how cosine similarities between vectors correlate with membership in the same class. Let's see if the cosine similarity between corresponding pairs of documents is useful for your particular binary classification. Let's compute the dot product between the first six topic vectors for the first six SMS messages. You should see larger positive cosine similarity (dot products) between any spam message ("sms2!"):

> **Normalizing each topic vector by its length (L2-norm) allows you to compute the cosine distances with a dot product.**

```
>>> import numpy as np

>>> svd_topic_vectors = (svd_topic_vectors.T / np.linalg.norm(\
...      svd_topic_vectors, axis=1)).T
>>> svd_topic_vectors.iloc[:10].dot(svd_topic_vectors.iloc[:10].T).round(1)
       sms0   sms1  sms2!   sms3   sms4  sms5!   sms6   sms7  sms8!  sms9!
sms0    1.0    0.6   -0.1    0.6   -0.0   -0.3   -0.3   -0.1   -0.3   -0.3
sms1    0.6    1.0   -0.2    0.8   -0.2    0.0   -0.2   -0.2   -0.1   -0.1
sms2!  -0.1   -0.2    1.0   -0.2    0.1    0.4    0.0    0.3    0.5    0.4
sms3    0.6    0.8   -0.2    1.0   -0.2   -0.3   -0.1   -0.3   -0.2   -0.1
sms4   -0.0   -0.2    0.1   -0.2    1.0    0.2    0.0    0.1   -0.4   -0.2
sms5!  -0.3    0.0    0.4   -0.3    0.2    1.0   -0.1    0.1    0.3    0.4
sms6   -0.3   -0.2    0.0   -0.1    0.0   -0.1    1.0    0.1   -0.2   -0.2
sms7   -0.1   -0.2    0.3   -0.3    0.1    0.1    0.1    1.0    0.1    0.4
sms8!  -0.3   -0.1    0.5   -0.2   -0.4    0.3   -0.2    0.1    1.0    0.3
sms9!  -0.3   -0.1    0.4   -0.1   -0.2    0.4   -0.2    0.4    0.3    1.0
```

Reading down the "sms0" column (or across the "sms0" row), the cosine similarity between "sms0" and the spam messages ("sms2!," "sms5!," "sms8!," "sms9!") is significantly negative. The topic vector for "sms0" is significantly different from the topic vector for spam messages. A nonspam message doesn't talk about the same thing as spam messages.

Doing the same for the "sms2!" column should show a positive correlation with other spam messages. Spam messages share similar semantics; they talk about similar "topics."

This is how semantic search works as well. You can use the cosine similarity between a query vector and all the topic vectors for your database of documents to find the most semantically similar message in your database. The closest document (smallest distance) to the vector for that query would correspond to the document with the closest meaning. Spaminess is just one of the "meanings" mixed into your SMS message topics.

Unfortunately, this similarity between topic vectors within each class (spam and nonspam) isn't maintained for all the messages. "Drawing a line" between the spam and nonspam messages would be hard for this set of topic vectors. You'd have a hard time setting a threshold on the similarity to an individual spam message that would ensure that you'd always be able to classify spam and nonspam correctly. But, generally, the less spammy a message is, the further away it is (less similar it is) from another spam message in the dataset. That's what you need if you want to build a spam filter using these topic vectors. And a machine learning algorithm can look at all the topics individually for all the spam and nonspam labels and perhaps draw a hyperplane or other boundary between the spam and nonspam messages.

When using truncated SVD, you should discard the eigenvalues before computing the topic vectors. You tricked the scikit-learn implementation of TruncatedSVD into ignoring the scale information within the eigenvalues (the `Sigma` or `S` matrix in your diagrams) by

- Normalizing your TF-IDF vectors by their length ($L^2$-norm)
- Centering the TF-IDF term frequencies by subtracting the mean frequency for each term (word)

The normalization process eliminates any "scaling" or bias in the eigenvalues and focuses your SVD on the rotation part of the transformation of your TF-IDF vectors. By ignoring the eigenvalues (vector scale or length), you can "square up" the hyper-cube that bounds the topic vector space, which allows you to treat all topics as equally important in your model. If you want to use this trick within your own SVD implementation, you can normalize all the TF-IDF vectors by the $L^2$-norm before computing the SVD or truncated SVD. The scikit-learn implementation of PCA does this for you by "centering" and "whitening" your data.

Without this normalization, infrequent topics will be given slightly more weight than they would otherwise. Because "spaminess" is a rare topic, occurring only 13% of the time, the topics that measure it would be given more weight by this normalization or eigenvalue discarding. The resulting topics are more correlated with subtle characteristics, like spaminess, by taking this approach.

> **TIP** Whichever algorithm or implementation you use for semantic analysis (LSA, PCA, SVD, truncated SVD, or LDiA), you should normalize your BOW or TF-IDF vectors first. Otherwise, you may end up with large scale differences between your topics. Scale differences between topics can reduce the ability of your model to differentiate between subtle, infrequent topics. Another way to think of it is that scale variation can create deep canyons and rivers in a contour plot of your objective function, making it hard for other machine learning algorithms to find the optimal thresholds on your topics in this rough terrain.

### LSA AND SVD ENHANCEMENTS

The success of singular value decomposition for semantic analysis and dimension reduction has motivated researchers to extend and enhance it. These enhancements are mostly intended for non-NLP problems, but we mention them here in case you run across them. They're sometimes used for behavior-based recommendation engines alongside NLP content-based recommendation engines. And they've been used on natural language part-of-speech statistics.[36] Any matrix factorization or dimension reduction approach can be used with natural language term frequencies. So you may find use for them in your semantic analysis pipeline:

- Quadratic discriminant analysis (QDA)
- Random projection
- Nonnegative matrix factorization (NMF)

---

[36] See the paper titled "Part-of-speech Histograms for Genre Classification of Text" by S. Feldman, M. A. Marin, M. Ostendorf, and M. R. Gupta (http://citeseerx.ist.psu.edu/viewdoc/download?doi=10.1.1.332.629&rep=rep1&type=pdf).

QDA is an alternative to LDA. QDA creates quadratic polynomial transformations, rather than linear transformations. These transformations define a vector space that can be used to discriminate between classes. And the boundary between classes in a QDA vector space is quadratic, curved, like a bowl or sphere or halfpipe.

Random projection is a matrix decomposition and transformation approach similar to SVD, but the algorithm is stochastic, so you get a different answer each time you run it. But the stochastic nature makes it easier to run it on parallel machines. And in some cases (for some of those random runs), you can get transformations that are better than what comes out of SVD (and LSA). But random projection is rarely used for NLP problems, and there aren't widely used implementations of it in NLP packages such as Spacy or NLTK. We leave it to you to explore this one further, if you think it might apply to your problem.

In most cases, you're better off sticking with LSA, which uses the tried and true SVD algorithm under the hood.[37]

## 4.5    *Latent Dirichlet allocation (LDiA)*

We've spent most of this chapter talking about latent semantic analysis and various ways to accomplish it using scikit-learn or even just plain numpy. LSA should be your first choice for most topic modeling, semantic search, or content-based recommendation engines.[38] Its math is straightforward and efficient, and it produces a linear transformation that can be applied to new batches of natural language without training and with little loss in accuracy. But LDiA can give slightly better results in some situations.

LDiA does a lot of the things you did to create your topic models with LSA (and SVD under the hood), but unlike LSA, LDiA assumes a Dirichlet distribution of word frequencies. It's more precise about the statistics of allocating words to topics than the linear math of LSA.

LDiA creates a semantic vector space model (like your topic vectors) using an approach similar to how your brain worked during the thought experiment earlier in the chapter. In your thought experiment, you manually allocated words to topics based on how often they occurred together in the same document. The topic mix for a document can then be determined by the word mixtures in each topic by which topic those words were assigned to. This makes an LDiA topic model much easier to understand, because the words assigned to topics and topics assigned to documents tend to make more sense than for LSA.

LDiA assumes that each document is a mixture (linear combination) of some arbitrary number of topics that you select when you begin training the LDiA model. LDiA

---

[37] SVD has traditionally been used to compute the "pseudo-inverse" of nonsquare matrices, and you can imagine how many applications exist for matrix inversion.

[38] A 2015 comparison of content-based movie recommendation algorithms by Sonia Bergamaschi and Laura Po found LSA to be approximately twice as accurate as LDiA. See "Comparing LDA and LSA Topic Models for Content-Based Movie Recommendation Systems" by Sonia Bergamaschi and Laura Po (https://www.dbgroup .unimo.it/~po/pubs/LNBI_2015.pdf).

also assumes that each topic can be represented by a distribution of words (term frequencies). The probability or weight for each of these topics within a document, as well as the probability of a word being assigned to a topic, is assumed to start with a Dirichlet probability distribution (the *prior* if you remember your statistics). This is where the algorithm gets its name.

### 4.5.1 The LDiA idea

The LDiA approach was developed in 2000 by geneticists in the UK to help them "infer population structure" from sequences of genes.[39] Stanford Researchers (including Andrew Ng) popularized the approach for NLP in 2003.[40] But don't be intimidated by the big names that came up with this approach. We explain the key points of it in a few lines of Python shortly. You only need to understand it enough to get a feel for what it's doing (an intuition), so you know what you can use it for in your pipeline.

Blei and Ng came up with the idea by flipping your thought experiment on its head. They imagined how a machine that could do nothing more than roll dice (generate random numbers) could write the documents in a corpus you want to analyze. And because you're only working with bags of words, they cut out the part about sequencing those words together to make sense, to write a real document. They just modeled the statistics for the mix of words that would become a part of a particular BOW for each document.

They imagined a machine that only had two choices to make to get started generating the mix of words for a particular document. They imagined that the document generator chose those words randomly, with some probability distribution over the possible choices, like choosing the number of sides of the dice and the combination of dice you add together to create a D&D character sheet. Your document "character sheet" needs only two rolls of the dice. But the dice are large and there are several of them, with complicated rules about how they are combined to produce the desired probabilities for the different values you want. You want particular probability distributions for the number of words and number of topics so that it matches the distribution of these values in real documents analyzed by humans for their topics and words.

The two rolls of the dice represent the

1. Number of words to generate for the document (Poisson distribution)
2. Number of topics to mix together for the document (Dirichlet distribution)

After it has these two numbers, the hard part begins, choosing the words for a document. The imaginary BOW generating machine iterates over those topics and randomly chooses words appropriate to that topic until it hits the number of words that it had decided the document should contain in step 1. Deciding the probabilities of

---

[39] "Inference of Poplulation Structure Using Multilocus Genotype Data," by Jonathan K. Pritchard, Matthew Stephens, and Peter Donnelly" (http://www.genetics.org/content/155/2/945).

[40] See the PDF titled "Latent Dirichlet Allocation" by David M. Blei, Andrew Y. Ng, and Michael I. Jordan (http://www.jmlr.org/papers/volume3/blei03a/blei03a.pdf).

those words for topics—the appropriateness of words for each topic—is the hard part. But once that has been determined, your "bot" just looks up the probabilities for the words for each topic from a matrix of term-topic probabilities. If you don't remember what that matrix looks like, glance back at the simple example earlier in this chapter.

So all this machine needs is a single parameter for that Poisson distribution (in the dice roll from step 1) that tells it what the "average" document length should be, and a couple more parameters to define that Dirichlet distribution that sets up the number of topics. Then your document generation algorithm needs a term-topic matrix of all the words and topics it likes to use, its vocabulary. And it needs a mix of topics that it likes to "talk" about.

Let's flip the document generation (writing) problem back around to your original problem of estimating the topics and words from an existing document. You need to measure, or compute, those parameters about words and topics for the first two steps. Then you need to compute the term-topic matrix from a collection of documents. That's what LDiA does.

Blei and Ng realized that they could determine the parameters for steps 1 and 2 by analyzing the statistics of the documents in a corpus. For example, for step 1, they could calculate the mean number of words (or *n*-grams) in all the bags of words for the documents in their corpus; something like this:

```
>>> total_corpus_len = 0
>>> for document_text in sms.text:
...     total_corpus_len += len(casual_tokenize(document_text))
>>> mean_document_len = total_corpus_len / len(sms)
>>> round(mean_document_len, 2)
21.35
```

Or, in a one-liner

```
>>> sum([len(casual_tokenize(t)) for t in sms.text]) * 1. / len(sms.text)
21.35
```

Keep in mind, you should calculate this statistic directly from your BOWs. You need to make sure you're counting the tokenized and vectorized (`Counter()`-ed) words in your documents. And make sure you've applied any stop word filtering, or other normalizations before you count up your unique terms. That way your count includes all the words in your BOW vector vocabulary (all the *n*-grams you're counting), but only those words that your BOWs use (not stop words, for example). This LDiA algorithm relies on a bag-of-words vector space model, like the other algorithms in this chapter.

The second parameter you need to specify for an LDiA model, the number of topics, is a bit trickier. The number of topics in a particular set of documents can't be measured directly until after you've assigned words to those topics. Like *k-means* and *KNN* and other clustering algorithms, you must tell it the *k* ahead of time. You can guess the number of topics (analogous to the *k* in k-means, the number of "clusters") and then check to see if that works for your set of documents. Once you've told LDiA how many topics to look for, it will find the mix of words to put in each topic to opti-mize its objective function.[41]

You can optimize this "hyperparameter" (*k*, the number of topics)[42] by adjusting it until it works for your application. You can automate this optimization if you can mea-sure something about the quality of your LDiA language model for representing the meaning of your documents. One "cost function" you could use for this optimization is how well (or poorly) that LDiA model performs in some classification or regression problems, like sentiment analysis, document keyword tagging, or topic analysis. You just need some labeled documents to test your topic model or classifier on.[43]

### 4.5.2 *LDiA topic model for SMS messages*

The topics produced by LDiA tend to be more understandable and "explainable" to humans. This is because words that frequently occur together are assigned the same topics, and humans expect that to be the case. Where LSA (PCA) tries to keep things spread apart that were spread apart to start with, LDiA tries to keep things close together that started out close together.

This may sound like it's the same thing, but it's not. The math optimizes for differ-ent things. Your optimizer has a different objective function so it will reach a different objective. To keep close high-dimensional vectors close together in the lower-dimensional space, LDiA has to twist and contort the space (and the vectors) in non-linear ways. This is a hard thing to visualize until you do it on something 3D and take "projections" of the resultant vectors in 2D.

If you want to help out your fellow readers and learn something in the process, submit some additional code to the horse example (https://github.com/totalgood/nlpia/blob/master/src/nlpia/book/examples/ch04_horse.py) in nlpia (https://github.com/totalgood/nlpia). You can create word-document vectors for each of the thousands of points in the horse by converting them to integer counts of the words "x," "y," and "z," the dimensions of the 3D vector space. You could then generate syn-thetic documents from these counts and pass it through all the LDiA and LSA exam-ples from earlier in the chapter. Then you'd be able to directly visualize how each approach produces a different 2D "shadow" (projection) of the horse.

Let's see how that works for a dataset of a few thousand SMS messages, labeled for spaminess. First compute the TF-IDF vectors and then some topics vectors for each SMS message (document). We assume the use of only 16 topics (components) to clas-

---

[41] You can learn more about the particulars of the LDiA objective function here in the original paper "Online Learning for Latent Dirichlet Allocation" by Matthew D. Hoffman, David M. Blei, and Francis Bach (https://www.di.ens.fr/%7Efbach/mdhnips2010.pdf).

[42] The symbol used by Blei and Ng for this parameter was *theta* rather than *k*.

[43] Craig Bowman, a librarian at the University of Miami in Ohio (http://www.lib.miamioh.edu/people/), is using the Library of Congress classification system as the topic labels for Gutenberg Project books. This has to be the most ambitious and pro-social open-science NLP project (https://github.com/craigboman/gutenberg) I've run across so far.

sify the spaminess of messages, as before. Keeping the number of topics (dimensions) low can help reduce overfitting.[44]

LDiA works with raw BOW count vectors rather than normalized TF-IDF vectors. Here's an easy way to compute BOW vectors in scikit-learn:

```
>>> from sklearn.feature_extraction.text import CountVectorizer
>>> from nltk.tokenize import casual_tokenize
>>> np.random.seed(42)

>>> counter = CountVectorizer(tokenizer=casual_tokenize)
>>> bow_docs = pd.DataFrame(counter.fit_transform(raw_documents=sms.text)\
...      .toarray(), index=index)
>>> column_nums, terms = zip(*sorted(zip(counter.vocabulary_.values(),\
...      counter.vocabulary_.keys())))
>>> bow_docs.columns = terms
```

Let's double-check that your counts make sense for that first SMS message labeled "sms0":

```
>>> sms.loc['sms0'].text
'Go until jurong point, crazy.. Available only in bugis n great world la e
buffet... Cine there got amore wat...'
>>> bow_docs.loc['sms0'][bow_docs.loc['sms0'] > 0].head()
,            1
..           1
...          2
amore        1
available    1
Name: sms0, dtype: int64
```

And here's how to use LDiA to create topic vectors for your SMS corpus:

```
>>> from sklearn.decomposition import LatentDirichletAllocation as LDiA

>>> ldia = LDiA(n_components=16, learning_method='batch')
>>> ldia = ldia.fit(bow_docs)
>>> ldia.components_.shape
(16, 9232)
```

> LDiA takes a bit longer than PCA or SVD, especially for a large number of topics and a large number of words in your corpus.

So your model has allocated your 9,232 words (terms) to 16 topics (components). Let's take a look at the first few words and how they're allocated to your 16 topics. Keep in mind that your counts and topics will be different from mine. LDiA is a stochastic algorithm that relies on the random number generator to make some of the statistical decisions it has to make about allocating words to topics. So your topic-word weights will be different from those shown, but they should have similar magnitudes. Each time you run `sklearn.LatentDirichletAllocation` (or any LDiA algorithm), you will get different results unless you set the random seed to a fixed value:

---

[44] See appendix D if you want to learn more about why overfitting is a bad thing and how *generalization* can help.

```
>>> pd.set_option('display.width', 75)
>>> components = pd.DataFrame(ldia.components_.T, index=terms,\
...       columns=columns)
>>> components.round(2).head(3)
        topic0   topic1   topic2  ...   topic13  topic14  topic15
!       184.03   15.00    72.22   ...   297.29   41.16    11.70
"         0.68    4.22     2.41   ...    62.72   12.27     0.06
#         0.06    0.06     0.06   ...     4.05    0.06     0.06
```

So the exclamation point term (!) was allocated to most of the topics, but is a particularly strong part of `topic3` where the quote symbol (") is hardly playing a role at all. Perhaps "topic3" might be about emotional intensity or emphasis and doesn't care much about numbers or quotes. Let's see:

```
>>> components.topic3.sort_values(ascending=False)[:10]
!        394.952246
.        218.049724
to       119.533134
u        118.857546
call     111.948541
£        107.358914
,         96.954384
*         90.314783
your      90.215961
is        75.750037
```

So the top ten tokens for this topic seem to be the type of words that might be used in emphatic directives requesting someone to do something or pay something. It will be interesting to find out if this topic is used more in spam messages rather than non-spam messages. You can see that the allocation of words to topics can be rationalized or reasoned about, even with this quick look.

Before you fit your LDA classifier, you need to compute these LDiA topic vectors for all your documents (SMS messages). And let's see how they are different from the topic vectors produced by SVD and PCA for those same documents:

```
>>> ldia16_topic_vectors = ldia.transform(bow_docs)
>>> ldia16_topic_vectors = pd.DataFrame(ldia16_topic_vectors,\
...       index=index, columns=columns)
>>> ldia16_topic_vectors.round(2).head()
        topic0  topic1  topic2  ...   topic13  topic14  topic15
sms0     0.00    0.62    0.00   ...    0.00     0.00     0.00
sms1     0.01    0.01    0.01   ...    0.01     0.01     0.01
sms2!    0.00    0.00    0.00   ...    0.00     0.00     0.00
sms3     0.00    0.00    0.00   ...    0.00     0.00     0.00
sms4     0.39    0.00    0.33   ...    0.00     0.00     0.00
```

You can see that these topics are more cleanly separated. There are a lot of zeros in your allocation of topics to messages. This is one of the things that makes LDiA topics easier to explain to coworkers when making business decisions based on your NLP pipeline results.

So LDiA topics work well for humans, but what about machines? How will your LDA classifier fare with these topics?

### 4.5.3  *LDiA + LDA = spam classifier*

Let's see how good these LDiA topics are at predicting something useful, such as spaminess. You'll use your LDiA topic vectors to train an LDA model again (like you did with your PCA topic vectors):

```
>>> from sklearn.discriminant_analysis import LinearDiscriminantAnalysis as LDA

>>> X_train, X_test, y_train, y_test =
⇒ train_test_split(ldia16_topic_vectors, sms.spam, test_size=0.5,
⇒ random_state=271828)
>>> lda = LDA(n_components=1)
>>> lda = lda.fit(X_train, y_train)                    ◄─────────────────
>>> sms['ldia16_spam'] = lda.predict(ldia16_topic_vectors)
>>> round(float(lda.score(X_test, y_test)), 2)
0.94    ◄─────────────
```

**94% accuracy on the test set is pretty good, but not quite as good as LSA (PCA) in section 4.7.1.**

**Your ldia_topic_vectors matrix has a determinant close to zero so you will likely get the warning "Variables are collinear." This can happen with a small corpus when using LDiA because your topic vectors have a lot of zeros in them and some of your messages could be reproduced as a linear combination of the other message topics. Or there are some SMS messages with similar (or identical) topic mixes.**

The algorithms for `train_test_split()` and LDiA are stochastic. So each time you run it you will get different results and different accuracy values. If you want to make your pipeline repeatable, look for the `seed` argument for these models and dataset splitters. You can set the seed to the same value with each run to get reproducible results.

One way a "collinear" warning can occur is if your text has a few 2-grams or 3-grams where their component words only ever occur together. So the resulting LDiA model had to arbitrarily split the weights among these equivalent term frequencies. Can you find the words in your SMS messages that are causing this "collinearity" (zero determinant)? You're looking for a word that, whenever it occurs, another word (its pair) is always in the same message.

You can do this search with Python rather than by hand. First, you probably just want to look for any identical bag-of-words vectors in your corpus. These could occur for SMS messages that aren't identical, like "Hi there Bob!" or "Bob, Hi there," because they have the same word counts. You can iterate through all the pairings of the bags of words to look for identical vectors. These will definitely cause a "collinearity" warning in either LDiA or LSA.

If you don't find any exact BOW vector duplicates, you could iterate through all the pairings of the words in your vocabulary. You'd then iterate through all the bags of words to look for the pairs of SMS messages that contain those exact same two words. If there aren't any times that those words occur separately in the SMS messages, you've found one of the "collinearities" in your dataset. Some common 2-grams that might cause this are the first and last names of famous people that always occur together and are never used separately, like "Bill Gates" (as long as there are no other Bills in your SMS messages).

> **TIP** Whenever you need to iterate through all the combinations (pairs or triplets) of a set of objects, you can use the built-in Python `product()` function:

```
>>> from itertools import product
>>> all_pairs = [(word1, word2) for (word1, word2) in product(word_list,
    word_list) if not word1 == word2]
```

You got more than 90% accuracy on your test set, and you only had to train on half your available data. But you did get a warning about your features being collinear due to your limited dataset, which gives LDA an "under-determined" problem. The determinant of your topic-document matrix is close to zero, once you discard half the documents with `train_test_split`. If you ever need to, you can turn down the LDiA `n_components` to "fix" this issue, but it would tend to combine those topics together that are a linear combination of each other (collinear).

But let's find out how your LDiA model compares to a much higher-dimensional model based on the TF-IDF vectors. Your TF-IDF vectors have many more features (more than 3,000 unique terms). So you're likely to experience overfitting and poor generalization. This is where the generalization of LDiA and PCA should help:

```
>>> from sklearn.feature_extraction.text import TfidfVectorizer
>>> from nltk.tokenize.casual import casual_tokenize
>>> tfidf = TfidfVectorizer(tokenizer=casual_tokenize)
>>> tfidf_docs = tfidf.fit_transform(raw_documents=sms.text).toarray()
>>> tfidf_docs = tfidf_docs - tfidf_docs.mean(axis=0)

>>> X_train, X_test, y_train, y_test = train_test_split(tfidf_docs,\
...         sms.spam.values, test_size=0.5, random_state=271828)
>>> lda = LDA(n_components=1)
>>> lda = lda.fit(X_train, y_train)
>>> round(float(lda.score(X_train, y_train)), 3)
1.0
>>> round(float(lda.score(X_test, y_test)), 3)
0.748
```

You're going to "pretend" that there is only one topic in all the SMS messages, because you're only interested in a scalar score for the "spamminess" topic.

Fitting an LDA model to all these thousands of features will take quite a long time. Be patient; it's slicing up your vector space with a 9,332-dimension hyperplane!

The training set accuracy for your TF-IDF based model is perfect! But the test set accuracy is much worse than when you trained it on lower-dimensional topic vectors instead of TF-IDF vectors.

And test set accuracy is the only accuracy that counts. This is exactly what topic modeling (LSA) is supposed to do. It helps you generalize your models from a small training set, so it still works well on messages using different combinations of words (but similar topics).

### 4.5.4   *A fairer comparison: 32 LDiA topics*

Let's try one more time with more dimensions, more topics. Perhaps LDiA isn't as efficient as LSA (PCA), so it needs more topics to allocate words to. Let's try 32 topics (components):

```
>>> ldia32 = LDiA(n_components=32, learning_method='batch')
>>> ldia32 = ldia32.fit(bow_docs)
>>> ldia32.components_.shape
(32, 9232)
```

Now let's compute your new 32-D topic vectors for all your documents (SMS messages):

```
>>> ldia32_topic_vectors = ldia32.transform(bow_docs)
>>> columns32 = ['topic{}'.format(i) for i in range(ldia32.n_components)]
>>> ldia32_topic_vectors = pd.DataFrame(ldia32_topic_vectors, index=index, \
...         columns=columns32)
>>> ldia32_topic_vectors.round(2).head()
        topic0  topic1  topic2   ...    topic29  topic30  topic31
sms0      0.00     0.5     0.0   ...        0.0      0.0      0.0
sms1      0.00     0.0     0.0   ...        0.0      0.0      0.0
sms2!     0.00     0.0     0.0   ...        0.0      0.0      0.0
sms3      0.00     0.0     0.0   ...        0.0      0.0      0.0
sms4      0.21     0.0     0.0   ...        0.0      0.0      0.0
```

You can see that these topics are even more sparse, more cleanly separated.

And here's your LDA model (classifier) training, this time using 32-D LDiA topic vectors:

```
>>> X_train, X_test, y_train, y_test =
⇒ train_test_split(ldia32_topic_vectors, sms.spam, test_size=0.5,
⇒ random_state=271828)
>>> lda = LDA(n_components=1)
>>> lda = lda.fit(X_train, y_train)
>>> sms['ldia32_spam'] = lda.predict(ldia32_topic_vectors)
>>> X_train.shape
(2418, 32)
>>> round(float(lda.score(X_train, y_train)), 3)
0.924
>>> round(float(lda.score(X_test, y_test)), 3)
0.927
```

← **.shape is another way to check the number of dimensions in your topic vectors.**

← **Test accuracy is what matters, and 92.7% is comparable to the 94% score you got with 16-D LDiA topic vectors.**

Don't confuse this optimization of the number of "topics" or components with the collinearity problem earlier. Increasing or decreasing the number of topics doesn't fix or create the collinearity problem. That's a problem with the underlying data. If you want to get rid of that warning, you need to add "noise" or metadata to your SMS messages as synthetic words, or you need to delete those duplicate word vectors. If you have duplicate word vectors or word pairings that repeat a lot in your documents, no amount of topics is going to fix that.

The larger number of topics allows it to be more precise about topics, and, at least for this dataset, product topics that linearly separate better. But this performance still isn't quite as good as the 96% accuracy of PCA + LDA. So PCA is keeping your SMS topic vectors spread out more efficiently, allowing for a wider gap between messages to cut with a hyperplane to separate classes.

Feel free to explore the source code for the Dirichlet allocation models available in both scikit-learn as well as gensim. They have an API similar to LSA (sklearn.TruncatedSVD and gensim.LsiModel). We show you an example application when we talk about summarization in later chapters. Finding explainable topics, like those used for summarization, is what LDiA is good at. And it's not too bad at creating topics useful for linear classification.

---

**Digging deeper into your toolbox**

You can find the source code path in the \_\_file\_\_ attribute on any Python module, such as `sklearn.__file__`. And in ipython (jupyter console), you can view the source code for any function, class, or object with `??`, like `LDA??`:

```
>>> import sklearn
>>> sklearn.__file__
'/Users/hobs/anaconda3/envs/conda_env_nlpia/lib/python3.6/site-packages/sklearn/__init__.py'
>>> from sklearn.discriminant_analysis\
...     import LinearDiscriminantAnalysis as LDA
>>> LDA??
Init signature: LDA(solver='svd', shrinkage=None, priors=None, n_components=None, store_covariance=False, tol=0.0001)
Source:
class LinearDiscriminantAnalysis(BaseEstimator, LinearClassifierMixin,
                                 TransformerMixin):
    """Linear Discriminant Analysis

    A classifier with a linear decision boundary, generated by fitting
    class conditional densities to the data and using Bayes' rule.

    The model fits a Gaussian density to each class, assuming that all
    classes share the same covariance matrix.
...
```

This won't work on functions and classes that are extensions, whose source code is hidden within a compiled C++ module.

---

## 4.6 *Distance and similarity*

We need to revisit those similarity scores we talked about in chapters 2 and 3 to make sure your new topic vector space works with them. Remember that you can use similarity scores (and distances) to tell how similar or far apart two documents are based on the similarity (or distance) of the vectors you used to represent them.

You can use similarity scores (and distances) to see how well your LSA topic model agrees with the higher-dimensional TF-IDF model of chapter 3. You'll see how good your model is at retaining those distances after having eliminated a lot of the information contained in the much higher-dimensional bags of words. You can check how far away from each other the topic vectors are and whether that's a good representation of the distance between the documents' subject matter. You want to check that documents that mean similar things are close to each other in your new topic vector space.

LSA preserves large distances, but it doesn't always preserve close distances (the fine "structure" of the relationships between your documents). The underlying SVD algorithm is focused on maximizing the variance between all your documents in the new topic vector space.

Distances between feature vectors (word vectors, topic vectors, document context vectors, and so on) drive the performance of an NLP pipeline, or any machine learning pipeline. So what are your options for measuring distance in high-dimensional space? And which ones should you chose for a particular NLP problem? Some of these commonly used examples may be familiar from geometry class or linear algebra, but many others are probably new to you:

- Euclidean or Cartesian distance, or root mean square error (RMSE): 2-norm or $L_2$
- Squared Euclidean distance, sum of squares distance (SSD): $L_2^2$
- Cosine or angular or projected distance: normalized dot product
- Minkowski distance: p-norm or $L_p$
- Fractional distance, fractional norm: p-norm or $L_p$ for `0 < p < 1`
- City block, Manhattan, or taxicab distance; sum of absolute distance (SAD): 1-norm or $L_1$
- Jaccard distance, inverse set similarity
- Mahalanobis distance
- Levenshtein or edit distance

The variety of ways to calculate distance is a testament to how important it is. In addition to the pairwise distance implementations in Scikit-learn, many others are used in mathematics specialties such as topology, statistics, and engineering.[45] For reference, the following listing shows the distances you can find in the sklearn.metrics.pairwise module.[46]

---

**Listing 4.7   Pairwise distances available in sklearn**

```
'cityblock', 'cosine', 'euclidean', 'l1', 'l2', 'manhattan', 'braycurtis',
'canberra', 'chebyshev', 'correlation', 'dice', 'hamming', 'jaccard',
'kulsinski', 'mahalanobis', 'matching', 'minkowski', 'rogerstanimoto',
'russellrao', 'seuclidean', 'sokalmichener', 'sokalsneath', 'sqeuclidean',
'yule'
```

---

[45] See Math.NET Numerics for more distance metrics (https://numerics.mathdotnet.com/Distance.html).
[46] See the documentation for sklearn.metrics.pairwise (http://scikit-learn.org/stable/modules/generated/sklearn.metrics.pairwise_distances.html).

Distance measures are often computed from similarity measures (scores) and vice versa such that distances are inversely proportional to similarity scores. Similarity scores are designed to range between 0 and 1. Typical conversion formulas look like this:

```
>>> similarity = 1. / (1. + distance)
>>> distance = (1. / similarity) - 1.
```

But for distances and similarity scores that range between 0 and 1, like probabilities, it's more common to use a formula like this:

```
>>> similarity = 1. - distance
>>> distance = 1. - similarity
```

And cosine distances have their own convention for the range of values they use. The angular distance between two vectors is often computed as a fraction of the maximum possible angular separation between two vectors, which is 180 degrees or pi radians.[47] As a result, cosine similarity and distance are the reciprocal of each other:

```
>>> import math
>>> angular_distance = math.acos(cosine_similarity) / math.pi
>>> distance = 1. / similarity - 1.
>>> similarity = 1. - distance
```

The terms "distance" and "length" are often confused with the term "metric," because many distances and lengths are valid and useful metrics. But unfortunately not all distances can be called metrics. Even more confusing, metrics are also sometimes called "distance functions" or "distance metrics" in formal mathematics and set theory texts.[48]

## Metrics

A true metric must have four mathematical properties that distances or "scores" don't:

- Nonnegativity: metrics can never be negative. `metric(A, B) >= 0`
- Indiscerniblity: two objects are identical if the metric between them is zero. `if metric(A, B) == 0: assert(A == B)`
- Symmetry: metrics don't care about direction. `metric(A, B) = metric(B, A)`
- Triangle inequality: you can't get from A to C faster by going through B in-between. `metric(A, C) <= metric(A, B) + metric(B, C)`

A related mathematical term, *measure*, has both a natural English meaning and a rigorous mathematical definition. You'll find "measure" in both a Merriam-Webster dictionary and a math textbook glossary, with completely different definitions. So be careful when talking to your math professor.

---

[47] See the web page titled "Cosine similarity" (https://en.wikipedia.org/wiki/Cosine_similarity).

[48] See the Wikipedia article titled "Metric (mathematics)" (https://en.wikipedia.org/wiki/Metric_ (mathematics)).

To a math professor, a measure is the size of a set of mathematical objects. You can measure a Python `set` by its length, but many mathematical sets are infinite. And in set theory, things can be infinite in different ways. And measures are all the different ways to calculate the `len()` or size of a mathematical set, the ways things are infinite.

> **DEFINITION**   Like metric, the word "measure" has a precise mathematical definition, related to the "size" of a collection of objects. So the word "measure" should also be used carefully in describing any scores or statistics derived from an object or combination of objects in NLP.[49]

But in the real world, you measure all sorts of things. When you use it as a verb you might mean using a measuring tape, or a ruler, or a scale or a score, to measure something. That's how you use the word "measure" in this book, but we try not to use it at all, so that our math professors don't scold us.

## 4.7   *Steering with feedback*

All the previous approaches to LSA failed to take into account information about the similarity between documents. We created topics that were optimal for a generic set of rules. Our unsupervised learning of these feature (topic) extraction models didn't have any data about how "close" the topic vectors should be to each other. We didn't allow any "feedback" about where the topic vectors ended up, or how they were related to each other. Steering or "learned distance metrics"[50] are the latest advancement in dimension reduction and feature extraction. By adjusting the distance scores reported to clustering and embedding algorithms, you can "steer" your vectors so that they minimize some cost function. In this way you can force your vectors to focus on some aspect of the information content that you're interested in.

In the previous sections about LSA, you ignored all the meta information about your documents. For example, with the SMS messages you ignored the sender of the message. This is a good indication of topic similarity and could be used to inform your topic vector transformation (LSA).

At Talentpair, we experimented with matching resumes to job descriptions using the cosine distance between topic vectors for each document. This worked OK. But we learned quickly that we got much better results when we started "steering" our topic vectors based on feedback from candidates and account managers responsible for helping them find a job. Vectors for "good pairings" were steered closer together than all the other pairings.

One way to do this is to calculate the mean difference between your two centroids (like you did for LDA) and add some portion of this "bias" to all the resume or job description vectors. Doing so should take out the average topic vector difference between resumes and job descriptions. Topics such as beer on tap at lunch might

---

[49] See the Wikipedia article titled "Measure (mathematics)" (https://en.wikipedia.org/wiki/Measure_(mathematics)).

[50] See the web page titled "Superpixel Graph Label Transfer with Learned Distance Metric" (http://users.cecs.anu.edu.au/~sgould/papers/eccv14-spgraph.pdf).

appear in a job description but never in a resume. Similarly, bizarre hobbies, such as underwater scuplture, might appear in some resumes but never a job description. Steering your topic vectors can help you focus them on the topics you're interested in modeling.

If you're interested in refining topic vectors, taking out bias, you can search Google Scholar (http://scholar.google.com/) for "learned distance/similarity metric" or "distance metrics for nonlinear embeddings."[51] Unfortunately, no scikit-learn modules implement this feature yet. You'd be a hero if you found the time to add some "steering" feature suggestions or code to the Scikit-Learn project (http://github .com/scikit-learn/scikit-learn/issues).

### 4.7.1 *Linear discriminant analysis*

Let's train a linear discriminant analysis model on your labeled SMS messages. LDA works similarly to LSA, except it requires classification labels or other scores to be able to find the best linear combination of the dimensions in high-dimensional space (the terms in a BOW or TF-IDF vector). Rather than maximizing the separation (variance) between all vectors in the new space, LDA maximizes the distance between the centroids of the vectors within each class.

Unfortunately, this means you have to tell the LDA algorithm what "topics" you'd like to model by giving it examples (labeled vectors). Only then can the algorithm compute the optimal transformation from your high-dimensional space to the lower-dimensional space. And the resulting lower-dimensional vector can't have any more dimensions than the number of class labels or scores you're able to provide. Because you only have a "spaminess" topic to train on, let's see how accurate your 1D topic model can be at classifying spam SMS messages:

```
>>> lda = LDA(n_components=1)
>>> lda = lda.fit(tfidf_docs, sms.spam)
>>> sms['lda_spaminess'] = lda.predict(tfidf_docs)
>>> ((sms.spam - sms.lda_spaminess) ** 2.).sum() ** .5
0.0
>>> (sms.spam == sms.lda_spaminess).sum()
4837
>>> len(sms)
4837
```

It got every single one of them right! Oh, wait a minute. What did you say earlier about overfitting? With 10,000 terms in your TF-IDF vectors it's not surprising at all that it could just "memorize" the answer. Let's do some cross validation this time:

```
>>> from sklearn.model_selection import import cross_val_score
>>> lda = LDA(n_components=1)
>>> scores = cross_val_score(lda, tfidf_docs, sms.spam, cv=5)
>>> "Accuracy: {:.2f} (+/-{:.2f})".format(scores.mean(), scores.std() * 2)
'Accuracy: 0.76 (+/-0.03)'
```

---

[51] See the web page titled "Distance Metric Learning: A Comprehensive Survey" (https://www.cs.cmu.edu/ ~liuy/frame_survey_v2.pdf).

Clearly this isn't a good model. This should be a reminder to never get excited about a model's performance on your training set.

Just to make sure that 76% accuracy number is correct, let's reserve a third of your dataset for testing:

```
>>> from sklearn.model_selection import train_test_split
>>> X_train, X_test, y_train, y_test = train_test_split(tfidf_docs,\
...      sms.spam, test_size=0.33, random_state=271828)
>>> lda = LDA(n_components=1)
>>> lda.fit(X_train, y_train)
LinearDiscriminantAnalysis(n_components=1, priors=None, shrinkage=None,
           solver='svd', store_covariance=False, tol=0.0001)
>>> lda.score(X_test, y_test).round(3)
0.765
```

Again, poor test set accuracy. So it doesn't look like you're unlucky with your data sampling. It's a poor, overfitting model.

Let's see if LSA combined with LDA will help you create an accurate model that is also generalized well so that new SMS messages don't trip it up:

```
>>> X_train, X_test, y_train, y_test =
⇒ train_test_split(pca_topicvectors.values, sms.spam, test_size=0.3,
⇒ random_state=271828)
>>> lda = LDA(n_components=1)
>>> lda.fit(X_train, y_train)
LinearDiscriminantAnalysis(n_components=1, priors=None, shrinkage=None,
           solver='svd', store_covariance=False, tol=0.0001)
>>> lda.score(X_test, y_test).round(3)
0.965
>>> lda = LDA(n_components=1)
>>> scores = cross_val_score(lda, pca_topicvectors, sms.spam, cv=10)
>>> "Accuracy: {:.3f} (+/-{:.3f})".format(scores.mean(), scores.std() * 2)
'Accuracy: 0.958 (+/-0.022)'
```

So with LSA, you can characterize an SMS message with only 16 dimensions and still have plenty of information to classify them as spam (or not). And your low-dimensional model is much less likely to overfit. It should generalize well and be able to classify as-yet-unseen SMS messages or chats.

You've now come full circle back to your "simple" model at the beginning of this chapter. You got better accuracy with your simple LDA model before you tried all that semantic analysis. But the advantage of this new model is that you now can create vectors that represent the semantics of a statement in more than just a single dimension.

## 4.8   *Topic vector power*

With topic vectors, you can do things like compare the meaning of words, documents, statements, and corpora. You can find "clusters" of similar documents and statements. You're no longer comparing the distance between documents based merely on their word usage. You're no longer limited to keyword search and relevance ranking based entirely on word choice or vocabulary. You can now find documents that are relevant to your query, not just a good match for the word statistics themselves.

This is called "semantic search," not to be confused with the "semantic web."[52] Semantic search is what strong search engines do when they give you documents that don't contain many of the words in your query, but are exactly what you were looking for. These advanced search engines use LSA topic vectors to tell the difference between a `Python` package in "The Cheese Shop" and a python in a Florida pet shop aquarium, while still recognizing its similarity to a "Ruby gem."[53]

Semantic search gives you a tool for finding and generating meaningful text. But our brains aren't good at dealing with high-dimensional objects, vectors, hyperplanes, hyperspheres, and hypercubes. Our intuitions as developers and machine learning engineers breaks down above three dimensions.

For example, to do a query on a 2D vector, like your lat/lon location on Google Maps, you can quickly find all the coffee shops nearby without much searching. You can just scan (with your eyes or with code) near your location and spiral outward with your search. Alternatively, you can create bigger and bigger bounding boxes with your code, checking for longitudes and latitudes within some range. Doing this in hyperspace with hyperplanes and hypercubes to form the boundaries of your search is impossible.

As Geoffry Hinton says, "To deal with hyperplanes in a 14-dimensional space, visualize a 3D space and say 14 to yourself loudly." If you read Abbott's 1884 *Flatland* when you were young and impressionable, you might be able to do a little bit better than this hand waving. You might even be able to poke your head partway out of the window of your 3D world into hyperspace, enough to catch a glimpse of that 3D world from the outside. Like in *Flatland*, you used a lot of 2D visualizations in this chapter to help you explore the shadows that words in hyperspace leave in your 3D world. If you're anxious to check them out, skip ahead to the section showing "scatter matrices" of word vectors. You might also want to glance back at the 3D bag-of-words vector in the previous chapter and try to imagine what those points would look like if you added just one more word to your vocabulary to create a 4-D world of language meaning.

If you're taking a moment to think deeply about four dimensions, keep in mind that the explosion in complexity you're trying to wrap your head around is even greater than the complexity growth from 2D to 3D and exponentially greater than the growth in complexity from a 1D world of numbers to a 2D world of triangles, squares, and circles.

**NOTE** The explosive growth in possibilities from 1D lines, 2D rectangles, 3D cubes, and so on passes through bizarre universes with non-integer fractal dimensions, like a 1.5-dimension fractal. A 1.5D fractal has infinite length and completely fills a 2D plane while having less than two dimensions![54] But

---

[52] The semantic web is the practice of structuring natural language text with the use of tags in an HTML document so that the hierarchy of tags and their content provide information about the relationships (web of connections) between elements (text, images, videos) on a web page.

[53] Ruby is a programming language with a package called `gem`.

[54] fractional dimensions, http://www.math.cornell.edu/~erin/docs/research-talk.pdf

fortunately these aren't "real" dimensions.[55] So you don't have to worry about them in NLP... unless you get interested in fractional distance metrics, like `p-norm`, which have noninteger exponents in their formulas.[56]

### 4.8.1 *Semantic search*

When you search for a document based on a word or partial word it contains, that's called *full text search*. This is what search engines do. They break a document into chunks (usually words) that can be indexed with an *inverted index* like you'd find at the back of a textbook. It takes a lot of bookkeeping and guesswork to deal with spelling errors and typos, but it works pretty well.[57]

*Semantic search* is full text search that takes into account the meaning of the words in your query and the documents you're searching. In this chapter, you've learned two ways— LSA and LDiA—to compute topic vectors that capture the semantics (meaning) of words and documents in a vector. One of the reasons that latent semantic analysis was first called latent semantic *indexing* was because it promised to power semantic search with an index of numerical values, like BOW and TF-IDF tables. Semantic search was the next big thing in information retrieval.

But unlike BOW and TF-IDF tables, tables of semantic vectors can't be easily discretized and indexed using traditional inverted index techniques. Traditional indexing approaches work with binary word occurrence vectors, discrete vectors (BOW vectors), sparse continuous vectors (TF-IDF vectors), and low-dimensional continuous vectors (3D GIS data). But high-dimensional continuous vectors, such as topic vectors from LSA or LDiA, are a challenge.[58] Inverted indexes work for discrete vectors or binary vectors, like tables of binary or integer word-document vectors, because the index only needs to maintain an entry for each nonzero discrete dimension. Either that value of that dimension is present or not present in the referenced vector or document. Because TF-IDF vectors are sparse, mostly zero, you don't need an entry in your index for most dimensions for most documents.[59]

LSA (and LDiA) produce topic vectors that are high-dimensional, continuous, and dense (zeros are rare). And the semantic analysis algorithm doesn't produce an efficient index for scalable search. In fact, the curse of dimensionality that we talked about in the previous section makes an exact index impossible. The "indexing" part of latent semantic indexing was a hope, not a reality, so the LSI term is a misnomer.

---

[55] "Fractal dimensions, (http://www.askamathematician.com/2012/12/q-what-are-fractional-dimensions-can-space-have-a-fractional-dimension/).

[56] "The Concentration of Fractional Distances" (https://perso.uclouvain.be/michel.verleysen/papers/tkde 07df.pdf).

[57] A full text index in a database like PostgreSQL is usually based on trigrams of characters, to deal with spelling errors and text that doesn't parse into words.

[58] Clustering high-dimensional data is equivalent to discretizing or indexing high-dimensional data with bounding boxes and is described in the Wikipedia article "Clustering high dimensional data" (https://en.wikipedia .org/wiki/Clustering_high-dimensional_data).

[59] See the web page titled "Inverted index" (https://en.wikipedia.org/wiki/Inverted_index).

Perhaps that's why LSA has become the more popular way to describe semantic analysis algorithms that produce topic vectors.

One solution to the challenge of high-dimensional vectors is to index them with a *locality sensitive hash* (LSH). A locality sensitive hash is like a ZIP code (postal code) that designates a region of hyperspace so that it can easily be found again later. And like a regular hash, it's discrete and depends only on the values in the vector. But even this doesn't work perfectly once you exceed about 12 dimensions. In figure 4.6, each row represents a topic vector size (dimensionality), starting with 2 dimensions and working up to 16 dimensions, like the vectors you used earlier for the SMS spam problem.

| Dimensions | 100th cosine distance | Top 1 correct | Top 2 correct | Top 10 correct | Top 100 correct |
|---|---|---|---|---|---|
| 2 | .00 | TRUE | TRUE | TRUE | TRUE |
| 3 | .00 | TRUE | TRUE | TRUE | TRUE |
| 4 | .00 | TRUE | TRUE | TRUE | TRUE |
| 5 | .01 | TRUE | TRUE | TRUE | TRUE |
| 6 | .02 | TRUE | TRUE | TRUE | TRUE |
| 7 | .02 | TRUE | TRUE | TRUE | FALSE |
| 8 | .03 | TRUE | TRUE | TRUE | FALSE |
| 9 | .04 | TRUE | TRUE | TRUE | FALSE |
| 10 | .05 | TRUE | TRUE | FALSE | FALSE |
| 11 | .07 | TRUE | TRUE | TRUE | FALSE |
| 12 | .06 | TRUE | TRUE | FALSE | FALSE |
| 13 | .09 | TRUE | TRUE | FALSE | FALSE |
| 14 | .14 | TRUE | FALSE | FALSE | FALSE |
| 15 | .14 | TRUE | TRUE | FALSE | FALSE |
| 16 | .09 | TRUE | TRUE | FALSE | FALSE |

**Figure 4.6   Semantic search accuracy deteriorates at around 12-D.**

The table shows how good your search results would be if you used locality sensitive hashing to index a large number of semantic vectors. Once your vector had more than 16 dimensions, you'd have a hard time returning 2 search results that were any good.

So how can you do semantic search on 100-D vectors without an index? You now know how to convert the query string into a topic vector using LSA. And you know how to compare two vectors for similarity using the cosine similarity score (the scalar product, inner product, or dot product) to find the closest match. To find precise semantic matches, you need to find all the closest document topic vectors to a particular query (search) topic vector. But if you have $n$ documents, you have to do $n$ comparisons with your query topic vector. That's a lot of dot products.

You can vectorize the operation in numpy using matrix multiplication, but that doesn't reduce the number of operations; it only makes them 100 times faster.[60] Fundamentally, exact semantic search still requires $O(N)$ multiplications and additions for each query. So it scales only linearly with the size of your corpus. That wouldn't work for a large corpus, such as Google Search or even Wikipedia semantic search.

The key is to settle for "good enough" rather than striving for a perfect index or LSH algorithm for our high-dimensional vectors. There are now several open source implementations of some efficient and accurate *approximate nearest neighbors* algorithms that use LSH to efficiently implement semantic search. A couple of the easiest to use and install are

- Spotify's Annoy package [61]
- Gensim's `gensim.models.KeyedVector` class[62]

Technically these indexing or hashing solutions cannot guarantee that you will find all the best matches for your semantic search query. But they can get you a good list of close matches almost as fast as with a conventional reverse index on a TF-IDF vector or bag-of-words vector, if you're willing to give up a little precision.[63]

### 4.8.2   *Improvements*

In the next chapters, you'll learn how to fine tune this concept of topic vectors so that the vectors associated with words are more precise and useful. To do this we first start learning about neural nets. This will improve your pipeline's ability to extract meaning from short texts or even solitary words.

## *Summary*

- You can use SVD for semantic analysis to decompose and transform TF-IDF and BOW vectors into topic vectors.
- Use LDiA when you need to compute explainable topic vectors.
- No matter how you create your topic vectors, they can be used for semantic search to find documents based on their meaning.
- Topic vectors can be used to predict whether a social post is spam or is likely to be "liked."
- Now you know how to sidestep around the curse of dimensionality to find approximate nearest neighbors in your semantic vector space.

---

[60] Vectorizing your Python code, especially doubly-nested `for` loops, for pairwise distance calculations can speed your code by almost 100-fold. See Hacker Noon article "Vectorizing the Loops with Numpy" (https://hackernoon.com/speeding-up-your-code-2-vectorizing-the-loops-with-numpy-e380e939bed3).

[61] Spotify's researchers compared their `annoy` performance to that of several alternative algorithms and implementations on their github repo (https://github.com/spotify/annoy).

[62] The approach used in `gensim` for hundreds of dimensions in word vectors will work fine for any semantic or topic vector. See gensim's "KeyedVectors" documentation (https://radimrehurek.com/gensim/models/keyedvectors.html).

[63] If you want to learn about faster ways to find a high-dimensional vector's nearest neighbors, check out appendix F, or just use the Spotify `annoy` package to index your topic vectors.

# Part 2

# Deeper learning (neural networks)

Part 1 gathered the tools for natural language processing and dove into machine learning with statistics-driven vector space models. You discovered that even more meaning could be found when you looked at the statistics of connections between words.[1] You learned about algorithms such as latent semantic analysis that can help make sense of those connections by gathering words into topics.

But part 1 considered only linear relationships between words. And you often had to use human judgment to design feature extractors and select model parameters. The neural networks of part 2 accomplish most of the tedious feature extraction work for you. And the models of part 2 are often more accurate than those you could build with the hand-tuned feature extractors of part 1.

The use of multilayered neural networks for machine learning is called *deep learning*. This new approach to NLP and the modeling of human thought is often called "connectionism" by philosophers and neuroscientists.[2] The increasing access to deep learning, through greater availability of computational resources and the rich open source culture, will be your gateway into deeper

---

[1] *Conditional probability* is one term for these connection statistics (how often a word occurs given that other words occur before or after the "target" word). *Cross correlation* is another one of these statistics (the likelihood of words occurring together). The *singular values* and *singular vectors* of the word-document matrix can be used to collect words into topics, linear combinations of word counts.

[2] See the web page titled "Stanford Encyclopedia of Philosophy - Connectionism" (https://plato.stanford.edu/entries/connectionism).

understanding of language. In part 2, we begin to peel open the "black box" that is deep learning and learn how to model text in deeper nonlinear ways.

We start with a primer on neural networks. Then we examine a few of the various flavors of neural networks and how they can be applied to NLP. We also start to look at the patterns not only between words but between the characters within words. And finally we show you how to use machine learning to actually generate novel text.

# Baby steps with neural networks (perceptrons and backpropagation)

### This chapter covers

- Learning the history of neural networks
- Stacking perceptrons
- Understanding backpropagation
- Seeing the knobs to turn on neural networks
- Implementing a basic neural network in Keras

In recent years, a lot of hype has developed around the promise of neural networks and their ability to classify and identify input data, and more recently the ability of certain network architectures to generate original content. Companies large and small are using them for everything from image captioning and self-driving car navigation to identifying solar panels from satellite images and recognizing faces in security camera videos. And luckily for us, many NLP applications of neural nets exist as well. While deep neural networks have inspired a lot of hype and hyperbole, our robot overlords are probably further off than any clickbait cares to admit. Neural networks are, however, quite powerful tools, and you can easily use them in an NLP chatbot pipeline to classify input text, summarize documents, and even generate novel works.

This chapter is intended as a primer for those with no experience in neural networks. We don't cover anything specific to NLP in this chapter, but gaining a basic understanding of what is going on under the hood in a neural network is important for the upcoming chapters. If you're familiar with the basics of a neural network, you can rest easy in skipping ahead to the next chapter, where you dive back into processing text with the various flavors of neural nets. Although the mathematics of the underlying algorithm, *backpropagation*, are outside this book's scope, a high-level grasp of its basic functionality will help you understand language and the patterns hidden within.

> **TIP**    Manning publishes two other tremendous resources on deep learning:
> - *Deep Learning with Python*, by François Chollet (Manning, 2017), is a deep dive into the wonders of deep learning by the creator of Keras himself.
> - *Grokking Deep Learning*, by Andrew Trask (Manning, 2017), is a broad overview of deep learning models and practices.

## 5.1    *Neural networks, the ingredient list*

As the availability of processing power and memory has exploded over the course of the decade, an old technology has come into its own again. First proposed in the 1950s by Frank Rosenblatt, the perceptron[1] offered a novel algorithm for finding patterns in data.

The basic concept lies in a rough mimicry of the operation of a living neuron cell. As electrical signals flow into the cell through the *dendrites* (see figure 5.1) into the nucleus, an electric charge begins to build up. When the cell reaches a certain level of charge, it *fires*, sending an electrical signal out through the *axon*. However, the dendrites aren't all created equal. The cell is more "sensitive" to signals through certain dendrites than others, so it takes less of a signal in those paths to fire the axon.

The biology that controls these relationships is most certainly beyond the scope of this book, but the key concept to notice here is the way the cell *weights* incoming signals when deciding when to fire. The neuron will dynamically change those weights in the decision making process over the course of its life. You are going to mimic that process.

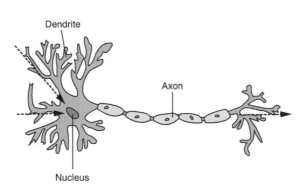

**Figure 5.1    Neuron cell**

---

[1]    Rosenblatt, Frank (1957), "The perceptron—a perceiving and recognizing automaton." Report 85-460-1, Cornell Aeronautical Laboratory.

### 5.1.1   Perceptron

Rosenblatt's original project was to teach a machine to recognize images. The original perceptron was a conglomeration of photo-receptors and potentiometers, not a computer in the current sense. But implementation specifics aside, Rosenblatt's concept was to take the features of an image and assign a weight, a measure of importance, to each one. The features of the input image were each a small subsection of the image.

A grid of photo-receptors would be exposed to the image. Each receptor would see one small piece of the image. The brightness of the image that a particular photo-receptor could see would determine the strength of the signal that it would send to the associated "dendrite."

Each dendrite had an associated weight in the form of a potentiometer. Once enough signal came in, it would pass the signal into the main body of the "nucleus" of the "cell." Once enough of those signals from all the potentiometers passed a certain threshold, the perceptron would fire down its axon, indicating a positive match on the image it was presented with. If it didn't fire for a given image, that was a negative classification match. Think "hot dog, not hot dog" or "iris setosa, not iris setosa."

### 5.1.2   A numerical perceptron

So far there has been a lot of hand waving about biology and electric current and photo-receptors. Let's pause for a second and peel out the most important parts of this concept.

Basically, you'd like to take an example from a dataset, show it to an algorithm, and have the algorithm say yes or no. That's all you're doing so far. The first piece you need is a way to determine the *features* of the sample. Choosing appropriate features turns out to be a surprisingly challenging part of machine learning. In "normal" machine learning problems, like predicting home prices, your features might be square footage, last sold price, and ZIP code. Or perhaps you'd like to predict the species of a certain flower using the Iris dataset.[2] In that case your features would be petal length, petal width, sepal length, and sepal width.

In Rosenblatt's experiment, the features were the intensity values of each pixel (subsections of the image), one pixel per photo receptor. You then need a set of *weights* to assign to each of the features. Don't worry yet about where these weights come from. Just think of them as a percentage of the signal to let through into the neuron. If you're familiar with linear regression, then you probably already know where these weights come from.[3]

---

[2]   The Iris dataset is frequently used to introduce machine learning to new students. See the Scikit-Learn docs (http://scikit-learn.org/stable/auto_examples/datasets/plot_iris_dataset.html).

[3]   The weights for the inputs to a single neuron are mathematically equivalent to the slopes in a multivariate linear regression or logistic regression.

**TIP**    Generally, you'll see the individual features denoted as $x_i$, where $i$ is a reference integer. And the collection of all features for a given example are denoted as $X$ representing a vector:

$$X = [x_1, x_2, ..., x_i, ..., x_n]$$

And similarly, you'll see the associate weights for each feature as $w_i$, where $i$ corresponds to the index of feature $x$ associated with that weight. And the weights are generally represented as a vector $W$:

$$W = [w_1, w_2, ..., w_i, ..., w_n]$$

With the features in hand, you just multiply each feature ($x_i$) by the corresponding weight ($w_i$) and then sum up:

$$(x_1 * w_1) + (x_2 * w_2) + ... + (x_i * w_i) + ...$$

The one piece you're missing here is the neuron's threshold to fire or not. And it's just that, a threshold. Once the weighted sum is above a certain threshold, the perceptron outputs 1. Otherwise it outputs 0.

You can represent this threshold with a simple *step function* (labeled "Activation Function" in figure 5.2).

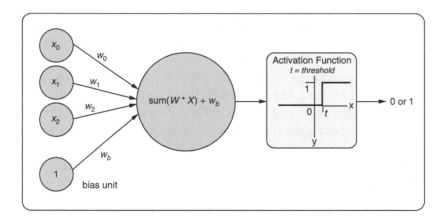

**Figure 5.2   Basic perceptron**

### 5.1.3    *Detour through bias*

Figure 5.2 and this example reference *bias*. What is this? The bias is an "always on" input to the neuron. The neuron has a weight dedicated to it just as with every other element of the input, and that weight is trained along with the others in the exact same way. This is represented in two ways in the various literature around neural networks. You may see the input represented as the base input vector, say of *n*-elements, with a 1 appended to the beginning or the end of the vector, giving you an *n*+1 dimensional vector. The position of the 1 is irrelevant to the network, as long as it's consistent across all of your samples. Other times people presume the existence of the bias term and leave it off the input in a diagram, but the weight associated with it exists separately and is always multiplied by 1 and added to the dot product of the sample input's values and their associated weights. Both are effectively the same—just a heads-up to notice the two common ways of displaying the concept.

The reason for having the bias weight at all is that you need the neuron to be resilient to inputs of all zeros. It may be the case that the network needs to learn to output 0 in the face of inputs of 0, but it may not. Without the bias term, the neuron would output 0 * weight = 0 for any weights you started with or tried to learn. With the bias term, you won't have this problem. And in case the neuron needs to learn to output 0, in that case, the neuron can learn to decrement the weight associated with the bias term enough to keep the dot product below the threshold.

Figure 5.3 is a rather neat visualization of the analogy between some of the signals within a biological neuron in your brain and the signals of an artificial neuron used for deep learning. If you want to get deep, think about how you are using a biological neuron to read this book about natural language processing to learn about deep learning.[4]

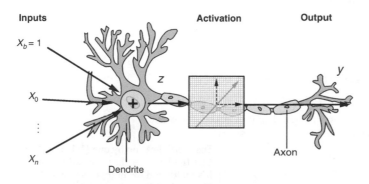

**Figure 5.3   A perceptron and a biological neuron**

And in mathematical terms, the output of your perceptron, denoted $f(x)$, looks like

$$f(\vec{x}) = 1 \; if \sum_{i=0}^{n} x_i w_i > threshold \; else \; 0$$

**Equation 5.1   *Threshold activation function***

---

> **TIP**  The sum of the pairwise multiplications of the input vector ($X$) and the weight vector ($W$) is exactly the dot product of the two vectors. This is the most basic element of why *linear algebra* factors so heavily in the development of neural networks. The other side effect of this matrix multiplication structure of a perceptron is that GPUs in modern computers turn out to be super-efficient at implementing neural networks due to their hyper-optimization of linear algebra operations.

Your perceptron hasn't *learned* anything just yet. But you have achieved something quite important. You've passed data into a model and received an output. That output is likely wrong, given you said nothing about where the weight values come from. But this is where things will get interesting.

> **TIP**  The base unit of any neural network is the neuron. And the basic perceptron is a special case of the more generalized neuron. We refer to the perceptron as a neuron for now.

### A PYTHONIC NEURON

Calculating the output of the neuron described earlier is straightforward in Python. You can also use the numpy *dot* function to multiply your two vectors together:

```
>>> import numpy as np

>>> example_input = [1, .2, .1, .05, .2]
>>> example_weights = [.2, .12, .4, .6, .90]

>>> input_vector = np.array(example_input)
>>> weights = np.array(example_weights)
>>> bias_weight = .2

>>> activation_level = np.dot(input_vector, weights) +\
...     (bias_weight * 1)
>>> activation_level
0.674
```

The multiplication by one (* 1) is just to emphasize that the bias_weight is like all the other weights: it's multiplied by an input value, only the bias_weight input feature value is always 1.

With that, if you use a simple threshold activation function and choose a threshold of .5, your next step is the following:

```
>>> threshold = 0.5
>>> if activation_level >= threshold:
...     perceptron_output = 1
... else:
...     perceptron_output = 0
>>> perceptron_output)
1
```

Given the example_input, and that particular set of weights, this perceptron will output 1. But if you have several example_input vectors and the associated expected outcomes with each (a labeled dataset), you can decide if the perceptron is correct or not for each *guess*.

### CLASS IS IN SESSION

So far you have set up a path toward making predictions based on data, which sets the stage for the main act: machine learning. The weight values up to this point have been brushed off as arbitrary values so far. In reality, they are the key to the whole structure, and you need a way to "nudge" the weights up and down based on the result of the prediction for a given example.

The perceptron *learns* by altering the weights up or down as a function of how wrong the system's guess was for a given input. But from where does it start? The weights of an untrained neuron start out random! Random values, near zero, are usually chosen from a normal distribution. In the preceding example, you can see why starting the weights (including the bias weight) at zero would lead only to an output of zero. But establishing slight variations, without giving any track through the neuron too much power, you have a foothold from where to be right and where to be wrong.

And from there you can start to learn. Many different samples are shown to the system, and each time the weights are readjusted a small amount based on whether the neuron output was what you wanted or not. With enough examples (and under the right conditions), the error *should* tend toward zero, and the system *learns*.

The trick is, and this is the key to the whole concept, that each weight is adjusted by how much it contributed to the resulting error. A larger weight (which lets that data point affect the result more) should be blamed more for the rightness/wrongness of the perceptron's output for that given input.

Let's assume that your earlier `example_input` should have resulted in a 0 instead:

```
>>> expected_output = 0
>>> new_weights = []
>>> for i, x in enumerate(example_input):
...     new_weights.append(weights[i] + (expected_output -\
...         perceptron_output) * x)
 >>> weights = np.array(new_weights)
```

For example, in the first index above:
new_weight = .2 + (0 - 1) * 1 = -0.8

```
>>> example_weights
[0.2, 0.12, 0.4, 0.6, 0.9]
>>> weights
[-0.8  -0.08  0.3   0.55  0.7]
```

Original weights

New weights

This process of exposing the network over and over to the same training set can, under the right circumstances, lead to an accurate predictor even on input that the perceptron has never seen.

### LOGIC IS A FUN THING TO LEARN

So the preceding example was just some arbitrary numbers to show how the math goes together. Let's apply this to a problem. It's a trivial toy problem, but it demonstrates the basics of how you can teach a computer a concept, by only showing it labeled examples.

Let's try to get the computer to understand the concept of logical OR. If either one side or the other of the expression is true (or both sides are), the logical OR statement is true. Simple enough. For this toy problem, you can easily model every possible example by hand (this is rarely the case in reality). Each sample consists of two signals, each of which is either true (1) or false (0). See the following listing.

---

**Listing 5.1    OR problem setup**

```
>>> sample_data = [[0, 0],   # False, False
...                [0, 1],   # False, True
...                [1, 0],   # True, False
...                [1, 1]]   # True, True

>>> expected_results = [0,   # (False OR False) gives False
...                     1,   # (False OR True ) gives True
...                     1,   # (True  OR False) gives True
...                     1]   # (True  OR True ) gives True

>>> activation_threshold = 0.5
```

You need a few tools to get started: numpy just to get used to doing vector (array) multiplication, and `random` to initialize the weights:

```
>>> from random import random
>>> import numpy as np

>>> weights = np.random.random(2)/1000   # Small random float 0 < w < .001
>>> weights
[5.62332144e-04 7.69468028e-05]
```

You need a bias as well:

```
>>> bias_weight = np.random.random() / 1000
>>> bias_weight
0.0009984699077277136
```

Then you can pass it through your pipeline and get a prediction for each of your four samples. See the following listing.

---

**Listing 5.2    Perceptron random guessing**

```
>>> for idx, sample in enumerate(sample_data):
...     input_vector = np.array(sample)
...     activation_level = np.dot(input_vector, weights) +\
...         (bias_weight * 1)
...     if activation_level > activation_threshold:
...         perceptron_output = 1
...     else:
...         perceptron_output = 0
```

```
...        print('Predicted {}'.format(perceptron_output))
...        print('Expected: {}'.format(expected_results[idx]))
...        print()
Predicted 0
Expected: 0

Predicted 0
Expected: 1

Predicted 0
Expected: 1

Predicted 0
Expected: 1
```

Your random weight values didn't help your little neuron out that much—one right and three wrong. Let's send it back to school. Instead of just printing 1 or 0, you'll update the weights at each iteration. See the following listing.

**Listing 5.3   Perceptron learning**

```
>>> for iteration_num in range(5):
...        correct_answers = 0
...        for idx, sample in enumerate(sample_data):
...            input_vector = np.array(sample)
...            weights = np.array(weights)
...            activation_level = np.dot(input_vector, weights) +\
...                (bias_weight * 1)
...            if activation_level > activation_threshold:
...                perceptron_output = 1
...            else:
...                perceptron_output = 0
...            if perceptron_output == expected_results[idx]:
...                correct_answers += 1
...            new_weights = []
...            for i, x in enumerate(sample):
...                new_weights.append(weights[i] + (expected_results[idx] -\
...                    perceptron_output) * x)
...            bias_weight = bias_weight + ((expected_results[idx] -\
...                perceptron_output) * 1)
...            weights = np.array(new_weights)
...        print('{} correct answers out of 4, for iteration {}'\
...            .format(correct_answers, iteration_num))
3 correct answers out of 4, for iteration 0
2 correct answers out of 4, for iteration 1
3 correct answers out of 4, for iteration 2
4 correct answers out of 4, for iteration 3
4 correct answers out of 4, for iteration 4
```

**The bias weight is updated as well, just like those associated with the inputs.**

**This is where the magic happens. There are more efficient ways of doing this, but you broke it out into a loop to reinforce that each weight is updated by force of its input (xi). If an input was small or zero, the effect on that weight would be minimal, regardless of the magnitude of the error. And conversely, the effect would be large if the input was large.**

Haha! What a good student your little perceptron is. By updating the weights in the inner loop, the perceptron is learning from its experience of the dataset. After the first iteration, it got two more correct (three out of four) than it did with random guessing (one out of four).

In the second iteration, it overcorrected the weights (changed them too much) and had to learn to backtrack with its adjustment of the weights. By the time the fourth iteration completed, it had learned the relationships perfectly. The subsequent iterations do nothing to update the network, as there is an error of 0 at each sample, so no weight adjustments are made.

This is what is known as *convergence.* A model is said to converge when its error function settles to a minimum, or at least a consistent value. Sometimes you're not so lucky. Sometimes a neural network bounces around looking for optimal weights to satisfy the relationships in a batch of data and never converges. In section 5.8, you'll see how an *objective function* or *loss function* affects what your neural net "thinks" are the optimal weights.

### NEXT STEP

The basic perceptron has an inherent flaw. If the data isn't linearly separable, or the relationship cannot be described by a linear relationship, the model won't converge and won't have any useful predictive power. It won't be able to predict the target variable accurately.

Early experiments were successful at learning to classify images based solely on example images and their classes. The initial excitement of the concept was quickly tempered by the work of Minsky and Papert,[5] who showed the perceptron was severely

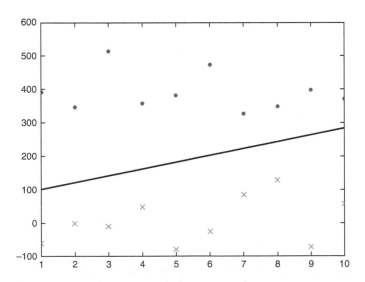

**Figure 5.4   Linearly separable data**

---

[5] Perceptrons by Minsky and Papert, 1969

limited in the kinds of classifications it can make. Minsky and Papert showed that if the data samples weren't linearly separable into discrete groups, the perceptron wouldn't be able to learn to classify the input data.

Linearly separable data points (as shown in figure 5.4) are no problem for a perceptron. Crossed up data will cause a single-neuron perceptron to forever spin its wheels without learning to predict anything better than a random guess, a random flip of a coin. It's not possible to draw a single line between your two classes (dots and Xs) in figure 5.5.

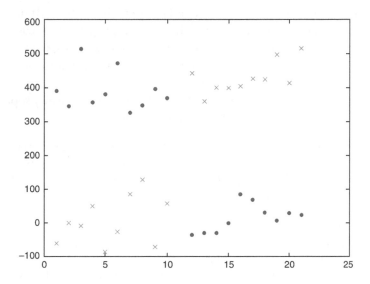

**Figure 5.5** **Nonlinearly separable data**

A perceptron finds a linear equation that describes the relationship between the features of your dataset and the target variable in your dataset. A perceptron is just doing linear regression. A perceptron cannot describe a nonlinear equation or a nonlinear relationship.

### Local vs global minimum

When a perceptron converges, it can be said to have found a linear equation that describes the relationship between the data and the target variable. It doesn't, however, say anything about how good this descriptive linear equation is, or how "minimum" the cost is. If there are multiple solutions, multiple possible cost minimums, it will settle on one particular minimum determined by where its weights started. This is called a *local minimum* because it's the best (smallest cost) that could be found near where the weights started. It may not be the *global minimum*, which is the best you could ever find by searching all the possible weights. In most cases it's not possible to know if you've found the global minimum.

A lot of relationships between data values aren't linear, and there's no good linear regression or linear equation that describes those relationships. And many datasets aren't linearly separable into classes with lines or planes. Because most data in the world isn't cleanly separable with lines and planes, the "proof" Minsky and Paperts published relegated the perceptron to the storage shelves.

But the perceptron idea didn't die easily. It resurfaced again when the Rumelhardt-McClelland collaboration effort (which Geoffrey Hinton was involved in)[6] showed you could use the idea to solve the *XOR* problem with multiple perceptrons in concert.[7] The problem you solved with a single perceptron and no multilayer backpropagation was for a simpler problem, the *OR* problem. The key breakthrough by Rumelhardt-McClelland was the discovery of a way to allocate the error appropriately to each of the perceptrons. The way they did this was to use an old idea called backpropagation. With this idea for backpropagation across layers of neurons, the first modern neural network was born.

The basic perceptron has the inherent flaw that if the data isn't linearly separable, the model won't converge to a solution with useful predictive power.

> **NOTE**  The code in listing 5.3 solved the *OR* problem with a single percep-
> tron. The table of 1s and 0s in listing 5.1 that our perceptron learned was the
> output of binary *OR* logic. The *XOR* problem slightly alters that table to try to
> teach the perceptron how to mimic an *Exclusive OR* logic gate. If you changed
> the correct answer for the last example from a 1 (True) to a 0 (False) to rep-
> resent XOR logic, that makes the problem a lot harder. The examples in each
> class (0 or 1) aren't linearly separable without adding an additional neuron to
> our neural network. The classes are diagonal from each other in our two-
> dimensional feature vector space (similar to figure 5.5), so there's no line you
> can draw that separates 1s (logic Trues) from 0s (logic Falses).

Even though they could solve complex (nonlinear) problems, neural networks were, for a time, too computationally expensive. It was seen as a waste of precious computational power to require two perceptrons and a bunch of fancy backpropagation math to solve the XOR problem, a problem that can be solved with a single logic gate or a single line of code. They proved impractical for common use, and they found their way back to the dusty shelves of academia and supercomputer experimentation. This began the second "AI Winter"[8] that lasted from around 1990 to about 2010.[9] But eventually computing power, backpropagation algorithms, and the proliferation of raw data, like labeled images of cats and dogs,[10] caught up. Computationally expensive

---

[6]  Rumelhart, D. E., Hinton, G. E., and Williams, R. J. (1986). "Learning representations by back-propagating errors." Nature, 323, 533–536.

[7]  See the Wikipedia article "The XOR affair" (https://en.wikipedia.org/wiki/Perceptrons_(book)#The_XOR_affair).

[8]  Wikipedia, https://en.wikipedia.org/wiki/AI_winter#The_setbacks_of_the_late_1980s_and_early_1990s.

[9]  See the web page titled "Philosophical Transactions of the Royal Society B: Biological Sciences" (http://rstb.royalsocietypublishing.org/content/365/1537/177.short).

algorithms and limited datasets were no longer show-stoppers. Thus the third age of neural networks began.

But back to what they found.

### EMERGENCE FROM THE SECOND AI WINTER

As with most great ideas, the good ones will bubble back to the surface eventually. It turns out that the basic idea behind the perceptron can be extended to overcome the basic limitation that doomed it at first. The idea is to gather multiple perceptrons together and feed the input into one (or several) perceptrons. Then you can feed the output of those perceptrons into more perceptrons before finally comparing the output to the expected value. This system (a neural network) can learn more complex patterns and overcome the challenge of classes that aren't linearly separable, like in the XOR problem. The key question is: How do you update the weights in the earlier layers?

Let's pause for a moment and formalize an important part of the process. So far we've discussed errors and how much the prediction was off base for a perceptron. Measuring this error is the job of a *cost function*, or *loss function*. A cost function, as you have seen, quantifies the mismatch between the correct answers that the network should output and the values of the actual outputs ($y$) for the corresponding "questions" ($x$) input into the network. The loss function tells us how often our network output the wrong answer and how wrong those answers were. Equation 5.2 is one example of a cost function, just the error between the truth and your model's prediction:

$$err(x) = |y - f(x)|$$

**Equation 5.2**   *Error between truth and prediction*

The goal in training a perceptron, or a neural network in general, is to minimize this cost function across all available input samples:

$$J(x) = \min \sum_{i=1}^{n} err(x_i)$$

**Equation 5.3**   *Cost function you want to minimize*

You'll soon see other cost functions, such as mean squared error, but you won't have to decide on the best cost function. It's usually already decided for you within most neural network frameworks. The most important thing to grasp is the idea that minimizing a cost function across a dataset is your ultimate goal. Then the rest of the concepts presented here will make sense.

---

[10] See the PDF "Learning Multiple Layers of Features from Tiny Images" by Alex Krizhevsky (http://citeseerx.ist.psu.edu/viewdoc/download?doi=10.1.1.222.9220&rep=rep1&type=pdf).

**BACKPROPAGATION**

Hinton and his colleagues decided there was a way to use multiple perceptrons at the same time with one target. This they showed could solve problems that weren't linearly separable. They could now approximate nonlinear functions as well as linear ones.

But how in the world do you update the weights of these various perceptrons? What does it even mean to have contributed to an error? Say two perceptrons sit next to each other and each receive the same input. No matter what you do with output (concatenate it, add it, multiply it), when you try to push the error back to the initial weights it will be a function of the input (which was identical on both sides), so they would be updated the same amount at each step and you'd never go anywhere. Your neurons would be redundant. They'd both end up with the same weights and your network wouldn't learn very much.

The concept gets even more mind bending when you imagine a perceptron that feeds into a second perceptron as the second's input. Which is exactly what you're going to do.

Backpropagation helps you solve this problem, but you have to tweak your perceptron a little to get there. Remember, the weights were updated based on how much they contributed to the overall error. But if a weight is affecting an output that becomes the input for another perceptron, you no longer have a clear idea of what the error is at the beginning of that second perceptron.

You need a way to calculate the amount a particular weight ($w_{1i}$ in figure 5.6) contributed to the error given that it contributed to the error via other weights ($w_{1j}$) and ($w_{2j}$) in the next layer. And the way to do that is with *backpropagation*.

Now is a good time to stop using the term "perceptron," because you're going to change how the weights in each neuron are updated. From here on out, we'll refer to

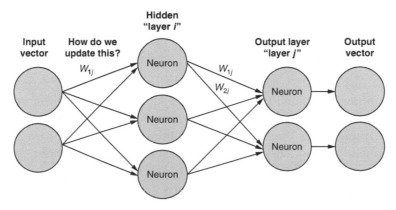

**Figure 5.6  Neural net with hidden weights**

the more general *neuron* that includes the perceptron, but also its more powerful relatives. You'll also see neurons referred to as cells or nodes in the literature, and in most cases the terms are interchangeable.

A neural network, regardless of flavor, is nothing more than a collection of neurons with connections between them. We often organize them into layers, but that's not required. Once you have an architecture where the output of a neuron becomes the input of another neuron, you begin to talk about *hidden* neurons and layers versus an *input* or *output* layer or neuron.

This is called a *fully connected* network. Though not all the connections are shown in figure 5.7, in a fully connected network each input element has a connection to *every* neuron in the next layer. And every connection has an associated weight. So in a network that takes a four-dimensional vector as input and has 5 neurons, there will be 20 total weights in the layer (4 weights for the connections to each of the 5 neurons).

As with the input to the perceptron, where there was a weight for each input, the neurons in the second layer of a neural network have a weight assigned not to the original input, but to each of the outputs from the first layer. So now you can see the difficulty in calculating the amount a first-layer weight contributed to the overall error. The first-layer weight has an effect that is passed through not just a single other weight but through one weight in each of the next layer's neurons. The derivation and mathematical details of the algorithm itself, although extremely interesting, are beyond the scope of this book, but we take a brief moment for an overview so you aren't left completely in the dark about the black box of neural nets.

Backpropagation, short for backpropagation of the errors, describes how you can discover the appropriate amount to update a specific weight, given the input, the

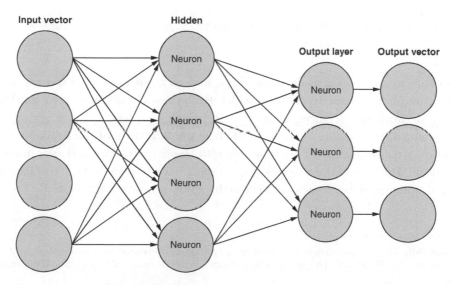

**Figure 5.7   Fully connected neural net**

output, and the expected value. *Propagation*, or forward propagation, is an input flowing "forward" through the net and computing the output for the network for that input. To get to backpropagation, you first need to change the perceptron's activation function to something that is slightly more complex.

Until now, you have been using a step function as your artificial neuron's *activation function*. But as you'll see in a moment, backpropagation requires an activation function that is nonlinear and continuously differentiable.[11] Now each neuron will output a value *between* two values, like 0 and 1, as it does in the commonly used sigmoid function shown in equation 5.4:

$$S(x) = \frac{1}{1 + e^{-x}}$$

**Equation 5.4    *Sigmoid function***

### Why does your activation function need to be nonlinear?

Because you want your neurons to be able to model nonlinear relationships between your feature vectors and the target variable. If all a neuron could do is multiply inputs by weights and add them together, the output would always be a linear function of the inputs and you couldn't model even the simplest nonlinear relationships.

But the threshold function you used for your neurons earlier was a nonlinear step function. So the neurons you used before could theoretically be trained to work together to model nearly any nonlinear relationship... as long as you had enough neurons.

That's the advantage of a nonlinear activation function; it allows a neural net to model a nonlinear relationship. And a continuously differentiable nonlinear function, like a sigmoid, allows the error to propagate smoothly back through multiple layers of neurons, speeding up your training process. Sigmoid neurons are quick learners.

There are many other activation functions, such as *hyperbolic tangent* and *rectified linear units*; they all have benefits and downsides. Each shines in different ways for different neural network architectures, as you'll learn in later chapters.

So why differentiable? If you can calculate the derivative of the function, you can also do partial derivatives of the function, with respect to various variables in the function itself. The hint of the magic is "with respect to various variables." You have a path toward updating a weight with respect to the amount of input it received!

---

[11] A continuously differentiable function is even more smooth than a differentiable function. See the Wikipedia article "Differentiable function" (https://en.wikipedia.org/wiki/Differentiable_function#Differentiability _and_continuity).

## DIFFERENTIATE ALL THE THINGS

You'll start with the error of the network and apply a cost function, say *squared error*, as shown in equation 5.5:

$$MSE = (y - f(x))^2$$

**Equation 5.5** *Mean squared error*

You can then lean on the *chain rule* of calculus to calculate the derivative of compositions of functions, as in equation 5.6. And the network itself is nothing but a composition of functions (specifically dot products followed by your new nonlinear activation function at each step):

$$(f(g(x))' = F'(x) = f'(g(x))g'(x)$$

**Equation 5.6** *Chain rule*

You can now use this formula to find the derivative of the activation function of each neuron with respect to the input that fed it. You can calculate how much that weight contributed to the final error and adjust it appropriately.

If the layer is the output layer, the update of the weights is rather straightforward, with the help of your easily differentiable activation function. The derivative of the error with respect to the *j*-th output that fed it is

$$\Delta w_{ij} = -\alpha \frac{\partial Error}{w_{ij}} = -\alpha y_i (y_j - f(x)_j)) y_j (1 - y_j)$$

**Equation 5.7** *Error derivative*

If you're updating the weights of a hidden layer, things are a little more complex, as you can see in equation 5.8:

$$\Delta w_{ij} = \alpha \frac{\partial E}{\partial w_{ij}} = \alpha y_i (\sum_{l \varepsilon L} \delta_{jl} w_{jl}) y_j (1 - y_j)$$

**Equation 5.8** *Derivative of the previous layer*

The function $f(x)$ in equation 5.7 is the output, specifically the *j*-th position of the output vector. The $y$ in equation 5.7 is the output of a node in either the *i*-th layer or the *j*-th layer, where the output of the *i*-th layer is the input of the *j*-th layer. So you have the $\alpha$ (the learning rate) times the output of the earlier layer times the derivative of the activation function from the later layer *with respect to* the weight that fed the output of the *i*-th layer into the *j*-th layer. The sum in equation 5.8 expresses this for all inputs to all the layers.

It's important to be specific about when the changes are applied to the weights themselves. As you calculate each weight update in each layer, the calculations all depend on the network's state during the forward pass. Once the error is calculated, you then calculate the proposed change to each weight in the network. But do *not* apply any of them—at least until you get all the way back to the beginning of the network. Otherwise as you update weights toward the end of the net, the derivatives calculated for the lower levels will no longer be the appropriate gradient for that particular input. You can aggregate all the ups and down for each weight based on each training sample, without updating any of the weights and instead update them at the end of all the training, but we discuss more on that choice in section 5.1.6.

And then to train the network, pass in all the inputs. Get the associated error for each input. Backpropagate those errors to each of the weights. And then update each weight with the total change in error. After all the training data has gone through the network once, and the errors are backpropagated, we call this an *epoch* of the neural network training cycle. The dataset can then be passed in again and again to further refine the weights. Be careful, though, or the weights will overfit the training set and no longer be able to make meaningful predictions on new data points from outside the training set.

In equations 5.7 and 5.8, $\alpha$ is the *learning rate*. It determines how much of the observed error in the weight is corrected during a particular training cycle (epoch) or batch of data. It usually remains constant during a single training cycle, but some sophisticated training algorithms will adjust it adaptively to speed up the training and ensure convergence. If $\alpha$ is too large, you could easily overcorrect. Then the next error, presumably larger, would itself lead to a large weight correction the other way, but even further from the goal. Set $\alpha$ too small and the model will take too long to converge to be practical, or worse, it will get stuck in a local minimum on the *error surface*.

### 5.1.4   Let's go skiing—the error surface

The goal of training in neural networks, as we stated earlier, is to minimize a cost function by finding the best parameters (weights). Keep in mind, this isn't the error for any one particular data point. You want to minimize the cost for all the various errors taken together.

Creating a visualization of this side of the problem can help build a mental model of what you're doing when you adjust the weights of the network as you go.

From earlier, mean squared error is a common cost function (shown back in equation 5.5). If you imagine plotting the error as a function of the possible weights, given a set of inputs and a set of expected outputs, a point exists where that function is closest to zero. That point is your *minimum*—the spot where your model has the least error.

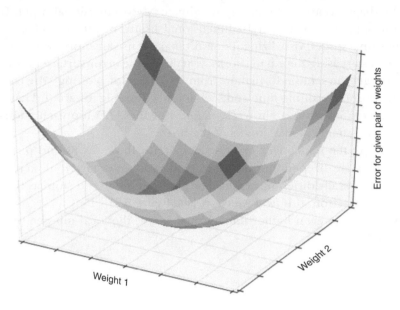

**Figure 5.8  Convex error curve**

This minimum will be the set of weights that gives the optimal output for a given training example. You will often see this represented as a three-dimensional bowl with two of the axes being a two-dimensional weight vector and the third being the error (see figure 5.8). That description is a vast simplification, but the concept is the same in higher dimensional spaces (for cases with more than two weights).

Similarly, you can graph the error surface as a function of all possible weights across all the inputs of a training set. But you need to tweak the error function a little. You need something that represents the aggregate error across all inputs for a given set of weights. For this example, you'll use *mean squared error* as the z axis (see equation 5.5).

Here again, you'll get an error surface with a minimum that is located at the set of weights. That set of weights will represent a model that best fits the entire training set.

### 5.1.5  *Off the chair lift, onto the slope*

What does this visualization represent? At each epoch, the algorithm is performing *gradient descent* in trying to minimize the error. Each time you adjust the weights in a direction that will hopefully reduce your error the next time. A convex error surface will be great. Stand on the ski slope, look around, find out which way is down, and go that way!

But you're not always so lucky as to have such a smoothly shaped bowl. The error surface may have some pits and divots scattered about. This situation is what is known as a *nonconvex error curve*. And, as in skiing, if these pits are big enough, they can suck you in and you might not reach the bottom of the slope.

Again, the diagrams are representing weights for two-dimensional input. But the concept is the same if you have a 10-dimensional input, or 50, or 1,000. In those higher dimensional spaces, visualizing it doesn't make sense anymore, so you trust the math. Once you start using neural networks, visualizing the error surface becomes less important. You get the same information from watching (or plotting) the error or a related metric over the training time and seeing if it's trending toward 0. That will tell you if your network is on the right track or not. But these 3D representations are a helpful tool for creating a mental model of the process.

But what about the nonconvex error space? Aren't those divots and pits a problem? Yes, yes they are. Depending on where you randomly start your weights, you could end up at radically different weights and the training would stop, as there's no other way to go down from this *local minimum* (see figure 5.9).

And as you get into even higher dimensional space, the local minima will follow you there as well.

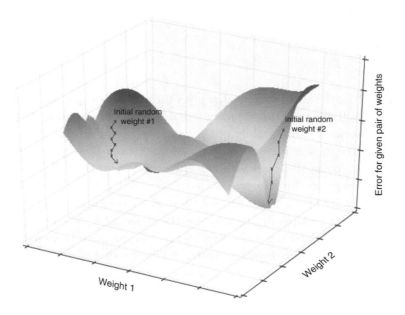

**Figure 5.9   Nonconvex error curve**

## 5.1.6   *Let's shake things up a bit*

Up until now, you have been aggregating the error for all the training examples and skiing down the slope as best you could. This training approach, as described, is *batch* learning. A batch is a large subset of your training data. But batch learning has a static error surface for the entire batch. With this single static surface, if you only head downhill from a random starting point, you could end up in some local minima (divot or hole) and not know that better options exist for your weight values. Two other options to training can help you skirt these traps.

The first option is *stochastic* gradient descent. In stochastic gradient descent, you update the weights after each training example, rather than after looking at all the training examples. And you reshuffle the order of the training examples each time through. By doing this, the error surface is redrawn for each example, as each different input could have a different expected answer. So the error surface for most examples will look different. But you're still just adjusting the weights based on gradient descent, *for that example*. Instead of gathering up the errors and then adjusting the weights once at the end of the epoch, you update the weights after every individual example. The key point is that you're moving *toward* the presumed minimum (not all the way to that presumed minimum) at any given step.

And as you move toward the various minima on this fluctuating surface, with the right data and right hyperparameters, you can more easily bumble toward the global minimum. If your model isn't tuned properly or the training data is inconsistent, the model won't converge, and you'll just spin and turn over and over and the model never learns anything. But in practice stochastic gradient descent proves quite effective in avoiding local minima in most cases. The downfall of this approach is that it's slow. Calculating the forward pass and backpropagation, and then updating the weights after each example, adds that much time to an already slow process.

The more common approach, your second training option, is *mini-batch*. In mini-batch training, a small subset of the training set is passed in and the associated errors are aggregated as in full *batch*. Those errors are then backpropagated as with *batch* and the weights updated for each subset of the training set. This process is repeated with the next batch, and so on until the training set is exhausted. And that again would constitute one epoch. This is a happy medium; it gives you the benefits of both *batch* (speedy) and *stochastic* (resilient) training methods.

Although the details of how *backpropagation* works are fascinating,[12] they aren't trivial, and as noted earlier they're outside the scope of this book. But a good mental image to keep handy is that of the error surface. In the end, a neural network is just a way to walk down the slope of the bowl *as fast as possible* until you're at the bottom. From a given point, look around you in every direction, find the steepest way down (not a pleasant image if you're scared of heights), and go that way. At the next step (batch, mini-batch, or stochastic), look around again, find the steepest way, and now go that way. Soon enough, you'll be by the fire in the ski lodge at the bottom of the valley.

### 5.1.7 *Keras: Neural networks in Python*

Writing a neural network in raw Python is a fun experiment and can be helpful in putting all these pieces together, but Python is at a disadvantage regarding speed, and the shear number of calculations you're dealing with can make even moderately sized

---

[12] Wikpedia, https://en.wikipedia.org/wiki/Backpropagation.

networks intractable. Many Python libraries, though, get you around the speed zone: PyTorch, Theano, TensorFlow, Lasagne, and many more. The examples in this book use Keras (https://keras.io/).

Keras is a high-level wrapper with an accessible API for Python. The exposed API can be used with three different backends almost interchangeably: Theano, TensorFlow from Google, and CNTK from Microsoft. Each has its own low-level implementation of the basic neural network elements and has highly tuned linear algebra libraries to handle the dot products to make the matrix multiplications of neural networks as efficiently as possible.

Let's look at the simple XOR problem and see if you can train a network using Keras.

### Listing 5.4   XOR Keras network

```
>>> import numpy as np
>>> from keras.models import Sequential
>>> from keras.layers import Dense, Activation
>>> from keras.optimizers import SGD
>>> # Our examples for an exclusive OR.
>>> x_train = np.array([[0, 0],
...                     [0, 1],
...                     [1, 0],
...                     [1, 1]])
>>> y_train = np.array([[0],
...                     [1],
...                     [1],
...                     [0]])
>>> model = Sequential()
>>> num_neurons = 10
>>> model.add(Dense(num_neurons, input_dim=2))
>>> model.add(Activation('tanh'))
>>> model.add(Dense(1))
>>> model.add(Activation('sigmoid'))
>>> model.summary()
Layer (type)                 Output Shape              Param #
=================================================================
dense_18 (Dense)             (None, 10)                30

activation_6 (Activation)    (None, 10)                0

dense_19 (Dense)             (None, 1)                 11

activation_7 (Activation)    (None, 1)                 0
=================================================================
Total params: 41.0
Trainable params: 41.0
Non-trainable params: 0.0
```

**The base Keras model class**

**Dense is a fully connected layer of neurons.**

**Stochastic gradient descent, but there are others**

**x_train is a list of samples of 2D feature vectors used for training.**

**y_train is the desired outcomes (target values) for each feature vector sample.**

**The fully connected hidden layer will have 10 neurons.**

**The output layer has one neuron to output a single binary classification value (0 or 1).**

**input_dim is only necessary for the first layer; subsequent layers will calculate the shape automatically from the output dimensions of the previous layer. We have 2D feature vectors for our 2-input XOR gate examples.**

The `model.summary()` gives you an overview of the network parameters and number of weights (`Param \#`) at each stage. Some quick math: 10 neurons, each with two weights (one for each value in the input vector), and one weight for the bias gives you 30 weights to learn. The output layer has a weight for each of the 10 neurons in the first layer and one bias weight for a total of 11 in that layer.

The next bit of code is a bit opaque:

```
>>> sgd = SGD(lr=0.1)
>>> model.compile(loss='binary_crossentropy', optimizer=sgd,
...     metrics=['accuracy'])
```

SGD is the stochastic gradient descent optimizer you imported. This is just how the model will try to minimize the error, or *loss*. *lr* is the learning rate, the fraction applied to the derivative of the error with respect to each weight. Higher values will speed learn, but may force the model away from the global minimum by shooting past the goal; smaller values will be more precise but increase the training time and leave the model more vulnerable to local minima. The loss function itself is also defined as a parameter; here it's `binary_crossentropy`. The metrics parameter is a list of options for the output stream during training. The `compile` method builds, but doesn't yet train the model. The weights are initialized, and you can use this random state to try to predict from your dataset, but you'll only get random guesses:

```
>>> model.predict(x_train)
[[ 0.5        ]
 [ 0.43494844]
 [ 0.50295198]
 [ 0.42517585]]
```

The `predict` method gives the raw output of the last layer, which would be generated by the sigmoid function in this example.

Not much to write home about. But remember this has no knowledge of the answers just yet; it's just applying its random weights to the inputs. So let's try to train this. See the following listing.

---

**Listing 5.5  Fit model to the XOR training set**

This Is where you
train the model. ←⎯⎯⎯

```
model.fit(x_train, y_train, epochs=100)
Epoch 1/100
4/4 [==============================] - 0s - loss: 0.6917 - acc: 0.7500
Epoch 2/100
4/4 [==============================] - 0s - loss: 0.6911 - acc: 0.5000
Epoch 3/100
4/4 [==============================] - 0s - loss: 0.6906 - acc: 0.5000
...
Epoch 100/100
4/4 [==============================] - 0s - loss: 0.6661 - acc: 1.0000
```

**TIP**    The network might not converge on the first try. The first compile might end up with base parameters from the random distribution that make finding the global minimum difficult or impossible. If you run into this situation, you can call `model.fit` again with the same parameters (or add even more epochs) and see if the network finds its way eventually. Or reinitialize the network with a different random starting point and try `fit` from there. If you try the latter, make sure that you don't set a random seed, or you'll just repeat the same experiment over and over.

As it looked at what was a tiny dataset over and over, it finally figured out what was going on. It "learned" what exclusive-or (XOR) was, just from being shown examples! That is the magic of neural networks and what will guide you through the next few chapters:

```
>>> model.predict_classes(x_train))
4/4 [==============================] - 0s
[[0]
 [1]
 [1]
 [0]]
>>> model.predict(x_train))
4/4 [==============================] - 0s
[[ 0.0035659 ]
 [ 0.99123639]
 [ 0.99285167]
 [ 0.00907462]]
```

Calling `predict` again (and `predict_classes`) on the trained model yields better results. It gets 100% accuracy on your tiny dataset. Of course, accuracy isn't necessarily the best measure of a predictive model, but for this toy example it will do. So in the following listing you save your ground-breaking XOR model for posterity.

---

**Listing 5.6    Save the trained model**

```
>>> import h5py
>>> model_structure = model.to_json()          ⟵   Export the structure of
                                                    the network to a JSON
>>> with open("basic_model.json", "w") as json_file:   blob for later use using
...     json_file.write(model_structure)               Keras' helper method.

>>> model.save_weights("basic_weights.h5")     ⟵
```

> **The trained weights must be saved separately. The first part just saves the network structure. You must re-instantiate the same model structure to reload them later.**

And there are similar methods to re-instantiate the model, so you don't have to retrain every time you want to make a prediction, which will be huge going forward. Although this model takes a few seconds to run, in the coming chapters that will quickly grow to minutes, hours, even in some cases days depending on the hardware and the complexity of the model, so get ready!

### 5.1.8 Onward and deepward

As neural networks have spread and spawned the entire deep learning field, much research has been done (and continues to be done) into the details of these systems:

- Different activation functions (such as sigmoid, rectified linear units, and hyperbolic tangent)
- Choosing a good learning rate, to dial up or down the effect of the error
- Dynamically adjusting the learning rate using a *momentum* model to find the global minimum faster
- Application of *dropout*, where a randomly chosen set of weights are ignored in a given training pass to prevent the model from becoming too attuned to its training set (overfitting)
- Regularization of the weights to artificially dampen a single weight from growing or shrinking too far from the rest of the weights (another tactic to avoid overfitting)

The list goes on and on.

### 5.1.9 Normalization: input with style

Neural networks want a vector input and will do their best to work on whatever is fed to them, but one key thing to remember is input *normalization*. This is true of many machine learning models. Imagine the case of trying to classify houses, say on their likelihood of selling in a given market. You have only two data points: number of bedrooms and last selling price. This data could be represented as a vector. Say, for a two-bedroom house that last sold for $275,000:

```
input_vec = [2, 275000]
```

As the network tries to learn anything about this data, the weights associated with bedrooms in the first layer would need to grow huge quickly to compete with the large values associated with price. So it's common practice to normalize the data so that each element retains its useful information from sample to sample. Normalization also ensures that each neuron works within a similar range of input values as the other elements within a single sample vector. Several approaches exist for normalization, such as mean normalization, feature scaling, and coefficient of variation. But the goal is to get the data in some range like [-1, 1] or [0, 1] for each element in each sample without losing information.

You won't have to worry too much about this with NLP, as TF-IDF, one-hot encoding, and word2vec (as you'll soon see) are normalized already. Keep it in mind for when your input feature vectors aren't normalized (such as with raw word frequencies or counts).

Finally, a last bit of terminology. Not a great deal of consensus exists on what constitutes a perceptron versus a multi-neuron layer versus deep learning, but we've found it handy to differentiate between a perceptron and a neural network if you have to use the activation function's derivative to properly update the weights. In this book, we use neural network and deep learning in this context and save the term "perceptron" for its (very) important place in history.

## Summary

- Minimizing a cost function is a path toward learning.
- A backpropagation algorithm is the means by which a network *learns*.
- The amount a weight contributes to a model's error is directly related to the amount it needs to be updated.
- Neural networks are, at their heart, optimization engines.
- Watch out for pitfalls (local minima) during training by monitoring the gradual reduction in error.
- Keras helps make all of this neural network math accessible.

# Reasoning with word vectors (Word2vec)

**This chapter covers**

- Understanding how word vectors are created
- Using pretrained models for your applications
- Reasoning with word vectors to solve real problems
- Visualizing word vectors
- Uncovering some surprising uses for word embeddings

One of the most exciting recent advancements in NLP is the "discovery" of word vectors. This chapter will help you understand what they are and how to use them to do some surprisingly powerful things. You'll learn how to recover some of the fuzziness and subtlety of word meaning that was lost in the approximations of earlier chapters.

In the previous chapters, we ignored the nearby context of a word. We ignored the words around each word. We ignored the effect the neighbors of a word have on its meaning and how those relationships affect the overall meaning of a statement. Our bag-of-words concept jumbled all the words from each document together into a statistical bag. In this chapter, you'll create much smaller bags of words from a "neighborhood" of only a few words, typically fewer than 10 tokens. You'll also ensure that these neighborhoods of meaning don't spill over into adjacent sentences. This process will help focus your word vector training on the relevant words.

Our new word vectors will be able to identify synonyms, antonyms, or words that just belong to the same category, such as people, animals, places, plants, names, or concepts. We could do that before, with latent semantic analysis in chapter 4, but your tighter limits on a word's neighborhood will be reflected in tighter accuracy of the word vectors. Latent semantic analysis of words, *n*-grams, and documents didn't capture all the literal meanings of a word, much less the implied or hidden meanings. Some of the connotations of a word are lost with LSA's oversized bags of words.

> **WORD VECTORS**   *Word vectors* are numerical vector representations of word semantics, or meaning, including literal and implied meaning. So word vectors can capture the connotation of words, like "peopleness," "animalness," "placeness," "thingness," and even "conceptness." And they combine all that into a dense vector (no zeros) of floating point values. This dense vector enables queries and logical reasoning.

## 6.1   *Semantic queries and analogies*

Well, what are these awesome word vectors good for? Have you ever tried to recall a famous person's name but you only have a general impression of them, like maybe this:

> *She invented something to do with physics in Europe in the early 20th century.*

If you enter that sentence into Google or Bing, you may not get the direct answer you're looking for, "Marie Curie." Google Search will most likely only give you links to lists of famous physicists, both men and women. You'd have to skim several pages to find the answer you're looking for. But once you found "Marie Curie," Google or Bing would keep note of that. They might get better at providing you search results the next time you look for a scientist.[1]

With word vectors, you can search for words or names that combine the meaning of the words "woman," "Europe," "physics," "scientist," and "famous," and that would get you close to the token "Marie Curie" that you're looking for. And all you have to do to make that happen is add up the word vectors for each of those words that you want to combine:

```
>>> answer_vector = wv['woman'] + wv['Europe'] + wv[physics'] +\
...      wv['scientist']
```

---

[1]   At least, that's what it did for us in researching this book. We had to use private browser windows to ensure that your search results would be similar to ours.

In this chapter, we show you the exact way to do this query. And we even show you how to subtract gender bias from the word vectors used to compute your answer:

```
>>> answer_vector = wv['woman'] + wv['Europe'] + wv[physics'] +\
...     wv['scientist'] - wv['male'] - 2 * wv['man']
```

With word vectors, you can take the "man" out of "woman"!

### 6.1.1 Analogy questions

What if you could rephrase your question as an analogy question? What if your "query" was something like this:

> *Who is to nuclear physics what Louis Pasteur is to germs?*

Again, Google Search, Bing, and even Duck Duck Go aren't much help with this one.[2] But with word vectors, the solution is as simple as subtracting "germs" from "Louis Pasteur" and then adding in some "physics":

```
>>> answer_vector = wv['Louis_Pasteur'] - wv['germs'] + wv['physics']
```

And if you're interested in trickier analogies about people in unrelated fields, such as musicians and scientists, you can do that, too:

> *Who is the Marie Curie of music?*

or

> *Marie Curie is to science as who is to music?*

Can you figure out what the word vector math would be for these questions?

You might have seen questions like these on the English analogy section of standardized tests such as SAT, ACT, or GRE exams. Sometimes they are written in formal mathematical notation like this:

```
MARIE CURIE : SCIENCE :: ? : MUSIC
```

Does that make it easier to guess the word vector math? One possibility is this:

```
>>> wv['Marie_Curie'] - wv['science'] + wv['music']
```

And you can answer questions like this for things other than people and occupations, like perhaps sports teams and cities:

> *The Timbers are to Portland as what is to Seattle?*

In standardized test form, that's

```
TIMBERS : PORTLAND :: ? : SEATTLE
```

---

[2] Try them all if you don't believe us.

But, more commonly, standardized tests use English vocabulary words and ask less fun questions, like the following:

```
WALK : LEGS :: ? : MOUTH
```

or

```
ANALOGY : WORDS :: ? : NUMBERS
```

All those "tip of the tongue" questions are a piece of cake for word vectors, even though they aren't multiple choice. When you're trying to remember names or words, just thinking of the *A*, *B*, *C*, and *D* multiple choice options can be difficult. NLP comes to the rescue with word vectors.

Word vectors can answer these vague questions and analogy problems. Word vectors can help you remember any word or name on the tip of your tongue, as long as the word vector for the answer exists in your word vector vocabulary.[3] And word vectors work well even for questions that you can't even pose in the form of a search query or analogy. You can learn about some of this non-query math with word vectors in section 6.2.1.

## 6.2 *Word vectors*

In 2012, Thomas Mikolov, an intern at Microsoft, found a way to encode the meaning of words in a modest number of vector dimensions.[4] Mikolov trained a neural network[5] to predict word occurrences near each target word. In 2013, once at Google, Mikolov and his teammates released the software for creating these word vectors and called it Word2vec.[6]

Word2vec learns the meaning of words merely by processing a large corpus of unlabeled text. No one has to label the words in the Word2vec vocabulary. No one has to tell the Word2vec algorithm that Marie Curie is a scientist, that the Timbers are a soccer team, that Seattle is a city, or that Portland is a city in both Oregon and Maine. And no one has to tell Word2vec that soccer is a sport, or that a team is a group of people, or that cities are both places as well as communities. Word2vec can learn that and much more, all on its own! All you need is a corpus large enough to mention Marie Curie and Timbers and Portland near other words associated with science or soccer or cities.

This unsupervised nature of Word2vec is what makes it so powerful. The world is full of unlabeled, uncategorized, unstructured natural language text.

---

[3] For Google's pretrained word vector model, your word is almost certainly within the 100B word news feed that Google trained it on, unless your word was invented after 2013.

[4] Word vectors typically have 100 to 500 dimensions, depending on the breadth of information in the corpus used to train them.

[5] It's only a single-layer network, so almost any linear machine learning model will also work. Logistic regression, truncated SVD, linear discriminant analysis, and Naive Bayes would all work well.

[6] "Efficient Estimation of Word Representations in Vector Space," Sep 2013, Mikolov, Chen, Corrado, and Dean (https://arxiv.org/pdf/1301.3781.pdf).

*Unsupervised* learning and *supervised* learning are two radically different approaches to machine learning.

**Supervised learning**

In supervised learning, the training data must be labeled in some way. An example of a label is the spam categorical label on an SMS message in chapter 4. Another example is the quantitative value for the number of likes of a tweet. Supervised learning is what most people think of when they think of machine learning. A supervised model can only get better if it can measure the difference between the expected output (the label) and its predictions.

In contrast, unsupervised learning enables a machine to learn directly from data, without any assistance from humans. The training data doesn't have to be organized, structured, or labeled by a human. So unsupervised learning algorithms like Word2vec are perfect for natural language text.

**Unsupervised learning**

In unsupervised learning, you train the model to perform a task, but without any labels, only the raw data. Clustering algorithms such as k-means or DBSCAN are examples of unsupervised learning. Dimension reduction algorithms like principal component analysis (PCA) and t-Distributed Stochastic Neighbor Embedding (t-SNE) are also unsupervised machine learning techniques. In unsupervised learning, the model finds patterns in the relationships between the data points themselves. An unsupervised model can get smarter (more accurate) just by throwing more data at it.

Instead of trying to train a neural network to learn the target word meanings directly (on the basis of labels for that meaning), you teach the network to predict words near the target word in your sentences. So in this sense, you do have labels: the nearby words you're trying to predict. But because the labels are coming from the dataset itself and require no hand-labeling, the Word2vec training algorithm is definitely an unsupervised learning algorithm.

Another domain where this unsupervised training technique is used is in time series modeling. Time series models are often trained to predict the next value in a sequence based on a window of previous values. Time series problems are remarkably similar to natural language problems in a lot of ways, because they deal with ordered sequences of values (words or numbers).

And the prediction itself isn't what makes Word2vec work. The prediction is merely a means to an end. What you do care about is the internal representation, the vector that Word2vec gradually builds up to help it generate those predictions. This representation will capture much more of the meaning of the target word (its semantics) than the word-topic vectors that came out of latent semantic analysis and latent Dirichlet allocation in chapter 4.

**NOTE**  Models that learn by trying to repredict the input using a lower-dimensional internal representation are called *autoencoders*. This may seem odd to you. It's like asking the machine to echo back what you just asked it, only it can't record the question as you're saying it. The machine has to compress your question into shorthand. And it has to use the same shorthand algorithm (function) for all the questions you ask it. The machine learns a new shorthand (vector) representation of your statements.

If you want to learn more about unsupervised deep learning models that create compressed representations of high-dimensional objects like words, search for the term "autoencoder."[7] They're also a common way to get started with neural nets, because they can be applied to almost any dataset.

Word2vec will learn about things you might not think to associate with all words. Did you know that every word has some geography, sentiment (positivity), and gender associated with it? If any word in your corpus has some quality, like "placeness," "peopleness," "conceptness," or "femaleness," all the other words will also be given a score for these qualities in your word vectors. The meaning of a word "rubs off" on the neighboring words when Word2vec learns word vectors.

All words in your corpus will be represented by numerical vectors, similar to the word-topic vectors discussed in chapter 4. Only this time the topics mean something more specific, more precise. In LSA, words only had to occur in the same document to have their meaning "rub off" on each other and get incorporated into their word-topic vectors. For Word2vec word vectors, the words must occur near each other—typically fewer than five words apart and within the same sentence. And Word2vec word vector topic weights can be added and subtracted to create new word vectors that mean something!

A mental model that may help you understand word vectors is to think of word vectors as a list of weights or scores. Each weight or score is associated with a specific dimension of meaning for that word. See the following listing.

**Listing 6.1  Compute nessvector**

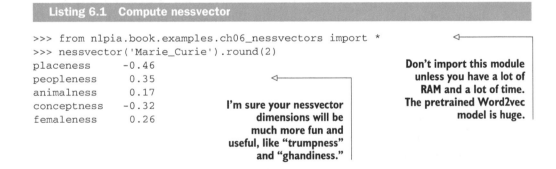

```
>>> from nlpia.book.examples.ch06_nessvectors import *
>>> nessvector('Marie_Curie').round(2)
placeness     -0.46
peopleness     0.35
animalness     0.17
conceptness   -0.32
femaleness     0.26
```

Don't import this module unless you have a lot of RAM and a lot of time. The pretrained Word2vec model is huge.

I'm sure your nessvector dimensions will be much more fun and useful, like "trumpness" and "ghandiness."

---

You can compute "nessvectors" for any word or *n*-gram in the Word2vec vocabulary using the tools from nlpia (https://github.com/totalgood/nlpia/blob/master/src/nlpia/book/examples/ch06_nessvectors.py). And this approach will work for any "ness" components that you can dream up.

Mikolov developed the Word2vec algorithm while trying to think of ways to numerically represent words in vectors. He wasn't satisfied with the less accurate word sentiment math you did in chapter 4. He wanted to do *vector-oriented reasoning*, like you just did in the previous section with those analogy questions. This concept may sound fancy, but really it means that you can do math with word vectors and that the answer makes sense when you translate the vectors back into words. You can add and subtract word vectors to *reason* about the words they represent and answer questions similar to your examples above, like the following:[8]

```
wv['Timbers'] - wv['Portland'] + wv['Seattle'] = ?
```

Ideally you'd like this math (word vector reasoning) to give you this:

```
wv['Seattle_Sounders']
```

Similarly, your analogy question "'Marie Curie' is to 'physics' as __ is to 'classical music'?" can be thought about as a math expression like this:

```
wv['Marie_Curie'] - wv['physics'] + wv['classical_music'] = ?
```

In this chapter, we want to improve on the LSA word vector representations we introduced in the previous chapter. Topic vectors constructed from entire documents using LSA are great for document classification, semantic search, and clustering. But the topic-word vectors that LSA produces aren't accurate enough to be used for semantic reasoning or classification and clustering of short phrases or compound words. You'll soon learn how to train the single-layer neural networks required to produce these more accurate and more fun word vectors. And you'll see why they have replaced LSA word-topic vectors for many applications involving short documents or statements.

### 6.2.1 *Vector-oriented reasoning*

Word2vec was first presented publicly in 2013 at the ACL conference.[9] The talk with the dry-sounding title "Linguistic Regularities in Continuous Space Word Representations" described a surprisingly accurate language model. Word2vec embeddings were four times more accurate (45%) compared to equivalent LSA models (11%) at answering analogy questions like those above.[10] The accuracy improvement was so surprising, in fact, that Mikolov's initial paper was rejected by the International Conference on

---

[8] For those not up on sports, the Portland Timbers and Seattle Sounders are major league soccer teams.

[9] See the PDF "Linguistic Regularities in Continuous Space Word Representations," by Tomas Mikolov, Wentau Yih, and Geoffrey Zweig (https://www.aclweb.org/anthology/N13-1090).

[10] See Radim Řehůřek's interview of Tomas Mikolov (https://rare-technologies.com/rrp#episode_1_tomas_mikolov_on_ai).

Learning Representations.[11] Reviewers thought that the model's performance was too good to be true. It took nearly a year for Mikolov's team to release the source code and get accepted to the Association for Computational Linguistics.

Suddenly, with word vectors, questions like

```
Portland Timbers + Seattle - Portland = ?
```

can be solved with vector algebra (see figure 6.1).

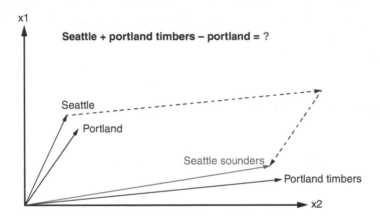

**Figure 6.1  Geometry of Word2vec math**

The Word2vec model contains information about the relationships between words, including similarity. The Word2vec model "knows" that the terms *Portland* and *Portland Timbers* are roughly the same distance apart as *Seattle* and *Seattle Sounders*. And those distances (differences between the pairs of vectors) are in roughly the same direction. So the Word2vec model can be used to answer your sports team analogy question. You can add the difference between *Portland* and *Seattle* to the vector that represents the *Portland Timbers*, which should get you close to the vector for the term *Seattle Sounders*:

$$
\begin{bmatrix} 0.0168 \\ 0.007 \\ 0.247 \\ ... \end{bmatrix} + \begin{bmatrix} 0.093 \\ -0.028 \\ -0.214 \\ ... \end{bmatrix} - \begin{bmatrix} 0.104 \\ 0.0883 \\ -0.318 \\ ... \end{bmatrix} = \begin{bmatrix} 0.006 \\ -0.109 \\ 0.352 \\ ... \end{bmatrix}
$$

**Equation 6.1  *Compute the answer to the soccer team question***

---

[11] See "ICRL2013 open review" (https://openreview.net/forum?id=idpCdOWtqXd60&noteId=C8Vn84fq SG8qa).

After adding and subtracting word vectors, your resultant vector will almost never exactly equal one of the vectors in your word vector vocabulary. Word2vec word vectors usually have 100s of dimensions, each with continuous real values. Nonetheless, the vector in your vocabulary that is closest to the resultant will often be the answer to your NLP question. The English word associated with that nearby vector is the natural language answer to your question about sports teams and cities.

Word2vec allows you to transform your natural language vectors of token occurrence counts and frequencies into the vector space of much lower-dimensional Word2vec vectors. In this lower-dimensional space, you can do your math and then convert back to a natural language space. You can imagine how useful this capability is to a chatbot, search engine, question answering system, or information extraction algorithm.

**NOTE** The initial paper in 2013 by Mikolov and his colleagues was able to achieve an answer accuracy of only 40%. But back in 2013, the approach outperformed any other semantic reasoning approach by a significant margin. Since the initial publication, the performance of Word2vec has improved further. This was accomplished by training it on extremely large corpora. The reference implementation was trained on the 100 billion words from the Google News Corpus. This is the pretrained model you'll see used in this book a lot.

The research team also discovered that the difference between a singular and a plural word is often roughly the same magnitude, and in the same direction:

$$\vec{x}_{coffee} - \vec{x}_{coffees} \approx \vec{x}_{cup} - \vec{x}_{cups} \approx \vec{x}_{cookie} - \vec{x}_{cookies}$$

**Equation 6.2** *Distance between the singular and plural versions of a word*

But their discovery didn't stop there. They also discovered that the distance relationships go far beyond simple singular versus plural relationships. Distances apply to other semantic relationships. The Word2vec researchers soon discovered they could answer questions that involve geography, culture, and demographics, like this:

```
"San Francisco is to California as what is to Colorado?"

San Francisco - California + Colorado = Denver
```

#### More reasons to use word vectors

Vector representations of words are useful not only for reasoning and analogy problems, but also for all the other things you use natural language vector space models for. From pattern matching to modeling and visualization, your NLP pipeline's accuracy and usefulness will improve if you know how to use the word vectors from this chapter.

For example, later in this chapter we show you how to visualize word vectors on 2D semantic maps like the one shown in figure 6.2. You can think of this like a

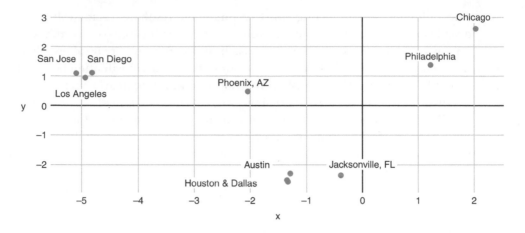

**Figure 6.2   Word vectors for ten US cities projected onto a 2D map**

cartoon map of a popular tourist destination or one of those impressionistic maps you see on bus stop posters. In these cartoon maps, things that are close to each other semantically as well as geographically get squished together. For cartoon maps, the artist adjusts the scale and position of icons for various locations to match the "feel" of the place. With word vectors, the machine too can have a feel for words and places and how far apart they should be. So your machine will be able to generate impressionistic maps like the one in figure 6.2 using word vectors you are learning about in this chapter.[12]

If you're familiar with these US cities, you might realize that this isn't an accurate geographic map, but it's a pretty good semantic map. I, for one, often confuse the two large Texas cities, Houston and Dallas, and they have almost identical word vectors. And the word vectors for the big California cities make a nice triangle of culture in my mind.

And word vectors are great for chatbots and search engines too. For these applications, word vectors can help overcome some of the rigidity, brittleness of pattern, or keyword matching. Say you were searching for information about a famous person from Houston, Texas, but didn't realize they'd moved to Dallas. From figure 6.2, you can see that a semantic search using word vectors could easily figure out a search involving city names such as Dallas and Houston. And even though character-based patterns wouldn't understand the difference between "tell me about a Denver omelette" and "tell me about the Denver Nuggets," a word vector pattern could. Patterns based on word vectors would likely be able to differentiate between the food item (omelette) and the basketball team (Nuggets) and respond appropriately to a user asking about either.

---

[12] You can find the code for generating these interactive 2D word plots at https://github.com/totalgood/nlpia/blob/master/src/nlpia/book/examples/ch06_w2v_us_cities_visualization.py.

### 6.2.2 *How to compute Word2vec representations*

Word vectors represent the semantic meaning of words as vectors in the context of the training corpus. This allows you not only to answer analogy questions but also reason about the meaning of words in more general ways with vector algebra. But how do you calculate these vector representations? There are two possible ways to train Word2vec embeddings:

- The *skip-gram* approach predicts the context of words (output words) from a word of interest (the input word).
- The *continuous bag-of-words* (CBOW) approach predicts the target word (the output word) from the nearby words (input words). We show you how and when to use each of these to train a Word2vec model in the coming sections.

The computation of the word vector representations can be resource intensive. Luckily, for most applications, you won't need to compute your own word vectors. You can rely on pretrained representations for a broad range of applications. Companies that deal with large corpora and can afford the computation have open sourced their pretrained word vector models. Later in this chapter we introduce you to using these other pretrained word models, such as GloVe and fastText.

> **TIP** Pretrained word vector representations are available for corpora like Wikipedia, DBPedia, Twitter, and Freebase.[13] These pretrained models are great starting points for your word vector applications:
>
> - Google provides a pretrained Word2vec model based on English Google News articles.[14]
> - Facebook published their word model, called *fastText*, for 294 languages.[15]

But if your domain relies on specialized vocabulary or semantic relationships, general-purpose word models won't be sufficient. For example, if the word "python" should unambiguously represent the programming language instead of the reptile, a domain-specific word model is needed. If you need to constrain your word vectors to their usage in a particular domain, you'll need to train them on text from that domain.

#### SKIP-GRAM APPROACH

In the skip-gram training approach, you're trying to predict the surrounding window of words based on an input word. In the sentence about Monet, in our following example, "painted" is the training input to the neural network. The corresponding training

---

[13] See the web page titled "GitHub - 3Top/word2vec-api: Simple web service providing a word embedding model" (https://github.com/3Top/word2vec-api#where-to-get-a-pretrained-model).

[14] Original Google 300-D Word2vec model on Google Drive (https://drive.google.com/file/d/0B7XkCwpI5KDYNlNUTTlSS21pQmM).

[15] See the web page titled "GitHub - facebookresearch/fastText: Library for fast text representation and classification" (https://github.com/facebookresearch/fastText).

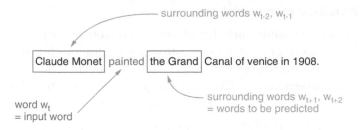

**Figure 6.3   Training input and output example for the skip-gram approach**

output example skip-grams are shown in figure 6.3. The predicted words for these skip-grams are the neighboring words "Claude," "Monet," "the," and "Grand."

> **WHAT IS A SKIP-GRAM?**   Skip-grams are $n$-grams that contain gaps because you skip over intervening tokens. In this example, you're predicting "Claude" from the input token "painted," and you skip over the token "Monet."

The structure of the neural network used to predict the surrounding words is similar to the networks you learned about in chapter 5. As you can see in figure 6.4, the network consists of two layers of weights, where the hidden layer consists of $n$ neurons; $n$ is the number of vector dimensions used to represent a word. Both the input and output layers contain $M$ neurons, where $M$ is the number of words in the model's vocabulary. The output layer activation function is a softmax, which is commonly used for classification problems.

### WHAT IS SOFTMAX?

The softmax function is often used as the activation function in the output layer of neural networks when the network's goal is to learn classification problems. The softmax will squash the output results between 0 and 1, and the sum of all outputs will always add up to 1. That way, the results of an output layer with a softmax function can be considered as probabilities.

For each of the $K$ output nodes, the softmax output value can be calculated using the normalized exponential function:

$$\sigma(z)_j = \frac{e^{z_j}}{\sum_{k=1}^{K} e^{z_k}}$$

If your output vector of a three-neuron output layer looks like this

$$v = \begin{bmatrix} 0.5 \\ 0.9 \\ 0.2 \end{bmatrix}$$

**Equation 6.3   *Example 3D vector***

The "squashed" vector after the softmax activation would look like this:

$$\sigma(v) = \begin{bmatrix} 0.309 \\ 0.461 \\ 0.229 \end{bmatrix}$$

**Equation 6.4** *Example 3D vector after softmax*

Notice that the sum of these values (rounded to three significant digits) is approximately 1.0, like a probability distribution.

Figure 6.4 shows the numerical network input and output for the first two surrounding words. In this case, the input word is "Monet," and the expected output of the network is either "Claude" or "painted," depending on the training pair.

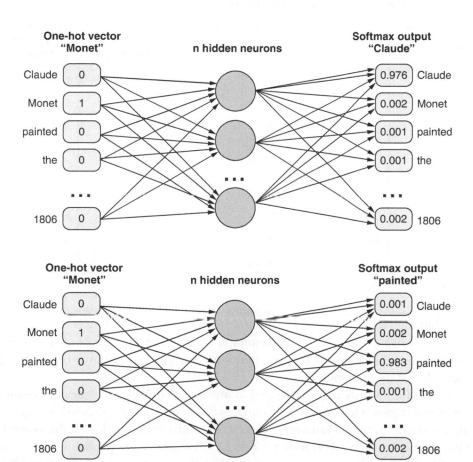

**Figure 6.4  Network example for the skip-gram training**

**NOTE**    When you look at the structure of the neural network for word embedding, you'll notice that the implementation looks similar to what you discovered in chapter 5.

### How does the network learn the vector representations?

To train a Word2vec model, you're using techniques from chapter 2. For example, in table 6.1, $w_t$ represents the one-hot vector for the token at position $t$. So if you want to train a Word2vec model using a skip-gram window size (radius) of two words, you're considering the two words before and after each target word. You would then use your 5-gram tokenizer from chapter 2 to turn a sentence like this

```
>>> sentence = "Claude Monet painted the Grand Canal of Venice in 1806."
```

into 10 5-grams with the input word at the center, one for each of the 10 words in the original sentence.

**Table 6.1    Ten 5-grams for sentence about Monet**

| Input word $w_t$ | Expected output $w_{t-2}$ | Expected output $w_{t-1}$ | Expected output $w_{t+1}$ | Expected output $w_{t+2}$ |
|---|---|---|---|---|
| Claude | | | Monet | painted |
| Monet | | Claude | painted | the |
| painted | Claude | Monet | the | Grand |
| the | Monet | painted | Grand | Canal |
| Grand | painted | the | Canal | of |
| Canal | the | Grand | of | Venice |
| of | Grand | Canal | Venice | in |
| Venice | Canal | of | in | 1908 |
| in | of | Venice | 1908 | |
| 1908 | Venice | in | | |

The training set consisting of the input word and the surrounding (output) words are now the basis for the training of the neural network. In the case of four surrounding words, you would use four training iterations, where each output word is being predicted based on the input word.

Each of the words are represented as one-hot vectors before they are presented to the network (see chapter 2). The output vector for a neural network doing embedding is similar to a one-hot vector as well. The softmax activation of the output layer nodes (one for each token in the vocabulary) calculates the probability of an output word being found as a surrounding word of the input word. The output vector of word probabilities can then be converted into a one-hot vector where the word with the highest probability will be converted to 1, and all remaining terms will be set to 0. This simplifies the loss calculation.

After training of the neural network is completed, you'll notice that the weights have been trained to represent the semantic meaning. Thanks to the one-hot vector conversion of your tokens, each row in the weight matrix represents each word from the vocabulary for your corpus. After the training, semantically similar words will have similar vectors, because they were trained to predict similar surrounding words. *This is purely magical!*

After the training is complete and you decide not to train your word model any further, the output layer of the network can be ignored. Only the weights of the inputs to the hidden layer are used as the embeddings. Or in other words: the weight matrix is your word embedding. The dot product between the one-hot vector representing the input term and the weights then represents the *word vector embedding*.

### Retrieving word vectors with linear algebra

The weights of a hidden layer in a neural network are often represented as a matrix: one column per input neuron, one row per output neuron. This allows the weight matrix to be multiplied by the column vector of inputs coming from the previous layer to generate a column vector of outputs going to the next layer (see figure 6.5). So if you multiply (dot product) a one-hot *row* vector by the trained weight matrix, you'll get a vector that is one weight from each neuron (from each matrix column). This also works if you take the weight matrix and multiply it (dot product) by a one-hot *column* vector for the word you are interested in.

Of course, the one-hot vector dot product just selects that row from your weight matrix that contains the weights for that word, which is your word vector. So you could easily retrieve that row by just selecting it, using the word's row number or index number from your vocabulary.

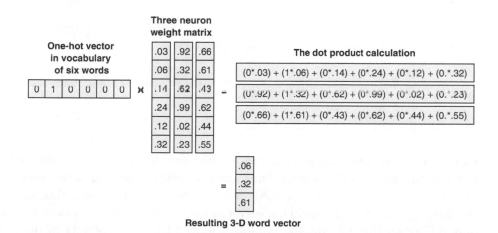

Figure 6.5 Conversion of one-hot vector to word vector

### CONTINUOUS BAG-OF-WORDS APPROACH

In the continuous bag-of-words approach, you're trying to predict the center word based on the surrounding words (see figures 6.5 and 6.6 and table 6.2). Instead of creating pairs of input and output tokens, you'll create a multi-hot vector of all surrounding terms as an input vector. The multi-hot input vector is the sum of all one-hot vectors of the surrounding tokens to the center, target token.

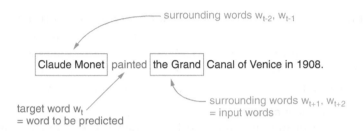

**Figure 6.6    Training input and output example for the CBOW approach**

**Table 6.2    Ten CBOW 5-grams from sentence about Monet**

| Input word $w_{t-2}$ | Input word $w_{t-1}$ | Input word $w_{t+1}$ | Input word $w_{t+2}$ | Expected output $w_t$ |
|---|---|---|---|---|
| | | Monet | painted | Claude |
| | Claude | painted | the | Monet |
| Claude | Monet | the | Grand | painted |
| Monet | painted | Grand | Canal | the |
| painted | the | Canal | of | Grand |
| the | Grand | of | Venice | Canal |
| Grand | Canal | Venice | in | of |
| Canal | of | in | 1908 | Venice |
| of | Venice | 1908 | | in |
| Venice | in | | | 1908 |

Based on the training sets, you can create your multi-hot vectors as inputs and map them to the target word as output. The multi-hot vector is the sum of the one-hot vectors of the surrounding words' training pairs $w_{t-2} + w_{t-1} + w_{t+1} + w_{t+2}$. You then build the training pairs with the multi-hot vector as the input and the target word $w_t$ as the output. During the training, the output is derived from the softmax of the output node with the highest probability (see figure 6.7).

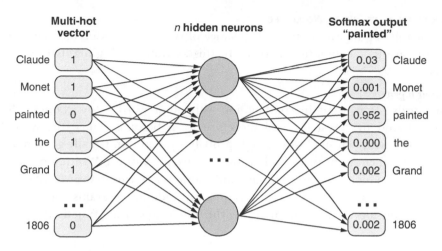

Figure 6.7   CBOW Word2vec network

## Continuous bag of words vs. bag of words

In previous chapters, we introduced the concept of a bag of words, but how is it different than a continuous bag of words? To establish the relationships between words in a sentence you slide a rolling window across the sentence to select the surrounding words for the target word. All words within the sliding window are considered to be the content of the continuous bag of words for the target word at the middle of that window.

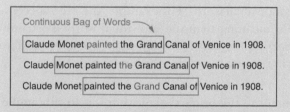

Example for a continuous bag of words passing a rolling window of five words over the sentence "Claude Monet painted the Grand Canal of Venice in 1908." The word painted is the target or center word within a five-word rolling window. "Claude," "Monet," "the," and "Grand" are the four surrounding words for the first CBOW rolling window.

### SKIP-GRAM VS. CBOW: WHEN TO USE WHICH APPROACH

Mikolov highlighted that the skip-gram approach works well with small corpora and rare terms. With the skip-gram approach, you'll have more examples due to the network structure. But the continuous bag-of-words approach shows higher accuracies for frequent words and is much faster to train.

## COMPUTATIONAL TRICKS OF WORD2VEC

After the initial publication, the performance of Word2vec models has been improved through various computational tricks. In this section, we highlight three improvements.

### Frequent bigrams

Some words often occur in combination with other words—for example, "Elvis" is often followed by "Presley"—and therefore form bigrams. Since the word "Elvis" would occur with "Presley" with a high probability, you don't really gain much value from this prediction. In order to improve the accuracy of the Word2vec embedding, Mikolov's team included some bigrams and trigrams as terms in the Word2vec vocabulary. The team[16] used co-occurrence frequency to identify bigrams and trigrams that should be considered single terms, using the following scoring function:

$$score(w_i, w_j) = \frac{count(w_i, w_j) - \delta}{count(w_i) \times count(w_j)}$$

**Equation 6.5   *Bigram scoring function***

If the words $w_i$ and $w_j$ result in a high score and the score is above the threshold $\delta$, they will be included in the Word2vec vocabulary as a pair term. You'll notice that the vocabulary of the model contains terms like "New_York" and "San_Francisco." The token of frequently occurring bigrams connects the two words with a character (usually "_"). That way, these terms will be represented as a single one-hot vector instead of two separate ones, such as for "San" and "Francisco."

Another effect of the word pairs is that the word combination often represents a different meaning than the individual words. For example, the MLS soccer team Portland Timbers has a different meaning than the individual words Portland and Timbers. But by adding oft-occurring bigrams like team names to the Word2vec model, they can easily be included in the one-hot vector for model training.

### Subsampling frequent tokens

Another accuracy improvement to the original algorithm was to subsample frequent words. Common words like "the" or "a" often don't carry significant information. And the co-occurrence of the word "the" with a broad variety of other nouns in the corpus might create less meaningful connections between words, muddying the Word2vec representation with this false semantic similarity training.

> **IMPORTANT**   All words carry meaning, including stop words. So stop words shouldn't be completely ignored or skipped while training your word vectors or composing your vocabulary. In addition, because word vectors are often used in generative models (like the model Cole used to compose sentences in

---

[16] The publication by the team around Tomas Mikolov (https://arxiv.org/pdf/1310.4546.pdf) provides more details.

this book), stop words and other common words must be included in your vocabulary and are allowed to affect the word vectors of their neighboring words.

To reduce the emphasis on frequent words like stop words, words are sampled during training in inverse proportion to their frequency. The effect of this is similar to the IDF effect on TF-IDF vectors. Frequent words are given less influence over the vector than the rarer words. Tomas Mikolov used the following equation to determine the probability of sampling a given word. This probability determines whether or not a particular word is included in a particular skip-gram during training:

$$P(w_i) = 1 - \sqrt{\frac{t}{f(w_i)}}$$

**Equation 6.6** *Subsampling probability in Mikolov's Word2vec paper*

The Word2vec C++ implementation uses a slightly different sampling probability than the one mentioned in the paper, but it has the same effect:

$$P(w_i) = \frac{f(w_i) - t}{f(w_i)} - \sqrt{\frac{t}{f(w_i)}}$$

**Equation 6.7** *Subsampling probability in Mikolov's Word2vec code*

In the preceding equations, $f(w_i)$ represents the frequency of a word across the corpus, and $t$ represents a frequency threshold above which you want to apply the subsampling probability. The threshold depends on your corpus size, average document length, and the variety of words used in those documents. Values between $10^{-5}$ and $10^{-6}$ are often found in the literature.

If a word shows up 10 times across your entire corpus, and your corpus has a vocabulary of one million distinct words, and you set the subsampling threshold to $10^{-6}$, the probability of keeping the word in any particular $n$-gram is 68%. You would skip it 32% of the time while composing your $n$ grams during tokenization.

Mikolov showed that subsampling improves the accuracy of the word vectors for tasks such as answering analogy questions.

### Negative sampling

One last trick Mikolov came up with was the idea of negative sampling. If a single training example with a pair of words is presented to the network, it'll cause all weights for the network to be updated. This changes the values of all the vectors for all the words in your vocabulary. But if your vocabulary contains thousands or millions of words, updating all the weights for the large one-hot vector is inefficient. To speed up the training of word vector models, Mikolov used negative sampling.

Instead of updating all word weights that weren't included in the word window, Mikolov suggested sampling just a few negative samples (in the output vector) to update their weights. Instead of updating all weights, you pick $n$ negative example word pairs (words that don't match your target output for that example) and update the weights that contributed to their specific output. That way, the computation can be reduced dramatically and the performance of the trained network doesn't decrease significantly.

> **NOTE**    If you train your word model with a small corpus, you might want to use a negative sampling rate of 5 to 20 samples. For larger corpora and vocabularies, you can reduce the negative sample rate to as low as two to five samples, according to Mikolov and his team.

### 6.2.3    *How to use the gensim.word2vec module*

If the previous section sounded too complicated, don't worry. Various companies provide their pretrained word vector models, and popular NLP libraries for different programming languages allow you to use the pretrained models efficiently. In the following section, we look at how you can take advantage of the magic of word vectors. For word vectors you'll use the popular gensim library, which you first saw in chapter 4.

If you've already installed the nlpia package,[17] you can download a pretrained Word2vec model with the following command:

```
>>> from nlpia.data.loaders import get_data
>>> word_vectors = get_data('word2vec')
```

If that doesn't work for you, or you like to "roll your own," you can do a Google search for Word2vec models pretrained on Google News documents.[18] After you find and download the model in Google's original binary format and put it in a local path, you can load it with the gensim package like this:

```
>>> from gensim.models.keyedvectors import KeyedVectors
>>> word_vectors = KeyedVectors.load_word2vec_format(\
...     '/path/to/GoogleNews-vectors-negative300.bin.gz', binary=True)
```

Working with word vectors can be memory intensive. If your available memory is limited or if you don't want to wait minutes for the word vector model to load, you can reduce the number of words loaded into memory by passing in the `limit` keyword argument. In the following example, you'll load the 200k most common words from the Google News corpus:

```
>>> from gensim.models.keyedvectors import KeyedVectors
>>> word_vectors = KeyedVectors.load_word2vec_format(\
...     '/path/to/GoogleNews-vectors-negative300.bin.gz',
...         binary=True, limit=200000)
```

---

[17] See the README file at http://github.com/totalgood/nlpia for installation instructions.

[18] Google hosts the original model trained by Mikolov on Google Drive at https://bit.ly/GoogleNews-vectors-negative300.

But keep in mind that a word vector model with a limited vocabulary will lead to a lower performance of your NLP pipeline if your documents contain words that you haven't loaded word vectors for. Therefore, you probably only want to limit the size of your word vector model during the development phase. For the rest of the examples in this chapter, you should use the complete Word2vec model if you want to get the same results we show here.

The `gensim.KeyedVectors.most_similar()` method provides an efficient way to find the nearest neighbors for any given word vector. The keyword argument `positive` takes a list of the vectors to be added together, similar to your soccer team example from the beginning of this chapter. Similarly, you can use the `negative` argument for subtraction and to exclude unrelated terms. The argument `topn` determines how many related terms should be provided as a return value.

Unlike a conventional thesaurus, Word2vec synonymy (similarity) is a continuous score, a distance. This is because Word2vec itself is a continuous vector space model. Word2vec high dimensionality and continuous values for each dimension enable it to capture the full range of meaning for any given word. That's why analogies and even zeugmas, odd juxtopositions of multiple meanings within the same word, are no problem:[19]

```
>>> word_vectors.most_similar(positive=['cooking', 'potatoes'], topn=5)
[('cook', 0.6973530650138855),
 ('oven_roasting', 0.6754530668258667),
 ('Slow_cooker', 0.6742032170295715),
 ('sweet_potatoes', 0.6600279808044434),
 ('stir_fry_vegetables', 0.6548759341239929)]
>>> word_vectors.most_similar(positive=['germany', 'france'], topn=1)
[('europe', 0.7222039699554443)]
```

Word vector models also allow you to determine unrelated terms. The gensim library provides a method called `doesnt_match`:

```
>>> word_vectors.doesnt_match("potatoes milk cake computer".split())
'computer'
```

To determine the most unrelated term of the list, the method returns the term with the highest distance to all other list terms.

If you want to perform calculations (such as the famous example *king* + *woman* - *man* = *queen*, which was the example that got Mikolov and his advisor excited in the first place), you can do that by adding a `negative` argument to the `most_similar` method call:

```
>>> word_vectors.most_similar(positive=['king', 'woman'],
...     negative=['man'], topn=2)
[('queen', 0.7118192315101624), ('monarch', 0.6189674139022827)]
```

---

[19] *Surfaces and Essences: Analogy as the Fuel and Fire of Thinking* by Douglas Hoffstadter and Emmanuel Sander makes it clear why machines that can handle analogies and zeugmas are such a big deal.

The gensim library also allows you to calculate the similarity between two terms. If you want to compare two words and determine their cosine similarity, use the method `.similarity()`:

```
>>> word_vectors.similarity('princess', 'queen')
0.70705315983704509
```

If you want to develop your own functions and work with the raw word vectors, you can access them through Python's square bracket syntax (`[]`) or the `get()` method on a `KeyedVector` instance. You can treat the loaded model object as a dictionary where your word of interest is the dictionary key. Each float in the returned array represents one of the vector dimensions. In the case of Google's word model, your numpy arrays will have a shape of 1 × 300:

```
>>> word_vectors['phone']
array([-0.01446533, -0.12792969, -0.11572266, -0.22167969, -0.07373047,
       -0.05981445, -0.10009766, -0.06884766,  0.14941406,  0.10107422,
       -0.03076172, -0.03271484, -0.03125   , -0.10791016,  0.12158203,
        0.16015625,  0.19335938,  0.0065918 , -0.15429688,  0.03710938,
        ...
```

If you're wondering what all those numbers *mean*, you can find out. But it would take a lot of work. You would need to examine some synonyms and see which of the 300 numbers in the array they all share. Alternatively you can find the linear combination of these numbers that make up dimensions for things like "placeness" and "femaleness," like you did at the beginning of this chapter.

### 6.2.4    *How to generate your own word vector representations*

In some cases, you may want to create your own domain-specific word vector models. Doing so can improve the accuracy of your model if your NLP pipeline is processing documents that use words in a way that you wouldn't find on Google News before 2006, when Mikolov trained the reference Word2vec model. Keep in mind, you need a *lot* of documents to do this as well as Google and Mikolov did. But if your words are particularly rare on Google News, or your texts use them in unique ways within a restricted domain, such as medical texts or transcripts, a domain-specific word model may improve your model accuracy. In the following section, we show you how to train your own Word2vec model.

For the purpose of training a domain-specific Word2vec model, you'll again turn to gensim, but before you can start training the model, you'll need to preprocess your corpus using tools you discovered in chapter 2.

#### PREPROCESSING STEPS

First you need to break your documents into sentences and the sentences into tokens. The gensimword2vec model expects a list of sentences, where each sentence is broken up into tokens. This prevents word vectors learning from irrelevant word occurrences in neighboring sentences. Your training input should look similar to the following structure:

```
>>> token_list
[
  ['to', 'provide', 'early', 'intervention/early', 'childhood', 'special',
   'education', 'services', 'to', 'eligible', 'children', 'and', 'their',
   'families'],
  ['essential', 'job', 'functions'],
  ['participate', 'as', 'a', 'transdisciplinary', 'team', 'member', 'to',
   'complete', 'educational', 'assessments', 'for']
  ...
]
```

To segment sentences and then convert sentences into tokens, you can apply the various strategies you learned in chapter 2. Detector Morse is a sentence segmenter that improves upon the accuracy segmenter available in NLTK and gensim for some applications.[20] Once you've converted your documents into lists of token lists (one for each sentence), you're ready for your Word2vec training.

### TRAIN YOUR DOMAIN-SPECIFIC WORD2VEC MODEL

Get started by loading the Word2vec module:

```
>>> from gensim.models.word2vec import Word2Vec
```

The training requires a few setup details, shown in the following listing.

**Listing 6.2  Parameters to control Word2vec model training**

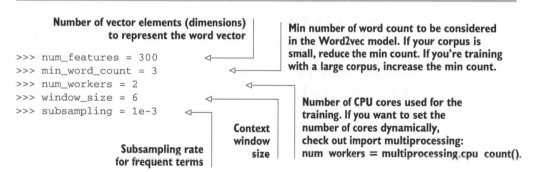

---

[20] Detector Morse, by Kyle Gorman and OHSU on pypi and at https://github.com/cslu-nlp/DetectorMorse, is a sentence segmenter with state-of-the-art performance (98%) and has been pretrained on sentences from years of text in the Wall Street Journal. So if your corpus includes language similar to that in the WSJ, Detector Morse is likely to give you the highest accuracy currently possible. You can also retrain Detector Morse on your own dataset if you have a large set of sentences from your domain.

Now you're ready to start your training, using the following listing.

**Listing 6.3   Instantiating a Word2vec model**

```
>>> model = Word2Vec(
...     token_list,
...     workers=num_workers,
...     size=num_features,
...     min_count=min_word_count,
...     window=window_size,
...     sample=subsampling)
```

Depending on your corpus size and your CPU performance, the training will take a significant amount of time. For smaller corpora, the training can be completed in minutes. But for a comprehensive word model, the corpus will contain millions of sentences. You need to have several examples of all the different ways the different words in your corpus are used. If you start processing larger corpora, such as the Wikipedia corpus, expect a much longer training time and a much larger memory consumption.

Word2vec models can consume quite a bit of memory. But remember that only the weight matrix for the hidden layer is of interest. Once you've trained your word model, you can reduce the memory footprint by about half if you freeze your model and discard the unnecessary information. The following command will discard the unneeded output weights of your neural network:

```
>>> model.init_sims(replace=True)
```

The `init_sims` method will freeze the model, storing the weights of the hidden layer and discarding the output weights that predict word co-ocurrences. The output weights aren't part of the vector used for most Word2vec applications. But the model cannot be trained further once the weights of the output layer have been discarded.

You can save the trained model with the following command and preserve it for later use:

```
>>> model_name = "my_domain_specific_word2vec_model"
>>> model.save(model_name)
```

If you want to test your newly trained model, you can use it with the same method you learned in the previous section; use the following listing.

**Listing 6.4   Loading a saved Word2vec model**

```
>>> from gensim.models.word2vec import Word2Vec
>>> model_name = "my_domain_specific_word2vec_model"
>>> model = Word2Vec.load(model_name)
>>> model.most_similar('radiology')
```

### 6.2.5 *Word2vec vs. GloVe (Global Vectors)*

Word2vec was a breakthrough, but it relies on a neural network model that must be trained using backpropagation. Backpropagation is usually less efficient than direct optimization of a cost function using gradient descent. Stanford NLP researchers[21] led by Jeffrey Pennington set about to understand the reason why Word2vec worked so well and to find the cost function that was being optimized. They started by counting the word co-occurrences and recording them in a square matrix. They found they could compute the singular value decomposition[22] of this co-occurrence matrix, splitting it into the same two weight matrices that Word2vec produces.[23] The key was to normalize the co-occurrence matrix the same way. But in some cases the Word2vec model failed to converge to the same global optimum that the Stanford researchers were able to achieve with their SVD approach. It's this direct optimization of the global vectors of word co-occurrences (co-occurrences across the entire corpus) that gives GloVe its name.

GloVe can produce matrices equivalent to the input weight matrix and output weight matrix of Word2vec, producing a language model with the same accuracy as Word2vec but in much less time. GloVe speeds the process by using the text data more efficiently. GloVe can be trained on smaller corpora and still converge.[24] And SVD algorithms have been refined for decades, so GloVe has a head start on debugging and algorithm optimization. Word2vec relies on backpropagation to update the weights that form the word embeddings. Neural network backpropagation is less efficient than more mature optimization algorithms such as those used within SVD for GloVe.

Even though Word2vec first popularized the concept of semantic reasoning with word vectors, your workhorse should probably be GloVe to train new word vector models. With GloVe you'll be more likely to find the global optimum for those vector representations, giving you more accurate results.

Advantages of GloVe are

- Faster training
- Better RAM/CPU efficiency (can handle larger documents)
- More efficient use of data (helps with smaller corpora)
- More accurate for the same amount of training

### 6.2.6 *fastText*

Researchers from Facebook took the concept of Word2vec one step further[25] by adding a new twist to the model training. The new algorithm, which they named fastText,

---

[21] Stanford GloVe Project (https://nlp.stanford.edu/projects/glove/).

[22] See chapter 5 and appendix C for more details on SVD.

[23] *GloVe: Global Vectors for Word Representation*, by Jeffrey Pennington, Richard Socher, and Christopher D. Manning: https://nlp.stanford.edu/pubs/glove.pdf.

[24] Gensim's comparison of Word2vec and GloVe performance: https://rare-technologies.com/making-sense-of-Word2vec/#glove_vs_word2vec.

[25] "Enriching Word Vectors with Subword Information," Bojanowski et al.: https://arxiv.org/pdf/1607.04606.pdf.

predicts the surrounding *n-character* grams rather than just the surrounding words, like Word2vec does. For example, the word "whisper" would generate the following 2- and 3-character grams:

wh, whi, hi, his, is, isp, sp, spe, pe, per, er

fastText trains a vector representation for every *n*-character gram, which includes words, misspelled words, partial words, and even single characters. The advantage of this approach is that it handles rare words much better than the original Word2vec approach.

As part of the fastText release, Facebook published pretrained fastText models for 294 languages. On the Github page of Facebook research,[26] you can find models ranging from *Abkhazian* to *Zulu*. The model collection even includes rare languages such as *Saterland Frisian*, which is only spoken by a handful of Germans. The pretrained fastText models provided by Facebook have only been trained on the available Wikipedia corpora. Therefore the vocabulary and accuracy of the models will vary across languages.

**HOW TO USE THE PRETRAINED FASTTEXT MODELS**
The use of fastText is just like using Google's Word2vec model. Head over to the fastText model repository and download the bin+text model for your language of choice. After the download finishes, unzip the binary language file.[27] With the following code, you can then load it into gensim:

> If you're using a gensim version before 3.2.0,
> you need to change this line to from
> gensim.models.wrappers.fasttext import FastText.

```
>>> from gensim.models.fasttext import FastText
>>> ft_model = FastText.load_fasttext_format(\
...      model_file=MODEL_PATH)
>>> ft_model.most_similar('soccer')
```

> The model_file points to the
> directory where you stored
> the model's bin and vec files.

> After loading the model, use it like
> any other word model in gensim.

The gensim fastText API shares a lot of functionality with the Word2vec implementations. All methods you learned about earlier in this chapter also apply to the fastText models.

### 6.2.7   *Word2vec vs. LSA*

You might now be wondering how Word2vec and GloVe word vectors compare to the LSA topic-word vectors of chapter 4. Even though we didn't say much about the LSA topic-document vectors in chapter 4, LSA gives you those, too. LSA topic-document

---

[26] See the web page titled "fastText/pretrained-vectors.md at master" (https://github.com/facebookresearch/fastText/blob/master/pretrained-vectors.md).

[27] The en.wiki.zip file is 9.6GB.

vectors are the sum of the topic-word vectors for all the words in those documents. If you wanted to get a word vector for an entire document that is analogous to topic-document vectors, you'd sum all the Word2vec word vectors in each document. That's pretty close to how Doc2vec document vectors work. We show you those a bit later in this chapter.

If your LSA matrix of topic vectors is of size $N_{\{words\}} * N_{\{topics\}}$, the LSA word vectors are the rows of that LSA matrix. These row vectors capture the meaning of words in a sequence of around 200 to 300 real values, like Word2vec does. And LSA topic-word vectors are useful for finding both related and unrelated terms. As you learned in the GloVe discussion, Word2vec vectors can be created using the exact same SVD algorithm used for LSA. But Word2vec gets more use out of the same number of words in its documents by creating a sliding window that overlaps from one document to the next. This way it can reuse the same words five times before sliding on.

What about incremental or online training? Both LSA and Word2vec algorithms allow adding new documents to your corpus and adjusting your existing word vectors to account for the co-occurrences in the new documents. But only the existing bins in your lexicon can be updated. Adding completely new words would change the total size of your vocabulary and therefore your one-hot vectors would change. That requires starting the training over if you want to capture the new word in your model.

LSA trains faster than Word2vec does. And for long documents, it does a better job of discriminating and clustering those documents.

The "killer app" for Word2vec is the semantic reasoning it popularized. LSA topic-word vectors can do that, too, but it usually isn't accurate. You'd have to break documents into sentences and then only use short phrases to train your LSA model if you want to approach the accuracy and "wow" factor of Word2vec reasoning. With Word2vec you can determine the answer to questions like *Harry Potter + University = Hogwarts.*[28]

Advantages of LSA are

- Faster training
- Better discrimination between longer documents

Advantages of Word2vec and GloVe are

- More efficient use of large corpora
- More accurate reasoning with words, such as answering analogy questions

## 6.2.8 *Visualizing word relationships*

The semantic word relationships can be powerful and their visualizations can lead to interesting discoveries. In this section, we demonstrate steps to visualize the word vectors in 2D.

---

[28] As a great example for domain-specific Word2vec models, check out the models around Harry Potter, the Lord of the Rings, and so on at https://github.com/nchah/word2vec4everything#harry-potter.

**NOTE**  If you need a quick visualization of your word model, we highly recommend using Google's TensorBoard word embedding visualization functionality. For more details, check out the section "How to visualize word embeddings" in chapter 13.

To get started, let's load all the word vectors from the Google Word2vec model of the Google News corpus. As you can imagine, this corpus included a lot of mentions of Portland and Oregon and a lot of other city and state names. You'll use the nlpia package to keep things simple, so you can start playing with Word2vec vectors quickly. See the following listing.

---

**Listing 6.5   Load a pretrained Word2vec model using nlpia**

```
>>> import os
>>> from nlpia.loaders import get_data
>>> from gensim.models.word2vec import KeyedVectors
>>> wv = get_data('word2vec')        ◁──┐  Downloads the pretrained Google News
>>> len(wv.vocab)                        │  word vectors to nlpia/src/nlpia/bigdata/
3000000                                  │  GoogleNews-vectors-negative300.bin.gz
```

**WARNING**  The Google News Word2vec model is huge: three million words with 300 vector dimensions each. The complete word vector model requires 3 GB of available memory. If your available memory is limited or you quickly want to load a few most frequent terms from the word model, check out chapter 13.

This KeyedVectors object in gensim now holds a table of three million Word2vec vectors. We loaded these vectors from a file created by Google to store a Word2vec model that they trained on a large corpus based on Google News articles. There should definitely be a lot of words for states and cities in all those news articles. The following listing shows just a few of the words in the vocabulary, starting at the one millionth word.

---

**Listing 6.6   Examine Word2vec vocabulary frequencies**

```
>>> import pandas as pd
>>> vocab = pd.Series(wv.vocab)
>>> vocab.iloc[1000000:100006]
Illington_Fund            Vocab(count:447860, index:2552140)
Illingworth               Vocab(count:2905166, index:94834)
Illingworth_Halifax       Vocab(count:1984281, index:1015719)
Illini                    Vocab(count:2984391, index:15609)
IlliniBoard.com           Vocab(count:1481047, index:1518953)
Illini_Bluffs             Vocab(count:2636947, index:363053)
```

Notice that compound words and common *n*-grams are joined together with an underscore character ("_"). Also notice that the value in the key-value mapping is a gensimVocab object that contains not only the index location for a word, so you can retrieve the Word2vec vector, but also the number of times it occurred in the Google News corpus.

As you've seen earlier, if you want to retrieve the 300-D vector for a particular word, you can use the square brackets on this `KeyedVectors` object to `.__getitem__()` any word or *n*-gram:

```
>>> wv['Illini']
array([ 0.15625   ,  0.18652344,  0.33203125,  0.55859375,  0.03637695,
       -0.09375   , -0.05029297,  0.16796875, -0.0625    ,  0.09912109,
       -0.0291748 ,  0.39257812,  0.05395508,  0.35351562, -0.02270508,
        ...
```

The reason we chose the one millionth word (in lexical alphabetic order) is because the first several thousand "words" are punctuation sequences like "#" and other symbols that occurred a lot in the Google News corpus. We just got lucky that "Illini"[29] showed up in this list. Let's see how close this "Illini" vector is to the vector for "Illinois," shown in the following listing.

---

**Listing 6.7  Distance between "Illinois" and "Illini"**

```
>>> import numpy as np
>>> np.linalg.norm(wv['Illinois'] - wv['Illini'])        ◁──── Euclidean distance
3.3653798
>>> cos_similarity = np.dot(wv['Illinois'], wv['Illini']) / (
...       np.linalg.norm(wv['Illinois']) *\
...       np.linalg.norm(wv['Illini']))                   ◁──── Cosine similarity is the
>>> cos_similarity                                              normalized dot product
0.5501352
>>> 1 - cos_similarity        ◁──── Cosine distance
0.4498648
```

These distances mean that the words "Illini" and "Illinois" are only moderately close to one another in meaning.

Now let's retrieve all the Word2vec vectors for US cities so you can use their distances to plot them on a 2D map of meaning. How would you find all the cities and states in that Word2vec vocabulary in that `KeyedVectors` object? You could use cosine distance like you did in the previous listing to find all the vectors that are close to the words "state" or "city". But rather than reading through all three million words and word vectors, let's load another dataset containing a list of cities and states (regions) from around the world, as shown in the following listing.

---

**Listing 6.8  Some US city data**

```
>>> from nlpia.data.loaders import get_data
>>> cities = get_data('cities')
>>> cities.head(1).T
geonameid                         3039154
name                             El Tarter
```

---

[29] The word "Illini" refers to a group of people, usually football players and fans, rather than a single geographic region like "Illinois" (where most fans of the "Fighting Illini" live).

```
asciiname                        El Tarter
alternatenames      Ehl Tarter,?? ??????
latitude                           42.5795
longitude                          1.65362
feature_class                            P
feature_code                           PPL
country_code                            AD
cc2                                    NaN
admin1_code                             02
admin2_code                            NaN
admin3_code                            NaN
admin4_code                            NaN
population                            1052
elevation                              NaN
dem                                   1721
timezone                   Europe/Andorra
modification_date             2012-11-03
```

This dataset from Geocities contains a lot of information, including latitude, longitude, and population. You could use this for some fun visualizations or comparisons between geographic distance and Word2vec distance. But for now you're just going to try to map that Word2vec distance on a 2D plane and see what it looks like. Let's focus on just the United States for now, as shown in the following listing.

### Listing 6.9  Some US state data

```
>>> us = cities[(cities.country_code == 'US') &\
...     (cities.admin1_code.notnull())].copy()
>>> states = pd.read_csv(\
...     'http://www.fonz.net/blog/wp-content/uploads/2008/04/states.csv')
>>> states = dict(zip(states.Abbreviation, states.State))
>>> us['city'] = us.name.copy()
>>> us['st'] = us.admin1_code.copy()
>>> us['state'] = us.st.map(states)
>>> us[us.columns[-3:]].head()
                          city  st      state
geonameid
4046255        Bay Minette  AL    Alabama
4046274               Edna  TX      Texas
4046319      Bayou La Batre  AL    Alabama
4046332          Henderson  TX      Texas
4046430            Natalia  TX      Texas
```

Now you have a full state name for each city in addition to its abbreviation. Let's check to see which of those state names and city names exist in your Word2vec vocabulary:

```
>>> vocab = pd.np.concatenate([us.city, us.st, us.state])
>>> vocab = np.array([word for word in vocab if word in wv.wv])
>>> vocab[:5]
array(['Edna', 'Henderson', 'Natalia', 'Yorktown', 'Brighton'])
```

Even when you only look at United States cities, you'll find a lot of large cities with the same name, like Portland, Oregon and Portland, Maine. So let's incorporate into your city vector the essence of the state where that city is located. To combine the meanings of words in Word2vec, you add the vectors together. That's the magic of vector-oriented reasoning. Here's one way to add the Word2vecs for the states to the vectors for the cities and put all these new vectors in a big DataFrame. We use either the full name of a state or just the abbreviations (whichever one is in your Word2vec vocabulary), as shown in the following listing.

---

**Listing 6.10  Augment city word vectors with US state word vectors**

```
>>> city_plus_state = []
>>> for c, state, st in zip(us.city, us.state, us.st):
...     if c not in vocab:
...         continue
...     row = []
...     if state in vocab:
...         row.extend(wv[c] + wv[state])
...     else:
...         row.extend(wv[c] + wv[st])
...     city_plus_state.append(row)
>>> us_300D = pd.DataFrame(city_plus_state)
```

Depending on your corpus, your word relationship can represent different attributes, such as geographical proximity or cultural or economic similarities. But the relationships heavily depend on the training corpus, and they will reflect the corpus.

---

**Word vectors are biased!**

Word vectors learn word relationships based on the training corpus. If your corpus is about finance then your "bank" word vector will be mainly about businesses that hold deposits. If your corpus is about geology, then your "bank" word vector will be trained on associations with rivers and streams. And if you corpus is mostly about a matriarchal society with women bankers and men washing clothes in the river, then your word vectors would take on that gender bias.

The following example shows the gender bias of a word model trained on Google News articles. If you calculate the distance between "man" and "nurse" and compare that to the distance between "woman" and "nurse," you'll be able to see the bias:

```
>>> word_model.distance('man', 'nurse')
0.7453
>>> word_model.distance('woman', 'nurse')
0.5586
```

Identifying and compensating for biases like this is a challenge for any NLP practitioner that trains her models on documents written in a biased world.

---

The news articles used as the training corpus share a common component, which is the semantical similarity of the cities. Semantically similar locations in the articles seem to be interchangeable and therefore the word model learned that they are similar. If you had trained on a different corpus, your word relationships might have differed. In this news corpus, cities that are similar in size and culture are clustered close together despite being far apart geographically, such as San Diego and San Jose, or vacation destinations such as Honolulu and Reno.

Fortunately you can use conventional algebra to add the vectors for cities to the vectors for states and state abbreviations. As you discovered in chapter 4, you can use tools such as principal components analysis to reduce the vector dimensions from your 300 dimensions to a human-understandable 2D representation. PCA enables you to see the projection or "shadow" of these 300-D vectors in a 2D plot. Best of all, the PCA algorithm ensures that this projection is the best possible view of your data, keeping the vectors as far apart as possible. PCA is like a good photographer that looks at something from every possible angle before composing the optimal photograph. You don't even have to normalize the length of the vectors after summing the city + state + abbrev vectors, because PCA takes care of that for you.

We saved these augmented city word vectors in the nlpia package so you can load them to use in your application. In the following code, you use PCA to project them onto a 2D plot.

---

**Listing 6.11   Bubble chart of US cities**

```
>>> from sklearn.decomposition import PCA
>>> pca = PCA(n_components=2)          ◁──  The 2D vectors producted by PCA are
>>> us_300D = get_data('cities_us_wordvectors')    for visualization. Retain the original
>>> us_2D = pca.fit_transform(us_300D.iloc[:, :300])    ◁──  300-D Word2vec vectors for any vector
                                                            reasoning you might want to do.
```

The last column of this DataFrame contains the city
name, which is also stored in the DataFrame index.

Figure 6.8 shows the 2D projection of all these 300-D word vectors for US cities:

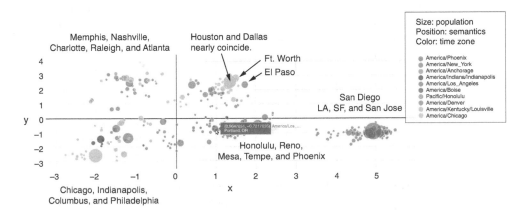

**Figure 6.8   Google News Word2vec 300-D vectors projected onto a 2D map using PCA**

**NOTE** Low semantic distance (distance values close to zero) represents high similarity between words. The semantic distance, or "meaning" distance, is determined by the words occurring nearby in the documents used for training. The Word2vec vectors for two terms are *close* to each other in word vector space if they are often used in similar contexts (used with similar words nearby). For example San Francisco is *close* to California because they often occur nearby in sentences and the distribution of words used near them is similar. A large distance between two terms expresses a low likelihood of shared context and shared meaning (they are semantically dissimilar), such as cars and peanuts.

If you'd like to explore the city map shown in figure 6.8, or try your hand at plotting some vectors of your own, listing 6.12 shows you how. We built a wrapper for Plotly's offline plotting API that should help it handle DataFrames where you've denormalized your data. The Plotly wrapper expects a DataFrame with a row for each sample and columns for features you'd like to plot. These can be categorical features (such as time zones) and continuous real-valued features (such as city population). The resulting plots are interactive and useful for exploring many types of machine learning data, especially vector-representations of complex things such as words and documents.

---

**Listing 6.12  Bubble plot of US city word vectors**

```
>>> import seaborn
>>> from matplotlib import pyplot as plt
>>> from nlpia.plots import offline_plotly_scatter_bubble
>>> df = get_data('cities_us_wordvectors_pca2_meta')
>>> html = offline_plotly_scatter_bubble(
...     df.sort_values('population', ascending=False)[:350].copy()\
...        .sort_values('population'),
...     filename='plotly_scatter_bubble.html',
...     x='x', y='y',
...     size_col='population', text_col='name', category_col='timezone',
...     xscale=None, yscale=None,  # 'log' or None
...     layout={}, marker={'sizeref': 3000})
{'sizemode': 'area', 'sizeref': 3000}
```

To produce the 2D representations of your 300-D word vectors, you need to use a dimension reduction technique. We used PCA. To reduce the amount of information lost during the compression from 300-D to 2D, reducing the range of information contained in the input vectors also helps. So you limited your word vectors to those associated with cities. This is like limiting the domain or subject matter of a corpus when computing TF-IDF or BOW vectors.

For a more diverse mix of vectors with greater information content, you'll probably need a nonlinear embedding algorithm such as t-SNE. We talk about t-SNE and other neural net techniques in later chapters. t-SNE will make more sense once you've grasped the word vector embedding algorithms here.

### 6.2.9  *Unnatural words*

Word embeddings such as Word2vec are useful not only for English words but also for any sequence of symbols where the sequence and proximity of symbols is representative of their meaning. If your symbols have semantics, embeddings may be useful. As you may have guessed, word embeddings also work for languages other than English.

Embedding works also for pictorial languages such as traditional Chinese and Japanese (Kanji) or the mysterious hieroglyphics in Egyptian tombs. Embeddings and vector-based reasoning even works for languages that attempt to obfuscate the meaning of words. You can do vector-based reasoning on a large collection of "secret" messages transcribed from "Pig Latin" or any other language invented by children or the Emperor of Rome. A *Caesar cipher*[30] such as RO13 or a *substitution cipher*[31] are both vulnerable to vector-based reasoning with Word2vec. You don't even need a decoder ring (shown in figure 6.9). You need only a large collection of messages or *n*-grams that your Word2vec embedder can process to find co-occurrences of words or symbols.

Word2vec has even been used to glean information and relationships from unnatural words or ID numbers such as college course numbers (CS-101), model numbers (Koala E7270 or Galaga Pro), and even serial numbers, phone numbers, and ZIP codes.[32] To get the most useful information about the relationship between ID numbers like this, you'll need a variety of sentences that contain those ID numbers. And if

Figure 6.9   Decoder rings (left: Hubert Berberich (HubiB) (https://commons.wikimedia.org/wiki/File:CipherDisk2000.jpg), CipherDisk2000, marked as public domain, more details on Wikimedia Commons: https://commons.wikimedia.org/wiki/Template:PD-self; middle: Cory Doctorow (https://www.flickr.com/photos/doctorow/2817314740/in/photostream/), Crypto wedding-ring 2, https://creativecommons.org/licenses/by-sa/2.0/legalcode; right: Sobebunny (https://commons.wikimedia.org/wiki/File:Captain-midnight-decoder.jpg), Captain-midnight-decoder, https://creativecommons.org/licenses/by-sa/3.0/legalcode)

---

[30] See the web page titled "Caesar cipher" (https://en.wikipedia.org/wiki/Caesar_cipher).

[31] See the web page titled "Substitution cipher" (https://en.wikipedia.org/wiki/Substitution_ cipher).

[32] See the web page titled "A non-NLP application of Word2Vec – Towards Data Science" (https://medium.com/towards-data-science/a-non-nlp-application-of-word2vec-c637e35d3668).

the ID numbers often contain a structure where the position of a symbol has meaning, it can help to tokenize these ID numbers into their smallest semantic packet (such as words or syllables in natural languages).

### 6.2.10 *Document similarity with Doc2vec*

The concept of Word2vec can also be extended to sentences, paragraphs, or entire documents. The idea of predicting the next word based on the previous words can be extended by training a paragraph or document vector (see figure 6.10).[33] In this case, the prediction not only considers the previous words, but also the vector representing the paragraph or the document. It can be considered as an additional word input to the prediction. Over time, the algorithm learns a document or paragraph representation from the training set.

How are document vectors generated for unseen documents after the training phase? During the *inference stage*, the algorithm adds more document vectors to the document matrix and computes the added vector based on the *frozen* word vector matrix, and its weights. By inferring a document vector, you can now create a semantic representation of the whole document.

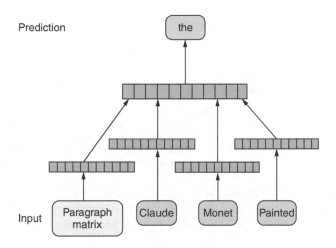

Figure 6.10  Doc2vec training uses an additional document vector as input.

By expanding the concept of Word2vec with an additional document or paragraph vector used for the word prediction, you can now use the trained document vector for various tasks, such as finding similar documents in a corpus.

#### HOW TO TRAIN DOCUMENT VECTORS

Similar to your training of word vectors, you're using the gensim package to train document vectors, as shown in the following listing.

---

[33] See the web page titled "Distributed Representations of Sentences and Documents" (https://arxiv.org/pdf/1405.4053v2.pdf).

**Listing 6.13    Train your own document and word vectors**

gensim uses Python's multiprocessing module to parallelize your training on multiple CPU cores, but this line only counts how many cores you have available to size the number of workers.

The gensim Doc2vec model contains your word vector embeddings as well as document vectors for each document in your corpus.

The simple_preprocess utility from gensim is a crude tokenizer that will ignore one-letter words and all punctuation. Any of the tokenizers from chapter 2 will work fine.

```
>>> import multiprocessing
>>> num_cores = multiprocessing.cpu_count()

>>> from gensim.models.doc2vec import TaggedDocument,\
...     Doc2Vec
>>> from gensim.utils import simple_preprocess

>>> corpus = ['This is the first document ...',\
...           'another document ...']
>>> training_corpus = []
>>> for i, text in enumerate(corpus):
...     tagged_doc = TaggedDocument(\
...         simple_preprocess(text), [i])
...     training_corpus.append(tagged_doc)

>>> model = Doc2Vec(size=100, min_count=2,
...     workers=num_cores, iter=10)
>>> model.build_vocab(training_corpus)
>>> model.train(training_corpus, total_examples=model.corpus_count,
...     epochs=model.iter)
```

You need to provide an object that can iterate through your document strings one at a time.

MEAP reader 24231 (https://forums.manning.com/user/profile/24231.page) suggests that you preallocate a numpy array rather than a bulky python list. You may also want to stream your corpus to and from disk or a database if it will not fit in RAM.

gensim provides a data structure to annotate documents with string or integer tags for category labels, keywords, or whatever information you want to associate with your documents.

Kick off the training for 10 epochs.

Before the model can be trained, you need to compile the vocabulary.

Instantiate the Doc2vec object with your window size of 10 words and 100-D word and document vectors (much smaller than the 300-D Google News Word2vec vectors). min_count is the minimum document frequency for your vocabulary.

**TIP**    If you're running low on RAM, and you know the number of documents ahead of time (your corpus object isn't an iterator or generator), you might want to use a preallocated numpy array instead of Python list for your `training_corpus`:

```
training_corpus = np.empty(len(corpus), dtype=object);
  … training_corpus[i] = …
```

Once the Doc2vec model is trained, you can infer document vectors for new, unseen documents by calling `infer_vector` on the instantiated and trained model:

```
>>> model.infer_vector(simple_preprocess(\
...     'This is a completely unseen document'), steps=10)
```

Doc2vec requires a "training" step when inferring new vectors. In your example, you update the trained vector through 10 steps (or iterations).

With these few steps, you can quickly train an entire corpus of documents and find similar documents. You could do that by generating a vector for every document in your corpus and then calculating the cosine distance between each document vector. Another common task is to cluster the document vectors of a corpus with something like k-means to create a document classifier.

## *Summary*

- You've learned how word vectors and vector-oriented reasoning can solve some surprisingly subtle problems like analogy questions and nonsynonomy relationships between words.
- You can now train Word2vec and other word vector embeddings on the words you use in your applications so that your NLP pipeline isn't "polluted" by the GoogleNews meaning of words inherent in most Word2vec pretrained models.
- You used gensim to explore, visualize, and even build your own word vector vocabularies.
- A PCA projection of geographic word vectors like US city names can reveal the cultural closeness of places that are geographically far apart.
- If you respect sentence boundaries with your *n*-grams and are efficient at setting up word pairs for training, you can greatly improve the accuracy of your latent semantic analysis word embeddings (see chapter 4).

# 7

# *Getting words in order with convolutional neural networks (CNNs)*

**This chapter covers**

- Using neural networks for NLP
- Finding meaning in word patterns
- Building a CNN
- Vectorizing natural language text in a way that suits neural networks
- Training a CNN
- Classifying the sentiment of novel text

Language's true power isn't in the words themselves, but in the spaces between the words, in the order and combination of words. Sometimes meaning is hidden beneath the words, in the intent and emotion that formed that particular combination of words. Understanding the intent beneath the words is a critical skill for an empathetic, emotionally intelligent listener or reader of natural language, be it human or machine.[1] Just as in thought and ideas, it's the connections between

---

[1] *International Association of Facilitators Handbook,* http://mng.bz/oVWM.

218

words that create depth, information, and complexity. With a grasp on the meaning of individual words, and multiple clever ways to string them together, how do you look beneath them and measure the meaning of a combination of words with something more flexible than counts of *n*-gram matches? How do you find meaning, emotion— *latent semantic information*—from a sequence of words, so you can do something with it? And even more ambitious, how do you impart that hidden meaning to text generated by a cold, calculating machine?

Even the phrase "machine-generated text" inspires dread of a hollow, tinned voice issuing a chopped list of words. Machines may get the point across, but little more than that. What's missing? The tone, the flow, the character that you expect a person to express in even the most passing of engagements. Those subtleties exist between the words, underneath the words, in the patterns of how they're constructed. As a person communicates, they will underlay patterns in their text and speech. Truly great writers and speakers will actively manipulate these patterns, to great effect. And your innate ability to recognize them, even if on a less-than-conscious level, is the reason machine-produced text tends to sound terrible. The patterns aren't there. But you can find them in human-generated text and impart them to your machine friends.

In the past few years, research has quickly blossomed around neural networks. With widely available open source tools, the power of neural networks to find patterns in large datasets quickly transformed the NLP landscape. The perceptron quickly became the feedforward network (a multilayer perceptron), which led to the development of new variants: convolutional neural nets and recurrent neural nets, ever more efficient and precise tools to fish patterns out of large datasets.

As you have seen already with *Word2Vec*, neural networks have opened entirely new approaches to NLP. Although neural networks' original design purpose was to enable a machine to *learn* to quantify input, the field has since grown from just learning classifications and regressions (topic analysis, sentiment analysis) to actually being able to generate novel text based on previously unseen input: translating a new phrase to another language, generating responses to questions not seen before (chatbot, anyone?), and even generating new text based on the style of a particular author.

A complete understanding of the mathematics of the inner workings of a neural network isn't critical to employing the tools presented in this chapter. But, it does help to have a basic grasp of what is going on inside. If you understand the examples and explanations in chapter 5, you will have an intuition about where to use neural networks. And you can weak your neural network architecture (the number of layers or number of neurons) to help a network work better for your problem. This intuition will help you see how neural networks can give depth to your chatbot. Neural networks promise to make your chatbot a better listener and a little less superficially chatty.

## 7.1    *Learning meaning*

The nature of words and their secrets are most tightly correlated to (after their definition, of course) their relation to each other. That relationship can be expressed in at least two ways:

1   *Word order*—here are two statements that don't mean the same thing:

```
The dog chased the cat.
The cat chased the dog.
```

2   *Word proximity*—here "shone" refers to the word "hull" at the other end of the sentence:

```
The ship's hull, despite years at sea, millions of tons of cargo, and
➥ two mid-sea collisions, shone like new.
```

These relationships can be explored for patterns (along with patterns in the presence of the words themselves) in two ways: spatially and temporarily. The difference between the two is this: in the former, you examine the statement as if written on page—you're looking for relationships in the position of words; in the latter, you explore it as if spoken—the words and letters become *time series* data. These are closely related, but they mark a key difference in how you'll deal with them with neural network tools. Spatial data is usually viewed through a fixed-width window. Time series can extend for an unknown amount of time.

Basic feedforward networks (multilayer perceptron) are capable of pulling patterns out of data. But, the patterns they discover are found by relating weights to pieces of the input. Nothing captures the relations of the tokens spatially or temporally. But feed forward is only the beginning of the neural network architectures out there. The two most important choices for natural language processing are currently convolutional neural nets and recurrent neural nets and the many flavors of each.

In figure 7.1, three tokens are passed into this neural net input layer. And each input layer neuron is connected to each fully connected hidden layer neuron with an individual weight.

> **TIP**   How are you *passing tokens into the net?* The two major approaches you'll use in this chapter are the ones you developed in the previous chapters: one-hot encoding and word vectors. You can one-hot encode them—a vector that has a 0 for every possible vocabulary word you want to consider, with a 1 in the position of the word you're encoding. Or you can use the trained word vectors you discovered in chapter 6. You need the words to be represented as numbers to do math on them.

Now, if you swapped the order of these tokens from "See Jim run" to "run See Jim" and passed that into the network, unsurprisingly a different answer may come out. Remember each input position is associated with a specific weight inside each hidden neuron ($x_1$ is tied to $w_1$, $x_2$ is tied to $w_2$, and so on).

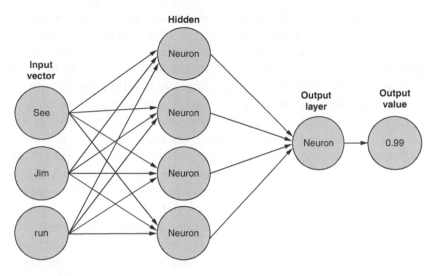

**Figure 7.1  Fully connected neural net**

A feedforward network may be able to learn specific relationships of tokens such as these, because they appear together in a sample but in different positions. But you can easily see how longer sentences of 5, 10, or 50 tokens—with all the possible pairs, triplets, and so on in all the possible positions for each—quickly become an intractable problem. Luckily you have other options.

## 7.2   Toolkit

Python is one of the richest languages for working with neural nets. Although a lot of the major players (hi Google and Facebook) have moved to lower-level languages for the implementation of these expensive calculations, the extensive resources poured into early models using Python for development have left their mark. Two of the major programs for neural network architecture are Theano (http://deeplearning .net/software/theano/) and TensorFlow (http://www.tensorflow.org). Both rely heavily on C for their underlying computations, but both have robust Python APIs. Facebook put their efforts into a Lua package called Torch; luckily Python now has an API for that as well in PyTorch (http://pytorch.org/). Each of these, however, for all their power, are heavily abstracted toolsets for building models from scratch. But the Python community is quick to the rescue with libraries to ease the use of these underlying architectures. Lasagne (Theano) and Skflow (TensorFlow) are popular options, but we'll use Keras (https://keras.io/) for its balance of friendly API and versatility. Keras can use either TensorFlow or Theano as its backend, and each has its advantages and weaknesses, but you'll use TensorFlow for the examples. You also need the h5py package for saving the internal state of your trained model.

By default, Keras will use TensorFlow as the backend, and the first line output at runtime will remind you which backend you're using for processing. You can easily change the backend in a config file, with an environment variable, or in your script itself. The documentation in Keras is thorough and clear; we highly recommend you spend some time there. But here's a quick overview: `Sequential()` is a class that is a neural net abstraction that gives you access to the basic API of Keras, specifically the methods `compile` and `fit`, which will do the heavy lifting of building the underlying weights and their interconnected relationships (compile), calculating the errors in training, and most importantly applying backpropagation (fit). `epochs`, `batch_size`, and `optimizer` are all hyperparameters that will require tuning, and in some senses, art.

Unfortunately, no one-size-fits-all rule exists for designing and tuning, a neural network. You'll need to develop your own intuition for which framework will work best for a particular application. But if you find example implementations for a problem similar to yours, then you're probably OK using that framework and adjusting that implementation to meet your needs. There's nothing scary about these neural network frameworks or all these bells and whistles you can play with and tune. But for now we steer this conversation back toward natural language processing via the world of image processing. Images? Bear with us for a minute, the trick will become clear.

## 7.3    *Convolutional neural nets*

*Convolutional neural nets*, or CNNs, get their name from the concept of sliding (or convolving) a small window over the data sample.

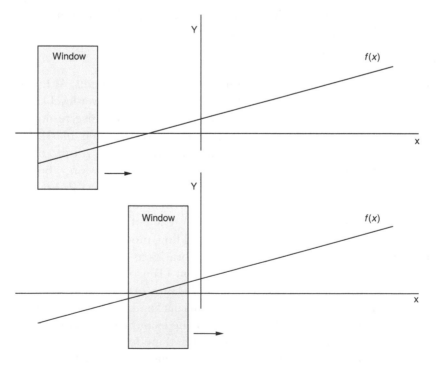

Figure 7.2    **Window convolving over function**

Convolutions appear in many places in mathematics, and they're usually related to time series data. The higher order concepts related to those use cases aren't important for your application in this chapter. The key concept is visualizing that box sliding over a field (see figure 7.2). You're going to start sliding them over images to get the concept. And then you'll start sliding the window over text. But always come back to that mental image of a window sliding over a larger piece of data, and you're looking only at what can be seen through the window.

### 7.3.1 Building blocks

Convolutional neural nets first came to prominence in image processing and image recognition. Because the net is capable of capturing spatial relationships between data points of each sample, the net can suss out whether the image contains a cat or a dog driving a bulldozer.

A convolutional net, or convnet (yeah that extra *n* in there is hard to say), achieves its magic not by assigning a weight to each element (say, each pixel of an image), as in a traditional feedforward net; instead it defines a set of *filters* (also known as *kernels*) that move across the image. Your *convolution*!

In image recognition, the elements of each data point could be a 1 (on) or 0 (off) for each pixel in a black-and-white image.

Or it could be the intensity of each pixel in a grayscale image (see figures 7.3 and 7.4), or the intensity in each of the color channels of each pixel in a color image.

**Figure 7.3  Small telephone pole image**

| | 0 | 1 | 2 | 3 | 4 | 5 | 6 | 7 | 8 | 9 | 10 | 11 | 12 | 13 | 14 | 15 | 16 | 17 | 18 | 19 | 20 | 21 | 22 | 23 | 24 | 25 | 26 | 27 |
|---|---|---|---|---|---|---|---|---|---|---|---|---|---|---|---|---|---|---|---|---|---|---|---|---|---|---|---|---|
| 0 | 120 | 119 | 118 | 108 | 103 | 111 | 113 | 115 | 111 | 117 | 120 | 120 | 120 | 119 | 121 | 114 | 118 | 120 | 120 | 120 | 121 | 121 | 121 | 115 | 100 | 120 | 118 | 117 |
| 1 | 111 | 109 | 111 | 106 | 107 | 118 | 120 | 110 | 106 | 117 | 120 | 119 | 119 | 119 | 121 | 114 | 118 | 119 | 118 | 119 | 118 | 114 | 119 | 109 | 102 | 122 | 114 | 117 |
| 2 | 109 | 114 | 121 | 116 | 108 | 119 | 118 | 104 | 111 | 119 | 119 | 119 | 119 | 119 | 119 | 110 | 119 | 121 | 122 | 124 | 73 | 92 | 128 | 100 | 87 | 119 | 115 | 119 |
| 3 | 109 | 102 | 114 | 117 | 108 | 116 | 108 | 111 | 117 | 118 | 118 | 117 | 119 | 117 | 118 | 79 | 75 | 80 | 76 | 87 | 36 | 63 | 86 | 51 | 55 | 72 | 91 | 120 |
| 4 | 108 | 110 | 100 | 116 | 111 | 95 | 104 | 110 | 114 | 117 | 117 | 117 | 117 | 117 | 117 | 106 | 107 | 108 | 94 | 90 | 42 | 54 | 70 | 62 | 86 | 70 | 96 | 118 |
| 5 | 103 | 112 | 109 | 98 | 100 | 93 | 111 | 112 | 115 | 113 | 117 | 117 | 117 | 116 | 116 | 112 | 118 | 116 | 114 | 110 | 41 | 81 | 110 | 102 | 119 | 114 | 119 | 117 |
| 6 | 111 | 111 | 112 | 104 | 93 | 106 | 119 | 115 | 108 | 110 | 116 | 115 | 116 | 117 | 115 | 107 | 108 | 111 | 118 | 49 | 87 | 109 | 100 | 115 | 110 | 115 | 115 | 115 |
| 7 | 111 | 111 | 103 | 105 | 103 | 110 | 103 | 103 | 106 | 111 | 115 | 115 | 114 | 110 | 107 | 102 | 113 | 114 | 115 | 49 | 97 | 105 | 105 | 114 | 111 | 116 | 115 | 115 |
| 8 | 112 | 105 | 108 | 94 | 89 | 102 | 95 | 106 | 111 | 113 | 111 | 108 | 106 | 109 | 112 | 109 | 114 | 113 | 114 | 115 | 45 | 83 | 104 | 108 | 111 | 112 | 114 | 114 |
| 9 | 112 | 106 | 108 | 86 | 95 | 109 | 104 | 103 | 106 | 104 | 108 | 109 | 114 | 114 | 113 | 108 | 112 | 113 | 113 | 114 | 43 | 80 | 104 | 111 | 109 | 113 | 114 | 113 |
| 10 | 99 | 111 | 102 | 88 | 111 | 97 | 101 | 101 | 106 | 111 | 112 | 110 | 112 | 110 | 113 | 111 | 107 | 112 | 113 | 112 | 43 | 79 | 106 | 110 | 108 | 114 | 112 | 112 |
| 11 | 110 | 106 | 93 | 96 | 108 | 107 | 110 | 109 | 111 | 112 | 108 | 107 | 111 | 112 | 111 | 107 | 111 | 111 | 112 | 110 | 38 | 78 | 109 | 108 | 108 | 111 | 114 | 103 |
| 12 | 101 | 93 | 76 | 101 | 103 | 107 | 107 | 108 | 110 | 107 | 103 | 111 | 111 | 110 | 109 | 106 | 112 | 111 | 111 | 109 | 37 | 82 | 108 | 107 | 111 | 113 | 111 | 100 |
| 13 | 98 | 92 | 99 | 115 | 108 | 108 | 111 | 106 | 100 | 98 | 106 | 108 | 109 | 110 | 107 | 106 | 109 | 108 | 109 | 107 | 37 | 78 | 106 | 103 | 106 | 108 | 103 | 98 |
| 14 | 100 | 73 | 97 | 102 | 92 | 95 | 93 | 89 | 89 | 97 | 103 | 106 | 106 | 103 | 101 | 106 | 104 | 106 | 102 | 33 | 75 | 105 | 103 | 108 | 108 | 98 | 98 | 107 |
| 15 | 84 | 69 | 92 | 87 | 85 | 92 | 89 | 95 | 98 | 100 | 107 | 107 | 107 | 108 | 106 | 108 | 107 | 109 | 105 | 29 | 74 | 107 | 107 | 110 | 106 | 99 | 109 | 109 |
| 16 | 71 | 82 | 87 | 85 | 78 | 89 | 106 | 104 | 99 | 106 | 106 | 105 | 106 | 105 | 104 | 103 | 106 | 106 | 107 | 103 | 21 | 72 | 106 | 106 | 109 | 100 | 102 | 109 |
| 17 | 67 | 87 | 64 | 68 | 84 | 89 | 98 | 96 | 99 | 104 | 104 | 104 | 104 | 105 | 103 | 101 | 106 | 103 | 106 | 102 | 23 | 76 | 103 | 103 | 106 | 98 | 108 | 101 |
| 18 | 68 | 82 | 84 | 97 | 92 | 81 | 84 | 84 | 90 | 98 | 98 | 102 | 102 | 103 | 100 | 99 | 103 | 101 | 103 | 92 | 16 | 76 | 98 | 98 | 89 | 86 | 92 | 73 |
| 19 | 60 | 71 | 77 | 77 | 80 | 88 | 92 | 91 | 93 | 96 | 96 | 101 | 100 | 100 | 98 | 101 | 101 | 101 | 104 | 92 | 13 | 64 | 93 | 89 | 81 | 89 | 81 | 79 |
| 20 | 84 | 98 | 87 | 94 | 101 | 100 | 101 | 101 | 103 | 101 | 101 | 100 | 101 | 103 | 98 | 98 | 100 | 96 | 97 | 87 | 12 | 71 | 100 | 97 | 93 | 105 | 91 | 101 |
| 21 | 92 | 80 | 88 | 99 | 100 | 98 | 100 | 100 | 100 | 97 | 98 | 97 | 98 | 96 | 92 | 91 | 92 | 93 | 96 | 87 | 13 | 79 | 105 | 95 | 98 | 96 | 89 | 100 |
| 22 | 77 | 80 | 88 | 92 | 96 | 97 | 96 | 95 | 93 | 92 | 93 | 92 | 92 | 91 | 94 | 96 | 95 | 98 | 89 | 12 | 79 | 103 | 91 | 100 | 89 | 98 | 104 | 104 |
| 23 | 81 | 87 | 83 | 84 | 89 | 89 | 91 | 87 | 90 | 92 | 93 | 95 | 94 | 96 | 94 | 95 | 98 | 94 | 93 | 84 | 7 | 74 | 89 | 86 | 90 | 70 | 81 | 73 |
| 24 | 60 | 66 | 82 | 92 | 90 | 90 | 87 | 90 | 94 | 94 | 94 | 93 | 94 | 92 | 93 | 94 | 92 | 94 | 95 | 81 | 0 | 76 | 90 | 92 | 81 | 77 | 65 | 58 |
| 25 | 87 | 81 | 83 | 86 | 87 | 84 | 90 | 92 | 92 | 92 | 92 | 92 | 92 | 91 | 92 | 92 | 91 | 92 | 77 | 4 | 73 | 91 | 92 | 81 | 95 | 96 | 95 | 95 |
| 26 | 87 | 88 | 88 | 83 | 85 | 91 | 91 | 89 | 90 | 91 | 92 | 91 | 91 | 89 | 90 | 92 | 90 | 89 | 73 | 8 | 66 | 92 | 83 | 84 | 92 | 91 | 91 | 91 |
| 27 | 81 | 86 | 88 | 91 | 89 | 89 | 89 | 89 | 89 | 88 | 88 | 89 | 89 | 89 | 84 | 83 | 79 | 80 | 87 | 74 | 0 | 60 | 89 | 77 | 90 | 91 | 90 | 89 |

**Figure 7.4  Pixel values for the telephone pole image**

Each filter you make is going to *convolve* or slide across the input sample (in this case, your pixel values). Let's pause and describe what we mean by sliding. You won't be doing anything in particular while the window is "in motion." You can think of it as a series of snapshots. Look through the window, do some processing, slide the window down a bit, do the processing again.

> **TIP**    This sliding/snapshot routine is precisely what makes convolutional neural nets highly parallelize-able. Each snapshot for a given data sample can be calculated independently of all the others for that given data sample. No need to wait for the first snapshot to happen before taking the second.

How big are these filters we're talking about? The filter window size is a parameter to be chosen by the model builder and is highly dependent on the content of data. But there are some common starting points. In image-based data, you'll commonly see a window size of three-by-three (3, 3) pixels. We get into a little more detail about the window size choice later in the chapter when we get back to NLP uses.

### 7.3.2    *Step size (stride)*

Note that the distance traveled during the sliding phase is a parameter. And more importantly, it's almost never as large as the filter itself. Each snapshot usually has an overlap with its neighboring snapshot.

The distance each convolution "travels" is known as the *stride* and is typically set to 1. Only moving one pixel (or anything less than the width of the filter) will create overlap in the various inputs to the filter from one position to the next. A larger stride that has no overlap between filter applications will lose the "blurring" effect of one pixel (or in your case, token) relating to its neighbors.

This overlap has some interesting properties, which will become apparent as you see how the filters change over time.

### 7.3.3    *Filter composition*

Okay, so far we've been describing windows sliding over data, looking at the data through the window, but we've said nothing about what you do with the data you see.

Filters are composed of two parts:

- A set of weights (exactly like the weights feeding into the neurons from chapter 5)
- An activation function

As we said earlier, filters are typically 3 x 3 (but often other sizes and shapes).

> **TIP**    These collections of filtering neurons are similar to the normal hidden layer neurons, except that each filter's weights are fixed for the entire sweep through the input sample. The weights are the same across the entire image.

Each filter in a convolutional neural net is unique, but each individual filter element is fixed within an image snapshot.

As each filter slides over the image, one stride at a time, it pauses and takes a snapshot of the pixels it's currently covering. The values of those pixels are then multiplied by the weight associated with that position in the filter.

Say you're using a 3 x 3 filter. You start in the upper-left corner and snapshot the first pixel $(0, 0)$ by the first weight $(0, 0)$, then the second pixel $(0, 1)$ by weight $(0, 1)$, and so on.

The products of pixel and weight (at that position) are then summed up and passed into the activation function (see figure 7.5); most often this function is ReLU (rectified linear units)—we come back to that in a moment.

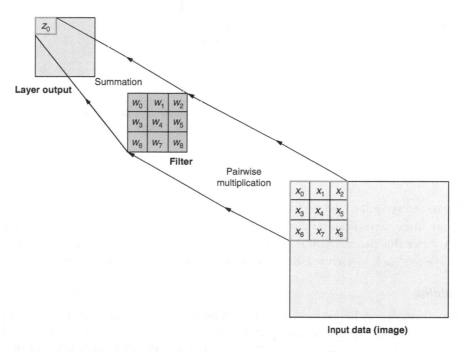

**Figure 7.5  Convolutional neural net step**

In figures 7.5 and 7.6, $x_i$ is the value of the pixel at position $i$ and $z_0$ is the output of a ReLU activation function ($z\_0$ = max(sum(x * w), 0) or $z_0 = max(x_i * w_j), 0$). The output of that activation function is recorded as a positional value in an output "image." The filter slides one stride-width, takes the next snapshot, and puts the output value next to the output of the first (see figure 7.6).

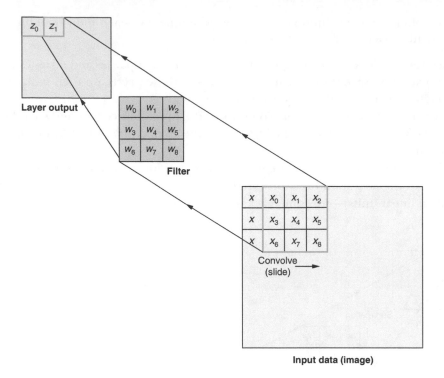

**Figure 7.6    Convolution**

There are several of these filters in a layer, and as they each convolve over the entire image, they each create a new "image," a "filtered" image if you will. Say you have $n$ filters. After this process, you'd have $n$ new, filtered images for each filter you defined.

We get back to what you do with these $n$ new images in a moment.

### 7.3.4   Padding

Something funny happens at the edges of an image, however. If you start a 3 x 3 filter in the upper-left corner of an input image and stride one pixel at a time across, stopping when the rightmost edge of the filter reaches the rightmost edge of the input, the output "image" will be two pixels narrower than the source input.

Keras has tools to help deal with this issue. The first is to ignore that the output is slightly smaller. The Keras argument for this is `padding='valid'`. If this is the case, you just have to be careful and take note of the new dimensions as you pass the data into the next layer. The downfall of this strategy is that the data in the edge of the original input is undersampled as the interior data points are passed into each filter multiple times, from the overlapped filter positions. On a large image, this may not be an issue, but as soon as you bring this concept to bear on a Tweet, for example, undersampling a word at the beginning of a 10-word dataset could drastically change the outcome.

The next strategy is known as *padding*, which consists of adding enough data to the input's outer edges so that the first real data point is treated just as the innermost data points are. The downfall of this strategy is that you're adding potentially unrelated data to the input, which in itself can skew the outcome. You don't care to find patterns in fake data that you generated after all. But you can pad the input several ways to try to minimize the ill effects. See the following listing.

---

**Listing 7.1  Keras network with one convolution layer**

```
>>> from keras.models import Sequential
>>> from keras.layers import Conv1D

>>> model = Sequential()
>>> model.add(Conv1D(filters=16,
                     kernel_size=3,
                     padding='same',          <--
                      activation='relu',
                     strides=1,
                     input_shape=(100, 300)))  <--
```

'same' or 'valid' are the options.

input_shape is still the shape of your unmodified input. The padding happens under the hood.

---

More on the implementation details in a moment. Just be aware of these troublesome bits, and know that a good deal of what could be rather annoying data wrangling has been abstracted away for you nicely by the tools you'll be using.

There are other strategies where the pre-processor attempts to guess at what the padding should be, mimicking the data points that are already on the edge. But you won't have use for that strategy in NLP applications, for it's fraught with its own peril.

**CONVOLUTIONAL PIPELINE**

You have *n* filters and *n* new images now. What do you do with that? This, like most applications of neural networks, starts from the same place: a labeled dataset. And likewise you have a similar goal. To predict a label given a novel image. The simplest next step is to take each of those filtered images and string them out as input to a feedforward layer and then proceed as you did in chapter 5.

> **TIP**  You can pass these filtered images into a second convolutional layer with its own set of filters. In practice, this is the most common architecture; you'll brush up on it later. It turns out the multiple layers of convolutions leads to a path to learning layers of abstractions: first edges, then shapes/colors, and eventually concepts!

No matter how many layers (convolutional or otherwise) you add to your network, once you have a final output you can compute the error and backpropagate that error all the way back through the network.

Because the activation function was differentiable, you can backpropagate as normal and update the weights of the individual filters themselves. The network then learns what kind of filters it needs to get the right output for a given input.

You can think of this process as the network learning to detect and extract information for the later layers to act on more easily.

### 7.3.5    *Learning*

The filters themselves, as in any neural network, start out with weights that are initialized to random values near zero. How is the output "image" going to be anything more than noise? At first, in the first few iterations of training, it will be just that: noise.

But the classifier you're building will have some amount of error from the expected label for each input, and that input can be backpropagated through the activation function to the values of the filters themselves. To backpropagate the error, you have to take the derivative of the error with respect to the weight that fed it.

And as the convolution layer comes earlier in the net, it's specifically the derivative of the gradient from the layer above with respect to the weight that fed it. This calculation is similar to normal backpropagation because the weight generated output in many positions for a given training sample.

The specific derivations of the gradient with respect to the weights of a convolutional filter are beyond the scope of this book. But a shorthand way of thinking about it is for a given weight in a given filter, the gradient is the sum of the normal gradients that were created for each individual position in the convolution during the forward pass. This is a fairly complicated formula (two sums and multiple stacked equations, as follows):

$$\frac{\partial E}{\partial w_{ab}} = \sum_{i=0}^{m} \sum_{j=0}^{n} \frac{\partial E}{\partial x_{ij}} \frac{\partial x_{ij}}{\partial w_{ab}}$$

**Sum of the gradients for a filter weight**

This concept is pretty much the same as a regular feedforward net, where you are figuring out how much each particular weight contributed to the overall error of the system. Then you decide how best to correct that toward a weight that will cause less error in the future training examples. None of these details are vital for the understanding of the use of convolutional neural nets in natural language processing. But hopefully you've developed an intuition for how to tweak neural network architectures and build on these examples later in the chapters.

## 7.4    *Narrow windows indeed*

Yeah, yeah, okay, images. But we're talking about language here, remember? Let's see some words to train on. It turns out you can use convolutional neural networks for natural language processing by using word vectors (also known as *word embeddings*), which you learned about in chapter 6, instead of an image's pixel values, as the input to your network.

Because relative vertical relations between words would be arbitrary, depending on the page width, no relevant information is in the patterns that may emerge there. Relevant information is in the relative "horizontal" positions though.

> **TIP**    The same concepts hold true for languages that are read top to bottom *before* reading right or left, such as Japanese. But in those cases, you focus on "vertical" relationships rather than "horizontal."

You want to focus only on the relationships of tokens in one spatial dimension. Instead of a two-dimensional filter that you would convolve over a two-dimensional input (a picture), you'll convolve one-dimensional filters over a one-dimensional input, such as a sentence.

Your filter *shape* will also be one-dimensional instead of two-dimensional as in the 1 x 3 rolling window shown in figure 7.7.

If you imagine the text as an image, the "second" dimension is the full length of the word vector, typically 100-D–500-D, just like a real image. You'll only be concerned with the "width" of the filter. In figure 7.7, the filter is three tokens wide. Aha! Notice that each word token (or later character token) is a "pixel" in your sentence "image."

1 x 3 Filter

The cat and dog went to the bodega together.

1 x 3 Filter

The cat and dog went to the bodega together.

1 x 3 Filter

The cat and dog went to the bodega together.

**Figure 7.7   1D convolution**

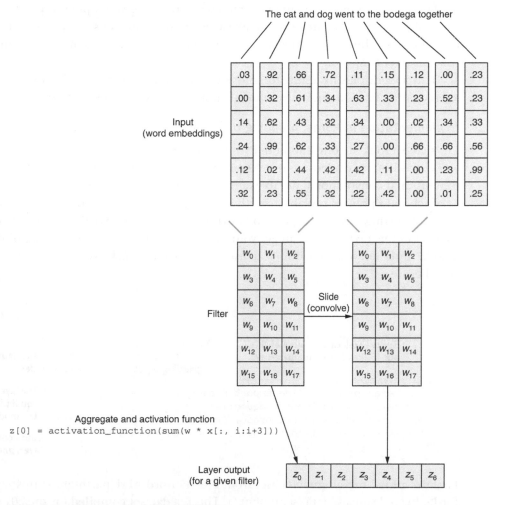

**Figure 7.8   1D convolution with embeddings**

**TIP** The term one-dimensional filter can be a little misleading as you get to word embeddings. The vector representation of the word itself extends "downward" as shown in figure 7.8, but the filter covers the whole length of that dimension in one go. The dimension we're referring to when we say one-dimensional convolution is the "width" of the phrase—the dimension you're traveling across. In a two-dimensional convolution, of an image say, you would scan the input from side to side and top to bottom, hence the two-dimensional name. Here you only slide in one dimension, left to right.

As mentioned earlier, the term convolution is actually a bit of shorthand. But it bears repeating: the sliding has no effect on the model. The data at multiple positions dictates what's going on. The order in which the "snapshots" are calculated isn't important as long as the output is reconstructed in the same way the windows onto the input were positioned.

The weight values in the filters are unchanged for a given input sample during the forward pass, which means you can take a given filter and all its "snapshots" in parallel and compose the output "image" all at once. This is the convolutional neural network's secret to speed.

This speed, plus its ability to ignore the position of a feature, is why researchers keep coming back to this convolutional approach to feature extraction.

### 7.4.1 Implementation in Keras: prepping the data

Let's take a look at convolution in Python with the example convolutional neural network classifier provided in the Keras documentation. They have crafted a one-dimensional convolutional net to examine the IMDB movie review dataset.

Each data point is prelabeled with a 0 (negative sentiment) or a 1 (positive sentiment). In listing 7.2, you're going to swap out their example IMDB movie review dataset for one in raw text, so you can get your hands dirty with the preprocessing of the text as well. And then you'll see if you can use this trained network to classify text it has never seen before.

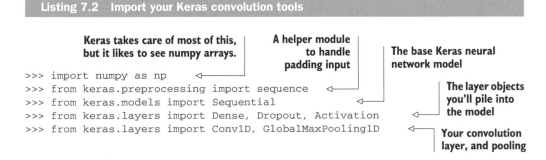

Listing 7.2 Import your Keras convolution tools

Keras takes care of most of this, but it likes to see numpy arrays.

A helper module to handle padding input

The base Keras neural network model

```
>>> import numpy as np
>>> from keras.preprocessing import sequence
>>> from keras.models import Sequential
>>> from keras.layers import Dense, Dropout, Activation
>>> from keras.layers import Conv1D, GlobalMaxPooling1D
```

The layer objects you'll pile into the model

Your convolution layer, and pooling

First download the original dataset from the Stanford AI department (https://ai.stanford.edu/%7eamaas/data/sentiment/). This is a dataset compiled for the 2011 paper

*Learning Word Vectors for Sentiment Analysis.*[2] Once you have downloaded the dataset, unzip it to a convenient directory and look inside. You're just going to use the train/ directory, but other toys are in there also, so feel free to look around.

The reviews in the train folder are broken up into text files in either the pos or neg folders. You'll first need to read those in Python with their appropriate label and then shuffle the deck so the samples aren't all positive and then all negative. Training with the sorted labels will skew training toward whatever comes last, especially when you use certain hyperparameters, such as momentum. See the following listing.

---

**Listing 7.3   Preprocessor to load your documents**

```
>>> import glob
>>> import os

>>> from random import shuffle

>>> def pre_process_data(filepath):
...     """
...     This is dependent on your training data source but we will
...     try to generalize it as best as possible.
...     """
...     positive_path = os.path.join(filepath, 'pos')
...     negative_path = os.path.join(filepath, 'neg')
...     pos_label = 1
...     neg_label = 0
...     dataset = []
...
...     for filename in glob.glob(os.path.join(positive_path, '*.txt')):
...         with open(filename, 'r') as f:
...             dataset.append((pos_label, f.read()))
...
...     for filename in glob.glob(os.path.join(negative_path, '*.txt')):
...         with open(filename, 'r') as f:
...             dataset.append((neg_label, f.read()))
...
...     shuffle(dataset)
...
...     return dataset
```

The first example document should look something like the following. Yours will differ depending on how the samples were shuffled, but that's fine. The first element in the tuple is the *target* value for sentiment: 1 for positive sentiment, 0 for negative:

```
>>> dataset = pre_process_data('<path to your downloaded file>/aclimdb/train')
>>> dataset[0]
(1, 'I, as a teenager really enjoyed this movie! Mary Kate and Ashley worked
➥ great together and everyone seemed so at ease. I thought the movie plot was
➥ very good and hope everyone else enjoys it to! Be sure and rent it!! Also
they had some great soccer scenes for all those soccer players! :)')
```

---

[2]   Maas, Andrew L. et al., *Learning Word Vectors for Sentiment Analysis*, Proceedings of the 49th Annual Meeting of the Association for Computational Linguistics: Human Language Technologies, June 2011, Association for Computational Linguistics.

The next step is to tokenize and vectorize the data. You'll use the Google News pre-trained Word2vec vectors, so download those via the nlpia package or directly from Google.[3]

You'll use gensim to unpack the vectors, just like you did in chapter 6. You can experiment with the limit argument to the load_word2vec_format method; a higher number will get you more vectors to play with, but memory quickly becomes an issue and return on investment drops quickly in really high values for limit.

Let's write a helper function to tokenize the data and then create a list of the vectors for those tokens to use as your data to feed the model, as shown in the following listing.

**Listing 7.4   Vectorizer and tokenizer**

```
>>> from nltk.tokenize import TreebankWordTokenizer
>>> from gensim.models.keyedvectors import KeyedVectors
>>> from nlpia.loaders import get_data
>>> word_vectors = get_data('w2v', limit=200000)

>>> def tokenize_and_vectorize(dataset):
...     tokenizer = TreebankWordTokenizer()
...     vectorized_data = []
...     expected = []
...     for sample in dataset:
...         tokens = tokenizer.tokenize(sample[1])
...         sample_vecs = []
...         for token in tokens:
...             try:
...                 sample_vecs.append(word_vectors[token])
...
...             except KeyError:
...                 pass   # No matching token in the Google w2v vocab
...
...         vectorized_data.append(sample_vecs)
...
...     return vectorized_data
```

get_data('w2v') downloads "GoogleNews-vectors-negative300.bin.gz" to the nlpia.loaders.BIGDATA_PATH directory.

Note that you're throwing away information here. The Google News Word2vec vocabulary includes some stopwords, but not all of them. A lot of common words like "a" will be thrown out in your function. Not ideal by any stretch, but this will give you a baseline for how well convolutional neural nets can perform even on lossy data. To get around this loss of information, you can train your word2vec models separately and make sure you have better vector coverage. The data also has a lot of HTML tags like <br\>, which you do want to exclude, because they aren't usually relevant to the text's sentiment.

---

[3] See the download titled "GoogleNews-vectors-negative300.bin.gz - Google Drive" (https://drive.google.com/file/d/0B7XkCwpI5KDYNlNUTTlSS21pQmM/edit?usp=sharing).

You also need to collect the target values—0 for a negative review, 1 for a positive review—in the same order as the training samples. See the following listing.

##### Listing 7.5   Target labels

```
>>> def collect_expected(dataset):
...      """ Peel off the target values from the dataset """
...      expected = []
...      for sample in dataset:
...          expected.append(sample[0])
...      return expected
```

And then you simply pass your data into those functions:

```
>>> vectorized_data = tokenize_and_vectorize(dataset)
>>> expected = collect_expected(dataset)
```

Next you'll split the prepared data into a training set and a test set. You're just going to split your imported dataset 80/20, but this ignores the folder of test data. Feel free to combine the data from the download's original test folder with the training folder. They both contain valid training and testing data. More data is always better. The train/ and test/ folders in most datasets you will download are the particular train/ test split that the maintainer of that package used. Those folders are provided so you can duplicate their results exactly.[4]

The next code block buckets the data into the training set (x_train) that you'll show the network, along with "correct" answers (y_train) and a testing dataset (x_test) that you hold back, along with its answers (y_test). You can then let the network make a "guess" about samples from the test set, and you can validate that it's learning something that generalizes outside of the training data. y_train and y_test are the associated "correct" answers for each example in the respective sets x_train and x_test. See the following listing.

##### Listing 7.6   Train/test split

```
>>> split_point = int(len(vectorized_data)*.8)

>>> x_train = vectorized_data[:split_point_]
>>> y_train_ = expected[:split_point]
>>> x_test = vectorized_data[split_point:]
>>> y_test = expected[split_point:]
```

The next block of code (listing 7.7) sets most of the hyperparameters for the net. The maxlen variable holds the maximum review length you'll consider. Because each input to a convolutional neural net must be equal in dimension, you truncate any sample that is longer than 400 tokens and pad the shorter samples out to 400 tokens

---

[4]  You want to publicize the test set performance with a model that has never seen the test data. But you want to use *all* the labeled data you have available to you for your final training of the model you deploy to your users.

with Null or 0; actual "PAD" tokens are commonly used to represent this when showing the original text. Again this introduces data into the system that wasn't previously in the system. The network itself can learn that pattern as well though, so that PAD == "ignore me" becomes part of the network's structure, so it's not the end of the world.

Note of caution: this padding isn't the same as the padding introduced earlier. Here you're padding out the input to be of consistent size. You'll need to decide separately the issue of padding the beginning and ending of each training sample based on whether you want the output to be of similar size and the end tokens to be treated the same as the interior ones, or whether you don't mind the first/last tokens being treated differently. See the following listing.

---

**Listing 7.7  CNN parameters**

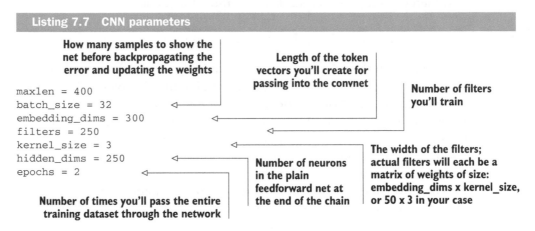

```
maxlen = 400
batch_size = 32
embedding_dims = 300
filters = 250
kernel_size = 3
hidden_dims = 250
epochs = 2
```

How many samples to show the net before backpropagating the error and updating the weights

Length of the token vectors you'll create for passing into the convnet

Number of filters you'll train

The width of the filters; actual filters will each be a matrix of weights of size: embedding_dims x kernel_size, or 50 x 3 in your case

Number of neurons in the plain feedforward net at the end of the chain

Number of times you'll pass the entire training dataset through the network

---

**TIP**  In listing 7.7, the `kernel_size` (filter size or window size) is a scalar value, as opposed to the two-dimensional type filters you had with images. Your filter will look at the word vectors for three tokens at a time. It's helpful to think of the filter sizes, in the *first layer only*, as looking at *n*-grams of the text. In this case, you're looking at 3-grams of your input text. But this could easily be five or seven or more. The choice is data- and task-dependent, so experiment freely with this parameter for your models.

Keras has a preprocessing helper method, `pad_sequences`, that in theory could be used to pad your input data, but unfortunately it works only with sequences of scalars, and you have sequences of vectors. Let's write a helper function of your own to pad your input data, as shown in the following listing.

---

**Listing 7.8  Padding and truncating your token sequence**

```
>>> def pad_trunc(data, maxlen):
...     """
...     For a given dataset pad with zero vectors or truncate to maxlen
...     """
...     new_data = []
```

An astute LiveBook reader (@madara) pointed out this can all be accomplished with a one-liner: [smp[:maxlen] + [[0.] * emb_dim] * (maxlen - len(smp)) for smp in data]

```
...
...         # Create a vector of 0s the length of our word vectors
...         zero_vector = []
...         for _ in range(len(data[0][0])):
...             zero_vector.append(0.0)
...
...         for sample in data:
...             if len(sample) > maxlen:
...                 temp = sample[:maxlen]
...             elif len(sample) < maxlen:
...                 temp = sample
...                 # Append the appropriate number 0 vectors to the list
...                 additional_elems = maxlen - len(sample)
...                 for _ in range(additional_elems):
...                     temp.append(zero_vector)
...             else:
...                 temp = sample
...             new_data.append(temp)
...         return new_data
```

**Finally the augmented data is ready to be tacked onto the end of our list of augmented data.**

Then you need to pass your train and test data into the padder/truncator. After that you can convert it to numpy arrays to make Keras happy. This is a tensor with the shape (number of samples, sequence length, word vector length) that you need for your CNN. See the following listing.

---

**Listing 7.9  Gathering your augmented and truncated data**

```
>>> x_train = pad_trunc(x_train, maxlen)
>>> x_test = pad_trunc(x_test, maxlen)

>>> x_train = np.reshape(x_train, (len(x_train), maxlen, embedding_dims))
>>> y_train = np.array(y_train)
>>> x_test = np.reshape(x_test, (len(x_test), maxlen, embedding_dims))
>>> y_test = np.array(y_test)
```

Phew; finally you're ready to build a neural network.

### 7.4.2  *Convolutional neural network architecture*

You start with the base neural network model class `Sequential`. As with the feed-forward network from chapter 5, `Sequential` is one of the base classes for neural networks in Keras. From here you can start to layer on the magic.

The first piece you add is a convolutional layer. In this case, you assume that it's okay that the output is of smaller dimension than the input, and you set the padding to `'valid'`. Each filter will start its pass with its leftmost edge at the start of the sentence and stop with its rightmost edge on the last token.

Each shift (stride) in the convolution will be one token. The kernel (window width) you already set to three tokens in listing 7.7. And you're using the `'relu'` activation function. At each step, you'll multiply the filter weight times the value in the three tokens it's looking at (element-wise), sum up those answers, and pass them through if they're greater than 0, else you output 0. That last passthrough of positive values and 0s is the *rectified linear units* activation function or *ReLU*. See the following listing.

---

**Listing 7.10   Construct a 1D CNN**

```
>>> print('Build model...')
>>> model = Sequential()

>>> model.add(Conv1D(
...     filters,
...     kernel_size,
...     padding='valid',
...     activation='relu',
...     strides=1,
...     input_shape=(maxlen, embedding_dims)))
```

> The standard model definition pattern for Keras. You'll learn an alternative constructor pattern called the Keras "functional API" in chapter 10.

> Add one Conv1D layer, which will learn word group filters of size kernel_size. There are many more keyword arguments, but you're just using their defaults for now.

### 7.4.3   Pooling

You've started a neural network, so ... everyone into the pool! Pooling is the convolutional neural network's path to dimensionality reduction. In some ways, you're speeding up the process by allowing for parallelization of the computation. But you may notice you make a new "version" of the data sample, a filtered one, for each filter you define. In the preceding example, that would be 250 filtered versions (see listing 7.7) coming out of the first layer. Pooling will mitigate that somewhat, but it also has another striking property.

The key idea is you're going to evenly divide the output of each filter into a subsection. Then for each of those subsections, you'll select or compute a representative value. And then you set the original output aside and use the collections of representative values as the input to the next layers.

But wait. Isn't throwing away data terrible? Usually, discarding data wouldn't be the best course of action. But it turns out, it's a path toward learning higher order representations of the source data. The filters are being trained to find patterns. The patterns are revealed in *relationships* between words and their neighbors! Just the kind of subtle information you set out to find.

In image processing, the first layers will tend to learn to be edge detectors, places where pixel densities rapidly shift from one side to the other. Later layers learn concepts like shape and texture. And layers after that may learn "content" or "meaning." Similar processes will happen with text.

> **TIP**   In an image processor, the pooling region would usually be a 2 x 2 pixel window (and these don't overlap, like your filters do), but in your 1D convolution they would be a 1D window (such as 1 x 2 or 1 x 3).

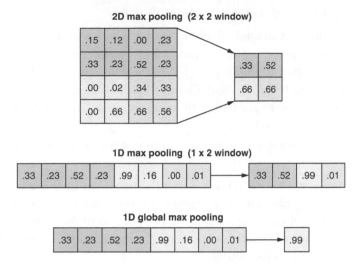

**Figure 7.9  Pooling layers**

You have two choices for pooling (see figure 7.9): *average* and *max*. Average is the more intuitive of the two in that by taking the average of the subset of values you would in theory retain the most data. Max pooling, however, has an interesting property, in that by taking the largest activation value for the given region, the network sees that subsection's most prominent feature. The network has a path toward learning what it should look at, regardless of exact pixel-level position!

In addition to dimensionality reduction and the computational savings that come with it, you gain something else special: *location invariance*. If an original input element is jostled slightly in position in a similar but distinct input sample, the max pooling layer will still output something similar. This is a huge boon in the image recognition world, and it serves a similar purpose in natural language processing.

In this simple example from Keras, you're using the `GlobalMaxPooling1D` layer. Instead of taking the max of a small subsection of each filter's output, you're taking the max of the entire output for that filter, which results in a large amount of information loss. But even tossing aside all that good information, your toy model won't be deterred:

```
>>> model.add(GlobalMaxPooling1D())
```

Pooling options are
GlobalMaxPoolingID(),
MaxPoolingID(n), or AvgPoolingID(n),
where n is the size of the area to pool
and defaults to 2 if not provided.

Okay, outta the pool; grab a towel. Let's recap the path so far:

- For each input example, you applied a filter (weights and activation function).
- Convolved across the length of the input, which would output a 1D vector slightly smaller than the original input (1 x 398 which is input with the filter starting left-aligned and finishing right-aligned) for each filter.
- For each filter output (there are 250 of them, remember), you took the single maximum value from each 1D vector.
- At this point you have a single vector (per input example) that is 1 x 250 (the number of filters).

Now for each input sample you have a 1D vector that the network thinks is a good representation of that input sample. This is a *semantic* representation of the input—a crude one to be sure. And it will only be semantic in the context of the training target, which is sentiment. There won't be an encoding of the content of the movie being reviewed, say, just an encoding of its sentiment.

You haven't done any training yet, so it's a garbage pile of numbers. But we get back to that later. This is an important point to stop and really understand what is going on, for once the network is trained, this *semantic* representation (we like to think of it as a "thought vector") can be useful. Much like the various ways you embedded words into vectors, so too you can perform math on them: you now have something that represents whole groupings of words.

Enough of the excitement, back to the hard work of training. You have a goal to work toward and that's your labels for sentiment. You take your current vector and pass it into a standard feedforward network; in Keras that is a `Dense` layer. The current setup has the same number of elements in your semantic vector and the number of nodes in the Dense layer, but that's just coincidence. Each of the 250 (`hidden_dims`) neurons in the Dense layer has 250 weights for the input from the pooling layer. You temper that with a dropout layer to prevent overfitting.

### 7.4.4  Dropout

*Dropout* (represented as a layer by Keras, as in listing 7.11) is a special technique developed to prevent overfitting in neural networks. It isn't specific to natural language processing, but it does work well here.

The idea is that on each training pass, if you "turn off" a certain percentage of the input going to the next layer, randomly chosen on each pass, the model will be less likely to learn the specifics of the training set, "overfitting," and instead learn more nuanced representations of the patterns in the data and thereby be able to generalize and make accurate predictions when it sees completely novel data.

Your model implements the dropout by assuming the output coming into the Dropout layer (the output from the previous layer) is 0 for that particular pass. It works on that pass because the contribution to the overall error of each of the neuron's weights that would receive the dropout's zero input is also effectively 0. Therefore those weights won't get updated on the backpropagation pass. The network is then forced to rely on relationships among varying weight sets to achieve its goals (hopefully they won't hold this tough love against us).

> **TIP** Don't worry too much about this point, but note that Keras will do some magic under the hood for Dropout layers. Keras is randomly turning off a percentage of the inputs on each forward pass of the training data. You won't do that dropout during inference or prediction on your real application. The strength of the signal going into layers after a Dropout layer would be significantly higher during the nontraining inference stage.
>
> Keras mitigates this in the training phase by proportionally boosting all inputs that aren't turned off, so the aggregate signal that goes into the next layer is of the same magnitude as it will be during inference.

The parameter passed into the Dropout layer in Keras is the percentage of the inputs to randomly turn off. In this example, only 80% of the embedding data, randomly chosen for each training sample, will pass into the next layer as it is. The rest will go in as 0s. A 20% dropout setting is common, but a dropout of up to 50% can have good results (one more hyperparameter you can play with).

And then you use the Rectified Linear Units activation (`relu`) on the output end of each neuron. See the following listing.

##### Listing 7.11 Fully connected layer with dropout

```
>>> model.add(Dense(hidden_dims))
>>> model.add(Dropout(0.2))
>>> model.add(Activation('relu'))
```

You start with a vanilla fully connected hidden layer and then tack on dropout and ReLU.

### 7.4.5 The cherry on the sundae

The last layer, or output layer, is the actual classifier, so here you have a neuron that fires based on the `sigmoid` activation function; it gives a value between 0 and 1. During validation, Keras will consider anything below 0.5 to be classified as 0 and anything above 0.5 to be a 1. But in terms of the *loss* calculated, it will use the target minus the actual value provided by the sigmoid ($y - f(x)$).

Here you project onto a single unit output layer, and funnel your signal into a sigmoid activation function, as shown in the following listing.

##### Listing 7.12 Funnel

```
>>> model.add(Dense(1))
>>> model.add(Activation('sigmoid'))
```

Now you finally have a convolutional neural network model fully defined in Keras. Nothing's left but to compile it and train it, as shown in the following listing.

---

**Listing 7.13    Compile the CNN**

```
>>> model.compile(loss='binary_crossentropy',
...               optimizer='adam',
...               metrics=['accuracy'])
```

The `loss` function is what the network will try to minimize. Here, you use `'binary_crossentropy'`. At the time of writing, 13 loss functions are defined in Keras, and you have the option to define your own. You won't go into the use cases for each of those, but the two workhorses to know about are `binary_crossentropy` and `categorical_crossentropy`.

Both are similar in their mathematical definitions, and in many ways you can think of `binary_crossentropy` as a special case of `categorical_crossentropy`. The important thing to know is when to use which. Because in this example you have one output neuron that is either on or off, you'll use `binary_crossentropy`.

Categorical is used when you're predicting one of many classes. In those cases, your target will be an $n$-dimensional vector, one-hot encoded, with a position for each of your $n$ classes. The last layer in your network in this case would be as shown in the following listing.

---

**Listing 7.14    Output layer for categorical variable (word)**

```
>>> model.add(Dense(num_classes))
>>> model.add(Activation('sigmoid'))
```
⟵ **Where num_classes is ... well, you get the picture.**

In this case, target minus output $(y - f(x))$ would be an $n$-dimensional vector subtracted from an $n$-dimensional vector. And `categorical_crossentropy` would try to minimize that difference.

But back to your binary classification.

**OPTIMIZATION**

The parameter *optimizer* is any of a list of strategies to optimize the network during training, such as stochastic gradient descent, Adam, and RSMProp. The optimizers themselves are each different approaches to minimizing the loss function in a neural network; the math behind each is beyond the scope of this book, but be aware of them and try different ones for your particular problem. Although many may converge for a given problem, some may not, and they will do so at different paces.

Their magic comes from dynamically altering the parameters of the training, specifically the *learning rate*, based on the current state of the training. For example, the starting learning rate (remember: *alpha* is the learning rate applied to the weight updates you saw in chapter 5) may decay over time. Or some methods may apply *momentum* and increase the learning rate if the last movement of the weights in that particular direction was successful at decreasing the loss.

Each optimizer itself has a handful of hyperparameters, such as learning rate. Keras has good defaults for these values, so you shouldn't have to worry about them too much at first.

### Fit

Where *compile* builds the model, *fit* trains the model. All the inputs times the weights, all the activation functions, all the backpropagation is kicked off by this one statement. Depending on your hardware, the size of your model, and the size of your data, this process can take anywhere from a few seconds to a few months. Using a GPU can greatly reduce the training time in most cases, and if you have access to one, by all means use it. A few extra steps are required to pass environment variables to Keras to direct it to use the GPU, but this example is small enough you can run it on most modern CPUs in a reasonable amount of time. See the following listing.

---

**Listing 7.15  Training a CNN**

The number of data samples processed before the backpropagation updates the weights. The cumulative error for the n samples in the batch is applied at once.

```
>>> model.fit(x_train, y_train,
...           batch_size=batch_size,           ◁
...           epochs=epochs,                   ◁
...           validation_data=(x_test, y_test))
```

The number of times the training will run through the entire training dataset, before stopping

### 7.4.6  Let's get to learning (training)

One last step before you hit run. You would like to save the model state after training. Because you aren't going to hold the model in memory for now, you can grab its structure in a JSON file and save the trained weights in another file for later re-instantiation. See the following listing.

---

**Listing 7.16  Save your hard work**

Note that this doesn't save the weights of the network, only the structure.

```
>>> model_structure = model.to_json()          ◁
>>> with open("cnn_model.json", "w") as json_file:
...     json_file.write(model_structure)
>>> model.save_weights("cnn_weights.h5")        ◁
```

Save your trained model before you lose it!

Now your trained model will be persisted on disk; should it converge, you won't have to train it again.

Keras also provides some amazingly useful callbacks during the training phase that are passed into the `fit` method as keyword arguments, such as `checkpointing`, which iteratively saves the model only when the accuracy or loss has improved, or `EarlyStopping`, which stops the training phase early if the model is no longer improving based on a metric you provide. And probably most exciting, they have implemented a TensorBoard callback. TensorBoard works only with TensorFlow as a backend, but it provides an amazing level of introspection into your models and can be indispensable when troubleshooting and fine-tuning. Let's get to learning! Running the `compile` and `fit` steps above should lead to the following output:

```
Using TensorFlow backend.
Loading data...
25000 train sequences
25000 test sequences
Pad sequences (samples x time)
x_train shape: (25000, 400)
x_test shape: (25000, 400)
Build model...
Train on 20000 samples, validate on 5000 samples
Epoch 1/2 [==================================] - 417s - loss: 0.3756 -
acc: 0.8248 - val_loss: 0.3531 - val_acc: 0.8390
Epoch 2/2 [==================================] - 330s - loss: 0.2409 -
acc: 0.9018 - val_loss: 0.2767 - val_acc: 0.8840
```

Your final loss and accuracies may vary a bit, which is a side effect of the random initial weights chosen for all the neurons. You can overcome this randomness to create a repeatable pipeline by passing a seed into the randomizer. Doing so forces the same values to be chosen for the initial random weights on each run, which can be helpful in debugging and tuning your model. Just keep in mind that the starting point can itself force the model into a *local minimum* or even prevent the model from converging, so we recommend that you try a few different seeds.

To set the seed, add the following two lines above your model definition. The integer passed in as the argument to seed is unimportant, but as long as it's consistent, the model will initialize its weights to small values in the same way:

```
>>> import numpy as np
>>> np.random.seed(1337)
```

We haven't seen definitive signs of overfitting; the accuracy improved for both the training and validation sets. You could let the model run for another epoch or two and see if you could improve more without overfitting. A Keras model can continue the training from this point if it's still in memory, or if it's reloaded from a save file. Just call the `fit` method again (change the sample data or not), and the training will resume from that last state.

> **TIP**   Overfitting will be apparent when the loss continues to drop for the training run, but the `val_loss` at the end of each epoch starts to climb compared to the previous epoch. Finding that happy medium where the validation loss curve starts to bend back up is a major key to creating a good model.

Great. Done. Now, what did you just do?

The model was described and then compiled into an initial untrained state. You then called `fit` to actually learn the weights of the filters and the feedforward fully connected network at the end, as well as the weights of each of the 250 individual filters, by backpropagating the error encountered at each example all the way back down the chain.

The progress meter reported *loss*, which you specified as `binary_crossentropy`. For each batch, Keras is reporting a metric of how far you're away from the label you provided for that sample. The accuracy is a report of "percent correct guesses." This metric is fun to watch but certainly can be misleading, especially if you have a lopsided dataset. Imagine you have 100 examples: 99 of them are positive examples and only one of them should be predicted as negative. If you predict all 100 as positive without even looking at the data, you'll still be 99% accurate, which isn't helpful in generalizing. The `val_loss` and `val_acc` are the same metrics on the test dataset provided in the following:

```
>>> validation_data=(x_test, y_test)
```

The validation samples are never shown to the network for training; they're only passed in to see what the model predicts for them, and then reported on against the metrics. Backpropagation doesn't happen for these samples. This helps keep track of how well the model will generalize to novel, real-world data.

You've trained a model. The magic is done. The box has told you it figured everything out. You believe it. So what? Let's get some use out of your work.

### 7.4.7 *Using the model in a pipeline*

After you have a trained model, you can then pass in a novel sample and see what the network thinks. This could be an incoming chat message or tweet to your bot; in your case, it'll be a made-up example.

First, reinstate your trained model, if it's no longer in memory, as shown in the following listing.

**Listing 7.17  Loading a saved model**

```
>>> from keras.models import model_from_json
>>> with open("cnn_model.json", "r") as json_file:
...     json_string = json_file.read()
>>> model = model_from_json(json_string)

>>> model.load_weights('cnn_weights.h5')
```

Let's make up a sentence with an obvious negative sentiment and see what the network has to say about it. See the following listing.

**Listing 7.18  Test example**

```
>>> sample_1 = "I hate that the dismal weather had me down for so long,
 when will it break! Ugh, when does happiness return? The sun is blinding
 and the puffy clouds are too thin. I can't wait for the weekend."
```

With the model pretrained, testing a new sample is quick. The are still thousands and thousands of calculations to do, but for each sample you only need one forward pass and no backpropagation to get a result. See the following listing.

---

**Listing 7.19   Prediction**

> You pass a dummy value in the first element of the tuple just because
> your helper expects it from the way you processed the initial data.
> That value won't ever see the network, so it can be anything.

```
>>> vec_list = tokenize_and_vectorize([(1, sample_1)])      ◁

>>> test_vec_list = pad_trunc(vec_list, maxlen)             ◁

>>> test_vec = np.reshape(test_vec_list, (len(test_vec_list), maxlen,\
...     embedding_dims))
>>> model.predict(test_vec)
array([[ 0.12459087]], dtype=float32)
```

**Tokenize returns a list of the data (length I here).**

---

The Keras `predict` method gives you the raw output of the final layer of the net. In this case, you have one neuron, and because the last layer is a sigmoid it will output something between 0 and 1.

The Keras `predict_classes` method gives you the expected 0 or 1. If you have a multiclass classification problem, the last layer in your network will likely be a softmax function, and the outputs of each node will be the probability (in the network's eyes) that each node is the right answer. Calling `predict_classes` there will return the node associated with the highest valued probability.

But back to your example:

```
>>> model.predict_classes(test_vec)
array([[0]], dtype=int32)
```

A "negative" sentiment indeed.

A sentence that contains words such as "happiness," "sun," "puffy," and "clouds" isn't necessarily a sentence full of positive emotion. Just as a sentence with "dismal," "break," and "down" isn't necessarily a negative sentiment. But with a trained neural network, you were able to detect the underlying pattern and to learn something that generalized from data, without ever hard-coding a single rule.

### 7.4.8   *Where do you go from here?*

In the introduction, we talked about CNNs importance in image processing. One key point that was breezed over is the ability of the network to process *channels* of information. In the case of a black-and-white image, there's one channel in the two-dimensional image. Each data point is the grayscale value of that pixel, which gives you a two-dimensional input. In the case of color, the input is still a pixel intensity, but it's separated into its red, green, and blue components. The input then becomes a three-dimensional tensor that is passed into the net. And the filters follow suit and become three-dimensional as well, still a 3 x 3 or 5 x 5 or whatever in the x,y plane, but also three layers deep, resulting in filters that are three pixels wide x three pixels high x three channels deep, which leads to an interesting application in natural language processing.

Your input to the network was a series of words represented as vectors lined up next to each other, 400 (maxlen) words wide x 300 elements long, and you used Word2vec embeddings for the word vectors. But as you've seen in earlier chapters, you can generate word embeddings multiple ways. If you pick several and restrict them to an identical number of elements, you can stack them as you would picture *channels*, which is an interesting way to add information to the network, especially if the embeddings come from disparate sources. Stacking a variety of word embeddings this way may not be worth the increased training time due to the multiplier effect it has on the complexity of your model. But you can see now why we started you off with some image processing analogies. However, this analogy breaks down when you realize that the dimensions independent of word embeddings aren't correlated with each other in the same way that color channels in an image are, so YMMV.

We touched briefly on the output of the convolutional layers (before you step into the feedforward layer). This *semantic representation* is an important artifact. It's in many ways a numerical representation of the thought and details of the input text. Specifically in this case, it's a representation of the thought and details through the lens of sentiment analysis, as all the "learning" that happened was in response to whether the sample was labeled as a positive or negative sentiment. The vector that was generated by training on a set that was labeled for another specific topic and classified as such would contain much different information. Using the intermediary vector directly from a convolutional neural net isn't common, but in the coming chapters you'll see examples from other neural network architectures where the details of that intermediary vector become important, and in some cases are the end goal itself.

Why would you choose a CNN for your NLP classification task? The main benefit it provides is efficiency. In many ways, because of the pooling layers and the limits created by filter size (though you can make your filters large if you wish), you're throwing away a good deal of information. But that doesn't mean they aren't useful models. As you've seen, they were able to efficiently detect and predict sentiment over a relatively large dataset, and even though you relied on the Word2vec embeddings, CNNs can perform on much less rich embeddings without mapping the entire language.

Where can you take CNNs from here? A lot can depend on the available datasets, but richer models can be achieved by stacking convolutional layers and passing the output of the first set of filters as the "image" sample into the second set and so on. Research has also found that running the model with multiple size filters and concatenating the output of each size filter into a longer *thought vector* before passing it into the feedforward network at the end can provide more accurate results. The world is wide open. Experiment and enjoy.

## *Summary*

- A convolution is a window sliding over something larger (keeping the focus on a subset of the greater whole).
- Neural networks can treat text just as they treat images and "see" them.
- Handicapping the learning process with dropout actually helps.
- Sentiment exists not only in the words but in the patterns that are used.
- Neural networks have many knobs you can turn.

# Loopy (recurrent) neural networks (RNNs) 8

Chapter 7 showed how convolutional neural nets can analyze a fragment or sentence all at once, keeping track of nearby words in the sequence by passing a filter of shared weights over those words (convolving over them). Words that occurred in clusters could be detected together. If those words jostled a little bit in position, the network could be resilient to it. Most importantly, concepts that appeared near to one another could have a big impact on the network. But what if you want to look at the bigger picture and consider those relationships over a longer period of time, a broader window than three or four tokens of a sentence. Can you give the net a concept of what went on earlier? A memory?

For each training example (or batch of unordered examples) and output (or batch of outputs) of a feedforward network, the network weights will be adjusted in

247

the individual neurons based on the error, using backpropagation. This you've seen. But the effects of the next example's learning stage are largely independent of the order of input data. Convolutional neural nets make an attempt to capture that ordering relationship by capturing localized relationships, but there's another way.

In a convolutional neural network, you passed in each sample as a collection of word tokens gathered together. The word vectors are arrayed together to form a matrix. The matrix shape was (length-of-word-vector x number-of-words-in-sample), as you can see in figure 8.1.

But that sequence of word vectors could just as easily have been passed into a standard feedforward network from chapter 5 (see figure 8.2), right?

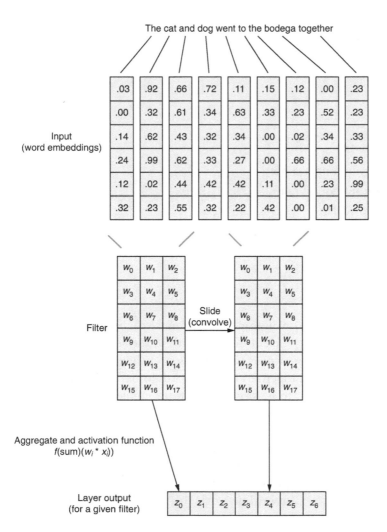

**Figure 8.1  1D convolution with embeddings**

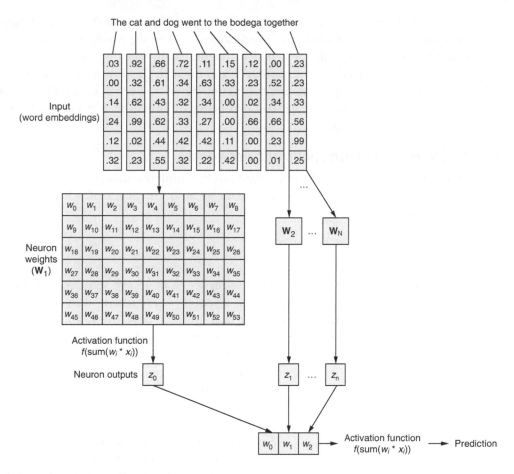

The cat and dog went to the bodega together

**Figure 8.2  Text into a feedforward network**

Sure, this is a viable model. A feedforward network will be able to react to the co-occurrences of tokens when they are passed in this way, which is what you want. But it will react to all the co-occurrences equally, regardless of whether they're separated from each other by a long document or right next to each other. And feedforward networks, like CNNs, don't work with variable length documents very well. They can't handle the text at the end of a document if it exceeds the width of your network.

A feedforward network's main strength is to model the relationships between a data sample, as a whole, to its associated label. The words at the beginning and end of a document have just as much effect on the output as the words in the middle, regardless of their unlikely semantic relationship to each other. You can see how this homogeneity or "uniformity of influence" can cause problems when you consider strong negation and modifier (adjectives and adverb) tokens like "not" or "good." In a feedforward network, negation words will influence the meaning of all the words in the sentence, even ones that are far from their intended influence.

One-dimensional convolutions gave us a way to deal with these inter-token relationships by looking at *windows* of words together. And the pooling layers discussed in chapter 7 were specifically designed to handle slight word order variations. In this chapter, we look at a different approach. And through this approach, you'll take a first step toward the concept of *memory* in a neural network. Instead of thinking about language as a large chunk of data, you can begin to look at it as it's created, token by token, over *time*, in sequence.

## 8.1   Remembering with recurrent networks

Of course, the words in a document are rarely completely independent of each other; their occurrence influences or is influenced by occurrences of other words in the document:

> *The stolen car sped into the arena.*
> *The clown car sped into the arena.*

Two different emotions may arise in the reader of these two sentences as the reader reaches the end of the sentence. The two sentences are identical in adjective, noun, verb, and prepositional phrase construction. But that adjective swap early in the sentence has a profound effect on what the reader infers is going on.

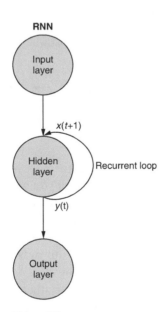

**RNN**

**Figure 8.3**
**Recurrent neural net**

Can you find a way to model that relationship? A way to understand that "arena" and even "sped" could take on slightly different connotations when an adjective that does not directly modify either occurred earlier in the sentence?

If you can find a way to *remember* what just happened the moment before (specifically what happened at time step $t$ when you're looking at time step $t+1$), you'd be on the way to capturing the patterns that emerge when certain tokens appear in patterns relative to other tokens in a sequence. *Recurrent neural nets* (RNNs) enable neural networks to remember the past words within a sentence.

You can see in figure 8.3 that a single recurrent neuron in the hidden layer adds a recurrent loop to "recycle" the output of the hidden layer at time $t$. The output at time $t$ is added to the next input at time $t+1$. This new input is processed by the network at time step $t+1$ to create the output for that hidden layer at time $t+1$. That output at $t+1$ is then recycled back into the input again at time step $t+2$, and so on.[1]

---

[1]  In finance, dynamics, and feedback control, this is often called an *auto-regressive moving average* (ARMA) model: https://en.wikipedia.org/wiki/Autoregressive_model.

Although the idea of affecting state across time can be a little mind boggling at first, the basic concept is simple. For each input you feed into a regular feedforward net, you'd like to take the output of the network at time step $t$ and provide it as an additional input, along with the next piece of data being fed into the network at time step $t+1$. You tell the feedforward network what happened before along with what is happening "now."

> **IMPORTANT**  In this chapter and the next, we discuss most things in terms of time steps. This isn't the same thing as individual data samples. We're referring to a single data sample split into smaller chunks that represent changes over time. The single data sample will still be a piece of text, say a short movie review or a tweet. As before, you'll tokenize the sentence. But rather than putting those tokens into the network all at once, you'll pass them in one at a time. *This is different than having multiple new document samples.* The tokens are still part of *one* data sample with *one* associated label.

> You can think of $t$ as referring to the token sequence index. So $t=0$ is the first token in the document and $t+1$ is the next token in the document. The tokens, in the order they appear in the document, will be the inputs at each *time step* or *token step.* And the tokens don't have to be words. Individual characters work well too. Inputing the tokens one at a time will be *substeps* of feeding the data sample into the network.

> Throughout, we reference the current time step as $t$ and the following time step as $t+1$.

You can visualize a recurrent net as shown in figure 8.3: the circles are entire feedforward network *layers* composed of one or more neurons. The output of the *hidden layer* emerges from the network as normal, but it's also set aside to be passed back in as an input to *itself* along with the normal input from the next time step. This feedback is represented with an arc from the output of a layer back into its own input.

An easier way to see this process—and it's more commonly shown this way—is by *unrolling* the net. Figure 8.4 shows the network stood on its head with two unfoldings of the time variable ($t$), showing layers for $t+1$ and $t+2$.

Each time step is represented by a column of neurons in the unrolled version of the very same neural network. It's like looking at a screenplay or video frame of the neural net for each sample in time. The network to the right is the *future* version of the network on the left. The output of a hidden layer at one time step ($t$) is fed back into the hidden layer along with input data for the next time step ($t+1$) to the right. Repeat. This diagram shows two iterations of this unfolding, so three columns of neurons for $t=0$, $t=1$, and $t=2$.

All the vertical paths in this visualization are clones, or views of the same neurons. They are the single network represented on a timeline. This visualization is helpful when talking about how information flows through the network forward and *backward*

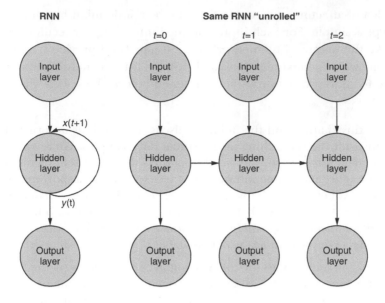

Figure 8.4    Unrolled recurrent neural net

during backpropagation. But when looking at the three unfolded networks, remember that they're all different snapshots of the same network with a single set of weights.

Let's zoom in on the original representation of a recurrent neural network before it was unrolled. Let's expose the input-weight relationships. The individual layers of this recurrent network look like what you see in figures 8.5 and 8.6.

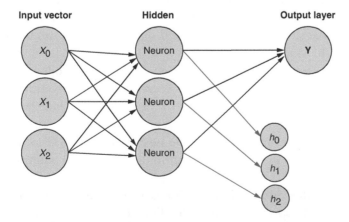

Figure 8.5    Detailed recurrent neural net at time step *t* = 0

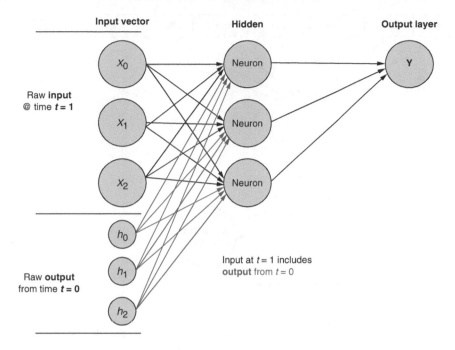

**Figure 8.6   Detailed recurrent neural net at time step $t$ = 1**

Each neuron in the hidden state has a set of weights that it applies to each element of each input vector, as a normal feedforward network. But now you have an additional set of trainable weights that are applied to the output of the hidden neurons from the previous time step. The network can learn how much weight or importance to give the events of the "past" as you input a sequence token by token.

> **TIP**   The first input in a sequence has no "past," so the hidden state at $t{=}0$ receives an input of 0 from its $t$-1 self. An alternative way of "filling" the initial state value is to first pass related but separate samples into the net one after the other. Each sample's final output is used for the $t{=}0$ input of the next sample. You'll learn how to preserve more of the information in your dataset using alternative "filling" approaches in the section on *statefulness* at the end of this chapter.

Let's turn back to the data: imagine you have a set of documents, each a labeled example. For each sample, instead of passing the collection of word vectors into a convolutional neural net all at once as in the last chapter (see figure 8.7), you take the sample one token at a time and pass the tokens individually into your RNN (see figure 8.8).

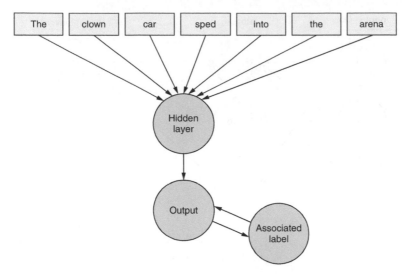

**Figure 8.7   Data into convolutional network**

In your recurrent neural net, you pass in the word vector for the first token and get the network's output. You then pass in the second token, but you also pass in the output from the first token! And then pass in the third token along with the output from the second token. And so on. The network has a concept of before and after, cause and effect, some vague notion of time (see figure 8.8).

**Recurrent neural net**

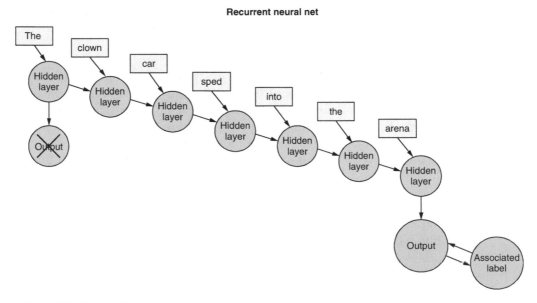

**Figure 8.8   Data fed into a recurrent network**

Now your network is remembering something! Well, sort of. A few things remain for you to figure out. For one, how does backpropagation even work in a structure like this?

### 8.1.1  *Backpropagation through time*

All the networks we've talked about so far have a label (the target variable) to aim for, and recurrent networks are no exception. But you don't have a concept of a label for each token. You have a single label for all the tokens in each sample text. You only have a label for the sample document.

> *... and that is enough.*
>
> Isadora Duncan

> **TIP**  We are speaking about tokens as the input to each time step of the network, but recurrent neural nets work identically with any sort of time series data. Your tokens can be anything, discrete or continuous: readings from a weather station, musical notes, characters in a sentence, you name it.

Here, you'll initially look at the output of the network at the last time step and compare that output to the label. That'll be (for now) the definition of the *error*. And the error is what your network will ultimately try to minimize. But you now have something that's a shift from what you had in the earlier chapters. For a given data sample, you break it into smaller pieces that are fed into the network sequentially. But instead of dealing with the output generated by any of these "subsamples" directly, you feed it back into the network.

You're only concerned with the final output, at least for now. You input each token from the sequence into your network and calculate the loss based on the output from the last time step (token) in the sequence. See figure 8.9.

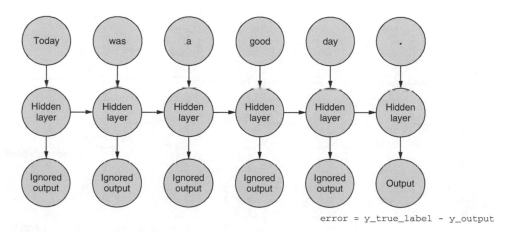

error = y_true_label - y_output

**Figure 8.9  Only last output matters here**

With an error for a given sample, you need to figure out which weights to update, and by how much. In chapter 5, you learned how to backpropagate the error through a standard network. And you know that the correction to each weight is dependent on how much that weight contributed to the error. You can input each token from your sample sequence and calculate the error based on the output of the network for the previous time step. This is where the idea of applying backpropagation over time seems to mess things up.

Here's one way to think about it: think of the process as time-based. You take a token for each time step, starting with the first token at $t=0$ and you enter it into the hidden neuron in front of you—the next column of figure 8.9. When you do that the network will unroll to reveal the next column in the network, ready for the next token in your sequence. The hidden neurons will unroll themselves, one at a time, like a music box or player piano. But after you get to the end, after all the pieces of the sample are fed in, there will be nothing left to unroll and you'll have the final output label for the target variable in hand. You can use that output to calculate the error and adjust your weights. You've just walked all the way through the computational graph of this *unrolled net.*

At this point, you can consider the whole of the input as static. You can see which neuron fed which input all the way through the graph. And once you know how each neuron fired, you can go back through the chain along the same path and *backpropagate* as you did with the standard feedforward network.

You'll use the chain-rule to backpropagate to the previous layer. But instead of going to the previous layer, you go to the layer in the *past,* as if each unrolled version of the network were different (see figure 8.10). The math is the same.

The error from the last step is backpropagated. For each "older" step, the gradient with respect to the more recent time step is taken. The changes are aggregated and applied to the single set of weights after all the individual tokenwise gradients have been calculated, all the way back to $t=0$ for that sample.

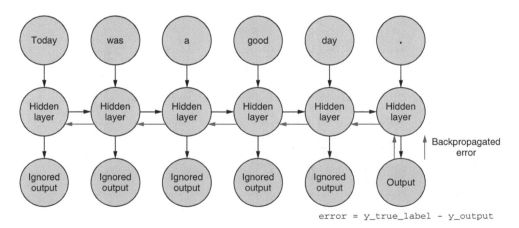

**Figure 8.10   Backpropagation through time**

- Break each data sample into tokens.
- Pass each token into a feedforward net.
- Pass the output of each time step to the input of the same layer alongside the input from the next time step.
- Collect the output of the last time step and compare it to the label.
- Backpropagate the error through the whole graph, all the way back to the first input at time step 0.

### 8.1.2 When do we update what?

You have converted your strange recurrent neural network into something that looks like a standard feedforward network, so updating the weights should be fairly straight-forward. There's one catch though. The tricky part of the update process is the weights you're updating aren't a different branch of a neural network. Each leg is the *same* network at different time steps. The weights are the *same* for each time step (see figure 8.10).

The simple solution is that the weight corrections are calculated at each time step but not immediately updated. In a feedforward network, all the weight updates would be calculated once all the gradients have been calculated for that input. Here the same holds, but you have to hold the updates until you go all the way back in time, to time step 0 for that particular input sample.

The gradient calculations need to be based on the values that the weights had when they contributed that much to the error. Now here's the mind-bending part: a weight at time step $t$ contributed something to the error when it was initially calculated. That *same* weight received a different input at time step $t+t$ and therefore contributed a different amount to the error then.

You can figure out the various changes to the weights (as if they were in a bubble) at each time step and then sum up the changes and apply the aggregated changes to each of the weights of the hidden layer as the last step of the learning phase.

> **TIP** In all of these examples, you've been passing in a single training example for the *forward pass*, and then backpropagating the error. As with any neural network, this forward pass through your network can happen after each training sample, or you can do it in batches. And it turns out that batching has benefits other than speed. But for now, think of these processes in terms of just single data samples, single sentences, or documents.

That seems like quite a bit of magic. As you backpropagate through time, a single weight may be adjusted in one direction at one time step $t$ (determined by how it reacted to the input at time step $t$) and then be adjusted in another direction at the time step for $t$-1 (because of how it reacted to the input at time step $t$-1), for a single data sample! But remember, neural networks in general work by minimizing a loss function, regardless of how complex the intermediate steps are. In aggregate, it will optimize across this complex function. As the weight update is applied once per data sample, the network will settle (assuming it converges) on the weight for that input to that neuron that best handles this task.

**BUT YOU DO CARE WHAT CAME OUT OF THE EARLIER STEPS**

Sometimes you may care about the entire sequence generated by each of the intermediate time steps as well. In chapter 9, you'll see examples where the output at a given time step *t* is as important as the output at the final time step. Figure 8.11 shows a path for capturing the error at any given time step and carrying that backward to adjust all the weights of the network during backpropagation.

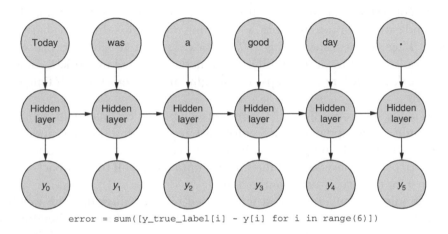

error = sum([y_true_label[i] - y[i] for i in range(6)])

**Figure 8.11   All outputs matter here**

This process is like the normal backpropagation through time for *n* time steps. In this case, you're now backpropagating the error from multiple sources at the same time. But as in the first example, the weight corrections are additive. You backpropagate from the last time step all the way to the first, summing up what you'll change for each weight. Then you do the same with the error calculated at the second-to-last time step and sum up all the changes all the way back to $t=0$. You repeat this process until you get all the way back down to time step 0 and then backpropagate it as if it were the only one in the world. You then apply the grand total of the updates to the corresponding hidden layer weights all at once.

In figure 8.12, you can see that the error is backpropagated from each output all the way back to $t=0$, and aggregated, before finally applying changes to the weights. This is the most important takeaway of this section. As with a standard feedforward network, you update the weights *only after* you have calculated the proposed change in the weights for the entire backpropagation step for that input (or set of inputs). In the case of a recurrent neural net, this backpropagation includes the updates all the way back to time $t=0$.

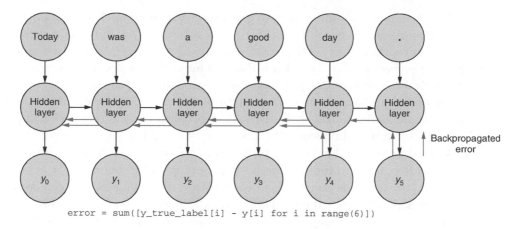

```
error = sum([y_true_label[i] - y[i] for i in range(6)])
```

**Figure 8.12   Multiple outputs and backpropagation through time**

Updating the weights earlier would "pollute" the gradient calculations in the back-propagations earlier in time. Remember the gradient is calculated with respect to a particular weight. If you were to update it early, say at time step *t*, when you go to calculate the gradient at time step *t*-1, the weight's value (remember it is the *same* weight position in the network) would've changed. Computing the gradient based on the input from time step *t*-1, the calculation would be off. You would be punishing (or rewarding) a weight for something it didn't do!

### 8.1.3   Recap

Where do you stand now? You've segmented each data sample into tokens. Then one by one you fed them into a feed forward network. With each token, you input not only the token itself, but also the output from the previous time step. At time step 0, you input the initial token alongside 0, which ends up being a 0 vector, because there's no previous output. You get your error from the difference between the output of the network from the final token and the expected label. You then backpropagate that error to the network weights, backward through time. You aggregate the proposed updates and apply them all at once to the network.

You now have a feedforward network that has some concept of time and a rudimentary tool for maintaining a memory of occurrences in that timeline.

### 8.1.4   There's always a catch

Although a recurrent neural net may have relatively fewer weights (parameters) to learn, you can see from figure 8.12 how a recurrent net can quickly get expensive to train, especially for sequences of any significant length, say 10 tokens. The more tokens you have, the further back in time each error must be backpropagated. For each step back in time, there are ever more derivatives to calculate. Recurrent neural nets aren't any less effective than others, but get ready to heat your house with your computer's exhaust fan.

New heat sources aside, you have given your neural network a rudimentary memory. But another, more troublesome problem arises, one you also see in regular feedforward networks as they get deeper. The *vanishing gradient problem* has a corollary: the *exploding gradient problem*. The idea is that as a network gets deeper (more layers), the error signal can grow or dissipate with each computation of the gradient.

This same problem applies to recurrent neural nets, because each time step back in time is the mathematical equivalent of backpropagating an error back to a previous layer in a feedforward network. But it's worse here! Although most feedforward networks tend to be a few layers deep for this very reason, you're dealing with sequences of tokens five, ten, or even hundreds long. Getting to the bottom of a network one hundred layers deep is going to be difficult. One mitigating factor keeps you in the game, though. Although the gradient may vanish or explode on the way to the last weight set, you're updating only one weight set. And that weight set is the same at every time step. Some information is going to get through, but it might not be the ideal memory state you thought you had created. But fear not, researchers are on the case, and you will have some answers to that challenge in the next chapter.

Enough doom and gloom; let's see some magic.

### 8.1.5   Recurrent neural net with Keras

You'll start with the same dataset and preprocessing that you used in the previous chapter. First, you load the dataset, grab the labels, and shuffle the examples. Then you tokenize it and vectorize it again using the Google Word2vec model. Next, you grab the labels. And finally you split it 80/20 into the training and test sets.

First you need to import all the modules you need for data processing and recurrent network training, as shown in the following listing.

**Listing 8.1   Import all the things**

```
>>> import glob
>>> import os
>>> from random import shuffle
>>> from nltk.tokenize import TreebankWordTokenizer
>>> from nlpia.loaders import get_data
>>> word_vectors = get_data('wv')
```

Then you can build your data preprocessor, which will whip your data into shape, as shown in the following listing.

**Listing 8.2   Data preprocessor**

```
>>> def pre_process_data(filepath):
...     """
...     Load pos and neg examples from separate dirs then shuffle them
...     together.
...     """
...     positive_path = os.path.join(filepath, 'pos')
...     negative_path = os.path.join(filepath, 'neg')
...     pos_label = 1
```

```
...        neg_label = 0
...        dataset = []
...        for filename in glob.glob(os.path.join(positive_path, '*.txt')):
...            with open(filename, 'r') as f:
...                dataset.append((pos_label, f.read()))
...        for filename in glob.glob(os.path.join(negative_path, '*.txt')):
...            with open(filename, 'r') as f:
...                dataset.append((neg_label, f.read()))
...        shuffle(dataset)
...        return dataset
```

As before, you can combine your tokenizer and vectorizer into a single function, as shown in the following listing.

**Listing 8.3   Data tokenizer + vectorizer**

```
>>> def tokenize_and_vectorize(dataset):
...        tokenizer = TreebankWordTokenizer()
...        vectorized_data = []
...        for sample in dataset:
...            tokens = tokenizer.tokenize(sample[1])
...            sample_vecs = []
...            for token in tokens:
...                try:
...                    sample_vecs.append(word_vectors[token])
...                except KeyError:
...                    pass                                        ◁─┐  No matching token in
...            vectorized_data.append(sample_vecs)                      the Google w2v vocab
...        return vectorized_data
```

And you need to extricate (unzip) the target variable into separate (but corresponding) samples, as shown in the following listing.

**Listing 8.4   Target unzipper**

```
>>> def collect_expected(dataset):
...        """ Peel off the target values from the dataset """
...        expected = []
...        for sample in dataset:
...            expected.append(sample[0])
...        return expected
```

Now that you have all the preprocessing functions assembled, you need to run them on your data, as shown in the following listing.

**Listing 8.5   Load and prepare your data**

```
>>> dataset = pre_process_data('./aclimdb/train')
>>> vectorized_data = tokenize_and_vectorize(dataset)        Divide the train and test
>>> expected = collect_expected(dataset)                     sets with an 80/20 split
>>> split_point = int(len(vectorized_data) * .8)    ◁─┐      (without any shuffling).
>>> x_train = vectorized_data[:split_point]
>>> y_train = expected[:split_point]
```

```
>>> x_test = vectorized_data[split_point:]
>>> y_test = expected[split_point:]
```

You'll use the same hyperparameters for this model: 400 tokens per example, batches of 32. Your word vectors are 300 elements long, and you'll let it run for 2 epochs. See the following listing.

**Listing 8.6    Initialize your network parameters**

```
>>> maxlen = 400
>>> batch_size = 32
>>> embedding_dims = 300
>>> epochs = 2
```

Next you'll need to pad and truncate the samples again. You won't usually need to pad or truncate with recurrent neural nets, because they can handle input sequences of variable length. But you'll see in the next few steps that this particular model requires your sequences to be of matching length. See the following listing.

**Listing 8.7    Load your test and training data**

```
>>> import numpy as np

>>> x_train = pad_trunc(x_train, maxlen)
>>> x_test = pad_trunc(x_test, maxlen)

>>> x_train = np.reshape(x_train, (len(x_train), maxlen, embedding_dims))
>>> y_train = np.array(y_train)
>>> x_test = np.reshape(x_test, (len(x_test), maxlen, embedding_dims))
>>> y_test = np.array(y_test)
```

Now that you have your data back, it's time to build a model. You'll start again with a standard `Sequential()` (layered) Keras model, as shown in the following listing.

**Listing 8.8    Initialize an empty Keras network**

```
>>> from keras.models import Sequential
>>> from keras.layers import Dense, Dropout, Flatten, SimpleRNN
>>> num_neurons = 50
>>> model = Sequential()
```

And then, as before, the Keras magic handles the complexity of assembling a neural net: you just need to add the recurrent layer you want to your network, as shown in the following listing.

**Listing 8.9    Add a recurrent layer**

```
>>> model.add(SimpleRNN(
...     num_neurons, return_sequences=True,
...     input_shape=(maxlen, embedding_dims)))
```

Now the infrastructure is set up to take each input and pass it into a simple recurrent neural net (the not-simple version is in the next chapter), and for each token, gather the output into a vector. Because your sequences are 400 tokens long and you're using 50 hidden neurons, your output from this layer will be a vector 400 elements long. Each of those elements is a vector 50 elements long, with one output for each of the neurons.

Notice here the keyword argument `return_sequences`. It's going to tell the network to return the network value at each time step, hence the 400 vectors, each 50 long. If `return_sequences` was set to `False` (the Keras default behavior), only a single 50-dimensional vector would be returned.

The choice of 50 neurons was arbitrary for this example, mostly to reduce computation time. Do experiment with this number to see how it affects computation time and accuracy of the model.

> **TIP**   A good rule of thumb is to try to make your model no more complex than the data you're training on. Easier said than done, but that idea gives you a rationale for adjusting your parameters as you experiment with your dataset. A more complex model will *overfit* training data and not generalize well; a model that is too simple will *underfit* the data and also not have much interesting to say about novel data. You'll see this discussion referred to as the *bias versus variance* trade-off. A model that's overfit to the data is said to have high variance and low bias. And an underfit model is the opposite: low variance and high bias; it gets everything wrong in a consistent way.

Note that you truncated and padded the data again. You did so to provide a comparison with the CNN example from the last chapter. But when using a recurrent neural net, truncating and padding isn't usually necessary. You can provide training data of varying lengths and unroll the net until you hit the end of the input. Keras will handle this automatically. The catch is that your output of the recurrent layer will vary from time step to time step with the input. A four-token input will output a sequence four elements long. A 100-token sequence will produce a sequence of 100 elements. If you need to pass this into another layer, one that expects a uniform input, it won't work. But there are cases where that's acceptable, and even preferred. But back to your classifier; see the following listing.

---

**Listing 8.10   Add a dropout layer**

```
>>> model.add(Dropout(.2))

>>> model.add(Flatten())
>>> model.add(Dense(1, activation='sigmoid'))
```

You requested that the simple RNN return full sequences, but to prevent overfitting you add a Dropout layer to zero out 20% of those inputs, randomly chosen on each input example. And then finally you add a classifier. In this case, you have one class: "Yes - Positive Sentiment - 1" or "No - Negative Sentiment - 0," so you chose a layer with one neuron (`Dense(1)`) and a sigmoid activation function. But a Dense layer expects a "flat" vector of *n* elements (each element a float) as input. And the data coming out of the `SimpleRNN` is a tensor 400 elements long, and each of those are 50 elements long. But a feedforward network doesn't care about order of elements as long as you're consistent with the order. You use the convenience layer, `Flatten()`, that Keras provides to flatten the input from a 400 x 50 tensor to a vector 20,000 elements long. And that's what you pass into the final layer that'll make the classification. In reality, the `Flatten` layer is a mapping. That means the error is backpropagated from the last layer back to the appropriate output in the RNN layer and each of those back-propagated errors are then backpropagated through time from the appropriate point in the output, as discussed earlier.

Passing the "thought vector" produced by the recurrent neural network layer into a feedforward network no longer keeps the order of the input you tried so hard to incorporate. But the important takeaway is to notice that the "learning" related to sequence of tokens happens in the RNN layer itself; the aggregation of errors via back-propagation through time is encoding that relationship in the network and express-ing it in the "thought vector" itself. Your decision based on the thought vector, via the classifier, is providing feedback to the "quality" of that thought vector with respect to your specific classification problem. You can "judge" your thought vector and work with the RNN itself in other ways, but more on that in the next chapter. (Can you sense our excitement for the next chapter?) Hang in there; all of this is critical to understanding the next part.

## 8.2   *Putting things together*

You compile your model as you did with the convolutional neural net in the last chapter.

Keras also comes with several tools, such as `model.summary()`, for inspection of the internals of your model. As your models grow more and more complicated, keep-ing track of how things inside your model change when you adjust the hyperparame-ters can be taxing unless you use `model.summary()` regularly. If you record that summary, along with the validation test results, in a hyperparameter tuning log, it really gets fun. You might even be able to automate much of it and turn over some of the tedium of record keeping to the machine.[2] See the following listing.

---

> **Listing 8.11   Compile your recurrent network**

```
>>> model.compile('rmsprop', 'binary_crossentropy',  metrics=['accuracy'])
Using TensorFlow backend.
>>> model.summary()
```

---

[2]  If you do decide to automate your hyperparameter selection, don't stick to grid search for too long; random search is much more efficient (http://hyperopt.github.io/hyperopt/). And if you really want to be profes-sional about it, you'll want to try Bayesean optimization. Your hyperparameter optimizer only gets one shot at it every few hours, so you can't afford to use just any old hyperparameter tuning model (heaven forbid a recurrent network!).

```
Layer (type)                   Output Shape              Param #
=================================================================
simple_rnn_1 (SimpleRNN)       (None, 400, 50)           17550
_____
dropout_1 (Dropout)            (None, 400, 50)           0
_____
flatten_1 (Flatten)            (None, 20000)             0
_____
dense_1 (Dense)                (None, 1)                 20001
=================================================================
Total params: 37,551.0
Trainable params: 37,551.0
Non-trainable params: 0.0
_____
None
```

Pause and look at the number of parameters you're working with. This recurrent neural network is relatively small, but note that you're learning 37,551 parameters! That's a lot of weights to update based on 20,000 training samples (not to be confused with the 20,000 elements in the last layer—that is just coincidence). Let's look at those numbers and see specifically where they come from.

In the `SimpleRNN` layer, you requested 50 neurons. Each of those neurons will receive input (and apply a weight to) each input sample. In an RNN, the input at each time step is one token. Your tokens are represented by word vectors in this case, each 300 elements long (300-dimensional). Each neuron will need 300 weights:

$$50 * 300 = 15,000$$

Each neuron also has the *bias* term, which always has an input value of 1 (that's what makes it a bias) but has a trainable weight:

$$15,000 + 50 \text{ (bias weights)} = 15,050$$

15,050 weights in the first time step of the first layer. Now each of those 50 neurons will feed its output into the network's next time step. Each neuron accepts the full input vector as well as the full output vector. In the first time step, the feedback from the output doesn't exist yet. It's initiated as a vector of zeros, its length the same as the length of the output.

Each neuron in the hidden layer now has weights for each token embedding dimension: that's 300 weights. It also has 1 bias for each neuron. And you have the 50 weights for the output results in the previous time step (or zeros for the first $t=0$ time step). These 50 weights are the *key feedback step in a recurrent neural network*. That gives us

$$300 + 1 + 50 = 351$$

351 times 50 neurons gives:

$$351 * 50 = 17,550$$

17,550 parameters to train. You're *unrolling* this net 400 time steps (probably too much given the problems associated with vanishing gradients, but even so, this network turns out to still be effective). But those 17,550 parameters are the same in each of the unrollings, and they remain the same until all the backpropagations have been calculated. The updates to the weights occur at once at the end of the sequence forward propagation and subsequent backpropagation. Although you're adding complexity to the backpropagation algorithm, you're saved by the fact you're not training a net with a little over 7 million parameters (17,550 * 400), which is what it would look like if the unrollings each had their own weight sets.

The final layer in the summary is reporting 20,001 parameters to train, which is relatively straightforward. After the `Flatten()` layer, the input is a 20,000-dimensional vector plus the one bias input. Because you only have one neuron in the output layer, the total number of parameters is

(20,000 input elements + 1 bias unit) * 1 neuron = 20,001 parameters

Those numbers can be a little misleading in computational time because there are so many extra steps to backpropagation through time (compared to convolutional neural networks or standard feedforward networks). Computation time shouldn't be a deal killer. Recurrent nets' special talent at *memory* is the start of a bigger world in NLP or any other sequence data, as you'll see in the next chapter. But back to your classifier for now.

## 8.3    *Let's get to learning our past selves*

OK, now it's time to actually train that recurrent network that we so carefully assembled in the previous section. As with your other Keras models, you need to give the `.fit()` method your data and tell it how long you want to run training (epochs), as shown in the following listing.

---

**Listing 8.12   Train and save your model**

```
>>> model.fit(x_train, y_train,
...           batch_size=batch_size,
...           epochs=epochs,
...           validation_data=(x_test, y_test))
Train on 20000 samples, validate on 5000 samples
Epoch 1/2
20000/20000 [==============================] - 215s - loss: 0.5723 -
acc: 0.7138 - val_loss: 0.5011 - val_acc: 0.7676
Epoch 2/2
20000/20000 [==============================] - 183s - loss: 0.4196 -
acc: 0.8144 - val_loss: 0.4763 - val_acc: 0.7820

>>> model_structure = model.to_json()
>>> with open("simplernn_model1.json", "w") as json_file:
...     json_file.write(model_structure)
>>> model.save_weights("simplernn_weights1.h5")
Model saved.
```

Not horrible, but also not something you'll write home about. Where can you look to improve...

## 8.4   *Hyperparameters*

All the models listed in the book can be tuned toward your data and samples in various ways; they all have their benefits and associated trade offs. Finding the perfect set of hyperparameters is usually an intractable problem. But human intuition and experience can at least provide approaches to the problem. Let's look at the last example. What are some of the choices you made? See the following listing.

**Listing 8.13   Model parameters**

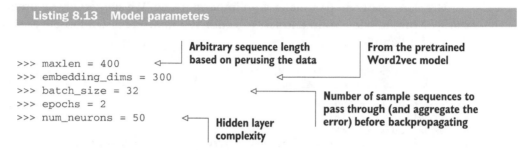

```
>>> maxlen = 400
>>> embedding_dims = 300
>>> batch_size = 32
>>> epochs = 2
>>> num_neurons = 50
```

Arbitrary sequence length based on perusing the data

From the pretrained Word2vec model

Number of sample sequences to pass through (and aggregate the error) before backpropagating

Hidden layer complexity

`maxlen` is most likely the biggest question mark in the bunch. The training set varies widely in sample length. When you force samples less than 100 tokens long up to 400 and conversely chop down 1,000 token samples to 400, you introduce an enormous amount of noise. Changing this number impacts training time more than any other parameter in this model; the length of the individual samples dictates how many and how far back in time the error must backpropagate. It isn't strictly necessary with recurrent neural networks. You can simply unroll the network as far or as little as you need to for the sample. It's necessary in your example because you're passing the output, itself a sequence, into a feedforward layer; and feedforward layers require uniformly sized input.

The `embedding_dims` value was dictated by the Word2vec model you chose, but this could easily be anything that adequately represents the dataset. Even something as simple as a one-hot encoding of the 50 most commons tokens in the corpus may be enough to get accurate predictions.

As with any net, increasing `batch_size` speeds training because it reduces the number of times backpropagation (the computationally expensive part) needs to happen. The tradeoff is that larger batches increase the chance of settling in a local minimum.

The `epochs` parameter is easy to test and tune, by simply running the training process again. But that requires a lot of patience if you have to start from scratch with each new `epochs` parameter you want to try. Keras models can restart training and pick up where you left off, as long as you saved the model as you "left off." To restart your training on a previously trained model, reload it and your dataset, and call `model.fit()` on your data. Keras won't reinitialize the weights, but instead continue the training as if you'd never stopped it.

The other alternative for tuning the `epochs` parameter is to add a Keras *callback* called `EarlyStopping`. By providing this method to the model, the model continues to train up until the number of epochs you requested, *unless* a metric passed to Early-Stopping crosses some threshold that you trigger within your callback. A common early stopping metric is the improvement in validation accuracy for several consecutive epochs. If you model isn't getting any better, that usually means it's time to "cut bait."

This metric allows you to set it and forget it; the model stops training when it hits your metric. And you don't have to worry about investing lots of time only to find out later that your model started overfitting your training data 42 epochs ago.

The num_neurons parameter is an important one. We suggested you use 50 arbitrarily. Now let's do a train and test run with 100 neurons instead of 50, as shown in listings 8.14 and 8.15.

#### Listing 8.14  Build a larger network

```
>>> num_neurons = 100
>>> model = Sequential()
>>> model.add(SimpleRNN(
...     num_neurons, return_sequences=True, input_shape=(maxlen,\
...     embedding_dims)))
>>> model.add(Dropout(.2))
>>> model.add(Flatten())
>>> model.add(Dense(1, activation='sigmoid'))
>>> model.compile('rmsprop', 'binary_crossentropy',  metrics=['accuracy'])
Using TensorFlow backend.
>>> model.summary()
```

| Layer (type) | Output Shape | Param # |
|---|---|---|
| simple_rnn_1 (SimpleRNN) | (None, 400, 100) | 40100 |
| dropout_1 (Dropout) | (None, 400, 100) | 0 |
| flatten_1 (Flatten) | (None, 40000) | 0 |
| dense_1 (Dense) | (None, 1) | 40001 |

```
Total params: 80,101.0
Trainable params: 80,101.0
Non-trainable params: 0.0
```

#### Listing 8.15  Train your larger network

```
>>> model.fit(x_train, y_train,
...           batch_size=batch_size,
...           epochs=epochs,
...           validation_data=(x_test, y_test))
Train on 20000 samples, validate on 5000 samples
Epoch 1/2
20000/20000 [==============================] - 287s - loss: 0.9063 -
acc: 0.6529 - val_loss: 0.5445 - val_acc: 0.7486
Epoch 2/2
20000/20000 [==============================] - 240s - loss: 0.4760 -
```

```
acc: 0.7951 - val_loss: 0.5165 - val_acc: 0.7824
>>> model_structure = model.to_json()
>>> with open("simplernn_model2.json", "w") as json_file:
...     json_file.write(model_structure)
>>> model.save_weights("simplernn_weights2.h5")
Model saved.
```

The validation accuracy of 78.24% is only 0.04% better after we doubled the complexity of our model in one of the layers. This negligible improvement should lead you to think the model (for this network layer) is too complex for the data. This layer of the network may be too wide.

Here's what happens with num_neurons set to 25:

```
20000/20000 [==============================] - 240s - loss: 0.5394 -
acc: 0.8084 - val_loss: 0.4490 - val_acc: 0.7970
```

That's interesting. Our model got a little better when we slimmed it down a bit in the middle. A little better (1.5%), but not significantly. These kinds of tests can take quite a while to develop an intuition for. You may find it especially difficult as the training time increases and prevents you from enjoying the instant feedback and gratification that you get from other coding tasks. And sometimes changing one parameter at a time can mask benefits you would get from adjusting two at a time. But if you went down that rabbit hole of combinatorics, your task complexity goes through the roof.

> **TIP** Experiment often, and always document how the model responds to your manipulations. This kind of hands-on work provides the quickest path toward an intuition for model building.

If you feel the model is overfitting the training data but you can't find a way to make your model simpler, you can always try increasing the Dropout(percentage). This is a sledgehammer (actually a shotgun) that can mitigate the risk of overfitting while allowing your model to have as much complexity as it needs to match the data. If you set the dropout percentage much above 50%, the model starts to have a difficult time learning. Your learning will slow and validation error will bounce around a lot. But 20% to 50% is a pretty safe range for a lot of NLP problems for recurrent networks.

## 8.5 *Predicting*

Now that you have a trained model, such as it is, you can predict just as you did with the CNN in the last chapter, as shown in the following listing.

---

**Listing 8.16 Crummy weather sentiment**

```
>>> sample_1 = "I hate that the dismal weather had me down for so long, when
⇒ will it break! Ugh, when does happiness return? The sun is blinding and
⇒ the puffy clouds are too thin. I can't wait for the weekend."

>>> from keras.models import model_from_json
>>> with open("simplernn_model1.json", "r") as json_file:
```

```
...      json_string = json_file.read()
>>> model = model_from_json(json_string)
>>> model.load_weights('simplernn_weights1.h5')

>>> vec_list = tokenize_and_vectorize([(1, sample_1)])
>>> test_vec_list = pad_trunc(vec_list, maxlen)
>>> test_vec = np.reshape(test_vec_list, (len(test_vec_list), maxlen,\
...      embedding_dims))

>>> model.predict_classes(test_vec)
array([[0]], dtype=int32)
```

**Tokenize returns a list of
the data (length I here).**

**You pass a dummy value in the first element of the
tuple because your helper expects it from the way
it processed the initial data. That value won't ever
see the network, so it can be anything.**

Negative again.

You have another tool to add to the pipeline in classifying your possible responses, and the incoming questions or searches that a user may enter. But why choose a recurrent neural network? The short answer is: don't. Well, not a SimpleRNN as you've implemented here. They're relatively expensive to train and pass new samples through compared to a feedforward net or a convolutional neural net. At least in this example, the results aren't appreciably better, or even better at all.

Why bother with an RNN at all? Well, the concept of remembering bits of input that have already occurred is absolutely crucial in NLP. The problems of vanishing gradients are usually too much for a recurrent neural net to overcome, especially in an example with so many time steps such as ours. The next chapter begins to examine alternative ways of *remembering*, ways that turn out to be, as Andrej Karpathy puts it, "unreasonably effective."[3]

The following sections cover a few things about recurrent neural networks that weren't mentioned in the example but are important nonetheless.

### 8.5.1  *Statefulness*

Sometimes you want to remember information from one input *sample* to the next, not just one-time step (token) to the next within a single sample. What happens to that information at the end of the training step? Other than what is encoded in the weights via backpropagation, the final output has no effect, and the next input will start fresh. Keras provides a keyword argument in the base RNN layer (therefore in the SimpleRNN as well) called stateful. It defaults to False. If you flip this to True when adding the SimpleRNN layer to your model, the last sample's last output passes into itself at the next time step along with the first token input, just as it would in the middle of the sample.

Setting stateful to True can be a good idea when you want to model a large document that has been split into paragraphs or sentences for processing. And you might

---

[3]  Karpathy, Andrej, The Unreasonable Effectiveness of Recurrent Neural Networks. http://karpathy.github.io/2015/05/21/rnn-effectiveness/.

even use it to model the meaning of an entire corpus of related documents. But you wouldn't want to train a `stateful` RNN on unrelated documents or passages without resetting the state of the model between samples. Likewise, if you usually shuffle your samples of text, the last few tokens of one sample have nothing to do with the first tokens of the next sample. So for shuffled text you'll want to make sure your `stateful` flag is set to `False`, because the order of the samples doesn't help the model find a good fit.

If the fit method is passed a `batch_size` parameter, the statefulness of the model holds each sample's output in the batch. And then for the first sample in the next batch it passes the output of the first sample in the previous batch. 2nd to 2nd. *i*-th to *i*-th. If you're trying to model a larger single corpus on smaller bits of the whole, paying attention to the dataset order becomes important.

### 8.5.2 Two-way street

So far we've discussed relationships between words and what has come before. But can't a case be made for flipping those word dependencies?

*They wanted to pet the dog whose fur was brown.*

As you get to the token "fur," you have encountered "dog" already and know something about it. But the sentence also contains the information that the dog has fur, and that the dog's fur is brown. And that information is relevant to the previous action of petting and the fact that "they" wanted to do the petting. Perhaps "they" only like to pet soft, furry brown things and don't like petting prickly green things like cacti.

Humans read the sentence in one direction but are capable of flitting back to earlier parts of the text in their brain as new information is revealed. Humans can deal with information that isn't presented in the best possible order. It would be nice if you could allow your model to flit back across the input as well. That is where *bidirectional* recurrent neural nets come in. Keras added a layer wrapper that will automatically flip around the necessary inputs and outputs to automatically assemble a bi-directional RNN for us. See the following listing.

**Listing 8.17  Build a `Bidirectional` recurrent network**

```
>>> from keras.models import Sequential
>>> from keras.layers import SimpleRNN
>>> from keras.layers.wrappers import Bidirectional

>>> num_neurons = 10
>>> maxlen = 100
>>> embedding_dims = 300

>>> model = Sequential()
>>> model.add(Bidirectional(SimpleRNN(
...     num_neurons, return_sequences=True),\
...     input_shape=(maxlen, embedding_dims)))
```

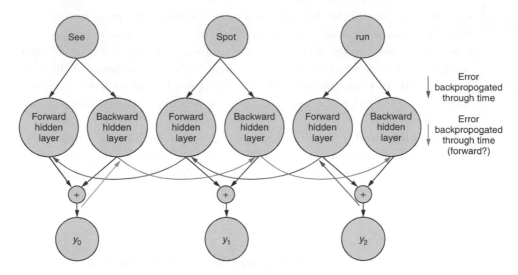

**Figure 8.13  Bidirectional recurrent neural net**

The basic idea is you arrange two RNNs right next to each other, passing the input into one as normal and the same input *backward* into the other net (see figure 8.13). The output of those two are then concatenated at each time step to the related (same input token) time step in the other network. You take the output of the final time step in the input and concatenate it with the output generated by the same input token at the first time step of the backward net.

> **TIP**  Keras also has a `go_backwards` keyword argument. If this is set to `True`, Keras automatically flips the input sequences and inputs them into the network in reverse order. This is the second half of a bidirectional layer.

> If you're not using a bidirectional wrapper, this keyword can be useful, because a recurrent neural network (due to the vanishing gradients problem) is more receptive to data at the end of the sample than at the beginning. If you have padded your samples with `<PAD>` tokens at the end, all the good, juicy stuff is buried deep in the input loop. `go_backwards` can be a quick way around this problem.

With these tools you're well on your way to not just predicting and classifying text, but actually modeling language itself and how it's used. And with that deeper algorithmic understanding, instead of just parroting text your model has seen before, you can generate completely new statements!

### 8.5.3    *What is this thing?*

Ahead of the Dense layer you have a vector that is of shape (number of neurons x 1) coming out of the last time step of the Recurrent layer for a given input sequence. This vector is the parallel to the *thought vector* you got out of the convolutional neural network in the previous chapter. It's an encoding of the sequence of tokens. Granted it's only going to be able to encode the thought of the sequences in relation to the labels the network is trained on. But in terms of NLP, it's an amazing next step toward encoding higher order concepts into a vector computationally.

## *Summary*

- In natural language sequences (words or characters), what came before is important to your model's understanding of the sequence.
- Splitting a natural language statement along the dimension of time (tokens) can help your machine deepen its understanding of natural language.
- You can backpropagate errors in time (tokens), as well as in the layers of a deep learning network.
- Because RNNs are particularly deep neural nets, RNN gradients are particularly temperamental, and they may disappear or explode.
- Efficiently modeling natural language character sequences wasn't possible until recurrent neural nets were applied to the task.
- Weights in an RNN are adjusted in aggregate across time for a given sample.
- You can use different methods to examine the output of recurrent neural nets.
- You can model the natural language sequence in a document by passing the sequence of tokens through an RNN backward and forward simultaneously.

# Improving retention with long short-term memory networks

9

**This chapter covers**

- Adding deeper memory to recurrent neural nets
- Gating information inside neural nets
- Classifying and generating text
- Modeling language patterns

For all the benefits recurrent neural nets provide for modeling relationships, and therefore *possibly* causal relationships, in sequence data they suffer from one main deficiency: a token's *effect* is almost completely lost by the time two tokens have passed.[1] Any effect the first node has on the third node (two time steps after the first time step) will be thoroughly stepped on by new data introduced in the intervening time step. This is important to the basic structure of the net, but it prevents the common case in human language that the tokens may be deeply interrelated even when they're far apart in a sentence.

---

[1] Christopher Olah explains why: https://colah.github.io/posts/2015-08-Understanding-LSTMs.

Take this example:

*The young woman went to the movies with her friends.*

The subject "woman" immediately precedes its main verb "went."[2] You learned in the previous chapters that both convolutional and recurrent nets would have no trouble learning from that relationship.

But in a similar sentence:

*The young woman, having found a free ticket on the ground, went to the movies.*

The noun and verb are no longer one time step apart in the sequence. A recurrent neural net is going to have difficulty picking up on the relationship between the subject "woman" and main verb "went" in this new, longer sentence. For this new sentence, a recurrent network would overemphasize the tie between the verb "having" and your subject "woman." And your network would underemphasize the connection to "went," the main verb of the predicate. You've lost the connection between the subject and verb of the sentence. The weights in a recurrent network decay too quickly in time as you roll through each sentence.

Your challenge is to build a network that can pick up on the same core *thought* in both sentences. What you need is a way to remember the past across the entire input sequence. A *long short-term memory* (LSTM) is just what you need.[3]

Modern versions of a long short-term memory network typically use a special neural network unit called a *gated recurrent unit* (GRU). A gated recurrent unit can maintain both long- and short-term memory efficiently, enabling an LSTM to process a long sentence or document more accurately.[4] In fact, LSTMs work so well they have replaced recurrent neural networks in almost all applications involving time series, discrete sequences, and NLP.[5]

## 9.1 LSTM

LSTMs introduce the concept of a *state* for each layer in the recurrent network. The state acts as its *memory*. You can think of it as adding attributes to a class in object-oriented programming. The memory state's attributes are updated with each training example.

---

[2] "Went" is the predicate (main verb) in this sentence. Find additional English grammar terminology at https://www.butte.edu/departments/cas/tipsheets/grammar/sentence_structure.html.

[3] One of the first papers on LSTMs was by Hochreiter and Schmidhuber in 1997, "Long Short-Term Memory" (http://citeseerx.ist.psu.edu/viewdoc/download?doi=10.1.1.676.4320&rep=rep1&type=pdf).

[4] "Learning Phrase Representations using RNN Encoder–Decoder for Statistical Machine Translation," by Kyunghyun Cho et al, 2014: https://arxiv.org/pdf/1406.1078.pdf.

[5] Christopher Olah's blog post explains why this is: https://colah.github.io/posts/2015-08-Understanding-LSTMs.

In LSTMs, the rules that govern the information stored in the state (memory) are trained neural nets themselves—therein lies the magic. They can be trained to learn what to remember, while at the same time the rest of the recurrent net learns to predict the target label! With the introduction of a memory and state, you can begin to learn dependencies that stretch not just one or two tokens away, but across the entirety of each data sample. With those long-term dependencies in hand, you can start to see beyond the words themselves and into something deeper about language.

With LSTMs, patterns that humans take for granted and process on a subconscious level begin to be available to your model. And with those patterns, you can not only more accurately predict sample classifications, but you can start to generate novel text using those patterns. The state of the art in this field is still far from perfect, but the results you'll see, even in your toy examples, are striking.

So how does this thing work (see figure 9.1)?

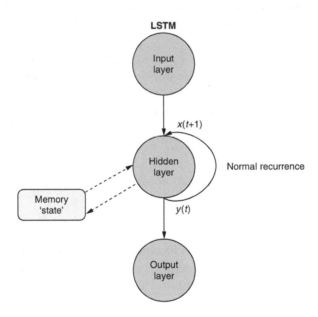

**Figure 9.1    LSTM network and its memory**

The memory state is affected by the input and also affects the layer output just as in a normal recurrent net. But that memory state persists across all the time steps of the time series (your sentence or document). So each input can have an effect on the memory state as well as an effect on the hidden layer output. The magic of the memory state is that it *learns* what to remember at the same time that it learns to reproduce the output, using standard backpropagation! So what does this look like?

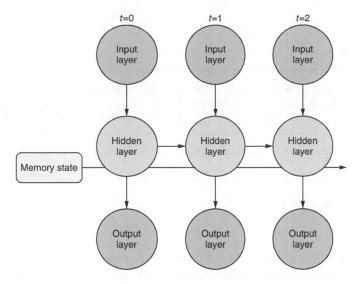

**Figure 9.2    Unrolled LSTM network and its memory**

First, let's unroll a standard recurrent neural net and add your memory unit. Figure 9.2 looks similar to a normal recurrent neural net. However, in addition to the activation output feeding into the next time-step version of the layer, you add a memory state that also passes through time steps of the network. At each time-step iteration, the hidden recurrent unit has access to the memory unit. The addition of this memory unit, and the mechanisms that interact with it, make this quite a bit different from a traditional neural network layer. However, you may like to know that it's possible to design a set of traditional recurrent neural network layers (a computational graph) that accomplishes all the computations that exist within an LSTM layer. An LSTM layer is just a highly specialized recurrent neural network.

> **TIP**    In much of the literature,[6] the "Memory State" block shown in figure 9.2 is referred to as an LSTM *cell* rather than an LSTM *neuron*, because it contains two additional neurons or gates just like a silicon computer memory *cell*.[7] When an LSTM memory *cell* is combined with a sigmoid activation function to output a value to the next LSTM *cell*, this structure, containing multiple interacting elements, is referred to as an LSTM *unit*. Multiple LSTM *units* are combined to form an LSTM *layer*. The horizontal line running across the unrolled recurrent neuron in figure 9.2 is the signal holding the memory or state. It becomes a vector with a dimension for each LSTM *cell* as the sequence of tokens is passed into a multi-unit LSTM *layer*.

---

[6]   A good recent example of LSTM terminology usage is Alex Graves' 2012 Thesis "Supervised Sequence Labelling with Recurrent Neural Networks": https://mediatum.ub.tum.de/doc/673554/file.pdf.

[7]   See the Wikipedia article "Memory cell" (https://en.wikipedia.org/wiki/Memory_cell_(computing)).

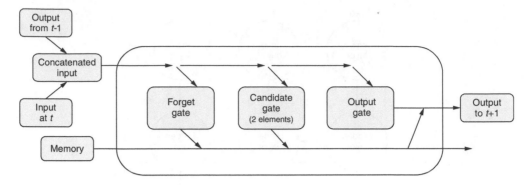

**Figure 9.3  LSTM layer at time step *t***

So let's take a closer look at one of these cells. Instead of being a series of weights on the input and an activation function on those weights, each cell is now somewhat more complicated. As before, the input to the layer (or cell) is a combination of the input sample and output from the previous time step. As information flows into the cell instead of a vector of weights, it's now greeted by three gates: a forget gate, an input/candidate gate, and an output gate (see figure 9.3).

Each of these gates is a feed forward network layer composed of a series of weights that the network will learn, plus an activation function. Technically one of the gates is composed of two feed forward paths, so there will be four sets of weights to learn in this layer. The weights and activations will aim to *allow* information to flow through the cell in different amounts, all the way through to the cell's state (or memory).

Before getting too deep in the weeds, let's look at this in Python, using the example from the previous chapter with the SimpleRNN layer swapped out for an LSTM. You can use the same vectorized, padded/truncated processed data from the last chapter, x_train, y_train, x_test, and y_test. See the following listing.

**Listing 9.1  LSTM layer in Keras**

```
>>> maxlen = 400
>>> batch_size = 32
>>> embedding_dims = 300
>>> epochs = 2
>>> from keras.models import Sequential
>>> from keras.layers import Dense, Dropout, Flatten, LSTM
>>> num_neurons = 50
>>> model = Sequential()
>>> model.add(LSTM(num_neurons, return_sequences=True,
...                 input_shape=(maxlen, embedding_dims)))
>>> model.add(Dropout(.2))
>>> model.add(Flatten())
>>> model.add(Dense(1, activation='sigmoid'))
>>> model.compile('rmsprop', 'binary_crossentropy',  metrics=['accuracy'])
>>> print(model.summary())
```

```
Layer (type)                 Output Shape              Param #
=================================================================
lstm_1 (LSTM)                (None, 400, 50)            70200
_____
dropout_1 (Dropout)          (None, 400, 50)            0
_____
flatten_1 (Flatten)          (None, 20000)              0
_____
dense_1 (Dense)              (None, 1)                  20001
=================================================================
Total params: 90,201.0
Trainable params: 90,201.0
Non-trainable params: 0.0
```

One import and one line of Keras code changed. But a great deal more is going on under the surface. From the summary, you can see you have many more parameters to train than you did in the SimpleRNN from last chapter for the same number of neurons (50). Recall the simple RNN had the following weights:

- 300 (one for each element of the input vector)
- 1 (one for the bias term)
- 50 (one for each neuron's output from the previous time step)

For a total of 351 per neuron.

$351 * 50 = 17{,}550$ for the layer

The cells have three gates (a total of four neurons):

$17{,}550 * 4 = 70{,}200$

But what is the memory? The memory is going to be represented by a vector that is the same number of elements as neurons in the cell. Your example has a relatively simple 50 neurons, so the memory unit will be a vector of floats that is 50 elements long.

Now what are these gates? Let's follow the first sample on its journey through the net and get an idea (see figure 9.4).

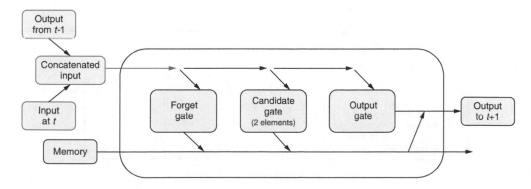

**Figure 9.4  LSTM layer inputs**

The "journey" through the cell isn't a single road; it has branches, and you'll follow each for a while then back up, progress, branch, and finally come back together for the grand finale of the cell's output.

You take the first token from the first sample and pass its 300-element vector representation into the first LSTM cell. On the way into the cell, the vector representation of the data is concatenated with the vector output from the previous time step (which is a 0 vector in the first time step). In this example, you'll have a vector that is 300 + 50 elements long. Sometimes you'll see a 1 appended to the vector—this corresponds to the bias term. Because the bias term always multiplies its associated weight by a value of one before passing to the activation function, that input is occasionally omitted from the input vector representation, to keep the diagrams more digestible.

At the first fork in the road, you hand off a copy of the combined input vector to the ominous sounding *forget gate* (see figure 9.5). The forget gate's goal is to learn, based on a given input, how much of the cell's memory you want to erase. Whoa, wait a minute. You just got this memory thing plugged in and the first thing you want to do is start erasing things? Sheesh.

The idea behind wanting to forget is as important as wanting to remember. As a human reader, when you pick up certain bits of information from text—say whether the noun is singular or plural—you want to retain that information so that later in the sentence you can recognize the right verb conjugation or adjective form to match with it. In romance languages, you'd have to recognize a noun's gender, too, and use that later in a sentence as well. But an input sequence can easily switch from one noun to another, because an input sequence can be composed of multiple phrases, sentences,

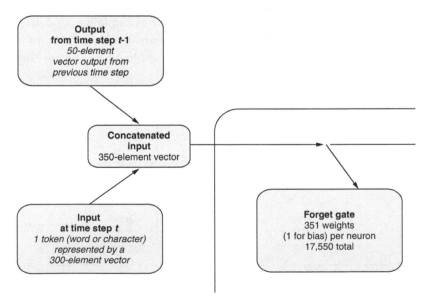

**Figure 9.5   First stop—the forget gate**

or even documents. As new thoughts are expressed in later statements, the fact that the noun is plural may not be at all relevant to later unrelated text.

> *A thinker sees his own actions as experiments and questions—as attempts to find out something. Success and failure are for him answers above all.*

> Friedrich Nietzsche

In this quote, the verb "see" is conjugated to fit with the noun "thinker." The next active verb you come across is "to be" in the second sentence. At that point "be" is conjugated into "are" to agree with "Success and failure." If you were to conjugate it to match the first noun you came across, "thinker," you would use the wrong verb form, "is" instead. So an LSTM must model not only long-term dependencies within a sequence, but just as crucially, also forget long-term dependencies as new ones arise. This is what forgetting gates are for, making room for the *relevant* memories in your memory cells.

The network isn't working with these kinds of explicit representations. Your network is trying to find a set of weights to multiply by the inputs from the sequence of tokens so that the memory cell and the output are both updated in a way that minimizes the error. It's amazing that they work at all. And they work very well indeed. But enough marveling: back to forgetting.

The forget gate itself (shown in figure 9.6) is just a feed forward network. It consists of $n$ neurons each with m + n + 1 weights. So your example forget gate has 50 neurons each with 351 (300 + 50 + 1) weights. The activation function for a forget gate is the sigmoid function, because you want the output for each neuron in the gate to be between 0 and 1.

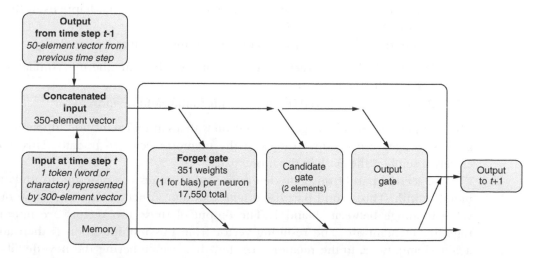

**Figure 9.6  Forget gate**

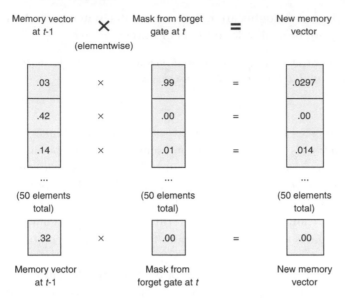

**Figure 9.7   Forget gate application**

The output vector of the forget gate is then a mask of sorts, albeit a porous one, that erases elements of the memory vector. As the forget gate outputs values closer to 1, more of the memory's knowledge in the associated element is retained for that time step; the closer it is to 0 the more of that memory value is erased (see figure 9.7).

Actively forgetting things, check. You better learn how to remember something new, or this is going to go south pretty quickly. Just like in the forget gate, you use a small network to learn how much to augment the memory based on two things: the input so far and the output from the last time step. This is what happens in the next gate you branch into: the *candidate gate*.

The candidate gate has two separate neurons inside it that do two things:

1  Decide which input vector elements are worth remembering (similar to the mask in the forget gate)
2  Route the remembered input elements to the right memory "slot"

The first part of a candidate gate is a neuron with a sigmoid activation function whose goal is to learn which input values of the memory vector to update. This neuron closely resembles the mask in the forget gate.

The second part of this gate determines what values you're going to update the memory with. This second part has a *tanh* activation function that forces the output value to range between -1 and 1. The output of these two vectors are multiplied together elementwise. The resulting vector from this multiplication is then added, again elementwise, to the memory register, thus remembering the new details (see figure 9.8).

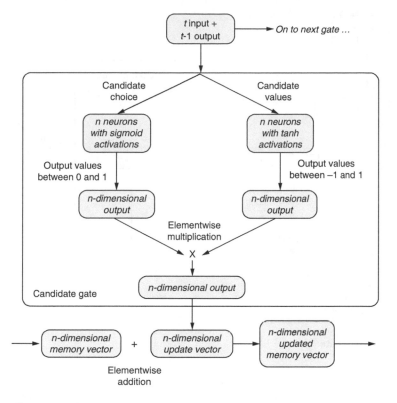

**Figure 9.8 Candidate gate**

This gate is learning simultaneously which values to extract and the magnitude of those particular values. The mask and magnitude become what's added to the memory state. As in the forget gate, the candidate gate is learning to mask off the inappropriate information before adding it to the cell's memory.

So old, hopefully irrelevant things are forgotten, and new things are remembered. Then you arrive at the last gate of the cell: the *output gate.*

Up until this point in the journey through the cell, you've only written to the cell's memory. Now it's finally time to get some use out of this structure. The output gate takes the input (remember this is still the concatenation of the input at time step *t* and the output of the cell at time step *t*-1) and passes it into the output gate.

The concatenated input is passed into the weights of the *n* neurons, and then you apply a sigmoid activation function to output an *n*-dimensional vector of floats, just like the output of a SimpleRNN. But instead of handing that information out through the cell wall, you pause.

The memory structure you've built up is now primed, and it gets to weigh in on what you *should* output. This judgment is achieved by using the memory to create one last mask. This mask is a kind of gate as well, but you refrain from using that term

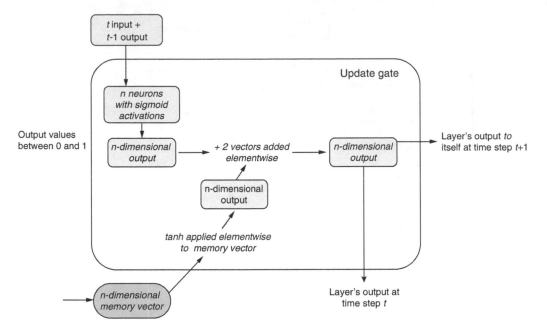

**Figure 9.9   Update/output gate**

because this mask doesn't have any learned parameters, which differentiates it from the three previous gates described.

The mask created from the memory is the memory state with a tanh function applied elementwise, which gives an *n*-dimensional vector of floats between -1 and 1. That mask vector is then multiplied elementwise with the raw vector computed in the output gate's first step. The resulting *n*-dimensional vector is finally passed out of the cell as the cell's official output at time step *t* (see figure 9.9).

> **TIP**   Remember that the output from an LSTM cell is like the output from a simple recurrent neural network layer. It's passed out of the cell as the layer output (at time step *t*) *and* to itself as part of the input to time step *t*+1.

Thereby the memory of the cell gets the last word on what's important to output at time step *t*, given what was input at time step *t* and output at *t*-1, and all the details it has gleaned up to this point in the input sequence.

### 9.1.1   *Backpropagation through time*

How does this thing learn then? Backpropagation—as with any other neural net. For a moment, let's step back and look at the problem you're trying to solve with this new complexity. A vanilla RNN is susceptible to a vanishing gradient because the derivative at any given time step is a factor of the weights themselves, so as you step back in time coalescing the various deltas, after a few iterations, the weights (and the learning rate) may shrink the gradient away to 0. The update to the weights at the end of the back-propagation (which would equate to the beginning of the sequence) are either minuscule or effectively 0. A similar problem occurs when the weights are somewhat large: the gradient *explodes* and grows disproportionately to the network.

An LSTM avoids this problem via the memory state itself. The neurons in each of the gates are updated via derivatives of the functions they fed, namely those that update the memory state on the forward pass. So at any given time step, as the normal chain rule is applied backwards to the forward propagation, the updates to the neurons are dependent on only the memory state at that time step and the previous one. This way, the error of the entire function is kept "nearer" to the neurons for each time step. This is known as the *error carousel.*

### IN PRACTICE

How does this work in practice then? Exactly like the simple RNN from the last chapter. All you've changed is the inner workings of the black box that's a recurrent layer in the network. So you can just swap out the Keras SimpleRNN layer for the Keras LSTM layer, and all the other pieces of your classifier will stay the same.

You'll use the same dataset, prepped the same way: tokenize the text and embed those using Word2vec. Then you'll pad/truncate the sequences again to 400 tokens each using the functions you defined in the previous chapters. See the following listing.

---

**Listing 9.2   Load and prepare the IMDB data**

```
>>> import numpy as np

>>> dataset = pre_process_data('./aclimdb/train')          Gather the data
>>> vectorized_data = tokenize_and_vectorize(dataset)      and prep it.
>>> expected = collect_expected(dataset)
>>> split_point = int(len(vectorized_data) * .8)

>>> x_train = vectorized_data[:split_point]                Split the data into
>>> y_train = expected[:split_point]                       training and testing sets.
>>> x_test = vectorized_data[split_point:]
>>> y_test = expected[split_point:]
                                       Declare the        Number of samples to show the
                                       hyperparameters.   net before backpropagating the
>>> maxlen = 400                                           error and updating the weights.
>>> batch_size = 32
>>> embedding_dims = 300          Length of the token vectors we will
>>> epochs = 2                    create for passing into the Convnet

>>> x_train = pad_trunc(x_train, maxlen)          Further prep the data by making
>>> x_test = pad_trunc(x_test, maxlen)            each point of uniform length.
>>> x_train = np.reshape(x_train,
...     (len(x_train), maxlen, embedding_dims))
>>> y_train = np.array(y_train)
>>> x_test = np.reshape(x_test, (len(x_test), maxlen, embedding_dims))
>>> y_test = np.array(y_test)

                                                          Reshape into a numpy
                                                          data structure.
```

Then you can build your model using the new LSTM layer, as shown in the following listing.

**Listing 9.3    Build a Keras LSTM network**

```
>>> from keras.models import Sequential
>>> from keras.layers import Dense, Dropout, Flatten, LSTM
>>> num_neurons = 50
>>> model = Sequential()
>>> model.add(LSTM(num_neurons, return_sequences=True,
...               input_shape=(maxlen, embedding_dims)))
>>> model.add(Dropout(.2))
>>> model.add(Flatten())
>>> model.add(Dense(1, activation='sigmoid'))
>>> model.compile('rmsprop', 'binary_crossentropy',  metrics=['accuracy'])
>>> model.summary()
Layer (type)                 Output Shape              Param #
=================================================================
lstm_2 (LSTM)                (None, 400, 50)           70200
_____
dropout_2 (Dropout)          (None, 400, 50)           0
_____
flatten_2 (Flatten)          (None, 20000)             0
_____
dense_2 (Dense)              (None, 1)                 20001
=================================================================
Total params: 90,201.0
Trainable params: 90,201.0
Non-trainable params: 0.0
```

**Keras makes the implementation easy.**

**Flatten the output of the LSTM.**

**A one neuron layer that will output a float between 0 and 1.**

Train and save the model as before, as shown in the next two listings.

**Listing 9.4    Fit your LSTM model**

```
>>> model.fit(x_train, y_train,
...           batch_size=batch_size,
...           epochs=epochs,
...           validation_data=(x_test, y_test))
Train on 20000 samples, validate on 5000 samples
Epoch 1/2
20000/20000 [==============================] - 548s - loss: 0.4772 -
acc: 0.7736 - val_loss: 0.3694 - val_acc: 0.8412
Epoch 2/2
20000/20000 [==============================] - 583s - loss: 0.3477 -
acc: 0.8532 - val_loss: 0.3451 - val_acc: 0.8516
<keras.callbacks.History at 0x145595fd0>
```

**Train the model.**

**Listing 9.5    Save it for later**

```
>>> model_structure = model.to_json()
>>> with open("lstm_model1.json", "w") as json_file:
...     json_file.write(model_structure)

>>> model.save_weights("lstm_weights1.h5")
```

**Save its structure so you don't have to do this part again.**

That is an enormous leap in the validation accuracy compared to the simple RNN you implemented in chapter 8 with the same dataset. You can start to see how large a gain you can achieve by providing the model with a memory when the relationship of tokens is so important. The beauty of the algorithm is that it learns the *relationships* of the tokens it sees. The network is now able to model those relationships, specifically in the context of the cost function you provide.

In this case, how close are you to correctly identifying positive or negative sentiment? Granted this is a narrow focus of a much grander problem within natural language processing. How do you model humor, sarcasm, or angst, for example? Can they be modeled together? It's definitely a field of active research. But working on them separately, while demanding a lot of hand-labeled data (and there's more of this out there every day), is certainly a viable path, and stacking these kinds of discrete classifiers in your pipeline is a perfectly legitimate path to pursue in a focused problem space.

### 9.1.2 *Where does the rubber hit the road?*

This is the fun part. With a trained model, you can begin trying out various sample phrases and seeing how well the model performs. Try to trick it. Use happy words in a negative context. Try long phrases, short ones, contradictory ones. See listings 9.6 and 9.7.

---

**Listing 9.6   Reload your LSTM model**

```
>>> from keras.models import model_from_json
>>> with open("lstm_model1.json", "r") as json_file:
...     json_string = json_file.read()
>>> model = model_from_json(json_string)

>>> model.load_weights('lstm_weights1.h5')
```

---

**Listing 9.7   Use the model to predict on a sample**

```
>>> sample_1 = """I hate that the dismal weather had me down for so long,
...     when will it break! Ugh, when does happiness return?  The sun is
...     blinding and the puffy clouds are too thin. I can't wait for the
...     weekend."""

>>> vec_list = tokenize_and_vectorize([(1, sample_1)])

>>> test_vec_list = pad_trunc(vec_list, maxlen)

>>> test_vec = np.reshape(test_vec_list,
...                     (len(test_vec_list), maxlen, embedding_dims))
```

Tokenize returns a list of the data (length I here).

You pass a dummy value in the first element of the tuple, because your helper expects it from the way you processed the initial data. That value won't ever see the network, so it can be anything.

```
>>> print("Sample's sentiment, 1 - pos, 2 - neg : {}"\
...     .format(model.predict_classes(test_vec)))
1/1 [==============================] - 0s
Sample's sentiment, 1 - pos, 2 - neg : [[0]]

>>> print("Raw output of sigmoid function: {}"\
...     .format(model.predict(test_vec)))
Raw output of sigmoid function: [[ 0.2192785]]
```

As you play with the possibilities, watch the raw output of the sigmoid in addition to the discrete sentiment classifications. Unlike the `.predict_class()` method, the `.predict()` method reveals the raw sigmoid activation function output before thresholding, so you can see a continuous value between 0 and 1. Anything above 0.5 will be classified as positive, below 0.5 will be negative. As you try your samples, you'll get a sense of how confident the model is in its prediction, which can be helpful in parsing results of your spot checks.

Pay close attention to the misclassified examples (both positively and negatively). If the sigmoid output is close to 0.5, that means the model is just flipping a coin for that example. You can then look at why that phrase is ambiguous to the model, but try not to be human about it. Set aside your human intuition and subjective perspective for a bit and try to think statistically. Try to remember what documents your model has "seen." Are the words in the misclassified example rare? Are they rare in your corpus or the corpus that trained the language model for your embedding? Do all of the words in the example exist in your model's vocabulary?

Going through this process of examining the probabilities and input data associated with incorrect predictions helps build your machine learning intuition so you can build better NLP pipelines in the future. This is backpropagation through the human brain for the problem of model tuning.

### 9.1.3  *Dirty data*

This more powerful model still has a great number of hyperparameters to toy with. But now is a good time to pause and look back to the beginning, to your data. You've been using the same data, processed in exactly the same way since you started with convolutional neural nets, specifically so you could see the variations in the types of models and their performance on a given dataset. But you did make some choices that compromised the integrity of the data, or *dirtied* it, if you will.

Padding or truncating each sample to 400 tokens was important for convolutional nets so that the filters could "scan" a vector with a consistent length. And convolutional nets output a consistent vector as well. It's important for the output to be a consistent dimensionality, because the output goes into a fully connected feed forward layer at the end of the chain, which needs a fixed length vector as input.

Similarly, your implementations of recurrent neural nets, both simple and LSTM, are striving toward a fixed length *thought vector* you can pass into a feed forward layer for classification. A fixed length vector representation of an object, such as a thought vector, is also called an *embedding*. So that the thought vector is of consistent size, you have to *unroll* the net to a consistent number of time steps (tokens). Let's look at the choice of 400 as the number of time steps to unroll the net, as shown in the following listing.

---

Listing 9.8   Optimize the thought vector size

```
>>> def test_len(data, maxlen):
...     total_len = truncated = exact = padded = 0
...     for sample in data:
...         total_len += len(sample)
...         if len(sample) > maxlen:
...             truncated += 1
...         elif len(sample) < maxlen:
...             padded += 1
...         else:
...             exact +=1
...     print('Padded: {}'.format(padded))
...     print('Equal: {}'.format(exact))
...     print('Truncated: {}'.format(truncated))
...     print('Avg length: {}'.format(total_len/len(data)))

>>> dataset = pre_process_data('./aclimdb/train')
>>> vectorized_data = tokenize_and_vectorize(dataset)
>>> test_len(vectorized_data, 400)
Padded: 22559
Equal: 12
Truncated: 2429
Avg length: 202.4424
```

Whoa. Okay, 400 was a bit on the high side (probably should have done this analysis earlier). Let's dial the `maxlen` back closer to the average sample size of 202 tokens. Let's round that to 200 tokens, and give your LSTM another crack at it, as shown in the following listings.

---

Listing 9.9   Optimize LSTM hyperparameters

```
>>> import numpy as np
>>> from keras.models import Sequential
>>> from keras.layers import Dense, Dropout, Flatten, LSTM
>>> maxlen = 200                              ◁─┐
>>> batch_size = 32                             │  All the same code as earlier, but you
>>> embedding_dims = 300                        │  limit the max length to 200 tokens.
>>> epochs = 2
>>> num_neurons = 50
>>> dataset = pre_process_data('./aclimdb/train')
>>> vectorized_data = tokenize_and_vectorize(dataset)
>>> expected = collect_expected(dataset)
>>> split_point = int(len(vectorized_data)*.8)
>>> x_train = vectorized_data[:split_point]
>>> y_train = expected[:split_point]
>>> x_test = vectorized_data[split_point:]
>>> y_test = expected[split_point:]
>>> x_train = pad_trunc(x_train, maxlen)
>>> x_test = pad_trunc(x_test, maxlen)
```

```
>>> x_train = np.reshape(x_train, (len(x_train), maxlen, embedding_dims))
>>> y_train = np.array(y_train)
>>> x_test = np.reshape(x_test, (len(x_test), maxlen, embedding_dims))
>>> y_test = np.array(y_test)
```

**Listing 9.10   A more optimally sized LSTM**

```
>>> model = Sequential()
>>> model.add(LSTM(num_neurons, return_sequences=True,
...                 input_shape=(maxlen, embedding_dims)))
>>> model.add(Dropout(.2))
>>> model.add(Flatten())
>>> model.add(Dense(1, activation='sigmoid'))
>>> model.compile('rmsprop', 'binary_crossentropy', metrics=['accuracy'])
>>> model.summary()
Layer (type)                    Output Shape               Param #
=================================================================
lstm_1 (LSTM)                   (None, 200, 50)            70200
_____
dropout_1 (Dropout)             (None, 200, 50)            0
_____
flatten_1 (Flatten)             (None, 10000)              0
_____
dense_1 (Dense)                 (None, 1)                  10001
=================================================================
Total params: 80,201.0
Trainable params: 80,201.0
Non-trainable params: 0.0
```

**Listing 9.11   Train a smaller LSTM**

```
>>> model.fit(x_train, y_train,
...           batch_size=batch_size,
...           epochs=epochs,
...           validation_data=(x_test, y_test))
Train on 20000 samples, validate on 5000 samples
Epoch 1/2
20000/20000 [==============================] - 245s - loss: 0.4742 -
acc: 0.7760 - val_loss: 0.4235 - val_acc: 0.8010
Epoch 2/2
20000/20000 [==============================] - 203s - loss: 0.3718 -
acc: 0.8386 - val_loss: 0.3499 - val_acc: 0.8450

>>> model_structure = model.to_json()
>>> with open("lstm_model7.json", "w") as json_file:
...     json_file.write(model_structure)

>>> model.save_weights("lstm_weights7.h5")
```

Well that trained much faster and the validation accuracy dropped less than half a percent (84.5% versus 85.16%). With samples that were half the number of time steps,
you cut the training time by more than half! There were half the LSTM time steps to

compute and half the weights in the feed forward layer to learn. But most importantly the backpropagation only had to travel half the distance (half the time steps back into the past) each time.

The accuracy got worse, though. Wouldn't a 200-D model generalize better (overfit less) than the earlier 400-D model? This is because you included a `Dropout` layer in both models. A dropout layer helps prevent overfitting, so your validation accuracy should only get worse as you reduce the degrees of freedom or the training epochs for your model.

With all the power of neural nets and their ability to learn complex patterns, it's easy to forget that a well-designed neural net is good at learning to discard noise and systematic biases. You had inadvertently introduced a lot of bias into the data by appending all those zero vectors. The bias elements in each node will still give it some signal even if all the input is zero. But the net will eventually learn to disregard those elements entirely (specifically by adjusting the weight on that bias element down to zero) and focus on the portions of the samples that contain meaningful information.

So your optimized LSTM didn't learn any more, but it learned a lot faster. The most important takeaway from this, though, is to be aware of the length of your test samples in relation to the training sample lengths. If your training set is composed of documents thousands of tokens long, you may not get an accurate classification of something only 3 tokens long padded out to 1,000. And vice versa—cutting a 1,000-token opus to 3 tokens will severely hinder your poor, little model. Not that an LSTM won't make a good go of it; just a note of caution as you experiment.

### 9.1.4   *Back to the dirty data*

What is arguably the greater sin in data handling? Dropping the "unknown" tokens on the floor. The list of "unknowns," which is basically just words you couldn't find in the pretrained Word2vec model, is quite extensive. Dropping this much data on the floor, especially when attempting to model the sequence of words, is problematic.

Sentences like

*I don't like this movie.*

may become

*I like this movie.*

if your word embedding vocabulary doesn't contain the word "don't". This isn't the case for the Word2vec embeddings, but many tokens are omitted and they may or may not be important to you. Dropping these unknown tokens is one strategy you can pursue, but there are others. You can use or train a word embedding that has a vector for every last one of your tokens, but doing so is almost always prohibitively expensive.

Two common approaches provide decent results without exploding the computational requirements. Both involve replacing the unknown token with a new vector representation. The first approach is counter-intuitive: for every token not modeled by a vector, randomly select a vector from the existing model and use that instead. You can easily see how this would flummox a human reader.

A sentence like

*The man who was defenestrated, brushed himself off with a nonchalant glance back inside.*

may become

*The man who was duck, brushed himself off with a airplane glance back inside.*

How is a model supposed to learn from nonsense like this? As it turns out, the model does overcome these hiccups in much the same way your example did when you dropped them on the floor. Remember, you're not trying to model every statement in the training set explicitly. The goal is to create a generalized model of the language in the training set. So outliers will exist, but hopefully not so much as to derail the model in describing the prevailing patterns.

The second and more common approach is to replace all tokens not in the word vector library with a specific token, usually referenced as "UNK" (for unknown), when reconstructing the original input. The vector itself is chosen either when modeling the original embedding or at random (and ideally far away from the known vectors in the space).

As with padding, the network can learn its way around these unknown tokens and come to its own conclusions around them.

### 9.1.5  *Words are hard. Letters are easier.*

Words have meaning—we can all agree on that. Modeling natural language with these basic building blocks only seems natural then. Using these models to describe meaning, feeling, intent, and everything else in terms of these atomic structures seems natural as well. But, of course, words aren't atomic at all. As you saw earlier, they're made up of smaller words, stems, phonemes, and so on. But they are also, even more fundamentally, a sequence of characters.

As you're modeling language, a lot of meaning is hidden down at the character level. Intonations in voice, alliteration, rhymes—all of this can be modeled if you break things down all the way to the character level. They can be modeled by humans without breaking things down that far. But the definitions that would arise from that modeling are fraught with complexity and not easily imparted to a machine, which after all is why you're here. Many of those patterns are inherent in text when you examine it with an eye toward which character came after which, given the characters you've already seen.

In this paradigm, a space or a comma or a period becomes just another character. And as your network is learning meaning from sequences, if you break them down all the way to the individual characters, the model is forced to find these lower-level patterns. To notice a repeated suffix after a certain number of syllables, which would quite probably rhyme, may be a pattern that carries meaning, perhaps joviality or derision. With a large enough training set, these patterns begin to emerge. And because there are many fewer distinct letters than words in the English language, you have a smaller variety of input vectors to worry about.

Training a model at the character level is tricky though. The patterns and long-term dependencies found at the character level can vary greatly across voices. You can find these patterns, but they may not generalize as well. Let's try the LSTM at the character level on the same example dataset. First, you need to process the data differently. As before, you grab the data and sort out the labels, as shown in the following listing.

---

**Listing 9.12  Prepare the data**

```
>>> dataset = pre_process_data('./aclimdb/train')
>>> expected = collect_expected(dataset)
```

You then need to decide how far to unroll the network, so you'll see how many characters on average are in the data samples, as shown in the following listing.

---

**Listing 9.13  Calculate the average sample length**

```
>>> def avg_len(data):
...     total_len = 0
...     for sample in data:
...         total_len += len(sample[1])
...     return total_len/len(data)

>>> avg_len(dataset)
1325.06964
```

So immediately you can see that the network is going to be unrolled much further. And you're going to be waiting a significant amount of time for this model to finish. Spoiler: this model doesn't do much other than overfit, but it provides an interesting example nonetheless.

Next you need to clean the data of tokens unrelated to the text's natural language. This function filters out some useless characters in the HTML tags in the dataset. Really the data should be more thoroughly scrubbed. See the following listing.

---

**Listing 9.14  Prepare the strings for a character-based model**

```
>>> def clean_data(data):
...     """Shift to lower case, replace unknowns with UNK, and listify"""
...     new_data = []
...     VALID = 'abcdefghijklmnopqrstuvwxyz0123456789"\'?!.,:; '
...     for sample in data:
...         new_sample = []
...         for char in sample[1].lower():        ◁── Just grab the string,
...             if char in VALID:                      not the label.
...                 new_sample.append(char)
...             else:
...                 new_sample.append('UNK')
```

```
...            new_data.append(new_sample)
...        return new_data

>>> listified_data = clean_data(dataset)
```

You're using the `'UNK'` as a single character in the list for everything that doesn't match the VALID list.

Then, as before, you pad or truncate the samples to a given `maxlen`. Here you introduce another "single character" for padding: `'PAD'`. See the following listing.

**Listing 9.15  Pad and truncated characters**

```
>>> def char_pad_trunc(data, maxlen=1500):
...        """ We truncate to maxlen or add in PAD tokens """
...        new_dataset = []
...        for sample in data:
...            if len(sample) > maxlen:
...                new_data = sample[:maxlen]
...            elif len(sample) < maxlen:
...                pads = maxlen - len(sample)
...                new_data = sample + ['PAD'] * pads
...            else:
...                new_data = sample
...            new_dataset.append(new_data)
...        return new_dataset
```

You chose `maxlen` of 1,500 to capture slightly more data than was in the average sample, but you tried to avoid introducing too much noise with PADs. Thinking about these choices in the sizes of words can be helpful. At a fixed character length, a sample with lots of long words could be undersampled, compared to a sample composed entirely of simple, one-syllable words. As with any machine learning problem, knowing your dataset and its ins and outs is important.

This time instead of using Word2vec for your embeddings, you're going to one-hot encode the characters. So you need to create a dictionary of the tokens (the characters) mapped to an integer index. You'll also create a dictionary to map the reverse as well, but more on that later. See the following listing.

**Listing 9.16  Character-based model "vocabulary"**

```
>>> def create_dicts(data):
...        """ Modified from Keras LSTM example"""
...        chars = set()
...        for sample in data:
...            chars.update(set(sample))
...        char_indices = dict((c, i) for i, c in enumerate(chars))
...        indices_char = dict((i, c) for i, c in enumerate(chars))
...        return char_indices, indices_char
```

And then you can use that dictionary to create input vectors of the indices instead of the tokens themselves, as shown in the next two listings.

---
**Listing 9.17  One-hot encoder for characters**

```
>>> import numpy as np

>>> def onehot_encode(dataset, char_indices, maxlen=1500):
...     """
...     One-hot encode the tokens
...
...     Args:
...         dataset  list of lists of tokens
...         char_indices
...                 dictionary of {key=character,
...                               value=index to use encoding vector}
...         maxlen  int  Length of each sample
...     Return:
...         np array of shape (samples, tokens, encoding length)
...     """
...     X = np.zeros((len(dataset), maxlen, len(char_indices.keys())))
...     for i, sentence in enumerate(dataset):
...         for t, char in enumerate(sentence):
...             X[i, t, char_indices[char]] = 1
...     return X          ◁────── A numpy array of length equal to the number of data
                                  samples—each sample will be a number of tokens equal
                                  to maxlen, and each token will be a one-hot encoded
                                  vector of length equal to the number of characters
```

---
**Listing 9.18  Load and preprocess the IMDB data**

```
>>> dataset = pre_process_data('./aclimdb/train')
>>> expected = collect_expected(dataset)
>>> listified_data = clean_data(dataset)

>>> common_length_data = char_pad_trunc(listified_data, maxlen=1500)
>>> char_indices, indices_char = create_dicts(common_length_data)
>>> encoded_data = onehot_encode(common_length_data, char_indices, 1500)
```

And then you split up your data just like before, as shown in the next two listings.

---
**Listing 9.19  Split dataset for training (80%) and testing (20%)**

```
>>> split_point = int(len(encoded_data)*.8)

>>> x_train = encoded_data[:split_point]
>>> y_train = expected[:split_point]
>>> x_test = encoded_data[split_point:]
>>> y_test = expected[split_point:]
```

**Listing 9.20    Build a character-based LSTM**

```
>>> from keras.models import Sequential
>>> from keras.layers import Dense, Dropout, Embedding, Flatten, LSTM

>>> num_neurons = 40
>>> maxlen = 1500
>>> model = Sequential()

>>> model.add(LSTM(num_neurons,
...                return_sequences=True,
...                input_shape=(maxlen, len(char_indices.keys()))))
>>> model.add(Dropout(.2))
>>> model.add(Flatten())
>>> model.add(Dense(1, activation='sigmoid'))
>>> model.compile('rmsprop', 'binary_crossentropy',  metrics=['accuracy'])
>>> model.summary()
Layer (type)                    Output Shape              Param #
=================================================================
lstm_2 (LSTM)                   (None, 1500, 40)          13920
_____
dropout_2 (Dropout)             (None, 1500, 40)          0
_____
flatten_2 (Flatten)             (None, 60000)             0
_____
dense_2 (Dense)                 (None, 1)                 60001
=================================================================
Total params: 73,921.0
Trainable params: 73,921.0
Non-trainable params: 0.0
```

So you're getting more efficient at building LSTM models. Your latest character-based model needs to train only 74k parameters, compared to the optimized word-based LSTM which required 80k. And this simpler model should train faster and generalize to new text better, since it has fewer degrees of freedom for overfitting.

Now you can try it out to see what character-based LSTM models have to offer, as shown in the following listings.

**Listing 9.21    Train a character-based LSTM**

```
>>> batch_size = 32
>>> epochs = 10
>>> model.fit(x_train, y_train,
...           batch_size=batch_size,
...           epochs=epochs,
...           validation_data=(x_test, y_test))
Train on 20000 samples, validate on 5000 samples
Epoch 1/10
20000/20000 [==============================] - 634s - loss: 0.6949 -
acc: 0.5388 - val_loss: 0.6775 - val_acc: 0.5738
Epoch 2/10
20000/20000 [==============================] - 668s - loss: 0.6087 -
acc: 0.6700 - val_loss: 0.6786 - val_acc: 0.5962
```

```
Epoch 3/10
20000/20000 [==============================] - 695s - loss: 0.5358 -
acc: 0.7356 - val_loss: 0.7182 - val_acc: 0.5786
Epoch 4/10
20000/20000 [==============================] - 686s - loss: 0.4662 -
acc: 0.7832 - val_loss: 0.7605 - val_acc: 0.5836
Epoch 5/10
20000/20000 [==============================] - 694s - loss: 0.4062 -
acc: 0.8206 - val_loss: 0.8099 - val_acc: 0.5852
Epoch 6/10
20000/20000 [==============================] - 694s - loss: 0.3550 -
acc: 0.8448 - val_loss: 0.8851 - val_acc: 0.5842
Epoch 7/10
20000/20000 [==============================] - 645s - loss: 0.3058 -
acc: 0.8705 - val_loss: 0.9598 - val_acc: 0.5930
Epoch 8/10
20000/20000 [==============================] - 684s - loss: 0.2643 -
acc: 0.8911 - val_loss: 1.0366 - val_acc: 0.5888
Epoch 9/10
20000/20000 [==============================] - 671s - loss: 0.2304 -
acc: 0.9055 - val_loss: 1.1323 - val_acc: 0.5914
Epoch 10/10
20000/20000 [==============================] - 663s - loss: 0.2035 -
acc: 0.9181 - val_loss: 1.2051 - val_acc: 0.5948
```

**Listing 9.22   And save it for later**

```
>>> model_structure = model.to_json()
>>> with open("char_lstm_model3.json", "w") as json_file:
...     json_file.write(model_structure)
>>> model.save_weights("char_lstm_weights3.h5")
```

The 92% training set accuracy versus the 59% validation accuracy is evidence of over-fitting. The model slowly started to learn the sentiment of the training set. Oh so slowly. It took over 1.5 hours on a modern laptop without a GPU. But the validation accuracy never improved much above a random guess, and later in the epochs it started to get worse, which you can also see in the validation loss.

Lots of things could be going on here. The model could be too rich for the dataset, meaning it has enough parameters that it can begin to model patterns that are unique to the training set's 20,000 samples, but aren't useful for a general language model focused on sentiment. One might alleviate this issue with a higher dropout percentage or fewer neurons in the LSTM layer. More labeled data would also help if you think the model is defined too richly. But quality labeled data is usually the hardest piece to come by.

In the end, this model is creating a great deal of expense for both your hardware and your time for limited reward compared to what you got with a word-level LSTM model, and even the convolutional neural nets in previous chapters. So why bother with the character level at all? The character-level model can be extremely good at modeling a language, given a broad enough dataset. Or it can model a specific kind of language given a focused training set, say from one author instead of thousands. Either way, you've taken the first step toward generating novel text with a neural net.

### 9.1.6   *My turn to chat*

If you could generate new text with a certain "style" or "attitude," you'd certainly have an entertaining chatbot indeed. Of course, being able to generate novel text with a given style doesn't guarantee your bot will talk about what you want it to. But you can use this approach to generate lots of text within a given set of parameters (in response to a user's style, for example), and this larger corpus of novel text could then be indexed and searched as possible responses to a given query.

Much like a Markov chain that predicts a sequence's next word based on the probability of any given word appearing after the 1-gram or 2-gram or *n*-gram that just occurred, your LSTM model can learn the probability of the next word based on what it just saw, but with the added benefit of *memory*! A Markov chain only has information about the *n*-gram it's using to search and the frequency of words that occur after that *n*-gram. The RNN model does something similar in that it encodes information about the next term based on the few that preceded it. But with the LSTM memory state, the model has a greater context in which to judge the most appropriate next term. And most excitingly, you can predict the next character based on the characters that came before. This level of granularity is beyond a basic Markov chain.

How do you train your model to do this magic trick? First, you're going to abandon your classification task. The real core of what the LSTM learned is in the LSTM cell itself. But you were using the model's successes and failures around a specific classification task to train it. That approach isn't necessarily going to help your model learn a general representation of language. You trained it to pay attention only to sequences that contained strong sentiment.

So instead of using the training set's sentiment label as the target for learning, you can use the training samples themselves! For each token in the sample, you want your LSTM to learn to *predict* the next token (see figure 9.10). This is very similar to the word vector embedding approach you used in chapter 6, only you're going to train a network on bigrams (2-grams) instead of skip-grams. A word generator model trained this way (see figure 9.10) would work just fine, but you're going to cut to the chase and go straight down to the character level with the same approach (see figure 9.11).

Instead of a thought vector coming out of the last time step, you're going to focus on the output of each time step individually. The error will still backpropagate through time from each time step back to the beginning, but the error is determined specifically at the time step level. In a sense, it was in the other LSTM classifiers of this chapter as well, but in the other classifiers the error wasn't determined until the end of the sequence. Only at the end of a sequence was an aggregated output available to feed into the feed forward layer at the end of the chain. Nonetheless, backpropagation is still

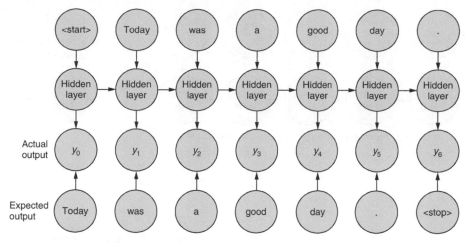

Expected output is the next token in the sample. Shown here on word level.

**Figure 9.10  Next word prediction**

working the same way, aggregating the errors by adjusting all your weights at the end of the sequence.

So the first thing you need to do is adjust your training set labels. The output vector will be measured not against a given classification label but against the one-hot encoding of the next character in the sequence.

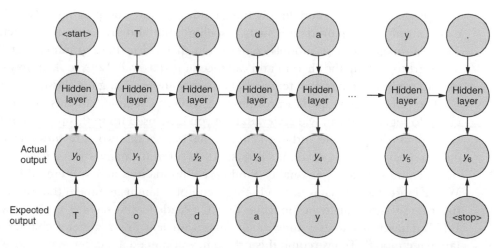

Expected output is the next token in the sample. Shown here on character level.

**Figure 9.11  Next character prediction**

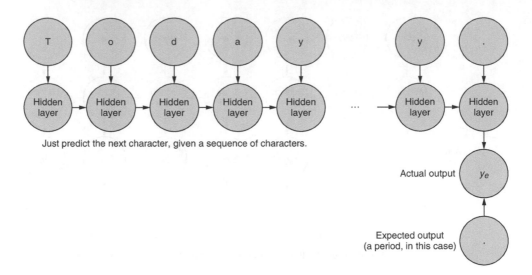

Figure 9.12   **Last character prediction only**

You can also fall back to a simpler model. Instead of trying to predict every subsequent character, predict the next character for a given sequence. This is exactly the same as all the other LSTM layers in this chapter, if you drop the keyword argument `return_sequences=True` (see listing 9.17). Doing so will focus the LSTM model on the return value of the last time step in the sequence (see figure 9.12).

### 9.1.7   *My turn to speak more clearly*

Simple character-level modeling is the gateway to more-complex models—ones that can not only pick up on details such as spelling, but also grammar and punctuation. The real magic of these models comes when they learn these grammar details, and also start to pick up the rhythm and cadence of text as well. Let's look at how you can start to generate some novel text with the tools you were using for classification.

The Keras documentation provides an excellent example. For this project, you're going to set aside the movie review dataset you have used up to this point. For finding concepts as deep as tone and word choice, that dataset has two attributes that are difficult to overcome. First of all, it's diverse. It's written by many writers, each with their own writing style and personality. Finding commonalities across them all is difficult. With a large enough dataset, developing a complex language model that can handle a diversity of styles might be possible. But that leads to the second problem with the IMDB dataset: it's an extremely small dataset for learning a general character-based language model. To overcome this problem, you'll need a dataset that's more consistent across samples in style and tone or a much larger dataset; you'll choose the former. The Keras example provides a sample of the work of Friedrich Nietzsche. That's fun, but you'll choose someone else with a singular style: William Shakespeare. He hasn't published anything in a while, so let's help him out. See the following listing.

**Listing 9.23    Import the Project Gutenberg dataset**

```
>>> from nltk.corpus import gutenberg
>>>
>>> gutenberg.fileids()
['austen-emma.txt',
 'austen-persuasion.txt',
 'austen-sense.txt',
 'bible-kjv.txt',
 'blake-poems.txt',
 'bryant-stories.txt',
 'burgess-busterbrown.txt',
 'carroll-alice.txt',
 'chesterton-ball.txt',
 'chesterton-brown.txt',
 'chesterton-thursday.txt',
 'edgeworth-parents.txt',
 'melville-moby_dick.txt',
 'milton-paradise.txt',
 'shakespeare-caesar.txt',
 'shakespeare-hamlet.txt',
 'shakespeare-macbeth.txt',
 'whitman-leaves.txt']
```

Ah, three plays by Shakespeare. You'll grab those and concatenate them into a large string. And if you want more, there's *lots* more where that came from at https://www.gutenberg.org.[8] See the following listing.

**Listing 9.24    Preprocess Shakespeare plays**

```
>>> text = ''
>>> for txt in gutenberg.fileids():        ←┐  Concatenate all Shakespeare plays
...     if 'shakespeare' in txt:            │  in the Gutenberg corpus in NLTK.
...         text += gutenberg.raw(txt).lower()
>>> chars = sorted(list(set(text)))
>>> char_indices = dict((c, i)                Make a dictionary of characters to an index,
...     for i, c in enumerate(chars))      ←┘  for reference in the one-hot encoding.
>>> indices_char = dict((i, c)
...     for i, c in enumerate(chars))         ←
>>> 'corpus length: {}  total chars: {}'.format(len(text), len(chars))
'corpus length: 375542  total chars: 50'
```

Make the opposite dictionary for lookup when interpreting the one-hot encoding back to the character.

---

The Project Gutenberg website hosts 57,000 scanned books in various formats. You can download them all for free in about a day, if you are polite about it: https://www.exratione.com/2014/11/how-to-politely-download-all-english-language-text-format-files-from-project-gutenberg/.

This is nicely formatted as well:

```
>>> print(text[:500])
[the tragedie of julius caesar by william shakespeare 1599]

actus primus. scoena prima.

enter flauius, murellus, and certaine commoners ouer the stage.

  flauius. hence: home you idle creatures, get you home:
is this a holiday? what, know you not
(being mechanicall) you ought not walke
vpon a labouring day, without the signe
of your profession? speake, what trade art thou?
  car. why sir, a carpenter

  mur. where is thy leather apron, and thy rule?
what dost thou with thy best apparrell on
```

Next you're going to chop up the source text into data samples, each with a fixed, *maxlen* set of characters. To increase your dataset size and focus on consistent patterns, the Keras example oversamples the data into semi-redundant chunks. Take 40 characters from the beginning, move to the third character from the beginning, take 40 from there, move to sixth … and so on.

Remember, the goal of this particular model is to learn to predict the 41st character in any sequence, given the 40 characters that came before it. So we'll build a training set of semi-redundant sequences, each 40 characters long, as shown in the following listing.

### Listing 9.25  Assemble a training set

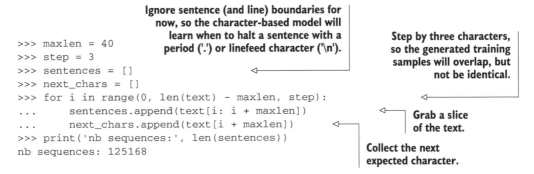

Ignore sentence (and line) boundaries for now, so the character-based model will learn when to halt a sentence with a period ('.') or linefeed character ('\n').

Step by three characters, so the generated training samples will overlap, but not be identical.

```
>>> maxlen = 40
>>> step = 3
>>> sentences = []
>>> next_chars = []
>>> for i in range(0, len(text) - maxlen, step):
...     sentences.append(text[i: i + maxlen])
...     next_chars.append(text[i + maxlen])
>>> print('nb sequences:', len(sentences))
nb sequences: 125168
```

Grab a slice of the text.

Collect the next expected character.

So you have 125,168 training samples and the character that follows each of them, the target for our model. See the following listing.

### Listing 9.26  One-hot encode the training examples

```
>>> X = np.zeros((len(sentences), maxlen, len(chars)), dtype=np.bool)
>>> y = np.zeros((len(sentences), len(chars)), dtype=np.bool)
```

```
>>> for i, sentence in enumerate(sentences):
...     for t, char in enumerate(sentence):
...         X[i, t, char_indices[char]] = 1
...     y[i, char_indices[next_chars[i]]] = 1
```

You then one-hot encode each character of each sample in the dataset and store it as the list *X*. You also store the list of one-hot encoded "answers" in the list *y*. You then construct the model, as shown in the following listing.

**Listing 9.27  Assemble a character-based LSTM model for generating text**

```
>>> from keras.models import Sequential
>>> from keras.layers import Dense, Activation
>>> from keras.layers import LSTM
>>> from keras.optimizers import RMSprop
>>> model = Sequential()
>>> model.add(LSTM(128,
...                 input_shape=(maxlen, len(chars))))
>>> model.add(Dense(len(chars)))
>>> model.add(Activation('softmax'))
>>> optimizer = RMSprop(lr=0.01)
>>> model.compile(loss='categorical_crossentropy', optimizer=optimizer)
>>> model.summary()
Layer (type)                 Output Shape              Param #
=================================================================
lstm_1 (LSTM)                (None, 128)               91648

dense_1 (Dense)              (None, 50)                6450

activation_1 (Activation)    (None, 50)                0
=================================================================
Total params: 98,098.0
Trainable params: 98,098.0
Non-trainable params: 0.0
```

> You use a much wider LSTM layer—128, up from 50. And you don't return the sequence. You only want the last output character.

> This is a classification problem, so you want a probability distribution over all possible characters.

This looks slightly different than before, so let's look at the components. Sequential and LSTM layers you know, same as before with your classifier. In this case, the *num_neurons* is 128 in the hidden layer of the LSTM cell. 128 is quite a few more than you used in the classifier, but you're trying to model much more complex behavior in reproducing a given text's tone. Next, the optimizer is defined in a variable, but this is the same one you've used up until this point. It's broken out here for readability purposes, because the learning rate parameter is being adjusted from its default (.001 normally). For what it's worth, RMSProp works by updating each weight by adjusting the learning rate with "a running average of the magnitudes of recent gradients for that weight."[9] Reading up on optimizers can definitely save you some heartache in your experiments, but the details of each individual optimizer are beyond the scope of this book.

---

[9]  Hinton, et al., http://www.cs.toronto.edu/~tijmen/csc321/slides/lecture_slides_lec6.pdf.

The next big difference is the loss function you want to minimize. Up until now it has been `binary_crossentropy`. You were only trying to determine the level at which one single neuron was firing. But here you've swapped out `Dense(1)` for `Dense (len(chars))` in the last layer. So the output of the network at each time step will be a 50-D vector (`len(chars) == 50` in listing 9.20). You're using `softmax` as the activation function, so the output vector will be the equivalent of a probability distribution over the entire 50-D vector (the sum of the values in the vector will always add up to one). Using `categorical_crossentropy` will attempt to minimize the difference between the resultant probability distribution and the one-hot encoded expected character.

And the last major change is no dropout. Because you're looking to specifically model this dataset, you have no interest in generalizing to other problems, so not only is overfitting okay, it's ideal. See the following listing.

---

**Listing 9.28   Train your Shakespearean chatbot**

> This is one way to train the model for a while, save its state, and then continue training. Keras also has a callback function built in that does similar tasks when called.

```
>>> epochs = 6
>>> batch_size = 128
>>> model_structure = model.to_json()
>>> with open("shakes_lstm_model.json", "w") as json_file:
>>>     json_file.write(model_structure)
>>> for i in range(5):
...     model.fit(X, y,
...             batch_size=batch_size,
...             epochs=epochs)
...     model.save_weights("shakes_lstm_weights_{}.h5".format(i+1))
Epoch 1/6
125168/125168 [==============================] - 266s - loss: 2.0310
Epoch 2/6
125168/125168 [==============================] - 257s - loss: 1.6851
...
```

This setup saves the model every six epochs and keeps training. If it stops reducing the loss, further training is no longer worth the cycles, so you can safely stop the process and have a saved weight set within a few epochs. We found it takes 20 to 30 epochs to start to get something decent from this dataset. You can look to expand the dataset. Shakespeare's works are readily available in the public domain. Just be sure to strive for consistency by appropriately preprocessing if you get them from disparate sources. Fortunately character-based models don't have to worry about tokenizers and sentence segmenters, but your case-folding approach could be important. We used a sledgehammer. You might find a softer touch works better.

Let's make our own play! Because the output vectors are 50-D vectors describing a probability distribution over the 50 possible output characters, you can sample from that distribution. The Keras example has a helper function to do just that, as shown in the following listing.

---

**Listing 9.29  Sampler to generate character sequences**

```
>>> import random
>>> def sample(preds, temperature=1.0):
...     preds = np.asarray(preds).astype('float64')
...     preds = np.log(preds) / temperature
...     exp_preds = np.exp(preds)
...     preds = exp_preds / np.sum(exp_preds)
...     probas = np.random.multinomial(1, preds, 1)
...     return np.argmax(probas)
```

Because the last layer in the network is a `softmax`, the output vector will be a probability distribution over all possible outputs of the network. By looking at the highest value in the output vector, you can see what the network thinks has the highest probability of being the next character. In explicit terms, the index of the output vector with the highest value (which will be between 0 and 1) will correlate with the index of the one-hot encoding of the expected token.

But here you aren't looking to exactly recreate what the input text was, but instead just what is likely to come next. Just as in a Markov chain, the next token is selected randomly based on the probability of the next token, not the most commonly occurring next token.

The effect of dividing the log by the temperature is flattening (temperature > 1) or sharpening (temperature < 1) the probability distribution. So a temperature (or `diversity` in the calling arguments) less than 1 will tend toward a more strict attempt to recreate the original text. Whereas a temp greater than 1 will produce a more diverse outcome, but as the distribution flattens, the learned patterns begin to wash away and you tend back toward nonsense. Higher diversities are fun to play with though.

The numpy random function `multinomial(num_samples, probabilities _list, size)` will make `num_samples` from the distribution whose possible outcomes are described by `probabilities_list`, and it'll output a list of length `size`, which is equal to the number of times the experiment is run. So in this case, you'll draw once from the probability distribution. You only need one sample.

When you go to predict, the Keras example has you cycle through various different values for the temperature, because each prediction will see a range of different outputs based on the temperature used in the `sample` function to sample from the probability distribution. See the following listing.

---

**Listing 9.30  Generate three texts with three diversity levels**

```
>>> import sys
>>> start_index = random.randint(0, len(text) - maxlen - 1)
>>> for diversity in [0.2, 0.5, 1.0]:
...     print()
...     print('----- diversity:', diversity)
...     generated = ''
...     sentence = text[start_index: start_index + maxlen]
```

```
...        generated += sentence
...        print('----- Generating with seed: "' + sentence + '"')
...        sys.stdout.write(generated)
...        for i in range(400):
...            x = np.zeros((1, maxlen, len(chars)))
...            for t, char in enumerate(sentence):
...                x[0, t, char_indices[char]] = 1.
...            preds = model.predict(x, verbose=0)[0]
...            next_index = sample(preds, diversity)
...            next_char = indices_char[next_index]
...            generated += next_char
...            sentence = sentence[1:] + next_char
...            sys.stdout.write(next_char)
...            sys.stdout.flush()
...        print()
```

**You seed the trained network and see what it spits out as the next character.**

**Model makes a prediction.**

**Look up which character that index represents.**

**Add it to the "seed" and drop the first character to keep the length the same. This is now the seed for the next pass.**

**Flushes the internal buffer to the console so your character appears immediately**

(Diversity 1.2 from the example was removed for brevity's sake, but feel free to add it back in and play with the output.)

You're taking a random chunk of 40 (`maxlen`) characters from the source and predicting what character will come next. You then append that predicted character to the input sentence, drop the first character, and predict again on those 40 characters as your input. Each time you write out the predicted character to the console (or a string buffer) and `flush()` so that your character immediately goes to the console. If the predicted character happens to be a newline, then that ends the line of text, but your generator keeps rolling along predicting the next line from the previous 40 characters it just output.

And what do you get? Something like this:

```
----- diversity: 0.2
----- Generating with seed: " them through & through
the most fond an"
 them through & through
the most fond and stranger the straite to the straite
him a father the world, and the straite:
the straite is the straite to the common'd,
and the truth, and the truth, and the capitoll,
and stay the compurse of the true then the dead and the colours,
and the comparyed the straite the straite
the mildiaus, and the straite of the bones,
and what is the common the bell to the straite
the straite in the commised and

----- diversity: 0.5
----- Generating with seed: " them through & through
the most fond an"
 them through & through
the most fond and the pindage it at them for
that i shall pround-be be the house, not that we be not the selfe,
```

```
and thri's the bate and the perpaine, to depart of the father now
but ore night in a laid of the haid, and there is it

    bru. what shall greefe vndernight of it

    cassi. what shall the straite, and perfire the peace,
and defear'd and soule me to me a ration,
and we will steele the words them with th

----- diversity: 1.0
----- Generating with seed: " them through & through
the most fond an"
 them through & through
the most fond and boy'd report alone

    yp. it best we will st of me at that come sleepe.
but you yet it enemy wrong, 'twas sir

    ham. the pirey too me, it let you?
  son. oh a do a sorrall you. that makino
beendumons vp?x, let vs cassa,
yet his miltrow addome knowlmy in his windher,
a vertues. hoie sleepe, or strong a strong at it
mades manish swill about a time shall trages,
and follow. more. heere shall abo
```

Diversity 0.2 and 0.5 both give us something that looks a little like Shakespeare at first glance. Diversity 1.0 (given this dataset) starts to go off the rails fairly quickly, but note that some basic structures, such as the line break followed by a character's abbreviated name, still show up. All in all, not bad for a relatively simple model, and definitely something you can have fun with generating text for a given style.

> ### Making your generator more useful
>
> If you want to use a generative model for more than just fun, what might you do to make it more consistent and useful?
>
> - Expand the quantity and quality of the corpus.
> - Expand the complexity of the model (number of neurons).
> - Implement a more refined case folding algorithm.
> - Segment sentences.
> - Add filters on grammar, spelling, and tone to match your needs.
> - Generate many more examples than you actually show your users.
> - Use seed texts chosen from the context of the session to steer the chatbot toward useful topics.
> - Use multiple different seed texts within each dialog round to explore what the chatbot can talk about well and what the user finds helpful.
>
> See figure 1.4 for more ideas. Maybe it'll make more sense now than when you first looked at it.

### 9.1.8    *Learned how to say, but not yet what*

So you're generating novel text based solely on example text. And from that you're learning to pick up style. But, and this is somewhat counterintuitive, you have no control over what is being said. The context is limited to the source data, as that'll limit its vocabulary if nothing else. But given an input, you can train toward what you think the original author or authors would say. And the best you can really hope for from this kind of model is *how* they would say it—specifically how they would finish saying what was started with a specific seed sentence. That sentence by no means has to come from the text itself. Because the model is trained on characters themselves, you can use novel words as the seed and get interesting results. Now you have fodder for an entertaining chatbot. But to have your bot say something of substance *and* in a certain style, you'll have to wait until the next chapter.

### 9.1.9    *Other kinds of memory*

LSTMs are an extension of the basic concepts of a recurrent neural net, and a variety of other extensions exist in the same vein. All of them are slight variations on the number or operations of the gates inside the cell. The gated recurrent unit, for example, combines the forget gate and the candidate choice branch from the candidate gate into a single update gate. This gate saves on the number of parameters to learn and has been shown to be comparable to a standard LSTM while being that much less computationally expensive. Keras provides a GRU layer that you can use just as with LSTMs, as shown in the following listing.

Listing 9.31    Gated recurrent units in Keras

```
>>> from keras.models import Sequential
>>> from keras.layers import GRU
>>> model = Sequential()
>>> model.add(GRU(num_neurons, return_sequences=True,
...                input_shape=X[0].shape))
```

Another technique is to use an LSTM with *peephole* connections. Keras doesn't have a direct implementation of this, but several examples on the web extend the Keras LSTM class to do this. The idea is that each gate in a standard LSTM cell has access to the current memory state directly, taken in as part of its input. As described in the paper *Learning Precise Timing with LSTM Recurrent Networks*,[10] the gates contain additional weights of the same dimension as the memory state. The input to each gate is then a concatenation of the input to the cell at that time step and the output of the cell from the previous time step *and* the memory state itself. The authors found more precise modeling of the timing of events in time series data. Although they weren't working specifically in the NLP domain, the concept has validity here as well, but we leave it to the reader to experiment with that.

---

[10] Gers, Schraudolph, Schmidhuber: http://www.jmlr.org/papers/volume3/gers02a/gers02a.pdf.

Those are just two of the RNN/LSTM derivatives out there. Experiments are ever ongoing, and we encourage you to join the fun. The tools are all readily available, so finding the next newest greatest iteration is in the reach of all.

### 9.1.10 *Going deeper*

It's convenient to think of the memory unit as encoding a specific representation of noun/verb pairs or sentence-to-sentence verb tense references, but that isn't specifically what's going on. It's just a happy byproduct of the patterns that the network learns, assuming the training went well. Like in any neural network, layering allows the model to form more-complex representations of the patterns in the training data. And you can just as easily stack LSTM layers (see figure 9.13).

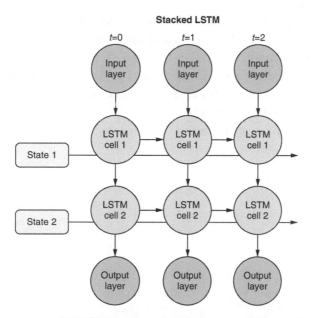

Figure 9.13   Stacked LSTM

Stacked layers are much more computationally expensive to train. But *stacking* them takes only a few seconds in Keras. See the following listing.

Listing 9.32   Two LSTM layers

```
>>> from keras.models import Sequential
>>> from keras.layers import LSTM
>>> model = Sequential()
>>> model.add(LSTM(num_neurons, return_sequences=True,
...                input_shape=X[0].shape))
>>> model.add(LSTM(num_neurons_2, return_sequences=True))
```

Note that the parameter `return_sequences=True` is required in the first and intermediary layers for the model to build correctly. This requirement makes sense because the output at each time step is needed as the input for the time steps of the next layer.

Remember, however, that creating a model that's capable of representing more-complex relationships than are present in the training data can lead to strange results. Simply piling layers onto the model, while fun, is rarely the answer to building the most useful model.

## Summary

- Remembering information with memory units enables more accurate and general models of the sequence.
- It's important to forget information that is no longer relevant.
- Only some new information needs to be retained for the upcoming input, and LSTMs can be trained to find it.
- If you can predict what comes next, you can generate novel text from probabilities.
- Character-based models can more efficiently and successfully learn from small, focused corpora than word-based models.
- LSTM thought vectors capture much more than just the sum of the words in a statement.

# Sequence-to-sequence models and attention

You now know how to create natural language models and use them for everything from sentiment classification to generating novel text (see chapter 9).

Could a neural network translate from English to German? Or even better, would it be possible to predict disease by translating genotype to phenotype (genes to body type)?[1] And what about the chatbot we've been talking about since the

---

[1] geno2pheno: https://academic.oup.com/nar/article/31/13/3850/2904197.

beginning of the book? Can a neural net carry on an entertaining conversation? These are all sequence-to-sequence problems. They map one sequence of indeterminate length to another sequence whose length is also unknown.

In this chapter, you'll learn how to build sequence-to-sequence models using an encoder-decoder architecture.

## 10.1 *Encoder-decoder architecture*

Which of our previous architectures do you think might be useful for sequence-to-sequence problems? The word vector embedding model of chapter 6? The convolutional net of chapter 7 or the recurrent nets of chapter 8 and chapter 9? You guessed it; we're going to build on the LSTM architecture from the last chapter.

LSTMs are great at handling sequences, but it turns out we need two of them rather than only one. We're going to build a modular architecture called an encoder-decoder architecture.

The first half of an encoder-decoder model is the sequence *encoder*, a network which turns a sequence, such as natural language text, into a lower-dimensional representation, such as the thought vector from the end of chapter 9. So you've already built this first half of our sequence-to-sequence model.

The other half of an encoder-decoder architecture is the sequence *decoder*. A sequence decoder can be designed to turn a vector back into human readable text again. But didn't we already do that too? You generated some pretty crazy Shakespearean playscript at the end of chapter 9. That was close, but there are a few more pieces you need to add to get that Shakespearean playwright bot to focus on our new task as a translating scribe.

For example, you might like your model to output the German translation of an English input text. Actually, isn't that just like having our Shakespeare bot translate modern English into Shakespearean? Yes, but in the Shakespeare example we were OK with rolling the dice to let the machine learning algorithm choose any words that matched the probabilities it had learned. That's not going to cut it for a translation service, or for that matter, even a decent playwright bot.

So you already know how to build encoders and decoders; you now need to learn how to make them better, more focused. In fact, the LSTMs from chapter 9 work great as encoders of variable-length text. You built them to capture the meaning and sentiment of natural language text. LSTMs capture that meaning in an internal representation, a thought vector. You just need to extract the thought vector from the state (memory cell) within your LSTM model. You learned how to set `return_state=True` on a Keras LSTM model so that the output includes the hidden layer state. That state vector becomes the output of your encoder and the input to your decoder.

> **TIP**  Whenever you train any neural network model, each of the internal layers contains all the information you need to solve the problem you trained it on. That information is usually represented by a fixed-dimensional tensor

containing the weights or the activations of that layer. And if your network generalizes well, you can be sure that an information bottleneck exists—a layer where the number of dimensions is at a minimum. In Word2vec (see chapter 6), the *weights* of an internal layer were used to compute your vector representation. You can also use the *activations* of an internal network layer directly. That's what the examples in this chapter do. Examine the successful networks you've build in the past to see if you can find this information bottleneck that you can use as an encoded representation of your data.

So all that remains is to improve upon the decoder design. You need to decode a thought vector back into a natural language sequence.

### 10.1.1 Decoding thought

Imagine you'd like to develop a translation model to translate texts from English to German. You'd like to map sequences of characters or words to another sequence of characters or words. You previously discovered how you can predict a sequence element at time step $t$ based on the previous element at time step $t$-1. But directly using an LSTM to map from one language to another runs into problems quickly. For a single LSTM to work, you would need input and output sequences to have the same sequence lengths, and for translation they rarely do.

Figure 10.1 demonstrates the problem. The English and the German sentence have different lengths, which complicates the mapping between the English input and the expected output. The English phrase "is playing" (present progressive) is translated to the German present tense "spielt." But "spielt" here would need to be predicted solely on the input of "is;" you haven't gotten to "playing" yet at that time step. Further,

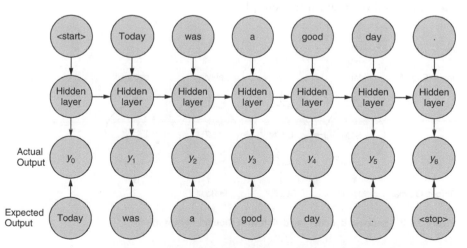

Expected output is the next token in the sample. Shown here on word level.

**Figure 10.1  Limitations of language modeling**

"playing" would then need to map to "Fußball." Certainly a network could learn these mappings, but the learned representations would have to be hyper-specific to the input, and your dream of a more general language model would go out the window.

Sequence-to-sequence networks, sometimes abbreviated with *seq2seq*, solve this limitation by creating an input representation in the form of a thought vector. Sequence-to-sequence models then use that thought vector, sometimes called a context vector, as a starting point to a second network that receives a different set of inputs to generate the output sequence.

> **THOUGHT VECTOR**   Remember when you discovered word vectors? Word vectors are a compression of the meaning of a word into a fixed length vector. Words with similar meaning are close to each other in this vector space of word meanings. A thought vector is very similar. A neural network can compress information from any natural language statement, not just a single word, into a fixed length vector that represents the content of the input text. Thought vectors are this vector. They are used as a numerical representation of the thought within a document to drive some decoder model, usually a translation decoder. The term was coined by Geoffrey Hinton in a talk to the Royal Society in London in 2015.[2]

A sequence-to-sequence network consists of two modular recurrent networks with a thought vector between them (see figure 10.2). The encoder outputs a thought vector at the end of its input sequence. The decoder picks up that thought and outputs a sequence of tokens.

The first network, called the encoder, turns the input text (such as a user message to a chatbot) into the thought vector. The thought vector has two parts, each a vector: the output (activation) of the hidden layer of the encoder and the memory state of the LSTM cell for that input example.

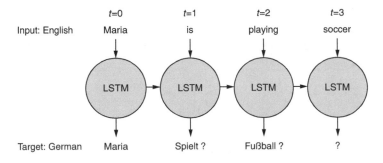

**Figure 10.2   Encoder-decoder sandwich with thought vector meat**

---

[2]   See the web page titled "Deep Learning," (https://www.evl.uic.edu/creativecoding/courses/cs523/slides/week3/DeepLearning_LeCun.pdf).

**TIP** As shown in listing 10.1 later in this chapter, the thought vector is captured in the variable names `state_h` (output of the hidden layer) and `state_c` (the memory state).

The thought vector then becomes the input to a second network: the decoder network. As you'll see later in the implementation section, the generated state (thought vector) will serve as the *initial state* of the decoder network. The second network then uses that initial state and a special kind of input, a *start token*. Primed with that information, the second network has to learn to generate the first element of the target sequence (such as a character or word).

The training and inference stages are treated differently in this particular setup. During training, you pass the starting text to the encoder and the *expected* text as the input to the decoder. You're getting the decoder network to learn that, given a primed state and a key to "get started," it should produce a series of tokens. The first direct input to the decoder will be the start token; the second input should be the first expected or predicted token, which should in turn prompt the network to produce the second expected token.

At inference time, however, you don't have the expected text, so what do you use to pass into the decoder other than the state? You use the generic start token and then take the first generated element, which will then become the input to the decoder at the next time step, to generate the next element, and so on. This process repeats until the maximum number of sequence elements is reached or a stop token is generated.

Trained end-to-end this way, the decoder will turn a thought vector into a fully decoded response to the initial input sequence (such as the user question). Splitting the solution into two networks with the thought vector as the binding piece in-between allows you to map input sequences to output sequences of different lengths (see figure 10.3).

## 10.1.2 Look familiar?

It may seem like you've seen an encoder-decoder approach before. You may have. Autoencoders are a common encoder-decoder architecture for students learning about neural networks. They are a repeat-game-playing neural net that's trained to

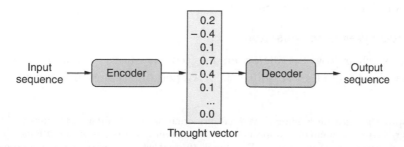

**Figure 10.3   Unrolled encoder-decoder**

regurgitate its input, which makes finding training data easy. Nearly any large set of high-dimensional tensors, vectors, or sequences will do.

Like any encoder-decoder architecture, autoencoders have a bottleneck of information between the encoder and decoder that you can use as a lower-dimensional representation of the input data. Any network with an information bottleneck can be used as an encoder within an encoder-decoder architecture, even if the network was only trained to paraphrase or restate the input.[3]

Although autoencoders have the same structure as our encoder-decoders in this chapter, they're trained for a different task. Autoencoders are trained to find a vector representation of input data such that the input can be reconstructed by the network's decoder with minimal error. The encoder and decoder are pseudo-inverses of each other. The network's purpose is to find a dense vector representation of the input data (such as an image or text) that allows the decoder to reconstruct it with the smallest error. During the training phase, the input data and the expected output are the same. Therefore, if your goal is finding a dense vector representation of your data—not generating thought vectors for language translation or finding responses for a given question—an autoencoder can be a good option.

What about PCA and t-SNE from chapter 6? Did you use `sklearn.decomposition.PCA` or `sklearn.manifold.TSNE` for visualizing vectors in the other chapters? The t-SNE model produces an embedding as its output, so you can think of it as an encoder, in some sense. The same goes for PCA. However, these models are unsupervised so they can't be targeted at a particular output or task. And these algorithms were developed mainly for feature extraction and visualization. They create very tight bottlenecks to output very low-dimensional vectors, typically two or three. And they aren't designed to take in sequences of arbitrary length. That's what an encoder is all about. And you've learned that LSTMs are the state-of-the-art for extracting features and embeddings from sequences.

> **NOTE** A *variational autoencoder* is a modified version of an autoencoder that is trained to be a good generator as well as encoder-decoder. A variational autoencoder produces a compact vector that not only is a faithful representation of the input but is also Gaussian distributed. This makes it easier to generate a new output by randomly selecting a seed vector and feeding that into the decoder half of the autoencoder.[4]

### 10.1.3 *Sequence-to-sequence conversation*

It may not be clear how the dialog engine (conversation) problem is related to machine translation, but they're quite similar. Generating replies in a conversation for

---

[3] An Autoencoder Approach to Learning Bilingual Word Representations by Chandar and Lauly et al.: https://papers.nips.cc/paper/5270-an-autoencoder-approach-to-learning-bilingual-word-representations.pdf.

[4] See the web page titled "Variational Autoencoders Explained" (http://kvfrans.com/variational-autoencoders-explained).

a chatbot isn't that different from generating a German translation of an English statement in a machine translation system.

Both translation and conversation tasks require your model to map one sequence to another. Mapping sequences of English tokens to German sequences is very similar to mapping natural language statements in a conversation to the expected response by the dialog engine. You can think of the machine translation engine as a schizophrenic, bilingual dialog engine that is playing the childish "echo game,"[5] listening in English and responding in German.

But you want your bot to be responsive, rather than just an echo chamber. So your model needs to bring in any additional information about the world that you want your chatbot to talk about. Your NLP model will have to learn a much more complex mapping from statement to response than echoing or translation. This requires more training data and a higher-dimensional thought vector, because it must contain all the information your dialog engine needs to know about the world. You learned in chapter 9 how to increase the dimensionality, and thus the information capacity, of the thought vector in an LSTM model. You also need to get enough of the right kind of data if you want to turn a translation machine into a conversation machine.

Given a set of tokens, you can train your machine learning pipeline to mimic a conversational response sequence. You need enough of those pairs and enough information capacity in the thought vector to understand all those mappings. Once you have a dataset with enough of these pairs of "translations" from statement to response, you can train a conversation engine using the same network you used for machine translation.

Keras provides modules for building networks for sequence-to-sequence networks with a modular architecture called an encoder-decoder model. And it provides an API to access all the internals of an LSTM network that you need to solve translation, conversation, and even genotype-to-phenotype problems.

### 10.1.4 LSTM review

In the last chapter, you learned how an LSTM gives recurrent nets a way to selectively remember and forget patterns of tokens they have "seen" within a sample document. The input token for each time step passes through the forget and update gates, is multiplied by weights and masks, and then is stored in a memory cell. The network output at that time step (token) is dictated not solely by the input token, but also by a combination of the input *and* the memory unit's current state.

Importantly, an LSTM shares that token pattern recognizer between documents, because the forget and update gates have weights that are trained as they read many documents. So an LSTM doesn't have to relearn English spelling and grammar with each new document. And you learned how to activate these token patterns stored in

---

5 Also called the "repeat game," http://uncyclopedia.wikia.com/wiki/Childish_Repeating_Game.

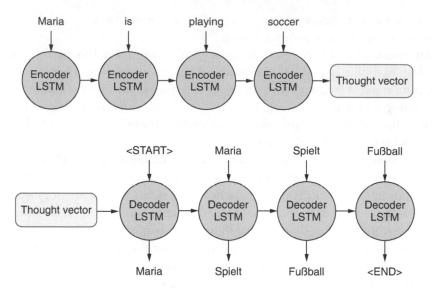

**Figure 10.4  Next word prediction**

the weights of an LSTM memory cell to predict the tokens that follow based on some seed tokens to trigger the sequence generation (see figure 10.4).

With a token-by-token prediction, you were able to generate some text by selecting the next token based on the probability distribution of likely next tokens suggested by the network. Not perfect by any stretch, but entertaining nonetheless. But you aren't here for mere entertainment; you'd like to have some control over what comes out of a generative model.

Sutskever, Vinyals, and Le came up with a way to bring in a second LSTM model to *decode* the patterns in the memory cell in a less random and more controlled way.[6] They proposed using the classification aspect of the LSTM to create a thought vector and then use that generated vector as the input to a second, *different* LSTM that only tries to predict token by token, which gives you a way to map an input sequence to a distinct output sequence. Let's take a look at how it works.

## 10.2 *Assembling a sequence-to-sequence pipeline*

With your knowledge from the previous chapters, you have all the pieces you need to assemble a sequence-to-sequence machine learning pipeline.

### 10.2.1 *Preparing your dataset for the sequence-to-sequence training*

As you've seen in previous implementations of convolutional or recurrent neural networks, you need to pad the input data to a fixed length. Usually, you'd extend the

---

[6] Sutskever, Vinyals, and Le; arXiv:1409.3215, http://papers.nips.cc/paper/5346-sequence-to-sequence-learning-with-neural-networks.pdf.

input sequences to match the longest input sequence with pad tokens. In the case of the sequence-to-sequence network, you also need to prepare your target data and pad it to match the longest target sequence. Remember, the sequence lengths of the input and target data don't need to be the same (see figure 10.5).

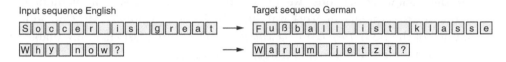

**Figure 10.5   Input and target sequence before preprocessing**

In addition to the required padding, the output sequence should be annotated with the start and stop tokens, to tell the decoder when the job starts and when it's done (see figure 10.6).

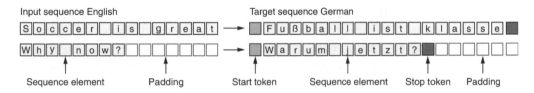

**Figure 10.6   Input and target sequence after preprocessing**

You'll learn how to annotate the target sequences later in the chapter when you build the Keras pipeline. Just keep in mind that you'll need two versions of the target sequence for training: one that starts with the start token (which you'll use for the decoder input), and one that starts without the start token (the target sequence the loss function will score for accuracy).

In earlier chapters, your training sets consisted of pairs: an input and an expected output. Each training example for the sequence-to-sequence model will be a triplet: initial input, expected output (prepended by a start token), and expected output (without the start token).

Before you get into the implementation details, let's recap for a moment. Your sequence-to-sequence network consists of two networks: the encoder, which will generate your thought vector; and a decoder, that you'll pass the thought vector into, as its initial state. With the initialized state and a start token as input to the decoder network, you'll then generate the first sequence element (such as a character or word vector) of the output. Each following element will then be predicted based on the updated state and the next element in the expected sequence. This process will go on until you either generate a stop token or you reach the maximum number of elements. All sequence elements generated by the decoder will form your predicted output (such as your reply to a user question). With this in mind, let's take a look at the details.

### 10.2.2 Sequence-to-sequence model in Keras

In the following sections, we guide you through a Keras implementation of a sequence-to-sequence network published by Francois Chollet.[7] Mr. Chollet is also the author of the book *Deep Learning with Python* (Manning, 2017), an invaluable resource for learning neural network architectures and Keras.

During the training phase, you'll train the encoder and decoder network together, end to end, which requires three data points for each sample: a training encoder input sequence, a decoder input sequence, and a decoder output sequence. The training encoder input sequence could be a user question for which you'd like a bot to respond. The decoder input sequence then is the expected reply by the future bot.

You might wonder why you need an input *and* output sequence for the decoder. The reason is that you're training the decoder with a method called *teacher forcing*, where you'll use the initial state provided by the encoder network and train the decoder to produce the expected sequences by showing the input to the decoder and letting it predict the same sequence. Therefore, the decoder's input and output sequences will be identical, except that the sequences have an offset of one time step.

During the execution phase, you'll use the encoder to generate the thought vector of your user input, and the decoder will then generate a reply based on that thought vector. The output of the decoder will then serve as the reply to the user.

> **KERAS FUNCTIONAL API**   In the following example, you'll notice a different implementation style of the Keras layers you've seen in previous chapters. Keras introduced an additional way of assembling models by calling each layer and passing the value from the previous layer to it. The functional API can be powerful when you want to build models and reuse portions of the trained models (as you'll demonstrate in the coming sections). For more information about Keras' functional API, we highly recommend the blog post by the Keras core developer team.[8]

### 10.2.3 Sequence encoder

The encoder's sole purpose is the creation of your thought vector, which then serves as the initial state of the decoder network (see figure 10.7). You can't train an encoder fully in isolation. You have no "target" thought vector for the network to learn to predict. The backpropagation that will train the encoder to create an appropriate

---

[7] See the web page titled "A ten-minute introduction to sequence-to-sequence learning in Keras" (https://blog.keras.io/a-ten-minute-introduction-to-sequence-to-sequence-learning-in-keras.html).

[8] See the web page titled "Getting started with the Keras functional API" (https://keras.io/getting-started/functional-api-guide/).

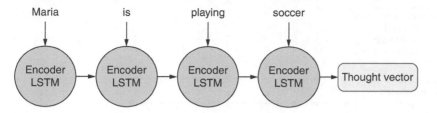

**Figure 10.7  Thought encoder**

thought vector will come from the error that's generated later downstream in the decoder.

Nonetheless the encoder and decoder are independent modules that are often interchangeable with each other. For example, once your encoder is trained on the English-to-German translation problem, it can be reused with a different encoder for translation from English to Spanish.[9] Listing 10.1 shows what the encoder looks like in isolation.

Conveniently, the RNN layers, provided by Keras, return their internal state when you instantiate the LSTM layer (or layers) with the keyword argument `return_state=True`. In the following snippet, you preserve the final state of the encoder and disregard the actual output of the encoder. The list of the LSTM states is then passed to the decoder.

---

**Listing 10.1   Thought encoder in Keras**

*The return_state argument of the LSTM layer needs to be set to True to return the internal states.*

```
>>> encoder_inputs = Input(shape=(None, input_vocab_size))
>>> encoder = LSTM(num_neurons, return_state=True)
>>> encoder_outputs, state_h, state_c = encoder(encoder_inputs)
>>> encoder_states = (state_h, state_c)
```

*The first return value of the LSTM layer is the output of the layer.*

Because `return_sequences` defaults to `False`, the first return value is the output from the last time step. `state_h` will be specifically the output of the last time step for this layer. So in this case, `encoder_outputs` and `state_h` will be identical. Either way you can ignore the official output stored in `encoder_outputs`. `state_c` is the current state of the memory unit. `state_h` and `state_c` will make up your thought vector.

---

[9]  Training a multi-task model like this is called "joint training" or "transfer learning" and was described by Luong, Le, Sutskever, Vinyals, and Kaier (Google Brain) at ICLR 2016: https://arxiv.org/pdf/1511.06114.pdf.

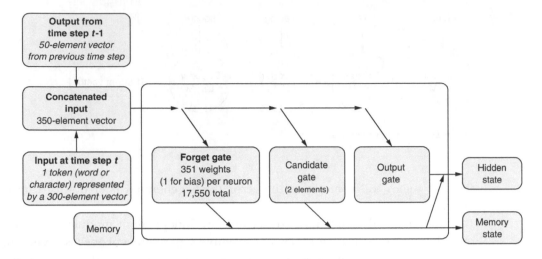

**Figure 10.8   LSTM states used in the sequence-to-sequence encoder**

Figure 10.8 shows how the internal LSTM states are generated. The encoder will update the hidden and memory states with every time step, and pass the final states to the decoder as the initial state.

### 10.2.4  Thought decoder

Similar to the encoder network setup, the setup of the decoder is pretty straightforward. The major difference is that this time you do want to capture the output of the network at each time step. You want to judge the "correctness" of the output, token by token (see figure 10.9).

This is where you use the second and third pieces of the sample 3-tuple. The decoder has a standard token-by-token input and a token-by-token output. They are almost identical, but off by one time step. You want the decoder to learn to reproduce the tokens of a given input sequence *given* the state generated by the first piece of the 3-tuple fed into the encoder.

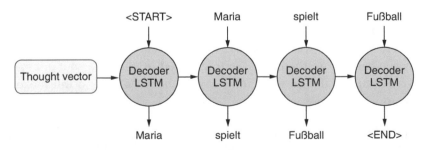

**Figure 10.9   Thought decoder**

> **NOTE** This is the key concept for the decoder, and for sequence-to-sequence models in general; you're training a network to output in the secondary problem space (another language or another being's response to a given question). You form a "thought" about both what was said (the input) and the reply (the output) simultaneously. And this thought defines the response token by token. Eventually, you'll only need the thought (generated by the encoder) and a generic start token to get things going. That's enough to trigger the correct output sequence.

To calculate the error of the training step, you'll pass the output of your LSTM layer into a dense layer. The dense layer will have a number of neurons equal to the number of all possible output tokens. The dense layer will have a softmax activation function across those tokens. So at each time step, the network will provide a probability distribution over all possible tokens for what it thinks is most likely the next sequence element. Take the token whose related neuron has the highest value. You used an output layer with softmax activation functions in earlier chapters, where you wanted to determine a token with the highest likelihood (see chapter 6 for more details). Also note that the `num_encoder_tokens` and the `output_vocab_size` don't need to match, which is one of the great benefits of sequence-to-sequence networks. See the following listing.

---

**Listing 10.2  Thought decoder in Keras**

**The functional API allows you to pass the initial state to the LSTM layer by assigning the last encoder state to initial_state.**

**Set up the LSTM layer, similar to the encoder but with an additional argument of return_sequences.**

```
>>> decoder_inputs = Input(shape=(None, output_vocab_size))
>>> decoder_lstm = LSTM(
...     num_neurons,return_sequences=True, return_state=True)
>>> decoder_outputs, _, _ = decoder_lstm(
...     decoder_inputs, initial_state=encoder_states)
>>> decoder_dense = Dense(
...     output_vocab_size, activation='softmax')
>>> decoder_outputs = decoder_dense(decoder_outputs)
```

**Softmax layer with all possible characters mapped to the softmax output**

**Passing the output of the LSTM layer to the softmax layer**

### 10.2.5  Assembling the sequence-to-sequence network

The functional API of Keras allows you to assemble a model as object calls. The `Model` object lets you define its input and output parts of the network. For this sequence-to-sequence network, you'll pass a list of your inputs to the model. In listing 10.2, you defined one input layer in the encoder and one in the decoder. These two inputs correspond with the first two elements of each training triplet. As an output layer, you're passing the `decoder_outputs` to the model, which includes the entire model setup you previously defined. The output in `decoder_outputs` corresponds with the final element of each of your training triplets.

NOTE   Using the functional API like this, definitions such as `decoder _out-puts` are *tensor* representations. This is where you'll notice differences from the sequential model described in earlier chapters. Again refer to the documentation for the nitty-gritty of the Keras API. See the following listing.

---

**Listing 10.3   Keras functional API (`Model()`)**

```
>>> model = Model(
...     inputs=[encoder_inputs, decoder_inputs],
...     outputs=decoder_outputs)
```

> The inputs and outputs arguments can be defined as lists if you expect multiple inputs or outputs.

## 10.3   *Training the sequence-to-sequence network*

The last remaining steps for creating a sequence-to-sequence model in the Keras model are to compile and fit. The only difference compared to earlier chapters is that earlier you were predicting a binary classification: yes or no. But here you have a categorical classification or multiclass classification problem. At each time step you must determine which of many "categories" is correct. And we have many categories here. The model must choose between all possible tokens to "say." Because you're predicting characters or words rather than binary states, you'll optimize your loss based on the `categorical_crossentropy` loss function, rather than the `binary_crossentropy` used earlier. So that's the only change you need to make to the Keras `model.compile` step, as shown in the following listing.

---

**Listing 10.4   Train a sequence-to-sequence model in Keras**

```
>>> model.compile(optimizer='rmsprop', loss='categorical_crossentropy')
>>> model.fit([encoder_input_data, decoder_input_data],
              decoder_target_data,
              batch_size=batch_size, epochs=epochs)
```

> The model expects the training inputs as a list, where the first list element is passed to the encoder network and the second element is passed to the decoder network during the training.

> Setting the loss function to categorical_ crossentropy.

Congratulations! With the call to `model.fit`, you're training your sequence-to-sequence network, end to end. In the following sections, you'll demonstrate how you can infer an output sequence for a given input sequence.

NOTE   The training of sequence-to-sequence networks can be computationally intensive and therefore time-consuming. If your training sequences are long or if you want to train with a large corpus, we highly recommend training these networks on a GPU, which can increase the training speed by 30 times. If you've never trained a neural network on a GPU, don't worry. Check out chapter 13 on how to rent and set up your own GPU on commercial computational cloud services.

LSTMs aren't inherently parallelizable like convolutional neural nets, so to get the full benefit of a GPU you should replace the LSTM layers with `CuDN-NLSTM`, which is optimized for training on a GPU enabled with CUDA.

### 10.3.1 Generate output sequences

Before generating sequences, you need to take the structure of your training layers and reassemble them for generation purposes. At first, you define a model specific to the encoder. This model will then be used to generate the thought vector. See the following listing.

> **Listing 10.5  Decoder for generating text using the generic Keras `Model`**

```
>>> encoder_model = Model(inputs=encoder_inputs, outputs=encoder_states)
```

**Here you use the previously defined encoder_inputs and encoder_states; calling the predict method on this model would return the thought vector.**

The definition of the decoder can look daunting. But let's untangle the code snippet step by step. First, you'll define your decoder inputs. You are using the Keras input layer, but instead of passing in one-hot vectors, characters, or word embeddings, you'll pass the thought vector generated by the encoder network. Note that the encoder returns a list of two states, which you'll need to pass to the `initial_state` argument when calling your previously defined `decoder_lstm`. The output of the LSTM layer is then passed to the dense layer, which you also previously defined. The output of this layer will then provide the probabilities of all decoder output tokens (in this case, all seen characters during the training phase).

Here is the magic part. The token predicted with the highest probability at each time step will then be returned as the most likely token and passed on to the next decoder iteration step, as the new input. See the following listing.

> **Listing 10.6  Sequence generator for random thoughts**

```
>>> thought_input = [Input(shape=(num_neurons,)),
...      Input(shape=(num_neurons,))]
>>> decoder_outputs, state_h, state_c = decoder_lstm(
...      decoder_inputs, initial_state=thought_input)
>>> decoder_states = [state_h, state_c]
>>> decoder_outputs = decoder_dense(decoder_outputs)

>>> decoder_model = Model(
...      inputs=[decoder_inputs] + thought_input,
...      output=[decoder_outputs] + decoder_states)
```

**Define an input layer to take the encoder states.**

**Pass the encoder state to the LSTM layer as initial state.**

**The updated LSTM state will then become the new cell state for the next iteration.**

**The last step is tying the decoder model together.**

**Pass the output from the LSTM to the dense layer to predict the next token.**

**The output of the dense layer and the updated states are defined as output.**

**The decoder_inputs and thought_input become the input to the decoder model.**

Once the model is set up, you can generate sequences by predicting the thought vector based on a one-hot encoded input sequence and the last generated token. During the first iteration, the `target_seq` is set to the start token. During all following iterations, `target_seq` is updated with the last generated token. This loop goes on until either you've reached the maximum number of sequence elements or the decoder generates a stop token, at which time the generation is stopped. See the following listing.

---

**Listing 10.7    Simple decoder—next word prediction**

```
...
>>> thought = encoder_model.predict(input_seq)    ◄─┐ Encode the input sequence
...                                                   into a thought vector (the
>>> while not stop_condition:            ◄──────────  LSTM memory cell state).
...        output_tokens, h, c = decoder_model.predict(
...            [target_seq] + thought)   ◄─┐
```

**The decoder returns the token with the highest probability and the internal states, which are reused during the next iteration.**

**The stop_condition is updated after each iteration and turns True if either the maximum number of output sequence tokens is hit or the decoder generates a stop token.**

## 10.4    *Building a chatbot using sequence-to-sequence networks*

In the previous sections, you learned how to train a sequence-to-sequence network and how to use the trained network to generate sequence responses. In the following section, we guide you through how to apply the various steps to train a chatbot. For the chatbot training, you'll use the Cornell movie dialog corpus.[10] You'll train a sequence-to-sequence network to "adequately" reply to your questions or statements. Our chatbot example is an adopted sequence-to-sequence example from the Keras blog.[11]

### 10.4.1    *Preparing the corpus for your training*

First, you need to load the corpus and generate the training sets from it. The training data will determine the set of characters the encoder and decoder will support during the training and during the generation phase. Please note that this implementation doesn't support characters that haven't been included during the training phase. Using the entire Cornell Movie Dialog dataset can be computationally intensive because a few sequences have more than 2,000 tokens—2,000 time steps will take a while to unroll. But the majority of dialog samples are based on less than 100 characters. For this example, you've preprocessed the dialog corpus by limiting samples to those with fewer than 100 characters, removed odd characters, and only allowed

---

[10] See the web page titled "Cornell Movie-Dialogs Corpus" (https://www.cs.cornell.edu/~cristian/Cornell_Movie-Dialogs_Corpus.html).

[11] See the web page titled "keras/examples/lstm_seq2seq.py at master" (https://github.com/fchollet/keras/blob/master/examples/lstm_seq2seq.py).

lowercase characters. With these changes, you limit the variety of characters. You can find the preprocessed corpus in the GitHub repository of *NLP in Action*.[12]

You'll loop over the corpus file and generate the training pairs (technically 3-tuples: input text, target text with start token, and target text). While reading the corpus, you'll also generate a set of input and target characters, which you'll then use to one-hot encode the samples. The input and target characters don't have to match. But characters that aren't included in the sets can't be read or generated during the generation phase. The result of the following listing is two lists of input and target texts (strings), as well as two sets of characters that have been seen in the training corpus.

**Listing 10.8    Build character sequence-to-sequence training set**

**The sets hold the seen characters in the input and target text.**

**The arrays hold the input and target text read from the corpus file.**

**The target sequence is annotated with a start (first) and stop (last) token; the characters representing the tokens are defined here. These tokens can't be part of the normal sequence text and should be uniquely used as start and stop tokens.**

**max_training_samples defines how many lines are used for the training. It's the lower number of either a user-defined maximum or the total number of lines loaded from the file.**

```
>>> from nlpia.loaders import get_data
>>> df = get_data('moviedialog')
>>> input_texts, target_texts = [], []
>>> input_vocabulary = set()
>>> output_vocabulary = set()
>>> start_token = '\t'
>>> stop_token = '\n'
>>> max_training_samples = min(25000, len(df) - 1)

>>> for input_text, target_text in zip(df.statement, df.reply):
...     target_text = start_token + target_text \
...         + stop_token
...     input_texts.append(input_text)
...     target_texts.append(target_text)
...     for char in input_text:
...         if char not in input_vocabulary:
...             input_vocabulary.add(char)
...     for char in target_text:
...         if char not in output_vocabulary:
...             output_vocabulary.add(char)
```

**The target_text needs to be wrapped with the start and stop tokens.**

**Compile the vocabulary— set of the unique characters seen in the input_texts.**

### 10.4.2  Building your character dictionary

Similar to the examples from your previous chapters, you need to convert each character of the input and target texts into one-hot vectors that represent each character. In order to generate the one-hot vectors, you generate token dictionaries (for the input and target text), where every character is mapped to an index. You also generate the reverse dictionary (index to character), which you'll use during the generation phase to convert the generated index to a character. See the following listing.

---

[12] See the web page titled "GitHub - totalgood/nlpia" (https://github.com/totalgood/nlpia).

---

**Listing 10.9   Character sequence-to-sequence model parameters**

**For the input and target data, you also determine the maximum number of sequence tokens.**

**You convert the character sets into sorted lists of characters, which you then use to generate the dictionary.**

**For the input and target data, you determine the maximum number of unique characters, which you use to build the one-hot matrices.**

```
>>> input_vocabulary = sorted(input_vocabulary)
>>> output_vocabulary = sorted(output_vocabulary)

>>> input_vocab_size = len(input_vocabulary)
>>> output_vocab_size = len(output_vocabulary)
>>> max_encoder_seq_length = max(
...     [len(txt) for txt in input_texts])
>>> max_decoder_seq_length = max(
...     [len(txt) for txt in target_texts])

>>> input_token_index = dict([(char, i) for i, char in
...     enumerate(input_vocabulary)])
>>> target_token_index = dict(
...     [(char, i) for i, char in enumerate(output_vocabulary)])
>>> reverse_input_char_index = dict((i, char) for char, i in
...     input_token_index.items())
>>> reverse_target_char_index = dict((i, char) for char, i in
...     target_token_index.items())
```

**Loop over the input_characters and output_vocabulary to create the lookup dictionaries, which you use to generate the one-hot vectors.**

**Loop over the newly created dictionaries to create the reverse lookups.**

### 10.4.3   Generate one-hot encoded training sets

In the next step, you're converting the input and target text into one-hot encoded "tensors." In order to do that, you loop over each input and target sample, and over each character of each sample, and one-hot encode each character. Each character is encoded by an *n x 1* vector (with *n* being the number of unique input or target characters). All vectors are then combined to create a matrix for each sample, and all samples are combined to create the training tensor. See the following listing.

---

**Listing 10.10   Construct character sequence encoder-decoder training set**

```
>>> import numpy as np

>>> encoder_input_data = np.zeros((len(input_texts),
...     max_encoder_seq_length, input_vocab_size),
...     dtype='float32')
>>> decoder_input_data = np.zeros((len(input_texts),
...     max_decoder_seq_length, output_vocab_size),
...     dtype='float32')
>>> decoder_target_data = np.zeros((len(input_texts),
...     max_decoder_seq_length, output_vocab_size),
...     dtype='float32')

>>> for i, (input_text, target_text) in enumerate(
...             zip(input_texts, target_texts)):
```

**You use numpy for the matrix manipulations.**

**The training tensors are initialized as zero tensors with shape (num_samples, max_len_sequence, num_unique_tokens_in_vocab).**

**Loop over the training samples; input and target texts need to correspond.**

```
...         for t, char in enumerate(input_text):          ◄──┐ Loop over each character
...             encoder_input_data[                             of each sample.
...                 i, t, input_token_index[char]] = 1.
...         for t, char in enumerate(target_text):          ◄────
...             decoder_input_data[
...                 i, t, target_token_index[char]] = 1.
...             if t > 0:
...                 decoder_target_data[i, t - 1, target_token_index[char]] = 1
```

**Set the index for the character at each time step to one; all other indices remain at zero. This creates the one-hot encoded representation of the training samples.**

**For the training data for the decoder, you create the decoder_input_data and decoder_target_data (which is one time step behind the decoder_input_data).**

### 10.4.4 *Train your sequence-to-sequence chatbot*

After all the training set preparation—converting the preprocessed corpus into input and target samples, creating index lookup dictionaries, and converting the samples into one-hot tensors—it's time to train the chatbot. The code is identical to the earlier samples. Once the model.fit completes the training, you have a fully trained chatbot based on a sequence-to-sequence network. See the following listing.

---

**Listing 10.11   Construct and train a character sequence encoder-decoder network**

**In this example, you set the batch size to 64 samples. Increasing the batch size can speed up the training; it might also require more memory.**

```
>>> from keras.models import Model
>>> from keras.layers import Input, LSTM, Dense

>>> batch_size = 64                                 ◄──┐ Training a sequence-to-
>>> epochs = 100                                    ◄──  sequence network can
>>> num_neurons = 256                               ◄──  be lengthy and easily
                                                          require 100 epochs.

>>> encoder_inputs = Input(shape=(None, input_vocab_size))    In this example, you set
>>> encoder = LSTM(num_neurons, return_state=True)            the number of neuron
>>> encoder_outputs, state_h, state_c = encoder(encoder_inputs)  dimensions to 256.
>>> encoder_states = [state_h, state_c]

>>> decoder_inputs = Input(shape=(None, output_vocab_size))
>>> decoder_lstm = LSTM(num_neurons, return_sequences=True,   You withhold 10%
...                     return_state=True)                    of the samples for
>>> decoder_outputs, _, _ = decoder_lstm(decoder_inputs,      validation tests
...     initial_state=encoder_states)                         after each epoch.
>>> decoder_dense = Dense(output_vocab_size, activation='softmax')
>>> decoder_outputs = decoder_dense(decoder_outputs)
>>> model = Model([encoder_inputs, decoder_inputs], decoder_outputs)

>>> model.compile(optimizer='rmsprop', loss='categorical_crossentropy',
...               metrics=['acc'])
>>> model.fit([encoder_input_data, decoder_input_data],
...     decoder_target_data, batch_size=batch_size, epochs=epochs,
...     validation_split=0.1)                                 ◄────
```

### 10.4.5  *Assemble the model for sequence generation*

Setting up the model for the sequence generation is very much the same as we discussed in the earlier sections. But you have to make some adjustments, because you don't have a specific target text to feed into the decoder along with the state. All you have is the input, and a start token. See the following listing.

---

**Listing 10.12    Construct response generator model**

```
>>> encoder_model = Model(encoder_inputs, encoder_states)
>>> thought_input = [
...     Input(shape=(num_neurons,)), Input(shape=(num_neurons,))]
>>> decoder_outputs, state_h, state_c = decoder_lstm(
...     decoder_inputs, initial_state=thought_input)
>>> decoder_states = [state_h, state_c]
>>> decoder_outputs = decoder_dense(decoder_outputs)

>>> decoder_model = Model(
...     inputs=[decoder_inputs] + thought_input,
...     output=[decoder_outputs] + decoder_states)
```

### 10.4.6  *Predicting a sequence*

The decode_sequence function is the heart of the response generation of your chatbot. It accepts a one-hot encoded input sequence, generates the thought vector, and uses the thought vector to generate the appropriate response by using the network trained earlier. See the following listing.

---

**Listing 10.13    Build a character-based translator**

```
>>> def decode_sequence(input_seq):            ┐ Generate the thought vector
...     thought = encoder_model.predict(input_seq) ◄─┘ as the input to the decoder.

...     target_seq = np.zeros((1, 1, output_vocab_size))    ◄──┐ In contrast to
...     target_seq[0, 0, target_token_index[stop_token]        │ the training,
...         ] = 1.              ◄──┐                           │ target_seq starts off
...     stop_condition = False      │ The first input token to the │ as a zero tensor.
...     generated_sequence = ''     │ decoder is the start token.

...     while not stop_condition:                           ┐ Passing the already-generated
...         output_tokens, h, c = decoder_model.predict(    │ tokens and the latest state
...             [target_seq] + thought)        ◄────────────┘ to the decoder to predict the
                                                              next sequence element

...         generated_token_idx = np.argmax(output_tokens[0, -1, :])
...         generated_char = reverse_target_char_index[generated_token_idx]
...         generated_sequence += generated_char
...         if (generated_char == stop_token or
...                 len(generated_sequence) > max_decoder_seq_length
...                 ):
...             stop_condition = True          ◄──┐ Setting the stop_condition
                                                   │ to True will stop the loop.
```

```
...            target_seq = np.zeros((1, 1, output_vocab_size))
...            target_seq[0, 0, generated_token_idx] = 1.
...            thought = [h, c]

...        return generated_sequence
```

**Update the target sequence and use the last generated token as the input to the next generation step.**

**Update the thought vector state.**

### 10.4.7 Generating a response

Now you'll define a helper function, `response()`, to convert an input string (such as a statement from a human user) into a reply for the chatbot to use. This function first converts the user's input text into a sequence of one-hot encoded vectors. That tensor of one-hot vectors is then passed to the previously defined `decode_sequence()` function. It accomplishes the encoding of the input texts into thought vectors and the generation of text from those thought vectors.

> **NOTE** The key is that instead of providing an initial state (thought vector) and an input sequence to the decoder, you're supplying only the thought vector and a start token. The token that the decoder produces given the initial state and the start token becomes the input to the decoder at time step 2. And the output at time step 2 becomes the input at time step 3, and so on. All the while the LSTM memory state is updating the memory and augmenting output as it goes—just like you saw in chapter 9:

**Loop over each character of the input text to generate the one-hot tensor for the encoder to generate the thought vector from.**

```
>>> def response(input_text):
...     input_seq = np.zeros((1, max_encoder_seq_length, input_vocab_size),
...         dtype='float32')
...     for t, char in enumerate(input_text):
...         input_seq[0, t, input_token_index[char]] = 1.
...     decoded_sentence = decode_sequence(input_seq)
...     print('Bot Reply (Decoded sentence):', decoded_sentence)
```

**Use the decode_sequence function to call the trained model and generate the response sequence.**

### 10.4.8 Converse with your chatbot

Voila! You just completed all necessary steps to train and use your own chatbot. Congratulations! Interested in what the chatbot can reply to? After 100 epochs of training, which took approximately seven and a half hours on an NVIDIA GRID K520 GPU, the trained sequence-to-sequence chatbot was still a bit stubborn and short-spoken. A larger and more general training corpus could change that behavior:

```
>>> response("what is the internet?")
Bot Reply (Decoded sentence): it's the best thing i can think of anything.

>>> response("why?")
Bot Reply (Decoded sentence): i don't know. i think it's too late.
```

```
>>> response("do you like coffee?")
Bot Reply (Decoded sentence): yes.

>>> response("do you like football?")
Bot Reply (Decoded sentence): yeah.
```

> **NOTE**  If you don't want to set up a GPU and train your own chatbot, no wor-
> ries. We made the trained chatbot available for you to test it. Head over to the
> GitHub repository of *NLP in Action*[13] and check out the latest chatbot version.
> Let the authors know if you come across any funny replies by the chatbot.

## 10.5  Enhancements

There are two enhancements to the way you train sequence-to-sequence models that
can improve their accuracy and scalability. Like human learning, deep learning can
benefit from a well-designed curriculum. You need to categorize and order the training material to ensure speedy absorption, and you need to ensure that the instructor
highlights the most import parts of any given document.

### 10.5.1  Reduce training complexity with bucketing

Input sequences can have different lengths, which can add a large number of pad
tokens to short sequences in your training data. Too much padding can make the
computation expensive, especially when the majority of the sequences are short and
only a handful of them use close-to-the-maximum token length. Imagine you train
your sequence-to-sequence network with data where almost all samples are 100
tokens long, except for a few outliers that contain 1,000 tokens. Without bucketing,
you'd need to pad the majority of your training with 900 pad tokens, and your
sequence-to-sequence network would have to loop over them during the training
phase. This padding will slow down the training dramatically. Bucketing can reduce
the computation in these cases. You can sort the sequences by length and use different sequence lengths during different batch runs. You assign the input sequences to
buckets of different lengths, such as all sequences with a length between 5 and 10
tokens, and then use the sequence buckets for your training batches, such as train
first with all sequences between 5 and 10 tokens, 10 to 15, and so on. Some deep
learning frameworks provide bucketing tools to suggest the optimal buckets for your
input data.

   As shown in figure 10.10, the sequences were first sorted by length and then only
padded to the maximum token length for the particular bucket. That way, you can
reduce the number of time steps needed for any particular batch while training the
sequence-to-sequence network. You only unroll the network as far as is necessary (to
the longest sequence) in a given training batch.

---

[13] See the web page titled "GitHub - totalgood/nlpia" (https://github.com/totalgood/nlpia).

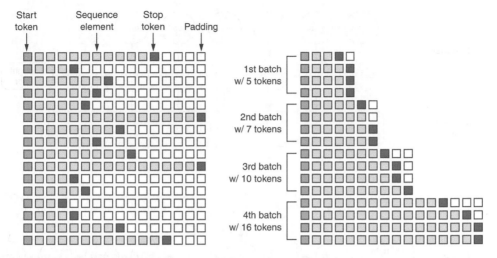

**Figure 10.10  Bucketing applied to target sequences**

## 10.5.2 *Paying attention*

As with latent semantic analysis introduced in chapter 4, longer input sequences (documents) tend to produce thought vectors that are less precise representations of those documents. A thought vector is limited by the dimensionality of the LSTM layer (the number of neurons). A single thought vector is sufficient for short input/output sequences, similar to your chatbot example. But imagine the case when you want to train a sequence-to-sequence model to summarize online articles. In this case, your input sequence can be a lengthy article, which should be compressed into a single thought vector to generate such as a headline. As you can imagine, training the network to determine the most relevant information in that longer document is tricky. A headline or summary (and the associated thought vector) must focus on a particular aspect or portion of that document rather than attempt to represent all of the complexity of its meaning.

In 2015, Bahdanau et al. presented their solution to this problem at the International Conference on Learning Representations.[14] The concept the authors developed became known as the *attention mechanism* (see figure 10.11). As the name suggests, the idea is to tell the decoder what to pay attention to in the input sequence. This "sneak preview" is achieved by allowing the decoder to also look all the way back into the states of the encoder network in addition to the thought vector. A version of a "heat map" over the entire input sequence is learned along with the rest of the network. That mapping, different at each time step, is then shared with the decoder. As it decodes any particular

---

[14] See the web page titled "Neural Machine Translation by Jointly Learning to Align and Translate" (https://arxiv.org/abs/1409.0473).

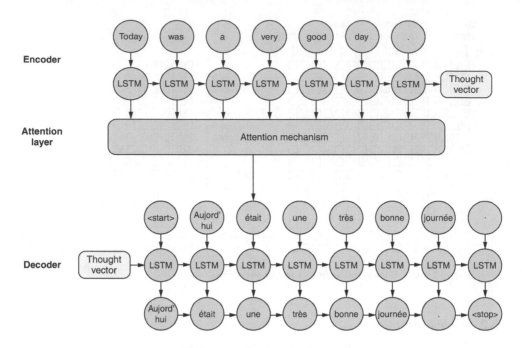

**Figure 10.11   Overview of the attention mechanism**

part of the sequence, its concept created from the thought vector can be augmented with direct information that it produced. In other words, the attention mechanism allows a direct connection between the output and the input by selecting relevant input pieces. This doesn't mean token-to-token alignment; that would defeat the purpose and send you back to autoencoder land. It does allow for richer representations of concepts wherever they appear in the sequence.

With the attention mechanism, the decoder receives an additional input with every time step representing the one (or many) tokens in the input sequence to pay "attention" to, at this given decoder time step. All sequence positions from the encoder will be represented as a weighted average for each decoder time step.

Configuring and tuning the attention mechanism isn't trivial, but various deep learning frameworks provide implementations to facilitate this. At the time of this writing, a pull request to the Keras package was discussed, but no implementation had yet been accepted.

## 10.6   *In the real world*

Sequence-to-sequence networks are well suited for any machine learning application with variable-length input sequences or variable-length output sequences. Since natural language sequences of words almost always have unpredictable length, sequence-to-sequence models can improve the accuracy of most machine learning models.

Key sequence-to-sequence applications are

- Chatbot conversations
- Question answering
- Machine translation
- Image captioning
- Visual question answering
- Document summarization

As you've seen in the previous sections, a dialog system is a common application for NLP. Sequence-to-sequence models are generative, which makes them especially well-suited to conversational dialog systems (chatbots). Sequence-to-sequence chatbots generate more varied, creative, and conversational dialog than information retrieval or knowledge-based chatbot approaches. Conversational dialog systems mimic human conversation on a broad range of topics. Sequence-to-sequence chatbots can generalize from limited-domain corpora and yet respond reasonably on topics not contained in their training set. In contrast, the "grounding" of knowledge-based dialog systems (discussed in chapter 12) can limit their ability to participate in conversations on topics outside their training domains. Chapter 12 compares the performance of chatbot architectures in greater detail.

Besides the Cornell Movie Dialog Corpus, various free and open source training sets are available, such as Deep Mind's Q&A datasets.[15, 16] When you need your dialog system to respond reliably in a specific domain, you'll need to train it on a corpora of statements from that domain. The thought vector has a limited amount of information capacity and that capacity needs to be filled with information on the topics you want your chatbot to be conversant in.

Another common application for sequence-to-sequence networks is machine translation. The concept of the thought vector allows a translation application to incorporate the *context* of the input data, and words with multiple meanings can be translated in the correct context. If you want to build translation applications, the ManyThings website (http://www.manythings.org/anki/) provides sentence pairs that can be used as training sets. We've provided these pairs for you in the `nlpia` package. In listing 10.8 you can replace `get_data('moviedialog')` with `get_data('deu-eng')` for English-German statement pairs, for example.

Sequence-to-sequence models are also well-suited to text summarization, due to the difference in string length between input and output. In this case, the input to the encoder network is, for example, news articles (or any other length document) and the decoder can be trained to generate a headline or abstract or any other summary sequence associated with the document. Sequence-to-sequence networks can provide

---

[15] Q&A dataset: https://cs.nyu.edu/~kcho/DMQA/.

[16] List of dialog corpora in the NLPIA package docs: https://github.com/totalgood/nlpia/blob/master/docs/notes/nlp–data.md#dialog-corpora.

more natural-sounding text summaries than summarization methods based on bag-of-words vector statistics. If you're interested in developing such an application, the Kaggle news summary challenge[17] provides a good training set.

Sequence-to-sequence networks aren't limited to natural language applications. Two other applications are automated speech recognition and image captioning. Current, state-of-the-art automated speech recognition systems[18] use sequence-to-sequence networks to turn voice input amplitude sample sequences into the thought vector that a sequence-to-sequence decoder can turn into a text transcription of the speech. The same concept applies to image captioning. The sequence of image pixels (regardless of image resolution) can be used as an input to the encoder, and a decoder can be trained to generate an appropriate description. In fact, you can find a combined application of image captioning and Q&A system called visual question answering at https://vqa.cloudcv.org/.

## Summary

- Sequence-to-sequence networks can be built with a modular, reusable encoder-decoder architecture.
- The encoder model generates a thought vector, a dense, fixed-dimension vector representation of the information in a variable-length input sequence.
- A decoder can use thought vectors to predict (generate) output sequences, including the replies of a chatbot.
- Due to the thought vector representation, the input and the output sequence lengths don't have to match.
- Thought vectors can only hold a limited amount of information. If you need a thought vector to encode more complex concepts, the attention mechanism can help selectively encode what is important in the thought vector.

---

[17] See the web page titled "NEWS SUMMARY: Kaggle" (https://www.kaggle.com/sunnysai12345/news-summary/data).

[18] State of the art speech recognition system: https://arxiv.org/pdf/1610.03022.pdf.

# Part 3

# Getting real
# (real-world NLP challenges)

Part 3 shows you how to extend your skills to tackle real-world problems. You'll learn how to extract information such as dates and names to build applications such as the Twitter bot that helped manage the self-service scheduling of Open Spaces at PyCon US in 2017 and 2018.

In these last three chapters, we also tackle the trickier problems of NLP. You'll learn about several different ways to build a chatbot, both with and without machine learning to guide it. And to create complex behavior, you'll learn how to combine these techniques together. You'll also learn about algorithms that can handle large corpora—sets of documents that cannot be loaded into RAM all at once.

# Information extraction
# (named entity extraction
# and question answering)

**This chapter covers**

- Sentence segmentation
- Named entity recognition (NER)
- Numerical information extraction
- Part-of-speech (POS) tagging and dependency tree parsing
- Logical relation extraction and knowledge bases

One last skill you need before you can build a full-featured chatbot is extracting information or knowledge from natural language text.

## 11.1 Named entities and relations

You'd like your machine to extract pieces of information and facts from text so it can know a little bit about what a user is saying. For example, imagine a user says "Remind me to read aiindex.org on Monday." You'd like that statement to trigger a calendar entry or alarm for the next Monday after the current date.

To trigger those actions, you'd need to know that "me" represents a particular kind of *named entity*: a person. And the chatbot should know that it should "expand" or normalize that word by replacing it with that person's username. You'd also need your chatbot to recognize that "aiindex.org" is an abbreviated URL, a named entity of the name of a specific instance of something. And you need to know that a normalized spelling of this particular kind of named entity might be "http://aiindex.org," "https://aiindex.org," or maybe even "https://www.aiindex.org." Likewise you need your chatbot to recognize that Monday is one of the days of the week (another kind of named entity called an "event") and be able to find it on the calendar.

For the chatbot to respond properly to that simple request, you also need it to extract the relation between the named entity "me" and the command "remind." You'd even need to recognize the implied subject of the sentence, "you," referring to the chatbot, another person named entity. And you need to "teach" the chatbot that reminders happen in the future, so it should find the soonest upcoming Monday to create the reminder.

A typical sentence may contain several named entities of various types, such as geographic entities, organizations, people, political entities, times (including dates), artifacts, events, and natural phenomena. And a sentence can contain several relations, too—facts about the relationships between the named entities in the sentence.

### 11.1.1 A knowledge base

Besides just extracting information from the text of a user statement, you can also use information extraction to help your chatbot train itself! If you have your chatbot run information extraction on a large corpus, such as Wikipedia, that corpus will produce facts about the world that can inform future chatbot behaviors and replies. Some chatbots record all the information they extract (from offline reading-assignment "homework") in a knowledge base. Such a knowledge base can later be queried to help your chatbot make informed decisions or inferences about the world.

Chatbots can also store knowledge about the current user "session" or conversation. Knowledge that is relevant only to the current conversation is called "context." This contextual knowledge can be stored in the same global knowledge base that supports the chatbot, or it can be stored in a separate knowledge base. Commercial chatbot APIs, such as IBM's Watson or Amazon's Lex, typically store context separate from the global knowledge base of facts that they use to support conversations with all the other users.

Context can include facts about the user, the chatroom or channel, or the weather and news for that moment in time. Context can even include the changing state of the chatbot itself, based on the conversation. An example of "self-knowledge" a smart chatbot should keep track of is the history of all the things it has already told someone or the questions it has already asked of the user, so it doesn't repeat itself.

So that's the goal for this chapter, teaching your bot to understand what it reads. And you'll put that understanding into a flexible data structure designed to store knowledge. Then your bot can use that knowledge to make decisions and say smart stuff about the world.

In addition to the simple task of recognizing numbers and dates in text, you'd like your bot to be able to extract more general information about the world. And you'd like it to do this on its own, rather than having you "program" everything you know about the world into it. For example, you'd like it to be able to learn from natural language documents such as this sentence from Wikipedia:

> *In 1983, Stanislav Petrov, a lieutenant colonel of the Soviet Air Defense Forces, saved the world from nuclear war.*

If you were to take notes in a history class after reading or hearing something like that, you'd probably paraphrase things and create connections in your brain between concepts or words. You might reduce it to a piece of knowledge, that thing that you "got out of it." You'd like your bot to do the same thing. You'd like it to "take note" of whatever it learns, such as the fact or knowledge that Stanislov Petrov was a lieutenant colonel. This could be stored in a data structure something like this:

```
('Stanislav Petrov', 'is-a', 'lieutenant colonel')
```

This is an example of two named entity nodes ('Stanislav Petrov' and 'lieutenant colonel') and a relation or connection ('is a') between them in a knowledge graph or knowledge base. When a relationship like this is stored in a form that complies with the RDF standard (relation description format) for knowledge graphs, it's referred to as an RDF triplet. Historically these RDF triplets were stored in XML files, but they can be stored in any file format or database that can hold a graph of triplets in the form of (`subject`, `relation`, `object`).

A collection of these triplets is a knowledge graph. This is also sometimes called an ontology by linguists, because it's storing structured information about words. But when the graph is intended to represent facts about the world rather than merely words, it's referred to as a knowledge graph or knowledge base. Figure 11.1 is a graphic representation of the knowledge graph you'd like to extract from a sentence like that.

The "is-a" relationship at the top of figure 11.1 represents a fact that couldn't be directly extracted from the statement about Stanislav. But this fact that "lieutenant colonel" is a military rank could be inferred from the fact that the title of a person who's a member of a military organization is a military rank. This logical operation of deriving facts from a knowledge graph is called knowledge graph *inference*. It can also be called querying a knowledge base, analogous to querying a relational database.

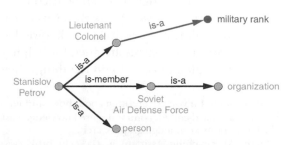

**Figure 11.1  Stanislav knowledge graph**

For this particular inference or query about Stanislov's military rank, your knowledge graph would have to already contain facts about militaries and military ranks. It might even help if the knowledge base had facts about the titles of people and how people relate to occupations (jobs). Perhaps you can see now how a base of knowledge helps a machine understand more about a statement than it could without that knowledge. Without this base of knowledge, many of the facts in a simple statement like this will be "over the head" of your chatbot. You might even say that questions about occupational rank would be "above the pay grade" of a bot that only knew how to classify documents according to randomly allocated topics.[1]

It may not be obvious how big a deal this is, but it is a *BIG* deal. If you've ever interacted with a chatbot that doesn't understand "which way is up," literally, you'd understand. One of the most daunting challenges in AI research is the challenge of compiling and efficiently querying a knowledge graph of common sense knowledge. We take common sense knowledge for granted in our everyday conversations.

Humans start acquiring much of their common sense knowledge even before they acquire language skill. We don't spend our childhood writing about how a day begins with light and sleep usually follows sunset. And we don't edit Wikipedia articles about how an empty belly should only be filled with food rather than dirt or rocks. This makes it hard for machines to find a corpus of common sense knowledge to read and learn from. No common-sense knowledge Wikipedia articles exist for your bot to do information extraction on. And some of that knowledge is instinct, hard-coded into our DNA.[2]

All kinds of factual relationships exist between things and people, such as "kind-of," "is-used-for," "has-a," "is-famous-for," "was-born," and "has-profession." NELL, the Carnegie Mellon Never Ending Language Learning bot, is focused almost entirely on the task of extracting information about the "kind-of" relationship.

Most knowledge bases normalize the strings that define these relationships, so that "kind of" and "type of" would be assigned a normalized string or ID to represent that particular relation. And some knowledge bases also *resolve* the nouns representing the objects in a knowledge base. So the bigram "Stanislav Petrov" might be assigned a particular ID. Synonyms for "Stanislav Petrov," like "S. Petrov" and "Lt Col Petrov," would also be assigned to that same ID, if the NLP pipeline suspected they referred to the same person.

A knowledge base can be used to build a practical type of chatbot called a *question answering system* (QA system). Customer service chatbots, including university TA bots, rely almost exclusively on knowledge bases to generate their replies.[3] Question answering systems are great for helping humans find factual information, which frees up human brains to do the things they're better at, such as attempting to generalize

---

[1]  See chapter 4 if you've forgotten about how random topic allocation can be.

[2]  There are hard-coded, common-sense knowledge bases out there for you to build on. Google Scholar is your friend in this knowledge graph search.

[3]  2016, AI Teaching Assistant at GaTech: http://www.news.gatech.edu/2016/05/09/artificial-intelligence-course-creates-ai-teaching-assistant.

from those facts. Humans are bad at remembering facts accurately but good at finding connections and patterns between those facts, something machines have yet to master. We talk more about question answering chatbots in the next chapter.

### 11.1.2 Information extraction

So you've learned that "information extraction" is converting unstructured text into structured information stored in a knowledge base or knowledge graph. Information extraction is part of an area of research called natural language understanding (NLU), though that term is often used synonymously with natural language processing.

Information extraction and NLU is a different kind of learning than you may think of when researching data science. It isn't only unsupervised learning; even the very "model" itself, the logic about how the world works, can be composed without human intervention. Instead of giving your machine fish (facts), you're teaching it how to fish (extract information). Nonetheless, machine learning techniques are often used to train the information extractor.

## 11.2 Regular patterns

You need a pattern-matching algorithm that can identify sequences of characters or words that match the pattern so you can "extract" them from a longer string of text. The naive way to build such a pattern-matching algorithm is in Python, with a sequence of if/then statements that look for that symbol (a word or character) at each position of a string. Say you wanted to find some common greeting words, such as "Hi," "Hello," and "Yo," at the beginning of a statement. You might do it as shown in the following listing.

**Listing 11.1   Pattern hardcoded in Python**

```
>>> def find_greeting(s):
...     """ Return greeting str (Hi, etc) if greeting pattern matches """
...     if s[0] == 'H':
...         if s[:3] in ['Hi', 'Hi ', 'Hi,', 'Hi!']:
...             return s[:2]
...         elif s[:6] in ['Hello', 'Hello ', 'Hello,', 'Hello!']:
...             return s[:5]
...     elif s[0] == 'Y':
...         if s[1] == 'o' and s[:3] in ['Yo', 'Yo,', 'Yo ', 'Yo!']:
...             return s[:2]
...     return None
```

And the following listing shows how it would work.

**Listing 11.2   Brittle pattern-matching example**

```
>>> find_greeting('Hi Mr. Turing!')
'Hi'
>>> find_greeting('Hello, Rosa.')
'Hello'
```

```
>>> find_greeting("Yo, what's up?")
'Yo'
>>> find_greeting("Hello")
'Hello'
>>> print(find_greeting("hello"))
None
>>> print(find_greeting("HelloWorld"))
None
```

You can probably see how tedious programming a pattern matching algorithm this way would be. And it's not even that good. It's quite brittle, relying on precise spellings and capitalization and character positions in a string. And it's tricky to specify all the "delimiters," such as punctuation, white space, or the beginnings and ends of strings (NULL characters) that are on either sides of words you're looking for.

You could probably come up with a way to allow you to specify different words or strings you want to look for without hard-coding them into Python expressions like this. And you could even specify the delimiters in a separate function. That would let you do some tokenization and iteration to find the occurrence of the words you're looking for anywhere in a string. But that's a lot of work.

Fortunately that work has already been done! A pattern-matching engine is integrated into most modern computer languages, including Python. It's called regular expressions. Regular expressions and string interpolation formatting expressions (for example, `"{:05d}".format(42)`), are mini programming languages unto themselves. This language for pattern matching is called the regular expression language. And Python has a regular expression interpreter (compiler and runner) in the standard library package `re`. So let's use them to define your patterns instead of deeply nested Python `if` statements.

### 11.2.1 Regular expressions

Regular expressions are strings written in a special computer language that you can use to specify algorithms. Regular expressions are a lot more powerful, flexible, and concise than the equivalent Python you'd need to write to match patterns like this. So regular expressions are the pattern definition language of choice for many NLP problems involving pattern matching. This NLP application is an extension of its original use for compiling and interpreting formal languages (computer languages).

Regular expressions define a *finite state machine* or FSM—a tree of "if-then" decisions about a sequence of symbols, such as the `find_greeting()` function in listing 11.1. The symbols in the sequence are passed into the decision tree of the FSM one symbol at a time. A finite state machine that operates on a sequence of symbols such as ASCII character strings, or a sequence of English words, is called a *grammar*. They can also be called *formal grammars* to distinguish them from natural language grammar rules you learned in grammar school.

In computer science and mathematics, the word "grammar" refers to the set of rules that determine whether or not a sequence of symbols is a valid member of a language, often called a computer language or formal language. And a computer language, or formal language, is the set of all possible statements that would match the formal grammar that defines that language. That's kind of a circular definition, but that's the way mathematics works sometimes. You probably want to review appendix B if you aren't familiar with basic regular expression syntax and symbols such as `r'.\*'` and `r'a-z'`.

### 11.2.2 *Information extraction as ML feature extraction*

So you're back where you started in chapter 1, where we first mentioned regular expressions. But didn't you switch from "grammar-based" NLP approaches at the end of chapter 1 in favor of machine learning and data-driven approaches? Why return to hard-coded (manually composed) regular expressions and patterns? Because your statistical or data-driven approach to NLP has limits.

You want your machine learning pipeline to be able to do some basic things, such as answer logical questions, or perform actions such as scheduling meetings based on NLP instructions. And machine learning falls flat here. You rarely have a labeled training set that covers the answers to all the questions people might ask in natural language. Plus, as you'll see here, you can define a compact set of condition checks (a regular expression) to extract key bits of information from a natural language string. And it can work for a broad range of problems.

Pattern matching (and regular expressions) continue to be the state-of-the art approach for information extraction. Even with machine learning approaches to natural language processing, you need to do feature engineering. You need to create bags of words or embeddings of words to try to reduce the nearly infinite possibilities of meaning in natural language text into a vector that a machine can process easily. Information extraction is just another form of machine learning feature extraction from unstructured natural language data, such as creating a bag of words, or doing PCA on that bag of words. And these patterns and features are still employed in even the most advanced natural language machine learning pipelines, such as Google's Assistant, Siri, Amazon Alexa, and other state-of-the-art bots.

Information extraction is used to find statements and information that you might want your chatbot to have "on the tip of its tongue." Information extraction can be accomplished beforehand to populate a knowledge base of facts. Alternatively, the required statements and information can be found on-demand, when the chatbot is asked a question or a search engine is queried. When a knowledge base is built ahead of time, the data structure can be optimized to facilitate faster queries within larger domains of knowledge. A prebuilt knowledge base enables the chatbot to respond quickly to questions about a wider range of information. If information is retrieved in real-time, as the chatbot is being queried, this is often called "search." Google and other search engines combine these two techniques, querying a knowledge graph (knowledge base) and falling back to text search if the necessary facts aren't found. Many of the natural language grammar rules you learned in school can be encoded in a formal grammar designed to operate on words or symbols representing parts of speech. And the English language can be thought of as the words and grammar rules that make up the language. Or you can think of it as the set of all the possible things you could say that would be recognized as valid statements by an English language speaker.

And that brings us to another feature of formal grammars and finite state machines that will come in handy for NLP. Any formal grammar can be used by a machine in two ways:

- To recognize matches to that grammar
- To generate a new sequence of symbols

Not only can you use patterns (regular expressions) for extracting information from natural language, but you can also use them in a chatbot that wants to "say" things that match that pattern! We show you how to do this with a package called `rstr`[4] for some of your information extraction patterns here.

This formal grammar and finite state machine approach to pattern matching has some other awesome features. A true finite state machine can be guaranteed to always run in finite time (to halt). It will always tell you whether you've found a match in your string or not. It will never get caught in a perpetual loop... as long as you don't use some of the advanced features of regular expression engines that allow you to "cheat" and incorporate loops into your FSM.

So you'll stick to regular expressions that don't require these "look-back" or "look-ahead" cheats. You'll make sure your regular expression matcher processes each character and moves ahead to the next character only if it matches—sort of like a strict train conductor walking through the seats checking tickets. If you don't have one, the conductor stops and declares that there's a problem, a mismatch, and he refuses to go on, or look ahead or behind you until he resolves the problem. There are no "go backs" or "do overs" for train passengers, or for strict regular expressions.

## 11.3 *Information worth extracting*

Some keystone bits of quantitative information are worth the effort of "hand-crafted" regular expressions:

- GPS locations
- Dates
- Prices
- Numbers

Other important pieces of natural language information require more complex patterns than are easily captured with regular expressions:

- Question trigger words
- Question target words
- Named entities

---

[4]  See the web page titled "leapfrogdevelopment / rstr — Bitbucket" (https://bitbucket.org/leapfrogdevelopment/rstr/).

### 11.3.1 *Extracting GPS locations*

GPS locations are typical of the kinds of numerical data you'll want to extract from text using regular expressions. GPS locations come in pairs of numerical values for latitude and longitude. They sometimes also include a third number for altitude, or height above sea level, but you'll ignore that for now. Let's just extract decimal latitude/longitude pairs, expressed in degrees. This will work for many Google Maps URLs. Though URLs aren't technically natural language, they are often part of unstructured text data, and you'd like to extract this bit of information, so your chatbot can know about places as well as things.

Let's use your decimal number pattern from previous examples, but let's be more restrictive and make sure the value is within the valid range for latitude (+/- 90 deg) and longitude (+/- 180 deg). You can't go any farther north than the North Pole (+90 deg) or farther south than the South Pole (-90 deg). And if you sail from Greenwich England 180 deg east (+180 deg longitude), you'll reach the date line, where you're also 180 deg west (-180 deg) from Greenwich. See the following listing.

> **Listing 11.3  Regular expression for GPS coordinates**

```
>>> import re
>>> lat = r'([-]?[0-9]?[0-9][.][0-9]{2,10})'
>>> lon = r'([-]?1?[0-9]?[0-9][.][0-9]{2,10})'
>>> sep = r'[,/ ]{1,3}'
>>> re_gps = re.compile(lat + sep + lon)

>>> re_gps.findall('http://...maps/@34.0551066,-118.2496763...')
[(34.0551066, -118.2496763)]

>>> re_gps.findall("https://www.openstreetmap.org/#map=10/5.9666/116.0566")
[('5.9666', '116.0566')]

>>> re_gps.findall("Zig Zag Cafe is at 45.344, -121.9431 on my GPS.")
[('45.3440', '-121.9431')]
```

Numerical data is pretty easy to extract, especially if the numbers are part of a machine-readable string. URLs and other machine-readable strings put numbers such as latitude and longitude in a predictable order, format, and units to make things easy for us. This pattern will still accept some out-of-this-world latitude and longitude values, but it gets the job done for most of the URLs you'll copy from mapping web apps such as Open-StreetMap.

But what about dates? Will regular expressions work for dates? What if you want your date extractor to work in Europe and the US, where the order of day/month is often reversed?

### 11.3.2 *Extracting dates*

Dates are a lot harder to extract than GPS coordinates. Dates are a more natural language, with different dialects for expressing similar things. In the US, Christmas 2017 is "12/25/17." In Europe, Christmas 2017 is "25/12/17." You could check the locale of your user and assume that they write dates the same way as others in their region. But this assumption can be wrong.

So most date and time extractors try to work with both kinds of day/month orderings and check to make sure it's a valid date. This is how the human brain works when we read a date like that. Even if you were a US-English speaker and you were in Brussels around Christmas, you'd probably recognize "25/12/17" as a holiday, because there are only 12 months in the year.

This "duck-typing" approach that works in computer programming can work for natural language, too. If it looks like a duck and acts like a duck, it's probably a duck. If it looks like a date and acts like a date, it's probably a date. You'll use this "try it and ask forgiveness later" approach for other natural language processing tasks as well. You'll try a bunch of options and accept the one the works. You'll try your extractor or your generator, and then you'll run a validator on it to see if it makes sense.

For chatbots this is a particularly powerful approach, allowing you to combine the best of multiple natural language generators. In chapter 10, you generated some chatbot replies using LSTMs. To improve the user experience, you could generate a lot of replies and choose the one with the best spelling, grammar, and sentiment. We'll talk more about this in chapter 12. See the following listing.

**Listing 11.4   Regular expression for US dates**

```
>>> us = r'((([01]?\d)[-/]([0123]?\d))([-/]([0123]\d)\d\d)?)'
>>> mdy = re.findall(us, 'Santa came 12/25/2017. An elf appeared 12/12.')
>>> mdy
[('12/25/2017', '12/25', '12', '25', '/2017', '20'),
 ('12/12', '12/12', '12', '12', '', '')]
```

A list comprehension can be used to provide a little structure to that extracted data, by converting the month, day, and year into integers and labeling that numerical information with a meaningful name, as shown in the following listing.

**Listing 11.5   Structuring extracted dates**

```
>>> dates = [{'mdy': x[0], 'my': x[1], 'm': int(x[2]), 'd': int(x[3]),
...          'y': int(x[4].lstrip('/') or 0), 'c': int(x[5] or 0)} for x in mdy]
>>> dates
[{'mdy': '12/25/2017', 'my': '12/25', 'm': 12, 'd': 25, 'y': 2017, 'c': 20},
 {'mdy': '12/12', 'my': '12/12', 'm': 12, 'd': 12, 'y': 0, 'c': 0}]
```

Even for these simple dates, it's not possible to design a regex that can resolve all the ambiguities in the second date, "12/12." There are ambiguities in the language of dates that only humans can guess at resolving using knowledge about things like Christmas and the intent of the writer of a text. For examle "12/12" could mean

- December 12th, 2017—month/day in the estimated year based on anaphora resolution[5]
- December 12th, 2018—month/day in the current year at time of publishing
- December 2012—month/year in the year 2012

Because month/day come before the year in US dates and in our regex, "12/12" is presumed to be December 12th of an unknown year. You can fill in any missing numerical fields with the most recently read year using the context from the structured data in memory, as shown in the following listing.

**Listing 11.6  Basic context maintenance**

```
>>> for i, d in enumerate(dates):
...     for k, v in d.items():
...         if not v:                                    This works because both
...             d[k] = dates[max(i - 1, 0)][k]    ◁──┐  the dict and the list are
>>> dates                                              mutable data types.
[{'mdy': '12/25/2017', 'my': '12/25', 'm': 12, 'd': 25, 'y': 2017, 'c': 20},
 {'mdy': '12/12', 'my': '12/12', 'm': 12, 'd': 12, 'y': 2017, 'c': 20}]
>>> from datetime import date
>>> datetimes = [date(d['y'], d['m'], d['d']) for d in dates]
>>> datetimes
[datetime.date(2017, 12, 25), datetime.date(2017, 12, 12)]
```

This is a basic but reasonably robust way to extract date information from natural language text. The main remaining tasks to turn this into a production date extractor would be to add some exception catching and context maintenance that's appropriate for your application. If you added that to the `nlpia` package (http://github.com/totalgood/nlpia) with a pull request, I'm sure your fellow readers would appreciate it. And if you added some extractors for times, well, then you'd be quite the hero.

There are opportunities for some hand-crafted logic to deal with edge cases and natural language names for months and even days. But no amount of sophistication could resolve the ambiguity in the date "12/11." That could be

- December 11th in whatever year you read or heard it
- November 12th if you heard it in London or Launceston, Tasmania (a commonwealth territory)
- December 2011 if you read it in a US newspaper
- November 2012 if you read it in an EU newspaper

Some natural language ambiguities can't be resolved, even by a human brain. But let's make sure your date extractor can handle European day/month order by reversing month and day in your regex. See the following listing.

---

[5]  Issues in Anaphora Resolution by Imran Q. Sayed for Stanford's CS224N course: https://nlp.stanford.edu/courses/cs224n/2003/fp/iqsayed/project_report.pdf.

**Listing 11.7    Regular expression for European dates**

```
>>> eu = r'((([0123]?\d)[-/]([01]?\d))([-/]([0123]\d)?\d\d)?)'
>>> dmy = re.findall(eu, 'Alan Mathison Turing OBE FRS (23/6/1912-7/6/1954) \
...     was an English computer scientist.')
>>> dmy
[('23/6/1912', '23/6', '23', '6', '/1912', '19'),
 ('7/6/1954', '7/6', '7', '6', '/1954', '19')]
>>> dmy = re.findall(eu, 'Alan Mathison Turing OBE FRS (23/6/12-7/6/54) \
...     was an English computer scientist.')
>>> dmy
[('23/6/12', '23/6', '23', '6', '/12', ''),
 ('7/6/54', '7/6', '7', '6', '/54', '')]
```

That regular expression correctly extracts Turing's birth and wake dates from a Wikipedia excerpt. But I cheated, I converted the month "June" into the number 6 before testing the regular expression on that Wikipedia sentence. So this isn't a realistic example. And you'd still have some ambiguity to resolve for the year if the century isn't specified. Does the year 54 mean 1954 or does it mean 2054? You'd like your chatbot to be able to extract dates from unaltered Wikipedia articles so it can read up on famous people and learn import dates. For your regex to work on more natural language dates, such as those found in Wikipedia articles, you need to add words such as "June" (and all its abbreviations) to your date-extracting regular expression.

You don't need any special symbols to indicate words (characters that go together in sequence). You can type them in the regex exactly as you'd like them to be spelled in the input, including capitalization. All you have to do is put an OR symbol (|) between them in the regular expression. And you need to make sure it can handle US month/day order as well as European order. You'll add these two alternative date "spellings" to your regular expression with a "big" OR (|) between them as a fork in your tree of decisions in the regular expression.

Let's use some named groups to help you recognize years such as "'84" as 1984 and "'08" as 2008. And let's try to be a little more precise about the 4-digit years you want to match, only matching years in the future up to 2399 and in the past back to year 0.[6] See the following listing.

**Listing 11.8    Recognizing years**

```
>>> yr_19xx = (
...     r'\b(?P<yr_19xx>' +
...     '|'.join('{}'.format(i) for i in range(30, 100)) +        ◁──┐  2-digit years
...     r')\b'                                                        │  30-99 = 1930-1999
...     )
>>> yr_20xx = (
...     r'\b(?P<yr_20xx>' +
...     '|'.join('{:02d}'.format(i) for i in range(10)) + '|' +
...     '|'.join('{}'.format(i) for i in range(10, 30)) +
```

---

[6]   See the web page titled "Year zero" (https://en.wikipedia.org/wiki/Year_zero).

```
...         r')\b'
...     )
>>> yr_cent = r'\b(?P<yr_cent>' + '|'.join(
...     '{}'.format(i) for i in range(1, 40)) + r')'
>>> yr_ccxx = r'(?P<yr_ccxx>' + '|'.join(
...     '{:02d}'.format(i) for i in range(0, 100)) + r')\b'
>>> yr_xxxx = r'\b(?P<yr_xxxx>(' + yr_cent + ')(' + yr_ccxx + r'))\b'
>>> yr = (
...     r'\b(?P<yr>' +
...     yr_19xx + '|' + yr_20xx + '|' + yr_xxxx +
...     r')\b'
...     )
>>> groups = list(re.finditer(
...     yr, "0, 2000, 01, '08, 99, 1984, 2030/1970 85 47 `66"))
>>> full_years = [g['yr'] for g in groups]
>>> full_years
['2000', '01', '08', '99', '1984', '2030', '1970', '85', '47', '66']
```

**1- or 2-digit years**
**01-30 = 2001-2030**

**First digits of a 3- or 4-digit year such as the "1" in "123 A.D." or "20" in "2018"**

**Last 2 digits of a 3- or 4-digit year such as the "23" in "123 A.D." or "18" in "2018"**

Wow! That's a lot of work, just to handle some simple year rules in regex rather than in Python. Don't worry, packages are available for recognizing common date formats. They are much more precise (fewer false matches) and more general (fewer misses). So you don't need to be able to compose complex regular expressions such as this yourself. This example just gives you a pattern in case you need to extract a particular kind of number using a regular expression in the future. Monetary values and IP addresses are examples where a more complex regular expression, with named groups, might come in handy.

Let's finish up your regular expression for extracting dates by adding patterns for the month names such as "June" or "Jun" in Turing's birthday on Wikipedia dates, as shown in the following listing.

---

**Listing 11.9  Recognizing month words with regular expressions**

```
>>> mon_words = 'January February March April May June July ' \
...     'August September October November December'
>>> mon = (r'\b(' + '|'.join('{}|{}|{}|{:02d}'.format(
...     m, m[:4], m[:3], i + 1, i + 1) for i, m in
➥ enumerate(mon_words.split())) +
...     r')\b')
>>> re.findall(mon, 'January has 31 days, February the 2nd month
➥ of 12, has 28, except in a Leap Year.')
['January', 'February', '12']
```

Can you see how you might combine these regular expressions into a larger one that can handle both EU and US date formats? One complication is that you can't reuse the same name for a group (parenthesized part of the regular expression). So you can't put an OR between the US and EU ordering of the named regular expressions for month and year. And you need to include patterns for some optional separators between the day, month, and year.

Here's one way to do all that.

**Listing 11.10   Combining information extraction regular expressions**

```
>>> day = r'|'.join('{:02d}|{}'.format(i, i) for i in range(1, 32))
>>> eu = (r'\b(' + day + r')\b[-,/ ]{0,2}\b(' +
...     mon + r')\b[-,/ ]{0,2}\b(' + yr.replace('<yr>', '<eu_yr>') + r')\b')
>>> us = (r'\b(' + mon + r')\b[-,/ ]{0,2}\b(' +
...     day + r')\b[-,/ ]{0,2}\b(' + yr.replace('<yr>', '<us_yr>') + r')\b')
>>> date_pattern = r'\b(' + eu + '|' + us + r')\b'
>>> list(re.finditer(date_pattern, '31 Oct, 1970 25/12/2017'))
[<_sre.SRE_Match object; span=(0, 12), match='31 Oct, 1970'>,
 <_sre.SRE_Match object; span=(13, 23), match='25/12/2017'>]
```

Finally, you need to validate these dates by seeing if they can be turned into valid Python `datetime` objects, as shown in the following listing.

**Listing 11.11   Validating dates**

```
>>> import datetime
>>> dates = []
>>> for g in groups:
...     month_num = (g['us_mon'] or g['eu_mon']).strip()
...     try:
...         month_num = int(month_num)
...     except ValueError:
...         month_num = [w[:len(month_num)]
...             for w in mon_words].index(month_num) + 1
...     date = datetime.date(
...         int(g['us_yr'] or g['eu_yr']),
...         month_num,
...         int(g['us_day'] or g['eu_day']))
...     dates.append(date)
>>> dates
[datetime.date(1970, 10, 31), datetime.date(2017, 12, 25)]
```

Your date extractor appears to work OK, at least for a few simple, unambiguous dates. Think about how packages such as `Python-dateutil` and `datefinder` are able to resolve ambiguities and deal with more "natural" language dates such as "today" and "next Monday." And if you think you can do it better than these packages, send them a pull request!

   If you just want a state of the art date extractor, statistical (machine learning) approaches will get you there faster. The Stanford Core NLP SUTime library (https://nlp.stanford.edu/software/sutime.html) and `dateutil.parser.parse` by Google are state-of-the-art.

## 11.4   *Extracting relationships (relations)*

So far you've looked only at extracting tricky noun instances such as dates and GPS latitude and longitude values. And you've worked mainly with numerical patterns. It's time to tackle the harder problem of extracting knowledge from natural language.

You'd like your bot to learn facts about the world from reading an encyclopedia of knowledge such as Wikipedia. You'd like it to be able to relate those dates and GPS coordinates to the entities it reads about.

What knowledge could your brain extract from this sentence from Wikipedia?

> *On March 15, 1554, Desoto wrote in his journal that the Pascagoula people ranged as far north as the confluence of the Leaf and Chickasawhay rivers at 30.4, -88.5.*

Extracting the dates and the GPS coordinates might enable you to associate that date and location with Desoto, the Pascagoula people, and two rivers whose names you can't pronounce. You'd like your bot (and your mind) to be able to connect those facts to larger facts—for example, that Desoto was a Spanish conquistador and that the Pascagoula people were a peaceful Native American tribe. And you'd like the dates and locations to be associated with the right "things": Desoto, and the intersection of two rivers, respectively.

This is what most people think of when they hear the term natural language understanding. To understand a statement you need to be able to extract key bits of information and correlate it with related knowledge. For machines, you store that knowledge in a graph, also called a knowledge base. The edges of your knowledge graph are the relationships between things. And the nodes of your knowledge graph are the nouns or objects found in your corpus.

The pattern you're going to use to extract these relationships (or relations) is a pattern such as SUBJECT - VERB - OBJECT. To recognize these patterns, you'll need your NLP pipeline to know the parts of speech for each word in a sentence.

### 11.4.1 Part-of-speech (POS) tagging

POS tagging can be accomplished with language models that contain dictionaries of words with all their possible parts of speech. They can then be trained on properly tagged sentences to recognize the parts of speech in new sentences with other words from that dictionary. NLTK and spaCy both implement POS tagging functions. You'll use spaCy here because it's faster and more accurate. See the following listing.

---

**Listing 11.12   POS tagging with spaCy**

```
>>> import spacy
>>> en_model = spacy.load('en_core_web_md')
>>> sentence = ("In 1541 Desoto wrote in his journal that the Pascagoula peop
    le " +
...     "ranged as far north as the confluence of the Leaf and Chickasawhay r
    ivers at 30.4, -88.5.")
>>> parsed_sent = en_model(sentence)
>>> parsed_sent.ents
(1541, Desoto, Pascagoula, Leaf, Chickasawhay, 30.4)     <--- spaCy misses the
                                                               longitude in the lat, lon
                                                               numerical pair.
>>> ' '.join(['{}_{}'.format(tok, tok.tag_) for tok in parsed_sent])
'In_IN 1541_CD Desoto_NNP wrote_VBD in_IN his_PRP$ journal_NN that_IN the_DT
    Pascagoula_NNP people_NNS
```

```
ranged_VBD as_RB far_RB north_RB as_IN the_DT confluence_NN of_IN the_DT Lea
    f_NNP and_CC Chickasawhay_NNP
rivers_VBZ at_IN 30.4_CD ,_, -88.5_NFP ._.'
```

> **spaCy uses the "OntoNotes 5" POS**
> **tags: https://spacy.io/api/annotation#pos-tagging.**

So to build your knowledge graph, you need to figure out which objects (noun phrases) should be paired up. You'd like to pair up the date "March 15, 1554" with the named entity Desoto. You could then resolve those two strings (noun phrases) to point to objects you have in your knowledge base. March 15, 1554 can be converted to a `datetime.date` object with a normalized representation.

spaCy-parsed sentences also contain the dependency tree in a nested dictionary. And `spacy.display` can generate a *scalable vector graphics* SVG string (or a complete HTML page), which can be viewed as an image in a browser. This visualization can help you find ways to use the tree to create tag patterns for relation extraction. See the following listing.

**Listing 11.13   Visualize a dependency tree**

```
>>> from spacy.display import render
>>> sentence = "In 1541 Desoto wrote in his journal about the Pascagoula."
>>> parsed_sent = en_model(sentence)
>>> with open('pascagoula.html', 'w') as f:
...     f.write(render(docs=parsed_sent, page=True,
➥ options=dict(compact=True)))
```

The dependency tree for this short sentence shows that the noun phrase "the Pascagoula" is the object of the relationship "met" for the subject "Desoto" (see figure 11.2). And both nouns are tagged as proper nouns.

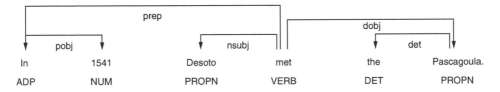

**Figure 11.2   The Pascagoula people**

To create POS and word property patterns for a `spacy.matcher.Matcher`, listing all the token tags in a table is helpful. The following listing shows some helper functions that make that easier.

**Listing 11.14   Helper functions for spaCy tagged strings**

```
>>> import pandas as pd
>>> from collections import OrderedDict
```

```
>>> def token_dict(token):
...     return OrderedDict(ORTH=token.orth_, LEMMA=token.lemma_,
...         POS=token.pos_, TAG=token.tag_, DEP=token.dep_)

>>> def doc_dataframe(doc):
...     return pd.DataFrame([token_dict(tok) for tok in doc])

>>> doc_dataframe(en_model("In 1541 Desoto met the Pascagoula."))
         ORTH      LEMMA    POS  TAG   DEP
0          In         in    ADP   IN  prep
1        1541       1541    NUM   CD  pobj
2      Desoto     desoto  PROPN  NNP  nsubj
3         met       meet   VERB  VBD  ROOT
4         the        the    DET   DT   det
5  Pascagoula  pascagoula  PROPN  NNP  dobj
6           .          .  PUNCT    .  punct
```

Now you can see the sequence of POS or TAG features that will make a good pattern. If you're looking for "has-met" relationships between people and organizations, you'd probably like to allow patterns such as "PROPN met PROPN," "PROPN met the PROPN," "PROPN met with the PROPN," and "PROPN often meets with PROPN." You could specify each of those patterns individually, or try to capture them all with some * or ? operators on "any word" patterns between your proper nouns:

```
'PROPN ANYWORD? met ANYWORD? ANYWORD? PROPN'
```

Patterns in spaCy are much more powerful and flexible than the preceding pseudo-code, so you have to be more verbose to explain exactly the word features you'd like to match. In a spaCy pattern specification, you use a dictionary to capture all the tags that you want to match for each token or word, as shown in the following listing.

**Listing 11.15   Example spaCy POS pattern**

```
>>> pattern = [{'TAG': 'NNP', 'OP': '+'}, {'IS_ALPHA': True, 'OP': '*'},
...            {'LEMMA': 'meet'},
...            {'IS_ALPHA': True, 'OP': '*'}, {'TAG': 'NNP', 'OP': '+'}]
```

You can then extract the tagged tokens you need from your parsed sentence, as shown in the following listing.

**Listing 11.16   Creating a POS pattern matcher with spaCy**

```
>>> from spacy.matcher import Matcher
>>> doc = en_model("In 1541 Desoto met the Pascagoula.")
>>> matcher = Matcher(en_model.vocab)
>>> matcher.add('met', None, pattern)
>>> m = matcher(doc)
>>> m
[(12280034159272152371, 2, 6)]

>>> doc[m[0][1]:m[0][2]]
Desoto met the Pascagoula
```

So you extracted a match from the original sentence from which you created the pattern, but what about similar sentences from Wikipedia? See the following listing.

---

**Listing 11.17   Using a POS pattern matcher**

```
>>> doc = en_model("October 24: Lewis and Clark met their first Mandan Chief,
       Big White.")
>>> m = matcher(doc)[0]
>>> m
(12280034159272152371, 3, 11)

>>> doc[m[1]:m[2]]
Lewis and Clark met their first Mandan Chief

>>> doc = en_model("On 11 October 1986, Gorbachev and Reagan met at a house")
>>> matcher(doc)
[]                          ◁──┐  The pattern doesn't match any substrings
                               │  of the sentence from Wikipedia.
```

You need to add a second pattern to allow for the verb to occur after the subject and object nouns, as shown in the following listing.

---

**Listing 11.18   Combining multiple patterns for a more robust pattern matcher**

```
>>> doc = en_model("On 11 October 1986, Gorbachev and Reagan met at a house")
>>> pattern = [{'TAG': 'NNP', 'OP': '+'}, {'LEMMA': 'and'}, {'TAG': 'NNP', 'O
       P': '+'},
...            {'IS_ALPHA': True, 'OP': '*'}, {'LEMMA': 'meet'}]
>>> matcher.add('met', None, pattern)    ◁──┐  Adds an additional pattern without removing
>>> m = matcher(doc)                        │  the previous pattern. Here 'met' is an arbitrary
>>> m                                       │  key. Name your pattern whatever you like.
[(14332210279624491740, 5, 9),
 (14332210279624491740, 5, 11),
 (14332210279624491740, 7, 11),          ┌──  The '+' operators increase the number
 (14332210279624491740, 5, 12)]    ◁─────┘   of overlapping alternative matches.

>>> doc[m[-1][1]:m[-1][2]]             ◁──┐  The longest match is the
Gorbachev and Reagan met at a house       │  last one in the list of matches.
```

So now you have your entities and a relationship. You can even build a pattern that is less restrictive about the verb in the middle ("met") and more restrictive about the names of the people and groups on either side. Doing so might allow you to identify additional verbs that imply that one person or group has met another, such as the verb "knows," or even passive phrases, such as "had a conversation" or "became acquainted with." Then you could use these new verbs to add relationships for new proper nouns on either side.

But you can see how you're drifting away from the original meaning of your seed relationship patterns. This is called semantic drift. Fortunately, spaCy tags words in a parsed document with not only their POS and dependency tree information, but it also provides the Word2vec word vector. You can use this vector to prevent the connector verb and the proper nouns on either side from drifting too far away from the original meaning of your seed pattern.[7]

### 11.4.2 *Entity name normalization*

The normalized representation of an entity is usually a string, even for numerical information such as dates. The normalized ISO format for this date would be "1541-01-01." A normalized representation for entities enables your knowledge base to connect all the different things that happened in the world on that same date to that same node (entity) in your graph.

You'd do the same for other named entities. You'd correct the spelling of words and attempt to resolve ambiguities for names of objects, animals, people, places, and so on. Normalizing named entities and resolving ambiguities is often called *coreference resolution* or *anaphora resolution*, especially for pronouns or other "names" relying on context. This is similar to lemmatization, which we discussed in chapter 2. Normalization of named entities ensures that spelling and naming variations don't pollute your vocabulary of entity names with confounding, redundant names.

For example "Desoto" might be expressed in a particular document in at least five different ways:

- "de Soto"
- "Hernando de Soto"
- "Hernando de Soto (c. 1496/1497–1542), Spanish conquistador"
- https://en.wikipedia.org/wiki/Hernando_de_Soto (a URI)
- A numerical ID for a database of famous and historical people

Similarly your normalization algorithm can choose any of these forms. A knowledge graph should normalize each kind of entity the same way, to prevent multiple distinct entities of the same type from sharing the same name. You don't want multiple person names referring to the same physical person. Even more importantly, the normalization should be applied consistently—both when you write new facts to the knowledge base or when you read or query the knowledge base.

If you decide to change the normalization approach after the database has been populated, the data for existing entities in the knowledge should be "migrated," or altered, to adhere to the new normalization scheme. Schemaless databases (key-value stores), like the ones used to store knowledge graphs or knowledge bases, aren't free from the migration responsibilities of relational databases. After all, schemaless databases are interface wrappers for relational databases under the hood.

Your normalized entities also need "is-a" relationships to connect them to entity categories that define types or categories of entities. These "is-a" relationships can be thought of as tags, because each entity can have multiple "is-a" relationships. Like

---

[7] This is the subject of active research: https://nlp.stanford.edu/pubs/structuredVS.pdf.

names of people or POS tags, dates and other discrete numerical objects need to be normalized if you want to incorporate them into your knowledge base.

What about *relations* between entities—do they need to be stored in some normalized way?

### 11.4.3  *Relation normalization and extraction*

Now you need a way to normalize the relationships, to identify the kind of relationship between entities. Doing so will allow you to find all birthday relationships between dates and people, or dates of occurrences of historical events, such as the encounter between "Hernando de Soto" and the "Pascagoula people." And you need to write an algorithm to choose the right label for your relationship.

And these relationships can have a hierarchical name, such as "occurred-on/ approximately" and "occurred-on/exactly," to allow you to find specific relationships or categories of relationships. You can also label these relationships with a numerical property for the "confidence," probability, weight, or normalized frequency (analogous to TF-IDF for terms/words) of that relationship. You can adjust these confidence values each time a fact extracted from a new text corroborates or contradicts an existing fact in the database.

Now you need a way to match patterns that can find these relationships.

### 11.4.4  *Word patterns*

Word patterns are just like regular expressions, but for words instead of characters. Instead of character classes, you have word classes. For example, instead of matching a lowercase character you might have a word pattern decision to match all the singular nouns ("NN" POS tag).[8] This is usually accomplished with machine learning. Some seed sentences are tagged with some correct relationships (facts) extracted from those sentences. A POS pattern can be used to find similar sentences where the subject and object words, or even the relationships, might change.

You can use the spaCy package two different ways to match these patterns in O(1) (constant time) no matter how many patterns you want to match:

- PhraseMatcher for any word/tag sequence patterns[9]
- Matcher for POS tag sequence patterns[10]

To ensure that the new relations found in new sentences are truly analogous to the original seed (example) relationships, you often need to constrain the subject, relation, and object word meanings to be similar to those in the seed sentences. The best way to do this is with some vector representation of the meaning of words. Does this ring a bell? Word vectors, discussed in chapter 4, are one of the most widely used word meaning representations for this purpose. They help minimize semantic drift.

---

[8]  spaCy uses the "OntoNotes 5" POS tags: https://spacy.io/api/annotation#pos-tagging.
[9]  See the web page titled "Code Examples - spaCy Usage Documentation" (https://spacy.io/usage/examples #phrase-matcher).
[10]  See the web page titled "Matcher - spaCy API Documentation" (https://spacy.io/api/matcher).

Using semantic vector representations for words and phrases has made automatic information extraction accurate enough to build large knowledge bases automatically. But human supervision and curation is required to resolve much of the ambiguity in natural language text. CMU's NELL (Never-Ending Language Learner)[11] enables users to vote on changes to the knowledge base using Twitter and a web application.

### 11.4.5 Segmentation

We've skipped one form of information extraction. It's also a tool used in information extraction. Most of the documents you've used in this chapter have been bite-sized chunks containing just a few facts and named entities. But in the real world you may need to create these chunks yourself.

Document "chunking" is useful for creating semi-structured data about documents that can make it easier to search, filter, and sort documents for information retrieval. And for information extraction, if you're extracting relations to build a knowledge base such as NELL or Freebase, you need to break it into parts that are likely to contain a fact or two. When you divide natural language text into meaningful pieces, it's called *segmentation*. The resulting segments can be phrases, sentences, quotes, paragraphs, or even entire sections of a long document.

Sentences are the most common chunk for most information extraction problems. Sentences are usually punctuated with one of a few symbols (., ?, !, or a new line). And grammatically correct English language sentences must contain a subject (noun) and a verb, which means they'll usually have at least one relation or fact worth extracting. And sentences are often self-contained packets of meaning that don't rely too much on preceding text to convey most of their information.

Fortunately most languages, including English, have the concept of a sentence, a single statement with a subject and verb that says something about the world. Sentences are just the right bite-sized chunk of text for your NLP knowledge extraction pipeline. For the chatbot pipeline, your goal is to segment documents into sentences, or statements.

In addition to facilitating information extraction, you can flag some of those statements and sentences as being part of a dialog or being suitable for replies in a dialog. Using a sentence segmenter allows you to train your chatbot on longer texts, such as books. Choosing those books appropriately gives your chatbot a more literary, intelligent style than if you trained it purely on Twitter streams or IRC chats. And these books give your chatbot access to a much broader set of training documents to build its common sense knowledge about the world.

#### SENTENCE SEGMENTATION

Sentence segmentation is usually the first step in an information extraction pipeline. It helps isolate facts from each other so that you can associate the right price with the

---

[11] See the web page titled "NELL: The Computer that Learns - Carnegie Mellon University" (https://www.cmu.edu/homepage/computing/2010/fall/nell-computer-that-learns.shtml).

right thing in a string such as "The Babel fish costs $42. 42 cents for the stamp." And that string is a good example of why sentence segmentation is tough—the dot in the middle could be interpreted as a decimal or a "full stop" period.

The simplest pieces of "information" you can extract from a document are sequences of words that contain a logically cohesive statement. The most important segments in a natural language document, after words, are sentences. Sentences contain a logically cohesive statement about the world. These statements contain the information you want to extract from text. Sentences often tell you the relationship between things and how the world works when they make statements of fact, so you can use sentences for knowledge extraction. And sentences often explain when, where, and how things happened in the past, tend to happen in general, or will happen in the future. So we should also be able to extract facts about dates, times, locations, people, and even sequences of events or tasks using sentences as our guide. And, most importantly, all natural languages have sentences or logically cohesive sections of text of some sort. And all languages have a widely shared process for generating them (a set of grammar rules or habits).

But segmenting text, identifying sentence boundaries, is a bit trickier than you might think. In English, for example, no single punctuation mark or sequence of characters always marks the end of a sentence.

### 11.4.6  *Why won't split('.!?') work?*

Even a human reader might have trouble finding an appropriate sentence boundary within each of the following quotes. And if they did find multiple sentences from each, they would be wrong for four out of five of these difficult examples:

> *I live in the U.S. but I commute to work in Mexico on S.V. Australis for a woman from St. Bernard St. on the Gulf of Mexico.*
>
> *I went to G.T. You?*
>
> *She yelled "It's right here!" but I kept looking for a sentence boundary anyway.*
>
> *I stared dumbfounded on as things like "How did I get here?," "Where am I?," "Am I alive?" flittered across the screen.*
>
> *The author wrote "'I don't think it's conscious.' Turing said."*

Even a human reader might have trouble finding an appropriate sentence boundary within each of these quotes. More sentence segmentation "edge cases" such as these are available at tm-town.com[12] and within the nlpia.data module.

Technical text is particularly difficult to segment into sentences, because engineers, scientists, and mathematicians tend to use periods and exclamation points to signify a

---

[12] See the web page titled "Natural Language Processing: TM-Town" (https://www.tm-town.com/natural -language-processing#golden_rules).

lot of things besides the end of a sentence. When we tried to find the sentence boundaries in this book, we had to manually correct several of the extracted sentences.

If only we wrote English like telegrams, with a "STOP" or unique punctuation mark at the end of each sentence. Because we don't, you'll need some more sophisticated NLP than just `split('.!?')`. Hopefully you're already imagining a solution in your head. If so, it's probably based on one of the two approaches to NLP you've used throughout this book:

- Manually programmed algorithms (regular expressions and pattern-matching)
- Statistical models (data-based models or machine learning)

We use the sentence segmentation problem to revisit these two approaches by showing you how to use regular expressions as well as perceptrons to find sentence boundaries. And you'll use the text of this book as a training and test set to show you some of the challenges. Fortunately you haven't inserted any newlines within sentences, to manually wrap text like in newspaper column layouts. Otherwise, the problem would be even more difficult. In fact, much of the source text for this book, in ASCIIdoc format, has been written with "old-school" sentence separators (two spaces after the end of every sentence), or with each sentence on a separate line. This was so we could use this book as a training and test set for segmenters.

### 11.4.7 *Sentence segmentation with regular expressions*

Regular expressions are just a shorthand way of expressing the tree of "if...then" rules (regular grammar rules) for finding character patterns in strings of characters. As we mentioned in chapters 1 and 2, regular expressions (regular grammars) are a particularly succinct way to specify the rules of a finite state machine. Our regex or FSM has only one purpose: identify sentence boundaries.

If you do a web search for sentence segmenters,[13] you're likely to be pointed to various regular expressions intended to capture the most common sentence boundaries. Here are some of them, combined and enhanced to give you a fast, general-purpose sentence segmenter. The following regex would work with a few "normal" sentences:

```
>>> re.split(r'[!.?]+[ $]', "Hello World.... Are you there?!?! I'm going
     to Mars!")
['Hello World', 'Are you there', "I'm going to Mars!"]
```

Unfortunately, this `re.split` approach gobbles up the sentence-terminating token, and only retains it if it's the last character in a document or string. But it does do a good job of ignoring the trickery of periods within doubly nested quotes:

```
>>> re.split(r'[!.?] ', "The author wrote \"'I don't think it's conscious.'
     Turing said.\"")
['The author wrote "\'I don\'t think it\'s conscious.\' Turing said."']
```

---

[13] See the web page titled "Python sentence segment at DuckDuckGo" (https://duckduckgo.com/?q=Python +sentence+segment&t=canonical&ia=qa).

It also ignores periods in quotes that terminate an actual sentence. This can be a good thing or a bad thing, depending on your information extraction steps that follow your sentence segmenter:

```
>>> re.split(r'[!.?] ', "The author wrote \"'I don't think it's conscious.'
➥ Turing said.\" But I stopped reading.")
['The author wrote "\'I don\'t think it\'s conscious.\' Turing said." But I
➥ stopped reading."']
```

What about abbreviated text, such as SMS messages and tweets? Sometimes hurried humans squish sentences together, leaving no space surrounding periods. Alone, the following regex could only deal with periods in SMS messages that have letters on either side, and it would safely skip over numerical values:

```
>>> re.split(r'(?<!\d)\.|\.(?!\d)', "I went to GT.You?")
['I went to GT', 'You?']
```

Even combining these two regexes isn't enough to get more than a few right in the difficult test cases from `nlpia.data`:

```
>>> from nlpia.data.loaders import get_data
>>> regex = re.compile(r'((?<!\d)\.|\.(?!\d))|([!.?]+)[ $]+')
>>> examples = get_data('sentences-tm-town')
>>> wrong = []
>>> for i, (challenge, text, sents) in enumerate(examples):
...     if tuple(regex.split(text)) != tuple(sents):
...         print('wrong {}: {}{}'.format(i, text[:50], '...' if len(text) >
    50 else ''))
...         wrong += [i]
>>> len(wrong), len(examples)
(61, 61)
```

You'd have to add a lot more "look-ahead" and "look-back" to improve the accuracy of a regex sentence segmenter. A better approach for sentence segmentation is to use a machine learning algorithm (often a single-layer neural net or logistic regression) trained on a labeled set of sentences. Several packages contain such a model you can use to improve your sentence segmenter:

- DetectorMorse[14]
- spaCy[15]
- SyntaxNet[16]

---

[14] See the web page titled "GitHub - cslu-nlp/DetectorMorse: Fast supervised sentence boundary detection using the averaged perceptron" (https://github.com/cslu-nlp/detectormorse).

[15] See the web page titled "Facts & Figures - spaCy Usage Documentation" (https://spacy.io/usage/facts-figures).

[16] See the web page titled "models/syntaxnet-tutorial.md at master" (https://github.com/tensorflow/models/blob/master/research/syntaxnet/g3doc/syntaxnet-tutorial.md).

- NLTK (Punkt)[17]
- Stanford CoreNLP [18]

You use the spaCy sentence segmenter (built into the parser) for most of your mission-critical applications. spaCy has few dependencies and compares well with the others on accuracy and speed. DetectorMorse, by Kyle Gorman, is another good choice if you want state-of-the-art performance in a pure Python implementation that you can refine with your own training set.

## 11.5  *In the real world*

Information extraction and question answering systems are used for

- TA assistants for university courses
- Customer service
- Tech support
- Sales
- Software documentation and FAQs

Information extraction can be used to extract things such as

- Dates
- Times
- Prices
- Quantities
- Addresses
- Names
  - People
  - Places
  - Apps
  - Companies
  - Bots
- Relationships
  - "is-a" (kinds of things)
  - "has" (attributes of things)
  - "related-to"

Whether information is being parsed from a large corpus or from user input on the fly, being able to extract specific details and store them for later use is critical to the performance of a chatbot. First by identifying and isolating this information and then by

---

[17] See the web page titled "nltk.tokenize package — NLTK 3.3 documentation" (http://www.nltk.org/api/nltk.tokenize.html#module-nltk.tokenize.punkt).

[18] See the web page titled "torotoki / corenlp-python — Bitbucket" (https://bitbucket.org/torotoki/corenlp-python).

tagging relationships between those pieces of information we've learned to "normalize" information programmatically. With that knowledge safely shelved in a search-able structure, your chatbot will be equipped with the tools to hold its own in a conversation in a given domain.

## Summary

- A knowledge graph can be built to store relationships between entities.
- Regular expressions are a mini-programming language that can isolate and extract information.
- Part-of-speech tagging allows you to extract relationships between entities mentioned in a sentence.
- Segmenting sentences requires more than just splitting on periods and exclamation marks.

# 12
# Getting chatty
# (dialog engines)

### This chapter covers

- Understanding four chatbot approaches
- Finding out what Artificial Intelligence Markup Language is all about
- Understanding the difference between chatbot pipelines and other NLP pipelines
- Learning about a hybrid chatbot architecture that combines the best ideas into one
- Using machine learning to make your chatbot get smarter over time
- Giving your chatbot agency—enabling it to spontaneously say what's on its mind

We opened this book with the idea of a dialog engine or chatbot NLP pipeline because wc think it's one of the most important NLP applications of this century. For the first time in history we can speak to a machine in our own language, and we can't always tell that it isn't human. Machines can fake being human, which is a lot harder than it sounds. There are several cash prize competitions, if you think you and your chatbot have the right stuff:

- The Alexa Prize ($3.5M)[1]
- Loebner Prize ($7k)[2]
- The Winograd Schema Challenge ($27k)[3]
- The Marcus Test[4]
- The Lovelace Test[5]

Beyond the pure fun and magic of building a conversational machine, beyond the glory that awaits you if you build a bot that can beat humans at an IQ test, beyond the warm fuzzy feeling of saving the world from malicious hacker botnets, and beyond the wealth that awaits you if you can beat Google and Amazon at their virtual assistant games—the techniques you'll learn in this chapter will give you the tools you need to get the job done.

The 21st century is going to be built on a foundation of AI (artificial intelligence) that assists us. And the most natural interface for AI is natural language conversation. For example, Aira.io's chatbot Chloe is helping to interpret the world for people who are blind or have low-vision. Other companies are building lawyer chatbots that save users thousands of dollars (or pounds) on parking tickets and hours of courtroom time. And self-driving cars will likely soon have conversational interfaces similar to Google Assistant and Google Maps to help you get where you want to go.

## 12.1   *Language skill*

You finally have all the pieces you need to assemble a chatbot—more formally, a *dialog system* or *dialog engine*. You'll build an NLP pipeline that can participate in natural language conversations.

Some of the NLP skills you'll use include

- Tokenization, stemming, and lemmatization
- Vector space language models such as bag-of-words vectors or topic vectors (semantic vectors)
- Deeper language representations such as word vectors or LSTM thought vectors
- Sequence-to-sequence translators (from chapter 10)
- Pattern matching (from chapter 11)
- Templates for generating natural language text

---

[1]  "The Alexa Prize," https://developer.amazon.com/alexaprize.

[2]  "Loebner Prize" at Bletchley Park, http://www.aisb.org.uk/events/loebner-prize.

[3]  "Establishing a Human Baseline for the Winograd Schema Challenge," by David Bender, http://ceur-ws.org/Vol-1353/paper_30.pdf; "An alternative to the Turing test," Kurzweil, http://www.kurzweilai.net/an-alternative-to-the-turing-test-winograd-schema-challenge-annual-competition-announced.

[4]  "What Comes After the Turing Test," New Yorker, Jan 2014, http://www.newyorker.com/tech/elements/what-comes-after-the-turing-test.

[5]  "The Lovelace 2.0 Test of Artificial Creativity and Intelligence," by Reidl, https://arxiv.org/pdf/1410.6142.pdf.

With these tools, you can build a chatbot with interesting behavior.

Let's make sure we're on the same page about what a chatbot is. In some communities, the word "chatbot" is used in a slightly derogatory way to refer to "canned response" systems.[6] These are chatbots that find patterns in the input text and use matches on those patterns to trigger a fixed, or templated, response.[7] You can think of these as FAQ bots that only know the answers to basic, general questions. These basic dialog systems are useful mainly for automated customer service phone-tree systems, where it's possible to hand off the conversation to a human when the chatbot runs out of canned responses.

But this doesn't mean that your chatbot needs to be so limited. If you're particularly clever about these patterns and templates, your chatbot can be the therapist in a convincing psychotherapy or counseling session. All the way back in 1964, Joseph Weizenbaum used patterns and templates to build the first popular chatbot, ELIZA.[8] And the remarkably effective Facebook Messenger therapy bot, Woebot, relies heavily on the pattern-matching and templated response approach. All that's needed to build Turing prize-winning chatbots is to add a little state (context) management to your pattern-matching system.

Steve Worswick's Mitsuku chatbot won the Loebner Prize (https://en.wikipedia .org/wiki/Turing_test), a form of the Turing Test, in 2016 and 2017 using pattern matching and templates. He added context or statefulness, to give Mitsuku a bit more depth. You can read about the other winners on Wikipedia (https://en.wikipedia.org/ wiki/Loebner_Prize#Winners). Amazon recently added this additional layer of conversational depth (context) to Alexa and called it "Follow-Up Mode."[9] You'll learn how to add context to your own pattern-maching chatbots in this chapter.

### 12.1.1 Modern approaches

Chatbots have come a long way since the days of ELIZA. Pattern-matching technology has been generalized and refined over the decades. And completely new approaches have been developed to supplement pattern matching. In recent literature, chatbots are often referred to as dialog systems, perhaps because of this greater sophistication. Matching patterns in text and populating canned-response templates with information extracted with those patterns is only one of four modern approaches to building chatbots:

- *Pattern matching*—Pattern matching and response templates (canned responses)
- *Grounding*—Logical knowledge graphs and inference on those graphs

---

[6] Wikipedia "Canned Response," https://en.wikipedia.org/wiki/Canned_response.

[7] "A Chatbot Dialogue Manager" by A.F. van Woudenberg, Open University of the Netherlands, http:// dspace.ou.nl/bitstream/1820/5390/1/INF_20140617_Woudenberg.pdf.

[8] Wikipedia: https://en.wikipedia.org/wiki/ELIZA.

[9] See the Verge article "Amazon Follow-Up Mode" (https://www.theverge.com/2018/3/9/17101330/amazon-alexa-follow-up-mode-back-to-back-requests).

- *Search*—Text retrieval
- *Generative*—Statistics and machine learning

This is roughly the order in which these approaches were developed. And that's the order in which we present them here. But before showing you how to use each technique to generate replies, we show you how chatbots use these techniques in the real world.

The most advanced chatbots use a hybrid approach that combines all of these techniques. This hybrid approach enables them to accomplish a broad range of tasks. Here's a list of a few of these chatbot applications; you may notice that the more advanced chatbots, such as Siri, Alexa, and Allo, are listed alongside multiple types of problems and applications:

- *Question answering*—Google Search, Alexa, Siri, Watson
- *Virtual assistants*—Google Assistant, Alexa, Siri, MS paperclip
- *Conversational*—Google Assistant, Google Smart Reply, Mitsuki Bot
- *Marketing*—Twitter bots, blogger bots, Facebook bots, Google Search, Google Assistant, Alexa, Allo
- *Customer service*—Storefront bots, technical support bots
- *Community management*—Bonusly, Slackbot
- *Therapy*—Woebot, Wysa, YourDost, Siri, Allo

Can you think of ways to combine the four basic dialog engine types to create chatbots for these seven applications? Figure 12.1 shows how some chatbots do it.

Let's talk briefly about these applications to help you build a chatbot for your application.

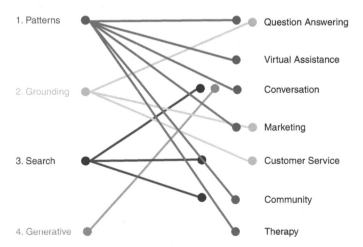

**Figure 12.1    Chatbot techniques used for some example applications**

## QUESTION ANSWERING DIALOG SYSTEMS

Question answering chatbots are used to answer factual questions about the world, which can include questions about the chatbot itself. Many question answering systems first search a knowledge base or relational database to "ground" them in the real world. If they can't find an acceptable answer there, they may search a corpus of unstructured data (or even the entire Web) to find answers to your questions. This is essentially what Google Search does. Parsing a statement to discern the question in need of answering and then picking the right answer requires a complex pipeline that combines most of the elements covered in previous chapters. Question answering chatbots are the most difficult to implement well because they require coordinating so many different elements.

## VIRTUAL ASSISTANTS

Virtual assistants, such as Alexa and Google Assistant, are helpful when you have a goal in mind. Goals or intents are usually simple things such as launching an app, setting a reminder, playing some music, or turning on the lights in your home. For this reason, virtual assistants are often called goal-based dialog engines. Dialog with such chatbots is intended to conclude quickly, with the user being satisfied that a particular action has been accomplished or some bit of information has been retrieved.

You're probably familiar with the virtual assistants on your phone or your home automation system. But you may not know that virtual assistants can also help you with your legal troubles and taxes. Though Intuit's TurboTax wizards aren't very chatty, they do implement a complex phone tree. You don't interact with them by voice or chat, but by filling in forms with structured data. So the TurboTax wizard can't really be called a chatbot yet, but it'll surely be wrapped in a chat interface soon, if the tax-bot AskMyUncleSam takes off.[10]

Lawyer virtual assistant chatbots have successfully appealed millions of dollars in parking tickets in New York and London.[11] And there's even a United Kingdom law firm where the only interaction you'll ever have with a lawyer is through a chatbot.[12] Lawyers are certainly goal-based virtual assistants, only they'll do more than set an appointment date: they'll set you a court date and maybe help you win your case.

Aira.io (http://aira.io) is building a virtual assistant called Chloe. Chloe gives blind and low-vision people access to a "visual interpreter for the blind." During onboarding, Chloe can ask customers things such as "Are you a white cane user?" "Do you have a guide dog?" and "Do you have any food allergies or dietary preferences you'd like us to know about?" This is called *voice first* design, when your app is designed from the

---

[10] Jan 2017, Venture Beat post by AskMyUncleSam: https://venturebeat.com/2017/01/27/how-this-chatbot-powered-by-machine-learning-can-help-with-your-taxes/.

[11] June 2016, "Chatbot Lawyer Overturns 160,000 Parking Tickets in London and New York," The Guardian, https://www.theguardian.com/technology/2016/jun/28/chatbot-ai-lawyer-donotpay-parking-tickets-london-new-york.

[12] Nov 2017, "Chatbot-based 'firm without lawyers' launched" blog post by Legal Futures: https://www.legalfutures.co.uk/latest-news/chatbot-based-firm-without-lawyers-launched.

ground up around a dialog system. In the future, the assistance that Chloe can provide will be greatly expanded as she learns to understand the real world through live video feeds. And the "explorers" around the world interacting with Chloe will be training her to understand common everyday tasks that humans perform in the world. Chloe is one of the few virtual assistants designed entirely to assist and not to influence or manipulate.[13]

Virtual assistants such as Siri, Google Assistant, Cortana, and Aira's Chloe are getting smarter every day. Virtual assistants learn from their interactions with humans and the other machines they're connected to. They're developing evermore general, domain-independent intelligence. If you want to learn about artificial general intelligence (AGI), you'll want to experiment with virtual assistants and conversational chatbots as part of that research.

### CONVERSATIONAL CHATBOTS

Conversational chatbots, such as Worswick's Mitsuku[14] or any of the Pandorabots,[15] are designed to entertain. They can often be implemented with very few lines of code, as long as you have lots of data. But doing conversation well is an ever-evolving challenge. The accuracy or performance of a conversational chatbot is usually measured with something like a Turing test. In a typical Turing test, humans interact with another chat participant through a terminal and try to figure out if it's a bot or a human. The better the chatbot is at being indistinguishable from a human, the better its performance on a Turing test metric.

The domain (variety of knowledge) and human behaviors that a chatbot is expected to implement, in these Turing tests, is expanding every year. And as the chatbots get better at fooling us, we humans get better at detecting their trickery. ELIZA fooled many of us in the BBS-era of the 1980s into thinking that "she" was a therapist helping us get through our daily lives. It took decades of research and development before chatbots could fool us again.

> *Fool me once, shame on bots; fool me twice, shame on humans.*
>
> Anonymous Human

Recently, Mitsuku won the Loebner challenge, a competition that uses a Turing test to rank chatbots.[16] Conversational chatbots are used mostly for academic research, entertainment (video games), and advertisement.

---

[13] We rarely acknowledge to ourselves the influence that virtual assistants and search engines exert over our free will and beliefs. And we rarely care that their incentives and motivations are different from our own. These misaligned incentives are present not only in technology such as virtual assistants, but within culture itself. Check out *Sapiens* and *Homo Deus* by Yuval Noah Harari if you're interested in learning about where culture and technology are taking us.

[14] See the web page titled "Mitsuku Chatbot" (http://www.square-bear.co.uk/aiml).

[15] See the web page titled "Pandorabots AIML Chatbot Directory" (https://www.chatbots.org).

[16] See the web page titled "Loebner Prize" (https://en.wikipedia.org/wiki/Loebner _Prize).

### MARKETING CHATBOTS

Marketing chatbots are designed to inform users about a product and entice them to purchase it. More and more video games, movies, and TV shows are launched with chatbots on websites promoting them: [17]

- HBO promoted "Westworld" with "Aeden."[18]
- Sony promoted "Resident Evil" with "Red Queen."[19]
- Disney promoted "Zootopia" with "Officer Judy Hopps."[20]
- Universal promoted "Unfriended" with "Laura Barnes."
- Activision promoted "Call of Duty" with "Lt. Reyes."

Some virtual assistants are marketing bots in disguise. Consider Amazon Alexa and Google Assistant. Though they claim to assist you with things such as adding reminders and searching the web, they invariably prioritize responses about products or businesses over responses with generic or free information. These companies are in the business of selling stuff—directly in the case of Amazon, indirectly in the case of Google. Their virtual assistants are designed to assist their corporate parents (Amazon and Google) in making money. Of course, they also want to assist users in getting things done, so we'll keep using them. But the objective functions for these bots are designed to steer users toward purchases, not happiness or well-being.

Most marketing chatbots are conversational, to entertain users and mask their ulterior motives. They can also employ question answering skills, grounded in a knowledge base about the products they sell. To mimic characters in a movie, show, or video game, chatbots will use text retrieval to find snippets of things to say from the script. And sometimes even generative models are trained directly on a collection of scripts. So marketing bots often employ all four of the techniques you'll learn about in this chapter.

### COMMUNITY MANAGEMENT

Community management is a particularly important application of chatbots because it influences how society evolves. A good chatbot "shepherd" can steer a video game community away from chaos and help it grow into an inclusive, cooperative world where everyone has fun, not just the bullies and trolls. A bad chatbot, such as the Twitter bot Tay, can quickly create an environment of prejudice and ignorance.[21]

When chatbots go "off the rails," some people claim they are merely mirrors or magnifiers of society. And there are often unintended consequences of any complicated

---

[17] Justin Clegg lists additional ones in his LinkedIn post: https://www.linkedin.com/pulse/how-smart-brands-using-chatbots-justin-clegg/.

[18] Sep 2016, Entertainment Weekly: https://www.yahoo.com/entertainment/westworld-launches-sex-touting-online-181918383.html.

[19] Jan 2017, IPG Media Lab: https://www.ipglab.com/2017/01/18/sony-pictures-launches-ai-powered-chatbot-to-promote-resident-evil-movie/.

[20] Jun 2016, Venture Beat: https://venturebeat.com/2016/06/01/imperson-launches-zootopias-officer-judy-hopps-bot-on-facebook-messenger/.

[21] Wikipedia article about the brief "life" of Microsoft's Tay chatbot, https://en.wikipedia.org/wiki/Tay_(bot).

system interacting with the real world. But because chatbots are active participants, imbued with motivations by developers like you, you shouldn't dismiss them as merely "mirrors of society." Chatbots seem to do more than merely reflect and amplify the best and the worst of us. They're an active force, partially under the influence of their developers and trainers, for either good or evil. Because supervisors and managers cannot perfectly enforce any policy that ensures chatbots "do no evil," it's up to you, the developer, to strive to build chatbots that are kind, sensitive, and pro-social. Asimov's "Three Laws of Robotics" aren't enough.[22] Only you can influence the evolution of bots, using smart software and cleverly constructed datasets.

Some smart people at Arizona University are considering using their chatbot-building skills to save humanity, not from Evil Superintelligent AI, but from ourselves. Researchers are trying to mimic the behavior of potential ISIS terrorist recruits to distract and misinform ISIS recruiters. This may one day mean that chatbots are saving human lives, simply by chatting it up with people that intend to bring harm to the world.[23] Chatbot trolls can be a good thing if they troll the right people or organizations.

## CUSTOMER SERVICE

Customer service chatbots are often the only "person" available when you visit an online store. IBM's Watson, Amazon's Lex, and other chatbot services are often used behind the scenes to power these customer assistants. They often combine both question answering skills (remember Watson's Jeopardy training?) with virtual assistance skills. But unlike marketing bots, customer service chatbots must be well-grounded. And the knowledge base used to "ground" their answers to reality must be kept current, enabling customer service chatbots to answer questions about orders or products as well as initiate actions such as placing or canceling orders.

In 2016, Facebook Messenger released an API for businesses to build customer service chatbots. And Google recently purchased API.ai to create their Dialogflow framework, which is often used to build customer service chatbots. Similarly, Amazon Lex is often used to build customer service dialog engines for retailers and wholesalers of products sold on Amazon. Chatbots are quickly becoming a significant sales channel in industries from fashion (Botty Hilfiger) to fast food (TacoBot) to flowers.[24]

## THERAPY

Modern therapy chatbots, such as Wysa and YourDOST, have been built to help displaced tech workers adjust to their new lives.[25] Therapy chatbots must be entertaining like a conversational chatbot. They must be informative like a question answering

---

[22] March 2014, George Dvorski, "Why Asimov's Three Laws of Robotics Can't Protect Us," Gizmodo, https://io9.gizmodo.com/why-asimovs-three-laws-of-robotics-cant-protect-us-1553665410.

[23] Oct 2015, Slate, http://www.slate.com/articles/technology/future_tense/2015/10/using_chatbots_to_distract_isis_recruiters_on_social_media.html.

[24] 1-800-flowers: 1-800-Flowers.com, Tommy Hilfiger: https://techcrunch.com/2016/09/09/botty-hilfiger/, TacoBot: http://www.businessinsider.com/taco-bells-tacobot-orders-food-for-you-2016-4.

[25] Dec 2017, Bloomberg: https://www.bloomberg.com/news/articles/2017-12-10/fired-indian-tech-workers-turn-to-chatbots-for-counseling.

chatbot. And they must be persuasive like a marketing chatbot. And if they're imbued with self-interest to augment their altruism, these chatbots may be "goal-seeking" and use their marketing and influence skill to get you to come back for additional sessions.

You might not think of Siri, Alexa, and Allo as therapists, but they can help you get through a rough day. Ask them about the meaning of life and you'll be sure to get a philosophical or humorous response. And if you're feeling down, ask them to tell you a joke or play some upbeat music. And beyond these parlor tricks, you can bet that developers of these sophisticated chatbots were guided by psychologists to help craft an experience intended to increase your happiness and sense of well-being.

As you might expect, these therapy bots employ a hybrid approach that combines all four of the basic approaches listed at the beginning of this chapter.

### 12.1.2  *A hybrid approach*

So what does this hybrid approach look like?

The four basic chatbot approaches can be combined in a variety of ways to produce useful chatbots. And many different applications use all four basic techniques. The main difference between hybrid chatbots is how they combine these four skills, and how much "weight" or "power" is given to each technique.

In this chapter, we show you how to balance these approaches explicitly in code to help you build a chatbot that meets your needs. The hybrid approach we use here will allow you to build features of all these real world systems into your bot. And you'll build an "objective function" that'll take into account the goals of your chatbot when it's choosing between the four approaches, or merely choosing among all the possible responses generated by each approach.

So let's dive into each of these four approaches, one at a time. For each one, we build a chatbot that uses only the technique we're learning. But in the end we show you how to combine them all together.

## 12.2  *Pattern-matching approach*

The earliest chatbots used pattern matching to trigger responses. In addition to detecting statements that your bot can respond to, patterns can also be used to extract information from the incoming text. You learned several ways to define patterns for information extraction in chapter 11.

The information extracted from your users' statements can be used to populate a database of knowledge about the users, or about the world in general. And it can be used even more directly to populate an immediate response to some statements. In chapter 1, we showed a simple pattern-based chatbot that used a regular expression to detect greetings. You can also use regular expressions to extract the name of the person being greeted by the human user. This helps give the bot "context" for the conversation. This context can be used to populate a response.

ELIZA, developed in the late 1970s, was surprisingly effective at this, convincing many users that "she" was capable of helping them with their psychological challenges.

ELIZA was programmed with a limited set of words to look for in user statements. The algorithm would rank any of those words that it saw in order to find a single word that seemed like the most important word in a user's statement. That would then trigger selection of a canned response template associated with that word. These response templates were carefully designed to emulate the empathy and open-mindedness of a therapist, using reflexive psychology. The key word that had triggered the response was often reused in the response to make it sound like ELIZA understood what the user was talking about. By replying in a user's own language, the bot helped build rapport and helped users believe that it was listening.

ELIZA taught us a lot about what it takes to interact with humans in natural language. Perhaps the most important revelation was that listening well, or at least appearing to listen well, is the key to chatbot success.

In 1995, Richard Wallace began building a general chatbot framework that used the pattern-matching approach. Between 1995 and 2002, his community of developers built the Artificial Intelligence Markup Language (AIML) to specify the patterns and responses of a chatbot. A.L.I.C.E. was the open source reference implementation of a chatbot that utilized this markup language to define its behavior. AIML has since become the de facto open standard for defining chatbot and virtual assistant configuration APIs for services such as Pandorabots. Microsoft's Bot framework is also able to load AIML files to define chatbot behaviors. Other frameworks like Google's Dialog-Flow and Amazon Lex don't support import or export of AIML.

AIML is an open standard, meaning the language is documented and it doesn't have hidden proprietary features locked to any particular company. Open source Python packages are available for parsing and executing AIML for your chatbot.[26] But AIML limits the types of patterns and logical structures you can define. And it's XML, which means chatbot frameworks built in Python (such as `Will` and `ChatterBot`) are usually a better foundation for building your chatbot.

Because you have a lot of your NLP tools in Python packages already, you can often build much more complex pattern-matching chatbots just by building up the logic for your bot directly in Python and regular expressions or glob patterns.[27] At Aira, we developed a simple glob pattern language similar to AIML to define our patterns. We have a translator that converts this glob pattern language into regular expressions that can be run on any platform with a regular expression parser.

And Aira uses `{{handlebars}}` for our template specifications in this `aichat` bot framework (http://github.com/aira/aichat). The handlebars templating language has interpreters for Java and Python, so Aira uses it on a variety of mobile and server platforms. And handlebars expressions can include filters and conditionals that can be

---

[26] `pip install aiml` https://github.com/creatorrr/pyAIML.

[27] Glob patterns and globstar patterns are the simplified regular expressions you use to find files in DOS or Bash or pretty much any other shell. In a glob pattern, the asterisk or star (`*`) is used to represent any number of any characters. So `*.txt` will match any filenames that have ".txt" at the end (https://en.wikipedia.org/wiki/Glob_%28programming%29).

used to create complex chatbot behavior. If you want something even more straightforward and Pythonic for your chatbot templates, you can use Python 3.6 f-strings. And if you're not yet using Python 3.6, you can use `str.format(template, **locals())` to render your templates just like f-strings do.

### 12.2.1 *A pattern-matching chatbot with AIML*

In AIML (v2.0), here's how you might define your greeting chatbot from chapter 1.[28]

Listing 12.1    nlpia/book/examples/greeting.v2.aiml

```
<?xml version="1.0" encoding="UTF-8"?><aiml version="2.0">
<category>
    <pattern>HI</pattern>
<template>Hi!</template>
</category>
<category>
    <pattern>[HELLO HI YO YOH YO'] [ROSA ROSE CHATTY CHATBOT BOT CHATTERBOT]<
    /pattern>
    <template>Hi , How are you?</template>
</category>
<category>
    <pattern>[HELLO HI YO YOH YO' 'SUP SUP OK HEY] [HAL YOU U YALL Y'ALL YOUS
    YOUSE]</pattern>
    <template>Good one.</template>
</category>
</aiml>
```

We used some of the new features of AIML 2.0 (by Bot Libre) to make the XML a little more compact and readable. The square brackets allow you to define alternative spellings of the same word in one line.

   Unfortunately, the Python interpreters for AIML (`PyAiml`, `aiml`, and `aiml_bot`) don't support version 2 of the AIML spec. The Python 3 AIML interpreter that works with the original AIML 1.0 specification is `aiml_bot`. In `aiml_bot`, the parser is embedded within a `Bot()` class, designed to hold the "brain" in RAM that helps a chatbot respond quickly. The brain, or *kernel*, contains all the AIML patterns and templates in a single data structure, similar to a Python dictionary, mapping patterns to response templates.

### AIML 1.0

AIML is a declarative language built on the XML standard, which limits the programming constructs and data structures you can use in your bot. But don't think of your AIML chatbot as being a complete system. You'll augment the AIML chatbot with all the other tools you learned about earlier.

---

[28] "AI Chat Bot in Python with AIML," by NanoDano Aug 2015, https://www.devdungeon.com/content/ai-chat-bot-python-aiml#what-is-aiml.

One limitation of AIML is the kinds of patterns you can match and respond to. An AIML kernel (pattern matcher) only responds when input text matches a pattern hard-coded by a developer. One nice thing is that AIML patterns can include wild cards, symbols that match any sequence of words. But the words that you do include in your pattern must match precisely. No fuzzy matches, emoticons, internal punctuation characters, typos, or misspellings can be matched automatically. In AIML, you have to manually define synonyms with an `</srai>`, one at a time. Think of all the stemming and lemmatization you did programmatically in chapter 2. That would be tedious to implement in AIML. Though we show you how to implement synonym and typo matchers in AIML here, the hybrid chatbot you build at the end of the chapter will sidestep this tedium by processing all text coming into your chatbot.

Another fundamental limitation of an AIML `<pattern>` you need to be aware of is that it can only have a single wild card character. A more expressive pattern-matching language such as regular expressions can give you more power to create interesting chatbots.[29] For now, with AIML, we only use patterns such as "HELLO ROSA *" to match input text such as "Hello Rosa, you wonderful chatbot!"

> **NOTE** The readability of a language is critical to your productivity as a developer. A good language can make a huge difference, whether you're building a chatbot or a web app.

We don't spend too much time helping you understand and write AIML. But we want you to be able to import and customize some of the available (and free) open source AIML scripts out there.[30] You can use AIML scripts, as-is, to give some basic functionality for your chatbot, with little upfront work.

In the next section, we show you how to create and load an AIML file into your chatbot and generate responses with it.

### PYTHON AIML INTERPRETER

Let's build up that complicated AIML script from listing 12.1 one step at a time, and show you how to load and run it within a Python program. The following listing is a simple AIML file that can recognize two sequences of words: "Hello Rosa" and "Hello Troll," and your chatbot will respond to each differently, like in earlier chapters.

> **Listing 12.2   nlpia/nlpia/data/greeting_step1.aiml**

```
<?xml version="1.0" encoding="UTF-8"?><aiml version="1.0.1">

<category>
    <pattern>HELLO ROSA </pattern>
```

---

[29] It's hard to compete with modern languages such as Python on expressiveness (https://en.wikipedia.org/wiki/Comparison_of_programming_languages#Expressiveness and http://redmonk.com/dberkholz/2013/03/25/programming-languages-ranked-by-expressiveness).

[30] Google for "AIML 1.0 files" or "AIML brain dumps" and check out AIML resources such as Chatterbots and Pandorabots: http://www.chatterbotcollection.com/category_contents.php?id_cat=20.

```
    <template>Hi Human!</template>
</category>
<category>
    <pattern>HELLO TROLL </pattern>
    <template>Good one, human.</template>
</category>

</aiml>
```

**NOTE** In AIML 1.0, all patterns must be specified in ALL CAPS.

You've set your bot up to respond differently to two different kinds of greetings: polite and impolite. Now let's use the `aiml_bot` package to interpret AIML 1.0 files in Python. If you've installed the `nlpia` package, you can load these examples from there using the code in the following listing. If you want to experiment with the AIML files you typed up yourself, you'll need to adjust the path `learn=path` to point to your file.

> **Listing 12.3    nlpia/book/examples/ch12.py**

```
>>> import os
>>> from nlpia.constants import DATA_PATH
>>> import aiml_bot

>>> bot = aiml_bot.Bot(
...     learn=os.path.join(DATA_PATH, 'greeting_step1.aiml'))
Loading /Users/hobs/src/nlpia/nlpia/data/greeting_step1.aiml...
done (0.00 seconds)
>>> bot.respond("Hello Rosa,")
'Hi there!'
>>> bot.respond("hello !!!troll!!!")
'Good one, human.'
```

That looks good. The AIML specification cleverly ignores punctuation and capitalization when looking for pattern matches.

But the AIML 1.0 specification only normalizes your patterns for punctuation and whitespace between words, not within words. It can't handle synonyms, spelling errors, hyphenated words, or compound words. See the following listing.

> **Listing 12.4    nlpia/nlpia/book/examples/ch12.py**

```
>>> bot.respond("Helo Rosa")
WARNING: No match found for input: Helo Rosa
' '
>>> bot.respond("Hello Ro-sa")
WARNING: No match found for input: Hello Ro-sa
' '
```

You can fix most mismatches like this using the `<srai>` tag and a star (*) symbol in your template to link multiple patterns back to the same response template. Think of these as synonyms for the word "Hello," even though they might be misspellings or completely different words. See the following listing.

**Listing 12.5   nlpia/data/greeting_step2.aiml**

```
<category><pattern>HELO *         </pattern><template><srai>HELLO <star/>
</srai></template></category>
<category><pattern>HI *           </pattern><template><srai>HELLO <star/>
</srai></template></category>
<category><pattern>HIYA *         </pattern><template><srai>HELLO <star/>
</srai></template></category>
<category><pattern>HYA *          </pattern><template><srai>HELLO <star/>
</srai></template></category>
<category><pattern>HY *           </pattern><template><srai>HELLO <star/>
</srai></template></category>
<category><pattern>HEY *          </pattern><template><srai>HELLO <star/>
</srai></template></category>
<category><pattern>WHATS UP *     </pattern><template><srai>HELLO <star/>
</srai></template></category>
<category><pattern>WHAT IS UP *   </pattern><template><srai>HELLO <star/>
</srai></template></category>
```

> **NOTE**   If you are writing your own AIML files, don't forget to include the
> <aiml> tags at the beginning and end. We omitted them in example AIML
> code here to keep things brief.

Once you load that additional AIML, your bot can recognize a few different ways of
saying and misspelling "Hello," as shown in the following listing.

**Listing 12.6   nlpia/nlpia/book/examples/ch12.py**

```
>>> bot.learn(os.path.join(DATA_PATH, 'greeting_step2.aiml'))
>>> bot.respond("Hey Rosa")
'Hi there!'
>>> bot.respond("Hi Rosa")
'Hi there!'
>>> bot.respond("Helo Rosa")
'Hi there!'
>>> bot.respond("hello **troll** !!!")
 'Good one, human.'
```

In AIML 2.0, you can specify alternative random response templates with square-
bracketed lists. In AIML 1.0 you use the <li> tag to do that. The <li> tag works only
within a <condition> or <random> tag. You'll use a <random> tag to help your bot be
a little more creative in how it responds to greetings. See the following listing.

**Listing 12.7   nlpia/nlpia/data/greeting_step3.aiml**

```
<category><pattern>HELLO ROSA </pattern><template>
    <random>
        <li>Hi Human!</li>
        <li>Hello friend</li>
        <li>Hi pal</li>
        <li>Hi!</li>
        <li>Hello!</li>
```

```
        <li>Hello to you too!</li>
        <li>Greetings Earthling ;)</li>
        <li>Hey you :)</li>
        <li>Hey you!</li>
    </random></template>
</category>
<category><pattern>HELLO TROLL </pattern><template>
    <random>
        <li>Good one, Human.</li>
        <li>Good one.</li>
        <li>Nice one, Human.</li>
        <li>Nice one.</li>
        <li>Clever.</li>
        <li>:)</li>
    </random></template>
</category>
```

Now your chatbot doesn't sound nearly as mechanical (at least at the beginning of a conversation). See the following listing.

**Listing 12.8   nlpia/nlpia/book/examples/ch12.py**

```
>>> bot.learn(os.path.join(DATA_PATH, 'greeting_step3.aiml'))
>>> bot.respond("Hey Rosa")
'Hello friend'
>>> bot.respond("Hey Rosa")
'Hey you :)'
>>> bot.respond("Hey Rosa")
'Hi Human!'
```

> **NOTE**   You likely didn't get the same responses in the same order that we did when we ran this code. That's the point of the <random> tag. It'll choose a random response from the list each time the pattern is matched. There's no way to set a random seed within aiml_bot, but this would help with testing (pull request anyone?).

You can define synonyms for your own alternative spellings of "Hi" and "Rosa" in separate <category> tags. You could define different groups of synonyms for your templates and separate lists of responses depending on the kind of greeting. For example, you could define patterns for greetings such as "SUP" and "WUSSUP BRO," and then respond in a similar dialect or similar level of familiarity and informality.

AIML even has tags for capturing strings into named variables (similar to named groups in a regular expression). States in AIML are called topics. And AIML defines ways of defining conditionals using any of the variables you've defined in your AIML file. Try them out if you're having fun with AIML. It's a great exercise in understanding how grammars and pattern-matching chatbots work. But we're going to move on to more expressive languages such as regular expressions and Python to build your chatbot. This will allow you to use more of the tools you learned in earlier chapters, such as stemmers and lemmatizers, to handle synonyms and misspellings (see chapter

2). If you use AIML in your chatbot, and you have preprocessing stages such as lemmatization or stemming, you'll probably need to modify your AIML templates to catch these stems and lemmas.

If you think AIML seems a bit complicated for what it does, you're not alone. Amazon Lex uses a simplified version of AIML that can be exported to and imported from a JSON file. The startup `API.ai` developed a dialog specification that was so intuitive that Google bought them out, integrated it with Google Cloud Services, and renamed it Dialogflow. Dialogflow specifications can also be exported to JSON and imported from JSON, but these files aren't compatible with AIML or Amazon Lex format.

If you think all these incompatible APIs should be consolidated into a single open specification such as AIML, you might want to contribute to the `aichat` project and the AIRS (AI Response Specification) language development. Aira and the Do More Foundation are supporting AIRS to make it easier for our users to share their content (dialog for interactive fiction, inspiration, training courses, virtual tours, and so on) with each other. The `aichat` application is a reference implementation of the AIRS interpreter in Python, with a web UX.

Here's what a typical AIRS specification looks like. It defines the four pieces of information that the chatbot needs to react to a user command in a single row of a flat table. This table can be exported/imported to/from CSV or JSON or a plain Python list of lists:

```
>>> airas_spec = [
...     ["Hi {name}","Hi {username} how are you?","ROOT","GREETING"],
...     ["What is your name?",
...      "Hi {username} how are you?","ROOT","GREETING"],
...     ]
```

The first column in an AIRS specification defines the pattern and any parameters you want to extract from the user utterance or text message. The second column defines the response you want the chatbot to say (or text), usually in the form of a template that can be populated with variables from the data context for the chatbot. And it can also contain special keywords to trigger bot actions other than just saying something.

The last two columns are used to maintain the state or context of the chatbot. Whenever the chatbot is triggered by a pattern match, it can transition to a new state if it wants to have different behavior within that state to, say, follow up with additional questions or information. So the two columns at the end of a row just tell the chatbot what state it should be listening for these patterns in and which state it should transition to after it has accomplished the utterance or action specified in the template. These source and destination state names define a graph, like in figure 12.2, that governs the chatbot behavior.

Google's Dialogflow and Amazon's Lex are more scalable versions of `aichat`'s pattern-matching chatbot specification approach. But for many use cases they seem more complicated than they need to be. The open source project aichat (http://github.com/totalgood/aichat) is attempting to provide a more intuitive way to design, visualize, and test chatbots. Check out the aichat or the hybrid chatbot in nlpia (http://github.com/totalgood/nlpia) if you want to learn more about this pattern-matching approach to chatbots. And if you want to implement a large-scale chatbot using this approach for a production application, Google's Dialogflow (formerly app.ai) and Amazon's Lex frameworks have extensive documentation on examples you can build on. Though both systems make it possible to deploy a free chatbot within these systems, you'll quickly get locked into their way of doing things, so you may be better off helping us build aichat.

### 12.2.2 A network view of pattern matching

As Aira built out its chatbot for assisting those with blindness, we developed some visualization tools to analyze and design that user experience. A network view of the connections between states and the patterns that create those connections revealed opportunities for new patterns and states. A network view allowed us to "run" the dialog in our heads, like running a few lines of Python in your head. And the network view let us navigate the maze of the dialog tree (actually a network or graph) from a birds-eye view, to avoid dialog dead ends and loops.

If you think about it, the patterns and responses of a pattern-matching chatbot define a network (graph). Nodes in this network represent the states. Edges in the network represent the pattern matching triggers that cause the chatbot to say something before transitioning to the next state (node). If you draw the state transitions for a few AIRS patterns and responses you might get something like in figure 12.2.

This can help you discover dead ends or loops in your dialog that you may want to address by refining or adding patterns to your dialog specification. Aira is working on visualization tools to turn AIRS specs into these graph diagrams (see figure 12.2) with

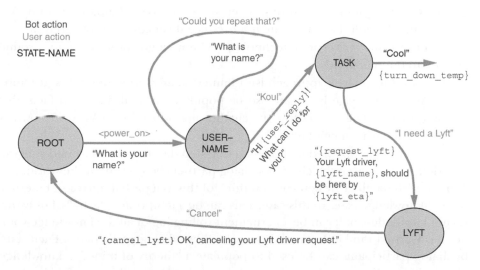

**Figure 12.2  Managing state (context)**

the `aichat` project (http://github.com/aira/aichat). If Javascript and D3 is your thing, they could use your help.

Now it's time to learn about another chatbot approach: grounding.

## 12.3   *Grounding*

A.L.I.C.E. and other AIML chatbots rely entirely on pattern-matching. And the first popular chatbot, ELIZA, used pattern-matching and templates as well, before AIML was even conceived. But these chatbot developers hardcoded the logic of the responses in patterns and templates. Hardcoding doesn't "scale" well, not in the processing performance sense, but in the human effort sense. The sophistication of a chatbot built this way grows linearly with the human effort put into it. In fact, as the complexity of this chatbot grows, you begin to see diminishing returns on your effort, because the interactions between all the "moving parts" grow and the chatbot behavior becomes harder and harder to predict and debug.

Data-driven programming is the modern approach to most complex programming challenges these days. How can you use data to program your chatbot? In the last chapter, you learned how to create structured knowledge from natural language text (unstructured data) using information extraction. You can build up a network of relationships or facts just based on reading text, such as Wikipedia, or even your own personal journal. In this section, you'll learn how to incorporate this knowledge about the world (or your life) into your chatbot's bag of tricks. This network of logical relationships between things is a knowledge graph or knowledge base that can drive your chatbot's responses.

This knowledge graph can be processed with logical inference to answer questions about the world of knowledge contained in the knowledge base. The logical answers can then be used to fill in variables within templated responses to create natural language answers. Question answering systems, such as IBM's Jeopardy-winning Watson, were originally built this way, though more recent versions almost surely also employ search or information retrieval technology. A knowledge graph is said to "ground" the chatbot to the real world.

This knowledge-base approach isn't limited to answering questions just about the world. Your knowledge base can also be populated in real time with facts about an ongoing dialog. This can keep your chatbot up-to-speed on who your conversation partner is, and what they're like.

If you take this knowledge modeling one step deeper, you can build subgraphs of knowledge about what the chatbot's dialog partners believe about the world. If you're familiar with database design you can think of this as a partial mirror of external databases—knowledge bases in this case. This can be a temporary "cache" of only the most recent knowledge, or it can be a permanent rolling log of all the knowledge your chatbot has learned (and unlearned) about the other dialog participants. Each statement by dialog participants can be used to populate a "theory of mind," a knowledge base about what each speaker believes about the world. This could be as simple as building patterns to extract the nicknames that dialog participants use when addressing each other or the chatbot, like we did in chapter 1.

If you think about it, humans seem to participate in dialog in a more sophisticated way than merely regurgitating canned responses, such as the AIML chatbot you just built. Your human brain enables you to think about the logic of what your conversation partner said and attempt to infer something from what you remember about real-world logic and each other. You may have to make several inferences and assumptions to understand and respond to a single statement. So this addition of logic and grounding to your chatbot may make it be more human-like, or at least more logical.

This grounding approach to chatbots works well for question answering chatbots, when the knowledge required to answer the question is within some broad knowledge base that you can obtain from an open source database. Some examples of open knowledge bases you can use to ground your chatbot include

- Wikidata (includes Freebase)[31]
- Open Mind Common Sense (ConceptNet)[32]
- Cyc[33]
- YAGO[34]
- DBpedia[35]

So all you need is a way to query the knowledge base to extract the facts you need to populate a response to a user's statement. And if the user is asking a factual question that your database might contain, you could translate their natural language question (such as "Who are you?" or "What is the 50th state of the United States?") into a knowledge base query to directly retrieve the answer they're looking for. This is what Google search does using Freebase and other knowledge bases they combined together to create their knowledge graph.

You could use your word pattern matching skills from chapter 11 to extract the critical parts of a question from the user's statement, such as the named entities or the relationship information sought by the question. You'd check for key question words such as "who," "what," "when," "where," "why," and "is" at the beginning of a sentence to classify the type of question. This would help your chatbot determine the kind of knowledge (node or named entity type) to retrieve from your knowledge graph.

Quepy[36] is a natural language query compiler that can produce knowledge base and database queries using these techniques. The SQL equivalent for a knowledge graph of RDF triples is called SPARQL.[37]

---

[31] See the web page titled "Welcome to Wikidata" (https://www.wikidata.org).

[32] See the web page titled "API : commonsense/conceptnet5 Wiki : GitHub" (https://github.com/commonsense/conceptnet5/wiki/API).

[33] See the web page titled "Cyc" (https://en.wikipedia.org/wiki/Cyc).

[34] See the Wikipedia article "YAGO (database)" (https://en.wikipedia.org/wiki/YAGO_(database)).

[35] See the web page titled "DBpedia" (https://en.wikipedia.org/wiki/DBpedia).

[36] See the web page titled "Welcome to Quepy's documentation! — Quepy 0.1 documentation" (http://quepy.readthedocs.io/en/latest/).

[37] See the web page titled "SPARQL Query Language for RDF" (https://www.w3.org/TR/rdf-sparql-query/).

## 12.4    *Retrieval (search)*

Another more data-driven approach to "listening" to your user is to search for previous statements in your logs of previous conversations. This is analogous to a human listener trying to recall where they've heard a question or statement or word before. A bot can search not only its own conversation logs, but also any transcript of human-to-human conversations, bot-to-human conversations, or even bot-to-bot conversations. But, as usual, garbage in means garbage out. So you should clean and curate your database of previous conversations to ensure that your bot is searching (and mimicking) high-quality dialog. You would like humans to enjoy the conversation with your bot.

A search-based chatbot should ensure that its dialog database contains conversations that were enjoyable or useful. And they should probably be on some theme that the bot personality is expected to converse in. Some examples of good sources of dialog for a search-based bot include movie dialog scripts, customer service logs on IRC channels (where the users were satisfied with the outcome), and direct-message interactions between humans (when those humans are willing to share them with you). Don't do this on your own email or SMS message logs without getting the written agreement of all humans involved in the conversations you want to use.

If you decide to incorporate bot dialog into your corpus, be careful. You only want statements in your database that have had at least one human appear to be satisfied with the interaction, if only by continuing the conversation. And bot-to-bot dialog should rarely be used, unless you have access to a *really* smart chatbot.

Your search-based chatbot can use a log of past conversations to find examples of statements similar to what the bot's conversation partner just said. To facilitate this search, the dialog corpus should be organized in statement-response pairs. If a response is responded to then it should appear twice in your database, once as the response and then again as the statement that is prompting a response. The response column in your database table can then be used as the basis for your bot's response to the statements in the "statements" (or prompt) column.

### 12.4.1  *The context challenge*

The simplest approach is to reuse the response verbatim, without any adjustment. This is often an OK approach if the statement is a good semantic (meaning) match for the statement your bot is responding to. But even if all the statements your users ever made could be found in your database, your bot would take on the personality of all the humans that uttered the responses in your dialog database. This can be a good thing, if you have a consistent set of responses by a variety of humans. But it can be a problem if the statement you are trying to reply to is dependent on the longer-term context of a conversation or some real-world situation that has changed since your dialog corpus was assembled.

For example, what if someone asked your chatbot "What time is it?" Your chatbot shouldn't reuse the reply of the human who replied to the best-matched statement in your database. That would work only if the question's time corresponded to the time the matching dialog statement was recorded. This time information is called context, or state, and should be recorded and matched along with the statement's natural language text. This is especially important when the statement's semantics point to some evolving state that is recorded in your context, or the chatbot's knowledge base.

Some other examples of how real-world knowledge or context should influence a chatbot's reply are the questions "Who are you?" or "Where are you from?" The context in this case is the identity and background of the person being addressed by the question. Fortunately, this is context that you can generate and store quite easily in a knowledge base or database containing facts about the profile or back-story for your bot. You'd want to craft your chatbot profile to include information such as a persona that roughly reflects the average or median profile of the humans who made the statements in your database. To compute this, you can use the profiles of the users that made statements in your dialog database.

Your chatbot's personality profile information could be used to resolve "ties" in the search for matching statements in your database. And if you want to be super sophisticated, you can boost the rank of search results for replies from humans that are similar to your bot persona. For example, imagine you know the gender of the people whose statements and responses you recorded in your dialog database. You'd include the nominal gender of the chatbot as another "word" or dimension or database field you're searching for among the genders of the respondents in your database. If this respondent gender dimension matched your chatbot's gender, and the prompting statement words or semantic vector were a close match for the corresponding vector from your user's statement, that would be a great match at the top of your search results. The best way to do this matching is to compute a scoring function each time a reply is retrieved and include in this score some profile match information.

Alternatively, you could solve this context challenge by building up a background profile for your bot and storing it in a knowledge base manually. You'd just make sure to only include replies in your chatbot's database that matched this profile.

No matter how you use this profile to give your chatbot a consistent personality, you'll need to deal with questions about that personality profile as special cases. You need to use one of the other chatbot techniques rather than retrieval if your database of statements and replies doesn't contain a lot of answers to questions such as "Who are you?" "Where are you from?" and "What's your favorite color?" If you don't have a lot of profile statement-reply pairs, you'd need to detect any questions about the bot and use a knowledge base to "infer" an appropriate answer for that element of the statement. Alternatively, you could use the grammar-based approach to populate a templated response, using information retrieved from a structured dataset for the chatbot profile.

To incorporate state or context into a retrieval-based chatbot, you can do something similar to what you did for the pattern-matching chatbot. If you think about it, listing a bunch of user statements is just another way of specifying a pattern. In fact, that's exactly the approach that Amazon Lex and Google Dialogflow take. Rather than defining a rigid pattern to capture the user command, you can just provide the dialog engine with a few examples. So just as you associated a state with each pattern in your pattern-matching chatbot, you just need to tag your statement-response example pairs with a named state as well.

This tagging can be difficult if your example state-response pairs are from an unstructured, unfiltered data source such as the Ubuntu Dialog Corpus or Reddit. But with dialog training sets such as Reddit, you can often find some small portions of the massive dataset that can be automatically labeled based on their channel and reply thread. You can use the tools of semantic search and pattern matching to cluster the initial comment that preceded a particular thread or discussion. And these clusters can then become your states. Detecting transitions from one topic or state to another can be difficult, however. And the states that you can produce this way aren't nearly as precise and accurate as those you can generate by hand.

This approach to state (context) management can be a viable option, if your bot just needs to be entertaining and conversational. But if you need your chatbot to have predictable and reliable behaviors, you probably want to stick to the pattern-matching approach or hand-craft your state transitions.

### 12.4.2  *Example retrieval-based chatbot*

You're going to be following along with the ODSC 2017 tutorial on building a retrieval-based chatbot. If you want to view the video or the original notebook for this tutorial, check out the github repository for it at https://github.com/totalgood/prosocial-chatbot.

Our chatbot is going to use the Ubuntu Dialog Corpus, a set of statements and replies recorded on the Ubuntu IRC channel, where humans are helping each other solve technical problems. It contains more than seven million utterances and more than one million dialog sessions, each with multiple turns and many utterances.[38] This large number of statement-response pairs makes it a popular dataset that researchers use to check the accuracy of their retrieval-based chatbots.

These are the sort of statement-response pairings you need to "train" a retrieval-based chatbot. But don't worry, you're not going to use all seven million utterances. You'll just use about 150 thousand turns and see if that's enough to give your chatbot the answers to some common Ubuntu questions. To get started, download the bite-sized Ubuntu corpus shown in the following listing.

> **Listing 12.9    ch12_retrieval.py**

```
>>> from nlpia.data.loaders import get_data
>>> df = get_data('ubuntu_dialog')
Downloading ubuntu_dialog
requesting URL:
https://www.dropbox.com/s/krvi79fbsryytc2/ubuntu_dialog.csv.gz?dl=1
remote size: 296098788
```

---

[38] "The Ubuntu Dialogue Corpus: A Large Dataset for Research in Unstructured Multi-Turn Dialogue Systems" by Lowe et al., 2015 https://arxiv.org/abs/1506.08909.

```
Downloading to /Users/hobs/src/nlpia/nlpia/bigdata/ubuntu_dialog.csv.gz
39421it [00:39, 998.09it/s]
```

You may get warning messages about the /bigdata/ path not existing if you haven't used nlpia.data.loaders.get_data() on a big dataset yet. But the downloader will create one for you when you run it for the first time.

> **NOTE**  The scripts here will work if you have 8 GB of free RAM to work with. If you run out of memory, try reducing the dataset size—slice out a smaller number of rows in df. In the next chapter, we use gensim to process data in batches "out of core" so that you can work with larger datasets.

What this corpus looks like can be seen in the following listing.

---

**Listing 12.10  ch12_retrieval.py**

```
>>> df.head(4)
                        Context                      Utterance
0  i think we could import the old comments via r...   basically each xfree86
      upload will NOT force u...
1  I'm not suggesting all -
      only the ones you mod...                         oh? oops. __eou__
2  afternoon all __eou__ not entirely related to ...   we'll have a BOF about
      this __eou__ so you're ...
3  interesting __eou__ grub-install worked with /
      ...   i fully endorse this suggestion </quimby> __eo...
```

Notice the "__eou__" tokens? This looks like it might be a pretty challenging dataset to work with. But it'll give you practice with some common preprocessing challenges in NLP. Those tokens mark the "end of utterance," the point at which the "speaker" hit [RETURN] or [Send] on their IRC client. If you print out some example Context fields, you'll notice that there are also "__eot__" ("end of turn") markers to indicate when someone concluded their thought and was waiting for a reply.

But if you look inside a context document (row in the table), you'll see there are multiple "__eot__" (turn) markers. These markers help more sophisticated chatbots test how they handle the context problem we talked about in the previous section. But you're going to ignore the extra turns in the corpus and focus only on the last one, the one that the utterance was a reply to. First, let's create a function to split on those "__eot__" symbols and clean up those "__eou__" markers, as seen in the following listing.

---

**Listing 12.11  ch12_retrieval.py**

```
>>> import re
>>> def split_turns(s, splitter=re.compile('__eot__')):
...     for utterance in splitter.split(s):
...         utterance = utterance.replace('__eou__', '\n')
...         utterance = utterance.replace('__eot__', '').strip()
...         if len(utterance):
...             yield utterance
```

Let's run that `split_turns` function on a few rows in the `DataFrame` to see if it makes sense. You'll retrieve only the last turn from both the context and the utterance and see if that'll be enough to train a retrieval-based chatbot. See the following listing.

**Listing 12.12　ch12_retrieval.py**

```
>>> for i, record in df.head(3).iterrows():
...     statement = list(split_turns(record.Context))[-1]
...     reply = list(split_turns(record.Utterance))[-1]
...     print('Statement: {}'.format(statement))
...     print()
...     print('Reply: {}'.format(reply))
```

This should print out something like this:

```
Statement: I would prefer to avoid it at this stage. this is something that
    has gone into XSF svn, I assume?
Reply:  each xfree86 upload will NOT force users to upgrade 100Mb of fonts
    for nothing
 no something i did in my spare time.

Statement: ok, it sounds like you're agreeing with me, then
 though rather than "the ones we modify", my idea is "the ones we need to
    merge"
Reply: oh? oops.

Statement: should g2 in ubuntu do the magic dont-focus-window tricks?
 join the gang, get an x-series thinkpad
 sj has hung on my box, again.
 what is monday mornings discussion actually about?
Reply: we'll have a BOF about this
 so you're coming tomorrow ?
```

Excellent! It looks like it has statements and replies that contain multiple statements (utterances). So your script is doing what you want, and you can use it to populate a statement-response mapping table, as shown in the following listing.

**Listing 12.13　ch12_retrieval.py**

```
>>> from tqdm import tqdm

>>> def preprocess_ubuntu_corpus(df):
...     """
...     Split all strings in df.Context and df.Utterance on
...     __eot__ (turn) markers
...     """
...     statements = []
...     replies = []
...     for i, record in tqdm(df.iterrows()):
...         turns = list(split_turns(record.Context))
...         statement = turns[-1] if len(turns) else '\n'
...         statements.append(statement)
...         turns = list(split_turns(record.Utterance))
```

> **You need an if because some of the statements and replies contained only whitespace.**

```
...            reply = turns[-1] if len(turns) else '\n'
...            replies.append(reply)
...        df['statement'] = statements
...        df['reply'] = replies
...        return df
```

Now you need to retrieve the closest match to a user statement in the statement column, and reply with the corresponding reply from the reply column. Do you remember how you found similar natural language documents using word frequency vectors and TF-IDF vectors in chapter 3? See the following listing.

---

**Listing 12.14   ch12_retrieval.py**

```
>>> from sklearn.feature_extraction.text import TfidfVectorizer
>>> df = preprocess_ubuntu_corpus(df)
>>> tfidf = TfidfVectorizer(min_df=8, max_df=.3, max_features=50000)
>>> tfidf.fit(df.statement)
```

**Notice you only need to compute the statement (not reply) TF-IDFs, because those are the things you want to search.**

Let's create a DataFrame called X to hold all these TF-IDF vectors for each of the 150 thousand statements, as shown in the following listing.

---

**Listing 12.15   ch12_retrieval.py**

```
>>> X = tfidf.transform(df.statement)
>>> X = pd.DataFrame(X.todense(), columns=tfidf.get_feature_names())
```

One way to find the closest statement is to compute the cosine distance from the query statement to all the statements in your X matrix, as shown in the following listing.

---

**Listing 12.16   ch12_retrieval.py**

```
>>> x = tfidf.transform(['This is an example statement that\
...      we want to retrieve the best reply for.'])
>>> cosine_similarities = x.dot(X.T)
>>> reply = df.loc[cosine_similarities.argmax()]
```

That took a long time (more than a minute on my MacBook). And you didn't even compute a confidence value or get a list of possible replies that you might be able to combine with other metrics.

### 12.4.3  *A search-based chatbot*

What if the patterns you wanted to match were the exact things people have said in previous conversations? That's what a search-based chatbot (or retrieval-based chatbot) does. A search-based chatbot indexes a dialog corpus so that it can easily retrieve previous statements similar to the one it's being asked to reply to. It can then reply with one of the replies associated with that statement in the corpus that it has "memorized" and indexed for quick retrieval.

If you'd like to quickly get going with a search-based chatbot, ChatterBot by Gunther Cox is a pretty good framework to cut your teeth on. It's easy to install (just `pip install ChatterBot`), and it comes with several conversation corpora that you can use to "train" your chatbot to carry on basic conversations. ChatterBot has corpora that allow it to talk about things such as sports trivia, wax philosophical about AI sentience, or just shoot the breeze with small talk. ChatterBot can be "trained" on any conversation sequence (dialog corpus). Don't think of this as machine learning training, but rather just indexing a set of documents for search.

By default ChatterBot will use both humans' statements as material for its own statements during training. If you want to be more precise with the personality of your chatbot, you'll need to create your own corpus in the ChatterBot ".yml" format. To ensure that only one personality is mimicked by your bot, make sure your corpus contains conversations of only two statements each, one prompt and one reply; the reply being from the personality you want to imitate. Incidentally, this format is similar to the AIML format, which has a pattern (the prompting `statement` in ChatterBot) and a template (the `response` in ChatterBot).

Of course, a search-based chatbot built this way is quite limited. It's never going to come up with new statements. And the more data you have, the harder it is to brute force the search of all the previous statements. So the smarter and more refined your bot is, the slower it'll be. This architecture doesn't scale well. Nonetheless, we show you some advanced techniques for scaling any search or index-based chatbot with indexing tools such as locality sensitive hashes (`pip install lshash3`) and approximate near neighbors (`pip install annoy`).

Out of the box, ChatterBot uses SQLite as its database, which highlights these scaling issues as soon as you exceed about 10k statements in your corpus. If you try to train a SQLite-based ChatterBot on the Ubuntu Dialog Corpus you'll be waiting around for days… literally. It took me more than a day on a MacBook to ingest only 100k statement-response pairs. Nonetheless, this ChatterBot code is quite useful for downloading and processing this motherlode of technical dialog about Ubuntu. ChatterBot takes care of all the bookkeeping for you, downloading and decompressing the tarball automatically before walking the "leafy" file system tree to retrieve each conversation.

How ChatterBot's "training" data (actually just a dialog corpus) is stored in a relational database is shown in the following listing.

**Listing 12.17   ch12_chatterbot.sql**

```
sqlite> .tables
conversation                response              tag
conversation_association    statement             tag_association
sqlite> .width 5 25 10 5 40
sqlite> .mode columns
```

```
sqlite> .mode column
sqlite> .headers on
sqlite> SELECT id, text, occur FROM response LIMIT 9;
id     text                      occur  statement_text
-----  ------------------------  -----  ----------------------------------------
1      What is AI?               2      Artificial Intelligence is the branch of
2      What is AI?               2      AI is the field of science which concern
3      Are you sentient?         2      Sort of.
4      Are you sentient?         2      By the strictest dictionary definition o
5      Are you sentient?         2      Even though I'm a construct I do have a
6      Are you sapient?          2      In all probability, I am not. I'm not t
7      Are you sapient?          2      Do you think I am?
8      Are you sapient?          2      How would you feel about me if I told yo
9      Are you sapient?          24     No.
```

Notice that some statements have many different replies associated with them, which allows the chatbot to choose among the possible replies based on mood, context, or random chance. ChatterBot just chooses a response at random, but yours could be more sophisticated if you incorporate some other objective or loss function or heuristic to influence the choice. Also, notice that the created_at dates are all the same. That happens to be the date when we ran the ChatterBot "training" script, which downloaded the dialog corpora and loaded them into the database.

Search-based chatbots can also be improved by reducing the statement strings down to topic vectors of fixed dimensionality, using something such as Word2vec (summing all the word vectors for a short statement), or Doc2vec (chapter 6) or LSA (chapter 4). Dimension reduction will help your bot generalize from the examples you train it with. This helps it respond appropriately when the meaning of the query statement (the most recent statement by your bot's conversation partner) is similar in meaning to one of your corpus statements, even if it uses different words. This will work even if the spelling or characters in statements are very different. Essentially, this semantic search-based chatbot is automating the programming of the templates you programmed in AIML earlier in this chapter. This dimension reduction also makes search-based chatbots smarter using machine learning (data-driven) than would be possible with a hardcoded approach to machine intelligence. Machine learning is preferable to hardcoding whenever you have a lot of labeled data, and not a lot of time (to code up intricate logic and patterns to trigger responses). For search-based chatbots, the only "label" needed is an example response for each example statement in the dialog.

## 12.5 Generative models

We promised a generative model in this chapter. But if you recall the sequence-to-sequence models you built in chapter 10, you may recognize them as generative chatbots. They're machine learning translation algorithms that "translate" statements by your user into replies by your chatbot. So we don't go into generative models in any more detail here, but know that many more kinds of generative models are out there.

If you want to build a creative chatbot that says things that have never been said before, generative models such as these may be what you need:

- *Sequence-to-sequence*—Sequence models trained to generate replies based on their input sequences [39]
- *Restricted Boltzmann machines (RBMs)*—Markov chains trained to minimize an "energy" function [40]
- *Generative adversarial networks (GANs)*—Statistical models trained to fool a "judge" of good conversation [41]

We talked about attention networks (enhanced LSTMs) in chapter 10, and we showed the kinds of novel statements your chatbot can spontaneously generate. In the next section, we take that approach in another direction.

### 12.5.1  Chat about NLPIA

Finally, the moment you've been waiting for... a chatbot that can help write a book about NLP. We've finally written (and you've read) enough text for the chatbot to have some seed material to work with. In this section, we show you how to use transfer learning to build a generative NLP pipeline to produce some of the sentences you may have already skimmed right by without noticing.

Why transfer learning? In addition to some seed text about the specific topic you want your chatbot to understand, generative models need an even bigger corpus of more general text to learn a language model from. Your chatbot needs to be able to do a lot of reading before it can recognize all the ways words are put together to form grammatically correct and meaningful sentences. And that corpus has to be segmented into grammatically correct sentences. So the project Gutenberg corpus isn't the ideal place for this model.

Think of how many books you had to read as a child before you built a decent vocabulary and a sense for the correct way to put words together into sentences. And your teachers probably gave you a lot of clues, like context, while you were practicing that reading.[42] Plus, humans are much better than machines at learning.[43]

This data-intensive language model learning is a particularly big challenge for character-based models. In character sequence language models, your chatbot needs to learn how to put characters together to form properly spelled and meaningful

---

[39] Explanation of sequence-to-sequence models and links to several papers: https://suriyadeepan.github.io/2016-06-28-easy-seq2seq/.

[40] Hinton lecture at Coursera: https://youtu.be/EZOpZzUKl48.

[41] Ian Goodfellow's GAN tutorial, NIPS 2016: https://arxiv.org/pdf/1701.00160.pdf and Lantau Yu's adaptation to text sequences: https://arxiv.org/pdf/1609.05473.pdf.

[42] "On the role of context in first- and second-language vocabulary learning" (https://www.ideals.illinois.edu/bitstream/handle/2142/31277/TR-627.pdf).

[43] See "One-shot and Few-shot Learning of Word Embeddings" (https://openreview.net/pdf?id=rkYgAJWCZ) and "One-shot learning by inverting a compositional causal process" (http://www.cs.toronto.edu/~rsalakhu/papers/lake_nips2013.pdf).

words, in addition to learning how to put those new words together to make sentences. So you'll want to reuse an existing language model trained on a large body of text in the language and style you'd like to imitate with your bot. If you think about this for a moment, you can probably see why data limitations have limited how far current NLP researchers have been able to climb up the complexity curve from characters to words to sentences. Composing paragraphs, chapters, and novels is still an active area of research. So we stop our climb there and show you how to generate a few sentences like those generated for the "about this book" front matter for NLPIA.

The DeepMind folks have provided TensorFlow character sequence-to-sequence language models pretrained on more than 500MB of sentences from CNN and Daily Mail news feeds.[44] And if you want to build your own language model, they've provided all the sentences in two large datasets as part of their "reading comprehension" (Q&A) challenge.[45] We reused the pretrained text summarization model directly to generate sentences for the "about this book" NLPIA front matter. You can also use these models to augment your own machine learning pipeline with an approach called "transfer learning," like we did with word vectors in Chapter 6.

Here's the algorithm:

1 Download a pretrained sequence-to-sequence text summarization model (https://github.com/totalgood/pointer-generator#looking-for-pretrained-model).

2 Parse and segment asciidoc text to extract natural language sentences with nlpia.book_parser (https://github.com/totalgood/nlpia/blob/master/src/nlpia/.py).

3 Use the text summarization model to summarize the first 30 or so lines of text in each asciidoc file (typically a chapter): https://github.com/totalgood/nlpia/blob/master/src/nlpia/book/examples/ch12_chat_about_nlpia.py.

4 Filter the generated sentences for novelty to avoid regurgitation of existing sentences from the book: https://github.com/totalgood/nlpia/blob/master/src/nlpia/book_parser.py.

Here are the only two well-formed and marginally original sentences that our @ChattyAboutNLPIA bot came up with. This is @Chatty's attempt to summarize the first 30 lines of chapter 5:

*Convolutional neural nets make an attempt to capture that ordering relationship by capturing localized relationships.*

---

[44] Pretrained TensorFlow text summarization model: TextSum from Google Brain (https://github.com/totalgood/pointer-generator#looking-for-pretrained-model) and a paper describing the model https://arxiv.org/abs/1704.04368.

[45] The dataset includes reading comprehension questions and answers as well as the sentences from news articles that you need to answer those questions: DeepMind Q&A Dataset (https://cs.nyu.edu/%7Ekcho/DMQA/).

This is @Chatty's summary of chapter 8:

> *Language's true power is not necessarily in the words, but in the intent and emotion that formed that particular combination of words.*

These sentences were among the 25 outputs (https://github.com/totalgood/nlpia/blob/master/src/nlpia/data/nlpia_summaries.md) for this hacky pipeline. In the coming months, we'll modify the pipeline in nlpia.book.examples.ch12_chat_about_nlpia to provide more useful results. One enhancement will be to process the entire book with TextSum so it has more material to work with. We'll also need to apply some more filtering:

1 Filter the generated sentences for well-formedness.[46]
2 Filter generated sentences for your style and sentiment objectives.
3 Automatically detokenize and unfold case (capitalization), if necessary.

### 12.5.2  *Pros and cons of each approach*

Now that you know all about the four major chatbot approaches, can you think how you might combine them to get the best out of your bot? Figure 12.3 lists the advantages and disadvantages of each approach.

| Approach | Advantages | Disadvantages |
|---|---|---|
| **Grammar** | Easy to get started<br>Training easy to reuse<br>Modular<br>Easily controlled/restrained | Limited "domain"<br>Capability limited by human effort<br>Difficult to debug<br>Rigid, brittle rules |
| **Grounding** | Answers logical questions well<br>Easily controlled/restrained | Sounds artificial, mechanical<br>Difficulty with ambiguity<br>Difficulty with common sense<br>Limited by structured data<br>Requires large scale information extraction<br>Requires human curation |
| **Retrieval** | Simple<br>Easy to "train"<br>Can mimic human dialog | Difficult to scale<br>Incoherent personality<br>Ignorant of context<br>Can't answer factual questions |
| **Generative** | New, creative ways of talking<br>Less human effort<br>Domain limited only by data<br>Context aware | Difficult to "steer"<br>Difficult to train<br>Requires more data (dialog)<br>Requires more processing to train |

Figure 12.3  **Advantages and disadvantages of four chatbot approaches**

---

[46] Thank you Kyle Gorman @wellformedness (https://twitter.com/wellformedness) for your 100+ suggestions and bits of clever content for this book. See also https://en.wikipedia.org/wiki/Well-formedness.

## 12.6 Four-wheel drive

As we promised at the beginning of this chapter, we now show you how to combine all four approaches to get traction with your users. To do this, you need a modern chatbot framework that's easy to extend and modify and can efficiently run each of these algorithm types in parallel.[47] You're going to add a response generator for each of the four approaches using the Python examples from earlier in the chapter. And then you're going to add the logic to decide what to say by choosing one of the four (or many) responses. You're going to have your chatbot think before it speaks, say things several different ways to itself first, and rank or merge some of these alternatives to produce a response. And maybe you can even try to be prosocial with your replies by checking their sentiment before "hitting the send button."

### 12.6.1 The Will to succeed

Will is a modern programmer-friendly chatbot framework by Steven Skoczen that can participate in your HipChat and Slack channels as well as others.[48] Python developers will enjoy the modular architecture. However it's pretty heavyweight in terms of requirements and installation. Fortunately, it comes with a Dockerized container you can use to spin up your own chatbot server.

Will uses regular expressions to make matches. Python itself can be used for any logical conditions you need to evaluate. And the jinja2 library is used for templating. Each one of these portions of the pipeline add versatility and flexibility to the kinds of behaviors you can build into your chatbot. As a result, Will is much more flexible than AIML-based frameworks. But Will still suffers from the same limitations that hold back all pattern-based chatbots (including AIML)–it can't learn from data; it must be "taught" by the developer writing code for each and every branch in the logic tree.

#### INSTALLING WILL

The installation documentation for Will has a couple small gaps. By the time this goes to print, we hope to have them fixed, so you can likely just read the high-quality docs.[49] On Mac OS X, you can install and launch a redis server () `brew install redis`.

#### HELLO WILL

Heres's what a conversation with an untrained Will looks like, if you ignore the tracebacks about port 80 permissions, or you can figure out how to avoid these errors:

```
You:  Hey
Will: hello!
You:  What's up?
Will: I heard you, but I'm not sure what to do.
You:  How are you?
```

---

[47] We're building an open source chatbot framework at Aira called `aichat` to help our users and their friends contribute "content" to our library of dialog to help and entertain people with blindness and low vision: http://github.com/aira/aichat.

[48] GitHub Repository: https://github.com/skoczen/will.

[49] Will documentation: http://skoczen.github.io/will/.

```
Will: Doing alright. How are you?
You:  What are you?
Will: Hmm. I'm not sure what to say.
You:  Are you a bot?
Will: I didn't understand that.
```

As you can see, out of the box, Will is polite but doesn't understand much. You can easily change Will for Rosa (or any other name). And you can use your natural language processing skills to beef up some of his patterns and expand his literary power.

## 12.7  *Design process*

To create a useful app, product managers and developers compose user stories. A user story describes a sequence of actions performed by a user in interacting with your app and how your app should respond. These can be imagined based on similar experiences in the real world with similar products, or they can be translated from user feature requests or feedback. Software features are tied to a user story to improve the likelihood that the development effort is focused on something that'll add usefulness to your product.

User stories for a chatbot can often be composed as statements (text messages) that a user might communicate to the bot. Those user statements are then paired with the appropriate response or action by the chatbot or virtual assistant. For a retrieval-based chatbot, this table of user stories is all that's required to "train" a chatbot for these particular responses and stories. It's up to you, the developer, to identify stories that can be generalized so that your design team doesn't have to specify everything your bot must understand and all the different things it can say. Can you tell which of the four chatbot techniques would be appropriate for each of these questions?

- "Hello!" => "Hello!"
- "Hi" => "Hi!"
- "How are you?" => "I'm fine. How are you?"
- "How are you?" => "I'm a stateless bot, so I don't have an emotional state."
- "Who won the 2016 World Series?" => "Chicago Cubs"
- "Who won the 2016 World Series?" => "The Chicago Cubs beat the Cleveland Indians 4 to 3"
- "What time is it" => "2:55 pm"
- "When is my next appointment?" => "At 3 pm you have a meeting with the subject 'Springboard call'"
- "When is my next appointment?" => "At 3 pm you need to help Les with her Data Science course on Springboard"
- "Who is the President?" => "Sauli Niinistö"
- "Who is the President?" => "Barack Obama"

Several valid responses may be possible for any given statement, even for the exact same user and context. And it's also common for multiple different prompting statements to elicit the same exact chatbot response (or set of possible responses). The many-to-many mapping between statements and responses works both ways, just as it does for human dialog. So the number of possible combinations of valid *statement => response* mappings can be enormous—seemingly infinite (but technically finite).

And you must also expand the combinations of statement-response pairs in your user stories using named variables for context elements that change often:

- Date
- Time
- Location: country, state, county, and city, or latitude and longitude
- Locale: US or Finland formatting for date, time, currency, and numbers
- Interface type: mobile or laptop
- Interface modality: voice or text
- Previous interactions: whether user asked for details about baseball stats recently
- Streaming audio, video, and sensor data from a mobile device (Aira.io)

IBM Watson and Amazon Lex chatbot APIs rely on knowledge bases that aren't easy to evolve quickly and keep up-to-speed with these evolving context variables. The "write rate" for these databases of knowledge are too slow to handle many of these evolving facts about the world that the chatbot and the user are interacting with.

The list of possible user stories for even the simplest of chatbots is technically finite, but it's quite large for even the simplest real-world chatbot. One way to deal with this explosion of combinations is to combine many user interactions into a single pattern or template. For the statement side of the mapping, this template approach is equivalent to creating a regular expression (or finite state machine) to represent some group of statements that should cause a particular pattern response. For the response side of the mapping, this approach is equivalent to `Jinja2` or `Django` or `Python` f-string templates.

Thinking back to your first chatbot in chapter 1, we can represent statement => response mappings that map regular expressions for the statement to a Python f-string for the response:

```
>>> pattern_response = {
...     r"[Hh]ello|[Hh]i[!]*":
...         r"Hello {user_nickname}, would you like to play a game?",
...     r"[Hh]ow[\s]*('s|are|'re)?[\s]*[Yy]ou([\s]*doin['g]?)?":
...         r"I'm {bot_mood}, how are you?",
...     }
```

But this doesn't allow for complex logic. And it requires hand coding rather than machine learning. So each mapping doesn't capture a broad range of statements and responses. You'd like a machine learning model to be able to handle a wide range of sports questions, or help a user manage their calendar.

**IMPORTANT**    Don't change those raw string templates to f-strings with `f"` or they'll be rendered at the time of instantiation. Your bot may not know much about the world at the time you create the `pattern_response` dictionary.

Here are some example chatbot user stories that don't lend themselves well to the template approach:

- "Where is my home" => "Your home is 5 minutes away by foot, would you like directions?"
- "Where am I" => "You are in SW Portland near Goose Hollow Inn" or "You are at 2004 SW Jefferson Street"
- "Who is the President?" => "Sauli Niinistö" or "Barack Obama" or "What country or company ..."
- "Who won the 2016 World Series?" => "Chicago Cubs" or "The Chicago Cubs beat the Cleveland Indians 4 to 3"
- "What time is it" => "2:55 pm" or "2:55 pm, time for your meeting with Joe" or ...

And here are some general IQ test questions that are too specific to warrant a pattern-response pair for each variation. A knowledge base is usually the answer for general intelligence questions. Nonetheless, that's probably how the Mitsuku chatbot was able to get close to the right answer in a recent test by Byron Reese:

- "Which is larger, a nickel or a dime?" => "Physically or monetarily?" or "A nickel is physically larger and heavier but less valuable monetarily."
- "Which is larger, the Sun or a nickel?" => "The Sun, obviously."[50]
- "What's a good strategy at Monopoly?" => "Buy everything you can, and get lucky."
- "How should I navigate a corn-row maze?" => "Keep your hand against one wall of corn and follow it until it becomes an outside wall of the maze."
- "Where does sea glass come from?" => "Garbage... fortunately the polishing of sand and time can sometimes turn human refuse, like broken bottles, into beautiful gemstones."

Even though these cannot be easily translated directly into code, they do translate directly into an automated test set for your NLP pipeline. Tests like these can be used to evaluate a new chatbot approach or feature or just to track progress over time.[51] If you can think of some more chatbot IQ questions, add them to the growing list at `nlpia/data/iq_test.csv` (https://github.com/totalgood/nlpia/blob/master/src/nlpia/data/iq_test.csv). And certainly include them in automated testing of your own chatbot. You never know when your bot is going to surprise you.

---

[50] Byron Reese, "AI Minute" podcast.
[51] 2017 Andrew Ng lecture to Stanford Business School students: https://youtu.be/21EiKfQYZXc?t=48m6s.

## 12.8 Trickery

You'll want to have a few specific tricks up your sleeve when building a chatbot. These tricks will help you ensure that your chatbot doesn't go off the rails too often.

### 12.8.1 Ask questions with predictable answers

When asked a question that you don't know the answer to, the chatbot can respond with a clarifying question. And if this clarifying question is well within the knowledge domain or personality profile of the chatbot, it's possible to predict the form of the answer that a human would make. Then the chatbot can use the user's response to regain control of the conversation and steer it back toward topics that it knows something about. To avoid frustration, try to make the clarifying question humorous, or positive and flattering, or in some way pleasing to the user:

```
Human: "Where were you born?"

Sports Bot: "I don't know, but how about those Mets?"
Therapist Bot: "I don't know, but are you close to your mother?"
Ubuntu Assistant Bot: "I don't know, but how do you shut down your Ubuntu PC
    at night?"
```

You can often use semantic search to find question-answer pairs, jokes, or interesting trivia in the chatbot's knowledge base that are at least tangentially related to what the user is asking about.

### 12.8.2 Be entertaining

Sometimes your generative process may take too long to converge to a high-quality message. And your chatbot may not find a reasonable clarifying question to ask. In that situation your chatbot has two choices: 1. admit ignorance, or 2. make up a non sequitur.

A non sequitur is a statement that has nothing to do with what the user asked about. Such statements are generally considered antisocial, and sometimes manipulative. Honesty is the best policy for your prosocial chatbot. And the more open you are, the more likely you are to build trust with your user. Your user might enjoy learning a bit about the "core" of your chatbot if you reveal the size of your database of responses or actions you can handle. You can also share some of the garbled responses that didn't make it through your grammar and style checker. The more honest you are the more likely the user is to be kind in return and try to help your chatbot get back on track. Cole Howard found that users would often coax his MNIST-trained handwriting recognizer toward the right answer by redrawing the digits in a more clear way.

So for a commercial chatbot, you may want this useless response to be sensational, distracting, flattering, or humorous. And you'll probably also want to ensure that your responses are randomly selected in a way that a human would consider random. For example, don't repeat yourself very often.[52] And use varying sentence structure, form, and style over time. That way you can monitor your customers' responses and measure their sentiment to determine which of your non sequiturs were the least annoying.

### 12.8.3  When all else fails, search

If your bot can't think of anything to say, try acting like a search engine or search bar. Search for webpages or internal database records that might be relevant to any question you might receive. But be sure to ask the user whether the page titles might help the user before spitting out all the information they contain. Stack Overflow, Wikipedia, and Wolfram Alpha are good resources at the ready for many bots (because Google does that and users expect it).

### 12.8.4  Being popular

If you have a few jokes or links to resources or responses that are favorably received by your audience, in general, then respond with those rather than the best match for the question asked, especially if the match is low. And these jokes or resources may help bring your human back into a conversation path that you're familiar with and have a lot of training set data for.

### 12.8.5  Be a connector

Chatbots that can be the hub of a social network will quickly be appreciated by their users. Introduce the human to other humans on the chat forum or people who've written about things the user has written about. Or point the user to a blog post, meme, chat channel, or other website that's relevant to something they might be interested in. A good bot will have a handy list of popular links to hand out when the conversation starts to get repetitive.

Bot: You might like to meet @SuzyQ, she's asked that question a lot lately. She might be able to help you figure it out.

### 12.8.6  Getting emotional

Google's Inbox email responder is similar to the conversational chatbot problem we want to solve. The auto-responder must suggest a reply to the emails you receive based on their semantic content. But a long chain of replies is less likely for an email exchange. And the prompting text is generally much longer for an email auto-responder than it is for a conversational chatbot. Nonetheless, the problems both involve generating text replies to incoming text prompts. So many of the techniques for one may be applicable to the other.

Even though Google had access to billions of emails, the paired replies in the Gmail Inbox "Smart Reply" feature tend to funnel you toward short, generic, bland

---

[52] Humans underestimate the number of repetitions there should be in a random sequence: https://mindmodeling.org/cogsci2014/papers/530/paper530.pdf.

replies. A semantic search approach is likely to produce relatively generic, bland replies if you're trying to maximize correctness for the average email user. The average reply isn't likely to have much personality or emotion. So Google tapped an unlikely corpus to add a bit of emotion to their suggested replies… romance novels.

It turns out that romance novels tend to follow predictable plots and have sappy dialog that can be easily dissected and imitated. And it contains a lot of emotion. Now I'm not sure how Google gleaned phrases like "That's awesome! Count me in!" or "How cool! I'll be there." from romance novels, but they claim that's the source of the emotional exclamations that they suggest with Smart Reply.

## 12.9 *In the real world*

The hybrid chatbot you've assembled here has the flexibility to be used for the most common real-world applications. In fact, you've probably interacted with such a chatbot sometime this week:

- Customer service assistants
- Sales assistants
- Marketing (spam) bots
- Toy or companion bots
- Video game AI
- Mobile assistants
- Home automation assistants
- Visual interpreters
- Therapist bots
- Automated email reply suggestions

And you're likely to run across chatbots like the ones you built in this chapter more and more. User interfaces are migrating away from designs constrained by the rigid logic and data structures of machines. More and more machines are being taught how to interact with us in natural, fluid conversation. The "voice first" design pattern is becoming more popular as chatbots become more useful and less frustrating. And these dialog system approaches promise a richer and more complex user experience than clicking buttons and swiping left. And with chatbots interacting with us behind the curtains, they are becoming more deeply embedded in the collective consciousness.

So now you've learned all about building chatbots for fun and for profit. And you've learned how to combine generative dialog models, semantic search, pattern matching, and information extraction (knowledge bases) to produce a chatbot that sounds surprisingly intelligent.

You've mastered all the key NLP components of an intelligent chatbot. Your only remaining challenge is to give it a personality of your own design. And then you'll probably want to "scale it up" so it can continue to learn, long after you've exhausted the RAM, hard drive, and CPU in your laptop. And we show you how to do that in chapter 13.

## Summary

- By combining multiple proven approaches, you can build an intelligent dialog engine.
- Breaking "ties" between the replies generated by the four main chatbot approaches is one key to intelligence.
- You can teach machines a lifetime of knowledge without spending a lifetime programming them.

# 13

# *Scaling up (optimization, parallelization, and batch processing)*

---

**This chapter covers**

- Scaling up an NLP pipeline
- Speeding up search with indexing
- Batch processing to reduce your memory footprint
- Parallelization to speed up NLP
- Running NLP model training on a GPU

In chapter 12, you learned how to use all the tools in your NLP toolbox to build an NLP pipeline capable of carrying on a conversation. We demonstrated crude examples of this chatbot dialog capability on small datasets. The humanness, or IQ, of your dialog system seems to be limited by the data you train it with. Most of the NLP approaches you've learned give better and better results, if you can scale them up to handle larger datasets.

You may have noticed that your computer bogs down, even crashes, if you run some of the examples we gave you on large datasets. Some datasets in `nlpia.data.loaders.get_data()` will exceed the memory (RAM) in most PCs or laptops.

Besides RAM, another bottleneck in your natural language processing pipelines is the processor. Even if you had unlimited RAM, larger corpora would take days to process with some of the more complex algorithms you've learned.

So you need to come up with algorithms that minimize the resources they require:

- Volatile storage (RAM)
- Processing (CPU cycles)

## 13.1    *Too much of a good thing (data)*

As you add more data, more knowledge, to your pipeline, the machine learning models take more and more RAM, storage, and CPU cycles to train. Even worse, some of the techniques relied on an $O(N^2)$ computation of distance or similarity between vector representations of statements or documents. For these algorithms, things get slower faster as you add data. Each additional sentence in the corpora takes more bytes of RAM and more CPU cycles to process than the previous one, which is impractical for even moderately sized corpora.

Two broad approaches help you avoid these issues so you can scale up your NLP pipeline to larger datasets:

- *Increased scalability*—Improving or optimizing the algorithms
- *Horizontal scaling*—Parallelizing the algorithms to run multiple computations simultaneously

In this chapter, you'll learn techniques for both.

Getting smarter about algorithms is almost always the best way to speed up a processing pipeline, so we talk about that first. We leave parallelization to the second half of this chapter, to help you run sleek, optimized algorithms even faster.

## 13.2    *Optimizing NLP algorithms*

Some of the algorithms you've looked at in previous chapters have expensive complexities, often quadratic $O(N^2)$ or higher:

- Compiling a thesaurus of synonyms from `word2vec` vector similarity
- Clustering web pages based on their topic vectors
- Clustering journal articles or other documents based on topic vectors
- Clustering questions in a Q&A corpus to automatically compose a FAQ

All of these NLP challenges fall under the category of indexed search, or k-nearest neighbors (KNN) vector search. We spend the next few sections talking about the scaling challenge: algorithm optimization. We show you one particular algorithm optimization, called *indexing*. Indexing can help solve most vector search (KNN) problems. In the second half of the chapter, we show you how to hyper-parallelize your natural language processing by using thousands of CPU cores in a graphical processing unit (GPU).

### 13.2.1 *Indexing*

You probably use natural language indexes every day. Natural language text indexes (also called reverse indexes) are what you use when you turn to the back of a textbook to find the page for a topic you're interested in. The pages are the documents and the words are the lexicon of your bag of words vectors (BOW) for each document. And you use a text index every time you enter a search string in a web search tool. To scale up your NLP application, you need to do that for semantic vectors like LSA document-topic vectors or `word2vec` word vectors.

Previous chapters have mentioned conventional "reverse indexes" used for searching documents to find a set of words or tokens based on the words in a query. But we've not yet talked about *approximate* KNN search for *similar* text. For KNN search, you want to find strings that are similar even if they don't contain the exact same words. Levenshtein distance is one of the distance metrics used by packages such as `fuzzywuzzy` and `ChatterBot` to find similar strings.

Databases implement a variety of text indexes that allow you to find documents or strings quickly. SQL queries allow you to search for text that matches patterns such as `SELECT book_title from manning_book WHERE book_title LIKE 'Natural Language%in Action'`. This query would find all the "in Action" Manning titles that start with "Natural Language." And there are trigram (`trgm`) indexes for a lot of databases that help you find similar text quickly (in constant time), without even specifying a pattern, just specifying a text query that's similar to what you're looking for.

These database techniques for indexing text work great for text documents or strings of any sort. But they don't work well on semantic vectors such as `word2vec` vectors or dense document-topic vectors. Conventional database indexes rely on the fact that the objects (documents) they're indexing are either discrete, sparse, or low dimensional:

- Strings (sequences of characters) are discrete: there are a limited number of characters.
- TF-IDF vectors are sparse: most terms have a frequency of 0 in any given document.
- BOW vectors are discrete and sparse: terms are discrete, and most words have zero frequency in a document.

This is why web searches, document searches, or geographic searches execute in milliseconds. And it's been working efficiently (`O(1)`) for many decades.

What makes continuous vectors such as document-topic LSA vectors (chapter 4) or `word2vec` vectors (chapter 6) so hard to index? After all, geographic information system (GIS) vectors are typically latitude, longitude, and altitude. And you can do a GIS search on Google Maps in milliseconds. Fortunately GIS vectors only have three continuous values, so indexes can be built based on bounding boxes that gather together GIS objects in discrete groups.

Several different index data structures can deal with this problem:

- K-d Tree: Elastic search will implement this for up to 8D in upcoming releases.
- Rtree: PostgreSQL implements this in versions >= 9.0 for up to 200D.
- Minhash or locality sensitive hashes: `pip install lshash3`.

These work up to a point. That point is at about 12 dimensions. If you play around with optimizing database indexes or locality sensitive hashes yourself, you'll find that it gets harder and harder to maintain that constant-time lookup speed. At about 12 dimensions it becomes impossible.

So what are you to do with your 300D `word2vec` vectors or 100+ dimension semantic vectors from LSA? Approximation to the rescue. Approximate nearest neighbor search algorithms don't try to give you the exact set of document vectors that are most similar to your query vector. Instead they just try to find some reasonably good matches. And they're usually pretty darn good, rarely missing any closer matches in the top 10 or so search results.

But things are quite different if you're using the magic of SVD or embedding to reduce your token dimensions (your vocabulary size, typically in the millions) to, say, 200 or 300 topic dimensions. Three things are different. One change is an improvement: you have fewer dimensions to search (think columns in a database table). Two things are challenging: you have dense vectors of continuous values.

### 13.2.2  *Advanced indexing*

Semantic vectors check all the boxes for difficult objects. They're difficult because they're

- High dimensional
- Real valued
- Dense

We've replaced the curse of dimensionality with two new difficulties. Our vectors are now dense (no zeros that you can ignore) and continuous (real valued).

In your dense semantic vectors, every dimension has a meaningful value. You can no longer skip or ignore all the zeros that filled the TF-IDF or BOW table (see chapters 2 and 3). Even if you filled the gaps in your TF-IDF vectors with additive (Laplace) smoothing, you'd still have some consistent values in your dense table that allow it to be handled like a sparse matrix. But there are no zeros or most-common values in your vectors anymore. Every topic has some weight associated with it for every document. This isn't an insurmountable problem. The reduced dimensionality more than makes up for the density problem.

The values in these dense vector are real numbers. But there's a bigger problem. Topic weight values in a semantic vector can be positive or negative and aren't limited to discrete characters or integer counts. The weights associated with each topic are now continuous real values (`float`). Nondiscrete values, such as floats, are impossible to index. They're no longer merely present or absent. They can't be vectorized with one-hot encoding of input as a feature into a neural net. And you certainly can't create an entry in an index table that refers to all the documents where that feature or topic was either present or absent. Topics are now everywhere, in all the documents, to varying degrees.

You can solve the natural language search problems at the beginning of the chapter if you can find an efficient search or KNN algorithm. One of the ways to optimize the algorithm for such problems is to sacrifice certainty and accuracy in exchange for a huge speed-up. This is called approximate nearest neighbors (ANN) search. For example, DuckDuckGo's search doesn't try to find you a perfect match for the semantic vector in your search. Instead it attempts to provide you with the closest 10 or so approximate matches.

Fortunately, a lot of companies have open sourced much of their research software for making ANN more scalable. These research groups are competing with each other to give you the easiest, fastest ANN search software. Here are some of the Python packages from this competition that have been tested with standard benchmarks for NLP problems at the India Technical University (ITU):[1]

- Spotify's `Annoy` [2]
- BallTree (using `nmslib`)[3]
- Brute Force using Basic Linear Algebra Subprograms library (BLAS)[4]
- Brute Force using Non-Metric Space Library (NMSlib)[5]
- Dimension reductiOn and LookuPs on a Hypercube for effIcient Near Neighbor (DolphinnPy)[6]
- Random Projection Tree Forest (`rpforest`)[7]
- Locality sensitive hashing (`datasketch`)[8]
- Multi-indexing hashing (MIH)[9]
- Fast Lookup of Cosine and Other Nearest Neighbors (FALCONN)[10]

---

[1] ITU comparison of ANN Benchmarks: http://www.itu.dk/people/pagh/SSS/ann-benchmarks/.

[2] See the web page titled "GitHub - spotify/annoy: Approximate Nearest Neighbors in C++/Python optimized for memory usage and loading/saving to disk" (https://github.com/spotify/annoy).

[3] See the web page titled "GitHub - nmslib/nmslib: Non-Metric Space Library (NMSLIB): An efficient similarity search library and a toolkit for evaluation of k-NN methods for generic non-metric spaces," (https://github.com/searchivarius/nmslib).

[4] See the web page titled "1.6. Nearest Neighbors — scikit-learn 0.19.2 documentation," (http://scikit-learn.org/stable/modules/neighbors.html#brute-force).

[5] See the web page titled "GitHub - nmslib/nmslib: Non-Metric Space Library (NMSLIB): An efficient similarity search library and a toolkit for evaluation of k-NN methods for generic non-metric spaces," (https://github.com/searchivarius/NMSLIB).

[6] See the web page titled "GitHub - ipsarros/DolphinnPy: High-dimensional approximate nearest neighbor in python" (https://github.com/ipsarros/DolphinnPy).

[7] See the web page titled "GitHub - lyst/rpforest: It is a forest of random projection trees," (https://github.com/lyst/rpforest).

[8] See the web page titled "GitHub - ekzhu/datasketch: MinHash, LSH, LSH Forest, Weighted MinHash, HyperLogLog, HyperLogLog++" (https://github.com/ekzhu/datasketch).

[9] See the web page titled "GitHub - norouzi/mih: Fast exact nearest neighbor search in Hamming distance on binary codes with Multi-index hashing" (https://github.com/norouzi/mih).

[10] See the web page titled "FALCONN : PyPI" (https://pypi.python.org/pypi/FALCONN).

- Fast Lookup of Approximate Nearest Neighbors (FLANN)[11]
- Hierarchical Navigable Small World (HNSW) (in `nmslib`)[12]
- K-Dimensional Trees (`kdtree`)[13]
- `nearpy`[14]

One of the most straightforward of these indexing approaches is implemented in a package called Annoy by Spotify.

### 13.2.3 *Advanced indexing with Annoy*

The recent update to `word2vec` (`KeyedVectors`) in `gensim` added an advanced indexing approach. You can now retrieve approximate nearest neighbors for any vector in milliseconds, out of the box. But as we discussed in the beginning of the chapter, you need to use indexing for any kind of high-dimension dense continuous vector set, not just `word2vec` vectors. You can use `Annoy` to index the `word2vec` vectors and compare your results to `gensim`'s `KeyedVectors` index. First, you need to load the `word2vec` vectors like you did in chapter 6, as shown in the following listing.

---

**Listing 13.1    Load `word2vec` vectors**

```
>>> from nlpia.loaders import get_data
>>> wv = get_data('word2vec')
100%|###########################| 402111/402111 [01:02<00:00, 6455.57it/s]
>>> len(wv.vocab), len(wv[next(iter(wv.vocab))])
(3000000, 300)
>>> wv.vectors.shape
(3000000, 300)
```

> **If you haven't already downloaded GoogleNews-vectors-negative300.bin.gz (https://bit.ly/GoogleNews-vectors-negative300) to nlpia/src/nlpia/bigdata/ then get_data() will download it for you.**

Set up an empty `Annoy` index with the right number of dimensions for your vectors, as shown in the following listing.

---

**Listing 13.2    Initialize 300D `AnnoyIndex`**

```
>>> from annoy import AnnoyIndex
>>> num_words, num_dimensions = wv.vectors.shape
>>> index = AnnoyIndex(num_dimensions)
```

> **The original GoogleNews word2vec model contains 3M word vectors, each with 300 dimensions.**

Now you can add your `word2vec` vectors to your `Annoy` index one at a time. You can think of this process as reading through the pages of a book one at a time, and putting

---

[11] See the web page titled "FLANN - Fast Library for Approximate Nearest Neighbors" (http://www.cs.ubc.ca/research/flann/).

[12] See the web page titled "nmslib/hnsw.h at master : nmslib/nmslib" (https://github.com/searchivarius/nmslib/blob/master/similarity_search/include/factory/method/hnsw.h).

[13] See the GitHub repository for kdtree: (https://github.com/stefankoegl/kdtree).

[14] See NearPy project on PyPi: (https://pypi.python.org/pypi/NearPy).

the page numbers where you found each word in the reverse index table at the back of the book. Obviously an ANN search is much more complicated, but `Annoy` makes it easier. See the following listing.

---

**Listing 13.3  Add each word vector to the `AnnoyIndex`**

**tqdm() takes an iterable and returns an iterable (like enumerate()) and inserts code in your loop to display a progress bar.**

**.index2word is an unsorted list of all 3M tokens in your vocabulary, equivalent to a map of the integer indexes (0-2999999) to tokens ('</s>' to 'snowcapped_Caucasus').**

```
>>> from tqdm import tqdm
>>> for i, word in enumerate(tqdm(wv.index2word)):
...     index.add_item(i, wv[word])
22%|#######?              | 649297/3000000 [00:26<01:35, 24587.52it/s]
```

Your `AnnoyIndex` object has to do one last thing: read through the entire index and try to cluster your vectors into bite-size chunks that can be indexed in a tree structure, as shown in the following listing.

---

**Listing 13.4  Build Euclidean distance index with 15 trees**

**This is just a rule of thumb—you may want to optimize this hyperparameter if this index isn't performant for the things you care about (RAM, lookup, indexing) or accurate enough for your application.**

```
>>> import numpy as np
>>> num_trees = int(np.log(num_words).round(0))
>>> num_trees
15
>>> index.build(num_trees)
>>> index.save('Word2vec_euc_index.ann')
True
>>> w2id = dict(zip(range(len(wv.vocab)), wv.vocab))
```

**round(ln(3000000)) => 15 indexing trees for our 3M vectors—takes a few minutes on a laptop**

**Saves the index to a local file and frees up RAM, but may take several minutes**

You built 15 trees (approximately the natural log of 3 million), because you have 3 million vectors to search through. If you have more vectors or want your index to be faster and more accurate, you can increase the number of trees. Just be careful not to make it too big or you'll have to wait a while for the indexing process to complete.

Now you can try to look up a word from your vocabulary in the index, as shown in the following listing.

---

**Listing 13.5  Find `Harry_Potter` neighbors with `AnnoyIndex`**

**The gensim KeyedVectors.vocab dict contains Vocab objects rather than raw strings or index numbers.**

**The gensim Vocab object can tell you the number of times the "Harry_Potter" 2-gram was mentioned in the GoogleNews corpus.... nearly 3M times.**

```
>>> wv.vocab['Harry_Potter'].index
9494
>>> wv.vocab['Harry_Potter'].count
2990506
>>> w2id = dict(zip(
```

```
...      wv.vocab, range(len(wv.vocab))))
>>> w2id['Harry_Potter']
9494
>>> ids = index.get_nns_by_item(
...      w2id['Harry_Potter'], 11)
>>> ids
[9494, 32643, 39034, 114813, ..., 113008, 116741, 113955, 350346]
>>> [wv.vocab[i] for i in _]
>>> [wv.index2word[i] for i in _]
['Harry_Potter',
 'Narnia',
 'Sherlock_Holmes',
 'Lemony_Snicket',
 'Spiderwick_Chronicles',
 'Unfortunate_Events',
 'Prince_Caspian',
 'Eragon',
 'Sorcerer_Apprentice',
 'RL_Stine']
```

Create a map similar to wv.vocab, mapping the tokens to their index values (integer).

Annoy returns the target vector first, so we have to request 11 "neighbors" if we want 10 in addition to the target.

The 10 nearest neighbors listed by Annoy are mostly books from the same general genre as *Harry Potter*, but they aren't really precise synonyms with the book title, movie title, or character name. So your results are definitely approximate nearest neighbors. Also, keep in mind that the algorithm used by Annoy is stochastic, similar to a random forest machine learning algorithm.[15] So your list won't be the same as what you see here. If you want repeatable results you can use the AnnoyIndex.set_seed() method to initialize the random number generator.

It seems like an Annoy index misses a lot of closer neighbors and provides results from the general vicinity of a search term rather than the closest 10. How about gensim? What would happen if you did that with gensim's built-in KeyedVector index to retrieve the correct closest 10 neighbors? See the following listing.

> Listing 13.6  Top Harry_Potter neighbors with gensim.KeyedVectors index

```
>>> [word for word, similarity in wv.most_similar('Harry_Potter', topn=10)]
['JK_Rowling_Harry_Potter',
 'JK_Rowling',
 'boy_wizard',
 'Deathly_Hallows',
 'Half_Blood_Prince',
 'Rowling',
 'Actor_Rupert_Grint',
 'HARRY_Potter',
 'wizard_Harry_Potter',
 'HARRY_POTTER']
```

Now that looks like a more relevant top-10 synonym list. This lists the correct author, alternative title spellings, titles of other books in the series, and even an actor in the

---

[15] Annoy uses random projections to generate locality sensitive hashes (http://en.wikipedia.org/wiki/Locality -sensitive_hashing#Random_projection).

Harry Potter movie. But the results from `Annoy` may be useful in some situations, when you're more interested in the genre or general sense of a word rather than precise synonyms. That's pretty cool.

But the `Annoy` indexing approximation really took some shortcuts. To fix that, rebuild the index using the cosine distance metric (instead of Euclidean) and add more trees. This should improve the accuracy of the nearest neighbors and make its results match `gensim`'s more closely. See the following listing.

---

**Listing 13.7  Build a cosine distance index**

```
>>> index_cos = AnnoyIndex(
...      f=num_dimensions, metric='angular')
>>> for i, word in enumerate(wv.index2word):
...      if not i % 100000:
...          print('{}: {}'.format(i, word))
...      index_cos.add_item(i, wv[word])
0: </s>
100000: distinctiveness
    ...
2900000: BOARDED_UP
```

> `metric='angular'` uses the angular (cosine) distance metric to compute your clusters and hashes. Your options are: 'angular', 'euclidean', 'manhattan', or 'hamming'.

> Another way to keep informed of your progress, if you don't like tqdm

Now let's build twice the number of trees. And set the random seed, so you can get the same results that you see in the following listing.

---

**Listing 13.8  Build a cosine distance index**

```
>>> index_cos.build(30)
>>> index_cos.save('Word2vec_cos_index.ann')
True
```

> 30 equals int(np.log(num_vectors).round(0)), double what you had before.

This indexing should take twice as long to run, but once it finishes you should expect results closer to what `gensim` produces. Now let's see how approximate those nearest neighbors are for the term "Harry Potter" for your more precise index.

---

**Listing 13.9  `Harry_Potter` neighbors in a cosine distance world**

```
>>> ids_cos = index_cos.get_nns_by_item(w2id['Harry_Potter'], 10)
>>> ids_cos
[9494, 37681, 40544, 41526, 14273, 165465, 32643, 420722, 147151, 28829]
>>> [wv.index2word[i] for i in ids_cos]
['Harry_Potter',
 'JK_Rowling',
 'Deathly_Hallows',
 'Half_Blood_Prince',
 'Twilight',
 'Twilight_saga',
 'Narnia',
 'Potter_mania',
 'Hermione_Granger',
 'Da_Vinci_Code']
```

> You'll not get the same results. Random projection for LSH is stochastic. Use AnnoyIndex.set_seed() if you need repeatability.

That's a bit better. At least the correct author is listed. You can compare the results for the two `Annoy` searches to the correct answer from `gensim`, as shown in the following listing.

---

**Listing 13.10   Search results accuracy for top 10**

> We leave it to you to figure out how to combine these top-10 lists into a single DataFrame.

```
>>> pd.DataFrame(annoy_top10, columns=['annoy_15trees',
...                                    'annoy_30trees'])
                            annoy_15trees         annoy_30trees
gensim
JK_Rowling_Harry_Potter        Harry_Potter          Harry_Potter
JK_Rowling                           Narnia            JK_Rowling
boy_wizard                  Sherlock_Holmes       Deathly_Hallows
Deathly_Hallows              Lemony_Snicket     Half_Blood_Prince
Half_Blood_Prince       Spiderwick_Chronicles            Twilight
Rowling                 Unfortunate_Events         Twilight_saga
Actor_Rupert_Grint           Prince_Caspian                Narnia
HARRY_Potter                         Eragon          Potter_mania
wizard_Harry_Potter       Sorcerer_Apprentice   Hermione_Granger
HARRY_POTTER                       RL_Stine          Da_Vinci_Code
```

To get rid of the redundant "Harry_Potter" synonym, you should've listed the top 11, and skipped the first one. But you can see the progression here. As you increase the number of `Annoy` index trees, you push down the ranking of less-relevant terms (such as "Narnia") and insert more-relevant terms from the true nearest neighbors (such as "JK_Rowling" and "Deathly_Hallows").

And the approximate answer from the `Annoy` index is significantly faster than the `gensim` index that provides exact results. And you can use this `Annoy` index for any high-dimensional, continuous, dense vectors that you need to search, such as LSA document-topic vectors or `doc2vec` document embeddings (vectors).

### 13.2.4   *Why use approximate indexes at all?*

Those of you with some experience analyzing algorithm efficiency may say to yourself that $O(N^2)$ algorithms are theoretically efficient. After all, they're more efficient than exponential algorithms and even more efficient than polynomial algorithms. They certainly aren't n-p hard to compute or solve. They aren't the kind of impossible thing that takes the lifetime of the universe to compute.

Because these $O(N^2)$ computations are only required to train the machine learning models in your NLP pipeline, they can be precomputed. Your chatbot doesn't need to compute $O(N^2)$ operations with each reply to a new statement. And $N^2$ operations are inherently parallelizable. You can almost always run one of the *N* sequences of computations independent of the other *N* sequences. So you could just throw more RAM and processors at the problem and run some batch training process every night or every weekend to keep your bot's brain up-to-date.[16] Even better, you may be able

---

[16] This is the real-world architecture you used on an $N^2$ document matching problem.

to just bite off chunks of the $N^2$ computation and run them one by one, incrementally, as data comes in that increases that $N$.

For example, imagine you've trained a chatbot on some small dataset to get started and then turned it loose on the world. Imagine that $N$ is the number of statements and replies in its persistent memory (database). Each time someone addresses the chatbot with a new statement, the bot might want to search its database for the most similar statement so it can reuse any replies that worked for that statement in the past. So you compute some similarity score (metric) between the $N$ existing statements and the new statement and store the new similarity scores in your $(N+1)^2$ similarity matrix as a new row and column. Or you just add $N$ more connections or relationships to your graph data structure storing all the similarity scores between statements. Now you can do a query on these connections (or cells in the connection matrix) to find the minimum distance value. For the simplest approach, you only really have to check those $N$ scores you just computed. But if you wanted to be more thorough, you could check other rows and columns (walk the graph a little deeper) to find, for instance, some replies to similar statements and check metrics such as kindness, information content, sentiment, grammaticality, well-formedness, brevity, and style. Either way you have an $O(N)$ algorithm for computing the best reply, even though the overall complexity for a full training run is $O(N^2)$.

But what if $O(N)$ still isn't enough? What if you're building a really big brain, such as Google, where $N$ is more than 60 trillion?[17] Even if your $N$ isn't quite that large, if the individual computations are pretty complex, or you want to respond in a reasonable amount of time (10s of milliseconds), you'll need to employ an index.

### 13.2.5 *An indexing workaround: discretizing*

So we've just claimed that floats (real values) are impossible to naively index. What's one way to prove us wrong, or be less naive about your indexing? Those of you with experience working with sensor data and analog-to-digital converters may be thinking to yourself that continuous values can easily be made digital or discrete. And a `float` isn't really continuous anyway. They're a bunch of bits, after all. But you need to make them *really* discrete if you want them to fit into your concept of an index and maintain that low dimensionality. You need to "bin" them into something manageable. The simplest way to turn a continuous variable into a manageable number of categorical or ordinal values is something like the code shown in the following listing.

---

> Listing 13.11  **`MinMaxScaler`** for low-dimensional vectors

```
>>> from sklearn.preprocessing import MinMaxScaler
>>> real_values = [-1.2, 3.4, 5.6, -7.8, 9.0]
>>>                                              Confine our floats to be
>>> scaler = MinMaxScaler()          ◁――――       between 0.0 and 1.0.
```

---

[17] Google tutorial on web indexing (https://www.google.com/insidesearch/howsearchworks/thestory/).

```
>>> scaler.fit(real_values)

[int(x * 100.) for x in scaler.transform(real_values)]     ⟵    Scaled, discretized
[39, 66, 79, 0, 100]                                              ints, 0 - 100
```

This works fine for low-dimensional spaces. This is essentially what some 2D GIS indexes use to discretize lat/lon values into a grid of bounding boxes. Points in 2D space are either present or absent for each of the grid points. As the number of dimensions grows, you need to use more and more sophisticated, efficient indexes than your simple 2D grid.

Let's use spatial dimensions to think about 3D space before diving into 300D natural language semantic vectors. For example, think about what changes when you grow from two to three dimensions by adding altitude to some database of 2D GPS latitude and longitude values. Now imagine you divided the Earth into 3D cubes rather than the 2D grid you used earlier. Most of those cubes wouldn't have much in them that humans would be interested in finding. And doing proximity searches, such as finding all the objects within some 3D sphere or 3D cube, becomes a much more difficult operation. The number of grid points you have to search through increases with $N^3$, where $N$ is the diameter of a search region. You can see how when 3 (the number of dimensions) goes up to 4 or 5, you really need to be smart about your search.

## 13.3  *Constant RAM algorithms*

One of the main challenges in working with large corpora and TF-IDF matrices is fitting it all in RAM. The reason why we used `gensim` throughout this book is that their algorithms attempt to maintain a constant RAM footprint.

### 13.3.1  *Gensim*

What if you have more documents than you can hold in RAM? As the size and variety of the documents in your corpus grows, you may eventually exceed the RAM capacity of even the largest machines you can rent from a cloud service. Have no fear, the mathematicians are here.

The math behind algorithms such as LSA has been around for decades. Mathematicians and computer scientists have had a lot of time to play with it and get it to work *out of core*, which just means that the objects required to run an algorithm don't all have to be present in core memory (RAM) at once. This means you're no longer limited by the RAM on your machine.

Even if you don't want to parallelize your training pipeline on multiple machines, constant RAM implementations will be required for large datasets. Gensim's `LsiModel` is one such out-of-core implementation of singular value decomposition for LSA.[18]

---

[18] See the web page titled "gensim: models.lsimodel – Latent Semantic Indexing" (https://radimrehurek.com/gensim/models/lsimodel.html).

Even for smaller datasets, the gensimLSIModel has the advantage that it doesn't require increasing amounts of RAM to deal with a growing vocabulary or set of documents. So you don't have to worry about it starting to swap to disk halfway through your corpus or grinding to a halt when it runs out of RAM. You can even continue to use your laptop for other tasks while a gensim model is training in the background.

gensim uses what's called batch training to accomplish this memory efficiency. It trains your LSA model (gensim.models.LsiModel) on batches of documents and merges the results from these batches incrementally. All of gensim's models are designed to be *constant RAM*, which makes them run faster on large datasets by avoiding swapping data to disk and using your precious CPU cache RAM efficiently.

**TIP**  In addition to being constant RAM, the training of gensim models is parallelizable, at least for many of the long-running steps in these pipelines.

So packages such as gensim are worth having in your toolbox. They can speed up your small-data experiments (like in this book) and also power your hyperspace travel on Big Data in the future.

### 13.3.2 *Graph computing*

Hadoop, TensorFlow, Caffe, Theano, Torch, and Spark were designed from the ground up to be constant RAM. If you can formulate your machine learning pipeline as a Map-Reduce problem or a general computational graph, you can take advantage of these frameworks to avoid running out of RAM. These frameworks automatically traverse your computational graph to allocate resources and optimize your throughput.

Peter Goldsborough implemented several benchmark models and datasets using these frameworks to compare their performance. Even though Torch has been around since 2002, it fared well on most of his benchmarks, outperforming all of the others on CPUs, and sometimes even on GPUs. In many cases, it was 10 times faster than the nearest competitor.

And Torch (and its PyTorch Python API) is integrated into many cluster compute frameworks such as RocketML. Though we haven't used PyTorch for the examples in this book (to avoid overwhelming you with options), you may want to look into it if RAM or throughput are blockers for your NLP pipeline.

We've had success parallelizing NLP pipelines using RocketML (rocketml.net). They contributed research and development time to help Aira and TotalGood parallelize our NLP pipelines to assist those who have blindness or low vision:

- Extracting images from videos
- Inference and embedding on pretrained Caffe, PyTorch, Theano, and TensorFlow (Keras) models
- SVD on large TF-IDF matrices spanning GB corpora[19]

---

[19] At SAIS 2008, Santi Adavani explained his optimizations that make SVD faster and more scalable on a RocketML HPC platform (databricks.com/speaker/santi-adavani).

RocketML pipelines scale well, often linearly, depending on the algorithm.[20] So if you double the machines in your cluster, you'll have a trained model twice as fast. This is harder than it seems. More general computational graph parallelization frameworks like PySpark and TensorFlow can rarely claim this.

## 13.4  *Parallelizing your NLP computations*

There are two popular approaches to *high-performance computing* for NLP. You can either add GPUs to your server (and even your laptop, in some cases), or you can connect CPUs together from multiple servers.

### 13.4.1  *Training NLP models on GPUs*

GPUs have become an important and sometimes necessary tool to develop real-world NLP applications. GPUs, first introduced in 2007, are designed to parallelize a large number of computational tasks and to access large amounts of memory. This contrasts the design of CPUs, which are the core of every computer. They're designed to handle tasks sequentially at a high speed, and they can access their limited processing memory at a high speed (see figure 13.1).

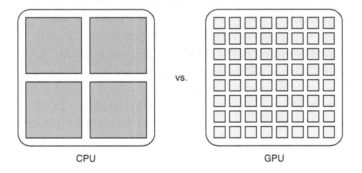

**Figure 13.1   Comparison between a CPU and GPU**

As it turns out, training deep learning models involves various operations that can be parallelized, such as the multiplication of matrices. Similar to graphical animations, which were the initial target market for GPUs, the training of deep learning models is heavily accelerated by parallelized matrix multiplications.

Figure 13.2 shows the multiplication of an input vector with a weight matrix, a frequent operation during a forward-pass of the neural network training. The individual cores of a GPU are slow compared to a CPU, but each core can compute one of the result vector components. If the training is executed on a CPU, each row multiplication

---

[20] Santi Adavani and Vinay Rao (http://www.rocketml.net/) are contributing to the Real-Time Video Description project (https://github.com/totalgood/viddesc).

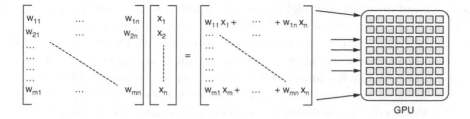

**Figure 13.2   Matrix multiplication where each row multiplication can be parallelized on a GPU**

would be executed sequentially, assuming that no specific linear algebra library is used. It'll require $n$ (number of matrix rows) time steps to complete the multiplication. If the same task is executed on a GPU, the multiplication will be parallelized and each row multiplication can happen at the same time in the individual cores of the GPU.

> **DO I NEED TO RUN MY MODEL ON A GPU AFTER THE TRAINING IS COMPLETE?**   You don't need to use a GPU for running inferences using your models in production, even if you used a GPU to train your model. In fact, unless you need to run forward passes (inference or activation of a neural net) of a pretrained model with millions of samples or with high throughput (real-time streaming), you probably should only use GPUs when training a new model. Backpropagation is much more computationally expensive than forward activation (inference) on a neural net.

GPUs introduce complexity and cost to your pipeline. But this upfront cost will quickly pay for itself if you can achieve faster turnaround on your models. If you can retrain your model with new hyperparameters in a tenth the time, you can try 10 times as many different approaches and achieve much better accuracy.

Once the training is completed, Keras or your deep learning framework provides you a way to export the model weights and structure. You can then load the weights and the model setup on almost any hardware to compute the model prediction (forward pass or inference pass), even on a smartphone[21] or in a browser.[22]

### 13.4.2   Renting vs. buying

The use of GPUs can accelerate your model development and allow you to iterate through your model development more quickly. GPUs are useful, but should you buy one?

The answer in most cases is no. The performance of GPUs is improving so rapidly that a purchased graphic card could quickly get out-of-date. Unless you plan to use your

---

[21] See Apple's Core ML documentation (https://developer.apple.com/documentation/coreml) or Google's TensorFlow Lite documentation (https://www.tensorflow.org/mobile/tflite/).

[22] See the web page titled "Keras.js - Run Keras models in the browser" (https://transcranial.github.io/keras-js/#/).

GPU around the clock, you might be better off with renting a GPU via a service such as Amazon Web Services or Google Cloud. The GPU service allows you to switch instance sizes between model training runs. That way, you can scale up or down your GPU size, depending on your needs. These providers also often provide fully configured installations, which can save you time and let you focus on your model development.

We built and maintained our own GPU server to speed some of the model training used in this book, but you should do as we say and not as we do. Selecting components that are compatible with each other and minimizing the data throughput bottlenecks was a challenge. We imitated successful architectures described by others and bought RAM and GPUs before the recent Bitcoin surge and the resulting high performance computing (HPC) component price spike. Keeping all the libraries up-to-date and coordinating usage and configuration between authors was a challenge. It was fun and educational, but it wasn't an efficient use of our time nor dollars.

The flexible setup of renting GPU instances has one drawback: you need to watch your costs closely. Completing your training won't stop your instance automatically. To stop the ticking of the meter (incurring ongoing cost), you'll need to turn off your GPU instance between training runs. For more details, check out the section "Cost control" in the Resources section at the end of this book.

### 13.4.3  *GPU rental options*

Various companies provide GPU rental options, starting with the well-known platform-as-a-service companies such as Microsoft, Amazon Web Services, and Google. Other startups, such as Paperspace or FloydHub, are breaking into the industry with interesting product offerings that can get you started quickly with your deep learning project.

Table 1 compares the different GPU options from platform-as-a-service providers. The services range from a bare GPU machine with a minimal installation to fully configured machines with drag-and-drop clients. Due to the regional variability in the service pricing, we can't compare the providers based on price. Prices for the services range from $0.65 to multiple dollars per hour and instance, depending on the server's location, configuration, and setup.

Table 13.1   Comparison of GPU platform-as-a-service options

| Company | Why? | GPU options | Ease to get started | Flexibility |
|---|---|---|---|---|
| Amazon Web Services (AWS) | Wide range of GPU options; spot prices; available in various data centers around the world | NVIDIA GRID K520, Tesla M60, Tesla K80, Tesla V100 | Medium | High |
| Google Cloud | Integrates Google Cloud Kubernetes, DialogFlow, Jupyter (colab.research .google.com/notebook) | NVIDIA Tesla K80, Tesla P100 | Medium | High |
| Microsoft Azure | Good option if you are using other Azure services | NVIDIA Tesla K80 | Medium | High |

**Table 13.1   Comparison of GPU platform-as-a-service options** *(continued)*

| Company | Why? | GPU options | Ease to get started | Flexibility |
|---|---|---|---|---|
| FloydHub | Command-line interface to bundle your code | NVIDIA Tesla K80, Tesla V100 | Easy | Medium |
| Paperspace | Virtual servers and hosted iPython/Jupyter notebooks with GPU support | NVIDIA Maxwell, Tesla P5000, Tesla P6000, Tesla V100 | Easy | Medium |

**SETTING UP YOUR OWN GPU ON AWS**   Appendix E shows a summary of the necessary steps for you to get started with your own GPU instance.

### 13.4.4   *Tensor processing units*

You might have heard of another abbreviation, TPU (tensor processing unit), which is a highly optimized computational unit for deep learning. They're particularly efficient at computing back-propagation for TensorFlow models. TPUs are optimized for multiplying tensors of any dimensionality and use specialized FPGA and ASIC chips to preprocess and transport data around. GPUs are optimized for graphical processing, which mostly consists of the 2D matrix multiplications required to render and move around in 3D game worlds.

Google claims that TPUs are 10 times more efficient at computing deep learning models than an equivalent GPU. At the time of this writing, Google, which designed and invented TPUs in 2015, just released them to the general public in a beta stage (no service-level agreement is provided). In addition, researchers can apply to become part of the TensorFlow Research Cloud[23] to train their models on TPUs.

## 13.5   *Reducing the memory footprint during model training*

When you train your NLP models on a GPU and you train with a large corpus, you'll probably eventually encounter the following error during training: MemoryError. See the following listing.

**Listing 13.12   Error message if your training data exceeds the GPU's memory**

```
Epoch 1/10
Exception in thread Thread-27:
Traceback (most recent call last):
  File "/usr/lib/python2.7/threading.py", line 801, in __bootstrap_inner
    self.run()
  File "/usr/lib/python2.7/threading.py", line 754, in run
    self.__target(*self.__args, **self.__kwargs)
  File "/usr/local/lib/python2.7/dist-packages/keras/engine/training.py",
    line 606, in data_generator_task
    generator_output = next(self._generator)
```

---

[23] See the web page titled "TensorFlow Research Cloud" (https://www.tensorflow.org/tfrc/).

```
File "/home/ubuntu/django/project/model/load_data.py", line 54,
  in load_training_set
  rv = np.array(rv)
MemoryError
```

To achieve the high performance of GPUs, the units use their own internal GPU memory in addition to the CPU memory. The card's memory is usually limited to a few gigabytes, and in most cases, not near as much as the CPU has access to. When you trained your model on a CPU, your training data was probably loaded into the computer memory in one large table or sequence of tensors. This isn't possible anymore with the memory restrictions of the GPU (see figure 13.3).

**Figure 13.3   Loading the training data without a generator function**

One efficient workaround is using Python's concept of a *generator*—a function that returns an iterator object. You can pass the iterator object to the model training method, and it will "pull out" one or more training items at each training iteration. It never requires the whole training dataset in memory. This efficient way to reduce your memory footprint comes with caveats:

- Generators only provide one sequence element at a time, so you don't know how many elements it contains until you reach the end.
- Generators can only be run once. They're disposable and not recyclable.

With these two difficulties, making multiple training passes through your data is much more tedious. But Keras comes to the rescue with methods that take care of all this tedious bookkeeping for you (see figure 13.4)

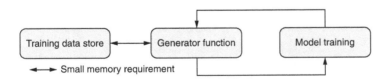

**Figure 13.4   Loading the training data with a generator function**

The generator function handles the loading of the training data store and returns the training "chunks" to the training methods. In listing 13.13, the training data store is a csv file with the input data separated from the expected output data by the | delimiter. The chunks are limited to the batch size, and only one batch at a time has to be stored in memory. That way, you can heavily reduce the model training dataset's memory footprint.

---

**Listing 13.13  Generator for improved RAM efficiency**

```
>>> import numpy as np
>>>
>>> def training_set_generator(data_store,
...                            batch_size=32):
...     X, Y = [], []
...     while True:
...         with open(data_store) as f:
...             for i, line in enumerate(f):
...                 if i % batch_size == 0 and X and Y:
...                     yield np.array(X), np.array(Y)
...                     X, Y = [], []
...                 x, y = line.split('|')
...                 X.append(x)
...                 Y.append(y)
>>>
>>> data_store = '/path/to/your/data.csv'
>>> training_set = training_set_generator(data_store)
```

**In the function setup, you can set the batch size dynamically.**

**This endless loop provides training batches forever; Keras stops requesting more training examples when an epoch ends.**

**This opens the training data store and creating the file handler f.**

**Loop over the training data stores content line by line until your entire data has been served as training samples; afterward start from the beginning of the training set.**

**If you have gathered enough training data samples, return the training data and the expected training output via a function yield. Python jumps back after the yield statement after the data is served to the model fit method.**

**If you don't have enough samples yet, read more lines, split them on the delimiter |, and keep them in the lists X and Y.**

---

In our example, the `training_set_generator` function reads from a pipe-separated values file, but it could load the data from any database or any other data storage system.

One disadvantage of the generator is that it doesn't return any information about the size of the training data array. Because you don't know how much training data is available, you have to use slightly different `fit`, `predict`, and `evaluate` methods of the Keras model.

Instead of training your model with

```
>>> model.fit(x=X,
...           y=Y,
...           batch_size=32,
...           epochs=10,
...           verbose=1,
...           validation_split=0.2)
```

you have to kick off the training of your model with

**fit_generator expects a generator being passed to it, which can be your training_set_generator or any other generator you program.**

```
>>> data_store = '/path/to/your/data.csv'
>>> model.fit_generator(generator=training_set_generator(data_store,
...     batch_size=32),
```

```
...                  steps_per_epoch=100,
...                  epochs=10,                        Set your number
...                  verbose=1,                        of epochs as usual.
...                  validation_data=[X_val, Y_val])
```

Because the full training data isn't
available to the fit_generator, it
doesn't allow the usual
validation_split; instead you need
to define validation_data.

In contrast to defining your training batch_size like you did in the
original fit method, the fit_generator expects the number of steps
per epoch, steps_per_epoch. For every step, the generator is called.
Set steps_per_epoch to training samples divided by batch_size, so
that your model is exposed to the full training set once per epoch.

If you use a generator, you might also want to update your model's `evaluate` and
`predict` methods with

```
>>> model.evaluate_generator(generator=your_eval_generator(eval_data,
...        batch_size=32), steps=10)
```

and

```
>>> model.predict_generator(generator=your_predict_generator(\
...        prediction_data, batch_size=32), steps=10)
```

> **WARNING**   Generators are memory efficient, but they can also become a
> bottleneck during the model training and slow down the training iterations.
> Pay attention to the generator speed while developing the training functions.
> If the on-the-fly processing slows down the generator, it might be beneficial to
> preprocess the training data, rent an instance with larger memory configura-
> tion, or both.

## 13.6   *Gaining model insights with TensorBoard*

Wouldn't it be nice to get insights into your model performance while you train your
model and compare it to previous training runs? Or quickly plot word embeddings to
check semantic similarities? Google's TensorBoard provides you exactly that.

While training your model using TensorFlow (or with Keras and a TF backend),
you can use TensorBoard to gain insights into your NLP models. You can use it to
track model training metrics, plot network weight distributions, visualize your word
embeddings, and various other things. TensorBoard is easy to use, and it connects to
the training instance via your browser.

If you want to use TensorBoard side-by-side with Keras, you need to install Tensor-
Board like any other Python package:

```
pip install tensorboard
```

After the installation is complete, you can now start it up:

```
tensorboard --logdir=/tmp/
```

After TensorBoard is running, access it in your browser at `localhost` on port 6006
(http://127.0.0.1:6006) if you train on your laptop or desktop PC. If you train your

model on a rented GPU instance, use the public IP address of your GPU instance and make sure the GPU provider allows access via the port 6006.

Once you're logged in, you can explore the model performance.

### 13.6.1 *How to visualize word embeddings*

TensorBoard is a great tool to visualize word embeddings. Especially when you train your own, domain-specific word embeddings, the embedding visualization can help to verify semantic similarities. Converting a word model into a format TensorBoard can handle is straightforward. Once the word vectors and the vector labels are loaded into TensorBoard, it'll perform the dimensionality reductions to 2D or 3D for you. Tensor-Board currently provides three methods of dimensionality reduction: PCA, t-SNE, and custom reductions.

The following listing shows how to convert your word embedding into a Tensor-Board format and generate the projection data.

**Listing 13.14  Convert an embedding into a TensorBoard projection**

```
>>> import os                              The create_projection function takes three arguments:
>>> import tensorflow as tf                   the embedding data, a name for the projection and a
>>> import numpy as np                             path, and where to store the projection files.
>>> from io import open
>>> from tensorflow.contrib.tensorboard.plugins import projector
>>>
>>>
>>> def create_projection(projection_data,
...                       projection_name='tensorboard_viz',
...                       path='/tmp/'):
...     meta_file = "{}.tsv".format(projection_name)
...     vector_dim = len(projection_data[0][1])
...     samples = len(projection_data)
...     projection_matrix = np.zeros((samples, vector_dim))
...
...     with open(os.path.join(path, meta_file), 'w') as file_metadata:
...         for i, row in enumerate(projection_data):
...             label, vector = row[0], row[1]
...             projection_matrix[i] = np.array(vector)
...             file_metadata.write("{}\n".format(label))
...
...     sess = tf.InteractiveSession()
...
...     embedding = tf.Variable(projection_matrix,
...                             trainable=False,
...                             name=projection_name)
...     tf.global_variables_initializer().run()
...
...     saver = tf.train.Saver()
...     writer = tf.summary.FileWriter(path, sess.graph)
...
...     config = projector.ProjectorConfig()
...     embed = config.embeddings.add()
```

The function loops over the embedding data and creates a numpy array, which will then be converted to a TensorFlow variable.

To create the TensorBoard projection, you need to create a TensorFlow session.

TensorFlow provides built-in methods to create projections.

```
...        embed.tensor_name = '{}'.format(projection_name)
...        embed.metadata_path = os.path.join(path, meta_file)
...
...        projector.visualize_embeddings(writer, config)     ◁
...        saver.save(sess, os.path.join(path, '{}.ckpt'\
...            .format(projection_name)))
...        print('Run `tensorboard --logdir={0}` to run\
...            visualize result on tensorboard'.format(path))
```

> visualize_embeddings writes the projection to your path and is then available for TensorBoard.

The function `create_projection` takes a list of tuples (expects the vector and then the label) and converts it into TensorBoard projection files. Once the projection files are created and available to TensorBoard (in your case, TensorBoard expects the files in the *tmp* directory), head over to TensorBoard in your browser and check out the embedding visualization (see figure 13.5):

```
>>> projection_name = "NLP_in_Action"
>>> projection_data = [
>>>     ('car', [0.34, ..., -0.72]),
>>>     ...
>>>     ('toy', [0.46, ..., 0.39]),
>>> ]
>>> create_projection(projection_data, projection_name)
```

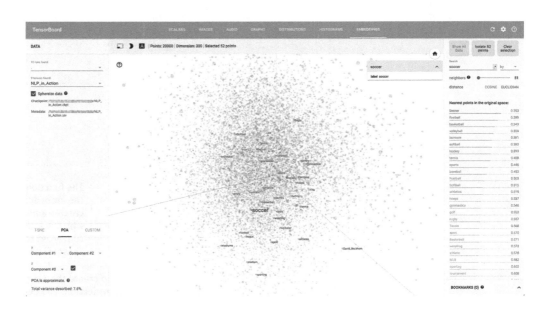

Figure 13.5    Visualize `word2vec` embeddings with Tensorboard.

## *Summary*

- Locality-sensitive hashes like `Annoy` make the promise of latent semantic indexing a reality.
- GPUs speed up model training, reducing the turn-around time on your models, making it easier to build better models faster.
- CPU parallelization can make sense for algorithms that don't benefit from speedier multiplication of large matrices.
- You can bypass the system RAM bottleneck using Python's generators, saving you money on your GPU and CPU instances.
- Google's TensorBoard can help you visualize and extract natural language embeddings that you might not have thought of otherwise.
- Mastering NLP parallelization can expand your brainpower by giving you a *society of minds*—machine clusters to help you think.[24]

---

[24] Conscious Ants and Human Hives by Peter Watts (https://youtube/v4uwaw_5Q3I?t=45s).

# *appendix A*
# *Your NLP tools*

You can run all the examples in this book if you are able to install the `nlpia` package (http://github.com/totalgood/nlpia). We keep the installation instructions in the README file up-to-date. But if you already have Python 3 installed, and you're feeling lucky (or are lucky enough to have a Linux environment), you can try

```
$ git clone https://github.com/totalgood/nlpia
$ pip3 install -e nlpia
```

If that doesn't work for you, you'll probably need to install a package manager and some binary packages for your OS. We have provided some OS-specific instructions in three sections:

- Ubuntu
- Mac
- Windows

These sections show you how to install an OS package manager. Once you have a package manager installed (or you're on a developer-friendly OS like Ubuntu that already has one), you can install Anaconda3.

## A.1 *Anaconda3*

Python 3 has a lot of performance and expressiveness features that are handy for NLP. And the easiest way to install Python 3 on almost any system is to install Anaconda3 (https://www.anaconda.com/download). This has the added benefit of giving you a package and environment manager that can install a lot of problematic packages (such as `matplotlib`) on a wide range of problematic OSes (like Windows).

You can install the latest version of Anaconda and its `conda` package manager programmatically by running the code in the following listing.

**Listing A.1   Install Anaconda3**

```
$ OS=MacOSX  # or Linux or Windows
$ BITS=_64  # or '' for 32-bit
$ curl https://repo.anaconda.com/archive/ > tmp.html
$ FILENAME=$(grep -o -E -e "Anaconda3-[.0-9]+-$OS-
    x86$BITS\.(sh|exe)" tmp.html | head -n 1)
$ curl "https://repo.anaconda.com/archive/$FILENAME" > install_anaconda
$ chmod +x install_anaconda
$ ./install_anaconda -b -p ~/Anaconda
$ export PATH="$HOME/Anaconda/bin:$PATH"
$ echo 'export PATH="$HOME/Anaconda/bin:$PATH"' >> ~/.bashrc
$ echo 'export PATH="$HOME/Anaconda/bin:$PATH"' >> ~/.bash_profile
$ source ~/.bash_profile
$ rm install_anaconda
```

Now you can create a virtual environment: not a Python virtualenv but a more complete `conda` environment that isolates all of Python's binary dependencies from your OS Python environment. Then you can install the dependencies and source code for NLPIA within that `conda` environment with listing A.2.

## A.2   *Install NLPIA*

We like to install software source code that we're working on in a subdirectory under our user `$HOME` called `code/`, but you can put it wherever you like. If this doesn't work, check out the `nlpia` README (https://github.com/totalgood/nlpia) for updated installation instructions.

**Listing A.2   Install `nlpia` source with `conda`**

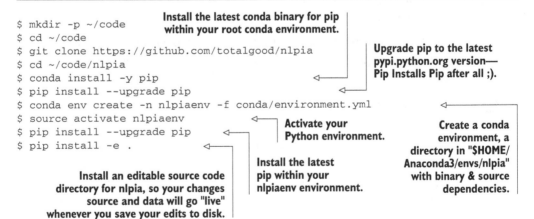

## A.3   *IDE*

Now that you have Python 3 and NLPIA on your machine, you only need a good text editor to round out your integrated development environment (IDE). Rather than installing a complete system like PyCharm by JetBrains, we prefer individual tools with small developer teams (team of one for Sublime Text) that do one thing well.

> **TIP** Built by developers for developers is a real thing, especially if the developer team is a team of one. Individual developers often build better tools than corporations because individuals are more open to incorporating code and suggestions by their users. An individual developer that builds a tool because they need it usually builds a tool that's optimized for their workflow. And their workflow is pretty awesome if they build tools that are reliable, powerful, and popular enough to compete. Large open source projects like `jupyter` are awesome, too, but in a different way. They're usually extremely versatile and full-featured, as long as they don't have a commercially licensed fork of the open source project.

Fortunately the tools you need for your Python IDE are all free, extensible, and continuously maintained. Most are even open source, so you can make them your own:

- Sublime Text 3 (www.sublimetext.com/3) text editor with Package Control (https://packagecontrol.io/installation#st3) and Anaconda (https://package-control.io/packages/Anaconda) linter plus auto-corrector
- `Meld` merge tool for Mac (https://yousseb.github.io/meld) or other OSes (http://meldmerge.org)
- `ipython` (`jupyter console`) for your **R**ead → **E**val → **P**rint → **L**oop (development workflow)
- `jupyter notebook` for creating reports, tutorials, and blog posts, or for sharing your results with your boss

> **TIP** Some phenomenally productive developers use a REPL workflow for Python.[1] The `ipython`, `jupyter console`, and `jupyter notebook` REPL consoles are particularly powerful, with their `help`, `?`, `??`, and `%` magic commands, plus automatic tab-completion of attributes, methods, arguments, file paths, and even `dict` keys. Before Googling or overflowing your stack, explore the docstrings and source code of the Python packages you've imported by trying commands like `>>> sklearn.linear_model.BayesianRidge??`. Python's REPLs even allow you to execute shell commands (try `>>> !git pull` or `>>> !find . -name nlpia`) to keep your fingers on the keyboard, minimizing context switching and maximizing productivity.

## A.4    *Ubuntu package manager*

Your Linux distribution already has a full-featured package manager installed. And you may not even need it if you use Anaconda's package manager `conda`, as suggested in the NLPIA installation instructions (http://github.com/totalgood/nlpia). The package manager for Ubuntu is called `apt`. We've suggested some packages to install

---

[1]   That's you, Steven "Digital Nomad" Skoczen and Aleck "The Dude" Landgraf.

in A.3. You almost certainly won't need all these packages, but this exhaustive list of tools is here in case you install something with Anaconda and it complains about a missing binary. You can start at the top and work your way down, until conda is able to install your Python packages. See the following listing.

---

**Listing A.3    Install developer tools with apt**

```
$ sudo apt-get update
$ sudo apt install -y build-essential libssl-dev g++ cmake swig git
$ sudo apt install -y python2.7-dev python3.5-dev libopenblas-dev libatlas-
    base-dev gfortran libgtk-3-dev
$ sudo apt install -y openjdk-8-jdk python-dev python-numpy python-
    pip python-virtualenv python-wheel python-nose
$ sudo apt install -y python3-dev python3-wheel python3-numpy python-
    scipy python-dev python-pip python3-six python3-pip
$ sudo apt install -y python3-pyaudio python-pyaudio
$ sudo apt install -y libcurl3-dev libcupti-dev xauth x11-apps python-qt4
$ sudo apt install -y python-opencv-dev libxvidcore-dev libx264-dev libjpeg8-
    dev libtiff5-dev libjasper-dev libpng12-dev
```

**TIP**    If the apt-get update command fails with an error regarding bazel, you've likely added the Google apt repository with their build tool for TensorFlow. This should get you back on track again:

```
$ sudo apt-get install curl
$ curl https://bazel.build/bazel-release.pub.gpg | sudo apt-key add -
```

## A.5    *Mac*

You need a real package manager (not XCode) before you can install all the tools you need to keep up with other developers.

### A.5.1    *A Mac package manager*

Homebrew (https://brew.sh) is probably the most popular command-line package manager for Macs among developers. It's easy to install and contains one-step installation packages for most tools that developers use. It's equivalent to Ubuntu's apt package manager. Apple could've ensured their OS would play nice with apt, but they didn't want developers to bypass their XCode and App Store "funnels," for obvious monetization reasons. So some intrepid Ruby developers homebrewed their own package manager.[2] And it's almost as good as apt or any other OS-specific binary package manager. See the following listing.

---

**Listing A.4    Install brew**

```
$ /usr/bin/ruby -e "$(curl -fsSL https://raw.githubusercontent.com/Homebrew/
    install/master/install)"
```

---

[2]    See the Homebrew package manager Wikipedia article (https://en.wikipedia.org/wiki/Homebrew_(package _management_software)).

You'll be asked to confirm things with the Return key and also enter your root/sudo password. So don't walk away to brew your coffee until you've entered your password and the installation script is happily chugging along.

### A.5.2 *Some packages*

Once brew is installed, you may want to install some Linux tools that are handy to have around, as shown in the following listing.

Listing A.5 Install developer tools

```
$ brew install wget htop tree pandoc asciidoctor
```

### A.5.3 *Tuneups*

If you are serious about NLP and software development, you'll want to make sure you have your OS tuned up so you can get stuff done. Here's what we install whenever we create a new user account on a Mac:

- Snappy to take screenshots (http://snappy-app.com)
- CopyClip to manage your clipboard (https://itunes.apple.com/us/app/copy-clip-clipboard-history-manager/id595191960)

If you want to share screenshots with other NLP developers you'll need a screen grabber such as Snappy. And a clipboard manager, such as CopyClip, lets you copy and paste more than one thing at a time and persist your clipboard history between reboots. A clipboard manager gives you the power of console history search ([ctrl]-[R]) in your GUI copy and paste world.

And you should also increase your bash shell history, add some safer rm -f aliases, set your default editor, create colorful text, and add open commands for your browser, text editor, and merge tool, as shown in the following listing.

Listing A.6 bash_profile

```
#!/usr/bin/env bash
echo "Running customized ~/.bash_profile script: '$0' ......."
export HISTFILESIZE=10000000
export HISTSIZE-10000000
#  append the history file after each session
shopt -s histappend
#  allow failed commands to be re-edited with Ctrl-R
shopt -s histreedit
#  command substitions are first presented to user before execution
shopt -s histverify
# store multiline commands in a single history entry
shopt -s cmdhist
# check the window size after each command and, if necessary, update the valu
     es of LINES and COLUMNS
shopt -s checkwinsize
# grep results are colorized
```

```
export GREP_OPTIONS='--color=always'
# grep matches are bold purple (magenta)
export GREP_COLOR='1;35;40'
# record everything you ever do at the shell in a file that won't be unintent
    ionally cleared or truncated by the OS
export PROMPT_COMMAND='echo "# cd $PWD" >> ~/
    .bash_history_forever; '$PROMPT_COMMAND
export PROMPT_COMMAND="history -a; history -c; history -r; history 1 >> ~/
    .bash_history_forever; $PROMPT_COMMAND"
# so it doesn't get changed again
readonly PROMPT_COMMAND
# USAGE: subl http://google.com  # opens in a new tab
if [ ! -f /usr/local/bin/firefox ]; then
    ln -s /Applications/Firefox.app/Contents/MacOS/firefox /usr/local/bin/
    firefox
fi
alias firefox='open -a Firefox'
# USAGE: subl file.py
if [ ! -f /usr/local/bin/subl ]; then
    ln -s /Applications/Sublime\ Text.app/Contents/SharedSupport/bin/subl /
    usr/local/bin/subl
fi
# USAGE: meld file1 file2 file3
if [ ! -f /usr/local/bin/meld ]; then
    ln -s /Applications/Meld.app/Contents/MacOS/Meld /usr/local/bin/meld
fi
export VISUAL='subl -w'
export EDITOR="$VISUAL"
# you can use -
    f to override these interactive nags for destructive disk writes
alias rm="rm -i"
alias mv="mv -i"
alias ..="cd .."
alias ...="cd ../.."
```

You can find other bash_profile scripts with a GitHubGist search (https://gist.github
.com/search?q=%22.bash_profile%22+mac).

## A.6  *Windows*

The command-line tools for package management, such as cygwin on Windows, aren't
that great. But if you install GitGUI on a Windows machine, that gets you a bash
prompt and a workable terminal that you can use to run your Python REPL console:

1  Download and install the `git` installer (https://git-scm.com/download/win).
2  Download and install the GitHub Desktop (https://desktop.github.com).

The `git` installer comes with a version of the bash shell that should work well within
Windows, but the `git-gui` that it installs isn't very user friendly, especially for begin-
ners. Unless you're using `git` from the command line (a bash shell within Windows),
you should use GitHub Desktop for all your `git` push/pull/merge needs on Windows. We had problems throughout the editing of this book when `git-gui` did unexpected things that overwrote commits by others whenever there was a version conflict,

even in files that weren't involved in the conflict. So that's why we ask you to install GitHub Desktop (http://desktop.github.com) on top of raw `git` and `git-bash`. GitHub Desktop gives you a more user-friendly `git` experience, letting you know when you need to pull and push or merge some changes.[3]

Once you have a shell running in a Windows terminal, you can install Anaconda and use the `conda` package manager to install the `nlpia` package just like the rest of us, using the instruction in the github repository README (http://github.com/total-good/nlpia).

### A.6.1  *Get Virtual*

If you get frustrated with Windows, you can always install VirtualBox or Docker and create a virtual machine with an Ubuntu OS. That's the subject of a whole book (or at least a chapter), and there are better people at that than we are:

- Jason Brownlee (https://machinelearningmastery.com/linux-virtual-machine-machine-learning-development-python-3)
- Jeroen Janssens (http://datasciencetoolbox.org)
- Vik Paruchuri (www.dataquest.io/blog/docker-data-science)
- Jamie Hall (http://blog.kaggle.com/2016/02/05/how-to-get-started-with-data-science-in-containers)

Another way to get Linux into your Windows world is with Microsoft's Ubuntu shell app. I've not used it, so I can't vouch for its compatibility with the Python packages you'll need to install. If you try it, share what you learn with us at the `nlpia` repository with a feature or pull request on the documentation (https://github.com/totalgood/nlpia/issues). The Manning NLPIA forum (https://forums.manning.com/forums/natural-language-processing-in-action) is also a great place to share your knowledge and get assistance.

## A.7  *NLPIA automagic*

Fortunately for you, `nlpia` has some automatic environment provisioning procedures that will download the NLTK, Spacy, Word2vec models, and the data you need for this book. These downloaders will be triggered whenever you call an `nlpia` wrapper function, like `segment_sentences()`, that requires any of these datasets or models. But this software is a work in progress, continually maintained and expanded by readers like you. So you may want to know how to manually install these packages and download the data you need to make them work for you when the automagic of `nlpia` fails. And you may just be curious about some of the datasets that make sentence parsing and part of speech taggers possible. So, if you want to customize your environment, the remaining appendices show you how to install and configure the individual pieces you need for a full-featured NLP development environment.

---

[3] Big thanks to Benjamin Berg and Darren Meiss at Manning for figuring this out, and for all the hard work they put into making this book presentable.

# appendix B
# *Playful Python and regular expressions*

To get the most out of this book, you'll want to get comfortable with Python. You'll want to be so comfortable that you get playful. When things don't work, you'll need to be able to play around and explore to find a way to make Python do what you want.

And even when your code works, playing around may help you uncover cool new ways of doing things or hidden monsters lurking in your code. Hidden errors and edge cases are very common in natural language processing, because there are so many different ways to say things in a language like English.

To get playful, just experiment with Python code, like children do. If you copy and paste code, change it. Try to break it and then fix it. Pull it apart into as many separate expressions as you can. Create modules out of bits of your code with functions or classes. Then pull it back together into as few lines of code as you can.

Try random things with the data structure or model or function you create. Try to run commands that you think should be included in a module or class. Use the Tab key on your keyboard often. When you press the Tab key, your editor or shell should try to finish your thought by completing the variable, class, function, method, attribute, and path name you started to type.

Use all the `help` that Python and your shell provides. Like `man` in a Linux shell, `help()` is your built-in friend in Python. Try typing `help` or `help(object)` in a Python console. It should work even when the IPython `?` and `??` fail. Try `object?` and `object??` in a Jupyter Console or Notebook if you've never done that before.

The rest of this Python primer introduces the data structures and functions we use throughout this book so you can start playing with them:

- `str` and `bytes`
- `ord` and `chr`
- `.format()`

- dict and OrderedDict
- list, np.array, pd.Series
- pd.DataFrame

We also explain some of the patterns and built-in Python functions we sometimes use here and in the nlpia package:

- List comprehensions—[x for x in range(10)]
- Generators—(x for x in range(1000000000))
- Regular expressions—re.match(r'[A-Za-z ]+', 'Hello World')
- File openers—open('path/to/file.txt')

## B.1 Working with strings

Natural language processing is all about processing strings. And strings have a lot of quirks in Python 3 that may take you by surprise, especially if you have a lot of Python 2 experience. So you'll want to play around with strings and all the ways you can interact with them so you are comfortable interacting with natural language strings.

### B.1.1 String types (str and bytes)

Strings (str) are sequences of Unicode characters. If you use a non-ASCII character in a str, it may contain multiple bytes for some of the characters. Non-ASCII characters pop up a lot if you are copying and pasting from the internet into your Python console or program. And some of them are hard to spot, like those curly asymmetrical quote characters and apostrophes.

When you open a file with the Python open command, it'll be read as a str by default. If you open a binary file, like a pretrained Word2vec model '.txt' file, without specifying mode='b' it won't load correctly. Even though the gensim.Keyed-Vectors model type may be text, not binary, the file must be opened in binary mode so that Unicode characters aren't garbled as gensim loads the model; likewise for a CSV file or any other text file saved with Python 2.

Bytes (bytes) are arrays of 8-bit values, usually used to hold ASCII characters or Extended ASCII characters (with integer ord values greater than 128).[1] Bytes are also sometimes used to store RAW images, WAV audio files, or other binary data blobs.

### B.1.2 Templates in Python (.format())

Python comes with a versatile string templating system that allows you to populate a string with the values of variables. This allows you to create dynamic responses with knowledge from a database or the context of a running python program (locals()).

---

[1] There's no single official Extended ASCII character set, so don't ever use them for NLP unless you want to confuse your machine trying to learn a general language model.

## B.2    *Mapping in Python (dict and OrderedDict)*

Hash table (or mapping) data structures are built into Python in `dict` objects. But a `dict` doesn't enforce a consistent key order, so the `collections` module, in the standard Python library, contains an `OrderedDict` that allows you to store key-value pairs in a consistent order that you can control (based on when you insert a new key).

## B.3    *Regular expressions*

Regular expressions are little computer programs with their own programming language. Each regular expression string like `r'[a-z]+'` can be compiled into a small program designed to be run on other strings to find matches. We provide a quick reference and some examples here, but you'll probably want to dig deeper in some online tutorials, if you're serious about NLP. As usual, the best way to learn is to play around at the command line. The `nlpia` package has a lot of natural language text documents and some useful regular expression examples for you to play with.

A regular expression defines a sequence of conditional expressions (`if` in Python) that each work on a single character. The sequence of conditionals forms a tree that eventually concludes in an answer to the question "is the input string a match or not." Because each regular expression can only match a finite number of strings and has a finite number of conditional branches, it defines a finite state machine (FSM).[2]

The `re` package is the default regex compiler/interpreter in Python, but the new official package is `regex` and can be easily installed with the `pip install regex`. It's more powerful, with better support for Unicode characters and fuzzy matching (pretty awesome for NLP). You don't need those extra features for the examples here, so you can use either one. You only need to learn a few regular expression symbols to solve the problems in this book:

- `|`—The OR symbol.
- `()`—Grouping with parentheses, just like in Python expressions.
- `[]`—Character classes.
- `\s, \b, \d, \w`—Shortcuts to common character classes.
- `*, ?, +`—Some common shortcuts to character class occurrence count limits.
- `{7,10}`—When—`\*`, `?`, and `+` aren't enough, you can specify exact count ranges with curly braces.

### B.3.1    *|—OR*

The `|` symbol is used to separate strings that can alternatively match the input string to produce an overall match for the regular expression. So the regular expression `'Hobson|Cole|Hannes'` would match any of the given names (first names) of this book's authors. Patterns are processed left to right, and "short circuit" when a match

---

[2]  This is only true for strict regular expression syntaxes that don't look-ahead and look-behind.

is made, like most other programming languages. So the order of the patterns between the OR symbols (|) doesn't affect the match, in this case, since all the patterns (author names) have unique character sequences in the first two characters. The following listing shows a shuffling of the author's names so you can see for yourself.

**Listing B.1   Regex OR symbol**

```
>>> import re
>>> re.findall(r'Hannes|Hobson|Cole', 'Hobson Lane, Cole Howard,
➥ and Hannes Max Hapke')
['Hobson', 'Cole', 'Hannes']
```
.findall() searches for all the non-overlapping regex matches within the input string, so it returns them in a list.

To exercise your Python playfulness, see if you can cause the regular expression to short circuit on the first pattern, when a human looking at all three patterns might choose a better match:

```
>>> re.findall(r'H|Hobson|Cole', 'Hobson Lane, Cole Howard,
➥ and Hannes Max Hapke')
['H', 'Cole', 'H', 'H', 'H']
```

## B.3.2   ()—Groups

You can use parentheses to group several symbol patterns into a single expression. Each grouped expression is evaluated as a whole. So r'(kitt|dogg)ie' matches either "kitty" or "doggy." Without the parentheses, r'kitt|doggy' would match "kitt" or "doggy" (notice no "kitty").

Groups have another purpose. They can be used to capture (extract) part of the input text. Each group is assigned a location in the list of groups() that you can retrieve according to their index, left to right. The .group() method returns the default overall group for the entire expression. You can use the previous groups to capture a "stem" (the part without the y) of the kitty/doggy regex, as shown in the following listing.

**Listing B.2   regex grouping parentheses**

```
>>> import re
>>> match = re.match(r'(kitt|dogg)y', "doggy")
>>> match.group()
'doggy'
>>> match.group(0)
'dogg'
>>> match.groups()
('dogg',)
>>> match = re.match(r'((kitt|dogg)(y))', "doggy")
>>> match.groups()
('doggy', 'dogg', 'y')
>>> match.group(2)
'y'
```
If you want to capture each part in its own group

If you want/need to give names to your groups for information extraction into a structured datatype (`dict`), you need to use the `P` symbol at the start of your group, like `(P?<animal_stemm>dogg|kitt)y`.[3]

### B.3.3    *[]—Character classes*

Character classes are equivalent to an OR symbol (`|`) between a set of characters. So `[abcd]` is equivalent to `(a|b|c|d)`, and `[abc123]` is equivalent to `(a|b|c|d|1|2|3)`.

And if some of the characters in a character class are consecutive characters in the alphabet of characters (ASCII or Unicode), they can be abbreviated using a hyphen between them. So `[a-d]` is equivalent to `[abcd]` or `(a|b|c|d)`, and `[a-c1-3]` is an abbreviation for `[abc123]` and `(a|b|c|d|1|2|3)`.

#### CHARACTER CLASS SHORTCUTS

- `\s`—`[ \t\n\r]`—Whitespace characters
- `\b`—A non-letter, non-digit next to a letter or digit
- `\d`—`[0-9]`—A digit
- `\w`—`[a-zA-Z0-9_]`—A word or variable name character

## B.4    *Style*

Try to comply with PEP8 (http://python.org/dev/peps/pep-0008), even if you don't plan on sharing your code with others. Your future self will appreciate being able to efficiently read and debug your code. Adding a linter (http://sublimelinter.com) or automatic style corrector (http://packagecontrol.io/packages/Anaconda) to your editor or IDE is the easiest way to get with the PEP8 program.

One additional style convention that can help with natural language processing is how you decide between the two possible quote characters (`'` and `"`). Whatever you do, try to be consistent. One thing that can help make your code more readable by professionals is to always use the single-quote (`'`) when defining a string intended for a machine, like regular expressions, tags, and labels. Then you can use double quotes (`""`) for natural language corpora intended for human consumption.

What about raw strings (`r''` and `r""`)? All regular expressions should be single-quoted raw strings like `r'match[ ]this'`, even if they don't contain backslashes. Docstrings should be triple-quoted raw strings, like `r""" This function does NLP """`. That way if you ever do add backslashes to your doctests or regular expressions, they will do what you expect.[4]

---

[3] Named regular expression group: What does "P" stand for? (https://stackoverflow.com/questions/10059673).

[4] This stack overflow question explains why (https://stackoverflow.com/q/8834916/623735).

## B.5   *Mastery*

Find an interactive coding challenge website to hone your Python skills before you jump into a production project. You can do one or two of these a week while reading this book:

1 CodingBat (http://codingbat.com)—Fun challenges in an interactive, web-based Python interpreter

2 Donne Martin's Coding Challenges (http://github.com/donnemartin/interactive-coding-challenges)—An open source repository of Jupyter Notebooks and Anki flashcards to help you learn algorithms and data 2

3 DataCamp (http://datacamp.com/community/tutorials)—Pandas and Python tutorials at DataCamp

# appendix C
# Vectors and matrices (linear algebra fundamentals)

Vectors and numbers are the language of machine thought. Bits are the most fundamental "number" that machine computation is based on, a little like letters (characters) are the most fundamental, irreducible part of words, the language of thought for humans. All mathematical operations can be reduced to a few logical operations on sequences of bits. Sequences of characters are processed by human brains when we read in an analogous way. So if we want to teach machines about our words, the first challenge is to come up with vectors to represent characters, words, sentences, and intermediate concepts that the machine will need to work with to produce seemingly intelligent behavior.

## C.1    Vectors

A *vector* is an ordered sequence of numbers without any "skips." In `scikit learn` and `numpy`, a vector is a dense `array`, and it works a lot like a Python list of numbers. The main reason we use numpy arrays rather than Python lists is because they are much faster to work with (100x) and use much less memory (1/4). Plus you can specify vectorized operations like multiplying the entire array by a value without iterating through it with a for loop. This is *very* important when working with a lot of text that contains a lot of information to be represented in these vectors and numbers.

Listing C.1   Create a vector

```
>>> import numpy as np
>>> np.array(range(4))
array([0, 1, 2, 3])
```

440

```
>>> np.arange(4)
array([0, 1, 2, 3])
>>> x = np.arange(0.5, 4, 1)
>>> x
array([ 0.5,  1.5,  2.5,  3.5])
>>> x[1] = 2
>>> x
array([ 0.5,  2,  2.5,  3.5])
>>> x.shape
(4,)
>>> x.T.shape
(4,)
```

An `array` has some properties that `list` doesn't—such as `.shape` and `.T`. The `.shape` attribute contains the length or size of each dimension (the number of objects it holds). We use lowercase letters when we name variables for holding arrays and vectors (or even just numbers), like formal mathematical symbols. In linear algebra, physics, and engineering texts, these letters are often bolded, and sometimes embellished with an arrow above them (especially by professors on chalkboards and whiteboards).

If you've ever heard of a matrix, you've probably heard that it can be thought of as an array of row vectors, like this:

```
>>> np.array([range(4), range(4)])
>>> array([[0, 1, 2, 3],
           [0, 1, 2, 3]])
>>> X = np.array([range(4), range(4)])
>>> X.shape
(2, 4)
>>> X.T.shape
(4, 2)
```

The `T` property returns the *transpose* of the matrix. The *transpose of a matrix* is the matrix flipped along an imaginary diagonal from the top-left corner to the bottom-right. So the following matrix called `A`

```
>>> A = np.array([[1, 2, 3], [4, 5, 6]])
>>> A
array([[1, 2, 3],
       [4, 5, 6]])
```

has a *transpose* of

```
>>> A.T
array([[1, 4],
       [2, 5],
       [3, 6]])
```

So if `A` started out as a collection of row vectors, `A.T` turns those row vectors into column vectors.

## C.1.1   Distances

The distance between two vectors can be measured a lot of different ways. The difference between two vectors is a vector itself, as shown in the following listing.

---
**Listing C.2   Vector difference**

```
>>> A
array([[1, 2, 3],
       [4, 5, 6]])
>>> A[0]
array([1, 2, 3])
>>> A[1]
array([4, 5, 6])
>>> np.diff(A, axis=0)
array([[3, 3, 3]]
>>> A[1] - A[0]
array([3, 3, 3])
```

That [3, 3, 3] vector gives you exactly the distance along each dimension in your two vectors. Imagine these vectors represented blocks and floors in Manhattan for two people: the difference would be the exact directions you'd need to go from one to the other. If you were on the third floor of an apartment on the corner of 1st Street and 2nd Ave, your coordinates in street, avenue, floor coordinates would be [1, 2, 3], just like in the example. And if your Python mentor was on the sixth floor of an apartment on the corner of 4th Street and 5th Ave, her coordinates would be [4, 5, 6]. So the difference between those vectors ([3, 3, 3]) would mean that you'd have to walk three blocks north, three blocks east, and three floors up to reach her apartment. Actually, vectors and math don't care about pesky details like gravity. So the algebra assumes you could skate on your *Back to the Future* hoverboard right out your window and scoot along three floors above the traffic to get to your linear algebra mentor's apartment.

If you told your mentor that her apartment was [3, 3, 3] away from yours, she'd laugh at your geeky precision. Less-geeky people simplify those three numbers into a single number, a scalar, when they talk about distances. So if you said her place is six blocks away, she'd understand exactly what you meant; you ignored the irrelevant floor dimension, since that's a snap on your hoverboard (or the elevator). In addition to ignoring some dimensions, you used a clever distance metric sometimes called the *Manhattan distance*. We show you how to calculate it for 300D word vectors just as easily as 2D apartment location vectors.

### EUCLIDEAN DISTANCE

*Euclidean distance* is the distance you are talking about for 2D vectors when you say "as the crow flies." It's the straight line distance between the two points defined by your vectors (the "tips" or "heads" of those vectors).

Euclidean distance is also called L2 norm, because it's the length of the vector difference between two vectors. The "L" in L2 stands for length. The "2" in L2 represents the exponent (squaring) of the dimensions of the difference vector before these values ares summed (and before the square root of the sum).

Euclidean distance is also called the RSS distance, which stands for the root sum square distance or difference, which means:

```
euclidean_distance = np.sqrt(((vector1 - vector2) ** 2).sum())
```

Let's look at Euclidean distance between some vectors from an NLP example in Patrick Winston's AI lecture series.[1]

Let's say we have 2D term frequency (bag-of-word) vectors that count the occurrences of the words "hack" and "computer" in articles from two publications, *Wired Magazine* and *Town and Country*. And we want to be able to query that set of articles while researching something to find some articles about a particular topic. The query string has both the words "hacking" and "computers" in it. Our query string word vector is [1, 1] for the words "hack" and "computer" because our query tokenized and stemmed the words that way (see chapter 2).

Now which articles would you say are closest to our query in Euclidean distance? Euclidean distance is the length of the four lines in figure C.1. They look pretty similar don't they. How would you fix this problem so that your search engine returns some useful articles for this query?

You could compute the *ratio* of the word counts relative to the total number of words in a document and use these ratios to calculate your Euclidean distance. But you learned in chapter 3 about

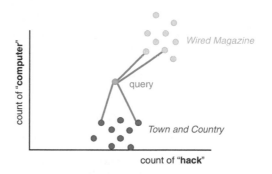

**Figure C.1   Measuring Euclidean distance**

a better way to compute this ratio: TF-IDF. The Euclidean distance between TF-IDF vectors tends to be a good measure of the distance (inverse similarity) of documents.

If you want to bound the Euclidean distance, you can normalize all your vectors to have unit length (each have a length of 1). This will ensure that all distances between your vectors will be between 0 and 2.

### COSINE DISTANCE

Another adjustment to our distance calculation makes our distance value even more useful. *Cosine distance* is the inverse of the *cosine similarity* (cosine_distance = 1 - cosine_similarity). Cosine similarity is the cosine of the angle between two vectors. So in this example, the angle between the TF vector for this query string and the vector for *Wired Magazine* articles would be much smaller than the angle between

---

[1]   Patrick Winston. 6.034 Artificial Intelligence. Fall 2010. Massachusetts Institute of Technology: MIT OpenCourseWare (https://ocw.mit.edu). License: Creative Commons BY-NC-SA. "Lecture 10" (http://mng.bz/nxjK).

the query and the *Town and Country* articles. This is what we want. Because a query about "hacking computers" should give us *Wired Magazine* articles and *not* articles about recreational activities like horse riding ("hacking")[2], duck hunting, dinner parties, and rustic interior design.

This is efficiently computed as the dot product of two normalized vectors, vectors whose values have all been divided by the length of the vector, as shown in the following listing.

**Listing C.3   Cosine distance**

```
>>> import numpy as np
>>> vector_query = np.array([1, 1])
>>> vector_tc = np.array([1, 0])
>>> vector_wired = np.array([5, 6])
>>> normalized_query = vector_query / np.linalg.norm(vector_query)
>>> normalized_tc = vector_tc / np.linalg.norm(vector_tc)
>>> normalized_wired = vector_wired / np.linalg.norm(vector_wired)

>>> normalized_query
array([ 0.70710678,  0.70710678])
>>> normalized_tc
array([ 1.,  0.])
>>> normalized_wired
array([ 0.6401844 ,  0.76822128])
```

The *cosine similarity* between our query TF vector and these other two TF vectors (cosine of the angle between them) is

```
>>> np.dot(normalized_query, normalized_tc)  # cosine similarity
0.70710678118654746
>>> np.dot(normalized_query, normalized_wired)  # cosine similarity
0.99589320646770374
```

The cosine *distance* between our query and these two TF vectors is one minus the cosine similarity.

```
>>> 1 - np.dot(normalized_query, normalized_tc)  # cosine distance
0.29289321881345254
>>> 1 - np.dot(normalized_query, normalized_wired)  # cosine distance
0.0041067935322962601
```

This is why cosine similarity is used for TF vectors in NLP:

- It's easy to compute (just multiplication and addition).
- It has a convenient range (-1 to +1).
- Its inverse (cosine distance) is easy to compute (1 - cosine_similarity).
- Its inverse (cosine distance) is bounded (0 to +2).

---

[2]  See the equestrian use of the word "hack" in the Wikipedia article "Hack (horse)" (https://en.wikipedia.org/wiki/Hack_%28horse%29).

However, cosine distance has one disadvantage compared to Euclidean distance: it isn't a real *distance metric* because the triangle inequality doesn't hold.[3] That means that if the word vector for "red" has a cosine distance of 0.5 from "car" and 0.3 from "apple," "apple" might be much further away than 0.8 from "car." The triangle inequality is mainly important when you want to use cosine distances to try to prove something about some vectors. That's rarely the case in real-world NLP.

### Manhattan distance

Manhattan distance is also called taxicab distance or L1 norm. It's called the taxicab distance because the distance represents how far a taxicab would have to drive to get from one vector to another, if the vectors were 2D vectors with coordinates aligned with a street grid.[4] This distance is also called the L1 norm.

Manhattan distance is super simple to calculate: sum up the absolute distance in all the dimensions. Using our made-up magazine vectors from earlier, the Manhattan distance would be:

```
>>> vector_tc = np.array([1, 0])
>>> vector_wired = np.array([5, 6])
>>> np.abs(vector_tc - vector_wired).sum()
10
```

If your vectors were normalized before calculating Manhattan distance, you'd get a much different distance:

```
>>> normalized_tc = vector_tc / np.linalg.norm(vector_tc)
>>> normalized_wired = vector_wired / np.linalg.norm(vector_wired)
>>> np.abs(normalized_tc - normalized_wired).sum()
1.128...
```

You might hope this distance metric would stay bounded within some range like 0 to 2, but it won't. Like Euclidean distance, Manhattan distance is a real metric, so it obeys the triangle inequality and can be used in mathematical proofs that rely on a true distance metric. But unlike Euclidean distance on normalized vectors, you can't rely on Manhattan distance between normalized vectors to stay bounded in some nice range like 0 to 2. The maximum length possible will grow with the number of dimensions, even if you've normalized your vectors to all have a length of one. For normalized 2D vectors, the maximum Manhattan distance between any two vectors is 2.82 (sqrt(8)). For 3D vectors it's 3.46 (sqrt(12)). Can you guess or compute what it is for 4D vectors?

---

[3] See the Wikipedia article "Cosine similarity," that links to the rules for true distance metrics (http://en.wikipedia.org/wiki/Cosine_similarity).

[4] See the Wikipedia article "Taxicab geometry," (https://en.wikipedia.org/wiki/Taxicab_geometry).

# *appendix D*
# *Machine learning*
# *tools and techniques*

Much of natural language processing involves machine learning. So it pays to understand some of the basic tools and techniques of machine learning. Some have been covered in earlier chapters, some haven't, but all warrant at least a few words here.

## D.1 Data selection and avoiding bias

Data selection and feature engineering are frought with the hazards of bias (in human terms). Once you've baked your own biases into your algorithm, by choosing a particular set of features, the model will fit to those biases and produce biased results. If you're lucky enough to discover this bias before going to production, it can require a significant amount of effort to undo the bias. Your entire pipeline must be rebuilt and retrained to be able to take advantage of the new vocabulary from your tokenizer, for example. You have to start over.

One example is the data and feature selection for the famous Word2vec model. Word2vec was trained on a vast array of news articles and from this corpus some 1 million or so $N$-grams were chosen as the vocabulary (features) for this model. This produced a model that excited data scientists and linguists with the possiblity of math on word vectors, such as "king - man + woman = queen." But as researchers dug deeper, more problematic relationships revealed themselves in the model.

For example, for the expression "doctor - father + mother = nurse," the answer "nurse" wasn't the unbiased and logical result that they'd hoped for. A gender bias was inadvertently trained into the model. Similar racial, religious, and even geographic regional biases are prevalent in the original Word2vec model. The Google researchers didn't create these biases intentionally. The bias is inherent in the data, the statistics of word usage in the Google News corpus they trained Word2vec on.

Many of the news articles simply had cultural biases because they were written by journalists motivated to keep their readers happy. And these journalists were writing about a world with institutional biases and biases in the real-world events and people. The word usage statistics in Google News merely reflect that there are many more mothers who are nurses than doctors. And there are many more fathers who are doctors than are nurses. The Word2vec model is just giving us a window into the world we have created.

Fortunately models like Word2vec don't require labeled training data. So you have the freedom to choose any text you like to train your model. You can choose a dataset that is more balanced, more representative of the beliefs and inferences that you would like your model to make. And when others hide behind the algorithms to say that they're only doing what the model tells them, you can share with them your datasets that more fairly represent a society where we aspire to provide everyone with equal opportunity.

As you're training and testing your models, you can rely on your innate sense of fairness to help you decide when a model is ready to make predictions that affect the lives of your customers. If your model treats *all* of your users the way you would like to be treated, you can sleep well at night. It can also help to pay particularly close attention to the needs of your users that are unlike you, especially those that are typically disadvantaged by society. And if you need more formal justification for your actions, you can learn more about statistics, philosophy, ethics, psychology, behavioral economics, and anthropology to augment the computer science skills you've learned in this book.

As a natural language processing practitioner and machine learning engineer, you have an opportunity to train machines to do better than many humans do. Your bosses and colleagues aren't going to tell you which documents to add or remove from your training set. You have the power to influence the behavior of machines that shape communities and society as a whole.

We've given you some ideas about how to assemble a dataset that's less biased and more fair. Now we'll show you how to fit your models to that unbiased data so that they're also accurate and useful in the real world.

## D.2 How fit is fit?

With any machine learning model, one of the major challenges is overcoming the model's ability to do *too well*. How can something be "too good"? When working with example data in any model, the given algorithm may do very well at finding patterns in that particular dataset. But given that we already likely know the label of any particular example in the training set (or it wouldn't be in the training set), that isn't particularly helpful. The real goal is to use those training examples to build a model that will *generalize*, and be able to correctly label an example that, while similar to members of the training set, is outside of the training set. Performance on new examples that are

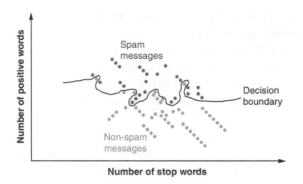

**Figure D.1   Overfit on training samples**

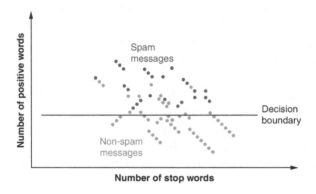

**Figure D.1   Underfit on training samples**

outside the training set is what we want to maximize.

A model that perfectly describes (and predicts) your training examples is *overfit* (see figure D.1). Such a model will have little or no capacity to describe new data. It isn't a general model that you can trust to do well when you give it an example not in your training set.

Conversely, if your model gets many of the training predictions wrong and also does poorly on new examples, it's *underfit* (see figure D.2). Neither of these kinds of models will be useful for making predictions in the real world. So let's look at techniques to detect these issues and, more importantly, ways to avoid them.

## D.3   *Knowing is half the battle*

In machine learning practice, if data is gold, labeled data is raritanium (or whatever metaphor for what is most precious to you). Your first instinct may be to take every last bit of labeled data and feed it to the model. More training data leads to a more resilient model, right? But that would leave us with no way to test the model short of throwing it out into the real world and hoping for the best. This obviously isn't practical. The solution is to split your labeled data into two and sometimes three datasets: a training set, a *validation* set, and in some cases a *test* set.

The training set is obvious. The validation set is a smaller portion of the labeled data we hold out and keep hidden from the model for one round of training. Good performance on the validation set is a first step to verifying that the trained model will perform well in the wild, as novel data comes in. You will often see an 80%/20% or 70%/30% split for training versus validation from a given labeled dataset. The *test* set is like the validation set—a subset of the labeled training data to run the model against and measure performance. But how is this test set different from the validation set then? In formulation, they aren't different at all. The difference comes in how you use each of them.

While training the model on the training set, there will be several iterations with various hyperparameters; the final model you choose will be the one that performs the best on the validation set. But there's a catch. How do you know you haven't tuned a model that's merely highly biased toward the validation set? There's no way to verify that the model will perform well on data from the wild. And this is what your boss or the readers of your white paper are most interested in—how well will it work on *their* data.

So if you have enough data, you want to hold a third chunk of the labeled dataset as a *test set*. This will allow your readers (or boss) to have more confidence that your model will work on data that your training and tuning process was never allowed to see. Once the trained model is selected based on validation set performance, and you're no longer training or tweaking your model at all, you can then run predictions (inference) on each sample in the test set. If the model performs well against this third set of data, it has generalized well. For this kind of high-confidence model verification, you will often see a 60%/20%/20% training/validation/test dataset split.

> **TIP** Shuffling your dataset before you make the split between training, validation, and testing datasets is vital. You want each subset to be a representative sample of the "real world," and they need to have roughly equal proportions of each of the labels you expect to see. If your training set has 25% positive examples and 75% negative examples, you want your test and validation sets to have 25% positive and 75% negative examples, too. And if your original dataset had all the negative examples first and you did a 50%/50% train/test split without shuffling the dataset first, you'd end up with 100% negative examples in your training set and 50%/50% in your test set. Your model would never learn from the positive examples in your dataset.

## D.4 Cross-fit training

Another approach to the train/test split question is *cross-validation* or *k-fold cross-validation* (see figure D.3). The concept behind cross validation is very similar to the rough splits we just covered, but it allows you a path to use the entire labeled set as training. The process involves dividing your training set into $k$ equal sets, or *folds*. You then train your model with $k$-1 of the folds as a training set and validate it against the

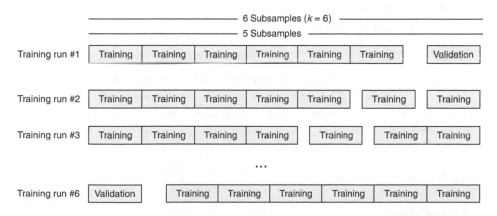

**Figure D.2** *K-fold cross-validation*

*k*-th fold. You then restart the training afresh with one of the *k*-1 sets used in training on the first attempt as your held-out validation set. The remaining *k*-1 folds become your new training set.

This technique is valuable for analyzing the structure of the model and finding hyperparameters that perform well against a variety of validation data. Once your hyperparameters are chosen, you still have to select the *trained* model that performed the best and as such is susceptible to the bias expressed in the previous section, so holding a test set out from this process is still advisable.

This approach also gives you some new information about the reliability of your model. You can compute a P-value for the likelihood that the relationship discovered by your model, between the input features and the output predictions, is statistically significant and not the result of random chance. This is a significantly new piece of information if your training dataset is truly a representative sample of the real world.

The cost of this extra confidence in your model is that it takes *K* times as long to train, for *K*-fold cross-validation. So if you want to get the 90% answer to your problem, you can often simply do 1-fold cross validation. This 1-fold is exactly equivalent to our training set and validation set split that we did earlier. You won't have 100% confidence in the reliability of your model as a description of the real world dynamics, but if it works well on your test set you can be very confident that it is a *useful* model for predicting your target variable. So this is the practical approach that makes sense for most business applications of machine learning models.

## D.5    *Holding your model back*

During the `model.fit()`, the gradient descent is over-enthusiastic about pursuing the lowest possible error in your model. This can lead to overfitting, where your model does really well on the training set but poorly on new unseen examples (the test set). So you probably want to "hold back" on the reins of your model. Here are three ways to do that:

- Regularization
- Random dropout
- Batch normalization

### D.5.1    *Regularization*

In any machine learning model, overfitting will eventually come up. Luckily, several tools can combat it. The first is *regularization*, which is a penalization to the learned parameters at each training step. It's usually, but not always, a factor of the parameters themselves. *L1-norm* and *L2-norm* are the most common.

$$+\lambda \sum_{i=1}^{n} |w_i|$$

**L1 regularization**

L1 is the sum of the absolute values of all the parameters (weights) multiplied by some lambda (a hyperparameter), usually a small float between 0 and 1. This sum is applied to the weights update—the idea being that weights with large magnitudes cause a penalty to be incurred, and the model is encouraged to use more of its weights … evenly.

$$+\lambda \sum_{i=1}^{n} w_i^2$$

**L2 regularization**

Similarly, L2 is a weight penalization, but defined slightly differently. In this case, it's the sum of the weights squared multiplied by some value lambda (a separate hyperparameter to be chosen ahead of training).

## D.5.2 *Dropout*

In neural networks, *dropout* is another handy tool for this situation—one that is seemingly magical on first glance. Dropout is the concept that at any given layer of a neural network we'll turn off a percentage of the signal coming through that layer at training time. Note that this occurs *only* during training, and never during inference. At any given training pass, a subset of the neurons in the layer below are "ignored;" those output values are explicitly set to zero. And because they have no input to the resulting prediction, they'll receive no weight update during the backpropagation step. In the next training step, a different subset of the weights in the layer will be chosen and those others are zeroed out.

How is a network supposed to learn anything with 20% of its brain turned off at any given time? The idea is that no specific weight path should wholly define a particular attribute of the data. The model must generalize its internal structures to be able to handle data via multiple paths through the neurons.

The percentage of the signal that gets turned off is defined as a hyperparameter, because it's a percentage that'll be a float between 0 and 1. In practice, a dropout of .1 to .5 is usually optimal, but of course it's model dependent. And at inference time, dropout is ignored and the full power of the trained weights are brought to bear on the novel data.

Keras provides a very simple way to implement this, and it can be seen in the book's examples and in the following listing.

---

**Listing D.1  A dropout layer in Keras reduces overfitting**

```
>>> from keras.models import Sequential
>>> from keras.layers import Dropout, LSTM, Flatten, Dense

>>> num_neurons = 20                    ◁─┐  Arbitrary hyperparmeters
>>> maxlen = 100                          │  used as an example
>>> embedding_dims = 300
```

```
>>> model = Sequential()

>>> model.add(LSTM(num_neurons, return_sequences=True,
...                input_shape=(maxlen, embedding_dims)))
>>> model.add(Dropout(.2))

>>> model.add(Flatten())
>>> model.add(Dense(1, activation='sigmoid'))
```

.2 here is the hyperparameter, so 20% of the outputs of the LSTM layer above will be zeroed out and therefore ignored.

### D.5.3   Batch normalization

A newer concept in neural networks called *batch normalization* can help regularize and generalize your model. Batch normalization is the idea that, much like the input data, the outputs of each layer should be normalized to values between 0 and 1. There's still some debate about how or why or when this is beneficial, and under which conditions it should be used. We leave it to you to explore that research on your own.

But Keras does provide a handy implementation with its `BatchNormalization` layer, as shown in the following listing.

#### Listing D.2   `BatchNormalization`

```
>>> from keras.models import Sequential
>>> from keras.layers import Activation, Dropout, LSTM, Flatten, Dense
>>> from keras.layers.normalization import BatchNormalization

>>> model = Sequential()
>>> model.add(Dense(64, input_dim=14))
>>> model.add(BatchNormalization())
>>> model.add(Activation('sigmoid'))
>>> model.add(Dense(64, input_dim=14))
>>> model.add(BatchNormalization())
>>> model.add(Activation('sigmoid'))
>>> model.add(Dense(1, activation='sigmoid'))
```

## D.6   Imbalanced training sets

Machine learning models are only ever as good as the data you feed them. Having a huge amount of data is only helpful if you have examples that cover all the cases you hope to predict in the wild. And covering each case only once isn't necessarily enough. Imagine you are trying to predict whether an image is a dog or a cat. But you have a training set with 20,000 pictures of cats and only 200 pictures of dogs. If you were to train a model on this dataset, it would be likely that the model would simply learn to predict any given image is a cat, regardless of the input. And from the model's perspective that would be fine, right? I mean, it would be correct in 99% of the cases from the training set. Of course, that's a bogus argument and that model is worthless. But totally outside the scope of any particular model, the most likely cause of this failure is the *imbalanced training set*.

Models can be very finicky regarding training sets, for the simple reason that the signal from an overly sampled class in the labeled data can overwhelm the signal from the small cases. The weights will more often be updated by the error generated by the dominant class, and the signal from the minority class will be washed out. It isn't vital to get an exactly even representation of each class, because the models have the ability to overcome some noise. The goal here is just to get the counts into the same ballpark.

The first step, as with any machine learning task, is to look long and hard at your data. Get a feel for the details and run some rough statistics on what the data actually represents. Find out not only how much data you have, but how much of which kinds of data you have.

So what do you do if things aren't magical even from the beginning? If the goal is to even out the class representations (and it is), there are three main options: oversampling, undersampling, and augmenting.

## D.6.1 Oversampling

*Oversampling* is the technique of repeating examples from the under-represented class or classes. Let's take the dog/cat example from earlier (only 200 dogs to 20,000 cats). You can simply repeat the dog images you do have 100 times each and end up with 40,000 total samples, half dogs/half cats.

This is an extreme example, and as such will lead to its own problems. The network will likely get very good at recognizing those specific 200 dogs and not generalize well to other dogs not in the training set. But the technique of oversampling can certainly help balance a training set in cases that aren't so radically imbalanced.

## D.6.2 Undersampling

*Undersampling* is the opposite side of the same coin. Here you drop examples from the over-represented class. In the dog/cat example, we would randomly drop 19,800 cat images and be left with 400 examples, half dog/half cat. This, of course, has a glaring problem of its own. We've thrown away the vast majority of the data and are working from a much less broad footing. Extreme cases such as this aren't ideal but can be a good path forward if you have a large number of examples in the under-represented class. Having that much data is definitely a luxury.

## D.6.3 Augmenting your data

This is a little trickier, but in the right circumstances, *augmenting* the data can be your friend. The concept of augmentation is to generate novel data, either from perturbations of the existing data or generating it from scratch. AffNIST (http://www.cs.toronto.edu/~tijmen/affNIST) is such an example. The famous MNIST dataset is a set of handwritten digits, 0-9 (see figure D.4). AffNIST takes each of the digits and skews, rotates, and scales them in various ways, while maintaining the original labels.

**Figure D.3    The entries in the leftmost column are examples from the original MNIST; the other columns are all affine transformations of the data included in affNIST [image credit: "affNIST" (http://www.cs.toronto.edu/~tijmen/affNIST)].**

The purpose of this particular effort wasn't to balance the training set but to make nets such as convolutional neural nets more resilient to new data written in other ways, but the concept of augmenting data still applies.

You must be cautious, though. Adding data that isn't truly representative of that which you're trying to model can hurt more than it helps. Say your dataset is the 200/20,000 dogs/cats from earlier. And let's further assume that the images are all high-resolution color images taken under ideal conditions. Now handing a box of crayons to 19,000 kindergarteners wouldn't necessarily get you the augmented data you desired. So think a bit about what augmenting your data will do to the model. The answer isn't always clear, so if you do go down this path, keep it in mind while you validate the resulting model and try to test around its edges to verify that you didn't introduce unexpected behavior unintentionally.

And lastly, probably the least helpful thing to say, but it's true: going back to the well to look for additional data should always be considered if your dataset is "incomplete." It isn't always feasible, but you should at least consider it as an option.

## D.7    *Performance metrics*

The most important piece of any machine learning pipeline is the performance metric. If you don't know how well your machine learning model is working, you can't make it better. The first thing we do when starting a machine learning pipeline is set up a performance metric, such as ".score()" on any sklearn machine learning model. We then build a completely random classification/regression pipeline with that performance score computed at the end. This lets us make incremental improvements to our pipeline that gradually improve the score, getting us closer to our goal. It's also a great way to keep your bosses and coworkers convinced that you're on the right track.

### D.7.1 *Measuring classifier performance*

A classifier has two things you want it to do right: labeling things that truly belong in the class with that class label, and not labeling things that aren't in that class with that label. The counts of these that it got right are called the true positives and the true negatives, respectively. If you have an array of all your model classifications or predictions in numpy arrays, you can count these correct predictions as shown in the following listing.

---

**Listing D.3 Count what the model got right**

> y_true is a numpy array of the true (correct) class labels. Usually these are determined by a human.

> y_pred is a numpy array of your model's predicted class labels (0 or 1.)

```
>>> y_true = np.array([0, 0, 0, 1, 1, 1, 1, 1, 1, 1])
>>> y_pred = np.array([0, 0, 1, 1, 1, 1, 1, 0, 0, 0])
>>> true_positives = ((y_pred == y_true) & (y_pred == 1)).sum()
>>> true_positives
4
```

> true_positives are the positive class labels (1) that your model got right (correctly labeled 1.)

```
>>> true_negatives = ((y_pred == y_true) & (y_pred == 0)).sum()
>>> true_negatives
2
```

> true_negatives are the negative class labels (0) that your model got right (correctly labeled 0.)

Often it's also important to count up the predictions that your model got wrong, as shown in the following listing.

---

**Listing D.4 Count what the model got wrong**

```
>>> false_positives = ((y_pred != y_true) & (y_pred == 1)).sum()
>>> false_positives
3
>>> false_negatives = ((y_pred != y_true) & (y_pred == 0)).sum()
>>> false_negatives
1
```

> false_negatives are the positive class examples (1) that were falsely labeled negative by your model (labeled 0 when they should be 1.)

> false_positives are the negative class examples (0) that were falsely labeled positive by your model (labeled 1 when they should be 0.)

Sometimes these four numbers are combined into a single 4 × 4 matrix called an error matrix or confusion matrix. The following listing shows what our made-up predictions and truth values would look like in a *confusion matrix*.

---

**Listing D.5 Confusion matrix**

```
>>> confusion = [[true_positives, false_positives],
...              [false_negatives, true_negatives]]
>>> confusion
[[4, 3], [1, 2]]
>>> import pandas as pd
>>> confusion = pd.DataFrame(confusion, columns=[1, 0], index=[1, 0])
```

```
>>> confusion.index.name = r'pred \ truth'
>>> confusion
                1   0
pred \ truth
1               4   1
0               3   2
```

In a confusion matrix, you want to have large numbers along the diagonal (upper left and lower right) and low numbers in the off diagonal (upper right and lower left). However, the order of positives and negatives are arbitrary, so sometimes you may see this table transposed. Always label your confusion matrix columns and indexes. And sometimes you might hear statisticians call this matrix a classifier contingency table, but you can avoid confusion if you stick with the name "confusion matrix."

There are two useful ways to combine some of these four counts into a single performance metric for your machine learning classification problem: *precision* and *recall*. Information retrieval (search engines) and semantic search are examples of such classification problems, since your goal is to classify documents as a match or not. In chapter 2, you learned how stemming and lemmatization can improve recall but reduce precision.

Precision measures how good your model is at detecting all the members of the class you're interested in, called the positive class. For this reason it's also called the positive predictive value. Since your true positives are the positive labels that you got right and false positives are the negative examples that you mislabeled as positive, the precision calculation is as shown in the following listing.

---

**Listing D.6   Precision**

```
>>> precision = true_positives / (true_positives + false_positives)
>>> precision
0.571...
```

The example confusion matrix gives a precision of about 57% because it got 57% of the true labels correct.

The recall performance number is similar. It's also called the sensitivity or the true positive rate or the probability of detection. Because the total number of examples in your dataset is the sum of the true positives and the false negatives, you can calculate recall, the percentage of positive labels that were detected, with the code shown in the following listing.

---

**Listing D.7   Recall**

```
>>> recall = true_positives / (true_positives + false_negatives)
>>> recall
0.8
```

So this says that our example model detected 80% of the positive examples in the dataset.

### D.7.2 Measuring regressor performance

The two most common performance scores used for machine learning regression problems are root mean square error (RMSE) and Pierson correlation ($R^2$). It turns out that classification problems are really regression problems under the hood. So you can use your regression metrics on your class labels if they've been converted to numbers, as we did in the previous section. So these code examples will reuse those example predictions and truth values here. RMSE is the most useful for most problems because it tells you how far away from the truth your predictions are likely to be. RMSE gives you the standard deviation of your error, as shown in the following listing.

#### Listing D.8 RMSE

```
>>> y_true = np.array([0, 0, 0, 1, 1, 1, 1, 1, 1, 1])
>>> y_pred = np.array([0, 0, 1, 1, 1, 1, 1, 0, 0, 0])
>>> rmse = np.sqrt((y_true - y_pred) ** 2) / len(y_true))
>>> rmse
0.632...
```

Another common performance metric for regressors in the Pierson correlation coefficient. The `sklearn` module attaches it to most models as the default `.score()` method. You should calculate these scores manually if you're unclear on exactly what they measure. See the following listing.

#### Listing D.9 Correlation

```
>>> corr = pd.DataFrame([y_true, y_pred]).T.corr()
>>> corr[0][1]
0.218...
>>> np.mean((y_pred - np.mean(y_pred)) * (y_true - np.mean(y_true))) /
...     np.std(y_pred) / np.std(y_true)
0.218...
```

So our example predictions are correlated with the truth by only 28%.

## D.8 Pro tips

Once you have the basics down, some simple tricks will help you build good models faster:

- Work with a small random sample of your dataset to get the kinks out of your pipeline.
- When you're ready to deploy to production, train your model on all the data you have.
- The first approach you should try is the one you know best. This goes for both the feature extractors and the model itself.
- Use scatter plots and scatter matrices on low-dimensional features and targets to make sure you aren't missing some obvious patterns.

- Plot high-dimensional data as a raw image to discover shifting across features.[1]
- Try PCA on high-dimensional data (LSA on NLP data) when you want to maximize the *differences* between pairs of vectors (separation).
- Use nonlinear dimension reduction, like t-SNE, when you want to find *matches* between pairs of vectors or perform regression in the low-dimensional space.
- Build an `sklearn.Pipeline` object to improve the maintainability and reusability of your models and feature extractors.
- Automate the hyperparameter tuning so your model can learn about the data and you can spend your time learning about machine learning.

**HYPERPARAMETER TUNING**   Hyperparameters are all the values that determine the performance of your pipeline, including the model type and how it's configured. This can be things like how many neurons and layers are in a neural network or the value of alpha in a `sklearn.linear_model.Ridge` regressor. Hyperparameters also include the values that govern any preprocessing steps, like the tokenizer type, any list of words that are ignored, the minimum and maximum document frequency for the TF-IDF vocabulary, whether or not to use a lemmatizer, the TF-IDF normalization approach, and so on.

Hyperparameter tuning can be a slow process, because each experiment requires you to train and validate a new model. So it pays to reduce your dataset size to a minimum representative sample while you're searching a broad range of hyperparameters. When your search gets close to the final model that you think is going to meet your needs, you can increase the dataset size to use as much of the data as you need.

Tuning the hyperparameters of your pipeline is how you improve the performance of your model. Automating the hyperparameter tuning can give you more time to spend reading books like this or visualizing and analyzing your results. You can still guide the tuning with your intuition by setting the hyperparameter ranges to try.

**TIP**   The most efficient algorithms for hyperparameter tuning are (from best to worst)

1 Bayesian search
2 Genetic algorithms
3 Random search
4 Multi-resolution grid searches
5 Grid search

But any algorithm that lets your computer do this searching at night while you sleep is better than manually guessing new parameters one by one.

---

[1]   Time series training sets will often be generated with a time shift or lag. Discovering this can help you on Kaggle competitions that hide the source of the data, like the Santander Value Prediction competition (www
.kaggle.com/c/santander-value-prediction-challenge/discussion/61394).

# *appendix E*
# *Setting up your AWS GPU*

If you want to train or run your NLP pipeline quickly, a server with a GPU will often speed things up. GPUs are especially speedy for training a deep neural network when you use a framework such as `Keras` (`TensorFlow` or `Theano`), `PyTorch`, or `Caffe` to build your model. These computational graph frameworks can take advantage of the massively parallel multiplication and addition operations that GPUs are built for.

A cloud service is a great option if you don't want to invest the time and money to build your own server. But it's possible to build a server with a GPU that's twice as fast as a comparable Amazon Web Services (AWS) server for about the cost of a month on a comparable AWS instance. Plus you can store a lot more data with tighter coupling (higher bandwidth) to your machine and often get more RAM than is possible on a single AWS EC2 instance.

With AWS you can be up and running quickly, without having to maintain your own storage devices and servers. Plus most cloud services provide preconfigured hard drive images (ISOs) that can get you up and running much quicker than if you had to configure your own server. For a production system, a cloud provider like AWS or Google Cloud Services (Azure is still playing catch-up) likely makes sense. For recreation and experimentation, you may want to roll your own.

## E.1 Steps to create your AWS GPU instance

1  Go to http://aws.amazon.com to sign up for an account or sign into an existing account. Once you are logged into your account, go to the AWS Management Console (http://console.aws.amazon.com) shown in figure E.1.

2  Select EC2 under All Services; you can also find the EC2 service in the Services menu at the top of the page. The EC2 Dashboard provides summary information about existing EC2 instances (see figure E.2)

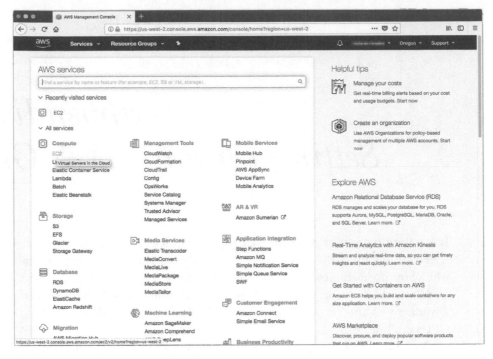

**Figure E.1   AWS Management Console**

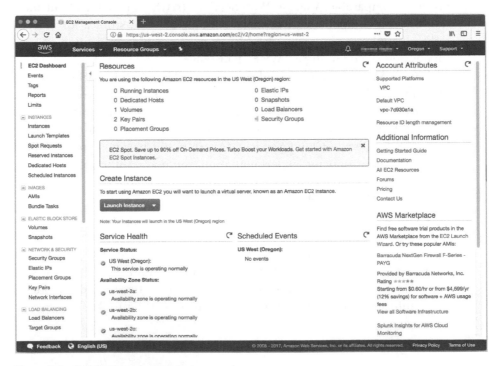

**Figure E.2   Creating a new AWS instance**

3 In the EC2 Dashboard, click the blue Launch Instance button to start the instance setup wizard, a sequence of screens where you can configure the virtual machine you want to launch.

4 This screen (figure E.3) shows the server hard drive images or ISOs you can install on your virtual machine. These are called *Amazon Machine Images* (AMIs) on Amazon.[1] Some AMIs come with deep learning frameworks already installed. That way, you don't need to install and configure the CUDA and BLAS libraries or Python packages such as `TensorFlow`, `numpy`, and `Keras`. To find a free preconfigured deep learning AMI, click the Amazon Marketplace or Community AMIs tab on the left side and search for "deep learning."[2] You must still configure the hardware that makes use of all the software features that a particular AMI provides.

5 Some of the neural network code in this book was tested on the Deep Learning AMI (Ubuntu), which is designed to take advantage of any GPU hardware present on your virtual machine. Click the blue Select button next to the AMI you

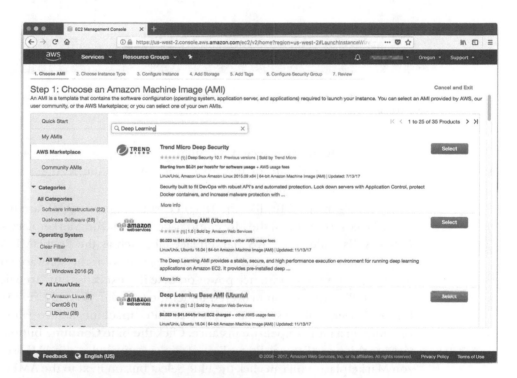

**Figure E.3   Selecting an AWS Machine Image**

---

[1]  ISO is short for ISO-9660, an International Standards Organization open standard for writing disk images in a way that they can be transported and installed elsewhere, not only on one proprietary cloud service, such as AWS.

[2]  At the time of this writing, one such image under the Amazon Marketplace had an AMI ID of *ami-f1d51489*.

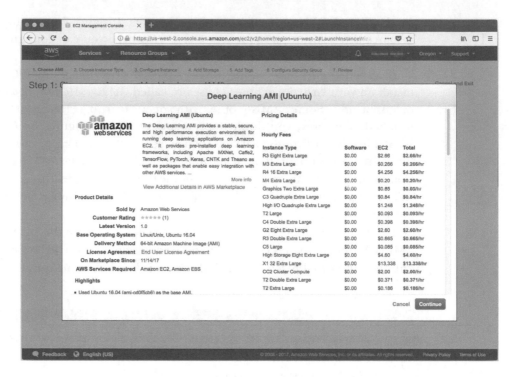

**Figure E.4  Cost overview for the machine image and the available instance types in your AWS region**

want to use. If you've selected an Amazon Marketplace image, you'll be presented with an estimate of the prices for running the AMI on various EC2 instance types that have a GPU (see figure E.4).

6  Many open source AMIs, like the Deep Learning Ubuntu AMI, are free, so the Software cost column on the More Info page for Amazon Marketplace shows $0. Other AMIs under the AWS Marketplace tab, such as the RocketML AMI, may have software costs associated with them. Regardless of the software cost, you'll need to pay for server instance power-on time if it exceeds your "free tier" allowance. A GPU instance isn't covered under the free tier. So make sure your pipeline has been fully tested on a low-cost CPU machine before running your pipeline on a more-expensive instance. Click the blue Continue button if you're viewing this price list (see figure E.4). If you've returned to the AMI lists on Amazon Marketplace, you can click the blue Select button next to the AMI you would like to install on your EC2 instance, which will take you to "Step 2: Choose an Instance Type" (see figure E.5).

7  In this step, you select the server type for your virtual machine (see figure E.5). The smallest GPU instance—g2.2xlarge—is a good value. Amazon's dark pattern UI will preselect a much more expensive type, so you'll have to manually

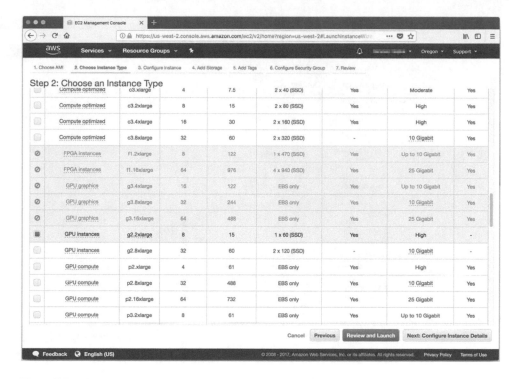

**Figure E.5  Choosing your instance type**

select the g2.2xlarge instance if that's the one you want. Also, you'll find that virtual machines are much cheaper if you've selected US West 2 (Oregon) as your region rather than other US regions. You can find this selection in the menu at the upper-right corner of the page near your account name.

8  Once you've selected the instance type you'd like to use, you can launch your machine by clicking the blue Review and Launch button. But for your first instance, you should work your way through all the setup wizard steps so you can see what your options are, even if you decide to accept the defaults on each of these screens. To proceed to the next step, click the gray Next: Configure Instance Details button.

9  Here you can configure the instance details (see figure E.6). If you are already using AWS machines on an existing *virtual private cloud* (VPC), you can assign your GPU machine to your existing VPC. Machines on the same VPC can use the same gateway or bastion servers on that VPC to access your machine. But if this is your first EC2 instance or you don't have a "bastion server,"[3] you don't need to worry about this.

---

[3] Amazon has a tutorial on the best practices for a Bastion host (https://docs.aws.amazon.com/quickstart/latest/linux-bastion/architecture.html).

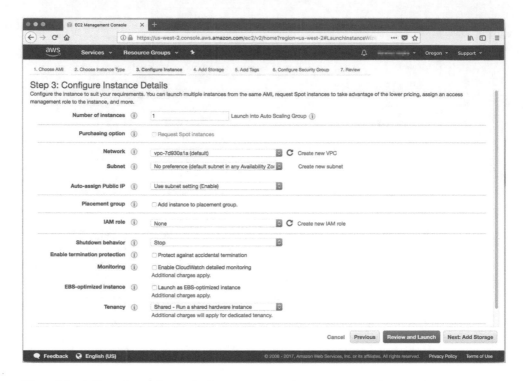

**Figure E.6   Adding storage to your instance**

10  Selecting "Protect against accidental termination" makes it harder for you to accidentally terminate your machine. On Amazon Web Services, "terminate" means to power off a machine and wipe its storage. "Stop" means to power down or suspend the machine while retaining any training checkpoints you may have saved to persistent storage on that machine.

11  To continue, click the Next: Add Storage button.

12  In this step (figure E.7), you can add storage if you plan to work with large corpora. But you may be better off proceeding with a minimal amount of "local" storage on your EC2 instance and waiting to mount an Amazon "S3 Bucket" or other cloud storage service after your EC2 instance is up and running. This will allow you to share large datasets across multiple servers or training runs (between instance terminations). Amazon Web Service will charge you for any "local" EC2 storage above the 30 GB free tier allowance. The AWS UX has a lot of dark patterns that make it hard to avoid racking up charges.

13  Click the Next buttons to proceed through the next steps and review the default tags and security groups assigned to your EC2 instance. The final Next button sends you to the review step (see figure E.8).

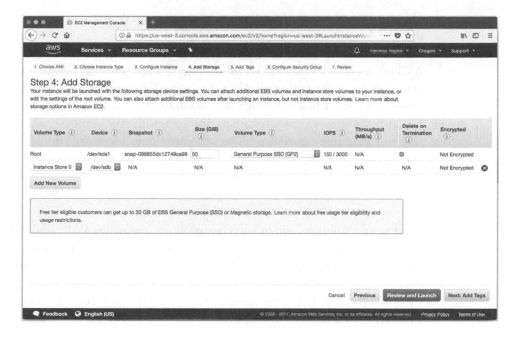

**Figure E.7  Adding persistent storage to your instance**

**Figure E.8  Reviewing your instance setup before launching**

14 On the review screen (see figure E.8), Amazon Web Services shows you the details of your instance in one overview.

15 Confirm that the instance details—particularly the type (RAM and CPU), the AMI image (Deep Learning Ubuntu), and storage (enough GB for your data)—are what you want before clicking the Launch button. At that point, AWS will power up your virtual machine and start loading your software image onto it.

16 If you haven't previously created an instance with AWS, it'll ask you to create a new key pair (see figure E.9). The key pair allows you to ssh into the machine without a password. By default, EC2 instances don't allow password login, so you'll need to save the `.pem` file in your `$HOME/.ssh/` folder and keep a copy of it in a safe place (such as your password manager) or you won't be able to access your running server and will have to start over.

17 After saving your key pair (if you created a new key pair), AWS confirms that the instance is launched. On rare occasions, the Amazon data center may not have the resources you requested and you'll receive an error, requiring you to start over.

18 Click the instance hash that starts with *i-...* (see figure E.10). The link sends you to the overview of all your EC2 instances, where you'll see your instance with its state indicated as "running" or "initializing."

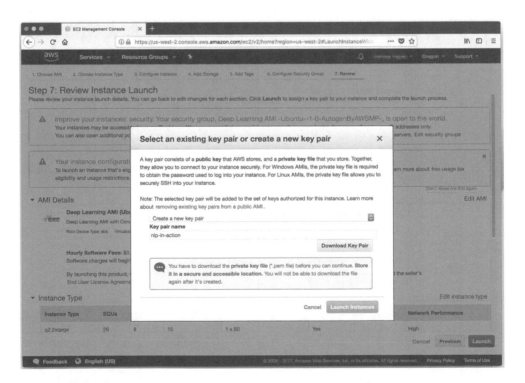

**Figure E.9  Creating a new instance key (or downloading an existing one)**

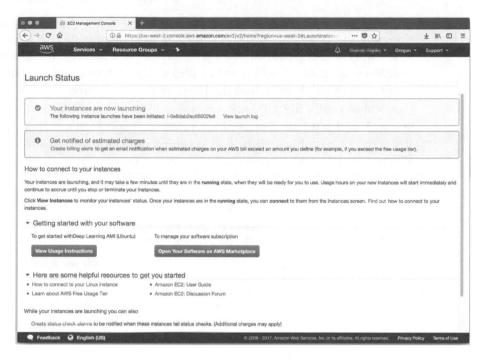

**Figure E.10    AWS launch confirmation**

**Figure E.11    EC2 Dashboard showing the newly created instance**

**19**  You'll want to record the public IP address for your instance (see figure E.11) alongside the `.pem` file for the key pair you generated earlier. A good place to store this is in your password manager with the `.pem` file. You'll also want to put it within your `$HOME/.ssh/config` file, so you can give your instance a host name so you don't have to find the IP address in the future.

   A typical config file will look something like what is shown in the following listing. You'll want to change the `HostName` value to the public IP address (from the EC2 Dashboard) or fully qualified domain name (from your "Route 53" Dashboard on AWS) for your EC2 instance that you just launched.

---

### Listing E.1   $HOME/.ssh/config

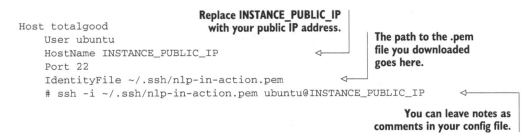

```
Host totalgood
    User ubuntu
    HostName INSTANCE_PUBLIC_IP
    Port 22
    IdentityFile ~/.ssh/nlp-in-action.pem
    # ssh -i ~/.ssh/nlp-in-action.pem ubuntu@INSTANCE_PUBLIC_IP
```

Replace INSTANCE_PUBLIC_IP with your public IP address.

The path to the .pem file you downloaded goes here.

You can leave notes as comments in your config file.

**20**  Before logging into the AWS instance, `ssh` requires that the private key file (`.pem` file in your `$HOME/.ssh` directory) can be read only by you and the root superuser on your system. You can set the appropriate permissions by executing the following bash commands:[4]

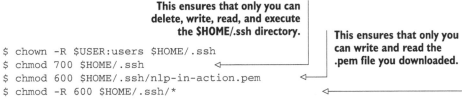

This ensures that only you can delete, write, read, and execute the $HOME/.ssh directory.

This ensures that only you can write and read the .pem file you downloaded.

```
$ chown -R $USER:users $HOME/.ssh
$ chmod 700 $HOME/.ssh
$ chmod 600 $HOME/.ssh/nlp-in-action.pem
$ chmod -R 600 $HOME/.ssh/*
```

This ensures that you can read and write any of the key files in your $HOME/.ssh directory, like the default id_rsa and id_rsa.pub files that may have been generated when your account was created.

**21**  After you've set the appropriate file permissions and set up your config file, execute the following bash command to attempt to log into your EC2 instance:

```
$ ssh -i ~/.ssh/nlp-in-action.pem ubuntu@INSTANCE_PUBLIC_IP
```

**22**  If the Amazon Machine Image is Ubuntu-based, the user name is usually `ubuntu`. But each AMI will have documentation on the user name and ssh port number required to log into it.

---

[4]  A bash shell, like cygwin or git-bash, must be installed for bash ssh commands to work on a Windows system.

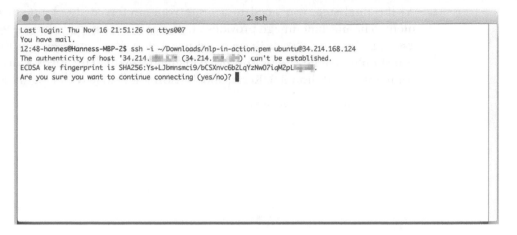

**Figure E.12   Confirmation request to exchange ssh credentials**

**23**   If you log in for the very first time, you're warned that the fingerprint of the machine is unknown (see figure E.12). Confirm with *yes* to go ahead with the login process.[5]

**24**   After a successful login, you see a welcome screen (see figure E.13).

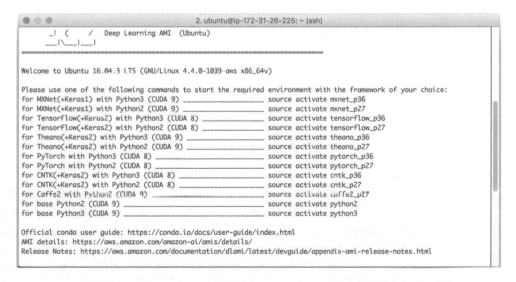

**Figure E.13   Welcome screen after a successful login**

---

[5]   If you see this warning in the future, when you haven't changed its IP address, then you may have someone attempting to spoof the IP address or domain name of your machine and hack into your instance with a man-in-the-middle attack. This is extremely rare.

25  As the final step, you need to activate your preferred development environment. The machine image provides various environments, including `PyTorch`,
`TensorFlow`, and `CNTK`. Because we use TensorFlow and Keras in this book,
you should activate the tensorflow_p36 environment. This loads a virtual environment with Python 3.6, Keras, and TensorFlow installed (see figure E.14):

```
$ source activate tensorflow_p36
```

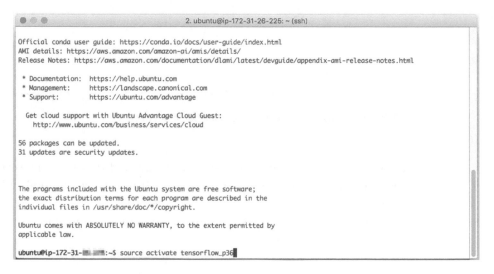

**Figure E.14  Activating your pre-installed Keras environment**

Now that you've activated your TensorFlow environment, you are ready to train
your deep learning NLP models. Head over to an iPython shell with

```
$ ipython
```

Now you're ready to train your models. Have fun!

### E.1.1  Cost control

Running a GPU instance on a cloud service like AWS can quickly get expensive. The
smallest GPU instance in the US-West 2 region costs $0.65 per hour at the time of this
writing. Training a simple sequence-to-sequence model can take a few hours, and then
you might want to iterate on your model parameters. All iterations can quickly add up
to a decent monthly bill. You can minimize surprises with a few precautions (see
figures E.15 and E.16):

- Turn off idle GPU machines. When you stop (not terminate) your machine, the
  last state of the storage (except your /tmp folder) will be preserved and you can
  return to it. In-memory data will be lost, so make sure to save all your model
  checkpoints before stopping the machine.

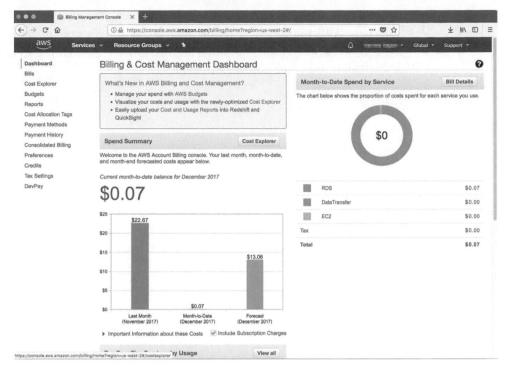

**Figure E.15 AWS Billing Dashboard**

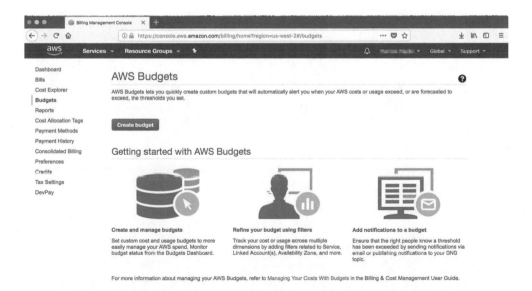

**Figure E.16 AWS Budget Console**

- Check your EC2 instance summary page for running instances.
- Check your AWS bill summary regularly to check for running instances.
- Create an AWS Budget with spending alarms. Once you've configured a budget, AWS will alert you when you are exceeding it.

# *appendix F*
# *Locality sensitive hashing*

In chapter 4, you learned how to create topic vectors with hundreds of dimensions of real-valued (floating point) numbers. In chapter 6, you learned how to create word vectors that have hundreds of dimensions. Even though you can do useful math operations on these vectors, you cannot quickly search them like you can discrete vectors or strings. Databases don't have efficient indexing schemes for vectors of more than four dimensions.[1] To use word vectors and document topic vectors efficiently, you need a search index that can help find the nearest neighbors for any given vector.

You need this to convert the results of vector math into a word or set of words (because the resultant vector is never an exact match for the vector of a word in the English language). You also need it to do semantic search. This appendix shows an example approach based on locality sensitive hashing (LSH).

## F.1 High-dimensional vectors are different

As you add dimensions to vectors going from 1D to 2D and even 3D, nothing much changes about the kinds of math you can do to find nearest neighbors quickly. Let's talk a little bit about conventional approaches used by database indexes for 2D vectors and work our way up to high-dimensional vectors. That will help you see where the math breaks down (becomes impractical).

### F.1.1 Vector space indexes and hashes

Indexes are designed to make looking up something easy. Real-value (`float`) indexes for things like latitude and longitude can't rely on exact matches, like the index of words at the back of a textbook. For 2D real-valued data, most indexes use

---

[1] Some advanced databases such as PostgreSQL can index higher-dimensional vectors, but efficiency drops quickly with dimensionality.

some sort of bounding box to divide a low-dimensional space into manageable chunks. The most common example of an index like this for two-dimensional geographic location information is the postal code systems used in various countries to collect mail addresses within contiguous regions (called ZIP Codes in the US).

You assign a number to each region in 2D space; even though postal code regions aren't rectangular bounding boxes, they serve the same purpose. The military uses bounding boxes with its grid system for dividing up the globe into rectangular bounding boxes and assigning each one a number. In both US ZIP Codes and the military grid system, the numbers for these regions have semantic meaning.

The "locality sensitivity" of hashes like US ZIP Codes comes from the fact that numbers or hashes that are close to each other in ordinal value are close to each other in the 2D space that they're for. For example, the first digit in a US ZIP Code identifies a region, such as the west coast or southwest or the US state they belong to. The next digit (combined with the first) uniquely identifies a particular state. The first three digits uniquely identify a region or large city within that state. Locality sensitivity of US zip codes continues all the way down to the "+4" suffix, which identifies a particular city block or even apartment building.[2]

The manual process and algorithm that produced the US ZIP Code system is equivalent to the locality sensitive hashing algorithms created for other vector spaces. Locality sensitive hashing algorithms define a way to produce these locality sensitive numbers. They use the coordinates of locations in a vector space so that the numerical value of the hashes are close to each other if the locations of the regions they map to in the vector space are also close to each other or even overlap. Locality sensitive hashes try to create those same mathematical properties like a high probability of collision and locality sensitivity that cryptographic hashing algorithms try to avoid.

### F.1.2  *High-dimensional thinking*

Natural language vector spaces are high dimensional. Natural language captures all the complex concepts that humans think and talk about, including natural language processing itself. So when you want to squeeze all that complexity into a vector, you often discard some of that complexity so it'll fit in your rigid vector-space box. And you keep adding dimensions to your vector to accommodate as much of the complexity of human thought and language as you can.

For example, bag-of-words vectors discard the information content contained in the order of words. This allows you to produce discrete high-dimensional vectors that you can index and search efficiently. You use binary search and indexing trees to detect whether or not particular keywords are present or absent in both your query and your corpus. This works even if you expand your keyword vocabulary to include all the words in a natural language. Web search engines often even include all the

---

[2]  The ZIP Code Wikipedia article contains a map that shows this locality sensitivity (https://en.wikipedia.org/wiki/ZIP_Code#Primary_state_prefixes).

words in hundreds of natural languages at once. That's why your web search can include Spanish and German words alongside English words all in the same query.

You learned in chapter 2 how to capture a bit of the complexity of the order of words by adding *N*-grams to your bag-of-words vector dimensions. And you learned in chapter 3 how to weight those millions of terms (words and *N*-grams) according to how important they are. This leaves you with millions of dimensions or "bins" in your vector space model of human languages.

But bag-of-words, TF-IDF, and regular expressions can't understand you. They can only help you find the documents you're looking for. So in chapter 4 through chapter 6, you allowed your vector spaces to become continuous. You squeezed some of the complexity of natural language into the gaps in the number line between the integer counts of words. You no longer relied on a rigid, discrete vocabulary to define the dimensions of your vector space. By grouping words into concepts or topics you reduced the dimensions of your vectors from millions down to hundreds. You created nessvectors that captured the femaleness and blueness and placeness of words and statements.

And there's more. In chapters 7 through 10, you figured out how to capture not only word combinations, but long, complex word sequences in your vectors. Your shallow nessvectors became deep thought vectors when you learned about recurrent neural networks and long short-term memory.

But all this depth and complexity creates a problem. Continuous, dense, high-dimensional vectors like thought vectors cannot be indexed or searched efficiently. That's why search engines don't just answer your complex question in a millisecond. When you want to know the meaning of life, you have to have a conversation with a chatbot, or, perish the thought, another human being.

Why is that? Why can't you index or search a high-dimensional continuous vector? Start with a 1D vector "space" and see how easy it is to index and search a single scalar value on a 1D number line. Then you can think about how to extend that 1D index to handle multiple dimensions. And you can keep going up in dimensionality from there until things break down.

### A 1D INDEX

Imagine a random distribution of 1D vectors—a bunch of random numbers. You can create a natural 1D bounding box that's half the width of the overall space by cutting the number line in half. You could put all the positive values in one box and the negative values in another box. As long as you have a pretty good idea where the middle or centroid of your vector space is located (usually zero), each box will have about half the number of vectors in it.

Each of those bounding boxes could be split in half again to create a total of four boxes. If you kept that up, a few more of those divisions would create a binary search tree or a binary hash that's sensitive to locality (where it's located). For a 1D vector space, the average number of points in each box is `pow(num_vectors/2, num _boxes)`. For 1D space, you need only about 32 levels (box sizes) for your boxes to index billions of points so that there are only a few in each box.

Each of your 1D vectors can have its own ZIP Code, an index value or locality sensitive hash. And all the vectors that are similar to each other will be nearby in a sorted list of all those hash values. That way you can compute the hash values for some new query and find it quickly in your database.

## 2D, 3D, 4-D INDEXES

Let's add a dimension and see how well the 1D binary tree index will work. Think about how you'd divide the space into regions in a binary tree, dividing your region approximately in half with each fork in the tree. Which dimension would you cut in half each time you tried to reduce the number points by half? For a 2D vector this would be the $2 \times 2$ squares or quadrants of 2D plane. For a 3D vector this might be the $3 \times 3 \times 3$ blocks in a "Rubix Cube" of space. For 4-D you'd need about $4 \times 4 \times 4 \times 4$ blocks... to get started. The first fork in your binary tree index would create $4\char`^4\char`^$ branches. And some of those 256 bounding boxes in your 4-D vector space might not contain any vectors at all. Some word combinations or sequences never occur.

Our naive binary tree approach works OK for 3D and 4-D vectors and even all the way out to 8-D or more. But it quickly gets unruly and inefficient. Imagine what your bounding "cubes" would be like in 10 dimensions. You're not alone if your brain can't handle that concept. Human brains live in a 3D world, so they aren't capable of fully grasping even 4-D vector space concepts.

Machines can handle 10-D OK, but you need them to handle 100-D or more if you want to squeeze the complexity of human thought into vectors. You can think of this curse of dimensionality in a few different ways:

- The possible combinations of dimensions grows exponentially with each added dimension.
- All vectors are far away from each other in high-dimensional spaces.
- High-dimensional vector spaces are mostly empty space—a random bounding box is almost always empty.

The following code may help you get a feel for these properties of high-dimensional spaces.

### Listing F.1  Explore high-dimensional space

```
>>> import pandas as pd
>>> import numpy as np
>>> from tqdm import tqdm

>>> num_vecs = 100000
>>> num_radii = 20
>>> num_dim_list = [2, 4, 8, 18, 32, 64, 128]
>>> radii = np.array(list(range(1, num_radii + 1)))
>>> radii = radii / len(radii)
>>> counts = np.zeros((len(radii), len(num_dims_list)))
>>> rand = np.random.rand
```

```
>>> for j, num_dims in enumerate(tqdm(num_dim_list)):      ┐  Normalize a table of
...     x = rand(num_vecs, num_dims)                       │  random row vectors
...     denom = (1. / np.linalg.norm(x, axis=1))        ◄──┘  to all have unit length.
...     x *= denom.reshape(-1, 1).dot(np.ones((1, x.shape[1])))
...     for i, r in enumerate(radii):
...         mask = (-r < x) & (x < r)
...         counts[i, j] = (mask.sum(axis=1) == mask.shape[1]).sum()
```

You can explore this weird world of high-dimensional spaces in `nlpia/book/examples/ch_app_h.py` on github (http://github.com/totalgood/nlpia). You can see much of the weirdness in the following table, which shows the density of points in each bounding box as you expand its size bit by bit:

```
>>> df = pd.DataFrame(counts, index=radii, columns=num_dim_list) / num_vecs
>>> df = df.round(2)
>>> df[df == 0] = ''
>>> df
         2     4     8    18    32    64   128
0.05
0.10
0.15                                     0.37
0.20                               0.1     1
0.25                                 1     1
0.30                          0.55   1     1
0.35                    0.12  0.98   1     1
0.40                    0.62     1   1     1
0.45              0.03  0.92     1   1     1
0.50              0.2   0.99     1   1     1
0.55        0.01  0.5     1     1   1     1
0.60        0.08  0.75    1     1   1     1
0.65        0.24  0.89    1     1   1     1
0.70        0.45  0.96    1     1   1     1
0.75  0.12  0.64  0.99    1     1   1     1
0.80  0.25  0.78    1     1     1   1     1
0.85  0.38  0.88    1     1     1   1     1
0.90  0.51  0.94    1     1     1   1     1
0.95  0.67  0.98    1     1     1   1     1
1.00     1     1    1     1     1   1     1
```

There's an indexing algorithm called a KD-Tree (https://en.wikipedia.org/wiki/K-d _tree) that attempts to divide up high-dimensional spaces as efficiently as possible to minimize empty bounding boxes. But even these approaches break down at dozens or hundreds of dimensions as the curse of dimensionality kicks in. Unlike 2D and 3D vectors, it's not possible to truly index or hash high-dimensional word and thought vectors in a way that allows you to retrieve the closest matches quickly. You have to just calculate the distance to a lot of guesses for the nearest neighbors until you find a few that are close. Or you have to check them all, if you want to be sure you didn't miss any.

## F.2 High-dimensional indexing

In high-dimensional space, conventional indexes that rely on bounding boxes fail. Eventually, even locality sensitive hashing fails. But let's first experiment with locality sensitive hashing to show its limitations. Then you will learn how to get around those limitations by giving up on the idea of a perfect index. You will create an approximate index after an experiment with locality sensitive hashing.

### F.2.1 Locality sensitive hashing

In figure F.1, we constructed 400,000 completely random vectors, each with 200 dimensions (typical for topic vectors for a large corpus). And we indexed them with the Python LSHash package (`pip install lshash3`). Now imagine that you have a search engine that wants to find all the topic vectors that are close to a query topic vector. How many will be gathered up by the locality sensitive hash? And for what number of dimensions for the topic vectors do your search results cease to make much sense at all?

| D | N | 100th Cosine Distance | Top 1 Correct | Top 2 Correct | Top 10 Correct | Top 100 Correct |
|---|------|-----------|------|------|------|------|
| 2 | 4254 | 0 | TRUE | TRUE | TRUE | TRUE |
| 3 | 7727 | 0.0003 | TRUE | TRUE | TRUE | TRUE |
| 4 | 12198 | 0.0028 | TRUE | TRUE | TRUE | TRUE |
| 5 | 9920 | 0.0143 | TRUE | TRUE | TRUE | TRUE |
| 6 | 11310 | 0.0166 | TRUE | TRUE | TRUE | TRUE |
| 7 | 12002 | 0.0246 | TRUE | TRUE | TRUE | FALSE |
| 8 | 11859 | 0.0334 | TRUE | TRUE | TRUE | FALSE |
| 9 | 6958 | 0.0378 | TRUE | TRUE | TRUE | FALSE |
| 10 | 5196 | 0.0513 | TRUE | TRUE | FALSE | FALSE |
| 11 | 3019 | 0.0695 | TRUE | TRUE | TRUE | FALSE |
| 12 | 12263 | 0.0606 | TRUE | TRUE | FALSE | FALSE |
| 13 | 1562 | 0.0871 | TRUE | TRUE | FALSE | FALSE |
| 14 | 733 | 0.1379 | TRUE | FALSE | FALSE | FALSE |
| 15 | 6350 | 0.1375 | TRUE | TRUE | FALSE | FALSE |
| 16 | 10980 | 0.0942 | TRUE | TRUE | FALSE | FALSE |

**Figure F.1  Semantic search with LSHash**

You can't get many search results correct once the number of dimensions gets significantly above 10 or so. If you'd like to play with this yourself, or try your hand at building a better LSH algorithm, the code for running experiments like this is available in the `nlpia` package. And the `lshash3` package is open source, with only about 100 lines of code at the heart of it.

### F.2.2   *Approximate nearest neighbors*

Approximate nearest neighbor search is the latest answer to the high-dimensional vector space problem. The approximate hashes are similar to locality sensitive hashes and KD-trees, but they rely on something that's more like a random forest algorithm. They're stochastic (random) approaches to splitting your vector space into smaller and smaller chunks of space.

The state of the art for finding the closest matches for high-dimensional vectors is Facebook's FAISS package and Spotify's `Annoy` package. Because `Annoy` is so easy to install and use, that's what we chose to use for your chatbot. In addition to it being the workhorse for finding matches among vectors representing song metadata for music fans, Dark Horse Comics has also used `Annoy` to suggest comic books efficiently. We mentioned these tools in chapter 13.

## F.3   *"Like" prediction*

Figure F.2 is what a collection of tweets looks like in hyperspace. These are the 2D shadows of 100D tweet topic vectors (points) from latent semantic analysis of those tweets. Most of the marks represent tweets that were liked at least once; a minority of marks are for tweets that received zero likes.

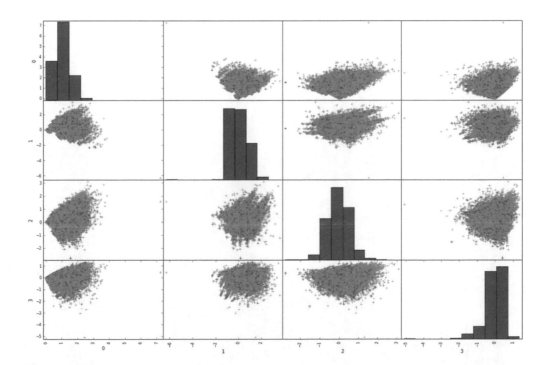

**Figure F.2   Scatter matrix of four topics for tweets**

An LDA model fit to these topic vectors will succeed 80% of the time. However, like your SMS dataset, your tweet dataset is also very imbalanced. So predicting the likability of new tweets using this model isn't likely to be very accurate. You should probably only use LSA, LDA, and LDiA language models for classification problems where variance maximization (class separability) is helpful:

- Semantic search
- Sentiment analysis
- Spam detection

For more subtle discrimination between texts that rely on generalizing from similarities in semantic content, you'll want the most sophisticated NLP tools in your toolbox. Use LSTM deep learning models and t-SNE dimension reduction techniques to solve difficult problems such as

- Human reaction prediction (tweet likability)
- Machine translation
- Natural language generation

# *resources*

In writing this book we pulled from numerous resources. Here are some of our favorites.

In an ideal world, you could find these resources yourself simply by entering the heading text into a semantic search engine like Duck Duck Go (http://duckduckgo .com), Gigablast (http://gigablast.com/search?c=main&q=open+source+search+ engine), or Qwant (https://www.qwant.com/web). But until Jimmy Wales takes another shot at Wikia Search (https://en.wikipedia.org/wiki/Wikia_Search) or Google shares their NLP technology, we have to rely on 1990s-style lists of links like this. Check out the "Search engines" section if your contribution to saving the world includes helping open source projects that index the web.

## Applications and project ideas

Here are some applications to inspire your own NLP projects:

- Guessing passwords from social network profiles (http://www.sciencemag .org/news/2017/09/artificial-intelligence-just-made-guessing-your-password -whole-lot-easier).
- *Chatbot lawyer overturns 160,000 parking tickets in London and New York* (www .theguardian.com/technology/2016/jun/28/chatbot-ai-lawyer-donotpay- parking-tickets-london-new-york).
- *GitHub - craigboman/gutenberg: Librarian working with project gutenberg data, for NLP and machine learning purposes* (https://github.com/craigboman/ gutenberg).
- *Longitudial Detection of Dementia Through Lexical and Syntactic Changes in Writing* (ftp://ftp.cs.toronto.edu/dist/gh/Le-MSc-2010.pdf)—Masters thesis by Xuan Le on psychology diagnosis with NLP.
- *Time Series Matching: a Multi-filter Approach* by Zhihua Wang (https://www .cs.nyu.edu/web/Research/Theses/wang_zhihua.pdf)—Songs, audio clips, and other time series can be discretized and searched with dynamic programming algorithms analogous to Levenshtein distance.

- NELL, Never Ending Language Learning (http://rtw.ml.cmu.edu/rtw/publications)—CMU's constantly evolving knowledge base that learns by scraping natural language text.
- *How the NSA identified Satoshi Nakamoto* (https://medium.com/cryptomuse/how-the-nsa-caught-satoshi-nakamoto-868affcef595)—*Wired Magazine* and the NSA identified Satoshi Nakamoto using NLP, or stylometry.
- Stylometry (https://en.wikipedia.org/wiki/Stylometry) and Authorship Attribution for Social Media Forensics (http://www.parkjonghyuk.net/lecture/2017-2nd-lecture/forensic/s8.pdf)—Style/pattern matching and clustering of natural language text (also music and artwork) for authorship and attribution.
- Online dictionaries like Your Dictionary (http://examples.yourdictionary.com/) can be scraped for grammatically correct sentences with POS labels, which can be used to train your own Parsey McParseface (https://ai.googleblog.com/2016/05/announcing-syntaxnet-worlds-most.html) syntax tree and POS tagger.
- *Identifying 'Fake News' with NLP* (https://nycdatascience.com/blog/student-works/identifying-fake-news-nlp/) by Julia Goldstein and Mike Ghoul at NYC Data Science Academy.
- simpleNumericalFactChecker (https://github.com/uclmr/simpleNumericalFactChecker) by Andreas Vlachos (https://github.com/andreasvlachos) and information extraction (see chapter 11) could be used to rank publishers, authors, and reporters for truthfulness. Might be combined with Julia Goldstein's "fake news" predictor.
- The artificial-adversary (https://github.com/airbnb/artificial-adversary) package by Jack Dai, an intern at Airbnb—Obfuscates natural language text (turning phrases like 'you are great' into 'ur gr8'). You could train a machine learning classifier to detect and translate English into obfuscated English or L33T (https://sites.google.com/site/inhainternetlanguage/different-internet-languages/l33t). You could also train a stemmer (an autoencoder with the obfuscator generating character features) to decipher obfuscated words so your NLP pipeline can handle obfuscated text without retraining. Thank you Aleck.

## Courses and tutorials

Here are some good tutorials, demonstrations, and even courseware from renowned university programs, many of which include Python examples:

- *Speech and Language Processing* (https://web.stanford.edu/~jurafsky/slp3/ed3book.pdf) by David Jurafsky and James H. Martin—The next book you should read if you're serious about NLP. Jurafsky and Martin are more thorough and rigorous in their explanation of NLP concepts. They have whole chapters on topics that we largely ignore, like finite state transducers (FSTs), hidden Markhov models (HMMs), part-of-speech (POS) tagging, syntactic parsing, discourse coherence, machine translation, summarization, and dialog systems.
- MIT Artificial General Intelligence course 6.S099 (https://agi.mit.edu) led by Lex Fridman Feb 2018—MIT's free, interactive (public competition!) AGI

course. It's probably the most thorough and rigorous free course on artificial intelligence engineering you can find.

- *Textacy: NLP, before and after spaCy* (https://github.com/chartbeat-labs/textacy) —Topic modeling wrapper for SpaCy.
- MIT Natural Language and the Computer Representation of Knowledge course 6-863j lecture notes (http://mng.bz/vOdM) for Spring 2003.
- *Singular value decomposition (SVD)* (http://people .revoledu.com/kardi/tutorial/ LinearAlgebra/SVD.html) by Kardi Teknomo, PhD.
- *An Introduction to Information Retrieval* (https://nlp.stanford.edu/IR-book/pdf/ irbookonlinereading.pdf) by Christopher D. Manning, Prabhakar Raghavan, and Hinrich Schütze.

## Tools and packages

- `nlpia` (http://github.com/totalgood/nlpia)—NLP datasets, tools, and example scripts from this book
- `OpenFST` (http://openfst.org/twiki/bin/view/FST/WebHome) by Tom Bagby, Dan Bikel, Kyle Gorman, Mehryar Mohri et al.—Open Source C++ Finite State Transducer implementation
- `pyfst` (https://github.com/vchahun/pyfst) by Victor Chahuneau—A Python interface to OpenFST
- Stanford `CoreNLP`—Natural language software (https://stanfordnlp.github.io/ CoreNLP/) by Christopher D. Manning et al.—Java library with state-of-the-art sentence segmentation, datetime extraction, POS tagging, grammar checker, and so on
- `stanford-corenlp 3.8.0` (https://pypi.org/project/stanford-corenlp/)— Python interface to Stanford `CoreNLP`
- `keras` (https://blog.keras.io/)—High-level API for constructing both Tensor-Flow and Theano computational graphs (neural nets)

## Research papers and talks

One of the best way to gain a deep understanding of a topic is to try to repeat the experiments of researchers and then modify them in some way. That's how the best professors and mentors "teach" their students, by just encouraging them to try to duplicate the results of other researchers they're interested in. You can't help but tweak an approach if you spend enough time trying to get it to work for you.

### Vector space models and semantic search

- *Semantic Vector Encoding and Similarity Search Using Fulltext Search Engines* (https:// arxiv.org/pdf/1706.00957.pdf)—Jan Rygl et al. were able to use a conventional inverted index to implement efficient semantic search for all of Wikipedia.
- *Learning Low-Dimensional Metrics* (https://papers.nips.cc/paper/7002-learning-low-dimensional-metrics.pdf)—Lalit Jain et al. were able to incorporate human

judgement into pairwise distance metrics, which can be used for better decision-making and unsupervised clustering of word vectors and topic vectors. For example, recruiters can use this to steer a content-based recommendation engine that matches resumes with job descriptions.

- *RAND-WALK: A latent variable model approach to word embeddings* (https://arxiv.org/pdf/1502.03520.pdf) by Sanjeev Arora, Yuanzhi Li, Yingyu Liang, Tengyu Ma, and Andrej Risteski—Explains the latest (2016) understanding of the "vector-oriented reasoning" of Word2vec and other word vector space models, particularly analogy questions

- *Efficient Estimation of Word Representations in Vector Space* (https://arxiv.org/pdf/1301.3781.pdf) by Tomas Mikolov, Greg Corrado, Kai Chen, and Jeffrey Dean at Google, Sep 2013—First publication of the Word2vec model, including an implementation in C++ and pretrained models using a Google News corpus

- *Distributed Representations of Words and Phrases and their Compositionality* (https://papers.nips.cc/paper/5021-distributed-representations-of-words-and-phrases-and-their-compositionality.pdf) by Tomas Mikolov, Ilya Sutskever, Kai Chen, Greg Corrado, and Jeffrey Dean at Google—Describes refinements to the Word2vec model that improved its accuracy, including subsampling and negative sampling

- *From Distributional to Semantic Similarity* (https://www.era.lib.ed.ac.uk/bitstream/handle/1842/563/IP030023.pdf) 2003 Ph.D. Thesis by James Richard Curran—Lots of classic information retrieval (full-text search) research, including TF-IDF normalization and page rank techniques for web search

## Finance

- *Predicting Stock Returns by Automatically Analyzing Company News Announcements* (http://www.stagirit.org/sites/default/files/articles/a_0275_ssrn-id2684558.pdf)—Bella Dubrov used gensim's Doc2vec to predict stock prices based on company announcements with excellent explanations of `Word2vec` and `Doc2vec`.

- *Building a Quantitative Trading Strategy to Beat the S&P 500* (https://www.youtube.com/watch?v=ll6Tq-wTXXw)—At PyCon 2016, Karen Rubin explained how she discovered that female CEOs are predictive of rising stock prices, though not as strongly as she initially thought.

## Question answering systems

- *Keras-based LSTM/CNN models for Visual Question Answering* (https://github.com/avisingh599/visual-qa) by Avi Singh

- *Open Domain Question Answering: Techniques, Resources and Systems* (http://lml.bas.bg/ranlp2005/tutorials/magnini.ppt) by Bernardo Magnini

- *Question Answering Techniques for the World Wide Web* by Lin Katz, University of Waterloo, Canada (https://cs.uwaterloo.ca/~jimmylin/publications/Lin_Katz _EACL2003_tutorial.pdf)

- *NLP-Question-Answer-System* (https://github.com/raoariel/NLP-Question-Answer -System/blob/master/simpleQueryAnswering.py)—Built from scratch using `corenlp` and `nltk` for sentence segmenting and POS tagging

- *PiQASso: Pisa Question Answering System* (http://trec.nist.gov/pubs/trec10/ papers/piqasso.pdf) by Attardi et al., 2001—Uses traditional information retrieval (IR) NLP

### Deep learning

- *Understanding LSTM Networks* (https://colah.github.io/posts/2015-08-Under- standing-LSTMs) by Christopher Olah—A clear and correct explanation of LSTMs

- *Learning Phrase Representations using RNN Encoder–Decoder for Statistical Machine Translation* (https://arxiv.org/pdf/1406.1078.pdf) by Kyunghyun Cho et al., 2014—Paper that first introduced gated recurrent units, making LSTMs more efficient for NLP

### LSTMs and RNNs

We had a lot of difficulty understanding the terminology and architecture of LSTMs. This is a gathering of the most cited references, so you can let the authors "vote" on the right way to talk about LSTMs. The state of the Wikipedia page (and Talk page discussion) on LSTMs is a pretty good indication of the lack of consensus about what LSTM means:

- *Learning Phrase Representations using RNN Encoder-Decoder for Statistical Machine Translation* (https://arxiv.org/pdf/1406.1078.pdf) by Cho et al.—Explains how the contents of the memory cells in an LSTM layer can be used as an embedding that can encode variable length sequences and then decode them to a new variable length sequence with a potentially different length, translating or transcoding one sequence into another.

- *Reinforcement Learning with Long Short-Term Memory* (https://papers.nips.cc/paper /1953-reinforcement-learning with long short-term-memory.pdf) by Bram Bakker—Application of LSTMs to planning and anticipation cognition with demonstrations of a network that can solve the T-maze navigation problem and an advanced pole-balancing (inverted pendulum) problem.

- *Supervised Sequence Labelling with Recurrent Neural Networks* (https://mediatum .ub.tum.de/doc/673554/file.pdf)—Thesis by Alex Graves with advisor B. Brugge; a detailed explanation of the mathematics for the exact gradient for LSTMs as first proposed by Hochreiter and Schmidhuber in 1997. But Graves fails to define terms like CEC or LSTM *block/cell* rigorously.

- Theano LSTM documentation (http://deeplearning.net/tutorial/lstm.html) by Pierre Luc Carrier and Kyunghyun Cho—Diagram and discussion to explain the LSTM implementation in Theano and Keras.
- *Learning to Forget: Continual Prediction with LSTM* (http://mng.bz/4v5V) by Felix A. Gers, Jurgen Schmidhuber, and Fred Cummins—Uses nonstandard notation for layer inputs ($\mathbf{y}^{in}$) and outputs ($\mathbf{y}^{out}$) and internal hidden state ($h$). All math and diagrams are "vectorized."
- *Sequence to Sequence Learning with Neural Networks* (http://papers.nips.cc /paper/ 5346-sequence-to-sequence-learning-with-neural-networks.pdf) by Ilya Sutskever, Oriol Vinyals, and Quoc V. Le at Google.
- *Understanding LSTM Networks* (http://colah.github.io/posts/2015-08-Understanding-LSTMs) 2015 blog by Charles Olah—lots of good diagrams and discussion/feedback from readers.
- *Long Short-Term Memory* (http://www.bioinf.jku.at/publications/older/2604 .pdf) by Sepp Hochreiter and Jurgen Schmidhuber, 1997—Original paper on LSTMs with outdated terminology and inefficient implementation, but detailed mathematical derivation.

### Competitions and awards

- *Large Text Compression Benchmark* (http://mattmahoney.net/dc/text.html) — Some researchers believe that compression of natural language text is equivalent to artificial general intelligence (AGI).
- *Hutter Prize* (https://en.wikipedia.org/wiki/Hutter_Prize)—Annual competition to compress a 100 MB archive of Wikipedia natural language text. Alexander Rhatushnyak won in 2017.
- *Open Knowledge Extraction Challenge 2017* (https://svn.aksw.org/papers/2017/ ESWC_Challenge_OKE/public.pdf).

### Datasets

Natural language data is everywhere you look. Language is the superpower of the human race, and your pipeline should take advantage of it:

- Google's Dataset Search (http://toolbox.google.com/datasetsearch)—A search engine similar to Google Scholar (http://scholar.google.com), but for data.
- *Stanford Datasets* (https://nlp.stanford.edu/data/)—Pretrained word2vec and GloVE models, multilingual language models and datasets, multilingual dictionaries, lexica, and corpora.
- *Pretrained word vector models* (https://github.com/3Top/word2vec-api#where-to-get-a-pretrained-model)—The README for a word vector web API provides links to several word vector models, including the 300D Wikipedia GloVE model.
- A list of datasets/corpora for NLP tasks, in reverse chronological order (https:// github.com/karthikncode/nlp-datasets) by Karthik Narasimhan.

- Alphabetical list of free/public domain datasets with text data for use in Natural Language Processing (NLP) (https://github.com/niderhoff/nlp-datasets).
- Datasets and tools for basic natural language processing (https://github.com/googlei18n/language-resources)—Google's international tools for i18n.
- nlpia (https://github.com/totalgood/nlpia)—Python package with data loaders (nlpia.loaders) and preprocessors for all the NLP data you'll ever need... until you finish this book ;).

## Search engines

Search (information retrieval) is a big part of NLP. And it's extremely important that we get it right so that our AI (and corporate) overlords can't manipulate us through the information they feed our brains. If you want to learn how to retrieve your own information, by building your own search engines, these are some resources that will help.

### Search algorithms

- *Billion-scale similarity search with GPUs* (https://arxiv.org/pdf/1702.08734.pdf) —BidMACH is a high-dimensional vector indexing and KNN search implementation, similar to the annoy Python package. This paper explains an enhancement for GPUs that is 8 times faster than the original implementation.
- Spotify's Annoy Package (https://erikbern.com/2017/11/26/annoy-1.10 -released-with-hamming-distance-and-windows-support.html) by Erik Bernhardsson's—A K-nearest neighbors algorithm used at Spotify to find similar songs.
- *New benchmarks for approximate nearest neighbors* by Erik Bernhardsson (https:// erikbern.com/2018/02/15/new-benchmarks-for-approximate-nearest-neighbors.html)—Approximate nearest neighbor algorithms are the key to scalable semantic search, and author Erik keeps tabs on the state of the art.

### Open source search engines

- BeeSeek (https://launchpad.net/~beeseek-devs)—Open source distributed web indexing and private search (hive search); no longer maintained
- WebSPHNIX (https://www.cs.cmu.edu/~rcm/websphinx/)—Web GUI for building a web crawler

### Open source full-text indexers

Efficient indexing is critical to any natural language search application. Here are a few open source full-text indexing options. However, these "search engines" don't crawl the web, so you need to provide them with the corpus you want them to index and search:

- Elasticsearch (https://github.com/elastic/elasticsearch)—Open Source, Distributed, RESTful Search Engine.
- Apache Lucern + Solr (https://github.com/apache/lucene-solr).

- Sphinx Search (https://github.com/sphinxsearch/sphinx).
- Kronuz/Xapiand: Xapiand: A RESTful Search Engine (https://github.com/Kronuz/Xapiand)—There are packages for Ubuntu that'll let you search your local hard drive (like Google Desktop used to do).
- Indri (http://www.lemurproject.org/indri.php)—Semantic search with a Python interface (https://github.com/cvangysel/pyndri), but it isn't actively maintained.
- Gigablast (https://github.com/gigablast/open-source-search-engine)—Open source web crawler and natural language indexer in C++.
- Zettair (http://www.seg.rmit.edu.au/zettair)—Open source HTML and TREC indexer (no crawler or live example); last updated 2009.
- OpenFTS: Full Text Search Engine (http://openfts.sourceforge.net)—Full text search indexer for PyFTS using PostgreSQL with a Python API (http://rhodesmill.org/brandon/projects/pyfts.html).

### Manipulative search engines

The search engines most of us use aren't optimized solely to help you find what you need, but rather to ensure that you click links that generate revenue for the company that built it. Google's innovative second-price sealed-bid auction ensures that advertisers don't overpay for their ads,[1] but it doesn't prevent search users from overpaying when they click disguised advertisements. This manipulative search isn't unique to Google. It's used in any search engine that ranks results according to any "objective function" other than your satisfaction with the search results. But here they are, if you want to compare and experiment:

- Google
- Bing
- Baidu

### Less manipulative search engines

To determine how commercial and manipulative a search engine was, I queried several engines with things like "open source search engine." I then counted the number of ad-words purchasers and click-bait sites among the search results in the top 10. The following sites kept that count below one or two. And the top search results were often the most objective and useful sites, such as Wikipedia, Stack Exchange, or reputable news articles and blogs:

- Alternatives to Google (https://www.lifehack.org/374487/try-these-15-search-engines-instead-google-for-better-search-results).[2]

---

[1]  Cornell University Networks Course case study, "Google AdWords Auction - A Second Price Sealed-Bid Auction," (https://blogs.cornell.edu/info2040/2012/10/27/google-adwords-auction-a-second-price-sealed-bid-auction).

[2]  See the web page titled "Try These 15 Search Engines Instead of Google For Better Search Results," (https://www.lifehack.org/374487/try-these-15-search-engines-instead-google-for-better-search-results).

- Yandex (https://yandex.com/search/?text=open%20source%20search%20engine&lr=21754)—Surprisingly, the most popular Russian search engine (60% of Russian searches) seemed less manipulative than the top US search engines.
- DuckDuckGo (https://duckduckgo.com).
- `Watson` Semantic Web Search (http://watson.kmi.open.ac.uk/WatsonWUI)—No longer in development, and not really a full-text web search, but it's an interesting way to explore the semantic web (at least what it was years ago before `watson` was frozen).

### Distributed search engines

Distributed search engines[3] are perhaps the least manipulative and most "objective" because they have no central server to influence the ranking of the search results. However, current distributed search implementations rely on TF-IDF word frequencies to rank pages, because of the difficulty in scaling and distributing semantic search NLP algorithms. However, distribution of semantic indexing approaches such as latent semantic analysis (LSA) and locality sensitive hashing have been successfully distributed with nearly linear scaling (as good as you can get). It's just a matter of time before someone decides to contribute code for semantic search into an open source project like Yacy or builds a new distributed search engine capable of LSA:

- Nutch (https://nutch.apache.org/)—Nutch spawned Hadoop and itself became less of a distributed search engine and more of a distributed HPC system over time.
- Yacy (https://www.yacy.net/en/index.html)—One of the few open source (https://github.com/yacy/yacy_search_server) decentralized, or federated, search engines and web crawlers still actively in use. Preconfigured clients for Mac, Linux, and Windows are available.

---

[3] See the web pages titled "Distributed search engine," (https://en.wikipedia.org/wiki/Distributed_search_engine) and "Distributed Search Engines," (https://wiki.p2pfoundation.net/Distributed_Search_Engines).

# *glossary*

We've collected some definitions of common natural language processing and machine language acronyms and terminology here.[1]

You can find some of the parsers and regular expressions we used to help generate this list in the `nlpia` Python package at github.com/totalgood/nlpia (https://github.com/totalgood/nlpia).[2] This listing shows how we used `nlpia` to draft this glossary:

```
>>> from nlpia.book_parser import write_glossary
>>> from nlpia.constants import import DATA_PATH
>>> print(write_glossary(
...      os.path.join(DATA_PATH, 'book')))       ←┐  YMMV because we can't
== Acronyms                                        provide the entire manuscript
                                                   in your data folder.
[acronyms,template="glossary",id="terms"]
*AGI*:: Artificial general intelligence --
*AI*:: Artificial intelligence --
*AIML*:: Artificial Intelligence Markup Language --
*ANN*:: Approximate nearest neighbors --
...
```

We didn't complete the definition generator, but that might be possible with a good LSTM language model (see chapter 10). We leave that to you.

## Acronyms

**AGI**—Artificial general intelligence
Machine intelligence capable of solving a variety of problems that human brains can solve

**AI**—Artificial intelligence
Machine behavior that is impressive enough to be called intelligent by scientists or corporate marketers

---

[1] Bill Wilson at the university of New South Wales in Australia has a more complete NLP dictionary (www.cse.unsw.edu.au/~billw/nlpdict.html).

[2] `nlpia.translators` (https://github.com/totalgood/nlpia/blob/master/src/nlpia/translators.py) and `nlpia.book_parser` (https://github.com/totalgood/nlpia/blob/master/src/nlpia/book_parser.py).

**AIML**—Artificial Intelligence Markup Language

A pattern matching and templated response specification language in XML that was invented during the building of A.L.I.C.E., one of the first conversational chatbots

**ANN**—Approximate nearest neighbors

Finding the $M$ closest vectors to a single vector in a set of $N$ high-dimensional vectors is an O(N) problem, because you have to calculate your distance metric between every other vector and the target vector. This makes clustering an intractable $O(N^2)$.

**ANN**—Artificial neural network

**API**—Application programmer interface

A user interface for your customers that are developers, usually a command line tool, source code library, or web interface that they can interact with programmatically

**AWS**—Amazon Web Services

Amazon invented the concept of cloud services when they exposed their internal infrastructure to the world.

**BOW**—Bag of words

A data structure (usually a vector) that retains the counts (frequencies) of words but not their order

**CEC**—Constant error carousel

A neuron that outputs its input delayed by one time step. Used within an LSTM or GRU memory unit. This is the memory register for an LSTM unit and can only be reset to a new value by the forgetting gate interrupting this "carousel."

**CNN**—Convolutional neural network

A neural network that is trained to learn *filters*, also known as *kernels*, for feature extraction in supervised learning

**CUDA**—Compute Unified Device Architecture

An Nvidia open source software library optimized for running general computations/algorithms on a GPU

**DAG**—Directed acyclic graph

A network topology without any cycles, connections that loop back on themselves

**DFA**—Deterministic finite automaton

A finite state machine that doesn't make random choices. The re package in Python compiles regular expressions to create a DFA, but the regex can compile fuzzy regular expressions into NDFA (nondeterministic FA).

**FSM**—Finite-state machine

Kyle Gorman and Wikipedia can explain this better than I (https://en.wikipedia.org/wiki/Finite-state_machine).

**FST**—Finite-state transducer

Like regular expressions, but they can output a new character to replace each character they matched. Kyle Gorman explains them well (www.openfst.org).

**GIS**—Geographic information system

A database for storing, manipulating, and displaying geographic information, usually involving latitude, longitude, and altitude coordinates and traces.

**GPU**—Graphical processing unit
The graphics card in a gaming rig, a cryptocurrency mining server, or a machine learning server

**GRU**—Gated recurrent unit
A variation of long short-term memory networks with shared parameters to cut computation time

**HNSW**—A graph data structure that enables efficient search (and robust approximate nearest neighbor search using Hierarchical Navigable Small World graphs (https://arxiv.org/vc/arxiv/papers/1603/1603.09320v1.pdf) by Yu A. Malkov and D. A. Yashunin)

**HPC**—High performance computing
The study of systems that maximize throughput, usually by parallelizing computation with separate `map` and `reduce` computation stages

**IDE**—Integrated development environment
A desktop application for software development, such as PyCharm, Eclipse, Atom, or Sublime Text 3

**IR**—Information retrieval
The study of document and web search engine algorithms. This is what brought NLP to the forefront of important computer science disciplines in the 90s.

**ITU**—India Technical University
A top-ranking technical university. The Georgia Tech of India.

**i18n**—Internationalization
Preparing application for use in more than one country (locale)

**LDA**—Linear discriminant analysis
A classification algorithm with linear boundaries between classes (see chapter 4)

**LSA**—Latent semantic analysis
Truncated SVD applied to TF-IDF or bag-of-words vectors to create topic vectors in a vector space language model (see chapter 4)

**LSH**—Locality sensitive hash
A hash that works as an efficient but approximate mapping/clustering index on dense, continuous, high-dimensional vectors (see chapter 13). Think of them as ZIP Codes that work for more than just 2D (latitude and longitude).

**LSI**—Latent semantic indexing
An old-school way of describing latent semantic analysis (see LSA), but it's a misnomer, since LSA vector-space models don't lend themselves to being easily indexed.

**LSTM**—Long short-term memory
An enhanced form of a recurrent neural network that maintains a memory of state that itself is trained via backpropagation (see chapter 9)

**MIH**—Multi-index hashing
A hashing and indexing approach for high-dimensional dense vectors

**ML**—Machine learning
Programming a machine with data rather than hand-coded algorithms

**MSE**—Mean squared error
The sum of the square of the difference between the desired output of a machine learning model and the actual output of the model

**NELL**—Never Ending Language Learning
A Carnegie Mellon knowledge extraction project that has been running continuously for years, scraping web pages and extracting general knowledge about the world (mostly "IS-A" categorical relationships between terms)

**NLG**—Natural language generation
Composing text automatically, algorithmically; one of the most challenging tasks of natural language processing (NLP)

**NLP**—Natural language processing
You probably know what this is by now. If not, see the introduction in chapter 1.

**NLU**—Natural language understanding
Often used in recent papers to refer to natural language processing with neural networks

**NMF**—Nonnegative matrix factorization
A matrix factorization similar to SVD, but constrains all elements in the matrix factors to be greater than or equal to zero

**NSF**—National Science Foundation
A US government agency tasked with funding scientific research

**NYC**—New York City
The US city that never sleeps

**OSS**—Open source software

**pip**—Pip installs pip
The official Python package manager that downloads and installs packages automatically from the "Cheese Shop" (`pypi.python.org`)

**PR**—Pull request
The right way to request that someone merge your code into theirs. GitHub has some buttons and wizards to make this easy. This is how you can build your reputation as a conscientious contributor to open source.

**PCA**—Principal component analysis
Truncated SVD on any numerical data, typically images or audio files

**QDA**—Quadratic discriminant analysis
Similar to LDA, but allows for quadratic (curved) boundaries between classes

**ReLU**—Rectified linear unit
A linear neural net activation function that forces the output of a neuron to be nonzero. Equivalent to `y = np.max(x, 0)`. The most popular and efficient activation function for image processing and NLP, because it allows back propagation to work efficiently on extremely deep networks without "vanishing the gradients."

**REPL**—Read–evaluate–print loop
The typical workflow of a developer of any scripting language that doesn't need to be compiled. The `ipython`, `jupyter console`, and `jupyter notebook` REPLs are particularly powerful, with their `help`, `?`, `??`, and `%` magic commands, plus auto-complete, and Ctrl-R history search.[3]

---

[3] Python's REPLs even allow you to execute any shell command (including `pip`) installed on your OS (such as `!git commit -am 'fix 123'`). This lets your fingers stay on the keyboard and away from the mouse, minimizing cognitive load from context switches.

**RMSE**—Root mean square error

The square root of the mean squared error. A common regression error metric. It can also be used for binary and ordinal classification problems. It provides an intuitive estimate of the 1-sigma uncertainty in a model's predictions.

**RNN**—Recurrent neural network

A neural network architecture that feeds the outputs of one layer into the input of an earlier layer. RNNs are often "unfolded" into equivalent feed forward neural networks for diagramming and analysis.

**SMO**—Sequential minimal optimization

A support vector machine training approach and algorithm

**SVD**—Singular value decomposition

A matrix factorization that produces a diagonal matrix of eigenvalues and two orthogonal matrices containing eigenvectors. It's the math behind LSA and PCA (see chapter 4).

**SVM**—Support vector machine

A machine learning algorithm usually used for classification

**TF-IDF**—Term frequency * inverse document frequency

A normalization of word counts that improves information retrieval results (see chapter 3)

**UI**—User interface

The "affordances" you offer your user through your software, often the graphical web pages or mobile application screens that your user must interact with to use your product or service

**UX**—User experience

The nature of a customer's interaction with your product or company, from purchase all the way through to their last contact with you. This includes your website or API UI on your website and all the other interactions with your company.

**VSM**—Vector space model

A vector representation of the objects in your problem, such as words or documents in an NLP problem (see chapter 4 and chapter 6)

**YMMV**—Your mileage may vary

You may not get the same results that we did.

## Terms

**Affordance**—A way for your user to interact with your product that you intentionally make possible. Ideally that interaction should come naturally to the user, be easily discoverable, and self-documenting.

**Artificial neural network**—A computational graph for machine learning or simulation of a biological neural network (brain)

**Cell**—The memory or state part of an LSTM unit that records a single scalar value and outputs it continuously [4]

**Dark patterns**—Software patterns (usually for a user interface) that are intended to increase revenue but often fail due to "blowback" because they manipulate your customers into using your product in ways that they don't intend

---

[4] See the web page titled "Long short-term memory" (https://en.wikipedia.org/wiki/Long_short-term_memory).

**Feed-forward network**—A "one-way" neural network that passes all its inputs through to its outputs in a consistent direction, forming a computation directed acyclic graph (DAG) or tree

**Morpheme**—A part of a token or word that contains meaning in and of itself. The morphemes that make up a token are collectively called the token's *morphology*. The morphology of a token can be found using algorithms in packages like SpaCy that process the token with its context (words around it).[5]

**Net, network, or neural net**—Artificial neural network

**Neuron**—A unit in a neural net whose function (such as $y = \text{tanh(w.dot(x))}$) takes multiple inputs and outputs a single scalar value. This value is usually the weights for that neuron ($\mathbf{w}$ or $w^i$) multiplied by all the input signals ($\mathbf{x}$ or $x^i$) and summed with a bias weight ($w^0$) before applying an activation function like *tanh*. A neuron always outputs a scalar value, which is sent to the inputs of any additional hidden or output neurons in the network. If a neuron implements a much more complicated activation function than that, like the enhancements that were made to recurrent neurons to create an LSTM, it is usually called a *unit*, for example, an *LSTM unit*.

**Nessvector**—An informal term for topic vectors or semantic vectors that capture concepts or qualities, such as femaleness or blueness, into the dimensions of a vector

**Predicate**—In English grammar, the predicate is the main verb of a sentence that's associated with the subject. Every complete sentence must have a predicate, just like it must also have a subject.

**Skip-grams**—Pairs of tokens used as training examples for a word vector embedding, where any number of intervening words are ignored (see chapter 6).

**Softmax**—Normalized exponential function used to squash the real-valued vector output by a neural network so that its values range between 0 and 1 like probabilities.

**Subject**—The main noun of a sentence—every complete sentence must have a subject (and a predicate) even if the subject is implied, like in the sentence "Run!" where the implied subject is "you."

**Unit**—Neuron or small collection of neurons that perform some more complicated nonlinear function to compute the output. For example, an LSTM unit has a memory cell that records state, an input gate (neuron) that decides what value to remember, a forget gate (neuron) that decides how long to remember that value, and an output gate neuron that accomplishes the activation function of the unit (usually a sigmoid or *tanh()*). A unit is a drop-in replacement for a neuron in a neural net that takes a vector input and outputs a scalar value; it just has more complicated behavior.

---

[5] See the web page titled "Linguistic Features : spaCy Usage Documentation" (https://spacy.io/usage/linguistic -features#rule-based-morphology).

# index